MW01629211

The Place of Many Moods

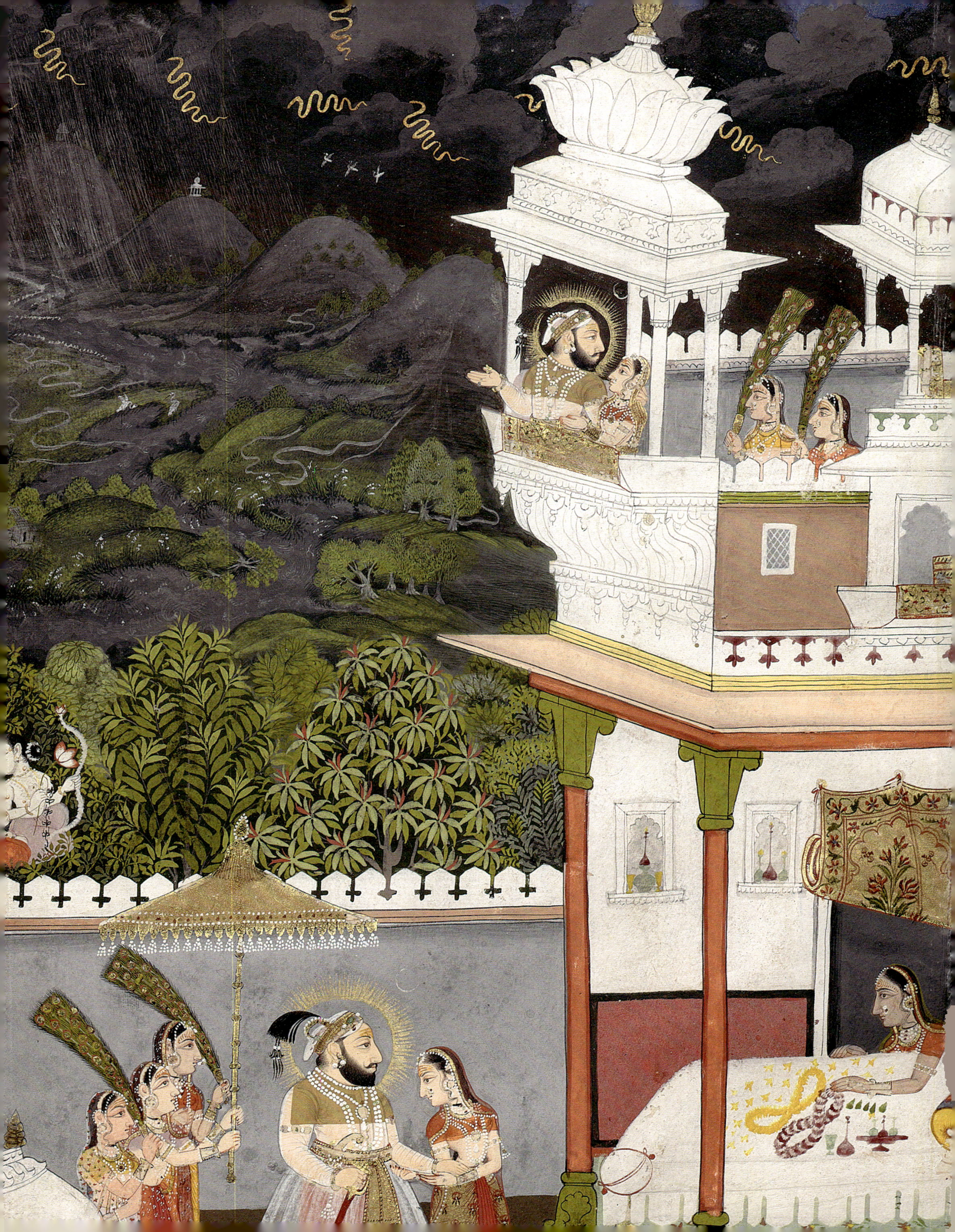

The Place of Many Moods

UDAIPUR'S PAINTED LANDS AND INDIA'S EIGHTEENTH CENTURY

Dipti Khera

PRINCETON UNIVERSITY PRESS
Princeton and Oxford

For Puneet, who makes my worlds possible.

In memory of Allison Busch,
who inspired inimitable moods for learning and listening.

Published by Princeton University Press, 41 William Street, Princeton, New Jersey 08540
In the United Kingdom: Princeton University Press, 6 Oxford Street, Woodstock, Oxfordshire OX20 1TR
press.princeton.edu

Jacket Illustrations (front and back): Maharana Sangram Singh II at the Gangaur Boat Procession, c. 1715–20, Udaipur. Gouache and gold on paper, 78.7 × 78.74 cm. The City Palace Museum, Udaipur; 2012.19.0014_R. Photography courtesy of the Freer Gallery of Art and Arthur M. Sackler Gallery, Smithsonian Institution. Photographer: Neil Greentree. © Maharana of Mewar Charitable Foundation, The City Palace Museum, Udaipur.
Illustrations in front matter: p. ii, detail of fig. 2.26; p. vi, detail of fig. 5.1; p. viii detail of fig. 2.15.

Library of Congress Cataloging-in-Publication Data
Names: Khera, Dipti, author.
Title: The place of many moods : Udaipur's painted lands and India's eighteenth century / Dipti Khera.
Description: Princeton : Princeton University Press, 2020. | Based on the author's thesis (Ph.D.)—Columbia University, 2013, under the title: Picturing India's "Land of Kings" between the Mughal and British empires : topographical imaginings of Udaipur and its environs. | Includes bibliographical references and index.
Identifiers: LCCN 2020002331 | ISBN 9780691201849 (hardback) | ISBN 9780691209111 (ebook)
Subjects: LCSH: Udaipur (Rajasthan, India)—In art. | Painting—Political aspects—India—Udaipur (Rajasthan)—History—18th century. | Art and society—India—Udaipur (Rajasthan)—History—18th century. | Udaipur (Rajasthan, India)—Intellectual life—18th century.
Classification: LCC ND1460.U33 K49 2020 | DDC 759.954/4—dc23
LC record available at https://lccn.loc.gov/2020002331

British Library Cataloging-in-Publication Data is available
Designed by Jo Ellen Ackerman / Bessas & Ackerman
This book has been composed in Vesper Pro, Frutiger Next Pro and Domaine Display Narrow
Printed on acid-free paper. ∞
Printed in Italy
10 9 8 7 6 5 4 3 2 1

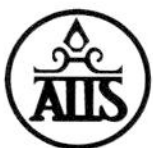

Awarded the Edward Cameron Dimock Jr. Prize
in the Indian Humanities
by the American Institute of Indian Studies and
published with the Institute's generous support.

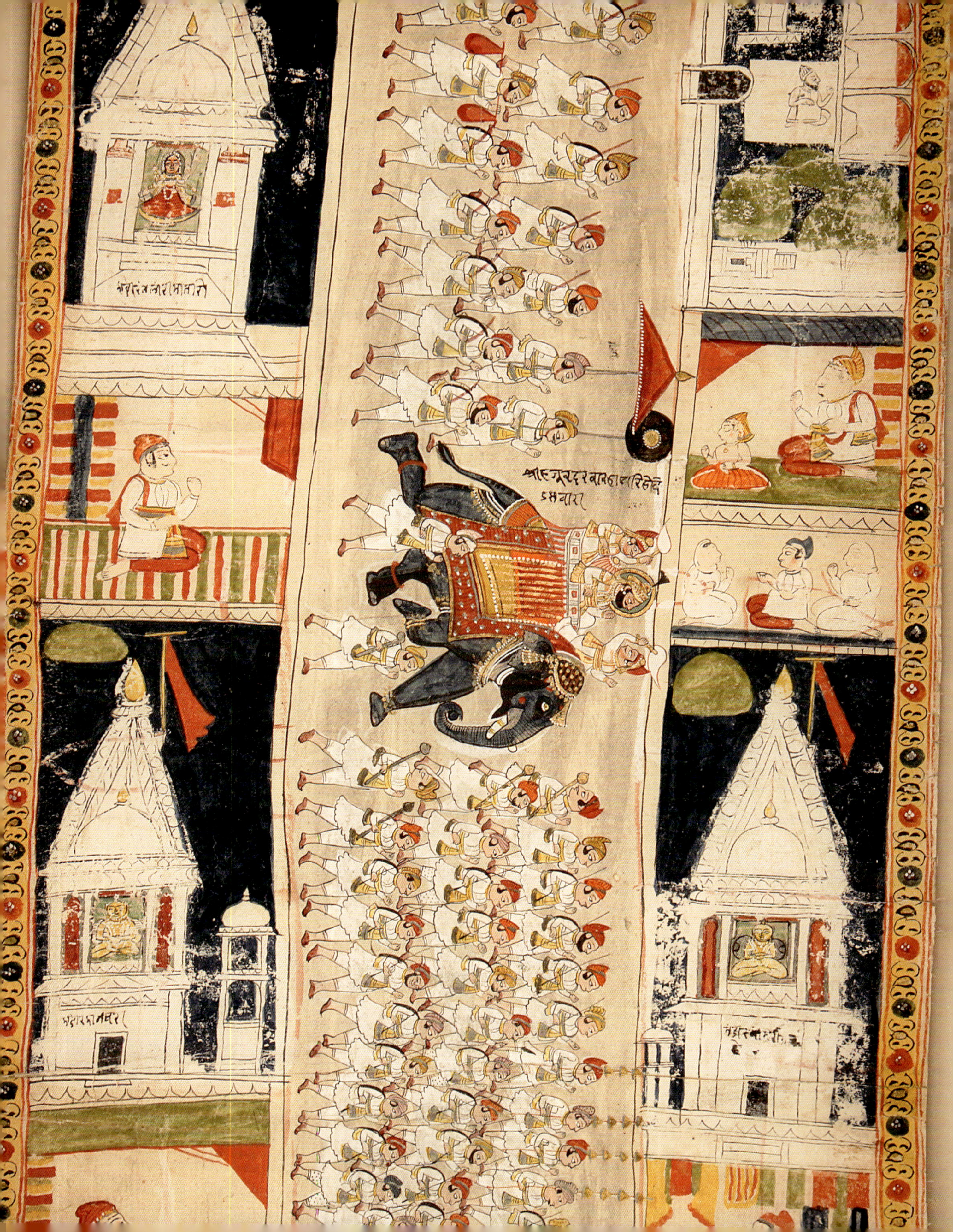

Contents

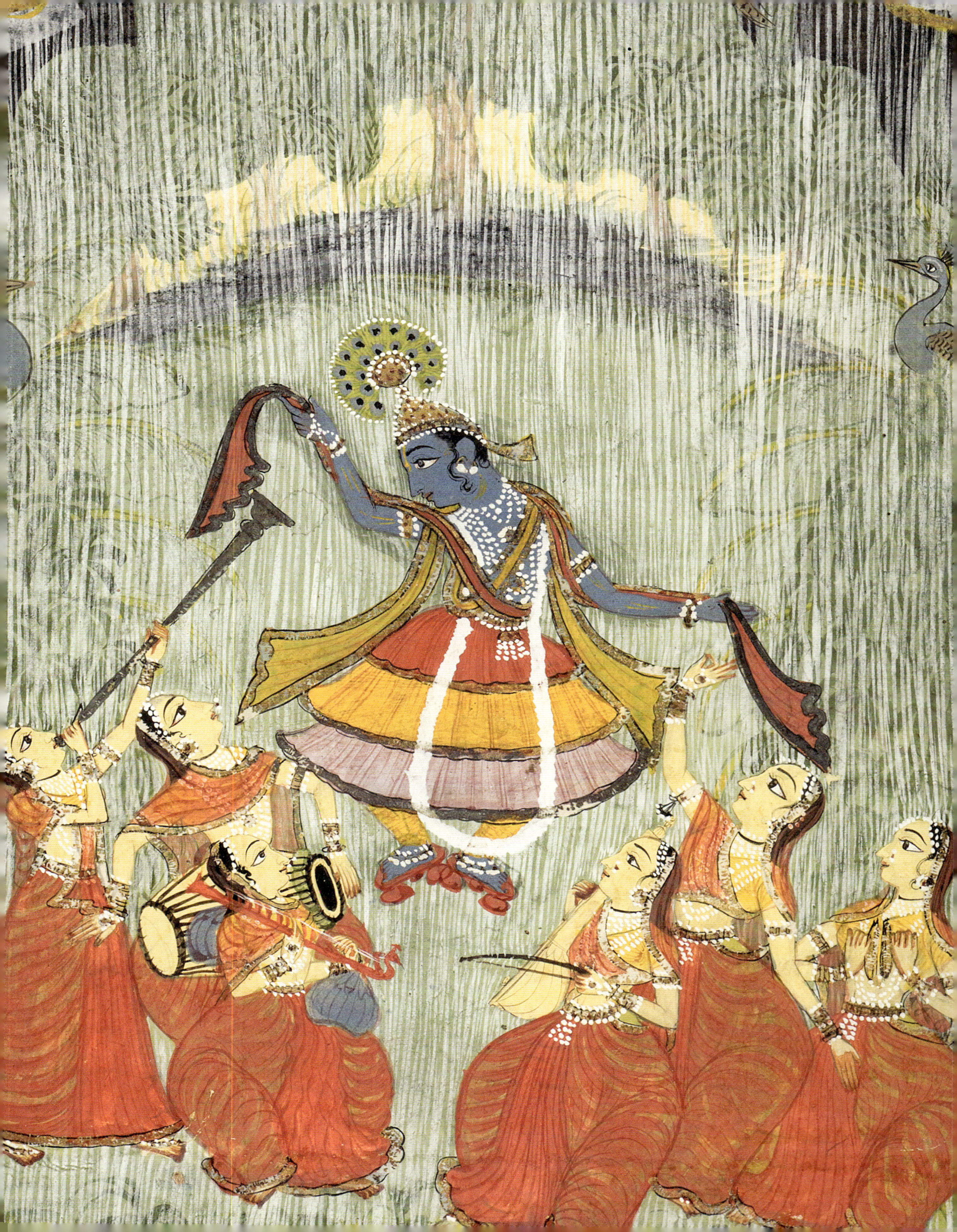

Acknowledgments

This is a book about artistic renderings of the moods of places. In recounting memorable times, why do we often start by describing the feel of a place where relevant episodes unraveled? We deploy stories and look for pictures. We turn to descriptions and tropes adopted by others, embedding our experiences and imaginings into their representations, even mixing times, actors, and vignettes. We exaggerate; we censor. We strive to capture the precise mood of the place conjured up in mental images, even if that means idealizing evocations, adapting details, and using imprecise associations. Nonetheless, each representation of moods and their effects is unmistakably historically contingent. *The Place of Many Moods* tells the story of such deep investments in picturing the moods of a place in the long eighteenth century. From the vantage point of Udaipur—India's city of lakes—it acknowledges the unacknowledged powerful emotional work of objects, images, places, and sustaining lands. The overpowering ability of the city's material and visual artifacts to make familiar places visible in unfamiliar ways reveals pasts, politics, and passions not always recorded in words.

Only upon the book's completion have I realized the enormity of my debts and the emotions bundled in between its covers. First and foremost, my thanks go out to the city of Udaipur itself—to its historical makers, its contemporary citizens, its painters, its poets, its scribes, its scholars, as well as to the custodians of its lakes, hills, streets, buildings, museums, archives, and the arts. My enchantment with Udaipur began more than two decades ago. To feel awestruck, inspired, enthralled, and flummoxed by it has been my good fortune.

The patrons and personnel of the city's institutions, especially the Maharana Mewar Charitable Foundation; City Palace Museum, Udaipur; and Maharana Mewar Research Institute, have enabled my research in ways big and small. Shriji Arvind Singh Mewar and his family have supported my intellectual endeavors for more than twenty years. I am ever grateful for their trust and warmth, and for Padmaja Kumari Parmar's enthusiasm for my research in recent years. I thank Mayank Gupta for facilitating my research in the City Palace Museum and across Udaipur institutions; Bhupendra Singh Auwa, Tarun Sukhwal, Janak Singh Chauhan, Giriraj Singh Rajput, Utesh Dungarwal, Prashant Lohar, Chayan Doshi, Ankit Mehta, and Priyanka Seth for their assistance in accessing archives, artifacts, and court documents; Hansmukh Patel for tracking down sources in Udaipur's libraries and private collections; Seema Srimal for correcting my transcriptions and for those memorable afternoons of poring over court records together; the formidable objects-conservation team of Girikumar, Saloni Guwalewala, Vasundhara PM, Bhasha Shah, and Anuja Mukherjee for their knowledge and unmatchable *masti*; and Shikha Jain for her many insights into architecture of the City Palace Museum and Rajasthan.

For their diligent assistance in locating research material, I sincerely thank the staffs of the following museums and archives: Rajasthan State Archives, Bikaner (especially Johiya-ji for teaching me to read eighteenth-century court records); Rajasthan Oriental Research Institute, Udaipur (Sharad Jawalia); Rajasthan Oriental Research Institute, Jaipur (especially Mr. Meena for reading the Chittor *gajal* with me); Rajasthan Oriental Research Institute, Jodhpur (especially Vasumati Sharma and Kamal Kishore); Mehrangarh Museum of Art, Jodhpur (Karni Singh Jasol); Sardar Government Museum, Jodhpur; City Palace Museum, Jaipur (especially Giles Tillotson and Sukbhir-ji for unrolling many maps in 2010); Prakrit Bharti Academy, Jaipur (especially Vinaysagar-ji and Surendra Bothda for introducing me to various Jain collections in India); Lalbhai Dalpatbhai Institute of Indology and Lalbhai Dalpatbhai Museum, Ahmedabad (especially Jayshree Lalbhai, Ratan Parimoo, and Jitendra Shah); Calico Museum of Textiles, Ahmedabad; Oriental Institute, Baroda; National Archives, New Delhi; National Museum, New Delhi; Chhatrapati Shivaji Maharaj Vastu Sangrahalaya, Mumbai; British Library, London; British Museum, London; Victoria and Albert Museum, London (especially Susan Stronge, Rosemary Crill, and Suhashini Sinha); Royal Asiatic Society, London (especially Camilla Larsen, Edward Weech, Kathy Lazenbatt, and Alice McEwan); Rijksmuseum, Amsterdam (Ching-Ling Wang and Anna Slaczka); Harvard Art Museum / Arthur M. Sackler Museum, Cambridge (Mary McWilliams); San Diego Museum of Art, San Diego (Cory Woodall); Yale Center for British Art (especially Gillian Forrester, David Thompson, and Adrianna Bates) and Yale University Art Gallery, New Haven (especially David Sensabaugh and Ami Potter); Fondation Custodia, Paris (Peter Furhring); Museum für Asiatische Kunst, Berlin (Rafael Gadebusch); Rietberg Museum, Zürich (especially Ebehard Fischer, Johannes Beltz, and Caroline Widmer); the Mignucci family (especially Aldo, Anna, and Marco for their enthusiastic support); Christen and Nandine Jürg (especially for welcoming me to their home and collection); Metropolitan Museum of Art, New York (especially John Guy, Navina Najat Haidar, Alison Clark, Hwai-lin Yeh-Lewis, and Yana Van Dyke); Asian Art Museum, San Francisco (Qamar Adamjee); Philadelphia Museum of Art (Darielle Mason, Leslie Essogolou); Museum of Fine Arts, Boston (Laura Weinstein); and the Brooklyn Museum of Art, New York (Joan Cummins).

Lengthy discussions with Carol Cains, formerly at the National Gallery of Victoria, Melbourne, in 2008 were among my first lessons in examining "real" Indian paintings. Along with her, I thank Wayne Crothers and Kathleen Burke for their assistance in recent years. The Freer Gallery of Art and the Arthur M. Sackler Gallery, Washington, DC, has been a pivotal learning lab. Its staff, conservators, and curators have indulged my many requests to research and teach with the collections. I thank Debra Diamond, Massumeh Farhad, Emily Jacobson, Simon Rettig, Amelia Meyer, Zeynep Simavi, Brian Abrams, Emma Natalya Stein, Nancy Micklewright, Sana Mirza, and David Horacio for their enthusiastic support. I am grateful to the members of the Nahata family residing in Bikaner and Assam, Mr. and Mrs. Vijaychand Nahata, and Chopra-ji for allowing me to study the 1830 painted letter-scroll (and to Jonas Spinoy for his photography). I hope the Agarchand Nahata Jain Granthalaya—a library assembled by the preeminent scholars Agarchand and Bhanwarlal Nahata—will remain open for generations of scholars to come. To Brajmohan Jawalia-ji, I am grateful for his scholarship on and preservation of a remarkable eighteenth-century manuscript on rains, droughts, and migrations.

Multiple institutions have generously supported my research. I thank the American Institute of Indian Studies (Chicago and New Delhi), Center for Advanced Study in the Visual Arts (National Gallery of Art, Washington, DC), Metropolitan Museum of Art, Yale Center for British Art, and South Asian Studies Council, Yale University. Special thanks go to Columbia University's Department of Art History and Archaeology for its graduate fellowships, and to librarians and allied staff at the Avery Library and the Visual Media Center who graciously enabled my work on this project, initially as a doctoral dissertation. I so wish I could continue to partake in the friendship and expertise of James Conlon and Caleb Smith, both who left us too soon. More recently, the Art Histories and Aesthetic Practices fellowship awarded by the Forum Transregionale Studien, Berlin and NYU's Goddard Junior Faculty Fellowship provided critical support for writing and research in 2015–16. I am grateful to all of the above institutions for providing a scholarly community and opportunities for constructive feedback.

I am honored and grateful to the American Institute of Indian Studies for awarding me the Edward Cameron Dimock Jr. Prize for the best book manuscript in the Indian humanities (2019) and the associated subvention for the subsequent production of the book. I am also grateful for the research stipend received from NYU's junior faculty mentoring program; the NYU Center for Humanities Book subvention grant; and Humanities Dean Carolyn Dinshaw's supplemental grants and sound advice. I thank the editors and journals that granted me permission to reproduce parts of "Jagvilasa: Picturing Worlds of Pleasure and Power in 18th-Century Udaipur Painting," from Marg Publications, Mumbai; of "Lakes within Lake-Palaces: A Material History of Pleasure in 18th-Century India," from Routledge, New Delhi; and of "Marginal, Mobile, Multilayered: Painted Invitation Letters as Bazaar Objects in Early Modern India," from *Journal18*.

Over the years, I have accrued several intellectual debts, mentors, and friends. I am grateful to Vidya Dehejia, who believed in this project from the very beginning during my doctoral studies. Her constant pursuit of new archival material motivated me. I feel lucky that Keith Moxey taught the proseminar in art history to my cohort at Columbia—I am yet to come across another art historian who begins his first class with "Provincializing Europe." The weight of Molly Aitken's work is exerted throughout this book. I am grateful for her engagement with my ideas and for pushing me to find precise ways to make my arguments. Ever since 2009, Tim Barringer's art of teaching with collections has enabled me to look at my material in new ways. In addition, his insistence that we learn about the relationship between art and empire from the viewpoint of multiple locales, his steadfast support at every stage of my academic career in the past ten years, including commentary on the book's introduction under tight time constraints, have expanded my horizons. If Allison Busch had not come to Columbia, I would never have gone down the current path. She opened my mind to things literary and early modern. Allison's passing and the lasting presence of her words and warmth have been a big part of writing *The Place of Many Moods*. For her mentorship and friendship, and shared sentiments on poetry and puzzles, baking and bhindi, I remain forever grateful.

The intellectual generosity that I have received from colleagues in South Asian art history and beyond has been truly enriching. I am particularly thankful to Debra Diamond for her sharp questions and comments, enthusiasm, and warm care as a generous colleague and friend. I am thrilled that we have embarked together on the next phase of *The Place of Many Moods*, to realize the *bhāva* of Udaipur in Washington, DC. For research advice, I sincerely thank Andrew Topsfield for his responses to my queries and for sharing images of inaccessible paintings on several occasions. To Cathy Benkaim, I am grateful for her help in locating several Udaipur paintings in private collections. To Susan Gole, I am most thankful for her work on Indian maps that made my journeys possible, and, in turn, I hope to share widely the image collection that she has entrusted to me.

The following colleagues, to whom I am incredibly grateful, generously devoted their time to reading and commenting on my book manuscript, which helped me clarify ideas on multiple instances: Molly Aitken, Manan Ahmad (especially for brainstorming the introduction), Allison Busch, Chanchal Dadlani, Debra Diamond, Finbarr Barry Flood, Sylvia Houghteling (for being the best outlining partner), Meredith Martin, Prita Meier, Sheldon Pollock (for believing in the project at a critical stage), and Nancy Um. I am enormously grateful to the two anonymous reviewers of the book manuscript for their incisive comments and questions. Of course, all errors that persist remain mine. I thank Lyla Halstead for her assistance with image procurement; Sophie Loring for her careful work on notes and bibliography; Janet Rauscher for editorial work; and Blair Simmons for digitally stitching together the 1830 scroll. It has been a pleasure to work with the team at Princeton University Press. First and foremost, I am immensely thankful to Michelle Komie for her enthusiasm, patience, and expedient work on my project, and I thank Sara Lerner, Kenneth Guay, and Pamela Weidman for their fine assistance and steadfast support at every stage. I am very grateful to Amy K. Hughes for her constructive questions and precise copyedits, and to Sarah Smith and Derek Gottlieb for their work on proofs and index. Steven Sears's and Jo Ellen Ackerman's attention to detail and design has been extraordinary. Thank you all, for making this book thing real!

For their genuine engagement, and for their comments and questions on various occasions that enriched my writing and thinking, I would like to thank Robert Skelton, Susan Stronge, Katherine Butler Schofield, Imre Bangha, Hannah Baader, Lamia Balafrej, Ned Cooke, Gerhard Wolf, Michele Mattieni, Deepali Dewan, Purnima Dhawan, Rima Hooja, Kajri Jain, Varsha Joshi, Sonal Khullar, Heeryoon Shin, Heidi Pauwels, Rashmi Poddar, Bhavani Raman, Sugata Ray, Tamara Sears, Avinoam Shalem, Sunil Sharma, Yuthika Sharma, Kavita Singh, Sumathi Ramaswamy, Cynthia Talbot, Audrey Truschke, Kishwar Rizvi, Zainab Bahrani, Jack Hawley, Richard Williams, Anand Yang, Pramod Kumar KG, Sarah Betzer, Holly Shaffer, Meredith Gamer, Katherine Kasdorf, Risha Lee, Anna Seastrand, Karin Zitzewitz, Dalpat Rajpurohit, Tyler Williams, Deborah Hutton, Varunika Saraf, Shailka Mishra, Chelsea Foxwell, Susan Babbaie, and Beate Fricke. I simply cannot imagine a CAA, ACSAA, AAS, or the Annual Conference on South Asia, Madison, without the presence and questions of Cathy and Rick Asher—thank you! John Cort and Phyllis Granoff also facilitated my forays into Jain collections and new sources, and I am thankful to both of them for the feedback they have provided along the way. I thank all my colleagues at the Department of Art History and the Insititute of Fine Arts at NYU for supporting my work. I am especially grateful to Dennis Geronimus, Kathryn Smith, Edward Sullivan, Christine Poggi, and Patricia Rubin for their support and advice in navigating my tenure-track years. Beyond art history, Fred Myers, Ulirich Baer, Ritty Lukose, Vasuki Nesiah, and Paula Chakravartty have always offered wise counsel.

There have been friends along the way who have enriched this journey in practical and inspirational ways. I am so thankful to Sylvia Houghteling for our intertwined friendship in which fun and work breathe seamlessly into each other. In many ways that I cannot describe, the presence and care of Jinee Lokaneeta and Sangay Mishra have nourished me through the highs and lows of the past three years. I feel extremely lucky that I could always call upon Lisa Lee, Daniel Bosch, Samira Sheikh, Aparna Balachandran, Ruchi Chaturvedi, Bhavani Raman, Karuna Mantena, Paula Chakravartty, Gianpaolo Biaocchi, Natasha Iskander, Maria Elosua, Arang Keshavarzian, Greta Scharnweber, Chanchal Dadlani, Meredith Gamer, Justin Gundlach, Brinda Kumar, Neil Greentree, Debra Diamond, Molly Aitken, and Meredith Martin. Finbarr Barry Flood, Srini Padmanabhan, Peyvand Firouzeh, Gül Kale, Rakhee Balaram, and Banu Karaca, who stood by me in the gray fog of Berlin (and beyond), all offered light in their unique ways. Various other friends have sustained me with their zest through the years at different stages—dearest Hana Elwell, Niko Higgins, Alok Arora, Amee Karnavat, Parul and Pranav Adurkar, Nobhojit Roy, Y. D. Pitkar (for the initial nudge during my "architecture days" to walk into areas unknown), and Ajit Rao (especially for the travels from Jaisalmer to the twenty-two *ṭhikānā*s of Mewar). In Udaipur, the Bohedas—(late Papa) Surinder Singh, Ajay, Anupama, Triambika, and Kartiki—have provided a home that has filled my research travels with warmth, relaxation, and laughter since the early 2000s. In Jaipur, the late Varsha Joshi and late Surjit Singh and in Berlin, Elisabeth and Avinoam Shalem generously opened their homes and neighborhoods. Thank you, all! I will always regret that I cannot place my book in Kavita Datla's hands. She would have expanded its horizons and indulged me with long conversations in New York's exclusive restaurants. Thank you for the everlasting gift—the feeling of your presence and thoughts—each time I visit a new exhibition!

My father was my staunchest supporter and would have been the proudest to hold this book. I thank Papa most for giving me the space to think freely and travel widely. I thank Mummy for her loving expression of support even when the writing came at the expense of spending time together and talking regularly. I am indeed fortunate that my parents and in-laws, Mummy and Papa-Rajkunj, have affirmed complete faith in my life choices. I thank them with all my heart. I hope to find ways to enjoy many more walks and talks with them than the past few years have allowed. I am particularly grateful for the love and care I continue to receive from my close family members, uncles, aunts, and cousins from the DLF, Panchsheel, Lokhandwala, Pleasantville, and Long Island households. Anjali and Harald, and my dearest Nehla, Nikian, and Maya, have added cheer to my New York life with their hugs, laughter, and scrumptious meals.

My final thanks are reserved for Puneet, who has been with me at every step. I am grateful to him for editing multiple chapters, often at the expense of his own writing time. When I complained about various complexities in finishing the book, he responded with supportive rebuttals, not losing his patience even once (well, once!), and with fresh-cooked meals and stories of why the "feeling of a place" resonated with him. I thank you for all that this page cannot record.

Note on Transliteration

I have followed conventions adopted in recent Hindi and Brajbhasha scholarship and preferred Hindi over Sanskrit for titles and terms, thus *Jagvilās*, not *Jagvilāsa*. Exceptions are representations of original Brajbhasha verse, which require the word-ending short *a* for metrical reasons, thus *vilāsa*, not *vilās*. For aesthetic terms that are more commonly used in secondary scholarship and spellings standardized per Sanskrit conventions, I follow those for consistency. Thus, *bhāva*, not *bhāv*, and *rasa*, not *ras*. I do not use diacritics for words such as *durbar*, now included in English-language dictionaries. And exception is made in the nonuse of diacritics for the titles of artworks following the norm adopted by most museums and libraries. For an illustration from a manuscript such as *Rasikpriyā*, *Rāmāyaṇa*, or a *bārah-māsa*, I have retained the diacritics to mantain consistency for indexing primary sources across text and captions. Similarly, I have used the spelling "Udaipur," rather than "Udayapura," in the poetry title *Udaipur rī gajal*, to avoid confusion in references to the place that most concerns the book. For the Hindi titles of primary sources, I have retained diacritics throughout the text. I have eschewed diacritics for the names of languages, people, and places. The appendix gives transliterated verses of literary works noted in the chapters, alongside my translations. Selected transliterated inscriptions related to artworks, paintings, and painted letters are included in the endnotes. I have followed the Library of Congress transliteration scheme. Calendric conversions from *vikram saṃvat* (VS) were calculated by subtracting fifty-seven and thus are only approximate.

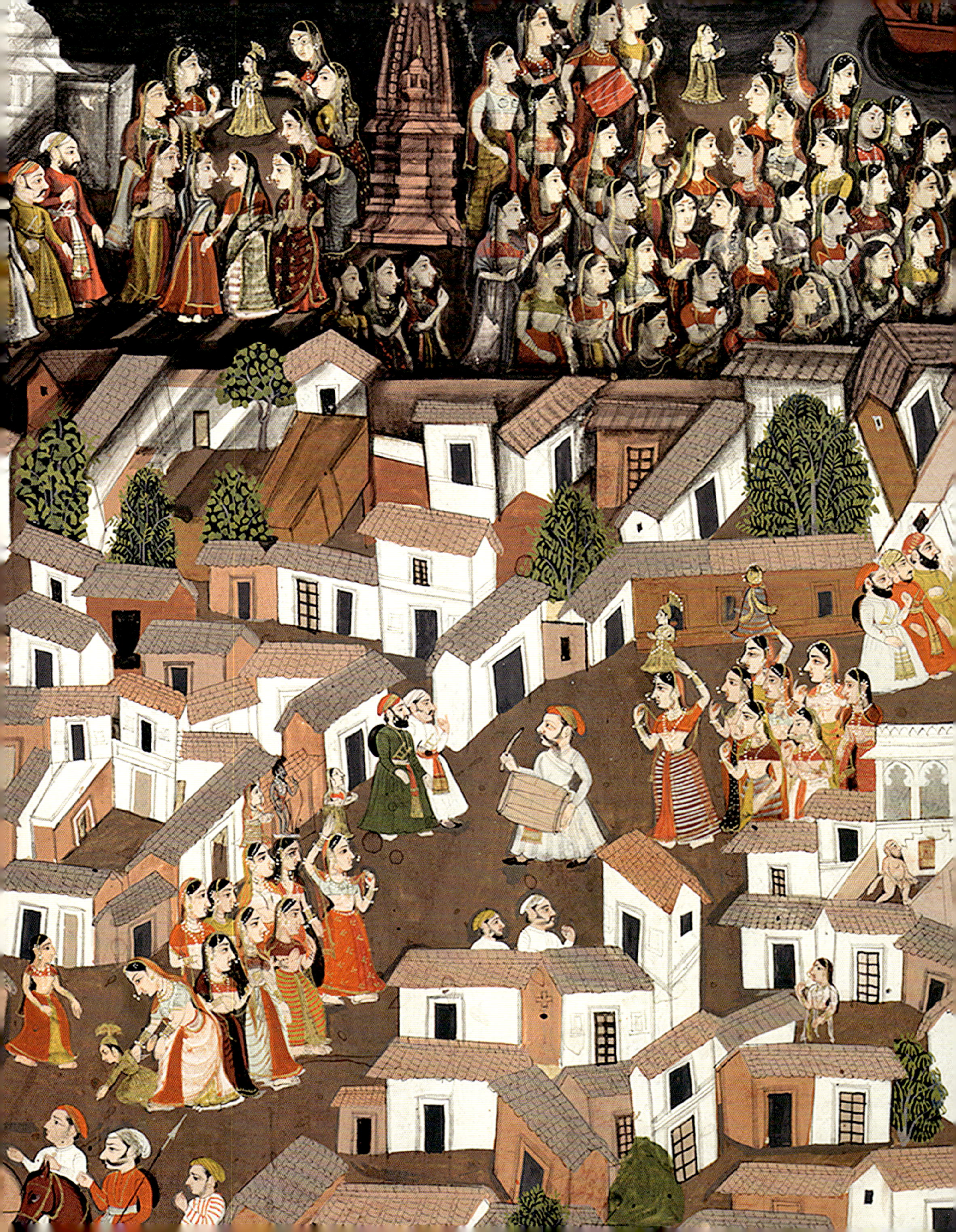

INTRODUCTION

Medium of Moods and Picturing of Place

AGRA, 1610

An invitation, painted and written on a paper scroll, opens with a depiction of the Mughal emperor Jahangir (r. 1605–27), seated under a white pavilion issuing a *farmān*, a decree (fig. I.1). Jahangir, at the request of Agra's merchants and monks, had proclaimed that all of his subjects were forbidden from killing animals during the twelve holy days of the Jain religious calendar. The painting's transregional audience includes imperial officers, aristocratic nobles, and erudite priests, dressed in distinguished attire and identified by scribal notations (fig. I.2). Both dress and text suggest they come from northern and western India, Persia, Bukhara, Europe, Arabia, and Turkic lands. Standing beside a white-clad Jain monk labeled "Pandit Vivekharsh," the raja Ramdas is shown holding aloft the rolled-up *farmān* in one hand.[1] The letter written on the scroll's other end includes the names of Agra's prominent merchants, who by sending the painted letter-scroll delivered the emperor's proclamation and invited the eminent Jain monk Shri Vijaysena Suri to inaugurate a new temple.[2] They hoped the letter would impress the monk, also depicted as the monarchical figure seated under a blue and gold umbrella, and motivate him to travel from the Gujarat coast to their inland city (fig. I.3).

The scribe writes that the painter, Usta Salivahana, who was in attendance at the court, has captured the mood (*bhāva*) of the moment that the drums sounded. The scribe invites the audience to "imagine the mood" of the durbar and city in one resonant instant by directing the recipient to "view the painted letter" to gain access to the momentous occasion.[3] Indeed, the painter drew the messenger monk unrolling and displaying a paper scroll to the invited monk.

UDAIPUR, 1715–20

Almost one hundred years after Salivahana represented the mood of Agra's durbar, by the late seventeenth century, painters hailing from the lake city of Udaipur in northwestern India had begun experimenting with picturing the sensorial, embodied experience of space. One such picture of spectacular moods, *Maharana Sangram Singh II at the Gangaur Boat Procession*, shows the Udaipur king and his companions viewing the springtime festival Gangaur, dedicated to the goddess Gauri, the wife of Shiva, which counted the joys of harvest

Detail of fig. I.4

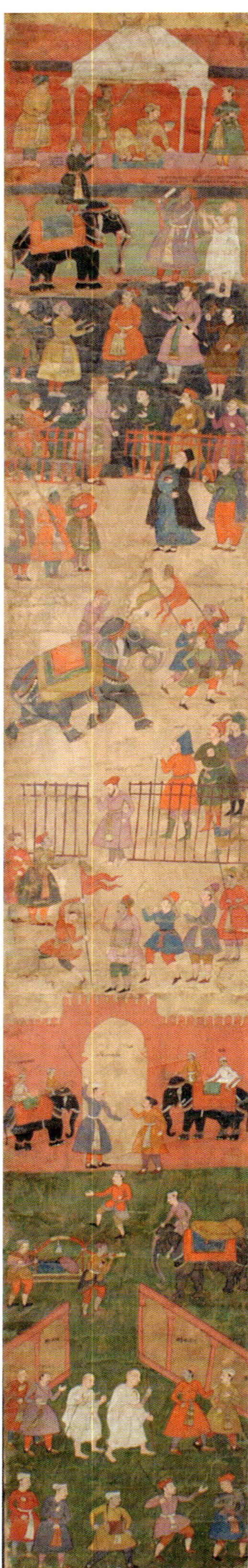

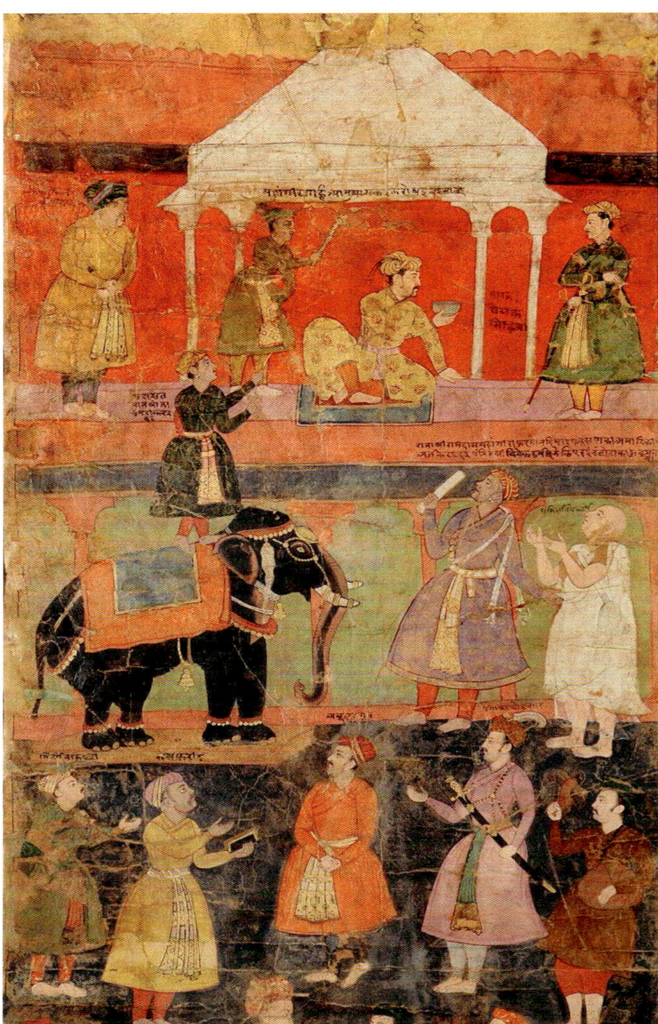

I.1. *Letter of Invitation to the Jain Monk Vijaysena Suri*, Usta Salivahana, 1610, Agra. Opaque watercolor and ink on paper, 284.7 × 32.2 cm. Lalbhai Dalpatbhai Institute of Indology, Ahmedabad; LDII.542.

I.2. Detail of fig. I.1. Depiction of Emperor Jahangir's durbar, with the Raja Ramdas and Pandit Vivekharsha receiving the scroll representing the imperial decree and invitation to travel.

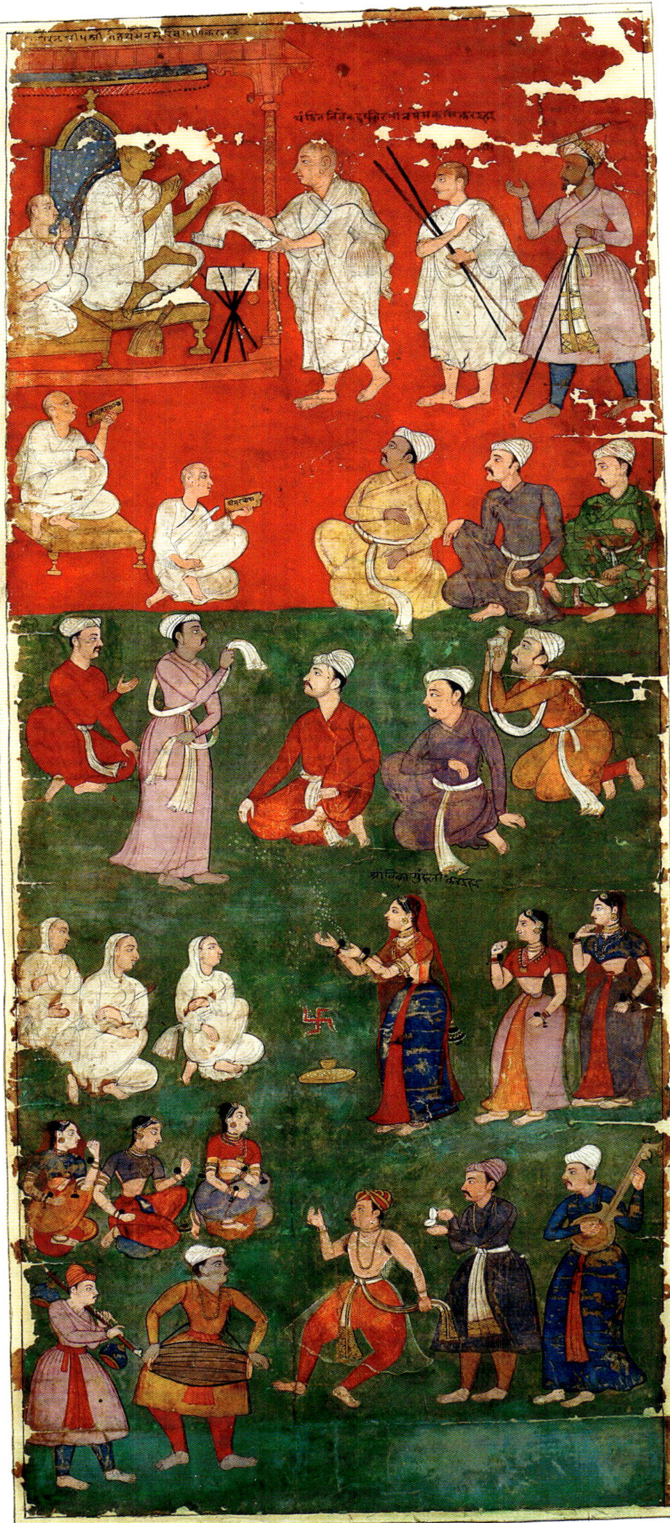

I.3. Detail of fig. I.1. Depiction of the messenger monk displaying the scroll to Shri Vijaysena Suri, shown seated at top left.

and matrimony (fig. I.4). The unnamed painter depicted the king Sangram Singh II (r. 1710–34), his visage easily identified by a gold nimbus painted around his head, and his courtiers on a royal barge three times, to denote the entourage's movement in Lake Pichola. In the upper register of the painting, the artist skillfully employed chiaroscuro to render a night view of the lake and the town on its opposite shore. Parts of the urban precincts are brightened to convey an effect of wall surfaces lit up by blazing torches and rockets. The delicate thin strokes, sprays, and dots in metallic gold sparkle against the dark-hued sky and water. The variety of pyrotechnic displays—including rockets, floating lamps, and radiating aureoles—creates the effect of a shimmering surface that glows in pockets. By contrast, the lower register, a busy urban landscape packed with colorful city dwellers and festivalgoers amid white houses and temples, lends the painting's surface fluorescent brightness. The throngs of women worshipping Gauri are seen carrying on their heads figurines that will soon be taken to the lakeside for ablutions, accompanied by performances of song and dance.

The scribe's inscription on the back of the painting identifies the painted subject as the king and his companions viewing the Gangaur spectacle.[4] The painter's strikingly distinguished renderings of the two registers, of the king's processional boat party in the lake and the commoners in the street, are equally elaborate, thus creating a picture of mutual admiration by each group of the other—and their enchanted immersion in the sparkling city's celebratory and convivial mood.

UDAIPUR, 1820

Another hundred years later, James Tod, the first senior British colonial administrator in northwestern India, who served with the East India Company in central and western India from 1799 to 1822, evocatively described the landscape of Udaipur's lakes and valley, noting the inability of words to match its real beauty.[5] Tod's assistant agent, Patrick Waugh, an amateur artist on their expeditions, renders a picturesque watercolor, *View of the Palace of Oodipoor*, in which the lake waters merge into bush-clad outcrops (fig. I.5). Tod's ekphrasis interweaves a historical narrative. First, he enumerates Udaipur's undulating mountains, the scented lake waters, and the sensuous materiality of the marble "columns, baths, reservoirs, fountains, often inlaid with mosaics," of the palace built in the middle of the lake.[6] Then he damns its royal patrons. In the lake palaces—from which Tod saw a

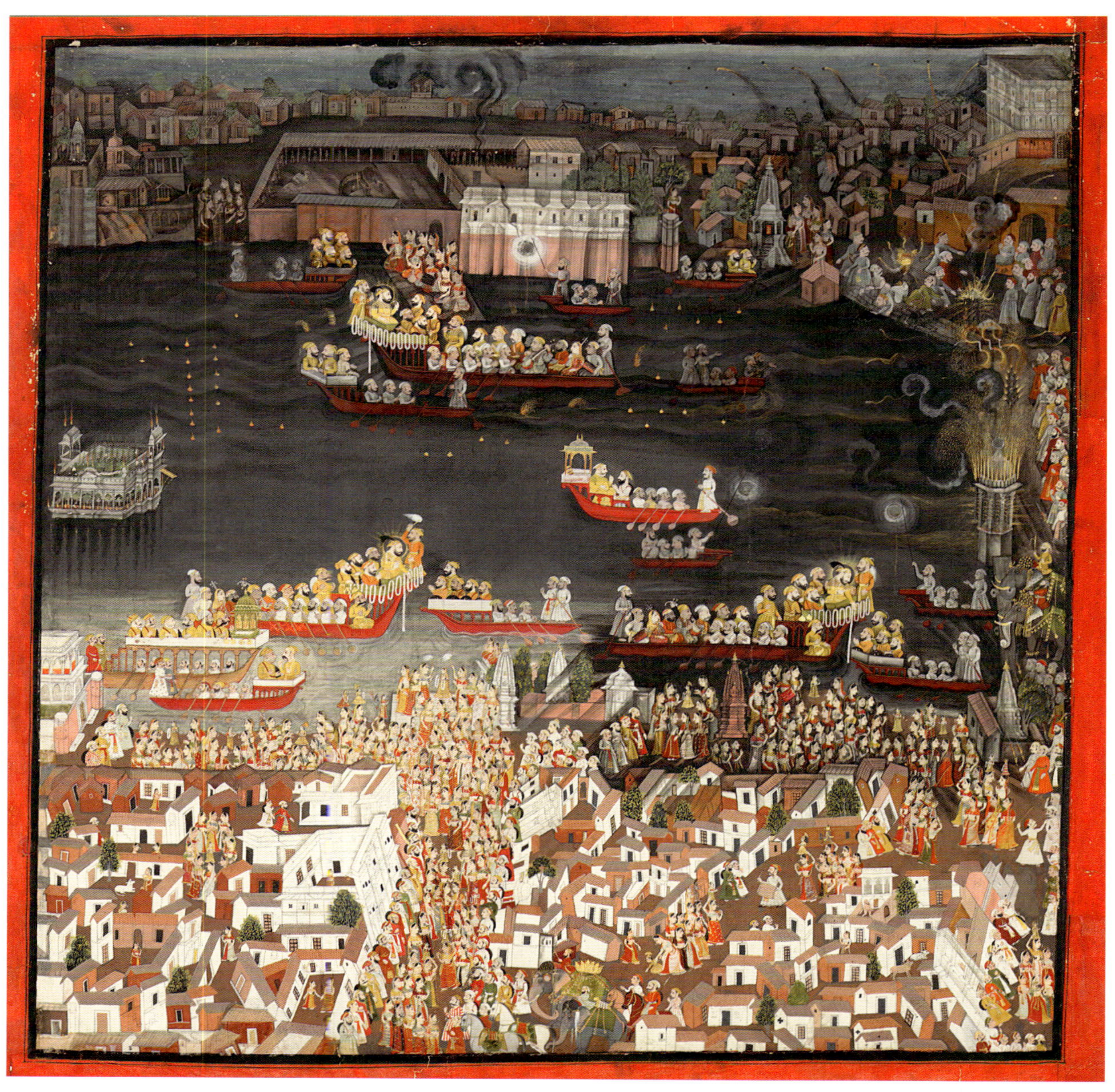

I.4. *Maharana Sangram Singh II at the Gangaur Boat Procession*, c. 1715–20, Udaipur. Gouache and gold on paper, 78.7 × 78.74 cm. The City Palace Museum, Udaipur; 2012.19.0014_R. Photography courtesy of the Freer Gallery of Art and Arthur M. Sackler Gallery, Smithsonian Institution. Photograph by Neil Greentree.

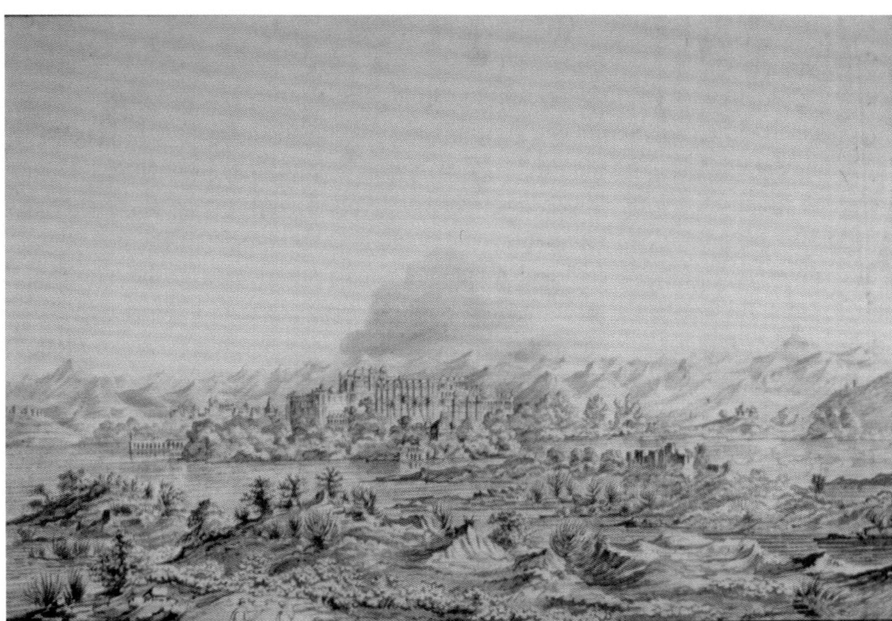

I.5. *View of the Palace of Oodipoor*, Patrick Waugh, 1820. Watercolor on paper, 27 × 37 cm. The Royal Asiatic Society, London; 037.003.

"landscape to which even its inspirations could frame an equal"—he reckoned, "the Seesodia princes and chieftains recreate[d] during two generations, exchanging the din of arms for *voluptuous inactivity*."[7] Tod's rhetoric of praise for Udaipur's lake environs destabilized the relation between reality and representation but also differentiated between the past and the present, seeking to underscore the shift in moods—from prosperity to exuberance to decadence to decline. The rocks, mounds, and shrubs in the foreground subsume Waugh's view of the lakefront palaces, suggesting a similar sentiment and a Lake Pichola that had almost dried out, desiccated of life.

Pictures of moods possess the overpowering ability to make places real and times memorable—to create worlds. Since the third century, the poets and intellectuals who shaped premodern aesthetics recognized the art of generating *bhāva*—a word encompassing moods, emotions, and feelings. Udaipur's painters expanded the conceptualization of *bhāva* in visual terms, rendering moods of the material world around them. What was implied in recognizing a painted vignette as a presentation of the mood of a real place at a historic time? How did painters compose the feel of spaces in a way that made places visible as exceptional, even desirable sites for travel or as places to proudly claim as one's own? How did audiences perceive pictorial moods, and how do we historicize their practice of sensing moods? Why did Udaipur's painters circulate across courtly and non-courtly worlds and repeat across highly valued artworks and objects hardly deemed as art the impression of eighteenth-century locales as plentiful, pleasurable, and pious? *The Place of Many Moods* attempts to answer these questions.

THE PLACE OF MANY MOODS

With its lime-washed white palaces overlooking lakes, Udaipur has stood since around 1559 as the capital city of the erstwhile regional court of Mewar.[8] As a site, it evokes the imaginary of an oasis within the dry desert landscape of the contemporary state of Rajasthan in northwestern India (fig. I.6). The city has captured the gaze of visitors from around the world for at least the past three centuries. Udaipur's early modern painters were the first to give visual form to their enchantment with the valley's sustaining lakes and flowing streams, revealing powerfully immersive and politically contingent conceptions of a place's *bhāva*. Over the course of the eighteenth century, they emerged as experts in devising new, imaginative ways to visualize historical moods, mining the aesthetics of idealized emotions, enduring natural and built environments, ephemeral atmospheres, and celebrated seasons. In their hundreds of artworks significantly larger than portraits or illustrated manuscripts, they represented the courtly worlds and cities of rajas, sacralized landscapes of many gods, and bazaars bustling with merchants, pilgrims, and craftspeople, thus creating urban imaginings of Udaipur's local streets and lake palaces as well as

I.6. View of the City Palace complex, overlooking Lake Pichola and the Jagniwas lake palace (today the Taj Lake-Palace Hotel), Udaipur, nestled in the Aravalli valley and established as the premodern Mewar court's capital in c. 1559. Photograph by Emma Natalya Stein.

I.7. (*Following spread*) Lake view of the City Palace, Udaipur. Media Office, Eternal Mewar, Udaipur.

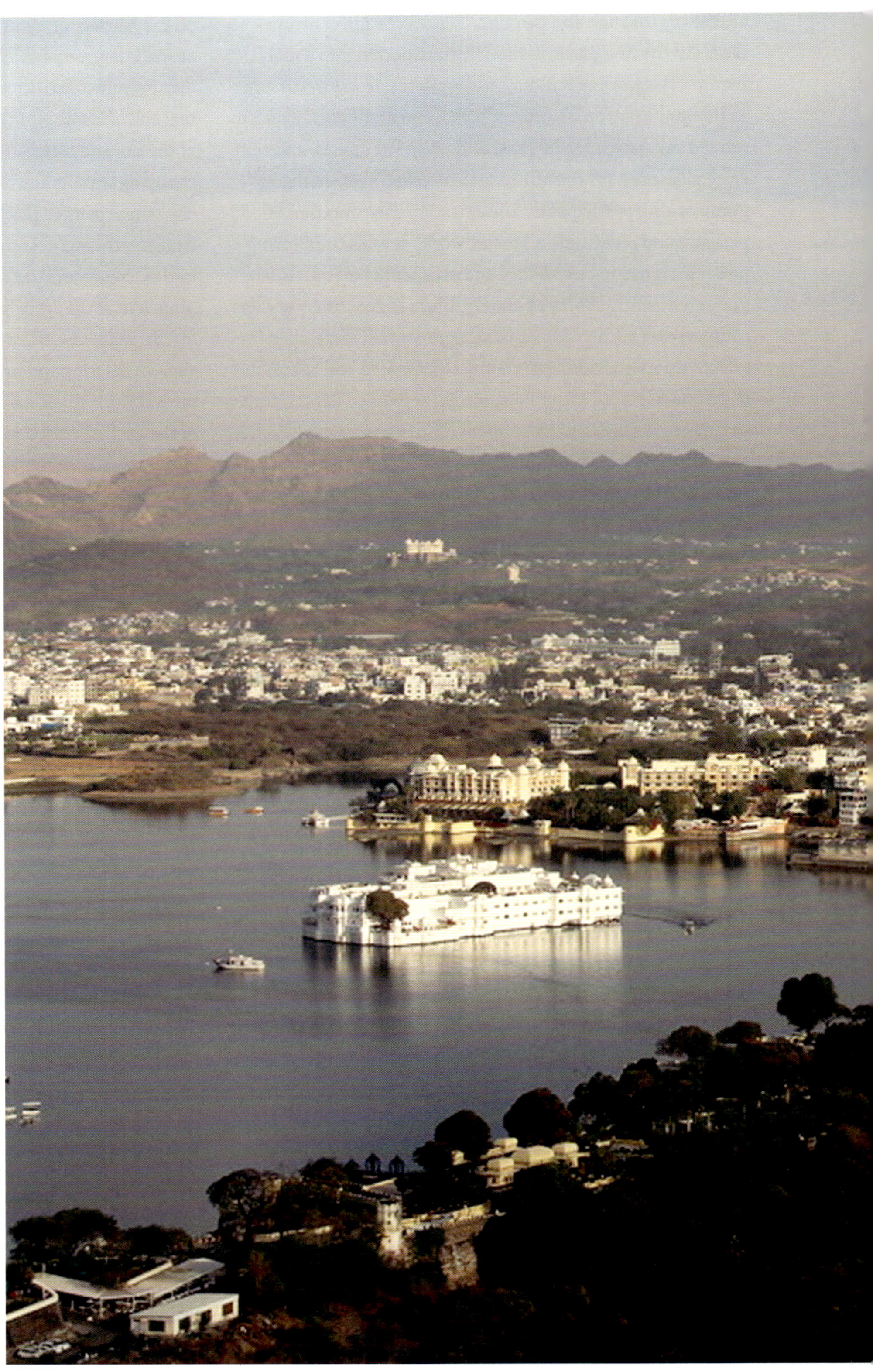

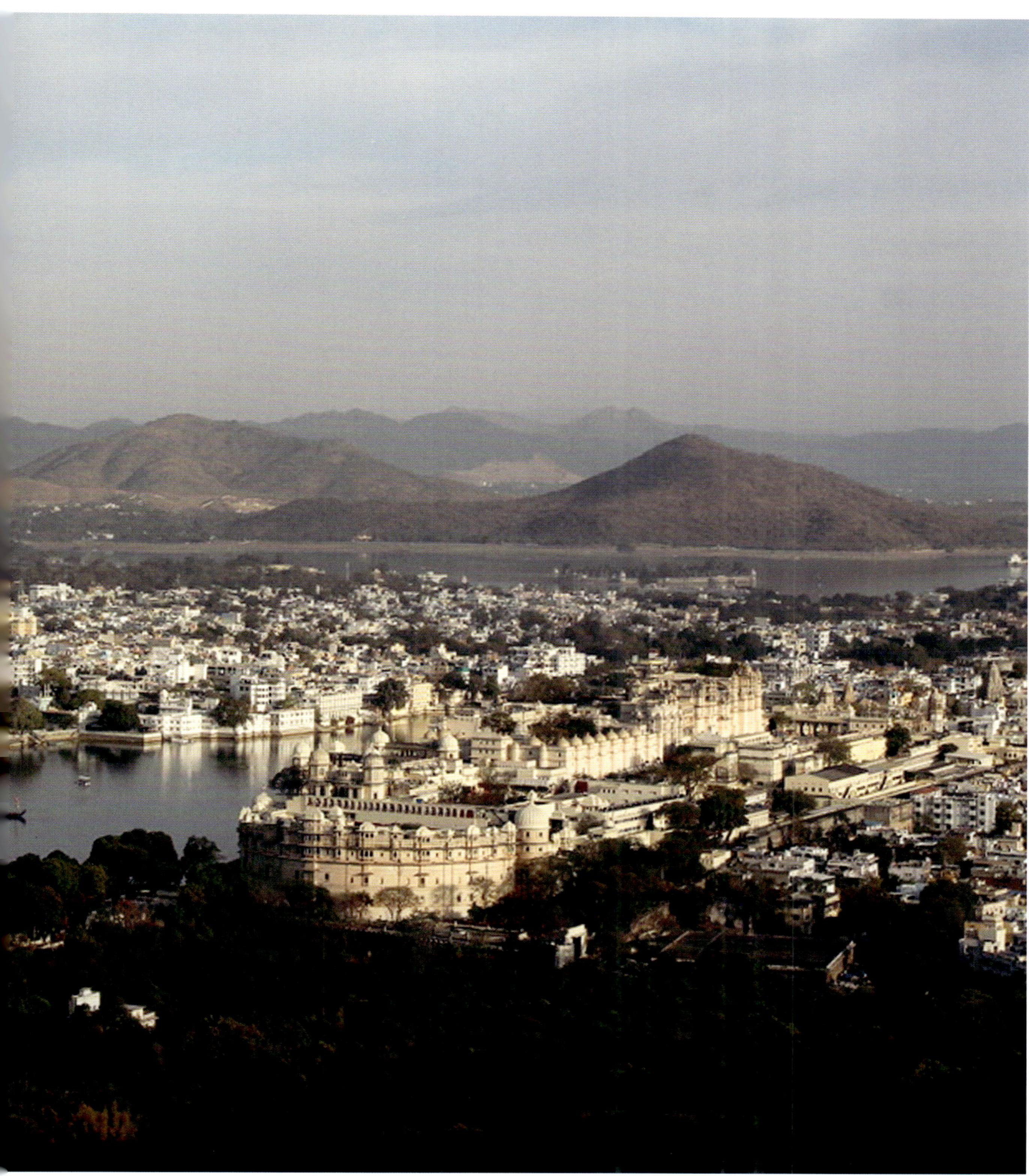

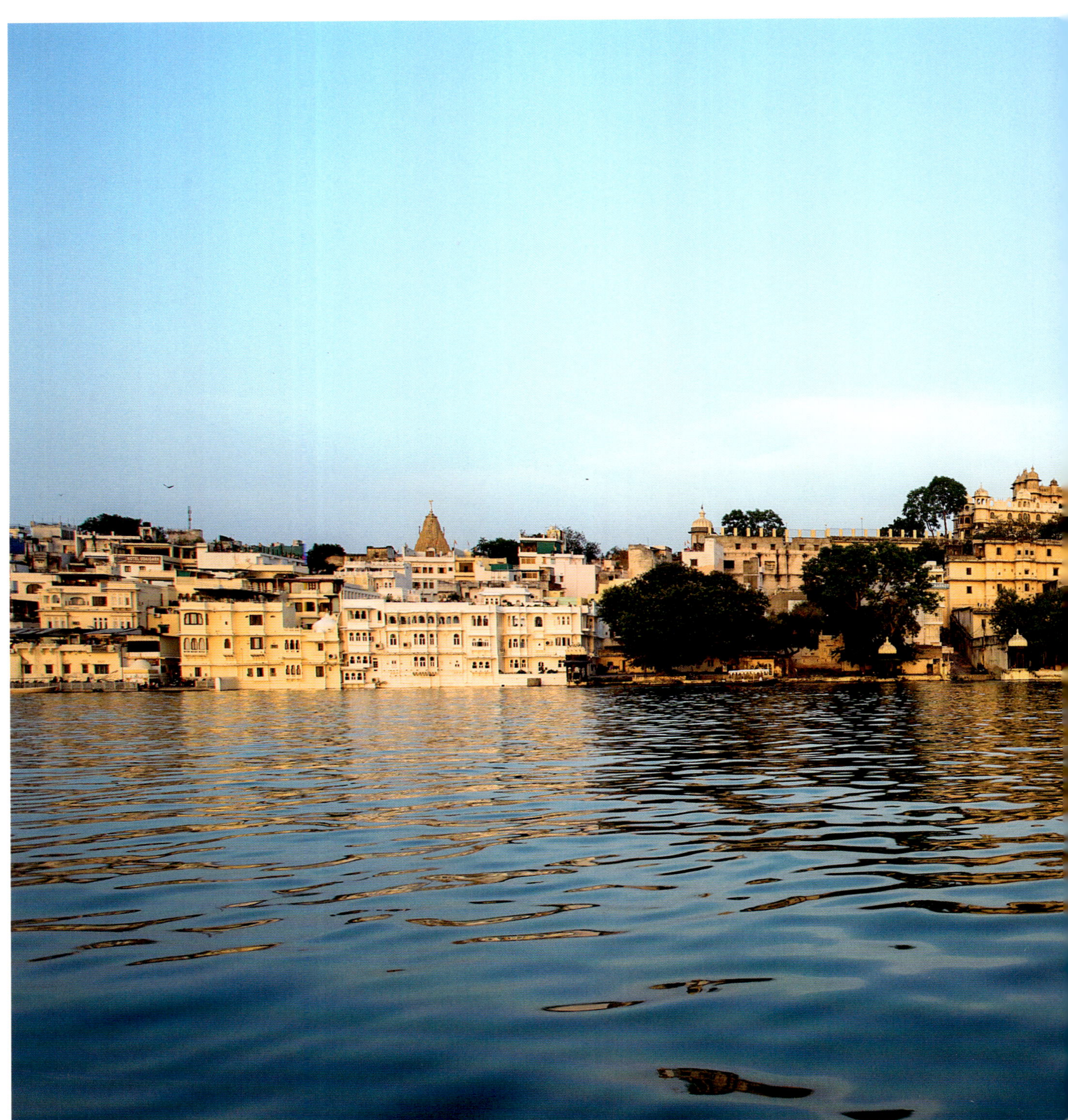

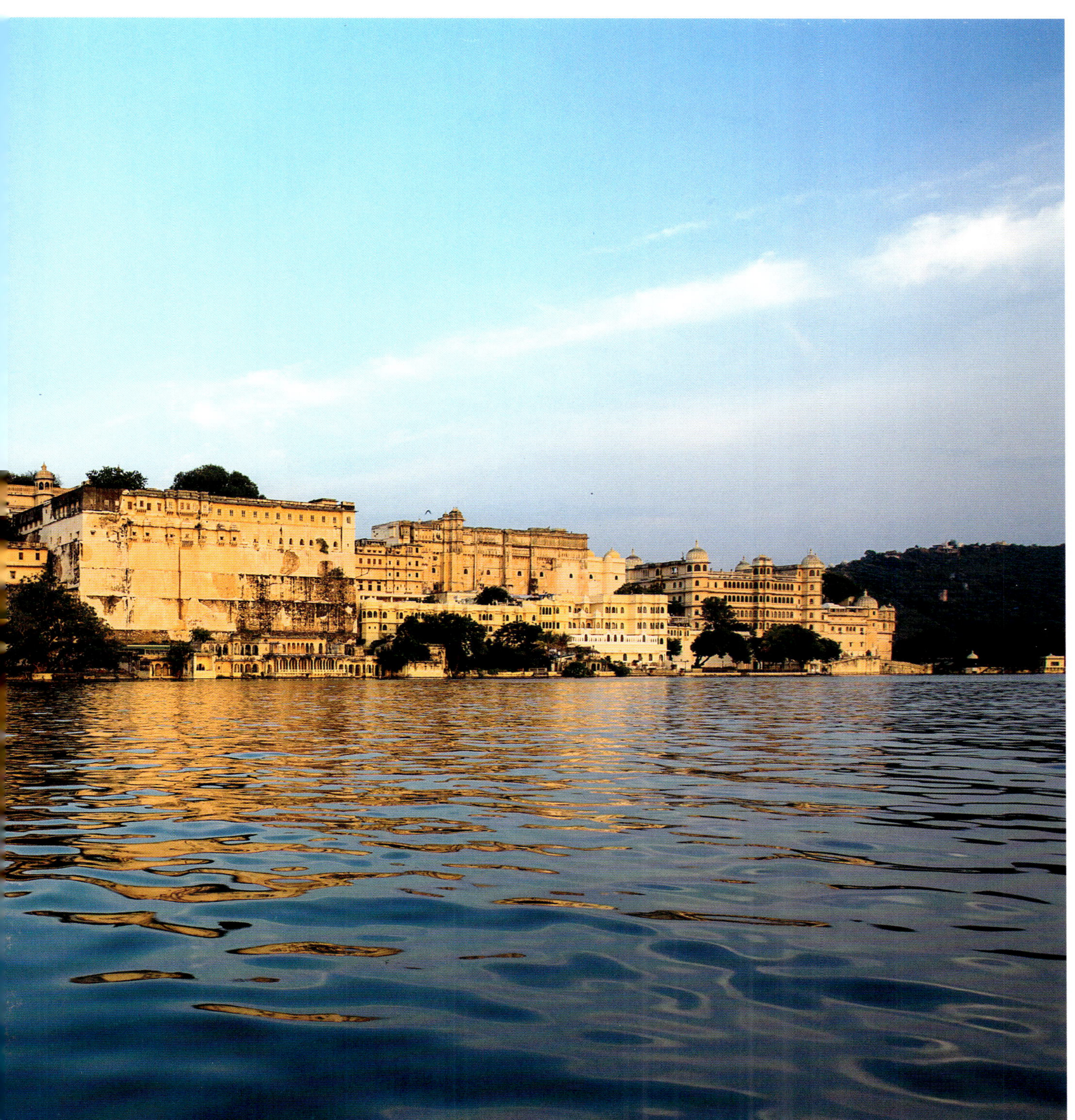

groups of works that reflect upon specific moods, celebrated across media such as poetry, music, and painting. Such groups of works explore the emotions and feelings invoked by the seasons and atmospheres of monsoon and spring or the pleasures generated by the sensate environments of gardens and lake palaces. Painters, like poets, saw *bhāva* as a malleable, multivalent, and valuable concept for seamlessly entwining the embodied, historicized experience of a place with the aesthetics of idealized spaces and times. Recognizing moods as a pictorial priority leads to fundamentally reconsidering the ontological role and the consumption of such artworks. The plurality of images and epistemic knowledge that informs their production implies that their efficacy was not bound to one genre.

Paintings that made moods of Udaipur's locales paramount illustrate the historical stakes for creating attuned communities in India's long eighteenth century. The engulfing of all the depicted figures in the entrancing sensorium of the scents, sounds, and sights suggested in the painting *Maharana Sangram Singh II at the Gangaur Boat Procession* creates a meta-picture. It invited courtly audiences to recall the immersive mood of the historical spectacle, the confab with friends in the lake city, while demanding that aficionados similarly immerse themselves in admiring the beauty of the painted picture itself. *The Place of Many Moods* explores moods of a place by considering what they do and their changing conceptions, contradictions, and ambitions. The artifacts considered present an emotional sensibility, which can be historicized to lead us to think about the sociability they produced.[24] Thus the challenge in addressing poetic and painted artifacts that idealize emotions, represent historical moods, and highlight sensorial experiences lies in identifying precisely the nature of their engagement with aesthetics and their affective work.[25] These strands collectively shaped intense "affective economies" within and attachments to the city of lakes.[26]

I view the multiple foci and painterly effects of *Maharana Sangram Singh II at the Gangaur Boat Procession*—almost dizzying at times and not instantly apparent—also seen in other painters' compositions of places, as making a formal argument about interpretation itself. This visual multiplicity asserts the plural nature of the artworks that presented the moods of places while also demanding that we adopt a methodological heterogeneity. To trace the aesthetic, epistemic, and political threads that run through the art of picturing moods, I have followed the environmental constituents—mountains, rivers, rains—that shaped Udaipur's lands and its experience. In researching this book I have inhabited the material world of lakes and lake palaces, architectures of courtyards, and altitudes of terraces, and I have dwelled upon their imaginings in expressive media: paintings, drawings, painted letters, daily court diaries, diplomatic correspondence, and the poetry of esteemed court poets and amateurs—traveling monks who illuminate the historical paths of strolling and point of views for admiring places. These eighteenth-century intellectuals' contemplations on the sensorial and the atmospheric gave voice to descriptive modes of world making that made affective images as important in rendering real places as they did in imagining mythical places. In yet other instances, I have tracked the political roles and personal bonds of represented participants—kings, nobles, and colonial officers; merchants, messengers and monks; and ordinary folk and court attendants—whom painters scrupulously included to create busy images of worlds immersed in praiseworthy moods.

The arguments of *The Place of Many Moods* concern the history of aesthetics, the history of affect, the history of painting places on paper, the history of the building of exceptional spaces, and the histories of eighteenth-century politics, literature, religion, and mobility to make sense of artifacts that yield new questions about Indian painters' visualization of deeply sensorial urban imaginaries. In between these lines of inquiry, mood of a place emerges as a phenomenon that was created to do enormous work, to be powerfully effective in making worlds feel alive on paper and cohere together on land. Beyond the intimacy of the story of a city, a region, or a subfield, *The Place of Many Moods* raises questions about relations between the sensorium and spatial knowledge, the affect and efficacy of artifacts, and the work, thinking, and agency embedded within meticulous aesthetic constructions of historical moods.

The representations of moods at Udaipur may not be shared symmetrically across South Asia, western Asia, and Europe. The creation of circumscribed assemblies, the building of spaces such as gardens, pleasure pavilions, and coffeehouses, and the consumption of material objects, books, and poetry, however, comprised activities central to cultivating friendships and the making of knowledge and beauty in the eighteenth century.[27] The artistic contemplation of passions and pleasures attached to places was integrated as much to concepts of sensorial immersion and practices of bonding as to artifacts and practices of mapping. *The Place of Many Moods* explicates the phenomenon of Udaipur's contribution of a novel art history form that was synchronic with interests across Eurasia in establishing sociability based on structures of feeling and experiences of emotions. Besides the trans-regional conversation on eighteenth-century pleasure, the affective turn across fields has generated comparative and intercultural historicized perspectives on the relation of senses to perception and to emotions.[28] For premodern India's intellectuals, this relationship never stopped being fascinating.

EMOTION, IMAGINATION, SENSATION

In common parlance today, we understand *bhāvanā*—a concept closely allied to the occurence and ability of sensing the *bhāva* of an event, conversation, or atmosphere—as an implication of one's feeling for something or someone or even a strong intuition or judgment. The prehistory of both terms, however, was tied to the enterprise of literary imagination and the actualization of literary emotions. In sixteenth-century southern India, David Shulman finds a particular self-awareness in the historical use of *bhāvanā*, especially for the "mind-born calling of a world, any world, into being."[29] The subtleties of *bhāvanā*, as debated by Sanskrit logicians and grammarians, infused the term with agency and potentiality, and in some cases also tied it to "mental generation of things such as memory."[30] Based on a corpus of classical texts on Sanskrit aesthetics, Sheldon Pollock translates *bhāva* as emotion that is less psychological and more affective and physical, a state that may incite emotions or may constitute emotions within it.[31] As such, the shifting intellectual history of *bhāva* and *bhāvanā* make static understandings untenable.[32] These theoretical traditions of aesthetics from Sanskrit literature were propelled by the seventeenth century in northern India's new courtly poetry in the vernacular of Brajbhasha, a literary dialect of classical Hindi. Aesthetic theory in Brajbhasha poetry included practice, which Allison Busch finds in the emphases placed on exemplification and description: these were equally incisive deliberations on *bhāva* as the stress laid on systematization and typology of *rasa* in Sanskrit treatises.[33] Hindi poets innovated by saturating their verses with "sound and sense" as well as a "wondrous rapture" with the world.[34] The scholarly emphases on poets' layered and varied engagements with emotion and imagination, especially in terms of how active processes of creation may reside in the root of *bhāvanā*, are instructive—not necessarily for directly translating the scribal iterations of *bhāva* in relation to paintings but for the methodological paths we may adopt for tracking the artistic constitution of *bhāva* in the picturing of the moods of places on paper.

Likewise, *rasikas*, or connoisseurs, were seen as astute men and women adept at experiencing *rasa*, the aesthetic taste, flavor, or essence of any art. While early thinkers generated theories of *rasa* in Sanskrit that focused on the arts of dance and drama, poetry and painting were considered allied arts. In his foundational *Nāṭyaśāstra* (Science of drama), dated to the third to fourth century, Bharata laid out eight types of *rasa*: love, mirth, wonder, anger, courage, compassion, fear, and disgust.[35] He drew analogies between aesthetic appreciation and the sense of taste, according to Pollock, "on the grounds both of the physicality of emotion—it is something we feel, not something we think—and of the blending of ingredients that complex tastes and aesthetic moods both evince."[36] From its very inception, the conceptualization of emotions was theorized as a temporal unraveling and kindling of feeling. The inclusion of somatic response gestured an intellectual interest in codifying the experience of real emotions and embodiment, and not the systematization of aesthetics alone. This explication was also a call to all artists—poets, performers, and painters—to create material, visual, textual, and sonic artifacts that invoked aesthetic emotions in ideal ways so that art offered moments of transformational experiences for a *rasika*.

Contemporaneous treatises dating to the third century defined *kama*, which literally means pleasure or desire, not simply an isolated practice of sex, but as a component of an aesthetically encoded world of the eponymous Hindu god of love and of the urbane man, the *rasika*.[37] The connoisseurs of this idealized world of delight, which Daud Ali calls the "'*kama* world' on earth," were courtly men.[38] For kings, a "properly lived worldly" life included "proper enjoyments" of material things like wines, perfumes, garlands, and jewelry. Consumption, likewise, was defined and refined by men in the Indo-Persianate worlds of pre-Mughal sultanates and imperial Mughal circles. The education of a mirza, the cultivated gentleman, outlined within the genre of *mīrzā nāmah*, the Persian conduct manuals written in India in the late seventeenth and early eighteenth century, speaks specifically, as Rosalind O'Hanlon argues, to the emergence of new nobility by the late seventeenth century.[39] A high value was placed on a variety of etiquette and knowledge, from cultivating new tastes to discerning artistic cultures, refining bodily manners, and acquiring hunting skills, within imperial durbars and regional courts. The connoisseurship ideals demanded of the mirza of

Indo-Persianate worlds echo those enlisted for the *rasika* of Sanskritic worlds. Both emphasized sensous, spiritual, and emotional experience.

The peculiarly affective language that suffused courtly life, aesthetics, and literature continued to be deployed and recast across religious, courtly, and intellectual milieus in medieval and early modern India. Poets engaged conceptions like *bhāva* and *rasa* in transcultural ways from the fourteenth to the eighteenth century in practices associated with Muslim, Hindu, and Jain patrons. The newness of late fourteenth-century Hindavi Sufi romances, such as the *Candāyan*, composed by Maulana Daud, lay in the combination of Persian verse narratives and Sanskrit aesthetics, and of classical languages and regional poetic and spoken forms of northern India.[40] By revealing layers of implication, Aditya Behl eloquently reads the poet's use of "*rasa* as the keystone" in romance verse stories to elicit emotional responses from audiences.[41] Similarly, the eminent poet Bhanudatta, under his patrons at the Nizamshahi court of Ahmadnagar in the Deccan, created the *Rasamañjarī* (Bouquet of literary emotion, c. 1500), which explores the nature of aesthetic emotions by describing heroines (*nāyikā*) and heroes (*nāyaka*) of Sanskrit literature.[42] At the Mughal court of the emperor Akbar (r. 1556–1605), Abu al-Fazl, the illustrious historian, in his *Ā'īn-i Akbarī* (Edicts of Akbar, c. 1595), written in Persian, acknowledged Bhanudatta's poetry as an exemplary work for its discussion of the nine sentiments associated with literature in Hindustan. The late sixteenth-century *Kitāb-i nauras* (Book of nine/new emotional essences), composed by Sultan Ibrahim Adil Shah II (r. 1580–1627) in Dakhni at the Bijapur court in the south, systematized an aesthetic interest in *nau* as "nine" or "new"—that is, the mixing of nine types of *rasa* or the making of a new *rasa*, thus emphasizing the feeling and emotional experience of art.[43] Ripe with tantalizing allusions to mixed audiences and interreligious devotional imagery, it generated an idealized vision of a new city, new music, new arts, new wines, and so on and so forth. This trajectory of literary *bhāva* displaces any neat divisions we may want to hold onto between medieval and early modern or between early modern and colonial. A major impetus for poets and patrons innovating practices of imagining lay in introducing established aesthetic ideas as centered on emotions and experience to new audiences.

One significant way by which painters engaged the concepts of *rasa* and *bhāva* was through representing aesthetic systematizations and erotic moods composed in poetry. For instance, Bhanudatta's poetic descriptions of types of heroines and emotions in his *Rasamañjarī* were artistically visualized by seventeenth-century painters from Udaipur as well as the courts of Punjab and the Deccan. In northern India, Mughal emperors, imperial officers, and Rajput kings patronized poetic texts in Sanskrit and *rītigrantha*—manuals on literary theory that elaborated *rasas* and *nāyikās*—in classical Hindi.[44] Both genres engaged the rhetoric of *rasa* as a literary emotion for imagining portraits of ideal emperors and for expressing imperial interest and connoisseurship in diverse literary and intellectual registers. One of the three works on aesthetic theory that the leading Brajbhasha poet Keshavdas composed between 1591 and 1602 at the sixteenth-century Rajput court of Orchha, the *Rasikpriyā* (Connoisseurs' delights, 1591), directly addressed *rasikas*.[45] The theoretic definition of each *rasa* was accompanied by an example that featured the love story of Radha and Krishna. These invited connoisseurs to imagine all the nine *rasas*—from how Krishna displayed the erotic mood (*śṛṅgāra*) by stealing the clothes of Radha and her friends to how even the gods were overcome by wonder (*adbhuta*) at seeing Krishna's play, while Krishna always embodied the emotional state of quiescence (*śānta*) at heart.

The aesthetic effects innovated in the terse verses of Keshavdas were especially savored by Udaipur's painters and patrons of the late sixteenth and seventeenth century. A painted page from Udaipur, made around 1640, depicts the non-illusionistic compartments dividing the spaces and emotional states occupied by the lovers, the blue god Krishna and his consort Radha (fig. I.8). Court paintings such as these, like other arts, Molly Aitken writes, were "designed to move viewers to experience feelings," to partake in the imagination of an emotional intensity of separation.[46] The turning of the folios of the illustrated *Rasikpriyā* serially evokes the expectation of Krishna and Radha's union and of the devotees' perception of a longing that is akin to their own desire for Krishna. In a page from the mid-seventeenth-century devotional and poetic manuscript of the *Gīta Govinda* (Song of Krishna), which praised the love of the Hindu god Krishna and his consort Radha, attributed to the Udaipur court artist Sahib Din, the lovers are seen within a red-colored space created by the arched bower, or *kuñj*, praised as the ideal place for lovemaking, where there was "forever spring" (fig. I.9).[47] As the image of the bower was reiterated in poetry, manuscripts, multiple folios of a single series, and across disparate genres, it became a devotional icon that carried along familiar associations of love and longing. The forest beyond the *kuñj* on the right in this image is equally resplendent: trees painted in greens, reds, oranges, and browns, which also hold the attention of

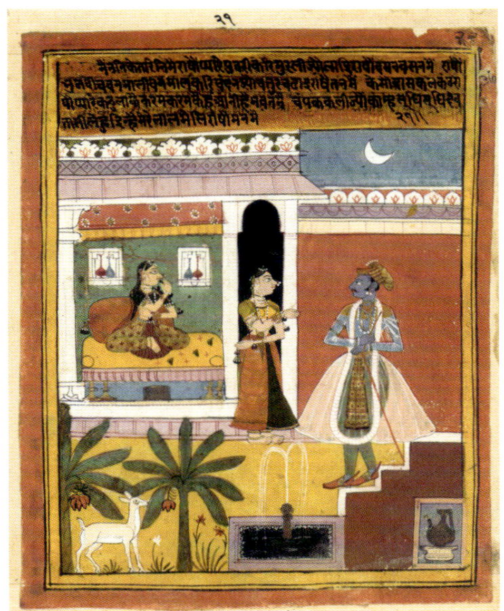

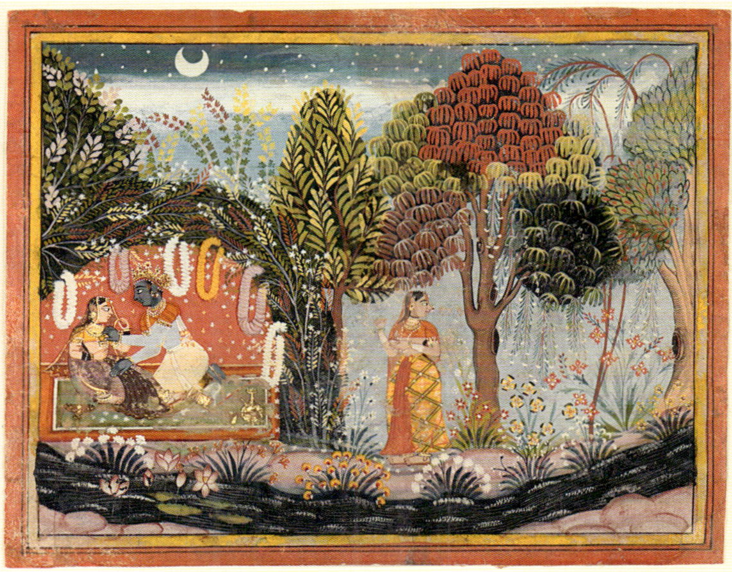

I.8. "Radha awaits Krishna," from the *Rasikpriyā*, by the poet Keshavdas, c. 1640, Udaipur. Opaque watercolor on paper, 25.7 × 21.6 cm. Freer Gallery of Art, Smithsonian Institution, Washington, DC; gift of Mr. and Mrs. Charles Page, F1991.91.

I.9. "Krishna and Radha in a Bower," from a dispersed *Gīta Govinda*, attributed to Sahib Din, c. 1665, Udaipur. Opaque watercolor on paper, 24.4 × 19.7 cm. The Metropolitan Museum of Art, New York; Gift of Ernest Erickson Foundation, 1988.103.

Radha's companion (*sakhī*). Her gaze, away from the lovers, toward the other direction, evokes the image of a deeper jungle beyond the physical page. Such immersive abstractions invited audiences to perceive the feeling invoked by forest beauty and the spring season; today they offer a glimpse into the interests of the mid-seventeenth century before Udaipur painters turned to admiring their city's lake environs.

Real places and the empirical world played a central role in reshaping the imaginations of painters and poets alike. When Keshavdas described the real-life gardens of his student Pravin Ray, a courtesan, he emphasized not only verisimilitude but also the stirring of *bhāva* and the activation of feelings and emotions that one feels in real and ideal places alike.[48] The views that the court poet Kavi Nandram and the traveling Jain monk poets Yati Jaichand and Kavi Khetal offered in their urban poetry suggest that evoking the many moods of the city of Udaipur and the broader region was meaningful for historical communities. These works of literature have barely been studied or even transcribed; this book introduces select verses in translation for the first time. Nandram, deeply immersed in the moods of the mid-eighteenth-century city, wrote a 405-verse-long poem, *Jagvilās* (World of pleasure), focused on the Udaipur lake palace Jagniwas.[49] It reveals multiple communities bound together by partaking in the delights of a newly built space in the middle of the lake. Many of these early modern poets of northern India drew upon various aesthetic topoi of urban praise, such as *nagara-varṇana*, seen in classical Hindi poetry, and *shahrāshūb*, seen in Persianate literary cultures, revealing the breadth of multilingual practices and mixed audiences.[50] That "*bhāva* of a place" was a meaningful category for historical communities is also evidenced by the sufficient number of instances we have of scribes at Udaipur deploying the term *bhāva* to describe ephemeral and emotive aspects of a place. Painting inventories and scribal accounts found on the backs of numerous paintings attest that scribes used the term to denote the mood and feel of places, of seasons, of momentous spectacles and festivals.[51] *Bhāva* was also used to refer to fleeting moments and the ephemeral sounds, sights, and scents that made places sensate. This scribal vocabulary is reminiscent of Keshavdas's prescriptions in *Kavipriyā* (1601) directed toward poets steeped in the Radha-Krishna universe, in which he examined the material qualities of colors and the feel of fleeting impressions.[52] Using the term for such varied descriptive purposes—across inscriptions and verses—demonstrates the centrality ascribed to *bhāva* for relating acts of imagination and perception.

Scholars have overlooked relationships between historical poetry and depictions of moods of worldly places because history traditionally separates manuscript illustration from other genres of painting, and the study of painting from studies of the other arts.[53] While the relations between *bhāva* and painters, as well as *bhāva* and connoisseurs, did not always result in one-to-one mappings across poetic and painted genres, the intermedial associations between painting, poetry, and places are clearly apparent. Evidence that eighteenth-century connoisseurs understood poetry and painting to be mutually dependent arts is also fairly abundant. The first painted page from the *Sundaraśṛṅgāra* (Beautiful adornments, 1726), for instance, depicts Maharana Sangram Singh II of Udaipur receiving the poet Kaviraj Jagannath and a painter, both of whom are pictured holding a page of writing and a page of painting between them. The verse on the depicted page indicates that the poet may be the supervisor of the manuscript and praises Sangram Singh as he "who understands with sweet discrimination [*sarasavicāra*] the joyous appreciation of pictures."[54] While the following chapters reveal the consumption of associated poetic and painted ideas, they also insist that formal departures seen in the constituting of *rasa* and *bhāva* on paper in precolonial India command our attention on material, compositional, and painterly terms.[55] In spite of silence in textual archives on the ways of knowing, making, and displaying large-scale pictures, instances of sophisticated visual thinking on emotions and places are discernible. By tracing the Udaipur painters' picturing—a tool for visualization that included ways of knowing, drawing, measuring, composing, coloring, layering, juxtaposing, citing, and adapting images—we learn about the actualizing of enchanting moods on paper.[56] The visualization of moods of real places created worlds that far superseded material and living examples, reflecting the ideational power of painters.

PICTURE, LAND, PLACE

The history of picturing lands, thereby producing places on paper, has always been tied to politics, poetics, and embodied practices on the ground. One of art history's founding preoccupations—the mimetic representation of worldly spaces, objects, and peoples—departs from excavating painted places. In one way, rethinking conceptions of landscape ties into older debates on the preoccupation with Cartesian vision in art history and the associated belief in the supremacy of a one-point perspective as a pictorial strategy.[57] As such, the gaze that rendered the concept of space as geometrically isotropic and the eye as singular led to, as Denis Cosgrove writes, "withdrawal of painters' emotional entanglement with the objects depicted in geometricized space."[58] Nonetheless, the shifts in recent years from an exclusive focus on illusionism to knowledge has been spurred by three historiographies that have been fairly trans-regional and not centered exclusively on Europe.

First, the intertwined nature of land and imaging of land with histories of ownership, territorial expansion, and colonialism has been addressed by scholars delving into multiple archives, formulating critical positions across fields from South Asian and African art to British and American art.[59] The more recent turn in humanities, art history included, toward pressing concerns of ecology and climate change has provided the ground for looking at familiar pictures of landscapes and seasons anew.[60] Lastly, integral to the above shifts are the approaches to senses and subjectivity taken up across the humanities and social sciences. They ask you to consider who has done the picturing, how terrains are encountered on the ground and negotiated with the aid of teams and technologies, and how the aesthetics of rendering lands in response to material worlds and to visual tropes reveal or conceal a sense of place. Painted places, as one author has put it, are "sensescapes" rather than landscapes.[61] With the interdisciplinary questions scholars have asked of India's painted lands, while looking anew at well-known artworks, all of the above shifts have made their mark. This book moves the field forward by introducing key questions about moods and affects into the discourse.

The Mughal emperor Babur's textual memoirs and copies of the illustrated *Bāburnāmah* constitute a watershed in the consideration of painted lands. Periods and places of hiatus structured the emperor's act of memorializing his journey into new lands within this first-person account.[62] Babur's writing vividly evokes the sensate, corporeal, and tactile experiences of travelers and arrivals "in and out of place," elucidating the function places perform in art historical inquiries.[63] The moods of these punctuated moments became the sites Akbar's painters illustrated. The well-known double folio depicting Babur as the first Mughal emperor, made around 1590, shows him directing the gardeners who are planting and plowing in the Bagh-i-vafa, the garden of fidelity, which the emperor built on newly acquired lands in Kabul (fig. I.10).[64] This image presents early Mughal gardens as significant

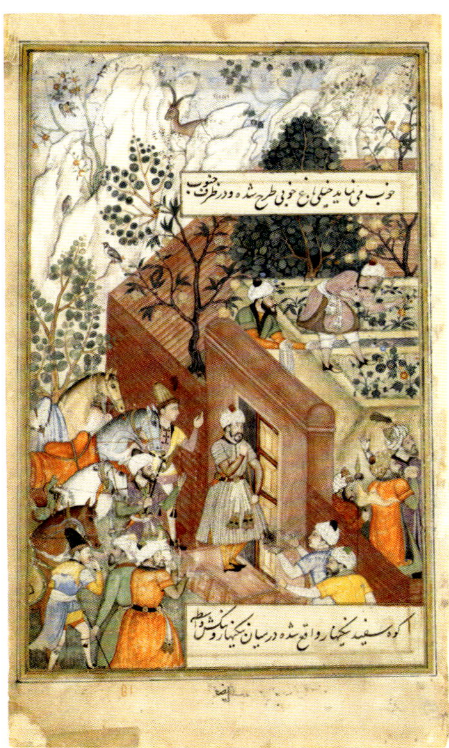

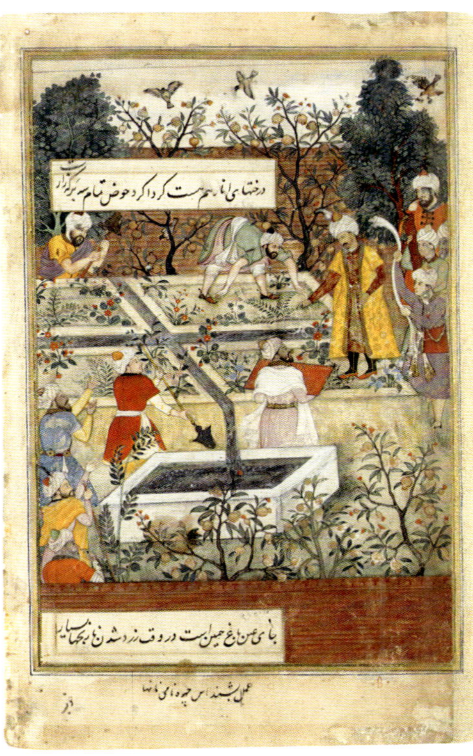

I.10. “Babur Supervises the Laying Out of the Garden of Fidelity in Kabul,” from a *Bāburnāmah* manuscript, Bishndas and Nanha, c. 1590. Opaque watercolor and gold on paper, each page 26.6 × 16.8 cm. Victoria and Albert Museum, London; IM.276A-1913 *(left)*, IM.276–1913 *(right)*.

painted, constructed, and ideated spaces. The painterly emphasis on the brick wall marking the garden’s boundaries from the wilderness, on the water flowing from the channels into the tank, on orange trees and blooming flowers, and on flying birds and laboring gardeners assembled elements from contemporaneous garden sites and from visions of idealized gardens. The personal voice of the memoir insists on accounting for the genre that shaped such described gardens and landscapes, but the material genre of the painted *Bāburnāmah* also creates a new text, image, and object by way of selection, commemoration, and collaboration among painters, calligraphers, and imperial historians, among others. There is no desire to re-create an indexical verisimilar picture of the world.[65]

The depictions of gardens and assemblies are significant, for both mirror the stakes in and the modes of depicting moods of places. Just as painted gardens emerge in every instance as heterotopias—spaces shaped by real places and historical practices as well as by ideal imaginaries and aesthetics—so do painted assemblies.[66] Painters intertwined purposeful compositions and painterly choices to evoke the immersive nature of both. More than a few pictures from the worlds of the Mughal, Deccan, and northern Indian courts certainly asked their courtly viewers to identify with the protagonists but also with the sensate spaces that sought to bind those assembled into a collective mood. A representation of Babur’s assembly emphasizes an outdoor setting’s sensorial overload (fig. I.11).[67] The curling lines of running and rippling water and the miniaturized trees near the lower edge of the painting become the central feature around which the painter assembles the seated group of musicians and elite men. This rendering of the portraits of the emperor, his attendants, and the men presenting poetry, playing music, holding books, or offering wine, as well as the hills and trees, in fine ink and gold, painted in two tones with a hint of pale greens and pinks, demands close looking and re-viewing. These kinds of painted assemblies potentially engaged historical viewers in acts of slow consumption, appreciation, and discernment. An etiquette manual, the fifteenth-century *Niʿmatnāmah-i Nāṣirshāhī* (Nasir Shah’s book of delights), commissioned at the Malwa sultanate of Mandu, includes concise textual instructions on recipes of delicacies and rules of courtly protocol that painters supplemented with images of the sultan and his friends and lovers partaking in shared tastes.[68] The painter’s artful abstractions iterate the feel of boundaries of

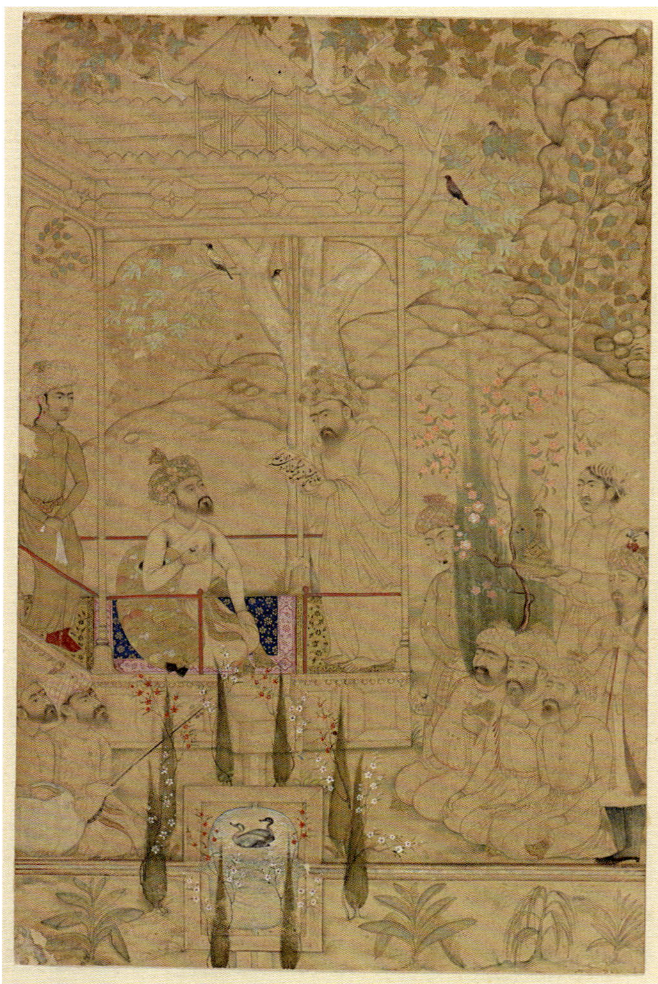

I.11. *Emperor Babur with Attendants in a Garden*, c. 1590. Opaque watercolor, ink, and gold on paper, 19.1 × 12.2 cm. Freer Gallery of Art, Smithsonian Institution, Washington, DC; purchase, Charles Lang Freer Endowment, F1954.27.

crenellated walls and interior chambers in illustration after illustration, reinforcing the division between those on the inside of the assembly and those left outside, as one turns the book's pages.

Even as the visual and haptic gain primacy when we examine the painted spaces emergent within books, manuscripts, albums, and independent folios, the immediacy of places and times can be felt only by reaching beyond what immediately meets the eye—in image and in verse. Among the lushest conceptions of painted lands, as seen above, were the illustrated *bhāva* of forests depicted within manuscripts praising the erotic beauty (*śṛṅgāra rasa*) of the blue god Krishna. From the creators of a thirty-six-foot-long painted scroll made from lightly primed cotton cloth in mid-fifteenth-century Gujarat of a *Vasantavilāsa*, a poem that celebrates the moods of *vāsanti*—the desired season of spring and the desired woman blooming in the spring of her youth—to the illustrators of leafs in the *Gīta Govinda*, painters responded to verses invoking the sounds, scents, and sights of the beauty of the forest.[69] Their resplendence reveals itself in alliance with poetry that saturated the season of spring with emotions of love. Similarly, Sunil Sharma finds the constitution of a "Mughal arcadia" in the reciprocal reinforcement of affect-saturated verses of Persian poets and images of painters that evoked Kashmir's highlands as a pastoral paradise.[70] These painted images of emperors' and courtly nobles' boat excursions on lakes and of windows looking onto vistas of scenery, included within illustrated books or as single folios, shifted the idealized landscape from city to countryside for Mughal elites in the mid-seventeenth century.[71] The proclivity toward courtly poetry that praised wondrous ideals at the Deccan court of Bijapur is thought to have shaped the mixing of miniature and gigantic elements as well as of otherworldly spatial and landscape settings in deeply contrasting colors.[72] Surely, painterly effects that suggested misty haze settling on lakes or manipulated the sizes of bees and butterflies invite the viewer to contemplate synesthetic experiences and patterns of poetic imaginings.[73] To gain access to painters' strategies of emplacing and idealizing places across courts and artifacts of early modern India thus demands paying astute attention to the tropes that defined genres across media.

The painter as witness within Mughal circles offers access to the subjective and affective experience of historical encounters—far more so than we have thus far acknowledged.[74] If we consider the circulation of images of landscapes that have shaped questions about painted lands in Mughal Hindustan, Europe has been at the heart of the debates. Following Ebba Koch's lead in evaluating architectural representation in seventeenth-century imperial manuscripts from two decades ago, Gregory Minissale and Kavita Singh have underscored the deliberate non-illusionism and selective mining of Europeanizing and Persianate visions within Mughal artworks.[75] Not that the primacy given to mimesis and naturalism in Europe were unitary: the calculative design of "tight handling of brush" and a paint surface built from "tiny units"—the facets that define seventeenth-century descriptive manner—was embedded in an aesthetic of curiosity tied to medieval Christian art that was not simply representative of newness or "independent" scientific curiosity.[76] Even the all-too-familiar images of castles, turrets, and bridges found in numerous sixteenth- and seventeenth-century examples, Mika Natif argues, do not exhibit Indian painters simply citing distant European lands or learning the subject of "landscape" from circulating Flemish engravings. Instead, they transformed distant European landscapes, in imperial productions as early as the 1580s, into renderings that sought to depict Mughal lands, dotted with red forts and village farms through which yogis traveled and farmers toiled.[77] To charm viewers into moods of wonderment, curiosity, and contemplation while observing depicted lands and landmarks was of consistent interest. It is worth considering that alongside the theme of the wondrous, the strange, the exotic, and the miraculous subsumed in the Perso-Arabic tradition of the *aja'ib*, Persian texts and inscriptions contain promising cues for pictorial *bhāva*.[78] Just as literary research has overturned the divide between "Mughal Islamic" and "non-Islamic, Hindu or Jain" sources and made space for multilingual conversations, the idiom of *bhāva* was part of drawing the sense of a place into Mughal pictures.[79] The Agra painted letter-scroll operates as an intermediary object to display the understanding of conceptions like *bhāva* within Mughal circles (figs. I.1–3). After all, emperors from Akbar onward were fluent in Hindi, the commonly spoken vernacular in northern India, and the associated learned literary idiom of Brajbhasha.[80]

Against these precursors, eighteenth-century painters intertwined the rendering of real places, aesthetic ideals, political claims, cartographic knowledge, and sensate encounters with natural and built environments. Moving away from the decline paradigm, Indian painting studies have followed understudied painters, manuscripts, styles, and patrons. For artists practicing in the courts of Kishangarh, Faizabad, and Lucknow, a predilection for lakeside terraces and fantastical gardens demonstrates a sensory immersion in beautiful places.[81] For other painters working at Kota, Udaipur, Delhi, and Jodhpur, exchanges with the notable cartography workshop of eighteenth-century Jaipur, as discussed in chapter 1, led them to revise their approaches to and conventions of observing, surveying, extracting planar and elevation forms, and incorporating recognizable built and natural environments in the early decades of the eighteenth century. In light of shrinking Mughal territories, Yuthika Sharma shows that artists such as Nidhamal, who worked for multiple patrons including European officers, deployed conventions to signify accuracy and beauty in the earliest cartographic representation of Shahjahanabad, Delhi's Red Fort, prepared around 1750.[82] Chanchal Dadlani has made a case for the historicisms established by eighteenth-century Mughal architecture and their commemoration within visually heterogeneous painted representations as related attempts that "effect" rather than "reflect" the "reality" of restricted Mughal authority.[83] Debra Diamond sees a similar purposefulness in early nineteenth-century monumental paintings of Jodhpur that combined planar map vignettes of temple spaces and royal portraits in order to define boundaries and make picture-viewing part of devotional practices.[84] The shapes and expressions of eighteenth-century vernaculars and localizations may look very different from one locale to the next, thus demanding assessments on individual terms of the continuities and discontinuities that rather mobile and urbane painters defined.

The sheer number of commissions at the Udaipur court that negotiate the dialectic of rendering the moods of real places and evoking idealized abodes far exceeded the corpus created at any of the other regional workshops. It cumulatively opens our minds to the artistic, intellectual, and historical capaciousness of "*bhāva* of a place" as a meaningful and pertinent conceptual category.

Emotions were at the heart of painted lands. The unnamed Udaipur painter's *Maharana Sangram Singh II at the Gangaur Boat Procession*, Tod's words on Indian princes' hedonist play in lake palaces, and Waugh's watercolor depicting a less aqueous Lake Pichola may seem entirely discrete on first glance. Indeed they were. Yet the way that the processes of each imagining were imbued with emotions and sensate encounters links them. That is, these artifacts not only are linked by a common place but also present a case of homologous aesthetic practices that sought to reveal places through the idiom of moods. Just as Romita Ray reminds us that the political underpinnings of the picturesque in colonial India were centrally made out of intense sensory encounters with new environments, Vittoria Di Palma has argued that pictorial landscapes in eighteenth-century Britain were ultimately not about representing architectures, pastoral grounds, or wilderness but essentially about mediating moods.[85] The emergence of landscape painting as a distinct kind of artwork underscores the new emphasis on affect. With the shift from the space of production to modes of reception in aesthetic theory, taste became central to defining beauty. What mattered most was the "emotional impact" of art, and thus, "objects capable of generating strong responses became those that were most highly esteemed."[86] Emotions such as wonder, fear, and disgust were central to the making of landscapes in the first place—and thereby, Di Palma emphasizes, "pastoral landscapes composed of verdant meadows, meandering brooks, and flowering shrubs were displaced in the cultural imagination by sublime landscapes featuring jagged rocks, desolate plans, towering cliffs, thundering cataracts, and exploding volcanoes."[87] By contrast, Udaipur's painters instead sought emotions such as longing, love, beauty, delight, pleasure, prosperity, devotion, piousness, and plentitude, especially of rain and lakes.

The ways that art history tells the story of landscape, via a history of empire and colonialism, critically motivated my initial forays into the archives, objects, texts, and travels that collectively suggest an intersecting, yet different, history of painted lands as well as of India's eighteenth century. I do not write about "moods of a place" as an emic textual category, especially since the act of painting moods of a place onto any surface is itself an imaginative, artistic, scientific, and embodied practice that requires artists to move between sensing moods and representing them. It is impossible to escape corporeal experiences and topographic terrains in navigating and picturing lands. Likewise, a stronger acknowledgment that ways of knowing were always sensate also means accounting for this centrality in the histories we write about historical moods and painted lands today. To write a trans-regional intellectual and material history of pictured moods that revealed places and mobilized new bonds between people, lands, spaces, and politics on emotional grounds, first and foremost necessitates a critical evaluation of each localized practice on its own terms. *The Place of Many Moods* takes precisely that step.

HISTORICIZING INDIA'S EIGHTEENTH CENTURY

How did Mughal Hindustan's cultures of mobility, sociability, and self-representation provide the basis for Rajput kings, nobles, merchants, and emergent elites to transform themselves into sophisticated patrons of distinguished localized cultures? While the rulers of Rajasthan's courts, who identified themselves as Hindu Rajputs, "sons of kings," had controlled small and large kingdoms since pre-Mughal times, by the late sixteenth century their political and artistic histories were transcultural, mutually transformed and entwined within Mughal networks.[88] The histories of aesthetics, sensation, and emotions, as embodied in the pictorial histories of painted lands in the early modern world, reveal the critical role of poets and painters, books and illustrated manuscripts, in expanding affect-saturated ideas and imaginings. These objects were consumed and exchanged by patrons and connoisseurs in impressive courtly interiors and gardens within convivial assemblies enlivened by the presence of learned men, poetry recitations, and music performances. I discuss the alliances and approaches, not only among kings and courts but also among non-courtly trans-regional agents, crucial for examining the sensibilities of belonging and the claims of territoriality that became significant in the long eighteenth century. In moving away from fetishizing marginality and mobility only in relation to Europe, the forthcoming chapters explore artifacts representing and circulating the moods of places among kings and nobles as well as merchants, monks, and British East India Company officers. Each chapter highlights the affective work performed by painted moods of places in shaping the efficacy of material culture from early modern letters to court paintings. The politics and powerbrokers emergent in eighteenth-century Udaipur speak to both continuities and changes in the *longue durée* and the broader context discussed below.

Far less opulent than numerous Mughal imperial productions, the painted letter-scroll sent from the emperor Jahangir's durbar with the support of Agra's rich local merchants is a revealing historical object, one that incisively presents the material, methodological, and historiographical ground on which this book stands. It offers a tantalizing glimpse into early seventeenth-century Agra (fig. I.2).[89] Jahangir holds an emerald bowl, exemplifying the delicately crafted and luxurious objects associated with the emperor's taste. Prince Khurram (the future emperor Shah Jahan) is shown standing opposite the emperor and his fan-bearing attendant, with the Persian noble Mirza Rustum Safavi behind them, while the Rajput raja Ramdas and the learned Jain monk Vivekharsha are receiving the scroll. The other identified persons of repute in Jahangir's assembly include a Jesuit priest, possibly the Goa-based Portuguese Father Xavier or the Florentine Father Corsi; a European man, likely William Hawkins, who is known to have posed as an ambassador of the king of England, seen removing his red hat as a sign of respect toward the court; and aides, identified by labels, including Farsat Khan Khoja, Shaikh Farid Bukhari (Murtaza Khan), and Kotwal Agha Nur.[90] Beyond the durbar, Salivahana rendered a red-colored gateway, emphasizing the fort's iconic imperial threshold, followed by arcades to denote Agra's bazaars that lay beyond. Merchants, musicians, laymen, and laywomen join the group that will collectively deliver the letter-scroll to the eminent Jain religious leader. His audience, too, is seen celebrating. The scroll's images ascertained that a prosperous city awaits the invited Jain monk Vijaysena Suri, who was residing in the town of Devapattan in Saurashtra, Gujarat's peninsular region, near the Arabian Sea. Both the letter's authors, the scribe and the painter, reinforced the scroll as a meta-object that tells the story of its own mobility and mediation while announcing a decree for the empire's citizens, particularly the Jains. The painted letter-scroll depicts people hailing from all these locales and regions—Persia, Arabia, the Mediterranean, Gujarat, Goa, Portugal, and courts and towns of northern India—assembled in the world commanded by Jahangir. In identifying each of these places, regions, peoples, and itineraries, the feel of the cosmopolitan Mughal durbar is perceptible.

The tracking of mobility, of knowledgeable individuals, and of influential intermediaries; the mining of vernacular artifacts; and the study of historical poetry and travelogues have cumulatively propelled the understanding of Mughal Hindustan as an early modern space shaped by local, regional, and trans-regional participants. One impetus is bringing the Mughal Empire into a broader conversation—charting the beginning of an early modern epoch across the world, not only in Europe.[91] That modernity, as seen through markers like historical consciousness, self-fashioning, travel narratives, and rise of the individual in Europe, was shaped not by exclusions but by connections. The period between the 1500s and the 1800s was characterized by new geographical discoveries, the expanding mercantile networks and imperial territories of the European East India companies, and the mobility of people and things and associated cross-cultural encounters. The travel routes to India, however, were not singularly imbricated by Mughal imperial presence or European mercantile presence. Merchants, pilgrims, scholars, and messengers who traveled from port towns in Gujarat, or from other ports such as Goa and Calicut, along the Malabar coast in the south, formed central nodes in the western Indian Ocean world and the global economy that expanded from the 1300s onward.[92] Since the sixteenth century, the Mughals and the Portuguese, who were powerful actors in the export of textiles and spices from Gujarat's port towns even before the arrival of the Dutch and British East India Companies in the early 1600s, found themselves continually negotiating with Jain mercantile networks.[93] By the eighteenth and nineteenth centuries, the expansion of pan-Indian and pan-Eurasian mercantile networks contributed to Jain merchants commissioning elaborate painted letters.[94] The moods of the thriving places featured within artifacts such as pilgrimage scrolls, maps, and invitation letters keep open the possibility that routes, apart from imperial and courtly networks, contributed to the innovation and proliferation of aesthetic sensibilities, embodied knowledge, and urban imaginaries.[95]

Professionals such as scribes, painters, poets, and pandits in the service of multiple patrons in the early modern world were among the most mobile.[96] While Mughal Hindustan may have been global at an unprecedented scale, the itinerary of Salivahana's painted letter from Agra to Gujarat makes clear the intensity of local and translocal travels and the vitality of imperial access to communities and networks of regional kings, nobles, merchants, and religious men. Salivahana was a painter from the Usta family, which claimed a trans-regional lineage from the region of Herat, who since the late sixteenth century had settled in Multan.[97] Along with one of Akbar's Rajput nobles stationed in Lahore, the Ustas arrived at the regional court of Bikaner in northern Rajasthan. Likewise, the Jains were key intellectual interlocutors, religious advisers, and political negotiators in the Mughal court.[98] One contemporaneous description of Agra's bazaars is recounted by the Jain poet, philosopher, and merchant Banarasidas, in his autobiography (composed in verse in 1641); Banarasidas arrived in the city the same year the painted letter was sent, with a consignment of precious stones and jewelry.[99] He described the merchants who were signatories on the painted letter as famous Jains who dealt in textiles, precious stones, oil, grain, rice, and indigo, and who supplemented their income as astute moneylenders in Akbar's and Jahangir's dominions.[100] In drawing India (and Asia) into an early modern world of "historical synchrony," scholars have argued for explicating the contours of humanistic thinking within microhistories penned down in Persian, the official language of the Mughal Empire, but also Sanskrit and the regional and vernacular registers of Hindi that flourished in northern India.[101] Others have questioned this search for "European cosmopolitanism" in every place. Mana Kia argues for the primacy of other modes of being a curious and astute cosmopolitan.[102] The Agra letter-scroll, as an object, text, and image, crossed multiple durbars and bazaars and connected imperial, vernacular, and popular domains, and thus demonstrates that to explore pictorial moods of a place we must step outside of courtly domains. This focus, pursued in chapter 5, also contributes to the limited conversations we have had thus far between courtly arts and bazaar arts in early modern India.

Within the domains of courtly spaces, both Mughal emperors and Rajput kings found it imperative to assert visions of local sovereignty within multiple idioms of language, aesthetics, and spaces. When Rajput kings entered into Mughal service, it impacted their political claims and historical narratives, the status of individual powerbrokers, their access to regions and resources, and the broader, heterogeneous populace on both ends. I surmise these relationships, seemingly distant from the perspective of eighteenth-century visions of Rajput kings, in order to pinpoint precisely the early modern pasts that mattered in the coming years. Abandoning center-periphery models to examine Mughal-Rajput exchanges on strictly hierarchical, religious, or ideological grounds, Catherine Asher's well-known work on Raja Man Singh's architectural patronage of forts, palaces, gardens, temples, and mosques establishes the Rajput raja's pivotal role in asserting Mughal authority and aesthetic taste across northern, western, and eastern India while expanding his own kingly status.[103]

Alliances with Rajput kings were prominent successes for the Mughals and one of the primary supporting pillars for imperial expansion in the north. Akbar instituted various forms, such as marriage (*sāgā*) and notions of brotherhood (*bhai-bandh*) to incorporate the Rajputs.[104] Raja Man Singh (r. 1590–1614), of the Kachhwaha clan, whose grandfather was the first king in alliance with Akbar after the Rajput princess of Amber (later Jaipur) became his queen as early as 1561, was the recipient of the Akbar's special affection. As a high-profile *manṣabdār*, a noble who held the *manṣab* rank in the Mughal court, which entitled him to land, salary, and protection in exchange for armies, Man Singh led many imperial conquests while operating as a king in his own right. Rao Surjan Singh of Bundi (r. 1558–1607), along with others, surrendered in 1569 to Akbar's army when the formidable Ranthambhor fort was attacked but rose to greater heights as a Mughal noble.[105] The expansion of Rajasthan's courts and Mughal authority gained political legitimacy from imperial capitals, and itinerant durbars set up in pilgrimage towns and gardens—thus, co-constituting territorial claims, social networks, and artistic cultures.

In contrast, Akbar's armies vehemently fought the Sisodia Rajputs at the fortress of Chittor in 1567–68—even though the Mewar king Udai Singh II (r. 1537–72) had escaped and established Udaipur as the new capital by 1559. The Sisodias of Mewar prided themselves on being the premier Hindu Rajputs, who did not surrender to the Mughals. The Sisodia king Rana Kumbha (r. 1433–68) was an avid patron of intellectual treatises on music and architecture and also an important builder of forts, who expanded the fortressed capital complex at Chittor in southwestern Rajasthan.[106] Ultimately, the signing of a Mughal-Mewar treaty in 1615, spearheaded by Prince Khurram before he became the emperor Shah Jahan, brought Mewar's Maharana Amar Singh I (r. 1597–1620) into Jahangir's ambit of authority—a significant victory for the Mughals, widely commemorated in texts and pictures.[107] While fully part of the empire, by the mid-seventeenth century the Mewar court had bolstered its genealogical histories (*vaṃśāvalī*) and martial tales.[108] The emphasis placed on noble descent and being a cultured participant at the Mughal court meant that Rajputs, in particular Mewar kings, felt more compelled than ever before, as Cynthia Talbot notes, "to demonstrate their connection to an illustrious past and dynastic history."[109] Additionally, the Mewar maharanas' patronage of grand books of the Hindu epic *Rāmāyaṇa* and of public works such as the Rajsamand Lake underwrote their attempts to assert "superiority" over the Mughals and the Kachhwaha Rajputs at Amber.[110] While the preference of Udaipur's painters for pre-Mughal visual archaisms in the mid-seventeenth century is well established, owing mainly to key differences between the genres of imperial portraiture and devotional manuscripts, painters, as discussed in chapter 1, also valued the formal vocabulary of Mughal imperial portraiture to praise gods as kingly men—as ethical, righteous, religious, and refined connoisseurs of aesthetic beauty and material pleasures.[111]

For both politics and culture, the grounds for loyalties, personal friendships, and representation had shifted by the late seventeenth century. The structure of nobility that strengthened the Mughal Empire ultimately contributed to larger numbers of high-ranking nobles with increased pay scales.[112] For a long time, eighteenth-century decentralization of Mughal authority was seen as an outcome of the emperor Aurangzeb's conservative turn toward religious orthodoxy, though historians have questioned such all-encompassing characterizations.[113] In reality, each assertion of independence over the course of the eighteenth century by former Mughal imperial officers, who had already operated as kings in their own right in Bengal, Awadh, Punjab, and Rajasthan, panned out distinctly based on the new alliances that emerged among regional powerbrokers, including the British East India Company, which expanded territorial operations across the subcontinent. The Marathas, a group that, like the Rajputs, claimed roots in warrior clans, had become powerful in seventeenth-century western India and were looking to expand their authority after the Mughals.[114] For instance, in the northwest, the Sisodias of Mewar and the Kachhwahas of Amber (later of Jaipur, after 1727, when the capital shifted), earlier considered staunch adversaries, forged an important political and marital alliance in 1708, when Sawai Jai Singh II married the sister of Udaipur king Sangram Singh II.[115] The Rajput kings of Udaipur, Amber, and Jodhpur came together again in 1734 at Hurda (near Ajmer) to form a political alliance against the Marathas. Within the city of Udaipur as well as in other regional courts, kings were increasingly dependent on relationships with estate holders (thakurs and *rāwats*)—elite men who populated their daily courts.[116] The positions of Rajput (and sometimes non-Rajput) estate holders were linked to their kings through complex kin-based relationships, political alliances, and estate lands (*ṭhikānā*) that can be understood as "little kingdoms" in their own right.[117] The Mewar court's thakurs of the 1730s–40s had begun to build forts and palaces in their independent territorial domains and, in such construction, patronized painters and poets, seen most strongly in the establishment of a painting workshop in the *ṭhikānā* of Devgarh.[118] Thus thakurs, quite apart from kings, employed cultural practices on their own terms to challenge the Udaipur court's centrality. It is this new community of friends that is seen accompanying Maharana Sangram Singh II in the depicted boat procession, collectively immersed in admiring a spectacular night (fig. I.4).

Closely allied to the innovations of transcultural forms and idioms lies the question of mobility and sociability among elite men. In the extensive field of Indian painting, work on the mobility of painters, patrons, and paintings in the early modern world, and Andrew Topsfield's scholarship on Udaipur's courtly arts especially, are indispensable for tracing the shift toward large-scale paintings containing a plurality of images that collectively present the mood of a place. Also key are the interdisciplinary turn toward understanding the centrality of arts in producing sociability among political men in the early modern world and the sensory turn, as discussed above, most notably in the study of the Deccan sultanates; both factors impact the major pictorial change *The Place of Many Moods* addresses. The stakes of accumulating cultural capital, aesthetic taste, and artistic expertise were serious—for patrons, painters, poets, and other skilled and intellectual men. Through patronage and refinement, Rajputs established their noteworthy position in the imperial circle and beyond. This included the dynamics of establishing intimate friendships—within assemblies held in itinerant camps or in the Mughal capital cities—through the exchange of books, painted albums, and manuscripts, among other material and musical and literary pleasures.[119] The creation of convivial moods was central to diplomacy but also enabled learning about new and unfamiliar objects, literature, and connoisseurship. The cultivation of curiosity, desires, and tastes was imperative to ultimately appreciate, admire, combine, reject, or adapt—whether it was painters drawing upon Persianate, classical pre-Mughal genres, European artifacts, or Flemish engravings; poets engaging in creative multilingual exchanges; or Muslim, Hindu, Jain, and Christian thinkers partaking in intellectual conversations. Inquiries in these directions have offered new historically contingent stories about personal intimacies and bodily experiences by interpreting texts concurrently with other material archives—books, paintings, verses, music, delicacies, and perfumes that were part of early modern elite sociality.

As individual eighteenth-century elites became increasingly powerful in the early colonial period, the Udaipur court's revenues declined. As the British colonial agent based in the city, Tod, who favored Mewar kings over other Rajputs, came to view the thakurs as responsible for the court's ruination—a view that supported his belief that the British should "protect" and "restore" the power of the Udaipur ruler Bhim Singh (r. 1778–1828).[120] While the British formally occupied Delhi in 1803, Tod's efforts resulted in individual treaties with Rajasthan's kings and led to proclamations of indirect British rule in northwestern India by 1818.[121] Ultimately, Tod's account enabled Lord William Bentinck, governor-general at Delhi, to establish the province of colonial Rajputana in 1832 and Rajasthan as the quintessential "place (*sthāna*) of kings (*rajas*)."[122] The Udaipur painter Ghasi's spectacular commemoration of the mood of Bentinck's monthlong durbar in Ajmer, discussed in chapter 4, suggests that Ghasi was reclaiming authority for his courtly patrons.

Querying the historical contours of India's long eighteenth century begins with questioning moods of decline. Tod's account bore the intense imprint of local encounters and ecumene; nonetheless, his narratives created persuasive Oriental stereotypes. By probing iterative tropes, historians have laid bare the evolutionary logic found in antiquarian projects such as Tod's *Annals and Antiquities of Rajast'han* (1829, 1832): the narrative arc of progress that culminated in the early nineteenth-century British present and the colonial future that was to come.[123] In part, *The Place of Many Moods* explores moods apart from decline, including also moods of celebratory spectacles and pleasurable assemblies that are recounted as such, thus historicizing the deliberate creation and agentive role of delightful, even decadent moods.

There is no doubt that the transpiring of spectacular moods in places and in pictures can dazzle audiences and generate lingering memories for a collective. Comprehending representations of people enchanted by wondrous and momentous moods, created in and shaped by extraordinary natural and built environments, however, is far from simple. The designation of Udaipur's large-scale court paintings as a corpus of "*tamasha* paintings" surely acknowledges their spectacular nature but otherwise as a descriptor raises issues of translation.[124] *Tamāśā* (or *tamasha*) may be approximately translated as "spectacle," likely meaningful to local audiences as modes of collective activity. Or, based on the circumstance and tenor of its use, the word may suggest a staged episode or the sense of a somewhat hollow and extravagant event. Interestingly, *Maharana Sangram Singh II at the Gangaur Boat Procession* is the only known Udaipur artwork with an inscription (on the verso) stating that the picture describes a *tamāśā*. That is, the inscription specifically refers to the painter's depiction of a spectacle of fireworks on the banks of Lake Pichola on a dark moonlit night.[125] In one way, Tod seems embedded in a longer tradition of smitten admiration of the city of lakes and lake palaces, though the valence of the mood strikes him as empty. That material consumption and celebratory extravaganzas could be open to interpretation—decried as meaningless or praised as meaningful—was, however, dependent on when and who did the looking, responding, and recalling.

PLAN OF THE BOOK

The evocation of *bhāva* in place-centric art is the unifying topic of inquiry across this book's five chapters. The following chapters unfold as a spatial and chronological journey. Each chapter traces the itinerancies of objects and people but more importantly of artistic practices and aesthetic ideas within and between media.[126] The chapters are sequenced so that the reader encounters the interrelated images of painted lands from the perspectives of courtly communities; officers, explorers, and artists connected with the British East India Company; and merchants, pilgrims, monks, laymen, and laywomen who intersect within bazaars. While the major pictorial changes heralded by Udaipur's court painters mark a critical point of departure for *The Place of Many Moods*, the unraveling opens a polysemous world. In the process, the book considers the methodological and historical problem of situating place-centric imagination, not as a peripheral anecdote to the history and historiography of South Asian art but as a central component that opens up broader questions for the field.

Chapter 1 explores the Udaipur painters' conceptions of moods of a place by using formal analysis to discern pictorial choices. The textual evidence available to understand the imagining of moods is plentiful, considering the copious inscribing on the backs of paintings by Udaipur's scribes as opposed to other courts, yet this evidence is limited in relating the picturing and the perception of moods. To understand the emergence of moods of a place as an operative category, this chapter thus accounts for the creation of Udaipur as a city of lakes; the urban, architectural, and political expansions of the early 1700s; the regional mobility of painters, patrons, and artworks; and cartographic practices. Chapter 2 examines the emphasis on rainfall and lakes seen in Udaipur's small and large paintings, poetry, history, and building of waterworks. It interprets historical perspectives offered on the emotions, ecology, and politics associated with rain and reservoirs in the early 1700s to find the multilayered significance attached to abundant monsoons and prosperous places. Closely connected to mediations on the moods of the monsoon, chapter 3 shifts our gaze from the lakeside city to the moods of pleasurable lake palaces. The myriad images of Udaipur's Jagniwas lake palace reveal the significance of aesthetics and affects of delight when examined alongside contemporaneous poetry that commemorated the lake palace as a "world of pleasure." Collectively, these three chapters illuminate the role of artifacts in shaping social histories of senses and sentiments, the material and visual means deployed to effect mid-eighteenth-century politics, and the role of moods in crafting lingering memories for a community.

The last two chapters address how the extraordinary interest among Udaipur painters to visualize real spaces as charismatic places across pictorial genres extended beyond courtly worlds. I have stressed courtly sociability for historicizing political, artistic, and cultural shifts at the turn of the eighteenth century and for constituting the moods of a place. The circulation of images featuring Udaipur's flourishing moods into vernacular objects such as painted letter-scrolls that traveled along mercantile and pilgrimage routes, and the itinerancy of non-courtly artworks and scraps of preparatory drawings among mixed publics, chiefly enable us to deliberate the efficacious potential of pictorial moods. Both chapters contribute to the revisionist histories of knowledge making at the interstices of the early modern world and the emergent colonial space in eighteenth-century India.

Chapter 4 turns to the artist Ghasi, who worked for Udaipur's rulers as a court painter and also for the British agent James Tod, as his artist-assistant. His corpus widens our understanding of changing artistic practices and attitudes toward the moods of place and the conventions of drawing, mapping, and recording architectural sites in the early nineteenth century. Ghasi forged critical conversations on the theme of picturing place, both within and between the visual and political worlds of the Udaipur court and the British East India Company. Chapter 5 focuses on a seventy-two-foot-long, eleven-inch-wide painted letter, the longest known scroll of this type of invitation, that regional merchants and the ruler of Udaipur jointly sent in 1830 to an eminent monk residing in the town of Bikaner. As expert panegyrists of urban places, Udaipur's painters, alongside iterating the established imagery of a lake-centered geography, extended the epistolary genre of painted invitation letters to function as an effective map of the city's shifting territoriality. By presenting the prosperous moods of the city's bazaars, the letter-scroll critically displaces the authority of the newly settled British agents of Udaipur and their letters, which reported a collapsing court and urban economy.

The excess inherent to panegyrical representations of place and the emphasis on emotions of plentitude and of pleasure reveal new histories of the eighteenth century. While praise as such is descriptive, with its aesthetics commonly standardized, the performance and interpretation of praise instead evokes subjective spaces of redolent historical moments that are under-studied and under-theorized. To consider any art of place is always to consider a practice of localization. The imagining, picturing, perceiving, composing, singing, and reciting of the moods of a place can never come from outside of an intense local experience. Thought of in this sense, places are made, always, from local and intimate worlds.

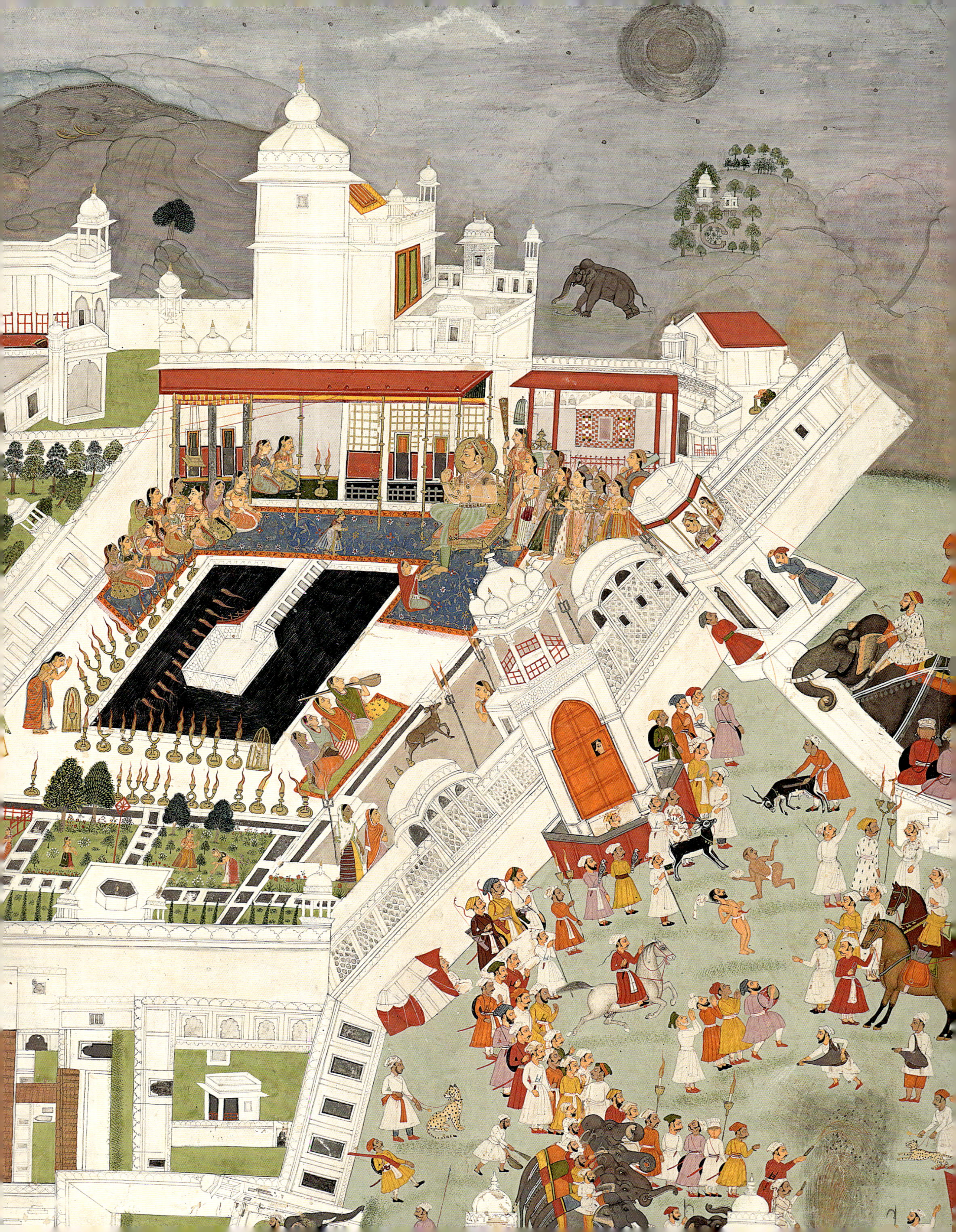

CHAPTER 1

Enlarging Painted Places and Imagining Moods Anew

WONDROUS IMMERSION

One side of the painting *Maharana Sangram Singh II at the Gangaur Boat Procession* is bathed in a flattening brightness and the other in a mysterious dimness (see fig. I.4). Simple, bold decorative patterns present the humbler quarter of Udaipur city. In streets lined by houses with white walls and tiled roofs, we see clusters of women and men painted against the emphatically two-dimensional space of the brown ground. On the far side of the lake, where tones of burnt umber, smoky gray, and Prussian blue dominate, shadows of projecting windowed balconies and the glow from blazing firecrackers reflect onto wall surfaces and human faces alike, creating a lakefront replete with modeled forms and fine outlines. Each side enhances the presence of the other, and together they co-constitute the painted place. This painting represents a new kind of artwork on paper, because it could not be held in a single hand, unlike a royal portrait, a page of illustrated poetry, or an album folio. The depiction of the mood of the spectacle unfolding against a starry night becomes the artwork's compositional and conceptual frame within which we search for portraits, places, and proceedings.

Fundamentally, this chapter asks one question: How did wondrous admiration of the city of lakes take form as a practice and as a painted subject on paper? To reconstruct the artistic shift toward the picturing of moods of places, this chapter examines visual precedents in painted epics and explores Udaipur's urban environs and architectural expansions in the city. It analyzes contemporaneous developments in architectural renderings and cartographic artifacts to demonstrate how the mobility of cartographers, painters, and paintings across Rajasthan shaped a new medium. These distinct strands cumulatively lead to insights into the painters' processes of delineating the visual *bhāva* of a place as a mutable and plural category in the early 1700s. We also learn of the value to be had in close looking for deciphering the formulation and perception of moods and the variations in inscriptions. The introduction to this volume presented the history of constituting emotions and sensations based on the aesthetic perspectives of intellectuals and poets in the early modern world. It discussed approaches painters established for picturing lands and architectures within the idioms of history, poetry, and devotion in early modern India more broadly. In this chapter, I analyze pictorial precursors,

Detail of fig. 1.19

experimentations, and departures that enabled the Udaipur painters to visually assemble images of moods and places. By following the contingent changes in the topographic, spatial, visual, pictorial, and cartographical arenas, I locate an increasing investment in knowing and describing places as well as in localizing moods.

Most interpretations of Udaipur's large-scale paintings stop after identifying buildings and portrait subjects. In contast, my inquiry seeks to comprehend from multiple perspectives the meaning of the rapture and affection on display in visualizations of moods of a place. To ask about the sensing of moods and the description of place on paper means to imagine and to historicize affective work and spatial encounters. To denaturalize places as somehow always there and to argue for the primacy of embodied experiences and not just chronology of building, geographers have looked to Heidegger's ideas on "dwelling" in spaces and landscapes.[1] Painted landscapes have been fruitful sites for historians across disciplines—as images to think with, to discover what places might have been, to "gather" meaning from what is shown of people's engagement with the world.[2] A place, Tim Ingold writes, "owes its character to the experiences it affords to those who spend time there—to the sights, sounds and indeed smells that constitute its specific ambience . . . [which depend] on the kinds of activities in which its inhabitants engage. It is from this relational context of people's engagement with the world, in the business of dwelling, that each place draws its unique significance."[3] Udaipur's painted lands invite an immersion into the featured moods that does not separate places, peoples, affects, and atmospheres. By looking at where painters took their keen eyes and pigments to generate *bhāva*, to kindle emotions and jog memories, I attempt to reconstruct their spatial skills and pictorial deliberations. The painters' embodied presence and walking paths can be detected in the collated vignettes of streets and buildings. Re-viewing well-known and lesser-known painted moods enables us to explore the "business of dwelling" that painters and patrons performed to sense and visualize moods of places.[4]

EPIC PLACES

The Mewar *Rāmāyaṇa*, also known as the Jagat Singh *Rāmāyaṇa* (1649–53), contains an expansive canon of painted moods of places—epic places. The seven-volume *Rāmāyaṇa*, one of the two major Sanskrit epics of ancient India, presents a formative moment in self-representation at the Mewar court and in the production of illustrated manuscripts at the court's painting workshop.[5] Alongside his support for cultural, architectural, and infrastructure projects, Jagat Singh I (r. 1628–52), patron of the *Rāmāyaṇa* manuscripts, sought to proclaim the higher Rajput status of Mewar kings, akin to that of the laudably ethical Hindu god-king Rama, and to define himself apart from the Mughal imperial network. The Udaipur court community was the *Rāmāyaṇa*'s primary space of consumption, though as scholars have extensively argued, the manuscript's paintings equally addressed a wider audience, including the emperor Shah Jahan (r. 1628–66) and the Kachhwaha rajas of Amber.[6] The project was spearheaded by the painters Sahib Din and Manohar, known by their names from the colophons, and equally shaped by the distinctive work of anonymous painters, including one in particular: known as the "Deccan Painter,"[7] he is thought to have been trained in one of the southern sultanates, due to a distinctive palette and style seen on the pages of books five and six. Less explicitly acknowledged is the emphasis across the manuscripts on painted locales and landscapes entwined with intense emotions, the awe of wondrous places, and the aesthetics of idealized courtly spaces and urban environs. I consider Jagat Singh's *Rāmāyaṇa* as one of the means by which a receptive courtly community of painters and patrons developed a taste for idealized painted places by the late seventeenth century.

The manuscript uses topographical and spatial vignettes to compose the visual story of the travels of the divine protagonists—the Hindu god Rama; his wife, Sita; and his brother, Lakshmana—and tracks their paths from courts and cities to forests and islands and then their return to urban places after the completion of the trio's exile and their combat with the demon-king Ravana. The spatial strategies both undergird and animate the epic's commentary on ethical kingship and the victory of good over evil within and across individual pages.[8] Udaipur's painters mined portrayals of ideal kingship from Mughal imperial painting, possibly from painted and textual translations of Hindu epics in the Mughal workshop, and from the depictions of the Hindu deity Krishna in Rajput court painting to render the mid-seventeenth-century version of the worlds of both Rama and Ravana.[9] On thick sheets of Indian paper that is slightly burnished, scribes wrote the poet Valmiki's version of the story on the verso of each preceding page so that the lines could be read or recited alongside their full-page illustration. Valmiki's poetry praises the lands through which the protagonists journeyed—the city of Ayodhya, from which the king

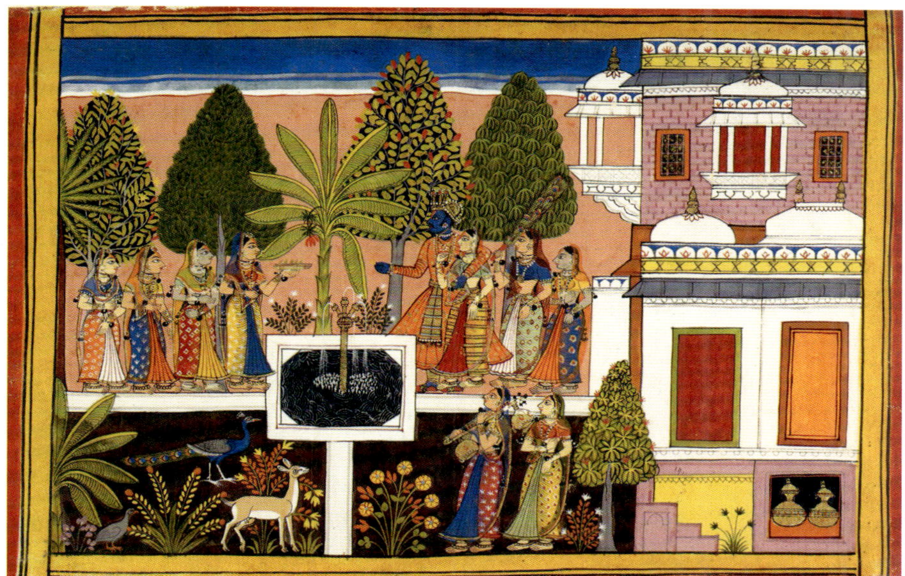

1.1. "Rama Enjoys the Gardens of Ayodhya with Sita," from book seven of Jagat Singh's *Rāmāyaṇa*, 1649–53, attributed to Sahib Din, Udaipur. Gouache on paper, 23 × 39.9 cm. British Library Board, London; Add. MS 15297(2), f.70.

Dasharatha (and later Rama) ruled; the island city of Lanka, from which the demon-king Ravana ruled; and Kishkindha, the capital of the monkey king Sugriva. Robert Goldman identifies how each of these three key cities becomes the setting for struggles over power and ideals: Ayodhya is embroiled in questions of "acquisition, maintenance, and execution of royal power," Kishkindha is the place where concerns with "fraternal struggles" play out, and Lanka is both "desirable and fearful."[10] Of the Jagat Singh *Rāmāyaṇa*'s three idealized cities, Lanka is unequaled for the wondrous admiration evident in its portrayal, though Ayodhya's presentation became an established ideal for the Udaipur court.

One folio depicting Ayodhya's palaces and gardens provides a commentary on connoisseurs, aesthetics, and beautiful spaces (fig. 1.1). Illustrated here is Valmiki's praise for the god-king as a model for ethical kingship par excellence; the poet describes Rama's enjoyment (*sukha*) of pleasures after having completed his kingly moral duties (*dharma*).[11] The painter visualized the king's private chambers and gardens as a space that delighted all the senses: a colorful courtly building with domes and balconies evokes Udaipur's palaces, while the painter's non-illusionistic use of bright colors and patterned forms calls upon us to imagine an otherworldly place. A blooming garden, a flowing fountain, a deer and a peacock with a transfixed gaze, a group of attendants who offer betel leaves, and musicians are all part of the audience that waits upon the royal couple. The cross-axial water channels call to mind Mughal folios that depicted imperial garden assemblies, and the springtime foliage connects with Sahib Din's paintings of the forests that Radha and Krishna inhabited. The idealized god-king Rama too strolls in his gardens, fashioned in the contemporaneous attire of Mughal elites.

The folio speaks to the emphasis on pleasure in seventeenth-century courtly society, both within advice manuals that theorize the roles of and relation between aesthetics and ethics and in the creation of convivial assemblies where political men bonded.[12] Udaipur's eighteenth-century painters adopted these ideals when they rendered moods of the pleasures offered by the city's lakes, palaces, and gardens. Unsurprisingly, given Mewar's interest in relating the story of the *Rāmāyaṇa* to contemporary courtiers, painters drew on the turrets, pavilions, and domes of seventeenth-century Udaipur's palaces for rendering Rama's capital city.[13] Although mimetic renderings of specific buildings do not occur, the white-colored doorways, interior chambers, and multistory palaces evoke the patron king's capital by virtue of iteration across the book. Such architectural depictions exhibit the skills and ideas for the picturing of spaces that were already operational in the mid-seventeenth-century court's workshop.

Ayodhya's spaces emerge as purposefully entangled in the story's emotional and ethical dilemmas. In book two, the departure of the royal trio from Ayodhya for their fourteen-year exile portrays one noticeably simple form of an entrance portal, where Dasharatha is caught between his roles as king and as Rama's father (fig. 1.2). The lamenting figure occupies the center of the arched gateway, the palace's threshold, and extends his hand beyond its frame to wave goodbye, as his family strives to pull him back inside. The verses recount the king's distress by conjuring the sounds of people wailing, women crying, and the "tumultuous clamor" of the citizenry, and through the figure of the charioteer, torn between the king's plea to stop and Rama's command to ride faster so as not to prolong his father's pain.[14] The painter's framing of the king's body, with its outstretched posture, intensifies his mediation not simply of the narrative moment but also of Dasharatha's feeling of being ripped apart—between the pain he felt as a father watching his eldest son's departure and the ethical conflict of a king fulfilling the promise made to his second queen, to banish Rama to the forest. The horizontality of the painted green ground outside the palace, which occupies two-thirds of the page's area, enhances the perception of the chariot's movement away from the structure. The painter elongated the somber mood in the subsequent folios by repeating the chariot's movement, expanding its distance from the capital of Ayodhya as it entered the forest of exile, perhaps even suggesting the deepening of pain for those left behind. The story of the epic is replete with a range of intense emotions—the pathos of departures, the joys of homecomings, the ferocity of combats—all of which were central to the story's praise for righteous kings. Each self-contained page of the manuscripts of Jagat Singh's *Rāmāyaṇa* can be imagined to have created opportunities for historical viewers reading, looking at, and relating across pages, but all while recalling from other media and time periods the epic's various recitations and retellings.[15]

Other folios of the Jagat Singh *Rāmāyaṇa* reveal the impact on painting of classical literary ideals of cities (*nagara-varṇana*) and the visual engagement with urban praise at the Udaipur court.[16] Both the poetry and the paintings described the demon-king Ravana's island of Lanka through the eyes of the monkey Hanuman, who is awestruck by its beauty. Valmiki's very first verse announcing the monkey's arrival compares Lanka to Amravati, the beautiful abode of the god Indra, just as the poet had compared Ayodhya to this very same city.[17] The Deccan Painter animates this place of wonder (fig. 1.3). The monkey depicted near the lower edge of this introductory page sits by the base of a hilly outcrop, gazing upward. An array of painted trees, flora, fauna, and the golden palace with multiple pavilions together reinforce the poet's verses that describe what the monkey saw: "lovely parklands and all kinds of lakes and pleasure groves completely covered with every sort of tree that blossomed and bore fruit in all seasons . . . with masses of blossoms and yet still budding . . . filled with birds, and their crowns waved gently in the breeze," and a city "adorned with moats covered with red and blue lotuses." Valmiki particularly emphasized a vision of Hanuman mesmerized, looking toward "the city of Laṅkā—like the city of the gods in heaven. . . . Laṅkā, set high on the mountain peak, looked to that majestic monkey like a city in the sky."[18]

The painter's response to the poet's praise of Lanka is simultaneously precise and flexible. The painter expands the pink-lotus-filled moat that surrounds the palace in verse and in the image by including the apparatus of a waterwheel attached to the boundary walls that splashes and sprays fresh water as it circulates. The dripping white paint gestures to the enchanting sounds of plentiful water. More than depicting the poet's evocative details, the painter emphasizes a poetic sense of abundance and fecundity, formally gathering together a density of sensorial delights. The scents and species that the verses highlight find their equals in the variegated, saturated colors and painterly textures. The curling waves of the ocean, awash with crocodiles, frame the island. Animals perched on its pink rocks—the monkey, pairs of colorful birds, white storks, and a lone peacock—gaze upward in the direction of the golden palace. The stillness captured in their awestruck poses is contrasted by flying white birds and swaying red flags painted against the undulating blue and white brushwork that evokes a resplendent sky. Beyond the looping patterns made of wavy lines that denote the churning water, and the oblong outlines of the topsy-turvy rocks and the rolling clouds, the palace's monumental, majestic presence is enhanced by the painter's flatly applied gold color for the walls and bright Indian yellow for the ground preceding the horizon.

In every way, the painting emphasizes the wondrous place. The poetry states that the monkey will embark on a reconnaissance mission at nightfall and hide during the daytime; to find Hanuman, the viewer must engage in the process of searching. The monkey's buff-colored body hides between the pink rocks, just as the Mughal-style palace guard's body remains almost hidden behind the barrier. Hanuman's vantage point, looking upward, provides a fish-eye perspective that suggests the position from which the painting's audiences are invited to gaze and to marvel at an endlessly enchanting place.

The beauty of natural and built environments is described and depicted in Jagat Singh's *Rāmāyaṇa*. Why, then, are the

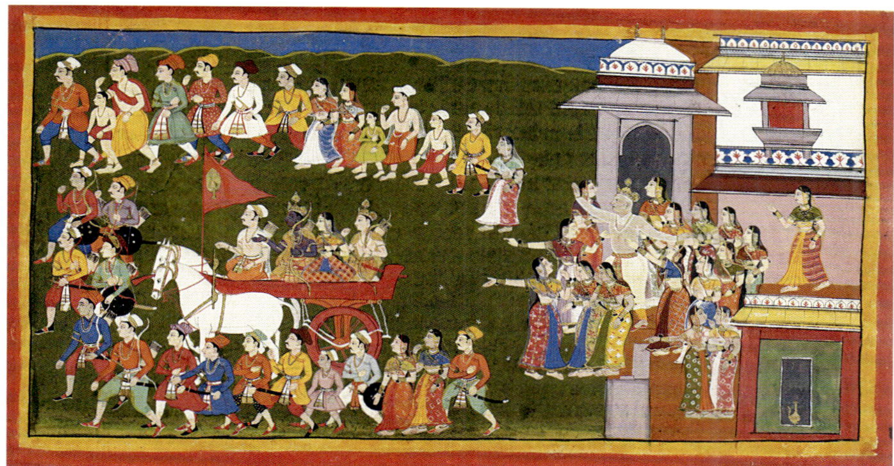

1.2. "Rama, His Wife, and Brother Ride off in a Chariot Driven by Sumantra," from book two of Jagat Singh's *Rāmāyaṇa*, 1649–53, attributed to Sahib Din, Udaipur. Gouache on paper, 23 × 39.9 cm. British Library Board, London; Add. 15296(1), f.56.

1.3. "Hanuman Arrives at the Island of Lanka and Admires the City from the Bottom of the Mountain," from book five of Jagat Singh's *Rāmāyaṇa*, 1649–53, attributed to the Deccan Painter, Udaipur. Gouache on paper, 23 × 39.9 cm. British Library Board, London; IO. San 3621, f.1

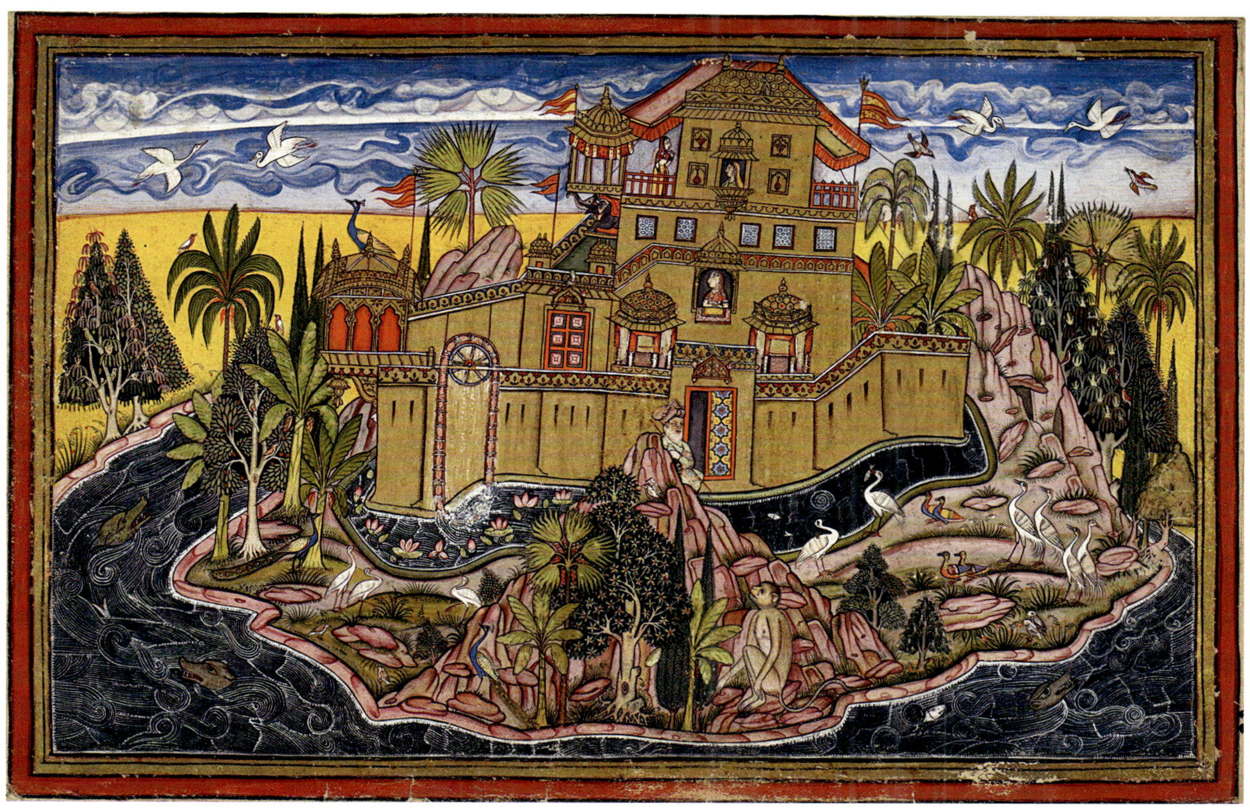

Deccan Painter's Lanka pages significant in charting the aesthetics of painted places? Lanka stands apart from the very beginning in Valmiki's *Rāmāyaṇa* as the poetic place idealized for its beauty and thoroughly observed by Hanuman from multiple vantage points. Indeed, multiple pages in book five depict the monkey perched on trees, hilltops, and temple towers, spying on the happenings below from his elevated viewpoint as he searches for Sita (fig. 1.4).[19] Valmiki praises Lanka's beauty, in contrast to his outlook on the other two locales, less in terms of the deeds of ideal kings and more for its geographical location as a remote island and for its natural riches, which predate the constructed palaces and gardens. Altogether Lanka made for an otherworldly, magical experience; a fantastical place, it was only enhanced in the hands of

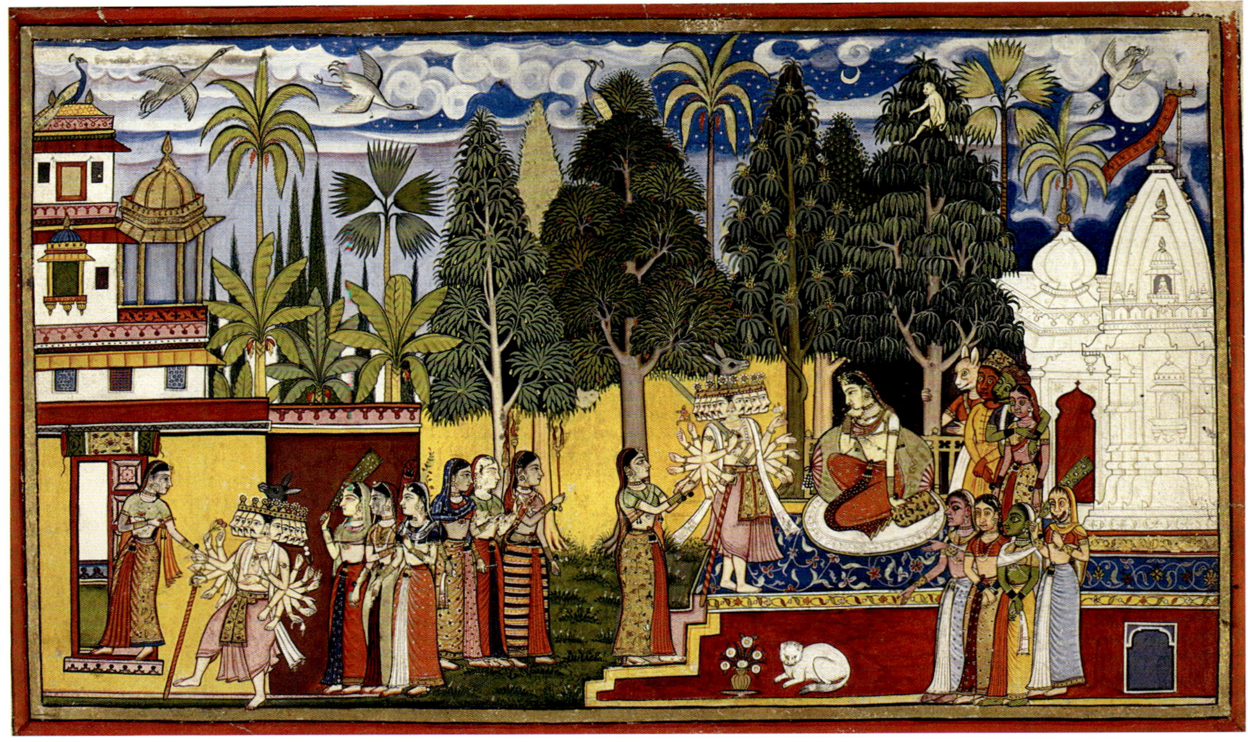

1.4. "Hanuman Thoroughly Explores the Palace of Lanka, Including Ravana's Bedchamber, while Perched atop a Tree," from book five of Jagat Singh's *Rāmāyaṇa*, 1649–53, attributed to the Deccan Painter, Udaipur. Gouache on paper, 23 × 39.9 cm. British Library Board, London; IO. San 3621, f.3.

the Deccan Painter.[20] The more ones gazes at the painted Lanka, the more monumental and impressive the palaces become, whereas the monkey's body asserts his position of belittlement in relation to Ravana's stature and strength. The text and image continue to develop the monkey's perspective, the mood of his watchful observation.

Jagat Singh's *Rāmāyaṇa* offers a pictorial genealogy for Udaipur's investment in painted moods of beautiful places and urban ideals. When eighteenth-century painters concentrated their gaze on the city of lakes in the early 1700s, they brought to bear already-established strategies for creating meta-pictures and immersive moods of admiration into a theme. By then court painters had created idealized images of lush forests, fragrant groves, wondrous islands, and beautiful gardens, palaces, and bazaars. Unlike the figure of the lone Hanuman, *Maharana Sangram Singh II at the Gangaur Boat Procession* is teeming with people immersed in wondrous admiration—within the lake and along the lakefront (see fig. I.4). The vantage point of one conspicuous lakeside bystander, painted in the center between the lake and the lower register,

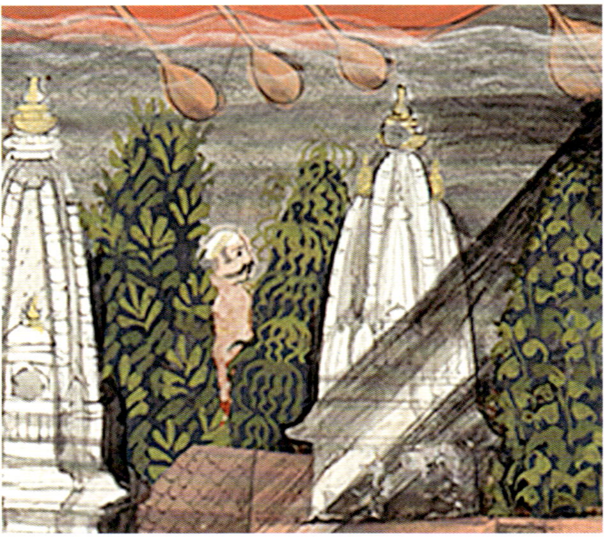

1.5. Detail of fig. I.4, *Maharana Sangram Singh II at the Gangaur Boat Procession*. A lakeside bystander inconspicuously depicted on the water edge delights in the nighttime beauty of the city.

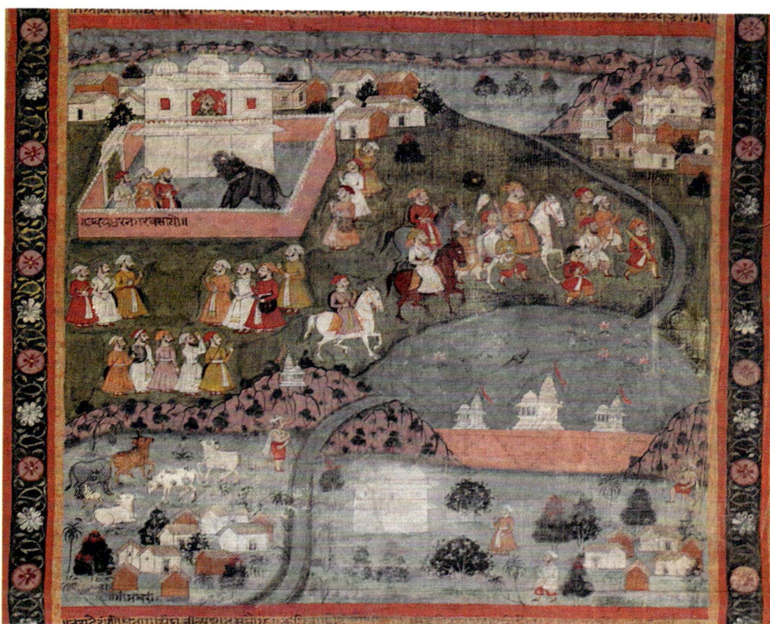

1.6. Maharana Udai Singh II's creation of lakes and palaces in Udaipur, part of a scroll painting depicting the history of the Mewar kings, 1732, Udaipur. Opaque watercolor on paper, width approx. 45 cm. Victoria and Albert Museum, London; 07965:1/(IS).

seems carefully composed to coincide almost exactly with the physical center of the prepared sheet of paper (fig. 1.5). He is hidden between trees, depicted in the patterned style typical of the foliage seen within the court's illustrated manuscripts. Such topographical renderings took the viewer delighting in the nighttime beauty of the city, an astute connoisseur, as their theme. The image included ordinary bystanders among the courtly men. Their presence reinforced the pleasures and enchantments of the lake city. Such constitutive strategies were used for the imagining of both moods and places, which were never discrete subjects.

BUILDING A CITY OF LAKES

Two painted scrolls made between 1730 and 1740 and commissioned by Sangram Singh II (r. 1710–34) depict the genealogy of Mewar's rulers.[21] Significantly, in terms of our explorations, one of the scrolls shows that the creation of lakes was central to the establishment of Udaipur as the court's new capital (fig. 1.6). Scroll painters highlight Udaipur's topography and status as a city built in a valley, rather than as a fort on a hilltop like Chittorgarh, the former capital of the Mewar court.[22] One section of the scroll presents a landscape of winding rivers and channels circulating silvery water into mountain-rimmed lakes. We see Maharana Udai Singh II (r. 1537–72) framed in the window of a white palace; its three domes likely represent Rai Angan (c. 1559), the palace block constructed around a courtyard that was among the first palaces Usai Singh built. On the boundary wall of the depicted courtyard, a scribe noted the Mewar court's settlement in Udaipur city (*udaypura nagara basāyo*). The painter, by drawing vignettes of temples with swaying red flags, marching processions of men on horseback and on foot, and modest homes with thatched roofs interspersed with herdsmen and cows, created a picture of settlement on the banks of the lakes complete with a portrait of the founder-king.[23]

If we take this painting momentarily as an objective document of built structures, the image reflects the care with which Udaipur was sited, by placing environmental and military concerns foremost. An earlier capital in the Debari valley, to which Udai Singh had first decided to relocate Mewar's capital, in 1553, lacked a perennial source of water (fig. 1.7).[24] In locating Udaipur on the Girwa plain, an area in the Aravalli hills with a radius of about ten miles, its founders carefully considered water supply and security. The royal personnel first tracked depressions in mountain passes and charted smaller lakes that were either natural to the region or had been created by previous settlers.[25] The hills to the west, near Lake Pichola, provided a natural barrier to the chosen site, and the expanse of land on the northeast was available for settlement and cultivation. To the south, the nearby mountain peak of Machla Magra, on which Udai Singh's personnel

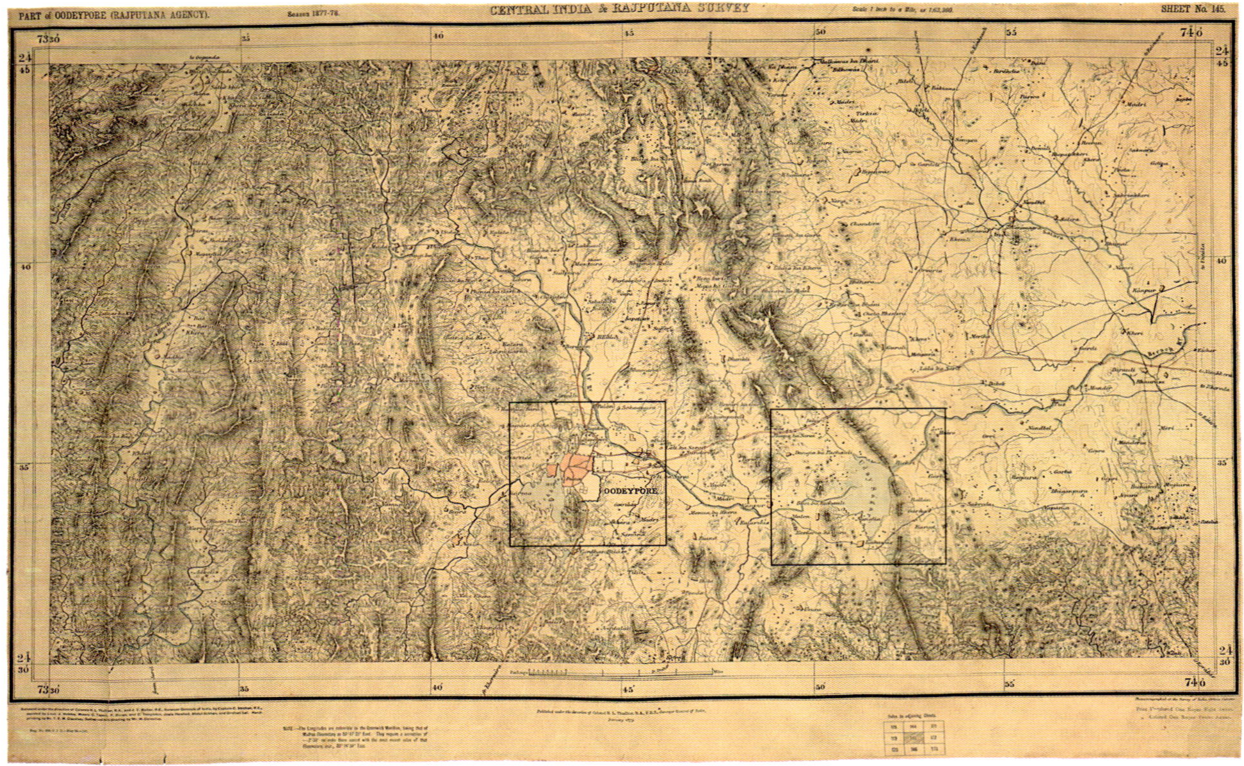

1.7. "Part of Oodeypore, Rajputana Agency. Central India and Rajputana Survey," sheet no. 145, season 1877–78. Nineteenth-century map of Udaipur and its environs, showing Lake Pichola and Lake Udaisagar. The City Palace Museum, Udaipur; MMRI Map no. MC 105.

created a water-holding tank called Dudh Talai, functioned as a defensive watchtower.[26] As the eastern frontier of the Girwa plain was not easily defended, Udai Singh created the lake of Udai Sagar between 1559 and 1564 to serve as a barrier to assailants. Over time, to ensure the well-being of their land and its inhabitants even after consecutive droughts, Udaipur's kings created even more lakes within the kingdom's broader territory. From the sixteenth century on, historical literary sources enumerate Udaipur's man-made lakes—Pichola, Udai Sagar, Fateh Sagar, Rup Sagar, Rang Sagar, and Jana Sagar, to name a few—as well as various dams (*bund* or *pāl*), stepwells (*baoṛi*), and broad steps and platforms (*ghāt*) that create the waterfronts on the banks of Lake Pichola.[27] The creation of an artificial lake was considered a visible demonstration of a sovereign's generosity. Mewar's citizens realized that the region's undulating topography limited access to perennial rivers, necessitating the construction of water tanks and lakes for the sustenance of life, livelihood, and, ultimately, the power and control of the king over both land and people.[28] The building of Udaipur's waterworks and lakes was thus already consolidated by the time painters and patrons turned toward representing and admiring the city's lakes, palaces, and gardens.

While the lakes, the lakefront, and the lake palaces nestled within the Aravalli valley shaped the city's planning and painted representations, the earliest palaces built on the mountain ridge constituted the core of Udaipur's other urban zone. With military considerations foremost in mind, the court's palaces were constructed on the ridge with their backs toward Lake Pichola, facing the west, and the city expanded toward its eastern and northern edges (figs. 1.8. and 1.9). Udai Singh built Rai Angan, the first palace block around a courtyard, atop a vaulted space that housed the royal armor; the enclosed courtyard has been associated with the most important royal functions and coronation ceremonies ever since.[29] The conglomeration of spaces added by successive kings, comprehensively studied by architecture historians Shikha Jain and Vanicka Arora, demonstrates that the royal builders maintained continuity in courtyard planning, linking buildings along a single spine, intersecting with the Rai Angan,

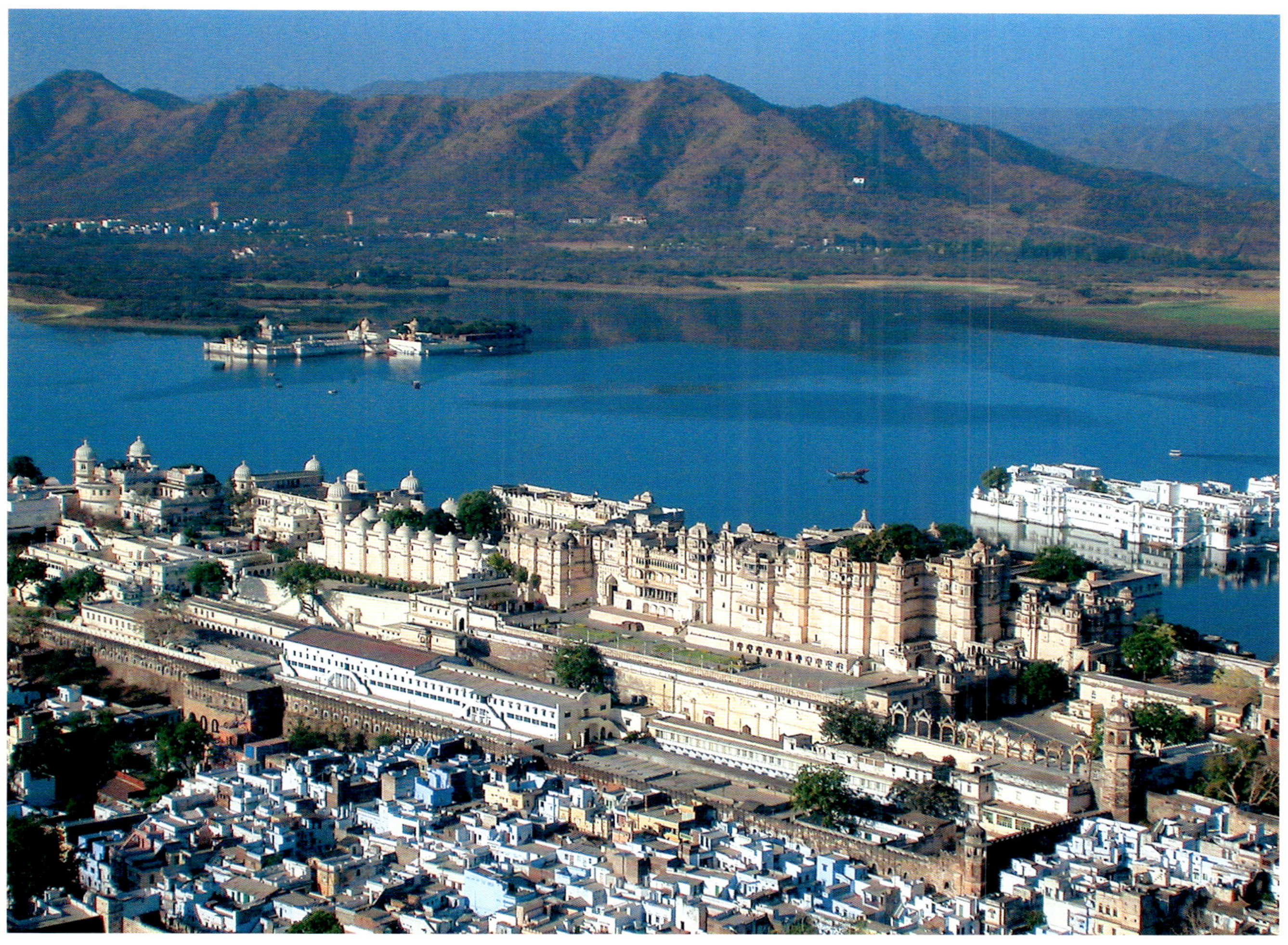

1.8. View of the eastern facade of the Men's and Women's Palaces, today part of the City Palace Museum, Udaipur. Media Office, Eternal Mewar, Udaipur.

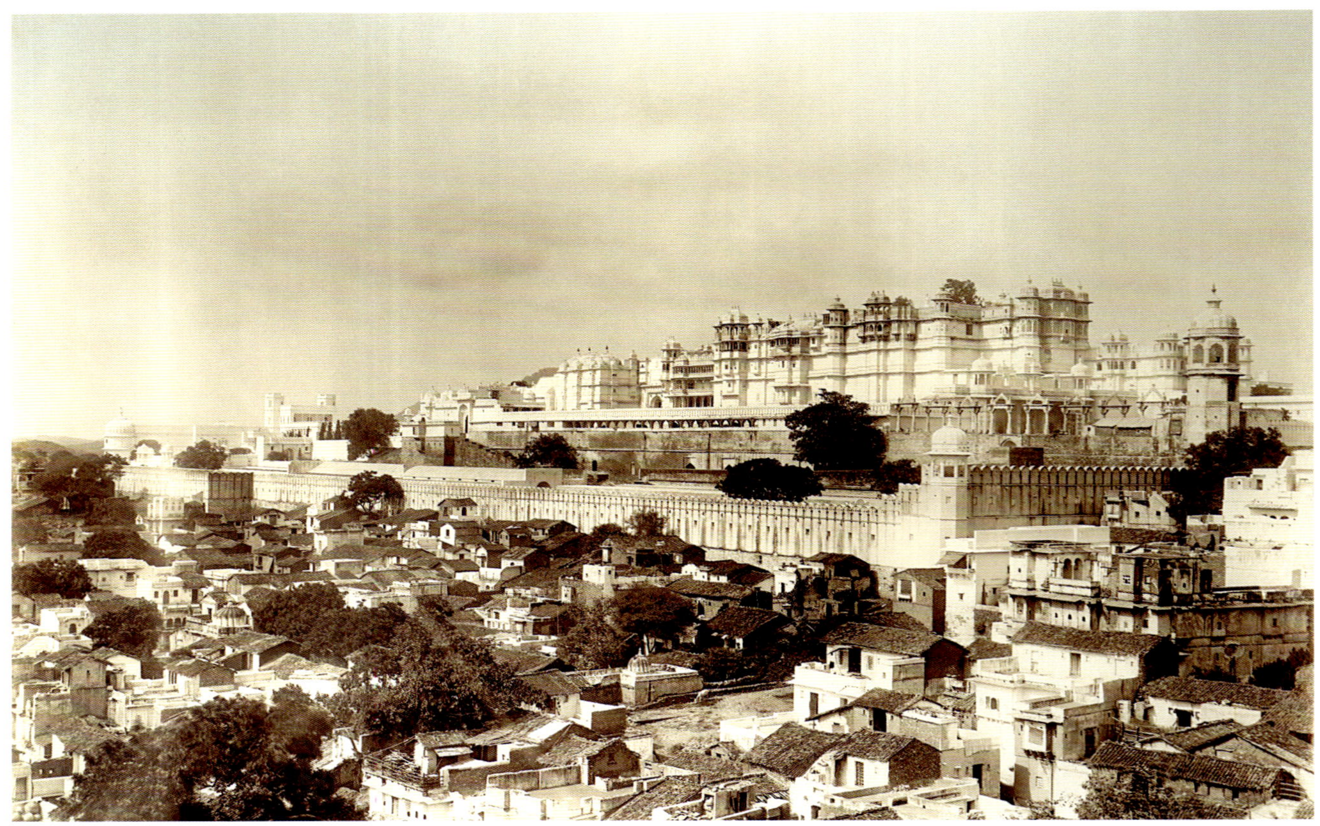

1.9. The eastern facade of the City Palace and the urban environs beyond its walls, Udaipur, photographed by N. Parasur, Ajmer and Kishangarh, c. 1910. Gelatin silver print. The City Palace Museum, Udaipur; 2008.07.0062_R.

until the late 1800s.[30] This mode of addition resulted in the formation of a large rectangular courtyard, the Manek Chowk, bounded by an imposing architectural facade on the west side. The linked palatial spaces are today collectively known as the Men's Palace (Mardana Mahal) (fig. 1.10). Parts of the substructure of the public courtyard of the Manek Chowk were in place by the mid-sixteenth century, during Udai Singh's reign, but Maharana Karan Singh (r. 1620–28) brought the area to completion in 1620.[31] Its boundaries, especially on the northern end, were also demarcated by the 1700s, though paintings demonstrate that the Tripoliya, the triple-arched gateway through which one enters the courtyard today, was built in 1711 during Sangram Singh II's reign (fig. 1.11).[32] By the early 1700s, a sprawling palatial complex had been constructed beyond the courtyard of the Manek Chowk as well as many apartments of the Women's Palace (Zenana Mahal) on all the four sides of the central courtyard Lakshmi Chowk (fig. 1.8). Historians of architecture have effectively deployed large-scale paintings, alongside archival information and analysis of building styles, to trace each of the individual palaces, telling stories of their structures, platforms, and colonnaded spaces, including many of the additions, especially on the higher levels, which cumulatively compose the seemingly unified facade of the City Palace.[33] The multiple courtyards, painted rooms, and terraces that lie behind the overpowering facade signal the interior worlds of the court and the patronage of successive kings, as well as the rich, layered history of styles and idioms continued and reinterpreted by architects and craftsmen.

The visualization of moods during the first three decades of the eighteenth century underscored both vistas—Udaipur's lakes nestled in the Aravalli valley and the Manek Chowk's palace facade. The first three kings of the century—Amar Singh II (r. 1698–1710), Sangram Singh II, and Jagat

Singh II (r. 1734–51)—did not patronize large-scale waterworks, as their predecessors did, but all added structures that impacted both spaces. Chapter 2 considers a key artwork, *Maharana Amar Singh II in Udaipur during a Monsoon Downpour*, in investigating Amar Singh II's architectural and painting commissions in the first decade of the 1700s (see fig. 2.1). Sangram Singh II built new palaces and gardens in the lake-island palace of Jagmandir (including the circular chamber known as the Gol Mahal, c. 1620–28), while Jagat Singh II built his own lake palace, Jagniwas (1746): both became key spaces for creating courtly assemblies, hosting regional kings, such as Sawai Jai Singh II (r. 1700–1743) of Jaipur, and Mewar's powerful nobles (see figs. 3.7 and 3.10). Each of these structures had architectural precursors, such as the Damdama Mahal at the Jagmandir island palace, built by the founder-king Udai Singh; the significance of each of these places is revealed not entirely in their founding dates but in their reclamation by eighteenth-century painters showcasing historical moods.[34]

The newfound motivation by patrons and painters to constitute Udaipur's sites as compelling was certainly part of the Udaipur kings' response to the expanding presence of nobles not only at the court but also in their city. In light of the increased decentralization of Mughal imperial systems, as discussed in the introduction, Maharana Amar Singh II consolidated his regional authority. At the turn of the eighteenth century, he institutionalized the status of various estate holders (thakurs) and estate lands (*ṭhikānās*), taking unto account each clan's ancestral services to the Mewar court in Udaipur.[35] Sacrifices made by a clan's forefathers in "protecting" Mewar's sovereignty in several conflicts, including those with the Mughals in the sixteenth century, were employed by each *ṭhikānā* to formulate the clan's status, genealogy, history, and identity. As this community staked its claims at the court, its

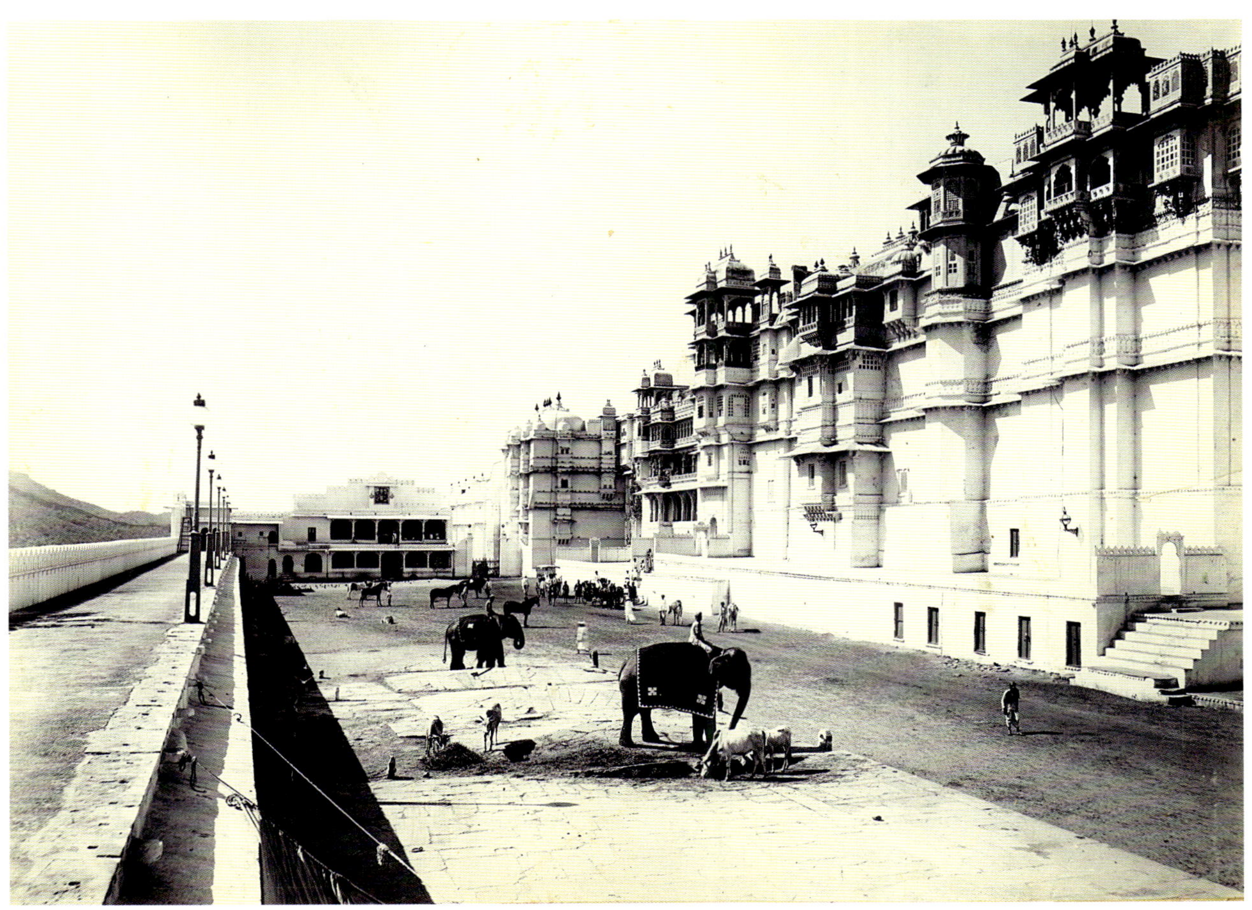

1.10. View of Manek Chowk and the Men's Palace facade, including the towering Baadi Mahal on the extreme right, City Palace, Udaipur, c. 1890–1905. Gelatin silver print. The City Palace Museum, Udaipur; 2009.10.0139-00046_R.

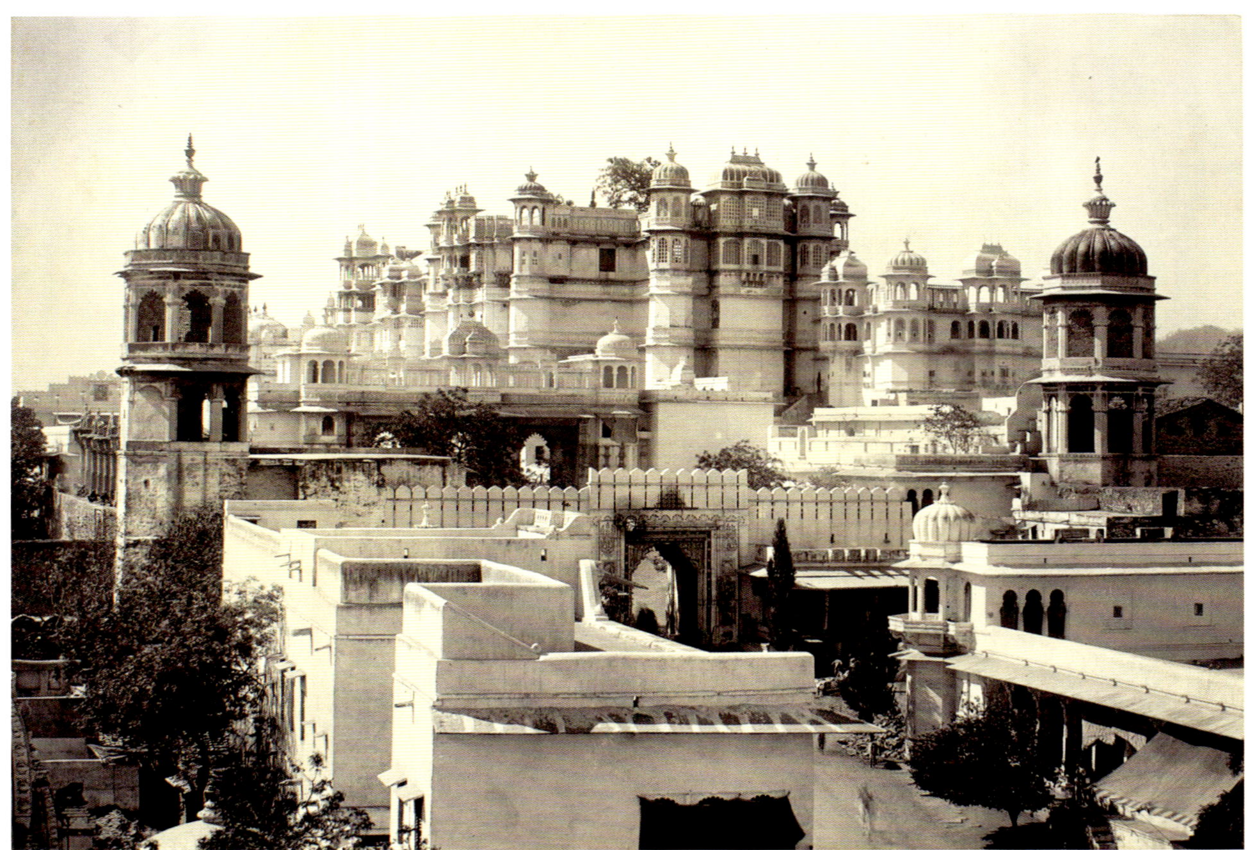

1.11. View of the City Palace and environs, with the northern facade of the Baadi Mahal overlooking the main gateway, Badi Pol, and the triple-arched entrance Tripoliya, Udaipur, c. 1895–1905. Gelatin silver print. The City Palace Museum, Udaipur; 2009.10.0139-00057_R.

members also started to build their own mansion (*haveli*) in the city, to the north beyond the palace entrance or, in some cases, around the lake as well. The official status of several of Mewar's *ṭhikānās* and the power each individual wielded at the Udaipur court changed continually over the course of the eighteenth century. The shifting status of the courtiers may be one of the reasons that patrons and painters focused less on pictorial genealogies and more on picturing the exceptional moods of Udaipur's lands, landmarks, and lakes, as well as on depicting the contemporary courtly audiences and specific courtiers immersed in these places.[36]

The championing of one's localized world—and its geographical, cultural, intellectual, and aesthetic distinctions—was not restricted to Udaipur. The emergence of new urban cultures in the neighboring Kachhwaha court at Jaipur (earlier Amber) may have contributed to the Udaipur kings' mode of adopting a distinctive approach. Already by the early 1700s, Sawai Jai Singh II of Amber had initiated plans for asserting his power and independence in northern India: he invited merchants and intellectuals, including astronomers and architects, to envision his new city of Jaipur.[37] He moved the Kachhwaha capital in 1727 from the fort of Amber to the new city of Jaipur, built on an unusual regular-grid plan. The planning and architecture of his new city, often singularly related with Shastric (that is, Hindu) canonical texts, was also informed by other factors, such as seventeenth-century Mughal cities, gardens, and imperial audience halls.[38] Even before moving to Jaipur, the Kachhwaha rajas commissioned their artists to make maps of prominent forts, towns, and urban routes in northern India while actively collecting maps as well. In short, while the Kachhwahas looked to create an urbane identity by shifting to a new place, Udaipur's Sisodia kings realized the potential their city's unique locale, microclimate, and natural resources offered to hold new communities together.

If Udaipur's painters of the early eighteenth century emerged at the forefront of establishing the taste for paintings mediating moods of place, then Jaipur's painters firmly established cartographic practices in eighteenth-century India. The 1708 political and marital alliance between the two courts, as noted in the introduction, was widely commemorated in paintings and resulted in the exchange of gifts (including works of art), travels of painters with their patrons, and a series of diplomatic and personal meetings in the following decades between Udaipur's Sangram Singh II and Jaipur's Sawai Jai Singh II. Despite the many exchanges between the two courts, and unlike the smaller, individual and group portraits that circulated as gifts sent from Udaipur to Jaipur, larger Udaipur paintings of place did not travel.[39] While direct citations of or adaptations from specific maps remain elusive, the shared visual conventions such as the use of planimetric views and composite viewpoints in the same picture suggest the mobility of productions, people, and practices related to cartographic knowledge. Pictures of maps and moods could have provoked somewhat similar conditions of viewing; both demand looking from a short distance (in order to observe the details) as well as from afar (to view the complete picture). If the pictorial and material shift at Udaipur in the 1700s involved both mapping of Mewar's terrain and describing of architecture, then in addition to considering the exchange of knowledge and practices on the ground, we must ask, what distinguished a map of a place (*taraha*) from the mood (*bhāva*) of a place?

MAPS AND MOODS

The workshops (*kārkhānā*) established at the Kachhwaha court capitals in Amber and Jaipur were highly systematized. Copious records reveal the organization of the court's artisanal economy for the production of wide-ranging material and intellectual cultures.[40] Maps feature in the records of both the painting workshop (*sūratkhānā*) and the library (*potikhānā*). Both the skills of the maker and the medium—paper and cloth on which drawings were made—were deemed important. According to Shailka Mishra's extensive reading of daily records of the *sūratkhānā*, the court artist (*chaterā*) at the turn of the eighteenth century could be as adept at drawing maps as he was at painting portraits, textiles, or illustrated manuscripts—the painter's skill was applicable across genres and media.[41] The mention of painters who created maps as well as portraits, such as Dwarak and Deepa, provides important clues for imagining their training and exposure to allied practices.[42] The Kachhwaha court amassed early modern India's most extensive cartographic collection. Wide-ranging map artifacts, while often titled with the same term, *taraha*, could refer to route maps, military maps, pilgrimage maps, construction drawings of individual buildings and gardens drawn on grid paper, maps depicting forts and palaces outside of Amber and Jaipur, and maps related to the purchasing of lands.[43] The launch of an early eighteenth-century project to conserve more than three hundred maps, the relation of drawings to specific construction projects, and the clues available about the lives of maps received as gifts from painters confirm that the social, symbolic, and historical roles of individual artifacts were varied and distinct.[44] I discuss cartographic artifacts from this corpus that mapped Udaipur's palaces as well as travel and territory in the Mewar region. Maps that commemorated singular landmarks, even those located beyond Mewar's boundaries, help us to tease out the affective and epistemic affinities between the painting of maps at Jaipur and of moods at Udaipur as well as their distinct operative roles as objects.

Maps representing Udaipur's palaces archived in Jaipur's collection attest that there were numerous opportunities for sharing of knowledge and techniques among painters and mapmakers working at both courts. An eighteenth-century plan of the palaces of Udaipur and Lake Pichola, likely made by an Udaipur artist and identified as a *taraha* by Jaipur's scribes and mapmakers, conveys the courtly precinct's architectural layout (fig. 1.12).[45] While the full map itself is now inaccessible to researchers, the scribe's notations of labeled spaces and a drawing based on a photograph of one section suggest an architectural plan conveying the function and ownership of various spaces. The drawing includes the public courtyard Manek Chowk, names of individual pavilions, colonnades, and buildings in the Men's and Women's Palaces, the stables for horses and elephants, and the broader environs of the Pichola lakefront. The scribe also identifies the mansions of several of Mewar's estate holders, Jagmandir island palace, the flight of steps that led to Jagniwas lake palace, and the dams that controlled the flow of water into Lake Pichola, thus providing us with a list of the broader urban precincts of note.[46] The inscriptions of painted rooms (*citrasāli*) related to Jagat Singh II and the colonnaded space (*darīkhānā*) associated with Pratap Singh II (r. 1752–55), who was married to Jaipur's

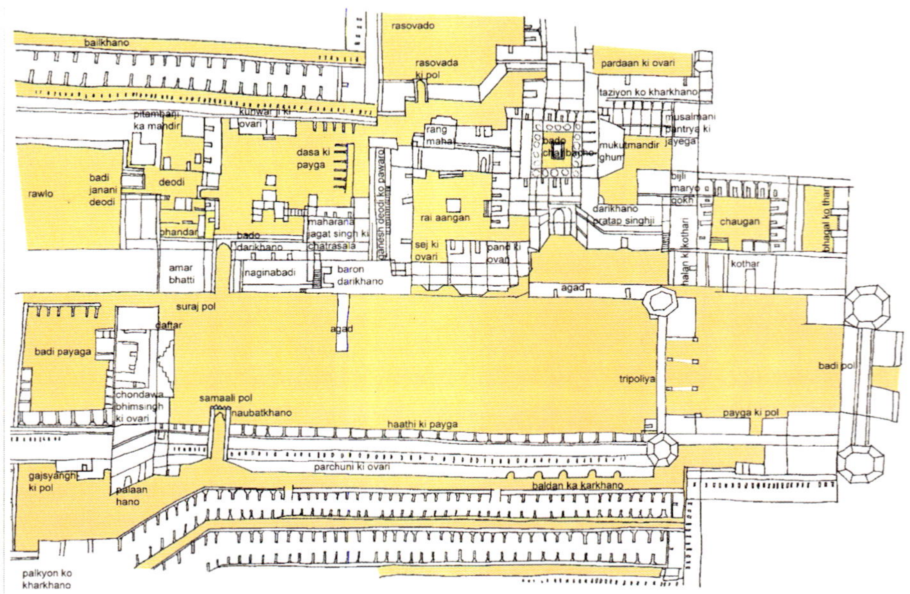

1.12. A representation of a plan of the City Palace, Udaipur, indicating the extent of the palace and its various courtyards. Based on an original plan of the palaces of Udaipur and Lake Pichola, c. 1755–65, Maharaja Sawai Man Singh II Museum, City Palace, Jaipur; Kapad Dwara Collection, cat. no. 158. Image courtesy of Shikha Jain and Vanicka Arora, *Living Heritage of Mewar: Architecture of the City Palace, Udaipur* (Ahmedabad: Mapin Publishing in association with Maharana Mewar Historical Publications Trust, 2017), 26.

Sawai Jai Singh II's daughter, allow us to date the drawing to Pratap Singh II's rule. It is very likely that familial associations led to the commission. The existence of another Udaipur map dated to 1792, noted as a customary gift (*nazar*) by painter Udairam to the Jaipur king, affirms that the commission of the Pratap Singh II–period plan was not an exception.[47]

Artists working across the painted genres of maps and portraits in the Kachhwaha workshops were not an anomaly. A similar fluidity must have been operable in Udaipur by the early 1700s, as evidenced by the rapid assimilation of new architectural precincts into larger artworks featuring the moods of place. This transformation of maps into a large-scale artwork can be seen in the drawing of lakeside architecture in *Maharana Sangram Singh II at the Gangaur Boat Procession* (see fig. I.4) and in an Udaipur painter's *The Mood of Kota Palace*, a work that at times has been discussed as a "large-scale map combining different perspectives" and that includes planimetric views of spaces (see fig. 1.19).[48] The juxtaposition of a bird's-eye view of the courtyard space, composed along an oblique axis in the center of the painting, and a quadripartite garden space defined by diagonal lines certainly demands that the viewer continuously negotiate differing vantage points. By contrast, the use of the planimetric and sectional elevation views of smaller courtyard spaces in the bottom half of the painting is absolutely clear. Interestingly, while no inscription on the back of place-centric Udaipur paintings identifies them as *taraha* (maps or cartographic images), the classification employed at Jaipur, no concomitant inscription related to the maps from Jaipur identifies a topographical or planar depiction as the *bhāva* of a place. Claims about architectural knowledge as well as topographical knowledge on a regional scale were made in both genres, and the decision to patronize one or the other emerges as a motivated choice at both neighboring courts.

The Jaipur collection's regional maps of present-day Rajasthan and Gujarat, to date studied to a lesser degree, further indicate that the routes to and from Udaipur were carefully surveyed and well traveled. The charting of mobility and territoriality was of consequence to the Kachhwahas, first as Rajput kings, who were high-ranking officers in service of Mughal emperors, and then as independent rajas over the course of the eighteenth century.[49] One Jaipur map depicting the Mewar territories across Rajasthan, described as the "Land of Ranaji," was made around 1654, when Jai Singh I of Jaipur took instructions from Shah Jahan for the campaign to dismantle Jagat Singh I's ordered repairs to the Chittor fort.[50] A second, late seventeenth- to early eighteenth-century regional representation, a map showing Ahmedabad, Ajmer, Udaipur, and Nagaur, represents routes connecting the four towns, as well as the forts of Jodhpur and Jaisalmer. Alongside the oblong lines and scalloped mounds that denote the mountainous terrain, routes connect diagrammatic representations of the major urban precincts (fig. 1.13).[51] Water bodies and tanks (*talāb*) of varying sizes are prominent, not due simply to the scribe's labels but also because of their sheer number and the painter's rendering of the water surface in wavy strokes that contrast with the dense enmeshing of the hills and the curving route lines. Scribal labels for each geographical landmark in Perso-Arabic and Devanagari script link this map (*taraha*) to the notating practices followed in the mid-seventeenth-century map of Mewar's territories described as the "Land of Ranaji."[52] Surely, such maps evoke an imaginary of the regional landscape—comprising forts and tanks nestled within hills and plains—and performed an epistemic role to ascertain knowledge of terrain and territories that lay beyond the court's boundaries. The functionality of the route map, however, seems to be underscored. It gives the distance from one place to the next, prioritizing directionality and sequence of travel on the ground. The network of small junctions, important stations (denoted by two concentric circles), and diagrammed urban landmarks creates a cartographic artifact ready for use.

The geographical expanse and the pictorial aspects of the map showing Ahmedabad, Ajmer, Udaipur, and Nagaur enable a classification of the types of expertise required to create it. The map provides as well evidence of the sharing of information between surveyors and painters that such a map would have demanded. The diagrammatic rendering of the towns signifies the natural and built profile of each precinct: for Ahmedabad, four gates and quadrants of the city suggest the urban layout of a city built in the plain (fig. 1.14). The drawing of a lake adjacent to an elevation view of clustered buildings is discernable as the profile of Udaipur—a palatial complex located in a hilly valley (fig. 1.15). The approximation evident in the schematic diagram suggests that the painters who made these kinds of regional maps were not necessarily the same ones who specialized in rendering painterly presentations of the individual forts and towns, seen in the specimen maps of Ranthambhor and Jodhpur forts discussed below. To create route maps, painters who specialized in rendering architecture, plans of individual buildings, and aerial views of urban precincts could have collaborated with others, especially those who specialized in measuring distances, plotting nodes, drawing the terrain, and incorporating information that could be culled from older sources.[53] We know that painters in Jaipur's workshops had access to professionals who as a team possessed the expertise to work across topographical and architectural scales. Such a map also invites us to imagine the exchanges among skilled professionals along the drawn routes, where painters and surveyors proficient in rendering regions and those specialized in delineating architecture intersected and plausibly would have exchanged skills and knowledge about instruments, mensuration, and drawing.

One of the earliest large-scale paintings on cloth made at the Udaipur court of comparable size to these regional and route maps, *Maharana Amar Singh II in Udaipur during a Monsoon Downpour* (discussed in chapter 2; see fig. 2.1), suggests that Udaipur's painters drew on the visual knowledge conveyed within maps. It is difficult to imagine that this early artwork's focus on mapping mountain streams and water bodies—an interest Udaipur's painters would transform into a major theme within depictions of the court's hunting expeditions over the course of the eighteenth century—could have been achieved without access to regional maps or the knowledge of how to map terrains. Such works give us reason to believe that specialists intersected but then continued on their own journeys and enriched their respective genres. In the map showing Ahmedabad, Ajmer, Udaipur, and Nagaur, curving lines operate as abstractions of the journeyed routes, and the indexical urban views function as landmarks punctuating the mapped travels and topography. This work demonstrates both the mobility of the map painters and their understanding of mobile vision. Within *Maharana Amar Singh II in Udaipur during a Monsoon Downpour*, as we will see, painters deployed representations of the city observed from multiple vantage points, thus constituting a mobile vision and establishing a relation with the landmarks depicted in the artwork itself—the new palaces built by the king and the exclusive views those offered. When Udaipur's painters sought to construct a locale's mood that praised its natural environment, they looked toward the material landscape and deployed navigational techniques of regional mapmakers.

In the Kachhwaha workshops, *taraha*, as a term and an artifact type, defined a capacious category. The subgenre of commemorative maps meaningfully connects empirical and aesthetic concerns. A sizable number of maps collected and commissioned feature fortified towns and cities of northern and western India and form a group of artifacts entirely ontologically distinct from the above-discussed map depicting the architectural layout of Udaipur's palaces. While the detailed accounts of measuring routes and land were in place, Susan Gole has argued, map painters juxtaposed views, asserted their affiliation based on stylistic choices, and emphasized painterly elements in commemorative maps to convey cartographic conceptions other than scale and size of built forms.[54] The study of one such map depicting

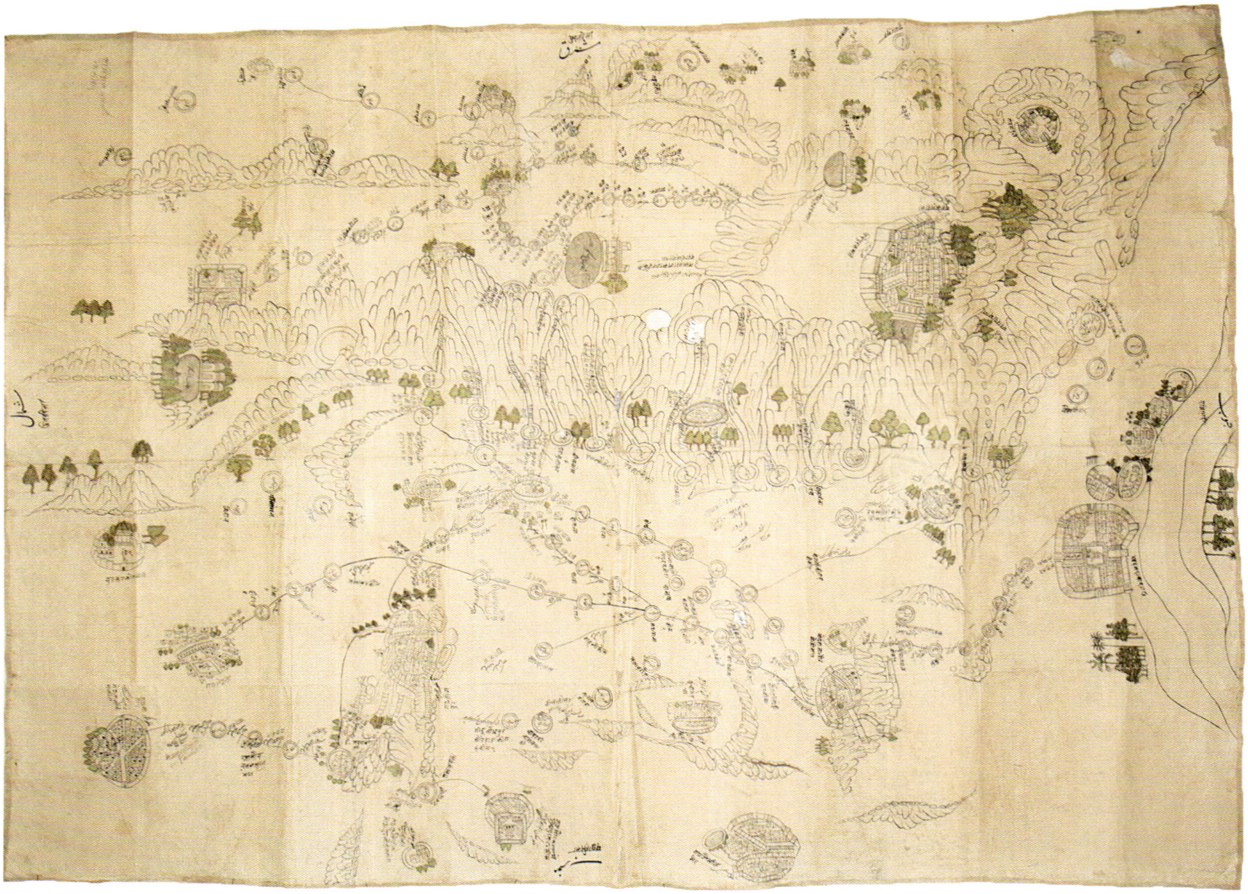

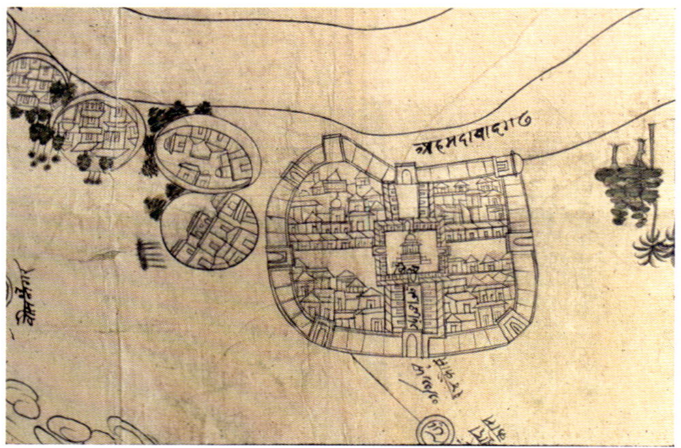

1.13. Map showing Ahmedabad, Ajmer, Udaipur, and Nagaur, late seventeenth to early eighteenth century. Opaque color and ink on paper lined with cloth, 109 × 152 cm. Maharaja Sawai Man Singh II Museum, City Palace, Jaipur; Potikhana (Map 119).

1.14. Detail of fig. 1.13. Depiction of the city plan of Ahmedabad.

1.15. Detail of fig. 1.13. Depiction of the topographical environs of Udaipur and Lake Pichola.

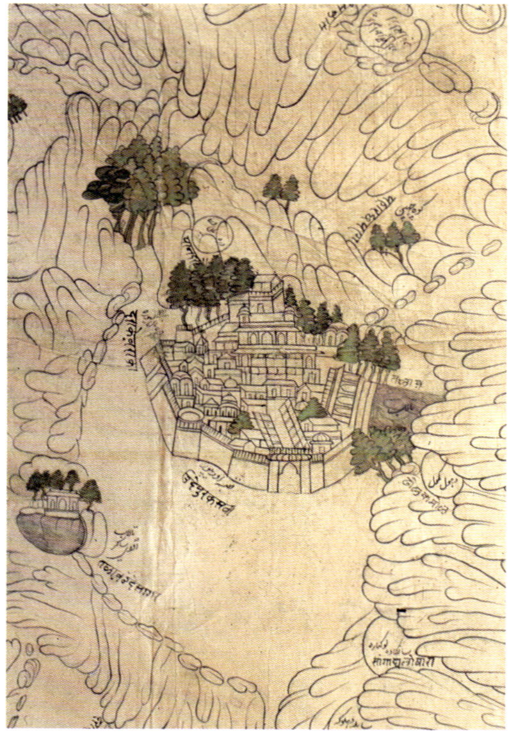

the Jodhpur fort, capital of the Rajput court of Marwar, underscores its construction on a hilly outcrop in a desert landscape and its critical access to routes and water resources. Its distinctive pink rocks connect with the court's painting style, suggesting that a local painter was part of the mapping team before the artifact was deposited in Jaipur during the 1730s–40s, when political tensions between the two courts heightened.[55] Another impressive map depicting an aerial view of the oval-shaped Ranthambhor fort is worth noting, not the least because Jaipur's painters were likely directly involved in this commission (fig. 1.16).[56] *Fortified City of Ranthambhor* is ascribed to the reign of Jagat Singh of Jaipur (r. 1786–1818), though it marks the fort's seizure in 1754 by his predecessor Madho Singh I (r. 1750–68), who desired to change parts of the fort's construction (*banwāṇā*).[57] Surrounded by moats, the fortress stands in the center of hills and forests; the turns and barriers along the main entrance path are carefully delineated in the planimetric view. All of the important buildings, hills, streets, gateways, neighborhoods, temples, lakes, and water tanks are labeled. The emphasis created by a chalky white layer on two of the major gateways suggests that conveying the fort's access route was imperative and that the over-painting represents either corrections by a supervisor or the proposed renovations. Known for its strong defensive walls, Ranthambhor was conquered by the Mughal emperor Akbar (r. 1556–1605) in 1569 and assigned to his noble Raja Ramdas Kachhwaha, the cousin of Amber's Raja Man Singh, who disliked him for his association with the Mughal emperor. Possessing the prestigious fort presumably made for a significant victory in the eyes of Amber's independent-minded mid-eighteenth-century successors who commissioned the artifact.

The *Fortified City of Ranthambhor* explicitly praises the depicted site as an impregnable fortress sited in an alluring landscape. The size and composition of the painted picture hardly suggests that it was made for the sole purpose of redesigning the fort. The scribe noted the height of the impermeable walls and the highest elevation for the firing of cannons, while the painter rendered a sense of invincibility by drawing numerous tiny white monkeys scaling the walls (fig. 1.17).[58] The monkeys are seen grabbing onto the hills and fortifications, but not one is painted as having climbed over the walls, heightening the thrill of this visual discovery. A restricted color palette further lends strength to the fortified boundaries, reminiscent of the strategies deployed by painters of the illustrated *Pādshāh-nāma* (Chronicle of Shah Jahan) more than a century earlier to render walls of forts. The painter Murar's depiction of the Deccan fort of Daulatabad's siege in 1633–34 in the following year commemorated a crucial imperial victory.[59] Ebba Koch flags Murar's topographical approach in this folio, manifested in his use of "maximum space" on the page for the "stunning depiction of the fortress," as unparalleled in Mughal painting.[60] While an engraved image, "'Würtzburg,' by Braun and Hogenberg," could have served as a model for Murar's rendering, his image also emphasizes the site's architectural specificity and visually proclaims the Daulatabad fort as a major triumph.[61] In the *Pādshāh-nāma* folio, we find a genealogy for the Jaipur *taraha* of the Ranthambhor fort, in which map painters sought to proclaim accuracy and beauty equally. The Jaipur painter's emphasis on subtle gradation in the use of darker browns and grays for the barrier is contrasted by the sparse colors in the fort's interiors. The slim translucent green strip denoting the surrounding flat land intensifies the perceived ramparts and the individual peaks that constitute a hilly border for the paper sheet, bolstering the fortifications. In contrast to the blue bodies of water inside the fort, which are inscribed and identified, the streams and lakes in the green plains on the outside contain floating lotus flowers, an established iconography in illustrated manuscripts. We have less clarity on the consumption of commemorative maps, compared to the established utility of route maps and construction drawings, though the painters of *Fortified City of Ranthambhor* were explicit in their formulation that it was possible to be both objective and subjective. It was imperative to be seen describing the feel of the place alongside the inscriptions conveying the heights of the fortification walls, thus shaping the perception of the landscape's beauty and plentitude through painterly effects alongside accurate planimetric representation.

As much as painted maps and paintings of moods had in common, the focus of each artifact type and the reasons for its production remained distinct. The affective insistences on display in commemorative maps have two meanings. First, the continuities and discontinuities between painted maps and moods may have more to offer than we have explored thus far. Certainly Jaipur's maps and mapmakers played a key role in Udaipur's painters acquiring the spatial skills to parse buildings and landscapes into representational idioms on multiple scales and in greater detail. But the tools of visualization deployed at Jaipur also argue for further research on the picturing of the perceptive feel of a place within maps and for in-depth analyses of specific historicisms at play. Ultimately, a question of audience emerges: toward whom were these

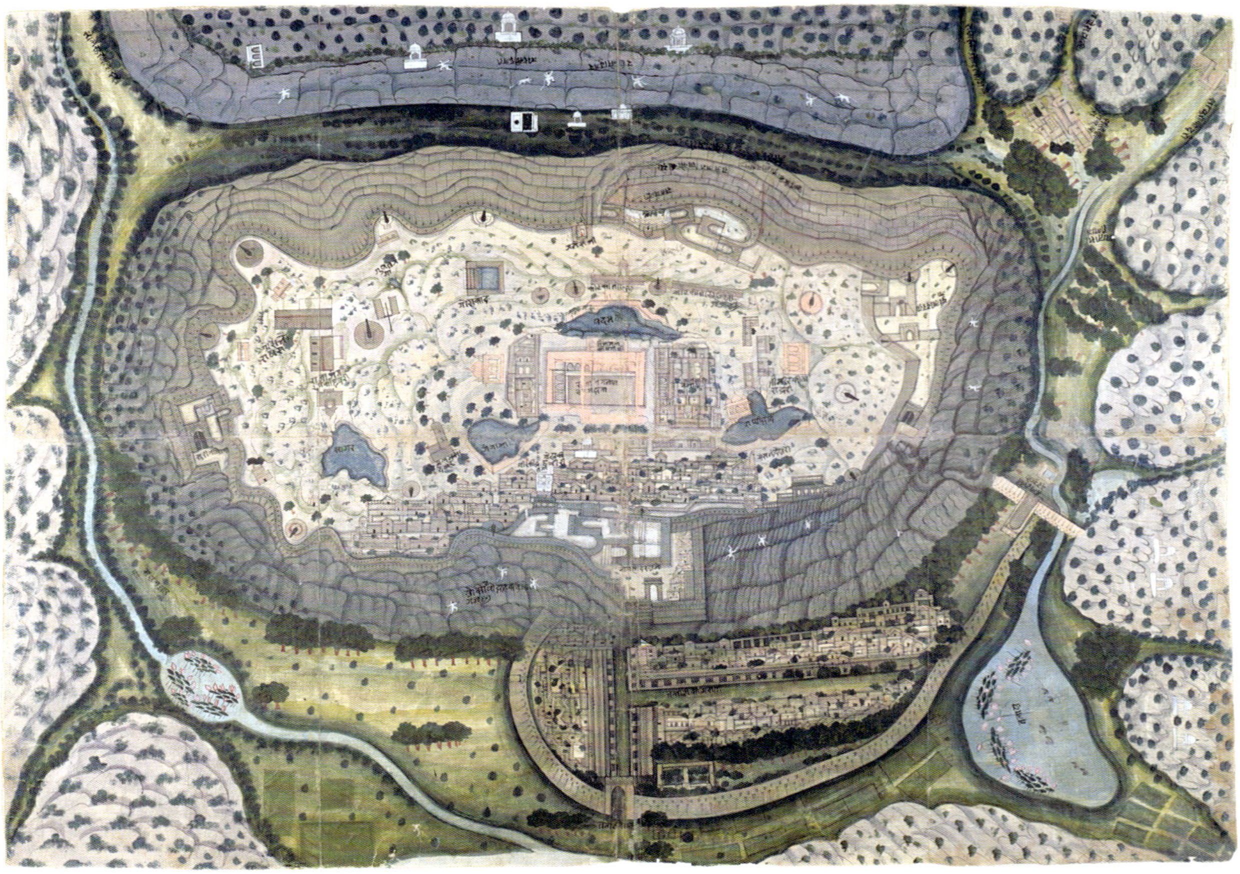

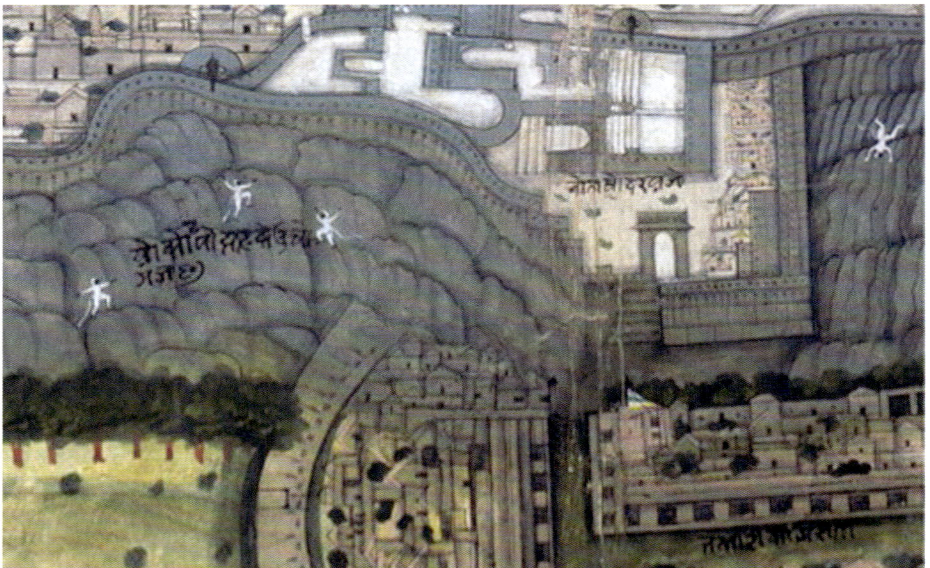

1.16. *Fortified City of Ranthambhor*, inscribed on reverse, dating to the reign of Jagat Singh of Jaipur (r. 1786–1818), Jaipur. Opaque watercolor and ink on paper, 73.7 × 103.2 cm. The Metropolitan Museum of Art, New York; Fletcher Fund, 1996, 1996.100.6.

1.17. Detail of fig. 1.16. View showing small monkeys scaling the fort's walls and the inscription indicating their height.

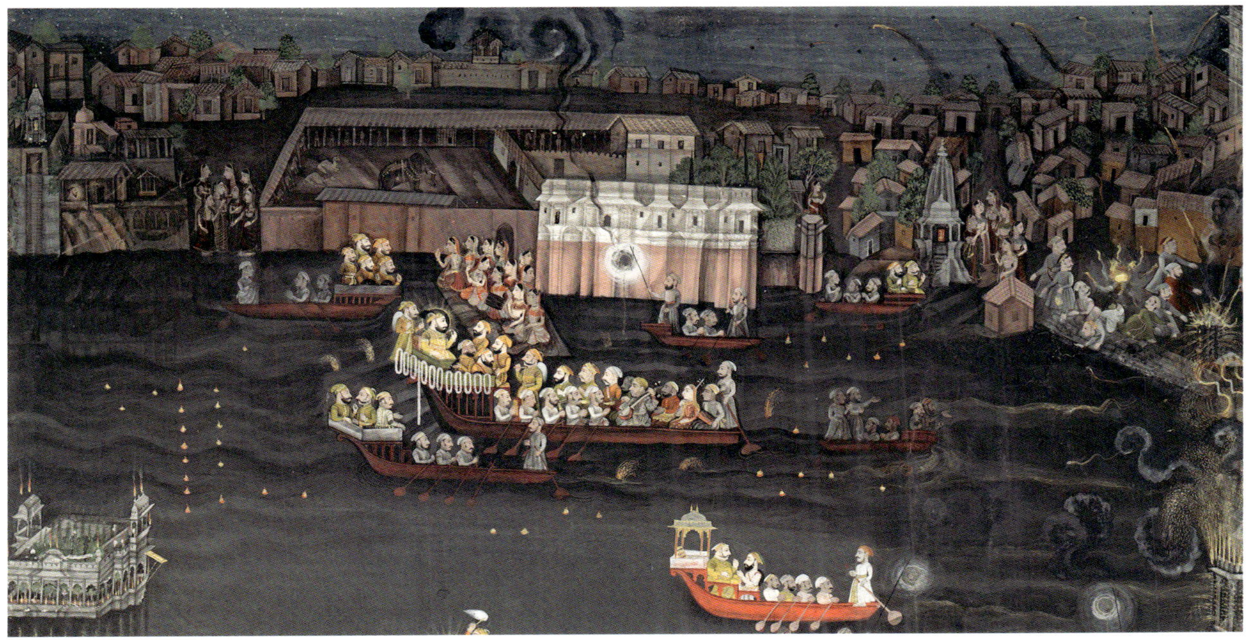

1.18. Detail of fig. I.4, *Maharana Sangram Singh II at the Gangaur Boat Procession*. Depiction of lakeside mansions and Gangaur festivities near the Hanuman temple and Hanuman *ghāt*.

enchanting images of new territories directed? This question ties into a second point. The absence of painted portraits in eighteenth-century commemorative maps makes the terminological and ontological distinctions between maps and moods all the more apparent. The courtiers who populated the boat procession presented in *Maharana Sangram Singh II at the Gangaur Boat Procession* were those whom the king desired to seduce. Admiration of the lakes and lakefronts of the city in the company of nobles, musicians, poets, and dancers was an established practice that features prominently in the court's archives.[62] Patrons hoped that the immersion in pleasurable moods offered by the lands, lakes, landmarks, and associated representations would enchant and enable meaningful attachments for the prominently featured courtly communities—in the changing seasons of courtly politics, land and feeling were held to be entirely interdependent. Udaipur's archive reveals the kinds of efficacy expected from images of alluring places. Jaipur's kings, such as Sawai Jai Singh II, were key consumers alongside Sangram Singh II of the depicted lakesides and lake palaces (see fig. 3.7). These insights from one locale that simultaneously emphasized spatial knowledge of and sociability centered on beautiful places have broader implications for understanding the affective work of mapping sensate encounters with sites.

The upper register of *Maharana Sangram Singh II at the Gangaur Boat Procession* reveals to us the painter's honing of his skills at representing spatial knowledge (fig. 1.18). Here we find evidence of his walking about and getting a sense of the lakeside activities and buildings, proceeding from studying the broad steps of the Hanuman *ghāt* and the adjoining Hanuman temple, coming to the prominent courtyard mansion with lakeside windowed pavilions and stables housing elephants, camels, and horses, and walking up a steep flight of steps leading to another, unidentified temple. The street on the upper edge of the painting is demarcated just as clearly as the lake frontage, its emptiness signaling that the residents are celebrating on the lakefront (or sleeping at home). The viewer searches for the outlines and forms hidden in the dark hues, finding the paths, courtyards, and corners that the painters of such urban descriptions, like mapmakers, traversed, building upon their spatial ability to hold images of the place from various angles and directions in the mind and fix them on paper.[63] In finding these details, we assume the position of the king and his courtiers on the boat, who were mobile, viewing the city from their vessel as it circles the lake. They were offered up-close views on both banks of Lake Pichola. The city residents in the lower registers are not privy to the king's view, nor are we privy to architectural details of their urban quarter in the same painting style or representational conventions (see fig. I.4). The lake's embankment near the festive gathering is barely visible. Silver-colored wavy lines bring the lake waters to the brown edge of the ground, yet the painter keeps them away from the bodies that jostle each other in the crowd. The painterly white and gray wavy brushstrokes denote the ripples created by the boats' movement. Diagonal lines in black, seen near the center of the painting, radiating from the base of the royal barge on the right toward the crowd, are suggestive of water lashing backward onto the lakefront as the boat moves forward. The deliberate use of shadows, shading, and translucency in the upper register, as opposed to the planar, bold, and pattern-like forms of buildings and bodies in the lower half, only enhances the simultaneity and the separateness, but it also asserts the insistent codependence of the two halves. Together, the two sections of the painting not only make the wondrous admiration of the mood of the Gangaur festival into a pictorial subject; they also showcase the artist's painterly effects and skills at urban description. Udaipur's painters had at their command the spatial skills, picturing skills, and painterly skills to offer these immersive moods.

PICTORIAL TRANSLATIONS—*THE MOOD OF KOTA PALACE*

In the preceding pages I have considered three visual, material, and spatial precedents that account for the abilities of Udaipur's early eighteenth-century painters to render the awe-inspiring moods of their lake city and its abundant hilly environs. First, I discussed Jagat Singh's *Rāmāyaṇa*, from the mid-seventeenth century, for its sophisticated intertwining of topographical description, emotional journeys, and formidable places. Second, I explicated the urban and political dynamics that prompted early eighteenth-century kings and painters to look anew at their established locale. Third, I considered the distinctions and overlaps between painted moods and maps alongside the routes through which ideas and practices traveled. I now turn to court paintings that inspired Udaipur's painters as they reimagined, circa 1700, their familiar streetscapes and local lakescapes. Like their seventeenth-century counterparts who painted the *Rāmāyaṇa*, these artists brought into their paintings Hanuman's smitten gaze as he admired Lanka.

A previously unexamined instance of exchange, an unnamed Udaipur painter's adaptation of a painting originally made at the Kota court, makes a persuasive case for the history of pictorial translations and the history of formal choices deployed for constituting the *bhāva* of a place. The formal departures seen in his version, *The Mood of Kota Palace* (fig. 1.19), reveal the particular kind of beholding with which the Udaipur artist encountered and adapted the original, a mediation that I attempt to recover by dwelling on its painted transformations. The Udaipur artist's looking and his making are given material form in *The Mood of Kota Palace*. Remarkably, the scribe who annotated the back of the painting asserted that it be received as a depiction of the *bhāva* of Kota palace.

Kota's paintings captured the imagination of Amar Singh II, introducing new techniques and visual effects to the Udaipur court workshop's repertoire.[64] Kota was originally part of the Bundi state, and although it was independently established in 1631, the development of painting at these two centers has largely been discussed in a related way, due to several artistic and political connections. Given the familial ties between Bundi-Kota and Udaipur, several paintings and artists circulated between the two Rajput courts even prior to Amar Singh II visiting Bundi or before he became king.[65] The mother of Amar Singh II of Udaipur was a Bundi princess, and the young prince stayed in Bundi around 1691, following a conflict with his father, Maharana Jai Singh (r. 1681–98). Upon his return to Udaipur, Amar Singh II resided for a few years at Rajnagar, near Rajsamand Lake, and held an independent court there. He likely patronized painters at Rajnagar, possibly attracting artists from Udaipur, Bundi, and Kota.[66] The portraits of Amar Singh II (made from 1690 through the 1710s) showcase the use of tinted *siyah kalam*—sepia tones, black, and gold combined with a hint of color.[67] This style emerged as a major interest at Udaipur—so much so that there are multiple surviving works, the evidence from which has led scholars to call the unnamed artist the "Stipple Master."[68] This artist's genius for tiny details and his minimalistic palette connect him to Kota court painters' portrayals of hunts.[69] His detailed stippling of the king's face with a distinctive handlebar mustache established Amar Singh II's portrait in the canon of Indian painting.

By way of these encounters and travels, Amar Singh II is thought to have acquired a taste for not only new, finely drawn and minimally colored paintings but also new painted subjects—in which portraits and places intertwined. *Kotā melā ro bhāva* (the mood or feel of Kota palace) is inscribed on the reverse of the painting I call *The Mood of Kota Palace*, completed by an unnamed artist hailing from Udaipur in about 1700. In depicting the courtly environs of the palace complex, its candlelit gardens and courtyards drenched in soothing moonlight, the painter evokes the palace as a sensuous phantasmagoria replete with visual spectacle: men bursting firecrackers, acrobats entertaining crowds, and female musicians and dancers performing for courtly audiences. One of the earliest Udaipur paintings to both expand in size and to depict the architecture of a palace, it adapts a painting with a radically different point of view and compositional focus, made at the neighboring regional court of Kota and now in the collection of the Rijksmuseum in Amsterdam (and hereafter called the "Rijksmuseum painting") (fig. 1.20). The grounds for such a reading can be found in tantalizing pictorial details within the painting depicting Kota palaces made by artists in Kota itself. On a vertically oriented sheet of paper, the Kota artist depicted a ruler within his courtly precinct, seen from an imaginary elevated viewpoint that looks into the palace courtyards. The Udaipur artist alludes to the Rijksmuseum painting made at Kota by citing several figures (for example, the two acrobats in the front courtyard and the water thrower) and by borrowing pictorial vignettes drawn in fine lines in the atmospheric background of the Kota painting, including, for example, the miniaturized trees, clusters of houses, and elephant (figs. 1.21 and 1.22). Several of these elements are visible only upon closely examining the Rijksmuseum painting under magnification, which reveals that the Udaipur artist studied the painting carefully.

The Udaipur artist transformed the Rijksmuseum painting by changing the position and angle of the elevated vantage point and by juxtaposing various representational conventions, including planimetric views and elevations. In *The Mood of Kota Palace*, the Udaipur painter relinquished every notion of the eye as constituting static, singular, and monocular vision. In a departure from his model, the artist set up myriad vantage points to present a complex and busy picture of a courtly world that is a product of anamorphic stretching of the architecture. As one's eyes move in and out of the pictorial spaces created by the white walls, one is enticed to imagine the sweet smell of the flowers and the sounds of men playing the drums under a canopy at the palace entrance. The painting invites the viewer to imaginatively wander through the palace, seeking the king. Tucked away in an upper corner of the bustling inner courtyard, he can be identified by a dazzling gold-colored halo.

In tracing the possible specificities of the routes by which the Rijksmuseum painting found its way into the hands of an Udaipur court artist, through the circulation of people and paintings across the network of Rajput kings and European merchants and collectors, we understand the related histories of the two artworks made at Kota and Udaipur. By gauging their relationship, we also attain a sharper sense of why the differences we see between *The Mood of Kota Palace* and its model must be studied carefully and how doing that may ultimately enable us to understand the Udaipur copy's focus on rendering moods. We know the Rijksmuseum painting is connected to the Kota court because the courtyard in which a royal figure with a golden halo is seated can be identified as the palatial quarters of Kota's Chattar Mahal; the painting's composition is connected to painted murals in the Kota palace, likely completed by 1701 (fig. 1.23).[70] Additionally, a European engraving by Bernard Picart entitled "Vue & description du palais du Grand Mogol . . ." (View and description of the palace of the grand Mughal . . .), which was based on the Rijksmuseum painting, provides an important connection to Udaipur (fig. 1.24). It was published by L'Honore & Chatelain in 1719, in the fifth volume of the *Atlas Historique*, which includes a section on the genealogy of Mughal emperors.[71] The publisher notes that this engraving, along with several other illustrations in the account of the Mughal Empire, was based on artworks in the collection of Conte Abate Giovanni Antonio Baldini (1654–1725), who acquired many objects from India in Amsterdam between 1710 and 1713.[72] Rajasthan's paintings may have reached Amsterdam through the Dutch delegation of J. J. Ketelaar that visited Udaipur in 1711. Several depictions of Ketelaar and the Dutch ambassadors are included in paintings made at Udaipur, although neither correspondence nor inscriptions that document the exchange of gifts or paintings between the two parties have been found to date.[73] Nevertheless, given the timing of Ketelaar's visit in 1711, Baldini's focus on collecting Indian paintings in Amsterdam between 1710 and 1713, and Picart's creation of the engraving in 1715,[74] it is highly likely that the Rijksmuseum painting that found its way to Amsterdam had circulated in the Udaipur court workshop at some point between 1700 and 1711.[75] When considered alongside the departures taken by the Udaipur painter in making his version of the Rijksmuseum painting—*The Mood of Kota Palace*—the circulation of works of art that I have briefly outlined makes it possible, even plausible, that this painting constituted a deliberated response.

The Udaipur artist transformed the Rijksmuseum painting in at least three significant ways, which become apparent when we look closely at the two paintings in relation to each other. First, the Udaipur artist changed the viewing point for the central courtyard and surrounding buildings, albeit while alluding to the oblique axis that dominates the composition in the Rijksmuseum painting. He presents us with a frontal view

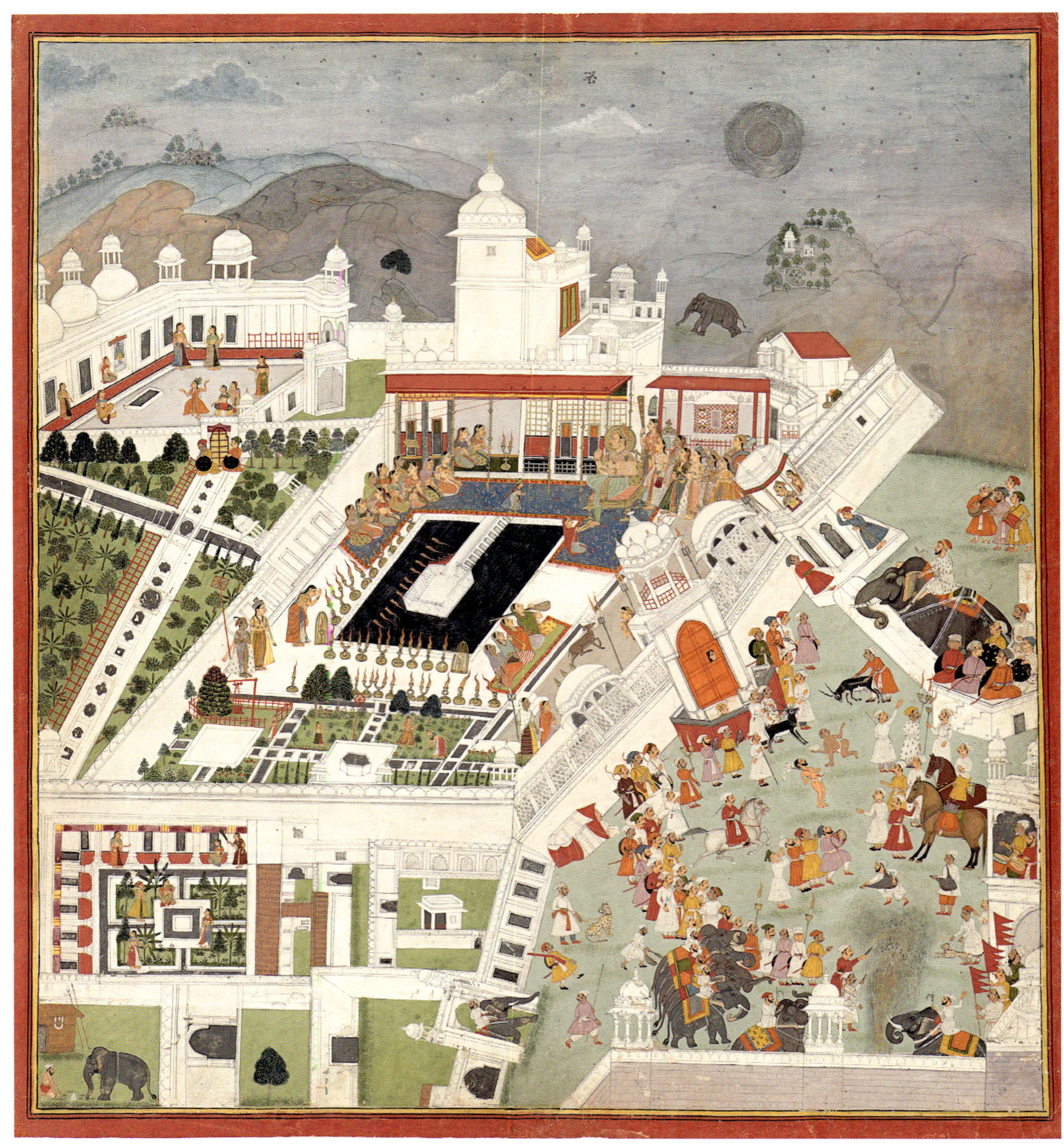

1.19. *The Mood of Kota Palace*, c. 1700, Udaipur. Opaque watercolor and gold on paper, 50.5 × 45.4 cm. National Gallery of Victoria, Melbourne; Felton Bequest, 1980, AS68- 1980.

1.20. *The Palace in Kota*, c. 1690–1700, Kota. Opaque watercolor and gold on paper, 59.1 × 41.2 cm. Rijksmuseum, Amsterdam; gift of P. Formijne, Amsterdam, 1993, RP-T-1993-277.

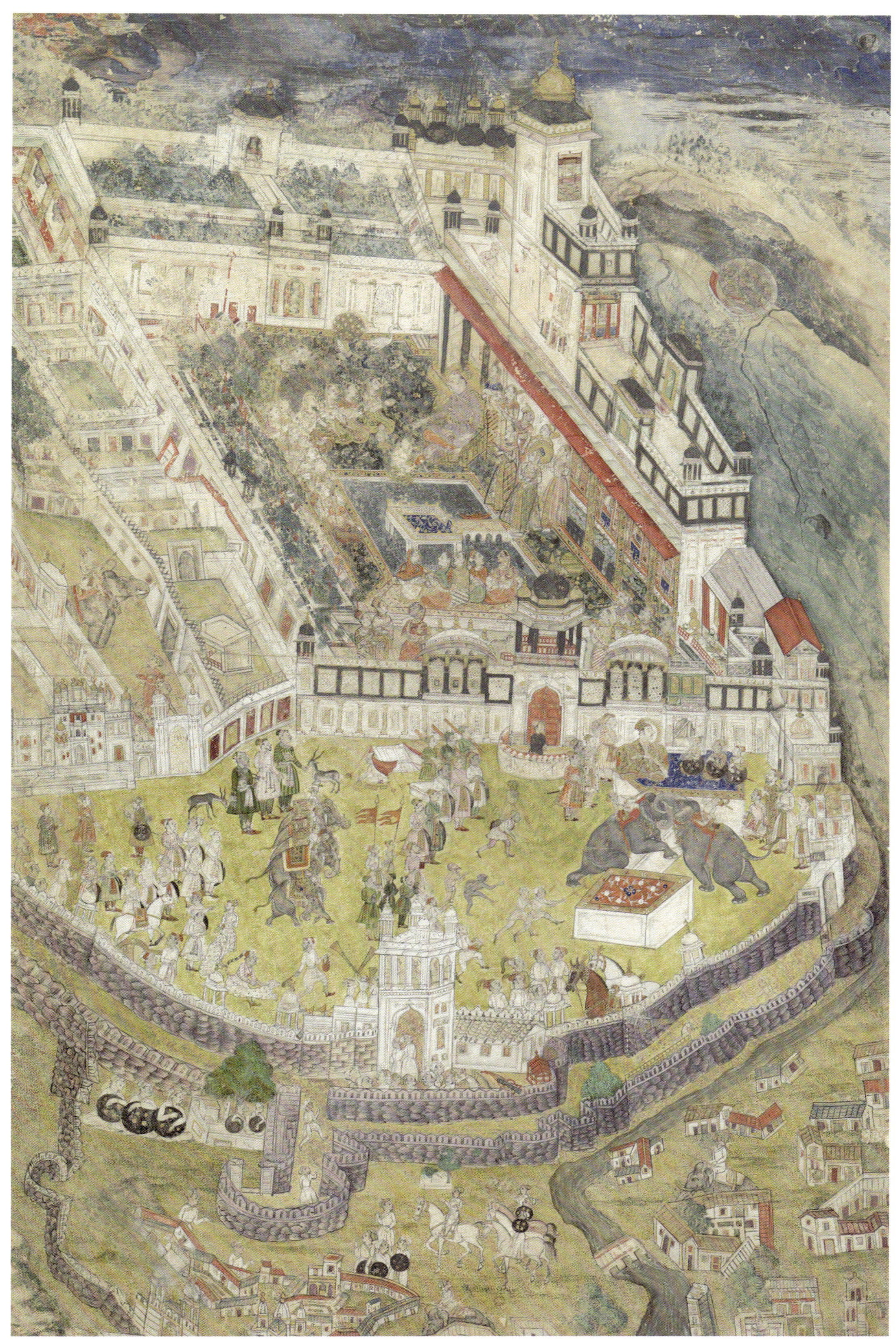

of the palace wall, next to which the ruler is portrayed in a profile view.[76] The artist thus altered the beholder's response, for the Udaipur composition directs one's vision from the left side of the painting toward the ruler, drawn approximately in the physical center of the paper. He also represented certain aspects of the palace in greater detail while eliminating many others, compressing and elongating the architecture as he saw fit. For example, he eliminated the carpet that covers the small pavilion within the water tank in the Rijksmuseum painting and added a red cloth canopy, supported on slender, gold-colored vertical supports, and a line of lamps with rising flames along and within the tank.

Second, the Udaipur artist employed a heterogeneous set of conventions. In the lower left corner, he depicted the smaller courtyards in a planimetric view combined with sectional elevations of select walls—a convention that was not employed by the Kota artist in the Rijksmuseum painting (figs. 1.25 and 1.26). The Udaipur artist also carefully imagined the plan of the depicted space from the bird's-eye view of these interlinked courtyards. This painting emphasizes the effect the artist achieved by means of this juxtaposition, which demands that the viewer make cognitive leaps by parsing out planar and isometric views. Such pictorial strategies would become one of the hallmarks of large-scale Udaipur paintings. In building the emotive content of a place in a work of art, painters not only populated their works with descriptive details but also combined shifting viewpoints. Such juxtapositions almost seem like invitations to their audiences, asking them to draw upon the suggestive power that the sense of a familiar place, such as Udaipur's courtyards and lakefronts, held for them, in order to reconstruct the represented place—to walk within it, to dwell in it.

Third, a distinct Udaipur palette and style informs the painter's adaptations. This is not only because of the preference given to applying gouache in bright reds, yellows, and whites, in stark contrast to the muted color palette of the Kota painting, but also because the Udaipur painter's minimal use of lines for shading the architecture and his preference for flatly applied gouache locate his pictorial translation within an Udaipuri idiom. In rendering the sky, the Udaipur artist rejected the Kota artist's use of several fine lines and an array of dark colors—ranging from shades of grays and cobalt blues to mauve mixed with streaks of red and gold, creating a textured effect—in favor of a monochromatic gray-blue wash (figs. 1.27 and 1.28). Furthermore, he transforms the delicately painted vignettes of mountainous topography and a body of

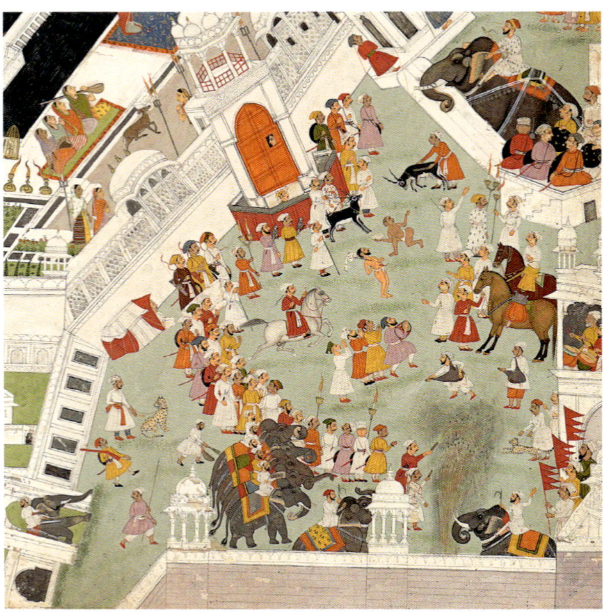

1.21. Detail of fig. 1.19. Depiction of festivities in the Kota palace's public courtyard.

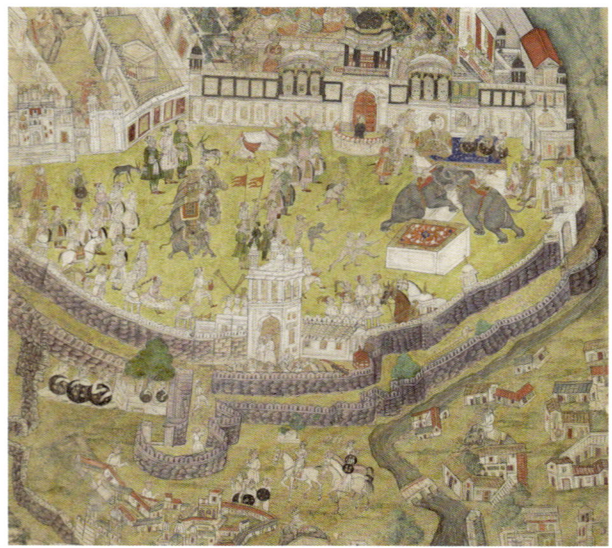

1.22. Detail of fig. 1.20. View displaying the Kota artist's emphasis on rendering fortified walls.

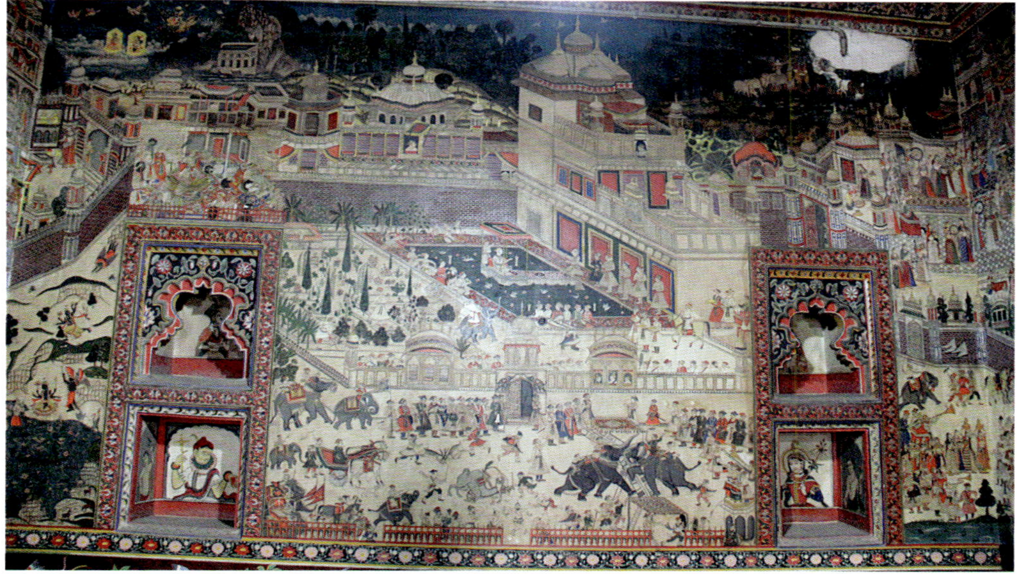

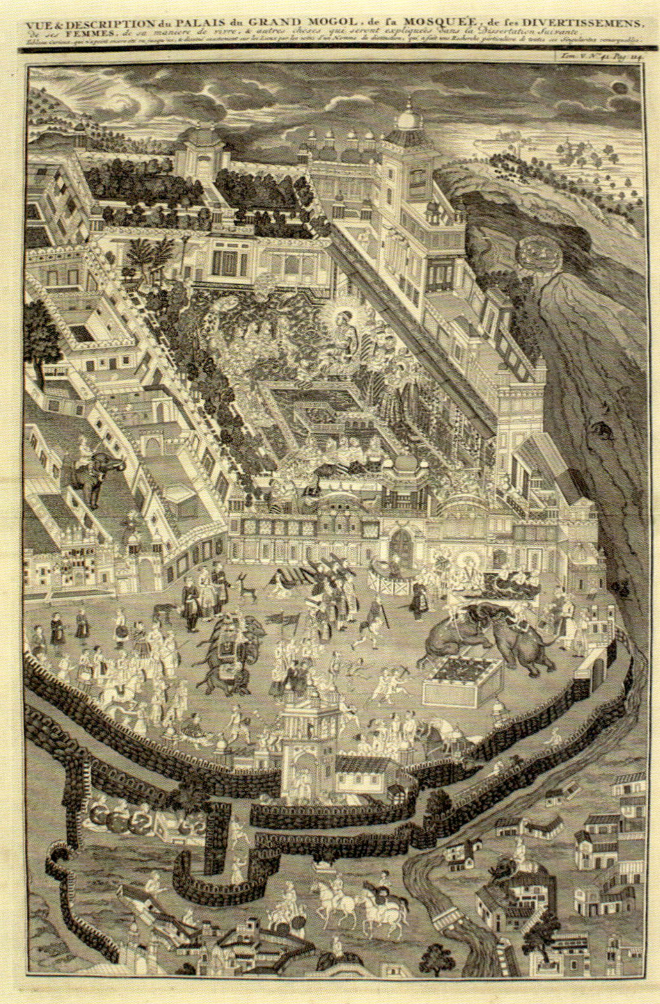

1.23. Mural depicting Kota palaces, suggested date 1701 based on an extant inscription, Chattar Mahal (part of the complex known today as the City Palace), Kota. Photograph by author.

1.24. "Vue & description du palais du Grand Mogol . . . ," Bernard Picart, 1715, after fig. 1.20, *The Palace in Kota*. Copperplate engraving on paper, 48.26 × 29.84 cm. Reproduced in *Atlas Historique*, vol. 5 (Amsterdam: L'Honore & Chatelain, 1719), 114, plate no. 41. Freer Gallery of Art and Arthur M. Sackler Gallery Archives, Smithsonian Institution, Washington, DC; gift of Robert J. del Bonta, FSA, A2014.06.

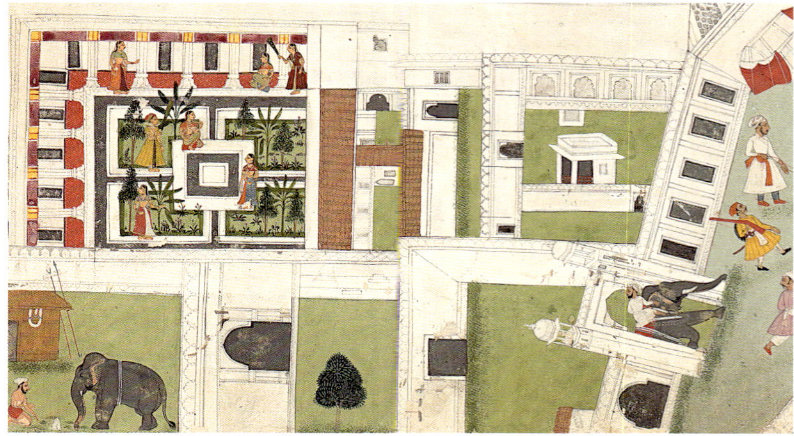

1.25. Detail of fig. 1.19. Udaipur painter's adaptation of the isometric view of the garden courtyard seen in fig. 1.26 into a combination of a plan and sectional elevation view.

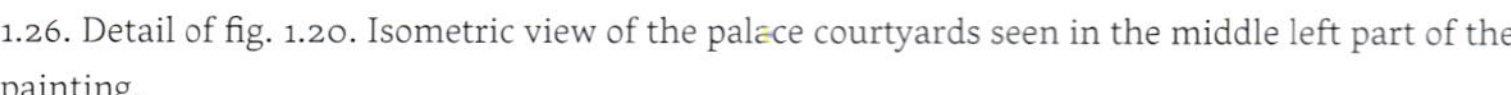

1.26. Detail of fig. 1.20. Isometric view of the palace courtyards seen in the middle left part of the painting.

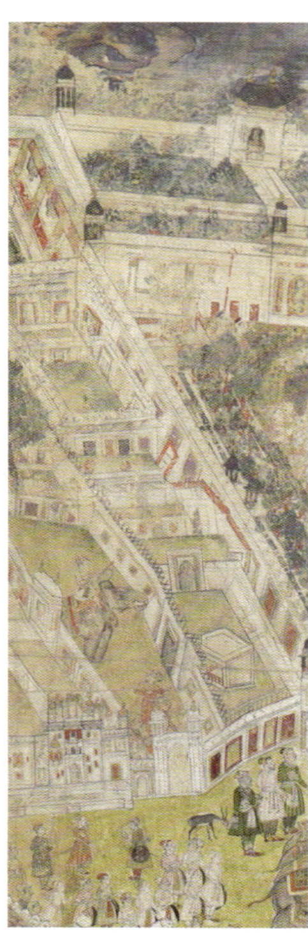

water, a cluster of tiny houses, a chained elephant, and the moon. Perhaps the most significant Udaipuri detail is an inconspicuous figure who holds a dagger and stands as if he has been nudged toward the right side of the picture (fig. 1.29). Cleverly painted, with a very deliberate, Amar Singh II–style face and distinctive handlebar mustache, his is the only visage in the painting assertively linked to an Udaipur ruler's portrait—forcefully bringing into play the stylistic distinctions in rendering royal portraits in such details as facial hair, eye shape, or turban style that were meaningful for historical audiences.[77]

What do we make of the pictorial translations and material transformations the Udaipur painter's version displays? The astute connoisseurs at the turn of the eighteenth century—painters themselves—were certainly open to mining circulating artworks in more ways than one. The Udaipur artist's eyes perused the world of Kota palaces not merely to replicate them but to make a world from *his* place at Udaipur. *The Mood of Kota Palace* exhibits an investment in reimagining the moods of depicted spaces. An example of reimagining is the Udaipur artist's inclusion of a tiny detail of the dancing figure of the blue god Krishna in one of the courtyards, depicted in the upper left corner of the palace, suggesting the presence of a small courtyard temple (fig. 1.30).[78] The artist could have been building upon the very faint suggestion of a figural icon of a deity rendered with a gold brushstroke, seen in the corresponding rendition of this space in the Rijksmuseum painting (fig. 1.31). Or he could have been depicting his subjective interpretation of how this temple courtyard was used, based on an act of imagination or his vivid recollection—or a combination of the two. The artist may or may not have encountered Kota palaces, but his additions and adaptations alongside the close pursuit of details from the original assert that mimetic rendering hardly seems to have been his aim.

Art historians have often found the visual juxtapositions of *The Mood of Kota Palace* confusing. This sense can be gleaned from writings about the painting, which variously describe it as a "large-scale map combining different perspectives" and, based on the painted lamps that line the water tank and the visual focus on the convivial mood of the gathering, as a depiction of "Diwali in India."[79] By contrast, I contend that its experiments opened up innovative material, aesthetic, and intellectual pathways for painters. It is exceptional for revealing the painter's close looking at a painted world and his imagination of its moods anew. For the painter, the process of making the painting was perhaps even more important than the final product. It is one among a range of new kinds of pictures in which thinking about moods was pursued in the visual realm. It is likely that, from an artist's perspective, such visual deliberations were easier to ponder in the absence of a

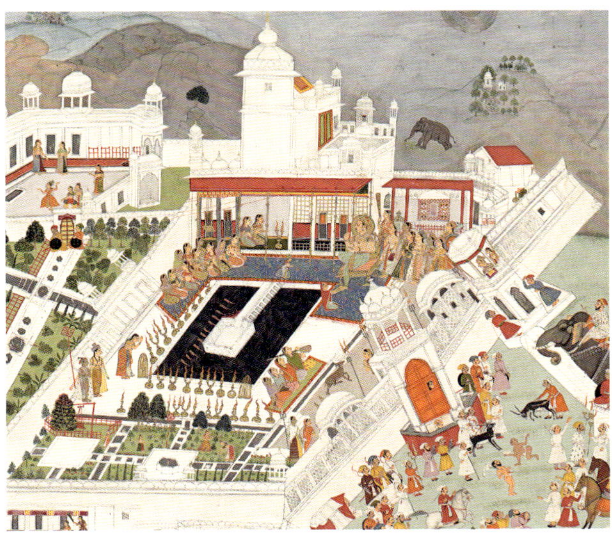

1.27. Detail of fig. 1.19. Udaipur painter's adaptation of the fine lines and deep cobalt and gray sky seen in fig. 1.28 into a monochromatic grayish-blue background in wash tones.

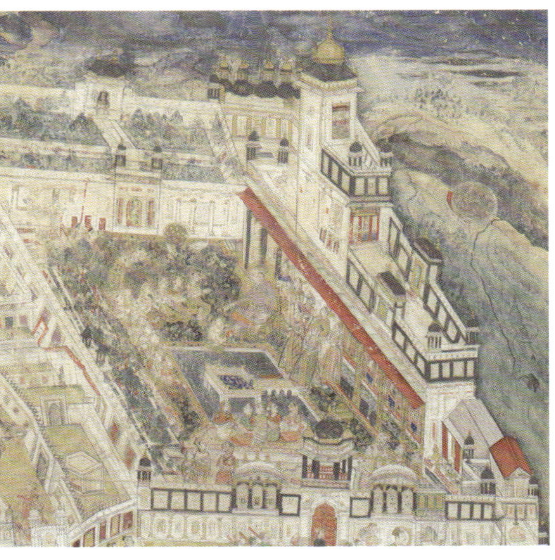

1.28. Detail of fig. 1.20. Rendering of the sky follows the Kota court workshop's preference for stippled effects and line work.

demand for a personality-oriented portrait of a patron.[80] My interpretation has included proposing a new title for the painting, *The Mood of Kota Palace*, based on the inscription on the verso—*kotā melā ro bhāva*—which further reinforces my argument for the painter's visual experiments (fig. 1.32). Scholars have usually translated *melā* as "festival" or "public revelry," based on what the word commonly means in modern Hindi.[81] Indeed, the painting as the "mood of Kota's revelry" explicates a parallel subject and constitutes a precedent for the painting of the festive spectacle of Gangaur admired by Sangram Singh II's court. However, several entries in Udaipur's court records show that *melā* in its regional dialect is the word used for "palaces." Seen in light of the Udaipur painter's concern with innovating new ways of depicting the palace, and the scribe's titling of the painting—as a picture that captures the mood of Kota palace—this artifact acquires an enhanced valence. The painter's constitution of a place's celebratory and praiseworthy moods—formed by interpreting pictures and material worlds—gives one the sense that perception results from the movements of a mobile body and vision that embeds itself within multiple planes and perspectives. Perhaps more important, the painting *The Mood of Kota Palace* is the result of a form of perception that is willing to recall scents, sights, sounds, spaces, memories, and intimacies from visual cues.

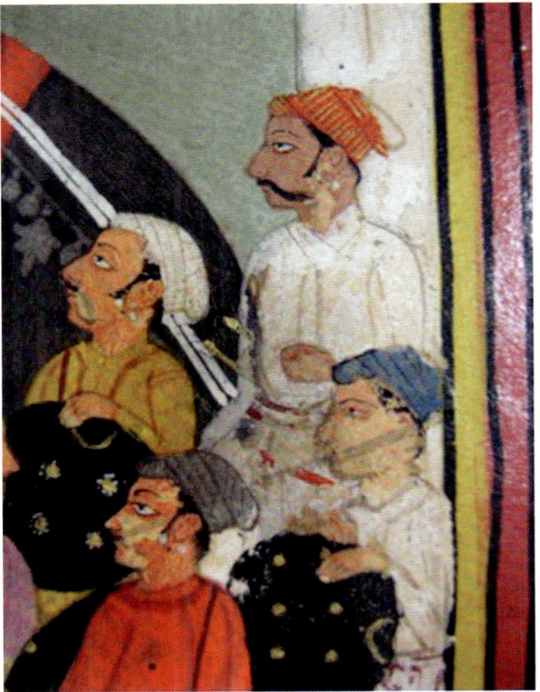

1.29. Detail of fig. 1.19. Figure with Amar Singh II–style face and distinctive handlebar mustache tucked away in the right-hand corner.

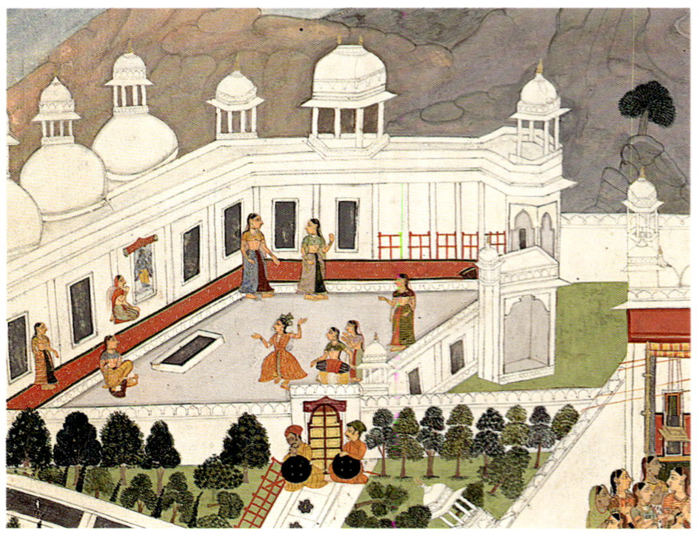

1.30. Detail of fig. 1.19. Udaipur painter's adaptation of the temple courtyard seen in fig. 1.31. The dancing figure drawn outside the shrine room with an icon of Krishna to the left suggests a performance of devotional dance and song dedicated to the blue god.

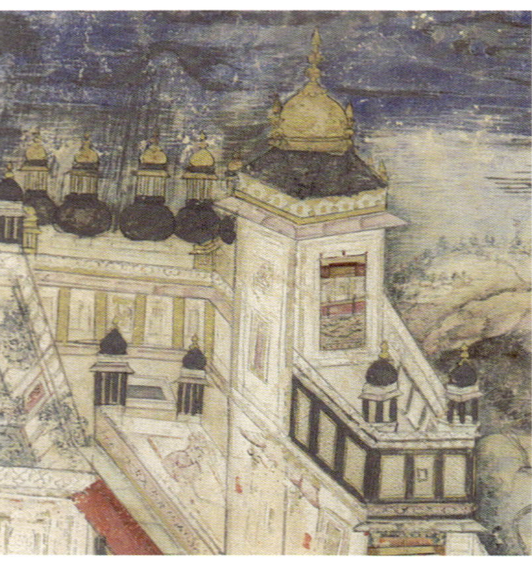

1.31. Detail of fig. 1.20. Temple courtyard with faint suggestion, in gold color, of an icon's presence in the shrine room.

1.32. Detail of fig. 1.19. Inscription on the verso: *kotā melā ro bhāva* (the mood of Kota palace).

Continuing with this anti-mimetic perspective, if we return one more time to the work *Maharana Sangram Singh II at the Gangaur Boat Procession*, this single painting lays bare questions that have not been raised by focusing only on vignettes and portraits identified in the inscriptions. Among the myriad details—heavy clouds, patterned stars, temple spires, and hidden faces—that come to the fore in the upper register of the dark night, the most dramatic is the hidden portrait of the king, sans his turban, framed by the window of a small hut in an obscure corner on the left-hand side of the painting (fig. 1.33). His shadowy presence, which has gone unnoticed by art historians thus far, and which I found only after many viewings, is confounding. The ghostly golden halo makes the royal presence definitive. He sits alone by the window but shines alongside other icons clustered in the corner. To his left, beneath a temple spire rendered in gray tones, is a gold-colored statue, and above the king's window, faint strokes suggest the presence of another shining idol within a domed building. These sanctums likely represent the temples on the opposite bank to which the women would bring their own icons of the goddess Gauri for the festival rituals, though the two small groups seen in the upper register are detached from the royal portrait. The king's portrait merges into the atmosphere. What do we make of this deliberate hidden portrait, one that is not caught in the scribe's inscription? Was it intended to generate a game of hide-and-seek for the audience?

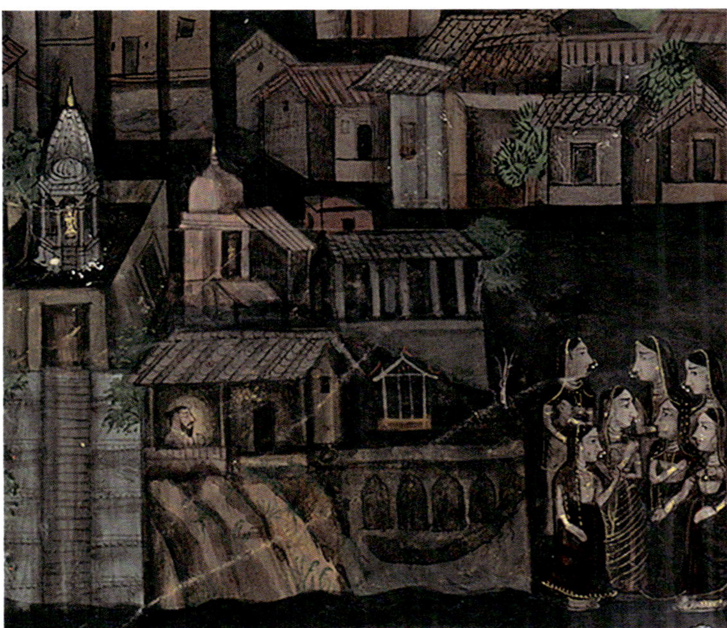

1.33. Detail of fig. I.4, *Maharana Sangram Singh II at the Gangaur Boat Procession*. Hidden portrait of the king framed by the window of a small lakeside hut in the painting's upper register.

The painting's two halves, though animated by contrasts, are also united by the painter's balcony view of the spectacle on the two lakefronts: we watch everything from an elevated level, such as an urban terrace or a balconied window (*jharokhā*) overlooking the lakeside's undulating streets, and may even imagine the painter hopping from one terrace to the next (fig. 1.34). Even if this perception is less heightened in the upper register, due to the absence of the teeming street crowd present in the lower half, the viewer still senses the path followed by the artist's mobile eye and body. The king's hidden portrait disrupts this feel. The singular Sangram Singh II commands a view of his city—a vista that seems amplified by the faintness and small size of his iconic presence, tucked into the corner. This is a perceptive move on the painter's behalf; from the shadowy vantage point of the king's icon, one hardly dwells in a depicted city divided between two banks. Rather, we perceive the image in a sweeping continuous view that offers a panoramic vision, an arc emanating from the king to the lake to the lakefront.

DESCRIBING, INSCRIBING, DWELLING

The expanded focus on presenting a city's moods belongs to a moment in history when innovations in urban cultures and in mensuration and mapping, emotional attachments to locales, and artistic assertions of locatedness were becoming important. Udaipur's topographical artworks inhabit and invent the location. My ground-up approach to find a located view from one place is not simply about pluralizing the map of art histories, asserting a peripheral urban identity. Rather, I understand "location" as an "itinerary rather than a bounded site—a series of encounters and translations," as James Clifford has noted.[82] In tracking a series of continuities, asymmetries, and entanglements, from painted epics to urban and political shifts, from routes of travel and cartographic artifacts to open-ended deliberation of circulating paintings, Udaipur's interpretation of painted moods of a place becomes a meaningful culminating point. Udaipur painters constituted *bhāva* on paper as a kind of place-centric immersion from which audiences may have gathered meanings in multiple ways, not all alike, and not all at the same time. The paintings invite the viewer to inhabit more than one subject, urban locale, architectural space, vantage point, and representational convention. On the one hand, by tracing questions of response and reception and evaluating moods and places across more than one genre or medium, we find that the locales themselves helped to formulate a sense of belonging that is then embedded within the objects themselves. On the other hand, I interpret the painter's image as a visual exegesis on the term *bhāva* and as an exploration of how moods, emotions, and sensations shape art. Moods of a place by their very definition create a picture by describing the world through juxtaposing

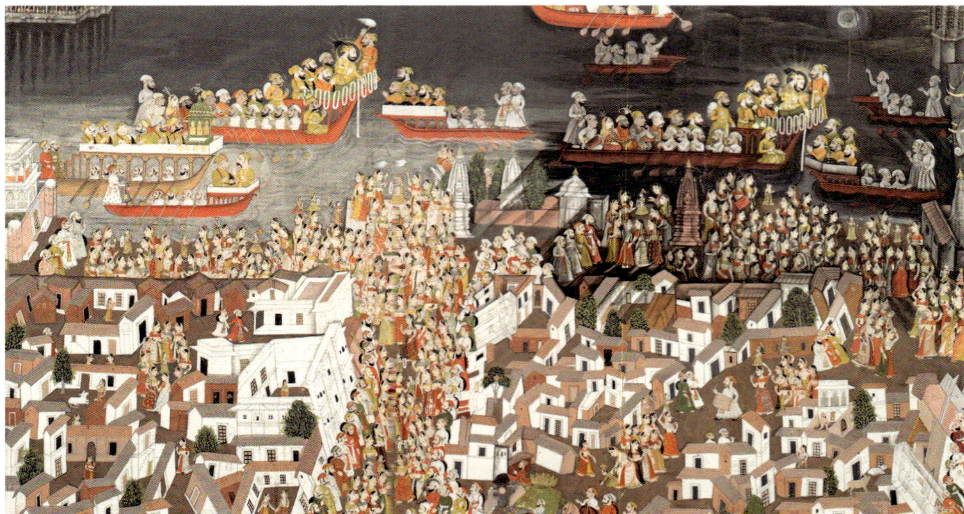

1.34. Detail of fig. I.4, *Maharana Sangram Singh II at the Gangaur Boat Procession*. Depiction of Udaipur city in the painting's lower register.

details, vignettes, and selections. Thus, one finds patterns in the painting of moods of place, as well as parallels with the visions of poets and a "mapping impulse."[83] We find that each world created by moods also contains, by way of hidden and myriad details, the painter's awareness that the perception of *bhāva* results from each viewer's own memories and associations.

The kind of situated analysis that has occurred in this chapter—the dwelling in and the thinking with artifacts—responds to the pictorial demands made by paintings of moods and place. The paintings also demand that we treat the inscriptional evidence as an instance of response to the artifact. A terse description like the "mood (*bhāva*) of Kota palace" was considered the painting's focus. However, a majority of the inscriptions on the backs of Udaipur paintings are longer. Even if they mention a specific *bhāva*, they, like the historical genres recounting the achievements of kings (*carita*) and the daily diaries of courts, tell us stories of the king's activities in the image.[84] Likewise, the prevalent cataloguing system reflected in the Udaipur court inventory of artworks from 1891, as well as the scribal marks behind the artworks, privileged the categories of kingly portraits—Udaipur kings, other (mostly Rajput) kings, Mughal emperors—and subcategories for images of foreigners (*fīrangī*), studies of elephants and horses, and the genres of poetic and devotional manuscripts.[85] This classification can help to contextualize the thirteen-line inscription on the reverse of the painting *Maharana Sangram Singh II at the Gangaur Boat Procession*. It provides the names of personnel in the king's party, a description of the movement of the boat—and a pithy note of admiration for the spectacle.[86]

An entry by one of the Udaipur court's scribes who recorded daily activities, excursions, and meetings of importance within official dairies (*haqiqat bahida*), dating to the last two decades of the eighteenth century, provides tantalizing glimpses of events of inscribing and looking at artworks in assemblies—of how descriptive inscriptions were produced. In one example, an account of Maharana Bhim Singh (r. 1778–1828) visiting the Jagniwas lake palace on a Tuesday in November 1780, we are told that after the king arrived at the lake palace he was presented (*nijar*) with paintings (*citrām*) in the painted room (*citrasāli*) and that scribes were called upon to write on the backs of completed artworks (*pāno pāche nām maṁdāyā*). Thus, we may look toward the inscribed texts as indices of gatherings in which the viewing of artworks created an event worthy of entry in the daily court diaries. These viewings preceded writing the names of the individuals who were part of the king's painted assembly and the court assembly at a later date—when the looking at and inscribing on the backs of paintings actually took place. Such a mode of reception and response reinforces the bonds of sociability on display in the paintings and the collectivities re-formed in the acts of inscribing. The distinct temporality of inscribing versus painting further destabilizes how we use the textual versus the painted evidence.

In another entry, from 1787, eight years later, we hear about an assembly admiring paintings and architecture while gathered in the *citrasāli* in the main palace. We can only speculate as to whether such viewing practices involved simultaneously appreciating both paintings and architecture and connecting representations and palaces. Long stretches of silent looking may not have been the norm in eighteenth-century courtly contexts, but the existence of collectives of people immersed in wondrous appreciation of paintings, texts, architecture, and courtly poetry (discussed in chapter 3) opens a space in which to consider the plurality of Udaipur's large-scale paintings. Such viewing events make the point to the wide variance in the inscriptional record, signifying conversations that may have unfolded from numerous visual leads.

The limits of describing moods found in eighteenth-century inscriptions on the backs of paintings parallels the limits art historians face in excavating sense and sentiments. The succinct use of the terminology of the *bhāva* of a place as ekphrasis throws light on the challenges of an art history that requires us to dwell in the painters' described moods of a space and time. Koch considers terms of description in her argument about *The Seige of Daulatabad in 1633–34*, painted by Murar in 1635 (discussed above), presenting a case of significant adaptation of cartographic knowledge within established visual genres. In Shah Jahan's mid-seventeenth-century letters, the architectural landmark and the painted Daulatabad fort were described as a *ṣūrat*. A mid-eighteenth-century Mughal historian writing on this imperial correspondence describes the fort's painting as a *naqśā (or naqsha)*. Koch writes, "*ṣūrat* is a term used in Mughal Persian for 'image' and *naqsha* for 'picture, design,'" which "can also refer to a portrait model, map, or plan."[87] This shift likely indicates the changing perceptions and genres of topographical artifacts between the 1630s and the 1710s. The flexibility inherent in each term—*ṣūrat, naqśā, taraha*, and *bhāva*—points to the plurality that engendered topographical imagery. In tracking the history of European city views, an established category of art making at the Hapsburg and Medici courts, Ryan Gregg discusses the use of the term *energia* as "a rhetorical concept used in antiquity for persuasion" for visual effects. He argues that *ekphrasis* and *energia* overlap somewhat in the process of visualization, but the former, which "in the classical and Renaissance worlds [could mean] the description of anything: place, person, thing, time," would have led "to the latter."[88] *Energia*, similar to *bhāva*, had a long-established conceptual presence across art and poetry and could be used in slightly different ways by authors writing at different times but "in general connoted both process and effect" and "could be translated as vividness or vision, and referred to the mental image in the audience's mind stimulated by ekphrasis, or detailed description."[89]

In the use of *bhāva*, it is worth considering how to encompass the description of the process of making a picture, the resultant image itself, and even perception and the kindling of emotions. The intellectual history on premodern aesthetics and emotions, as discussed in the introduction, included from the very beginning the emphasis on the process of aesthetic experience, feelings developing over time.[90] To discern the depicted mood of a place means to perceive and alternate between picture, place, and the people represented within, and to consider the experience of the connoisseurs who are shown experiencing this mood. The conception of *bhāva* also counts for process. Immersing himself in the mood of Gangaur might have been necessary for the artist to render such effective juxtapositions of places and people, sites and sounds, brightness and dimness. For courtly audiences, the perception of such atmospheric renderings of urban spectacles, and the recalling of spatial and sensorial associations, could have accumulated over a longer stretch of time, through the experience of many seasons and spectacles.[91] The painted Gangaur springtime festival signals the sensory overload of sights, sounds, smells—from the burning firecrackers that illuminate the night to the heady scent of jasmine garlands adorning the goddess Gauri and the melodies and rhythms of music and dance that accompanied the groups of women performing rituals on the king's barge. The jostling crowds on a festive night like the ones represented here might have found themselves constantly shifting their attention among the myriad happenings, just as we are drawn to multiple details and points of interest in the painting.

Consider another powerfully enchanting painted spring, *Maharana Amar Singh II's Holi Durbar with Sixteen Nobles in the Sarvaritu (Sarbat) Vilas Garden*.[92] It depicts Amar Singh II and his sixteen nobles in the garden of Sarbat Vilas, at play with red powder (*gulāl*) during Holi, the spring festival of colors (fig. 1.35). The artwork indexes a pivotal moment—when painters changed the subjects and size of their paintings, when a new political system was put in place, when new palaces and gardens were built, when new paintings and painters arrived from other courts, and when new cartographic workshops and regional alliances were emerging. It is noteworthy for the scribe's lengthy inscription.[93] The scribe positions the names on the verso to match the seating arrangement on the front, transforming the painting into a document of Amar Singh II's recent rearrangement of the elite positions that the nobles in his court occupied (fig. 1.36).[94] Along with the names and positions of the musicians (*kalāvant*), the scribe also included the positions of

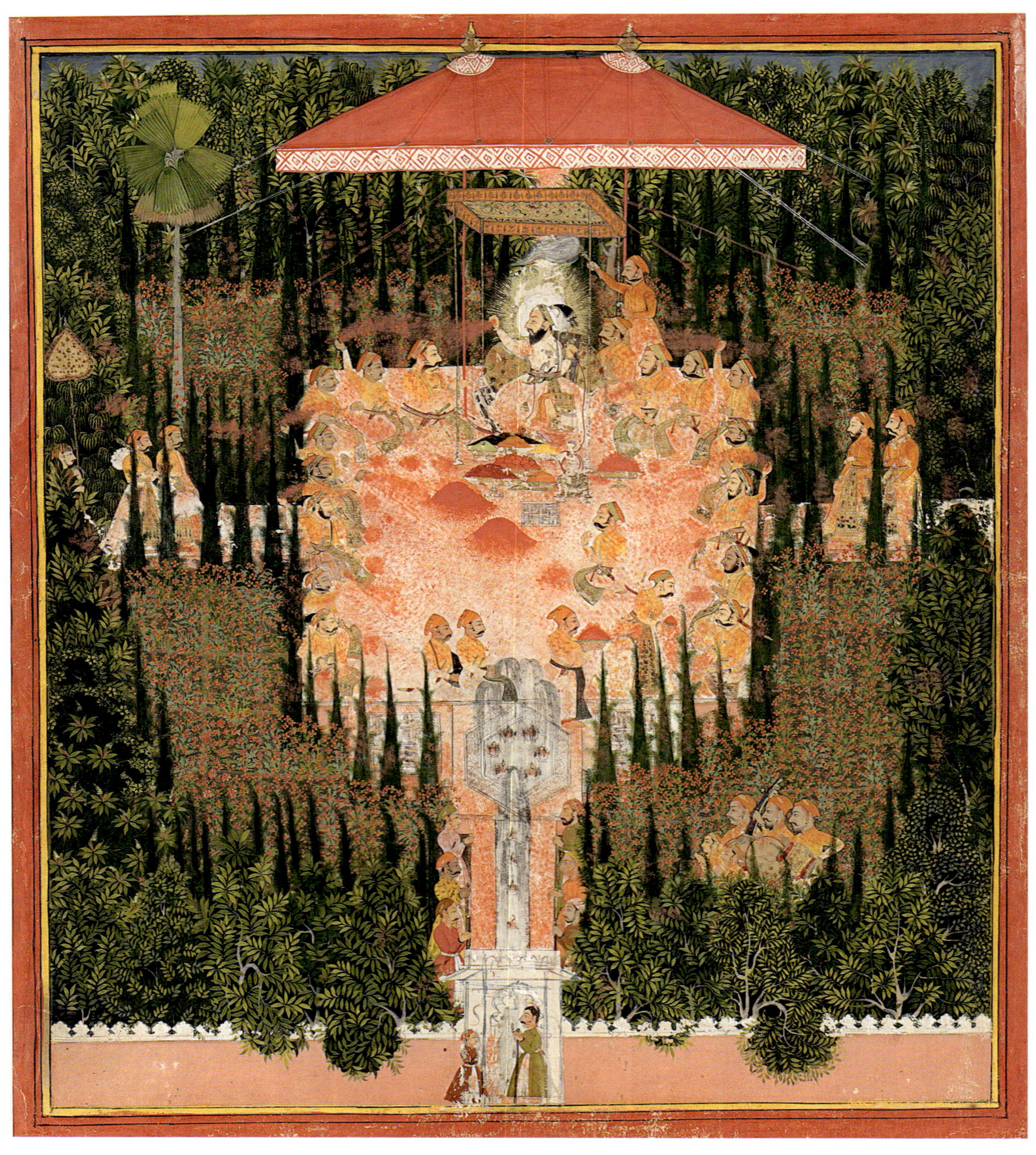

1.35. *Maharana Amar Singh II's Holi Durbar with Sixteen Nobles in the Sarvaritu (Sarbat) Vilas Garden*, attributed to the Stipple Master, c. 1708–10, Udaipur. Opaque watercolor and gold on paper, 47 × 41.5 cm. National Gallery of Victoria, Melbourne; Felton Bequest, 1980, AS74- 1980.

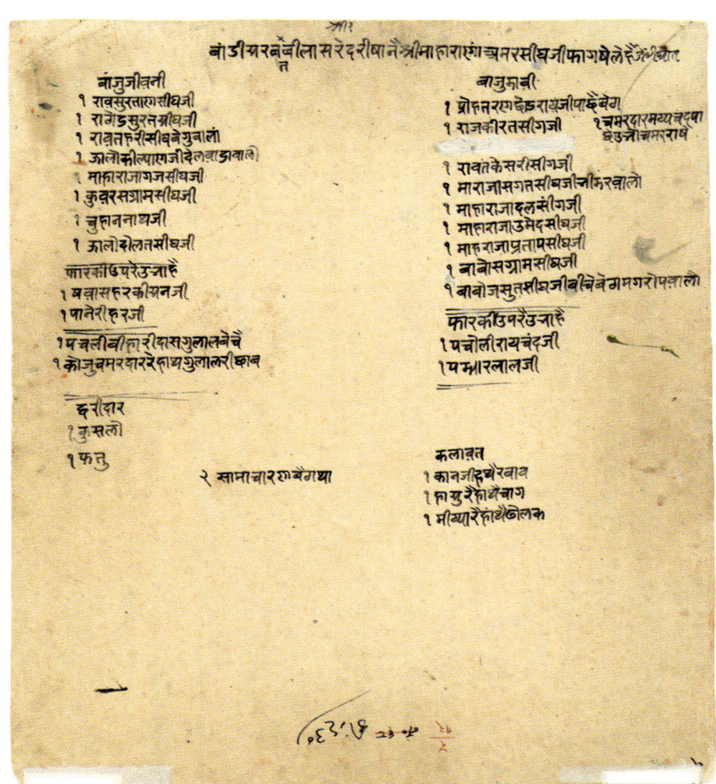

1.36. Detail of fig. 1.35. Inscription on the verso describing the seating arrangement and names of all the nobles who were part of the king's newly institutionalized network.

the two bards (each identified by his role as *cāran* rather than by name) who recited royal histories. The inscription is also among the earliest paintings to name the place that is pictured in the painting, the pavilion of the garden of Sarbat Vilas (*bādī sarabata bilāsa re darīkhānai*). Through its inscription, which refers to music and poetry, its detailing of a specific architectural structure, and the names of the nobility, this painting makes the point that the imaginings of moods and places were never discrete activities.

The artwork is also noteworthy for presenting Mewar's new courtly community as unitary on aesthetic terms. A band of lush green foliage bounds red flowers in full bloom, and a square of slim, tall trees surrounds the portraits of the Udaipur king Amar Singh II and his sixteen nobles. The men of the court are shown throwing *gulāl*, which the artist rendered by frottage, from their seated positions. The resultant concentric squares in hues of green, red, and white help focus the viewer's gaze on the center of the page, underscoring the designed formality of the seated collective—and of the painting—that exists in tension with its scenes of courtly play. The textural presence constituted by the trees and the individual portraits with distinctive features deepens the observation of and immersion into details. The contrast between the red clouds of the *gulāl* and the thick red blobs of the flowers animates the dryness of the powder and its spread on the ground, in the air, on clothing and faces (fig. 1.37). It colors the king and his courtly assembly in the red tinge of the spring bloom and of the Holi festival. The graphic and painterly effects intertwine to render the mood of a spring garden party that lingers in our imagination, composing the nobles and kings into a collective. The king's portrait provides a chronological time frame to the artwork, but the moods of his assemblies held in the Sarbat Vilas garden are remembered in the years that followed.[95] The artwork may not be reflective of a political reality of absolute unity among nobles and king, but the rendering of a Holi festival effectively positions Amar Singh II's kingship as a stabilizing force. In forging a new kind of artwork, the artist has immersed the portraits of competing nobles in the oneness of spring.

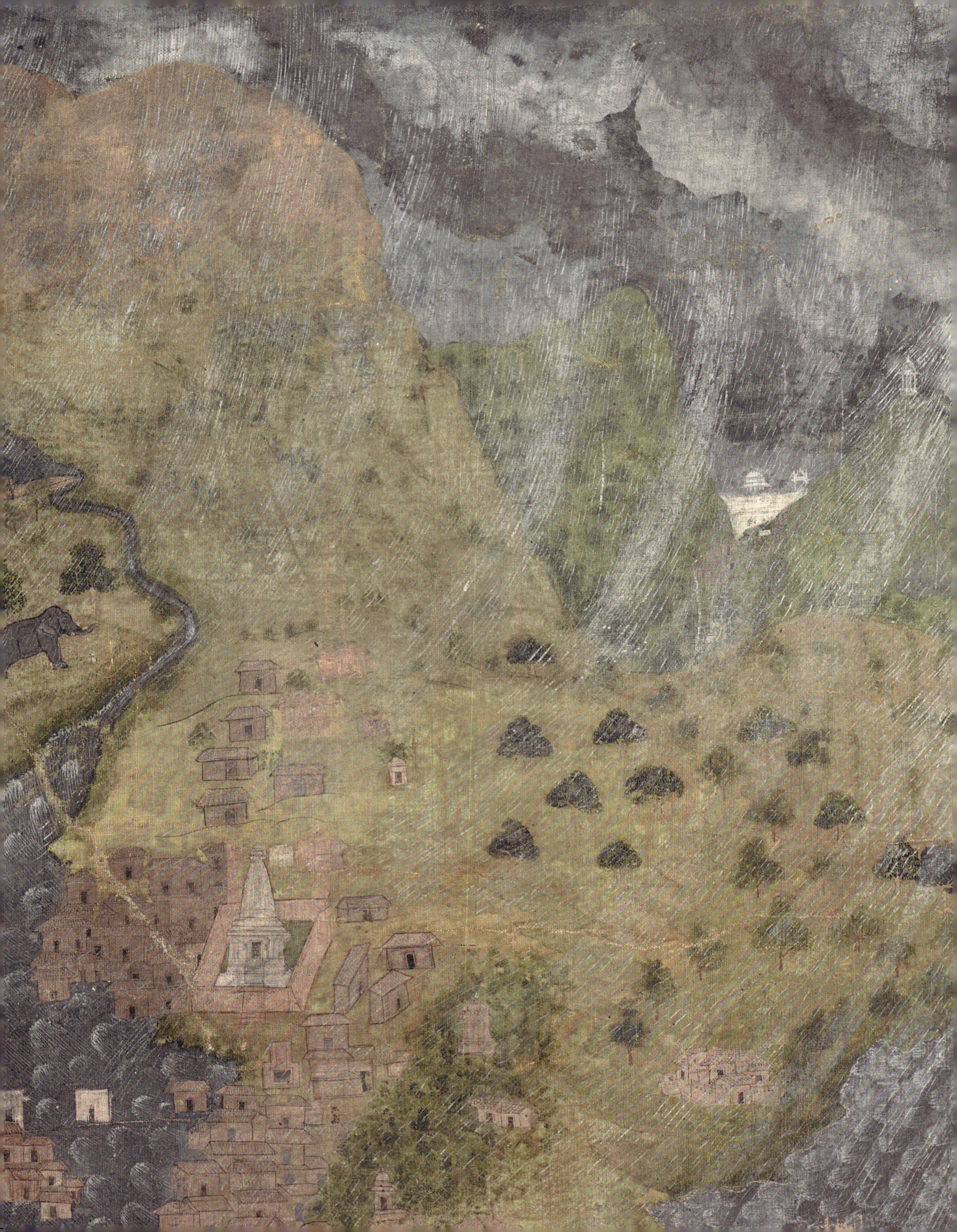

CHAPTER 2

Passionate Monsoons and Monumental Paintings

THE MOOD OF THE MONSOON

A painting on cotton cloth dated to around 1700, measuring nearly six feet wide and four feet high, *Maharana Amar Singh II in Udaipur during a Monsoon Downpour* was likely among the earliest large-scale paintings created by Udaipur artists (fig. 2.1). Beyond the palace precincts, slate-gray clouds and stormy rain engulf the city's hills and lakes. Against this topographic envisioning, Maharana Amar Singh II sits in the public hall, alongside his nobles, watching the spectacle of an elephant running amok, depicted nine times to denote its swift motions. The painter composed the eastern facade of the palace from a fish-eye point of view; he presents the outer courtyard from bird's-eye perspective, and he stretches the width of the courtly hall where the ruler is seated such that the viewer's eye is drawn to the king's entourage (fig. 2.2). Yet, these multiple perspectives prevent a simple, singular focus on the royal party.

We perceive acutely the shifts in viewpoint that are present here but not in other large-scale works made around the same time. We are invited to imagine the sweeping mountains, lakes, streams, and bursting clouds that could be viewed from the palatial terraces (fig. 2.3). We also ponder the palace elevation, its pavilions and balconies rising into the sky, curving around its edges and bent like a paper model. The painter accentuated the palace facade with black outlines, rendering the details of windows and balconies and exaggerating the oblique lines that denote the northern walls of the palace. We wonder about the pictorial highlighting of specific urban precincts: in the bottom half of the painting, the planar elevations of houses in brown and buff hues, combined with isometric views of temples, gateways, and larger buildings in white, are deliberate artistic juxtapositions of representational conventions (fig. 2.4).

The painting's painters blurred the boundaries between foreground and background, setting and subject. Looking to the right, we race to understand a landscape bursting with minute illusionary details (fig. 2.5). In the courtyard, the

2.1. *(following spread) Maharana Amar Singh II in Udaipur during a Monsoon Downpour*, c. 1705, Udaipur. Opaque watercolor and gold on cloth, 109.2 × 175.2 cm. Freer Gallery of Art, Smithsonian Institution, Washington, DC; purchase and partial gift made in 2012 from the Catherine and Ralph Benkaim Collection, Charles Lang Freer Endowment, F2012.4.2.

Detail of fig. 2.1

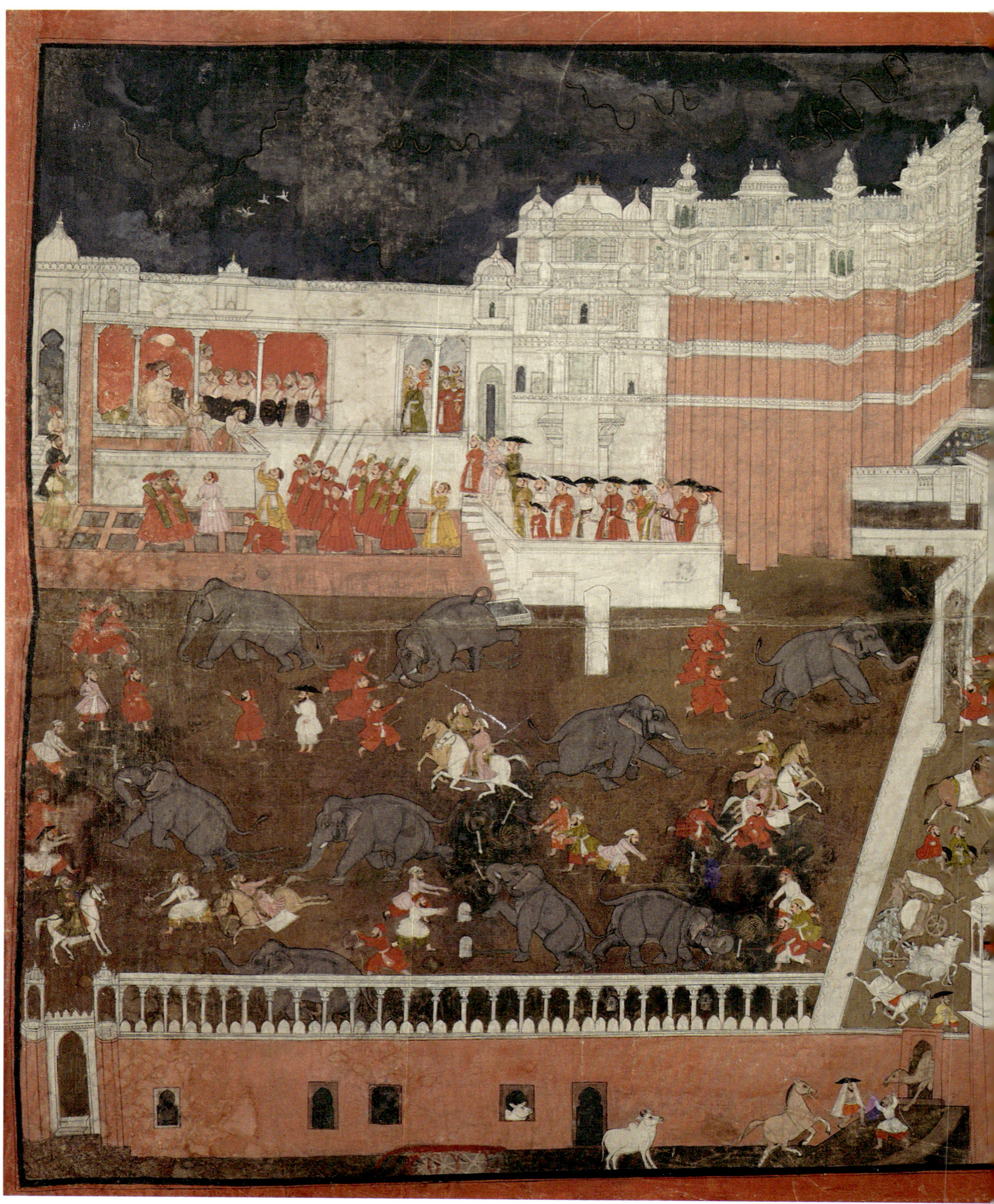

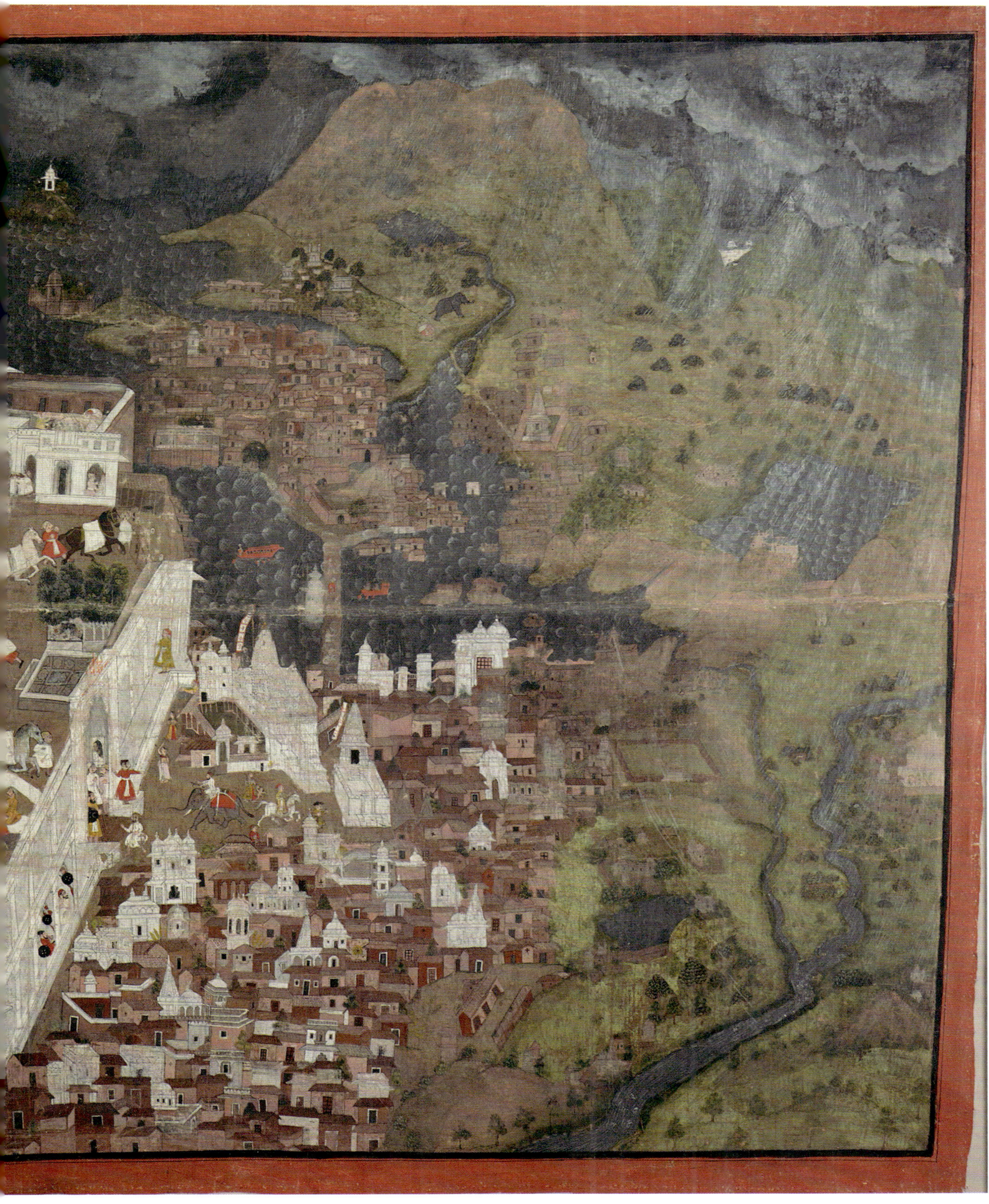

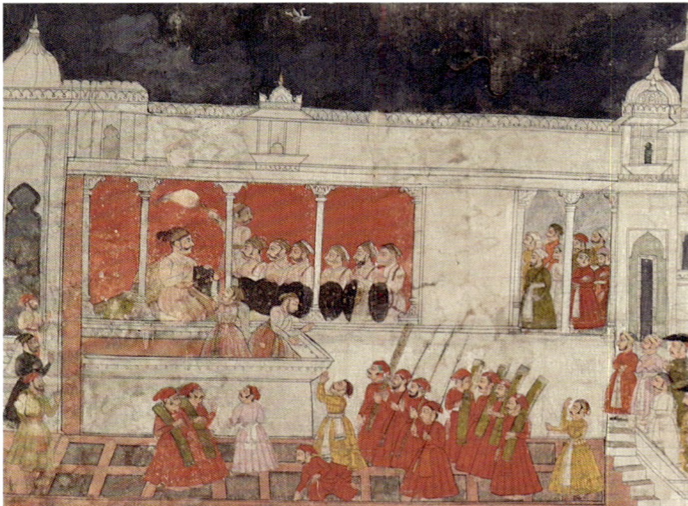

2.2. Detail of fig. 2.1. Amar Singh II, seated in the colonnaded pavilion for the court's public public assemblies, along with his nobles, watching the spectacle.

2.3. Detail of fig. 2.1. Painter's rendition of the mood of the monsoon—rains, clouds, mountains, lakes, rivers, and streams.

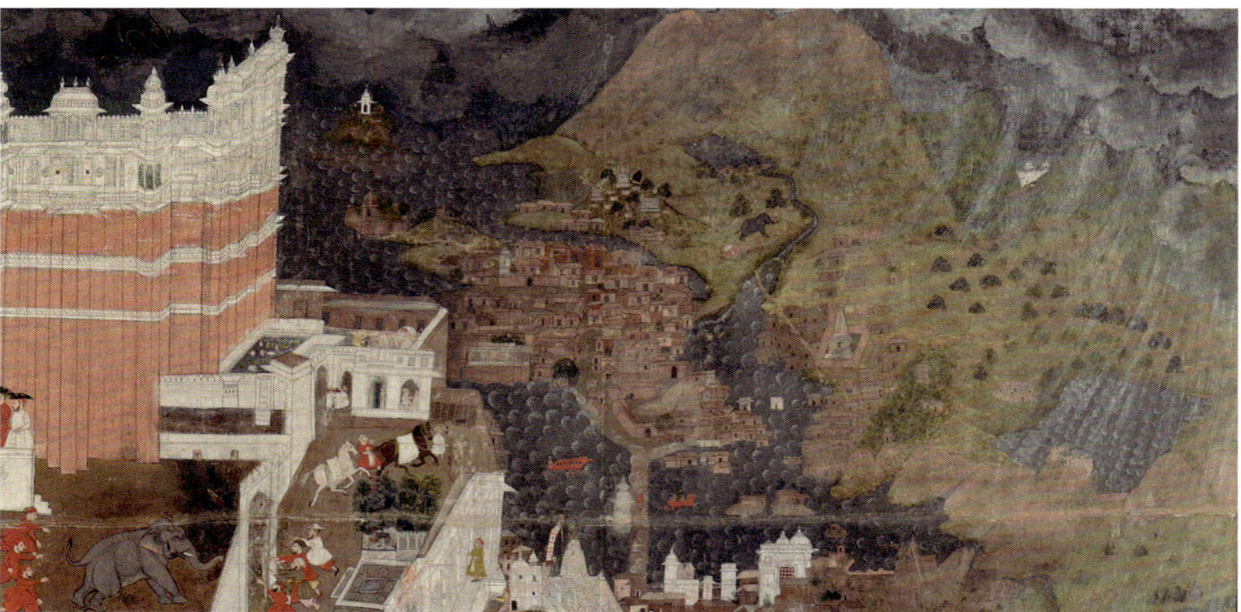

courtly staff, carrying fireworks, chases a running elephant, provoking him beyond the excitement (*masti*) an elephant might normally experience at the coming of the rains. Our Udaipur painter exaggerated the frenzy of the elephant by means of its repetition in the courtyard, an artistic choice based on the use of similar strategies to denote movement in smaller, mid-seventeenth-century illustrated manuscripts.[1] The spectacular scurry of the animal is enhanced by its contrast to a miniaturized solo elephant seen by the streams in the hills, calmly enjoying the rain, a motif and metaphor that courtly audiences would have recognized from poetic visions of the monsoon; the painter likely employed this elephant as a motif to connect the setting and the spectacle (fig. 2.6). We observe the layer of white-painted strokes of pouring rain that flows into the silvery-gray lakes and streams and feel the movement of waves created by feather-like semicircular paint strokes. The sense that the scene depicts a specific moment, the unfolding of a temporal spectacle, is reinforced by the view of a city nestled in the Aravalli hills being overtaken by the rain pouring from dark, heavy clouds painted in thick layers of gouache.

Udaipur's artists employed rain as a key feature in creating portraits of Amar Singh II. Just as we sense the feeling of heavy monsoon clouds and pouring rain in the large-scale

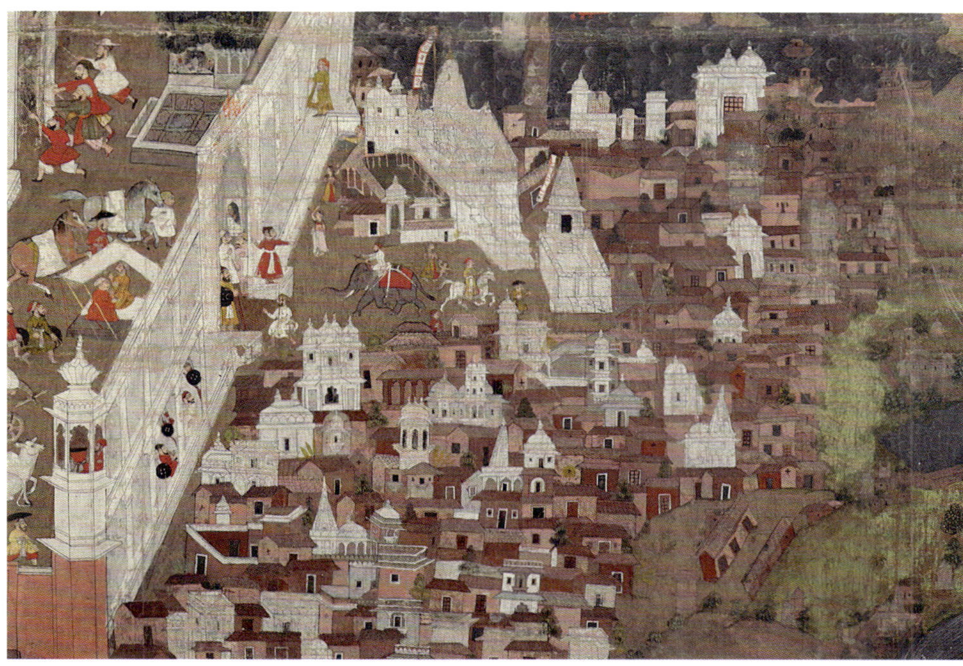

2.4. Detail of fig. 2.1. Planar elevations of houses juxtaposed with isometric views of prominent temples, gateways, and buildings in white.

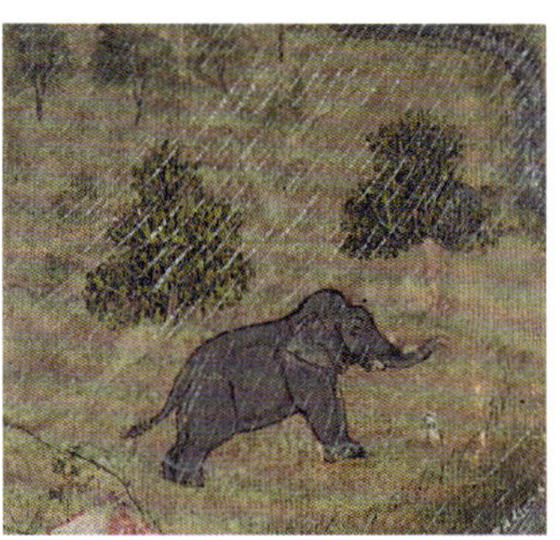

2.5. Detail of fig. 2.1. Miniaturized lone elephant by the streams.

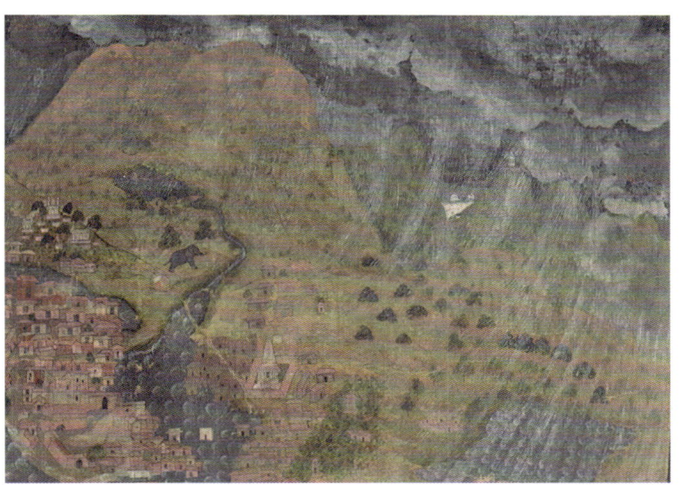

2.6. Detail of fig. 2.1. Strokes of white paint denote pouring rain, and feather-like, semicircular patterns suggest waves in the water.

painting on cloth, so too do these smaller portraits on paper stir in us the *bhāva* of being caught in a deluge. In one example, the material qualities of the painted rainwater displace the young nobleman, likely the prince Amar Singh II, as the painting's subject (fig. 2.7). The artist, thought to be the Stipple Master, delighted in how water pours and sprays from a brilliantly painted dark monsoon sky that is heavy with paint and water, how it splatters from the hat of the prince, how it drenches his austere white garment, and how it drips, thickening into dense rivulets before falling on the ground.[2] In another painting of the same subject, the artist rendered pouring rain in linear strokes that delicately curve against the sky and flow into the small rivulets that we see on the green ground along the bottom edge of the painting (fig. 2.8). Amar Singh's horse walks and floats in these grayish-white puddles and streams painted on the blue surface.

Following in the footsteps of Udaipur's eighteenth-century citizens and travelers, this chapter turns to the seductive and sustaining power of aqueous elements in early modern India. It explores how painters and patrons thematized rain to create a powerful images of Udaipur as a prosperous place, emphasizing the city's lake environs, which starkly contrast with the region's desert lands. To praise Udaipur as the city of lakes and rain, painters materially exalted their artistic practice

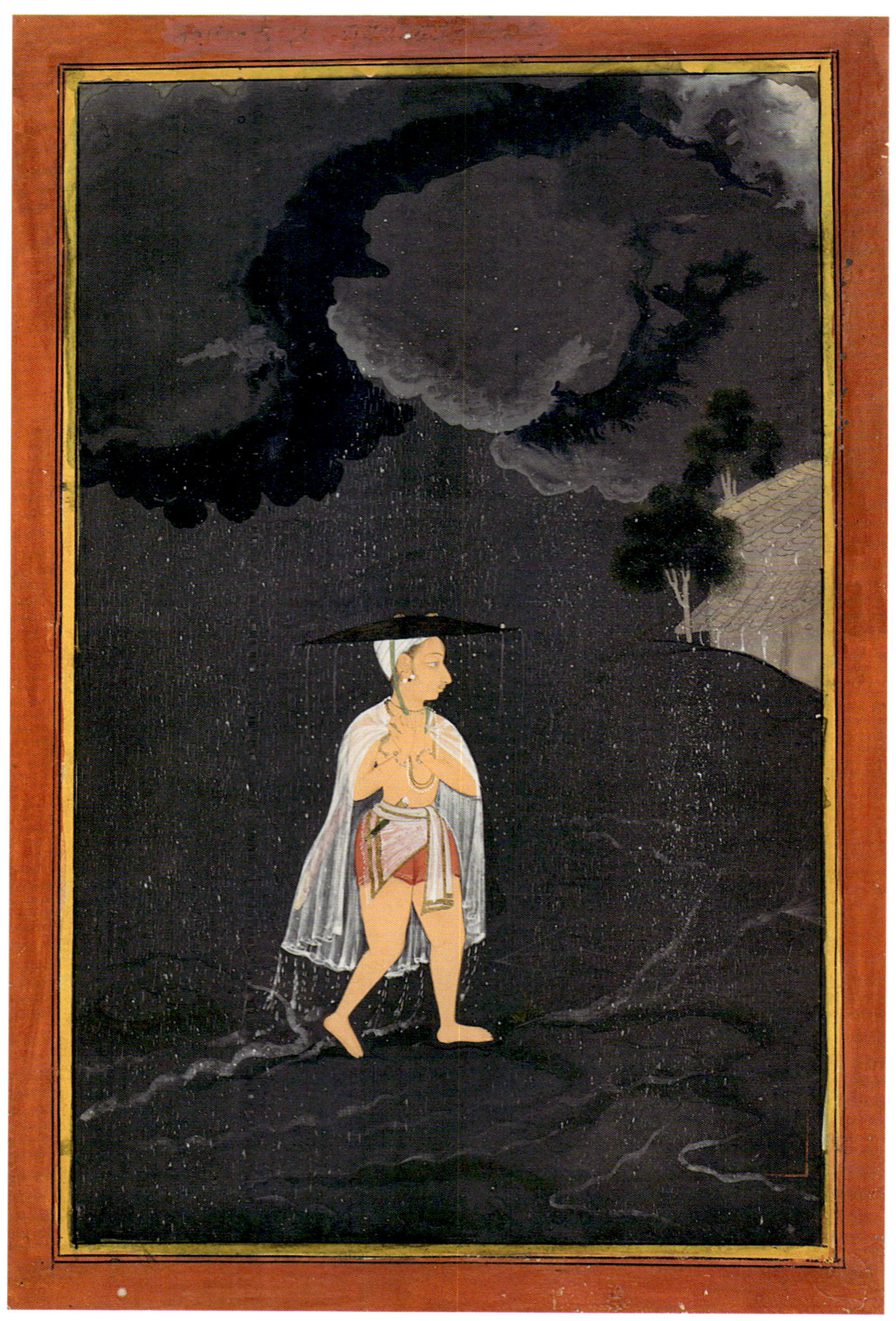

2.7. *Prince Amar Singh Walking in the Rain*, attributed to the Stipple Master, c. 1690, Rajnagar, Mewar. Opaque watercolor on paper, 34.4 × 21.3 cm. Freer Gallery of Art, Smithsonian Institution, Washington, DC; purchase and partial gift made in 2012 from the Catherine and Ralph Benkaim Collection, Charles Lang Freer Endowment, F2012.4.3.

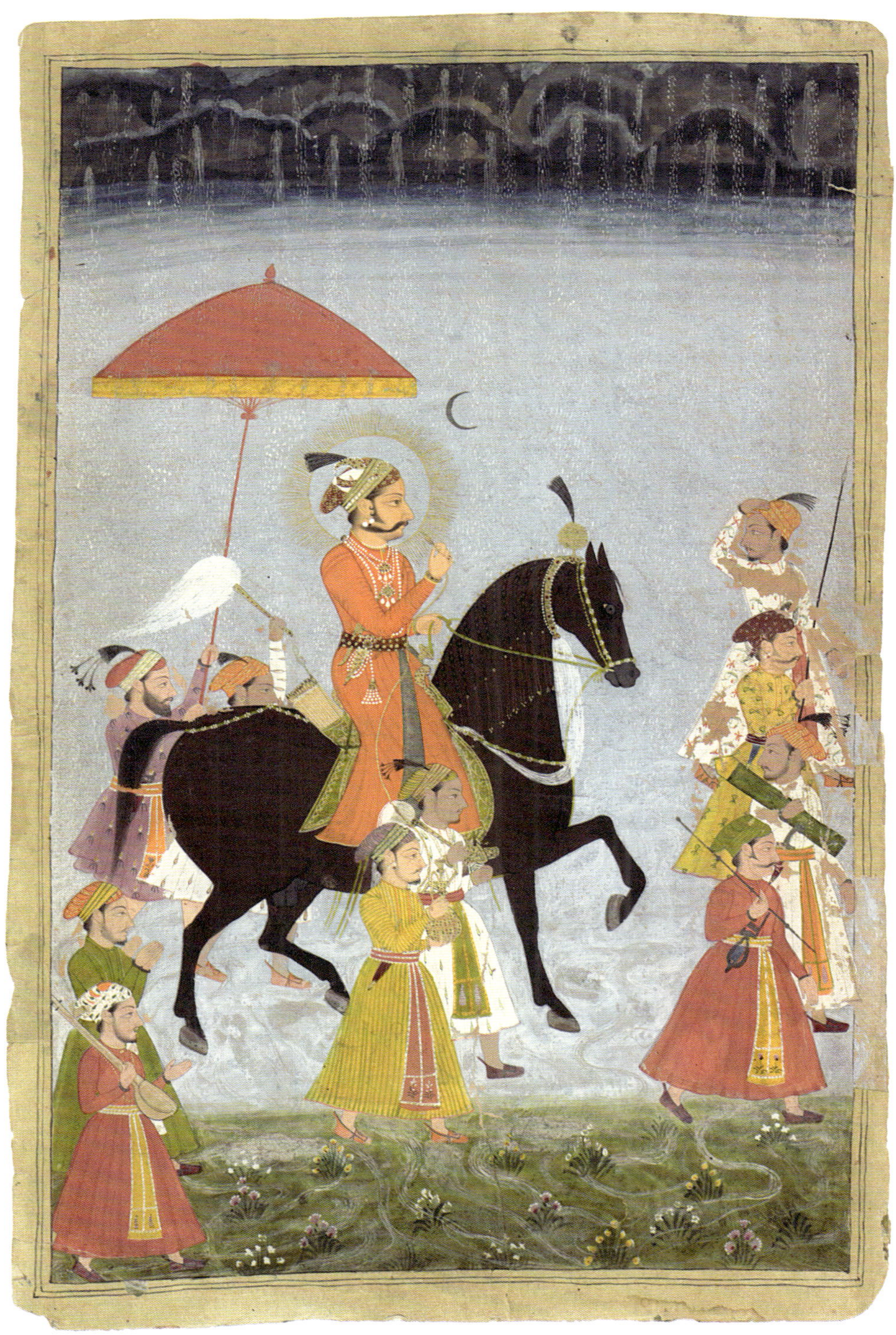

2.8. *Maharana Amar Singh II Riding in the Rain*, attributed to the Stipple Master, c. 1698, Udaipur. 31 × 26.7 cm. Fondation Custodia, Collection Frits Lugt, Paris, 2002-T.3.

by creating large works on both cloth and paper. They also combined and refracted the genres of small-scale portraits and poetic paintings of the seasons and musical melodies. In the process, artists constituted the *bhāva* of a place as a meaningful aesthetic and epistemic category that connects aspects of ecology, scale, and temporality. The tracking of intermedial practices—how painters, poets, and scribes invoked the sensorially powerful mood of the monsoon—is revealing. It traverses the analytical paths that constitute the art of picturing the *bhāva* of a place. In featuring thriving moods of urban places a potentiality was actualized in such painted artifacts. These representations cultivated a sense of bonding to places, keeping the image of forever plentiful rain and the lakes of Udaipur close to the heart and mind.

INTERMEDIALITY AND MONSOONS

Pictorial imaginings of rain and lakes were deeply tied to geography, to architecture, to history, to larger aesthetic currents, and to economic well-being. The painterly emphasis on rain finds its parallel in literary realms Poets and singers across regions and time periods in premodern South Asia described the transformation of human emotions with the onset of the monsoons. In Udaipur, bards also offered historical and ecological perspectives as they chronicled the rains that were central to the prosperity of early modern kings and territories. The celebration of the rainy season in the poetic genres of the *rāgamālā* (garland of musical notes) and *bārahmāsa* (twelve-month sequence)—as well as in chronicles like the Jain monk-poet Jaichand's *Saīkī* (A history of a hundred years), which I discuss further below—raises questions about how painters connected with their ever-changing environment, and how a painting presenting the feel of a monsoon downpour at Udaipur, not circumscribed by one text or genre, could have been received at the court.

These early modern perspectives on rain, whether in abundance or scarcity, provide, moreover, a context for the work of the architects and craftsmen who designed and built channels that guided limited rainwater into reservoirs as envisioned by their royal patrons—as well as the context of the poets and painters who represented them. Recent interdisciplinary scholarship on monsoon as an "emotional concept" dives into the rainy season's historical representations as "artefacts of emotional practices" to explore the season's role in development of feelings, memories, and knowledge systems in the early modern world.[3] The material reality of rain, however, remains difficult to access, which this chapter emphasizes by exploring poetry and painting across genres, alongside urban, architectural, and political shifts.[4] Longing for the lover and the expression of desire during the monsoon season are among the better-known aesthetic ideas circulated by poets, painters, and singers. In contrast, Jaichand's *Saīkī* includes an unusually detailed account of rainfall as it related to economics and politics during select years in the reigns of the Mughal emperor Aurangzeb (r. 1658–1707) and the Udaipur Maharanas Raj Singh (r. 1652–80) and Amar Singh II (r. 1698–1710). The poet recounts that the arrival of rains in extremes, more or less—the paucity or abundance of rainwater—could also lead to an experience of betokened feelings of precariousness. In other words, rains were multivalent, both aesthetically and in lived experience, which bears importantly on Udaipur painters' picturing of the city as the place of rain and lakes and the choices they made in responding to the city's unique lake-centered geography.

In the eighteenth century, as Udaipur's elites were expanding their presence in the lake city and realizing its potential as a place with a unique microclimate and rich natural resources, the city's painters were experimenting of their own accord. They appear to have been among the supremely enchanted inhabitants of Udaipur—the inspired ones who had knowledge of an established canon of painting and who also admired the verdant hills in the Aravalli valley, the descent of heavy clouds upon the hills, and the replenishing of streams as the rains came. These painters surely crossed bridges that spanned lakes and climbed mountains to survey the city nestled in the valley. They studied palace buildings intimately, and they walked the city's streets to collect vignettes of domestic facades. They display their acumen as keen architectural and topographical observers. But any attempt to privilege empirical observation and architectural knowledge as a key pictorial concern is stymied by the myriad associations among overlapping genres that painters established through affectively powerful pictorial means.

THE POETRY OF RAINS

Lotus-filled lakes and streams coursing with rainwater were ubiquitous aesthetic spaces in the pictorial and poetic imaginaries of early modern northern India. A late eighteenth-century painting, likely made in the kingdom of Udaipur's neighbor Bundi, reveals the elements and emotions associated with the monsoon (fig. 2.9).[5] Along with the standard tropes of

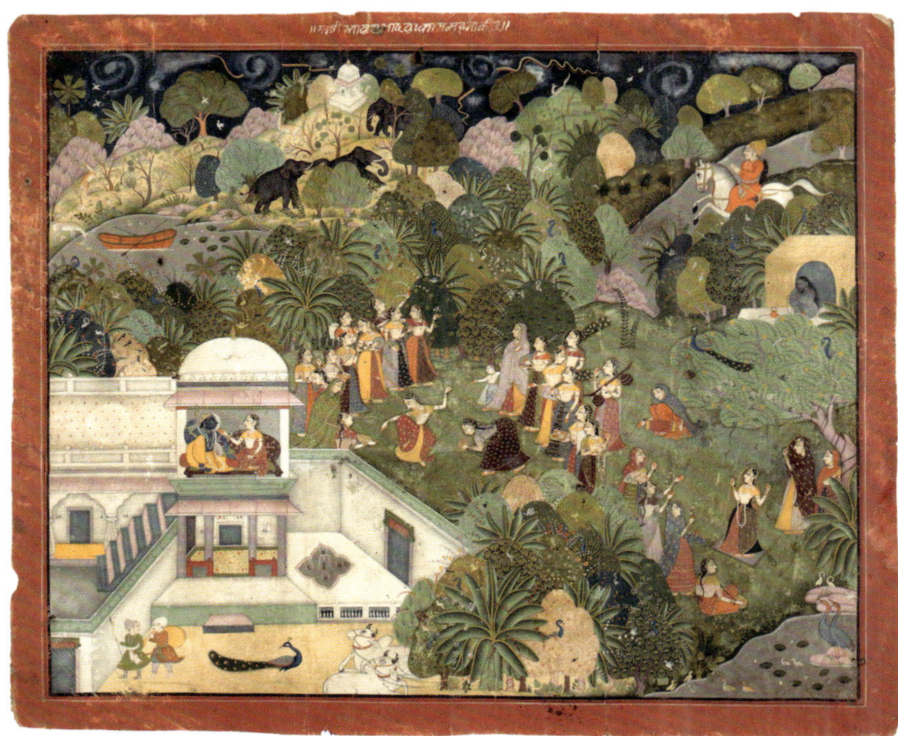

2.9. *A Bārah-māsa Painting Depicting the Late Summer Rainy Season*, c. 1780, Bundi. Opaque watercolor with gold on paper, 46.67 × 55.25 cm. Virginia Museum of Fine Arts, Richmond; Adolph D. and Wilkins C. Williams Fund, 2015.311.

besotted lovers, lightning streaks, thundering clouds, crying peacocks, roaring lions, and charging elephants, the painter invites us to savor the lotus-filled lakes created by the onslaught of rain. Blue-hued Krishna and his lover sit together in a courtly pavilion while a group of ladies celebrates the rainy season with dance and song or enjoys its cool breezes, playing on the swings in the verdant landscape. Because ascetic wandering and travel were forbidden during these rainy months, in the right corner the painter includes images of a mendicant, who takes shelter in a dwelling, and a nobleman astride a white horse. The artist's goal was to convey the emotional, social, atmospheric, and sensorial experience of the monsoon season. On the painting's border, a scribe notes that the picture (*sabī*) depicts the months of Savan (July and August) and Bhadon (August and September), covering the anticipated weather cycle of the rains, starting from late summer leading up to the wetter days.[6] The inscription identifies the painting's presentation of the *bhāva* of the rainy months.

Poetic verses associated with the rainy months of Savan and Bhadon were not always inscribed on monsoon paintings. However, the citation of familiar images and tropes across innumerable paintings persuades us that historical viewers, like contemporary art historians, plausibly related these painterly visions to the literary descriptions that circulated within courtly contexts and beyond. The poetic genre of the *bārah-māsa* was the paramount expression of the moods of people, places, flora, and fauna in the rainy season. The *bārah-māsa* is always structured as a lament divided into descriptions of the twelve months, each expressing the pain of separation when the lover of a *nāyikā*, the female heroine or lover in the Sanskrit and Hindi courtly literary tradition, goes abroad.[7] The poet Keshavdas, one of northern India's most prominent exponents on aesthetic theory in Brajbhasha, composed an extensive *bārah-māsa* in his acclaimed *Kavipriyā* (1601).[8] His verses describing the rainy months of Savan and Bhadon are in the voice of a woman desperately trying to convince her lover to stay:

> The swollen rivers merge into the sea, delighting him [the lover].
> The beautiful vines are locked in splendid embrace with youthful trees.
> The dazzle of lightning mingles with the clouds as far as the eye can see.
> The cry of the peacock is actually the earth making love with the rain.

And so all couples delight one another.
What's this talk of leaving?
It's simply unheard of to leave in Savan.

Thunder crashes and booms from every direction, overwhelming village huts.
Clouds take hold of the earth and unleash torrential rain.
The air fills with the din of crickets, the wind gusts and roars.
Lions and tigers roar, herds of elephants stampede through the forest, uprooting trees.
The difference between day and night vanishes completely.
You have to cover yourself against the rain.
In Bhadon, staying home with your beloved is nectar—being abroad is poison.
It's not a time to leave home.[9]

2.10. "The Month of Savan (July–August)," from a *Bārah-māsa* (twelve-month sequence), c. 1675–1700, Bundi. Opaque watercolor on paper, 30.5 × 21.7 cm. British Museum, London. 1999,1202,0.5.5.

2.11. "The Month of Savan (July–August)," from a *Bārah-māsa* (twelve-month sequence), c. 1800, Jaipur. Gouache painting on paper, 31.6 × 22.5 cm. British Museum, London. 1940,0713,0.5.

2.12. "The Month of Bhadon (August–September)," from a *Bārah-māsa* (twelve-month sequence), c. 1675, Bundi. Opaque watercolor with gold on paper, 30.5. × 21.3 cm. Art Gallery of New South Wales, Sydney; Margaret Hannah Olley Art Trust, 1991, 370.1991.

2.13. "The Month of Bhadon (August–September)," from a *Bārah-māsa* (twelve-month sequence), c. 1700–1725, Kota. Opaque watercolor, gold and ink on paper, 32.39 × 21.59 cm. Los Angeles County Museum of Art; from the Nasli and Alice Heeramaneck Collection, Museum Associates Purchase, M.71.1.25.

Rajasthan's court painters visualized these affect-saturated verses in manifold ways. A Bundi court painter who responded to Keshavdas's Savan verse depicts climbing creepers entangled with the bark of trees and serpentine streaks of gold-colored lightning intertwined with thick gray clouds (fig. 2.10). The rhythmic, wavelike brushstrokes of the clouds echo the sway of tall green grasses in the lush landscape. In another illustrated copy of Keshavdas's poetry, a painter at Jaipur, in depicting the same verse on Savan, included the customary dark clouds, rain, lightning, and peacocks. By placing the blue-hued Krishna inside the threshold of his lover's home, he emphasized the *nāyikā*'s wish to keep her beloved from leaving (fig. 2.11). He also devoted painterly attention to Keshavdas's verse describing the streams of water flowing from all directions that collect in a larger body of water. The radiating spokes and shining silver direct attention toward the dazzling lower register of the page. Thus we see that painted responses selected and accentuated varied aspects of the verses. In a companion to the Savan page from the *bārah-māsa* set illustrated at the Bundi court around 1670–75, the painter responded to the Bhadon verse by emphasizing the rising ferocity of the storm and the season, the madness of elephants uprooting trees and dogs running and leaping in the monsoon's billowing winds (fig. 2.12). About two decades later, a Bhadon page associated with the Hada court workshop established at Kota suggests that its painter modeled the composition on the Bundi page: the lovers sit in matching pictorial pavilions and the streams flow along similarly curving paths. What strikes the viewer is the enraged posture and snarling face of the second elephant in the Kota example (fig. 2.13). Set among the swaying trees and plants, he stares straight at the viewer. Unlike the Bundi composition's rearward elephant, seen standing steady behind the action of his accomplice, the Kota example displays the charged attitude of a stampeding elephant, also implied in Keshavdas's verses. In another, final instance, a mid-seventeenth-century painter at Malwa distinctively captured the destructive movements of Bhadon; his animals—an elephant, a dog, and a tiger—the foremost quite literally walking over the painted roof, tilt the building and render the bluster of an unmitigated storm (fig. 2.14).

While Keshavdas sought to evoke the sounds of Savan and Bhadon through alliteration, painters exploited the visual and painterly potential of atmospheric feeling and the physical movement of nature's elements. The affect of roaring thunder clouds we hear in the words *ghorata ghana* when spoken in a loud and heavy voice, or the feel of land being soaked by the rapidly falling downpour unleashed by rain clouds that the phrase *dhārādhara dhari dharani* implies, is very difficult to evoke in reading a translated Bhadon verse.[10] Busch urges "listening for context" and for the "aural landscape" of Keshavdas's highly scholastic poetry to conjure an early modern assembly of connoisseurs savoring verses recited by poets and at times sung by musicians.[11] Like poets and musicians, painters and paintings were essential participants in the courtly assembly of patrons. Across courts and between pages belonging to the same set, painted responses to Keshavdas's monsoon poetry imbibe these feelings heard only in sound and song. Painters not only chose among

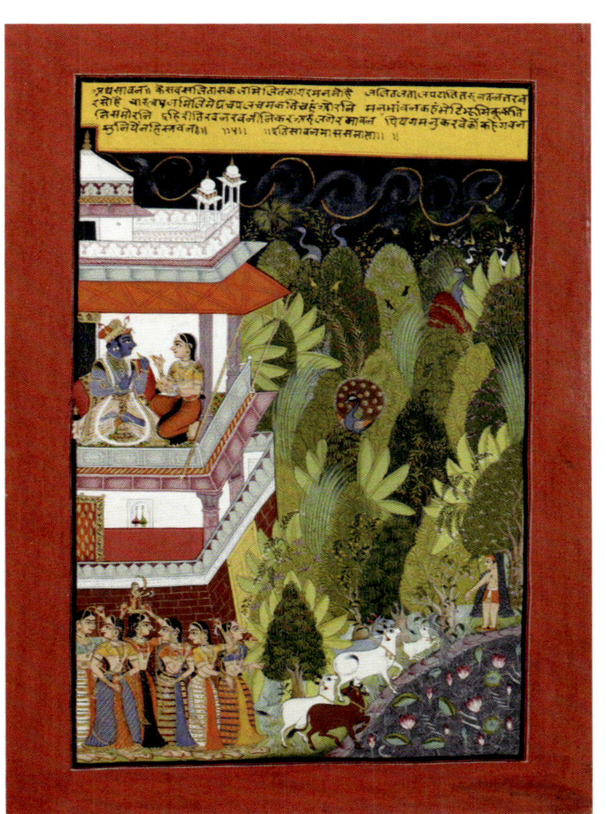

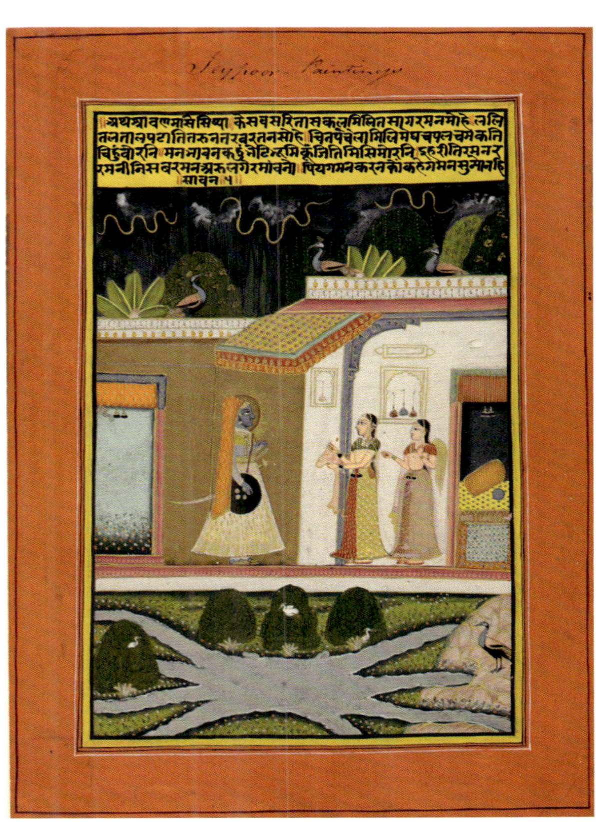
Jeypoor Paintings

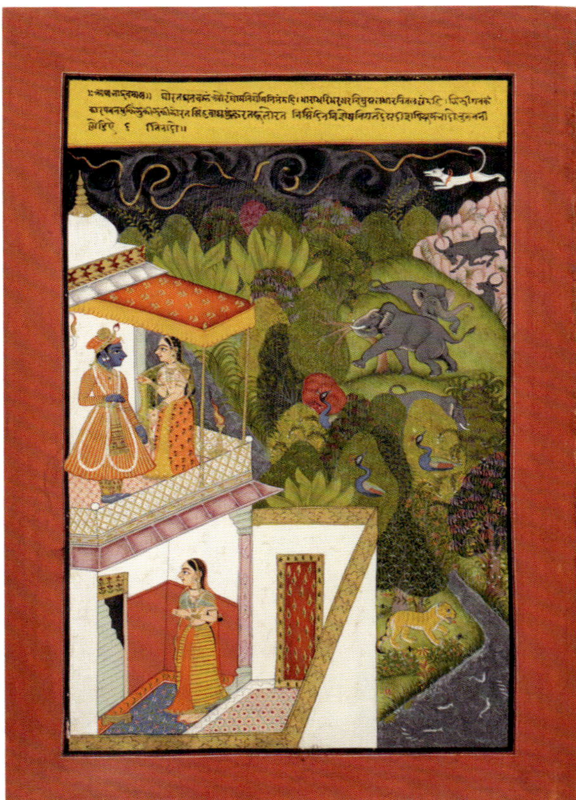

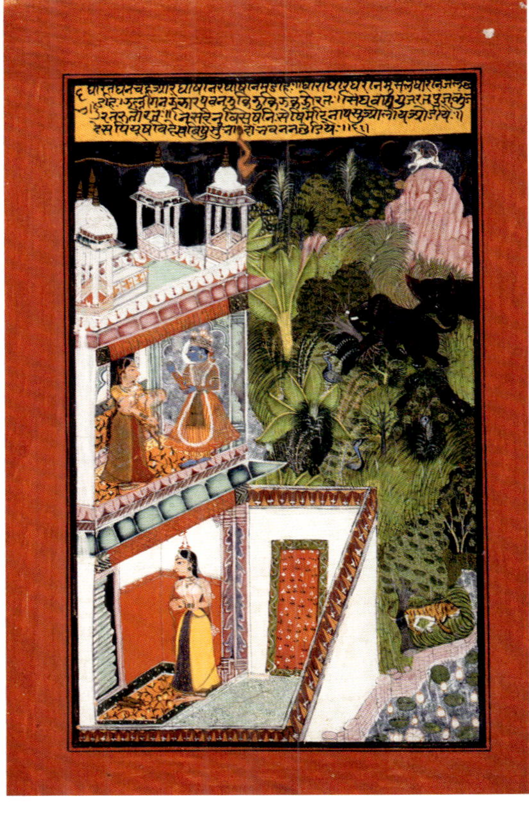

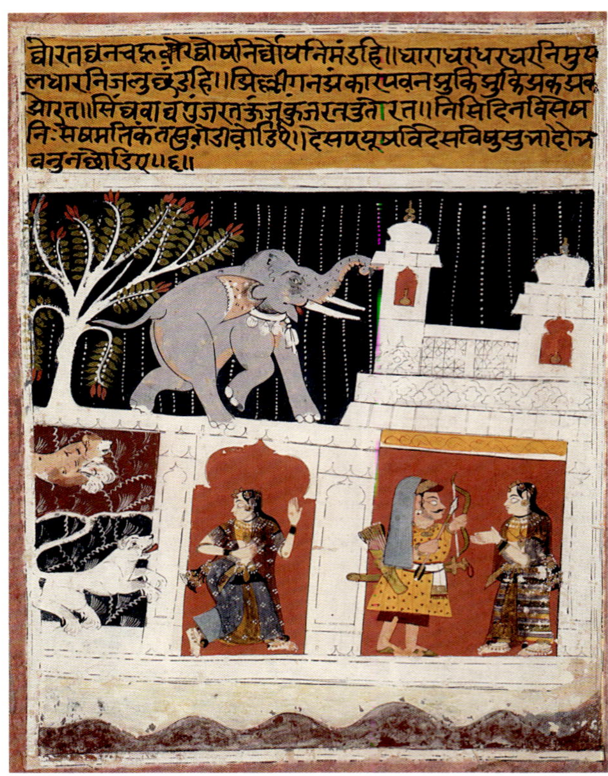

2.14. "The Month of Bhadon (August–September)," from a *Bārah-māsa* (twelve-month sequence), c. 1640–50, Malwa. Opaque watercolor, ink and gold on paper, 24.44 × 18.41 cm. Los Angeles County Museum of Art; from the Nasli and Alice Heeramaneck Collection, Museum Associates Purchase, M.71.1.15.

iconographic elements—the entangling of creepers or the joining of rivulets—in the poetry on Savan but also mediated their own experiences to create painterly effects that sought to evoke embodied feelings for viewers. A roof steeply inclined in one direction may make one strain the neck to one side or gesture to others through hand movements where the painted lines and animals are headed. A polished color reflecting light may demand tilting the painted artwork or straining our eyes to view its effects, just as literary compositions called for our ears to tune in to hear them.

The sounds of monsoon rain reverberate in painted iconography associated with contemplative poetic moods created out of sonic and lyrical ingredients. Another genre in which rains were important is the *rāgamālā*, the "garland" of musical compositions that evokes the *bhāva* of classical melodies.[12] By the seventeenth century, a complete *rāgamālā* set included between thirty-six and forty-two melodies codified as iconographies and accompanied with poetic verses that describe the mood, time of day or night, and often the particular season associated with each melody. Like other poetic and musical endeavors in Brajbhasha from the northern Indian courts, the genre of *rāgamālā* was concerned with provoking the connoisseur to experience emotional states of melancholy, longing, or peacefulness.[13] Each musical composition was personified, often as a lover enjoying—or longing for—the beloved. Some *rāgamālā* iconographies were also connected to sounds in nature, such as the hiss of a snake or the singing of birds, and to the sounds of human activity, like the washing of clothes near the river or the churning of milk. Increasing numbers of *rāgamālā* paintings from the fifteenth to the nineteenth centuries standardized the iconographies of lush or stormy landscapes that enhanced, respectively, the moods of love in union or separation. The singing of musical notes associated with the monsoon and belonging to the "Malhar family," such as the *megh raga* (literally, "the cloud melody"), had the power to affect—the atmosphere and audience, the physical and psychological.[14] The monsoon ragas, "sung correctly," could effectively not only transform the mood of an assembly of aficionados but also bring rains to a place—restoring the well-being of humans and nature.[15]

In depictions of raga celebrating the rains, known as *megh* or *megh malhār* (cloud thunder), we often see Krishna and his lovers dancing to tunes played by musicians and to the sounds of raindrops and rumbling clouds. Until the seventeenth century, the monsoon as depicted in paintings was largely iconic. That is, we as viewers see the iconographic elements of the peacocks, rain, and clouds collated onto the page, but we do not find painterly allusions to the texture of raindrops and the fleeting sense of a rain shower.[16] By 1700, the focus was starkly different: in a *rāgamālā* folio titled *Megh Malhar Raga*, likely made in Pratapgarh, the artist painted dense vertical lines of rain that coalesce into sheets of water falling forcefully over the hills, trees, and earth, overtaking the material surface of the painted page (fig. 2.15).[17] The painter pictorially collected the pouring rain—which one can imagine to have been caused by the singing of the *megh malhār raga*, depicted in the form of Krishna surrounded by a group of *nāyikās*, each playing a distinct instrument—into a lotus-filled stream at the bottom of the page. Both the materiality of water—the speed with which rain falls in droplets or sheets, how it collects, swirls into waves, splatters, puddles, and transforms into shimmering bodies dotted with blooming lotus flowers—and the sensorial and physical changes in monsoon landscapes garnered the attention of painters of *rāgamālā* sets. As these rainy compositions mediated "monsoon feelings" more and more on atmospheric terms, they also became harbingers of painted images that sought to describe the monsoon moods of particular places.

Paintings made at the Udaipur court, more so than artworks from any other region in early modern India, affixed for viewers a gamut of images and emotions of the rains and lakes evoked in poetry—longing, peril, plentitude. Iconic, non-illusionistic renderings, in colors tied to the Udaipur court's painting palette, meet a painterly interest in evoking watery textures, moist atmospheres, and cooling effects. For example, in the 1660s an Udaipur painter depicted a poet reciting verse to a lone *nāyikā* (fig. 2.16). The blooming lotuses that brighten dark-colored lakes, trees that sway ever so slightly, and lines of rain that fall from watery clouds appear to cool the red heat of summer. Even in the absence of literary verse, such painted visions compel us to imagine two contrasting atmospheres: intense heat and its imminent transformation by rain and breeze—and, by implication, the pain of longing and the anticipation of reunion encountered in *bārah-māsa* poetry. The painting *Krishna Raising Mount Govardhan*, an early 1700s rendering of the deity raising the mountain to protect the citizens of Mathura from torrential rain, centralizes nature's menace (fig. 2.17). The raindrops fall in clustered intensity from the hands of the rain gods residing in the clouds; however, the drops are obstructed by the mass of the mountain, and so a considerably smaller volume of water lashes the earth. The pleasure of viewing arises from deciphering the compositional dexterity of the cave-like cloths in which people take shelter, which echo the shape of the large mountain that weighs heavily on the composition even as it resists perception as a planar or elevation view. A sense unfolds of the tensed physical and affective experience of being caught in, shielded from, and caressed by a monsoon downpour.

More than the ethic of protection tied to peril, the emotion of plenty invoked the world of the blue god Krishna. Abundant and beautiful places were created and re-created by the coming of the rains in the real world as well as in the myriad recitations and representations that celebrated Krishna. Even before Udaipur painters turned to their city as an object of affection, at least one page belonging to a mid-seventeenth-century dispersed manuscript of the *Bhāgavata Purāṇa* (Ancient tales of Lord Vishnu), visually contemplates the flora and fauna of the monsoon landscape sans its inhabitants (fig. 2.18).[18] All of nature's elements that turned on the mood of

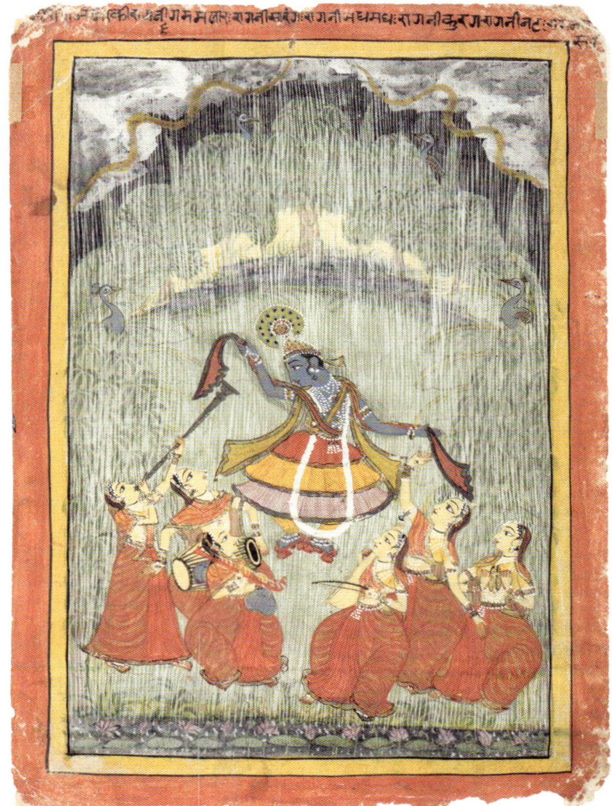

2.15. *Megh Malhar Raga* (The cloud thunder musical melody), c. 1720, Pratapgarh. Opaque watercolor on paper, 26.2 × 18.9 cm. San Diego Museum of Art; Edwin Binney 3rd Collection, 1990.654.

monsoons in Indian aesthetic traditions are depicted: the dense clouds in watery paint, the streaks of lightning, the chirping birds mounted atop trees and hills, the toads by the riverbank, the fish that float in the running streams of water, and the long lines of white raindrops painted on the dark gray ground of a monsoon night and on the verdant green ground of a land radiant in the rains. The painter juxtaposes styles as well: trees, replete in Mewar's poetic manuscripts, frame two mountain peaks that adapt the forms and colors of the craggy rocks that were hallmarks of albums and Persianate manuscripts of Mughal India and beyond. A later scribe complements the Sanskrit poetry on the back of the painting with a vernacular Hindi inscription written in red ink on the border of the painted vignette.[19] His response lists the sights and sounds of the monsoon and identifies the place depicted as the bank of the Yamuna River. The riverbank of the Yamuna was both a real and an idealized fluvial plain in the stories of

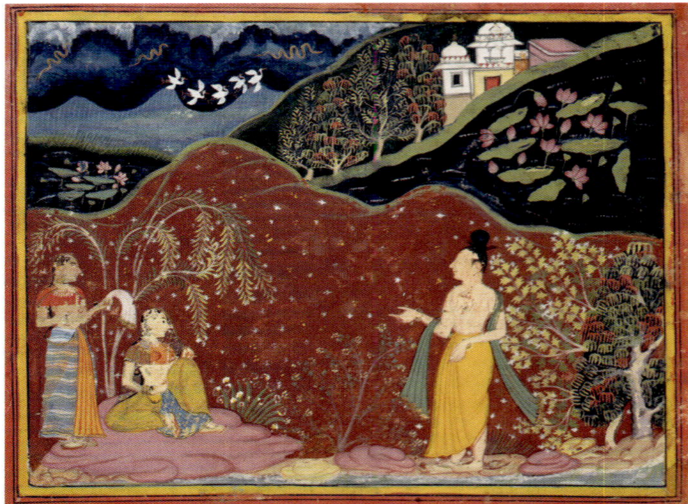

2.16. *The Poet Approaches Radha under a Monsoon Sky*, c. 1665, Udaipur. Opaque watercolor and gold on paper, 19.3 × 24.4 cm. Museum of Fine Arts, Boston; gift of John Goelet, 66.118.

2.17. *Krishna Raises Mount Govardhana*, c. 1700, Udaipur. Opaque watercolor, red and black inks, gold, and silver or tin on paper, 21.9 × 41.9 cm. Philadelphia Museum of Art; Stella Kramrisch Collection, 1994-148-428.

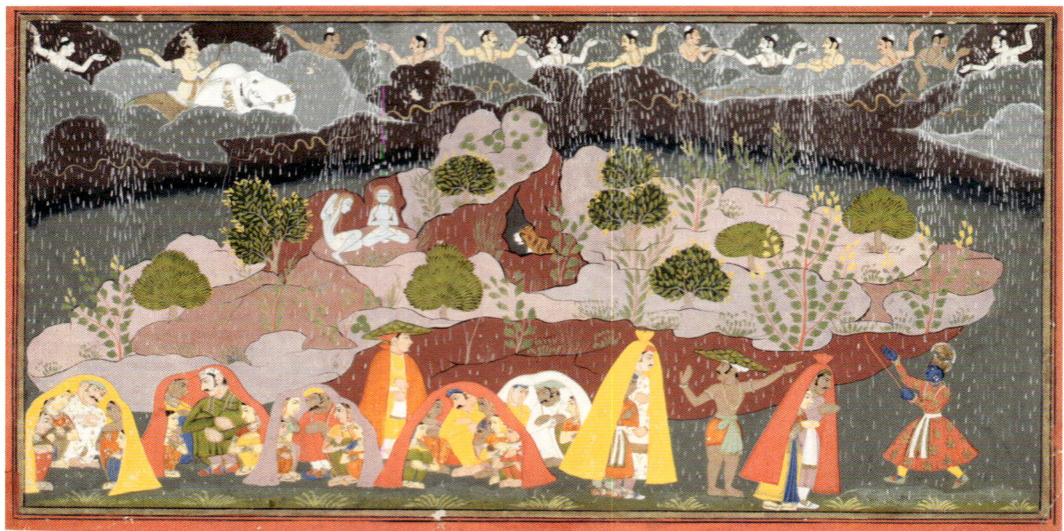

Krishna. Historical viewers would have comprehended this folio in material, narrative, and perceptual terms as part of the sequence of folios in a manuscript that combined text, commentaries, and paintings. Yet, it is noteworthy that the painter devotes a complete folio to the change of seasons that could possibly convey multiple stories. The white of the rain clouds touching the mountain peaks is suggestive of the descent of heavy clouds, prompting viewers, particularly from Udaipur, one can expect, to imagine the mood of monsoons as witnessed from the hills.

As we turn to the poetic and painted visions of rain and lakes in the landscape of Udaipur, it becomes clear that all monsoon imagery was highly charged with allusions. Just as the genre of the *bārah-māsa* moved across classical poetry, religious texts, and folk songs, the pictorial motifs of clouds, rain, streams, and lakes transformed renderings of ordinary settings into landscapes drenched in water and in love.[20] Whereas poets consistently drew upon the pining of heroines and the traits of seasons to create alternate registers of desire and pleasure, Udaipur's painters deployed the atmospheric effects of the monsoon season to embellish worldly places.[21] In the process, they created new genres and expanded the meanings that viewers could find within paintings such as *Maharana Amar Singh II in Udaipur during a Monsoon Downpour* from their immediate experiences of rains and monsoons. They intertwined the emotional intensity of love and desire with the ideals of prosperity and protection within the courtly genres of royal portraiture, poetic histories, and praiseworthy

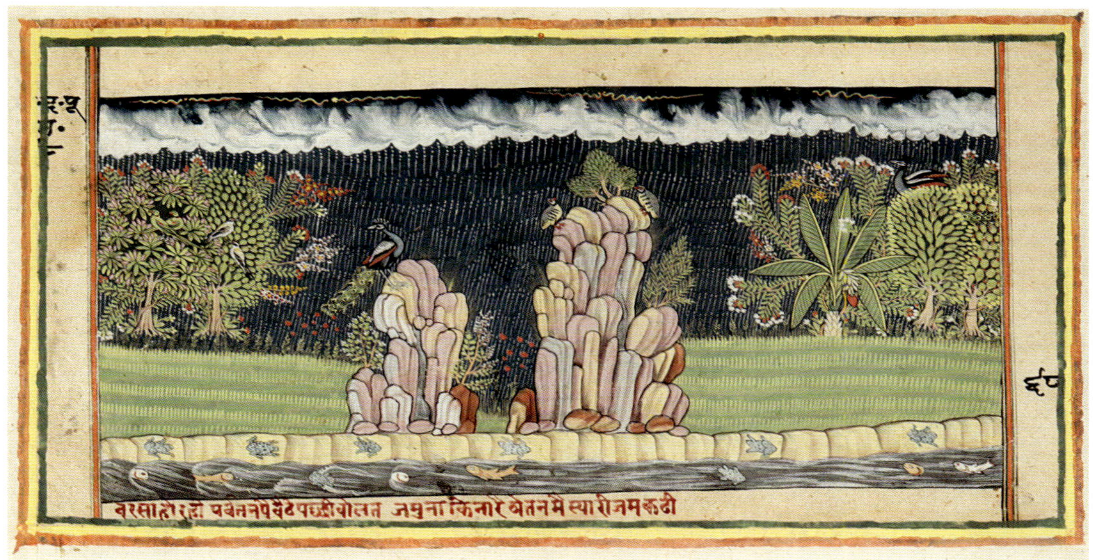

2.18. "The Rainy Season," page from a dispersed *Bhāgavata Purāṇa*, c. 1630–50, probably Udaipur. Opaque watercolor and ink on paper, 23.3 × 40 cm. Philadelphia Museum of Art; 125th Anniversary Acquisition, Alvin O. Bellak Collection, 2004-149-18.

places. What could be more joyful than admiring an expanding city of lakes? Especially when one was located in the arid landscape of northwestern India, what could be more powerful than ruling from a city of lakes drenched in monsoon rain?

THE HISTORY OF RAINS AND LAKES

Departing from poetic visions of the monsoon season, the Jain monk-traveler Jaichand offered an ecological perspective on rains and droughts in his chronicle. Almost each one of the 188 verses in Jaichand's *Saīkī* begins with an abbreviated reference to the years it chronicles, which span from 1658 to 1723—or 1715 to 1780 on the *vikram saṃvat* (VS) calendar.[22] Brajmohan Jawalia, the only historian to have studied the manuscript thus far, suggests that the *Saīkī* belongs to a wider genre of historical writing practiced by non-courtly scribes and travelers.[23] While Jaichand does not claim to belong to a specific region, the genre of the *Saīkī* and his language suggest that he came from Marwar.[24] Jaichand fashions himself as a traveler and gatherer of information from local people and historical sources. His six-line verses are often written in a conversational manner and refer to "information that [the poet] has heard," especially in passages about the east and the south beyond the regions of Rajasthan and Gujarat.[25] Jaichand's account is a treasure trove for those wishing to gain an understanding of political dynamics and negotiations between regional polities in northern, western, and southern India from the mid-seventeenth to the mid-eighteenth century. The discussion here focuses on the relations established between Jaichand's telling of history and the arrival of the rains.[26] The mid-seventeenth-century lakes constructed in the Mewar region to remedy water scarcity caused by successive seasons of drought certainly comprise critical evidence that connected ecological crisis to public benefaction. The creation of Rajsamand Lake, forty miles north of Udaipur, for instance, the most ambitious building project of the Udaipur king Raj Singh, was completed in 1680, toward the end of his reign.[27] It was intended to provide relief to Mewar citizens suffering from extreme drought.[28] The Udaipur court poet Ranchoda Bhatta composed an extensive genealogy in the introductory cantos of the *Rajpraśasti*, a Sanskrit poem inscribed on twenty-five stone slabs along the shores of Rajsamand Lake, which also describes the seven-day consecration ceremony and the king's circumambulation of the lake.[29] The lens offered, however, was exclusively kingly, aimed at memorializing Rajput pasts.[30]

Jaichand neither dedicated his work to a sole royal or mercantile patron nor sang the praises of a single figure.[31] Instead, in his verses we find critiques of the Mughal emperor Aurangzeb and the Rajput kings alike for the atrocities they inflicted on the common people; he criticizes Jain merchants for manipulating prices in the grain market, and he questions the integrity of his own monastic community for manipulating the sentiments of laymen and laywomen during difficult times.[32] In recounting the Udaipur king Raj Singh's destruction of crops in Malpura in verse 16, which focuses on the ecological story of the year 1697 (VS 1754), the author suggests that distressing times could be brought upon by gods or by men seeking to control nature. Prosperity and morality are linked to ecology and politics, respectively: both are steeped in crisis, and both change from year to year.

The *Saīkī* narrates a history that interweaves political events and ecological changes. This rhythmic narrative structure alerts us to the centrality of rain in the telling of Udaipur's history: typically, five to six verses on political conflicts and alliances are followed by three or four verses on annual rains and the associated state of agricultural production, the economy of the grain markets, the migration patterns of people, and the social behavior of people from various classes and castes. For instance, the introductory verses (7–15) cover several intertwined political events in the year 1658 (VS 1715): the military conquests of Maharana Raj Singh of Mewar, the emperor Aurangzeb's territorial outposts and inheritance woes, and the political negotiations and fierce battles that ensued among Mughal princes and Rajput kings.[33] Jaichand concludes this segment by turning to the environmental, economic, and societal happenings from the years 1658 to 1664 (VS 1715 to 1721).

1658
In [seventeen] fifteen there was famine, in sixteen all grain decayed
In seventeen, it cost sixteen for a *pailī* weight in grain; neither cloud nor rain from the beginning to the end
Many grain markets in Malpura were destroyed by the Rana in those days
For three consecutive years, there were no grains and people were pained
The sons of merchants and moneylenders became the followers of monks
Jaichand says, who can control these conditions, prosperity is created by God (16)

1661
In [seventeen] eighteen there was abundant rain, in nineteen there was lots of millet
In twenty the clouds did not burst, the entire earth dried up
The cost of grain for twenty *tolas* was now the same as for one and a half *mana*
Two and a half *sers* of ghee could not be brought even with one rupee paid in cash
Cows and buffalos died; one does not even find buttermilk to soothe
In the vast region of Bikaner, how do people hope for the future? (17)

1664
In [seventeen] twenty-one, abundant and sweet grains flourished aplenty
There were two monsoons, both poured abundant rains
Sojat did not see this abundance, there many people were sold
Many people felt pained, roamed here and there, or suffered at home
Says Jaichand after giving deep thought, good days will come back again
All must sit and take God's name, fulfill all your hearts' desires (18)[34]

Jaichand's verses partake in a culture of reportage and critique. He employed words from Brajbhasha, though his verses rarely engage aesthetic motifs. The historian-poet was likely aware of the *bārah-māsa*, but his concerns remained tied to the world around him rather than to the world of imagination. Jaichand adopted an enumerative strategy: we sense his insistence on years, chronology, and facticity—who killed whom in small and big wars; who became the next king; the names of key ministers and political players who constantly moved between courts; whether there were fewer or more rains, floods, and droughts; comparing droughts that occurred in different regions and different years; the quantity and quality of agricultural produce and the fluctuations in the prices of grains and butter across regions; and the constant movement of people from the regions of Rajasthan to the lush central lands in northern and western India due to the lack of rain. It is possible that the genre of the *Saīkī* had much in common with the newsletters (*akhbhārāt*) that circulated in the information network of eighteenth-century India.[35] In the *Saīkī*'s verses, on limited occasions, during a season of good monsoons, we read celebratory phrases proclaiming that the earth is now *sarasa* (full of *rasa*), while in drought years it was *nīrasa* (without any *rasa*).[36] The parallels between the water drenching the soil and one sense of the *rasa*, which refers to the liquid materiality of juice, are unmistakable but do not necessarily connect with aesthetic notions of *rasa* as the vital essence of art and one of the types of affective sentiments.[37] The suggestion here is one of both favorable and difficult conditions for farmers, merchants, kings, and society at large.

Ultimately, Jaichand creates a picture of *dukāḷa* (dark times) and *sukāḷa* (good times). In writing about 1700 (VS 1757)—the dawn of Maharana Amar Singh II's reign, around the time when the large-scale painting on cloth featuring Udaipur's king, court, and city in a monsoon was made—Jaichand specifies *sukāḷa*:

> 1700:
> [Seventeen] fifty-seven saw good times in all regions of Marwar
> Sujan Singh of Bikaner embarked to the Deccan on a horse
> Rana Amar Singh ruled in Udaipur and Chittor Fort
> Jaswant Singh at Jaisalmer, Sawai Jai Singh controlled Amber
> Crops were abundant on the earth; Raos and Ranas were happy
> Says Jaichand, on their good fortune, well earned through past deeds (103)[38]

Jaichand's narrative structure conveys kings as extremely dependent on both the availability of water—for the smooth functioning of their country—and the friendships and networks of their political compatriots, for enacting their political authority with goodwill. The poet enumerates rulers across Rajasthan and highlights their rightful deeds, abundant crops, and joyous, successful kingships. There are several reasons these might have come to be entangled. One possible impetus for intertwining the positive expressions of humankind and nature may be the passing of the old political order in 1698 (VS 1756) across the regional courts of Rajasthan—Udaipur, Amber, Jaisalmer, and Bikaner.[39] Another impetus could have been the diplomatic negotiations between the above-mentioned kings in the ensuing years, which Jaichand continues to highlight in the following verses.[40] Jaichand's assembly of Rajput kings within verse 103 is matched only by his assembly of the seasons of summer and monsoon in verse 112 on the year 1704; it celebrates prodigious rains that arrived across the months of Jyestha, Savan, Bhadon, and Asad.

> 1704:
> [Seventeen] sixty-one saw extensive rains, beginning in the months of Jyestha [May–June]
> Lakes filled up in Savana [July–August], rivers and streams were filled in Bhadon [August–September]
> In the months of Asad [June–July] hopes bloomed further, all grains were in abundance
> Corn, Bajra, Udad, all the crops thrived
> There was abundance in the entire country, inexpensive crops made all people happy
> Says Jaichand, do enjoy, all thieves and thugs have withdrawn! (112)[41]

His recounting in verse 103 of a ruler marching on horseback through a country bestowed with plentiful rain—in this case Sujan Singh of the Bikaner court, another early modern court in Rajasthan—invokes a trope made visible in the painted portrayals of Rajput kings, as seen in the painting of Amar Singh II riding his horse in the rain (fig. 2.8). Both are powerful reminders of how patrons, poets, and painters seized opportunities to intertwine the beginnings of new reigns and prosperous, bountiful times.

It is impossible to determine whether the large-scale painting depicting *Maharana Amar Singh II in Udaipur during a Monsoon Downpour*, which can be dated by style to around 1700, commemorated a particular season of good rains or a general condition of prosperity. Most of the paintings—small and large—depicting Amar Singh walking and riding in the rain or presiding over assemblies in palaces and gardens under thunderous skies are devoid of inscriptions. If the painting was made between 1700 (VS 1757) and 1704 (VS 1761), then it might parallel the season of good rains, good crops, and good times that Jaichand chronicled in those years. If the painting was made in 1705, then it may have commemorated flourishing times that were highly desired in the years to come, for we learn of yet another season of drought in 1705 (VS 1762) and uneven rains in the ensuing years up to 1709 (VS 1766).[42] In bringing Jaichand's telling of the history of rains in around 1700 to bear on our interpretation of the monumental painting featuring Amar Singh's court and Udaipur city in a monsoon downpour, my point is not simply about painting as historical documentation. Rather, I seek to demonstrate that this impressive picture, like Jaichand's *Saīkī*, underscores the critical influence that rain and lakes had on urban, economic, agrarian, and political futures. The stakes of idealizing monsoon moods were high and associating their seasonal pleasures with a protracted kingly temporality rather than annual chronological time could have been an expedient move on behalf of painters, patrons, and scribes.

That rain and lakes could stir emotions of longing and belonging augmented their allure for Udaipur's painters. In a

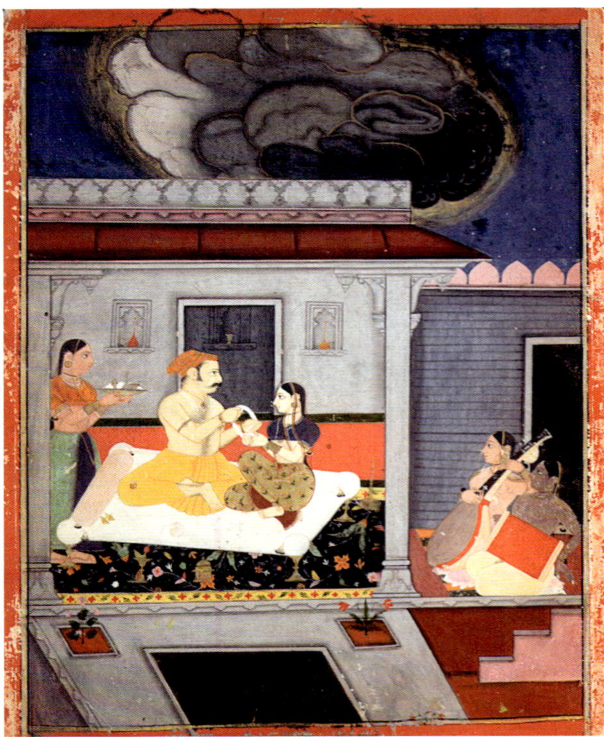

2.19. *Maharana Raj Singh and a Lady in a Courtyard Pavilion*, c. 1670, Udaipur. Opaque watercolor and gold on paper, 24 × 19 cm. Private collection.

circa-1670 portrait depicting Raj Singh, Amar Singh II's grandfather, a brilliantly rendered dark monsoon cloud, contained in a gold outline, appears attached to the bedchamber of the trysting king, who sits bare-chested with a woman in an intimate setting (fig. 2.19).[43] On the basis of the facial types and their pinkish complexions, Topsfield attributes the artwork to an artist trained at the Bundi court and remarks that the portrait's extraordinary "emotional charge [is] more redolent of a *rāgamālā* subject."[44] Indeed, the erotic mood (*śṛṅgāra*) inside the chamber is shaped by the presence of the cloud mass and the musicians outside the royal chamber. This historical portrait praised the king by conjuring an idealized poetic place where the entwined moods of rain and love were celebrated. More so, the rain-filled feel of the amorphous shapes of dark gray subtly changing into whiter tones creates a sense of texture, moisture, and imminent rain by taking the viewer inside a visible mass of watery gouache blotting the paper surface. An interest in creating ephemeral effects that demanded immersion can be sensed here. The atmospheric immediacy in this painted cloudburst anticipates the formal and thematic threads Udaipur's painters chose to pursue, even as they turned toward shifting the locale of idealized monsoon moods.

In the early eighteenth-century, patrons and painters imprinted their mark in Udaipur's intellectual and cultural arena by imagining, commissioning, and representing a city built on the lakeshore. They foregrounded this new approach to the aesthetics and knowledge of a place with a strikingly new kind of painted picture on a dramatically expanded scale, evoking Udaipur—the city of lakes ruled by Amar Singh II—as a real, specific place by including details of the palace architecture, royal portraits, and the urban topography of hills, lakes, and bridges. Through the painterly rendering of an abundant monsoon, painters transformed the land that was for them "the here and now" into an idealized image. The painting *Maharana Amar Singh II in Udaipur during a Monsoon Downpour* could have been commissioned to commemorate a good monsoon season in around 1700 and to associate it with Amar Singh II, or it could have represented the collective desire of patrons and painters for the mood of the monsoon—an imagining of the beauty and plentitude a good rainy season would bring to the city of Udaipur in the future.

THE PLACE OF RAINS AND LAKES

By the time rain arrived with full gusto in paintings that feature the city of Udaipur, its emotive potential and painterly pleasures were familiar to artists and audiences. For Udaipur's court painters, the rainy season was imbued with captivating potential that could be deployed to create new kinds of pictures and meaningful associations—whether within small-scale portraits on paper or large-scale works on cloth. Looking at historical archives, it becomes difficult to determine the precise process through which a feeling of longing for and belonging to the lake city was shaped. Did the sense of connection that the architecture and environs of the lake city evoked for its citizens work as a tour de force for poets, painters, and patrons? Or did works of art that connected spaces and senses play a stronger role than the material landscape and buildings in how courtly communities came to imagine and admire local landscapes? Indeed, the incomparable locale of Udaipur has been called both an inspiration for artistic genius and a reason for artistic conservatism and isolation.[45] The shaping of new viewing experiences in looking at paintings, in looking at architecture, and in looking out from newly built structures had been appearing with increasing frequency since the early 1700s. The large-scale cloth painting *Maharana*

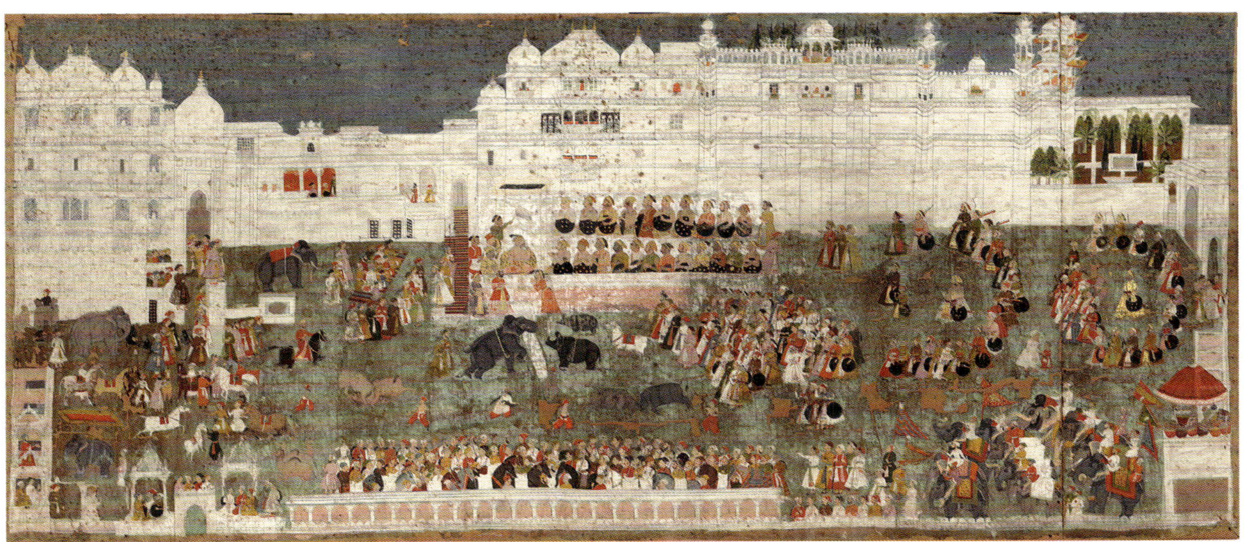

2.20. *Maharana Amar Singh II and His Court Watching Animal Fights at the Manek Chowk*, c. 1705, Udaipur. Opaque watercolor and gold on cloth, width approx. 100 cm. The City Palace Museum, Udaipur; 2012.20.0012_R.

Amar Singh II in Udaipur during a Monsoon Downpour is exceptional because its painters align these three experiences in one artwork, thereby making dwelling in the moods of an Udaipur monsoon possible and the arousing of a sense of place all the more powerful.

One way to parse how Udaipur became the place of rain and lakes in the courtly imaginary is to recognize the central relationship painters established between the enduring and the ephemeral. In three large-scale paintings on cloth, each measuring approximately forty to fifty inches in width and thought to have been created in the first decade of the eighteenth century, around the same time as *Maharana Amar Singh II in Udaipur during a Monsoon Downpour*, painters depicted the Udaipur king Amar Singh II and created an iconic image of the enduring nature of the Manek Chowk, the large courtyard in front of the facade of his palace. This rectangular courtyard, bounded by the imposing architecture of the Mardana Mahal (Men's Palace) on the west side, as discussed in chapter 1, was a significant space even before the early 1700s (see fig. 1.10). The early eighteenth-century painters, though, seem mesmerized by the palace's monumentality—enlarging their canvases as if to accommodate both its spell and its size. One of these cloth paintings, *Maharana Amar Singh II and His Court Watching Animal Fights at the Manek Chowk*, depicts multiple staged fights, between an elephant and a rhinoceros, a pair of camels, and a pair of bulls (fig. 2.20). The painters deployed elevation to distinguish the plane of the green foreground, denoting the palace courtyard, from the background of the blue sky.[46] The contiguity of the Mardana Mahal facade—constituted by agglutinated individual courtyards, roofs, and terraces facing the east—is one of the key pictorial experiences offered in this artwork. The painting suggests a meaningful alignment of the rectangle of the picture plane and the shape of the buildings.

Amar Singh II's patronage for these large artworks seems decidedly tied to his best-known building project, the Shivprasana Amar Vilas Mahal, completed in 1699. Popularly called the Baadi Mahal (literally "the garden palace") and built such that a hillock sixty feet high was enclosed within its retaining walls, it became a part of the contiguous palatial facade overlooking the Manek Chowk.[47] On the inside, the garden palace includes a courtyard with a large, raised square pool in the center, which is experienced effectively as the ground level though it is in fact elevated.[48] Nestled amid towering trees and surrounded by colonnaded spaces made of 104 carved marble columns, the Baadi Mahal courtyard alludes to earlier Mughal and Rajput gardens (see fig. 3.5). From the outside, of the several additions made to the Men's Palace over the course of the seventeenth and eighteenth centuries, the Baadi Mahal is the building that most impacts the frontage overlooking the Manek Chowk (fig. 2.21). Its towering pavilions, punctuated with domes, prominent octagonal domed turrets (*chatrī*), projecting balconies, pierced screens, and windows with colored glass, form the highest story on the northern end of the palace, altering the skyline for the palace's and city's inhabitants alike.

In viewing the actual palace, one feels the loftiness of the facade while walking near its plinth, craning one's neck to admire the balconies on the upper story, and senses the facade's impact when moving away from it to the edge of the courtyard, grasping its monumentality (see fig. 1.10). Udaipur painters, in creating an elevation view of the palace facade in these Amar Singh II–period large-scale cloth paintings such as the one discussed above, deployed two-dimensional drawing and selectively used oblique lines to create three-dimensional foci that highlighted the pavilions, turrets, and projections of the Baadi Mahal. Such choices combine visual perspectives, of a viewer moving away, to the edge of the courtyard, with one moving ever so close, revealing the painter's intimate knowledge of the architecture (fig. 2.22). Further, the decision to create multiple large-scale works on cloth employing this architectural facade as a compositional device reiterated the spatial impact of the courtyard's grandiosity. The expanded scale of the paintings potentially magnified the experience of the courtyard for audiences. Both repetition and expansion establish the architectural facade that dominates Manek Chowk as an enduring feature in pictorial and spatial experience alike.

What makes the artworks depicting the Manek Chowk unique is that each example features ephemeral moods, distinct from each other and created by separate events staged at different times. Not all paintings featuring the *bhāva* of the valley, lakes, and palaces of Udaipur present the mood of a monsoon downpour. From the inscriptions on the fronts of these cloth paintings we know that both the spectacle of animal fights and the identities of particular elephants, rhinoceroses, and bulls mattered to contemporaneous scribes and audiences. Painters, as we see in *Maharana Amar Singh II in Udaipur during a Monsoon Downpour*, foregrounded these staged events in ways that highlight the Manek Chowk's purpose at its best. The king and his retinue admire the animal fights from their vantage point on a platform projecting from the palatial facade. Thus, the painting's audiences are called upon to admire a representation of this courtly community's act of viewing a spectacle. Indeed, we are all invited to inhabit the body of the represented spectators because the painting situates us in the space of historical consumers of such paintings. Positioned between the courtly spectators represented inside the frame of the painting and the borders of the artwork, audiences then and now could and can immerse themselves in the mood of the fight, as mediated by the artists. The temporal unfolding is suggested through the repeated elephants and the busy movements of the brightly garbed courtly staff. Movement and excitement, rather than the desire to map a contiguous sequence of events, seem to have been the artist's point. We gain a sense of swift, momentary, and uncontrollable changes—ones that could provoke a sense of excitement in the audience.

If the Manek Chowk paintings situate and thus immerse historical and contemporary viewers in the mood of the animal fights, the enchantments elevated in *Maharana Amar Singh II in Udaipur during a Monsoon Downpour* stand apart. Rather than large-scale artworks that favored compositions that focus only the palace facade overlooking the Manek Chowk (fig. 2.20), painters eschewed the all-encompassing immersion on display in the former painting—the plurality, of an audience engrossed by an elephant spectacle while an equally spectacular monsoon descends on the city of lakes, was highlighted. The composition calls upon layers of affective referents: pangs of love and longing incited by the rainy season; aesthetic emotions that historical connoisseurs learned from appreciating poetry, painting, and music; and the feelings of belonging that a land of lakes with abundant rains shaped for its citizens in sensorially, ecologically, and economically powerful ways. To enhance the affective import of an elephant fight staged in the Manek Chowk during a season of joyful and plentiful rains, the painter divided the cloth into precise quadrants. The upper left quarter of the painting contains the palace elevation defining the boundary and shape of the courtyard. The bottom register of the left half evokes the fast-changing and fearsome sensations ignited by a heavy elephant's body running from fireworks, two chasing horsemen, and crowds of people. The right half of the painting, both the upper and lower quarters, is devoted to the rains, clouds, thunder, lightning, and streams that not only kindle the elephant's excitement but also engulf the city. The many moods of the *Maharana Amar Singh II in Udaipur during a Monsoon Downpour* thus established a systematically designed new panoramic vision. Its painters' collated views drawn and observed from multiple vantage points—centered on ephemeral subjects, from the elephant spectacle to rains, streams, clouds—to collectively suggest a radically new viewing experience.

The panoramic plentitude of a monsoon downpour was made possible by the newly built Baadi Mahal. Alongside the

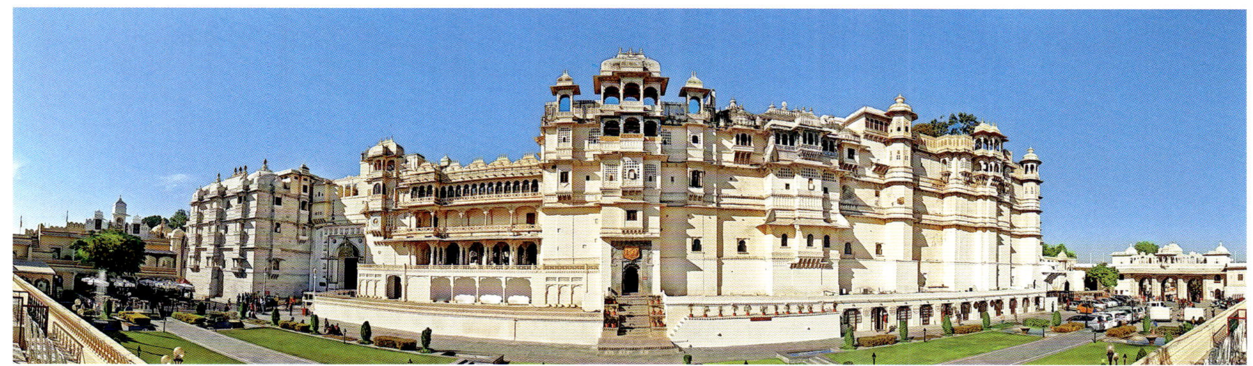

2.21. View of the eastern facade of the City Palace, including the Baadi Mahal (1699), overlooking the Manek Chowk, Udaipur. Media Office, Eternal Mewar, Udaipur.

impact of the Baadi Mahal on the palace skyline, its three wings offered consummate views of Udaipur's mountains, lakes, and environs beyond the palaces. From the corner turrets and wide projecting balconies on the east side, one looks down at the Manek Chowk (fig. 2.23); from the rear windows on the west side lies Lake Pichola (fig. 2.24); and from the windows of the north wing, which was built as a colonnaded hall for courtly gatherings, the city spreads out beyond the triple-arched Tripoliya entrance (fig. 2.25). It is not the case that significant urban and topographical vistas were entirely unavailable to Udaipur's painters before—from other hilltops or from parts of the Men's Palace, such as the Karan Mahal, built in 1620s, which overlooked Lake Pichola.[49] However, the distinctive viewing opportunities from the higher altitudes that Baadi Mahal's windows and terraces offered were simply unavailable earlier. If we examine the painter's drawing of the profile of the Baadi Mahal in *Maharana Amar Singh II in Udaipur during a Monsoon Downpour*, the northern walls of the structure are oriented in the direction of the view one would see from being high up in the space of the garden palace—the town toward the north (the painting's right side) encircling the palace complex from the northwest to the west as the clouds descend on the valley. The effect of depicting the walls of the Baadi Mahal that curve along the right-hand edge of the facade is accentuated in this artwork precisely because the painter offers us the panoramic vision of Udaipur's landscape. The bird's-eye view of the white-colored Jagdish (or Jaganath Rai) temple and the steep incline of the oblique lines of the entrance gateways give further evidence on the use of the Baadi Mahal as a vantage point for composing the view. The pink-buff color the painters deployed to denote the retaining walls of the Baadi Mahal demarcates the vantage point from which the monsoon moods of Udaipur could be best observed and sensed (fig. 2.3). As one dwells on the painted moods of the artwork, the design of the composition seems even more deliberate and methodical. The views of Amar Singh II, admiring the spectacle from his seated position with the courtiers in the Manek Chowk in the left-hand lower

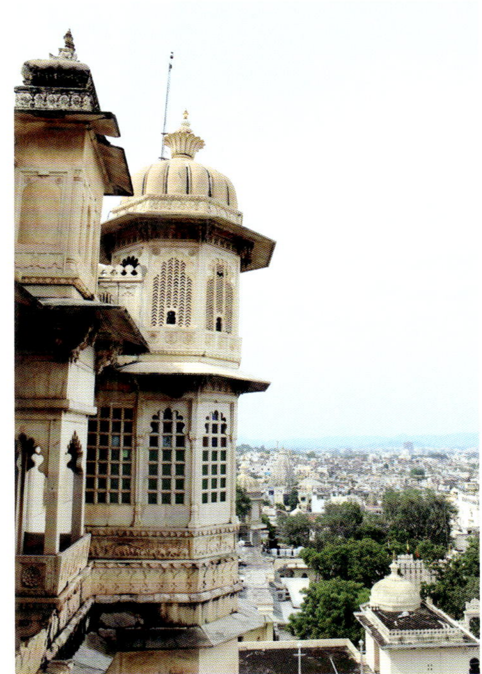

2.22. Exterior of the octagonal turret of the Baadi Mahal (1699), Udaipur. Media Office, Eternal Mewar, Udaipur.

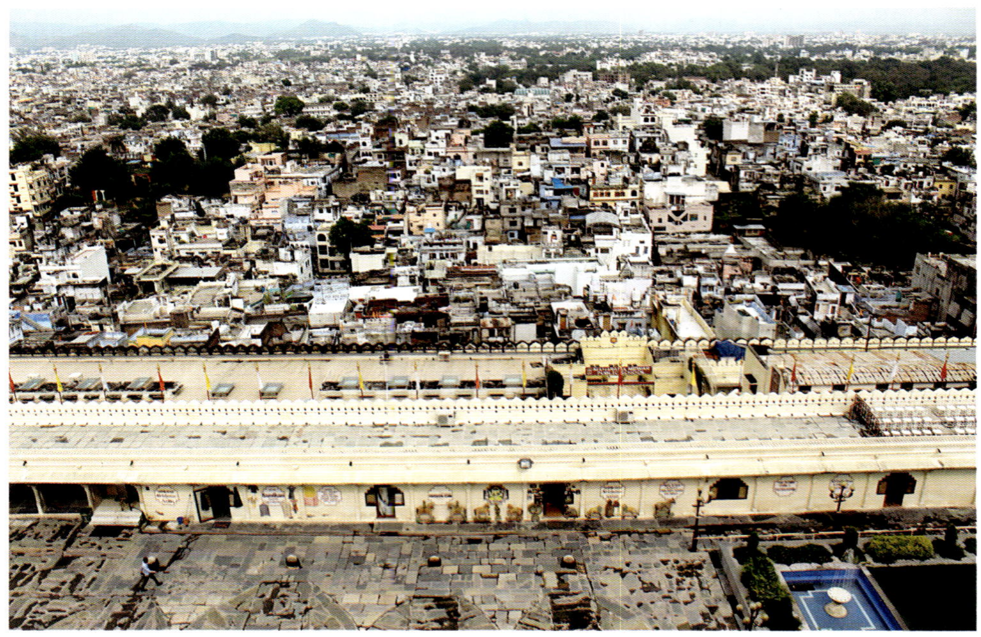

2.23. View from east wing of the Baadi Mahal (1699), overlooking the Manek Chowk courtyard, Udaipur. Media Office, Eternal Mewar, Udaipur.

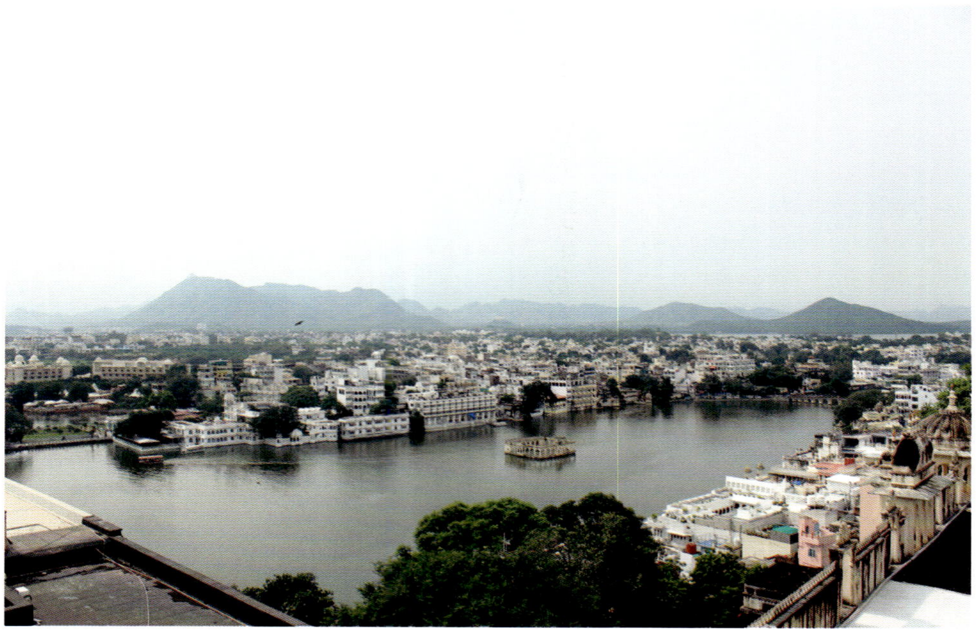

2.24. View from west wing of the Baadi Mahal (1699), overlooking Lake Pichola, Udaipur. Media Office, Eternal Mewar, Udaipur.

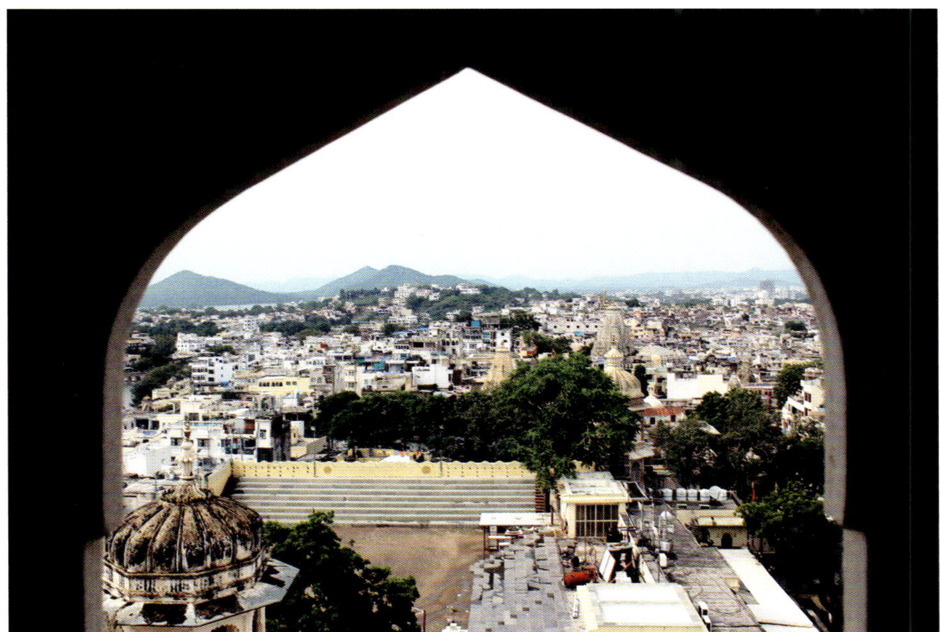

2.25. View from the Mukut Mandir pavilion, north wing of the Baadi Mahal (1699), overlooking the city, Udaipur. Media Office, Eternal Mewar, Udaipur.

quadrant, and of the Baadi Mahal, standing for the kingly presence at the edge of the right-hand upper quadrant from which the commanding view of Udaipur's valley and lakes could be admired, seem reinforced in this panoramic vision.

The aligning of the immersion offered by panoramic vision in place and in representation in the early 1700s in order to sense moods of a place is new. It is certainly not seen before at this scale or imbibing in such plurality in early modern Indian maps or paintings. The picturing of panoramic vision became popular in the eighteenth century across trans-regional geographies. In the case of late eighteenth-century Britain, new panoramas depicting the river Thames present a "continuity," according to Vittoria Di Palma, between the riverine routes and the multiple views these offered along the way, drawing upon both cartographic practices and "fundamentally new kinds of viewing experiences."[50] These new kinds of images, Di Palma argued, present a "convergence between landmarks and landscapes" and the rejection of the singular viewpoint privileged in British picturesque renderings.[51] At Udaipur as well, pictorially, the kind of mobile vision seen in *Maharana Amar Singh II in Udaipur during a Monsoon Downpour* seems enabled by Jaipur's cartographic practices, as discussed in chapter 1, especially those adopted for creating maps depicting routes and regions (see fig. 1.13). Udaipur's painters drew the curving lines of flowing rivers and the expanding water bodies from an aerial perspective. The operational role of represented landmarks as indexical diagrams, as seen within Jaipur's route maps, however, seems radically transformed in the Udaipur painters' drawing of the elevation profile of the Baadi Mahal's turned edge in close proximity to the planar forms of the landscape. This juxtaposition invites viewers to inhabit the depicted landmark, the Baadi Mahal in *Maharana Amar Singh II in Udaipur during a Monsoon Downpour*, signaling the novelty, enormity, and affect of the view afforded by the actual place.

Concurrently, Udaipur painters, who combined landmarks and lands—the Manek Chowk and the Baadi Mahal with the Aravalli valley's lakes, streams, and mountains—tap into the power of the aesthetic emotions of longing for the monsoon and feelings of acute dependency on the water ecology of the region. Monsoons are sensually overwhelming: the air becomes dense, the sky darkens, the sounds of rutting elephants change, rain wets skin and tongues, lakes fill. Like the heavily pounding monsoon rain, like the building of architecture that created the possibility to admire breathtaking vistas in fundamentally new ways, the stupendous size of *Maharana Amar Singh II in Udaipur during a Monsoon Downpour* affects on its own monumental terms. This kind of pictorial imagining and innovating also situates the history of engagement with *bhāva* more broadly within Indian art, material culture, and aesthetics. In medieval and early modern poetry from southern India, according to David

Shulman, the elements of visionary, meditative, or imaginative creativity beget places and events that often are superior to the sites and sights of the real world.[52] When the Udaipur painters applied the concept of *bhāva* to the depiction of actual architectural and urban precincts, their artworks revealed the visual and material mechanisms of praise through which affective power and sovereign claims operated. Enlarging the size of the canvas must have been pertinent to accommodate such convergence of maps, moods, panoramic views, and the momentousness associated with the arrival of rains.

By representing real-world places as sites for the contemplation of idealized monsoons, Udaipur painters assertively expanded the acts and genres of emotional imagining. Consider the citation of panoramic vision in a smaller painting on paper, from before 1730, which makes striking meaning of Udaipur as the idealized place of rain and lakes that was established in the early 1700s (fig. 2.26). We see Maharana Sangram Singh II, the successor of Amar Singh II, represented as a *nāyaka* who is welcomed by his beloved into a bedroom prepared for lovemaking. Outside the room, Kamadev (or Kama), the god of love, desire, and pleasure—with his wife, Rati, by his side—lifts his bow to shoot lotus arrows of love. Bees hover under rain clouds; rain flows through the streams that collect across the mountains and spill into lakes; and Sangram Singh II gestures toward the beauty of the monsoon night. In this second iteration on the terrace, the royal beholder features as the one admiring his beautiful and abundant territory. The painting has been cropped at its top edge, so we can decipher only a partial verse, but it tells us that the poet, like the painter, combined portrait, place, and emotion in his composition:

> Sangram Singh rests inside the Manak [Mahal]
> My beloved! By meeting during the monsoon my heart is
> enchanted and filled with boundless love.[53]

Both painter and poet convey the romantic mood of the monsoon precisely as it is felt *in* Udaipur. This is not the rainy season of Bhadon in every place or in a generic place. The small painting, moreover, harks back to the memory of the large-scale monsoon downpour on cloth. We see similar strokes—feathery lines—indicating the turns of streams and the rain pouring into the rivulets between the hills that made the Udaipur valley. The speed and scale of our gaze at the monsoon, as we follow the king's vantage point from the palace, are different from the gaze demanded by the large-scale painting. In the cloth painting, we see a view of the rains arriving in the valley—a perspective that would have been available only from palatial terraces—juxtaposed alongside the two-dimensional elevation view of the palatial facade. In the painting on paper, the layers of hills and the arrival of the rains—the place and the seasonal spectacle Sangram Singh II is seen admiring—are made visible from the king's vantage point for the benefit of Udaipur's courtly connoisseurs and citizens.

URBAN, MATERIAL, AND EMOTIONAL EXPANSIONS

Udaipur painters thus asserted a series of pathways—urban, material, and emotional—by which courtly connoisseurs might have felt a sense of belonging to their city of lakes and perhaps even become adept at the art of feeling emotional attachment to a place. By imagining the transformational effects of rain on the landscape, and evoking the abundance of a well-regulated kingdom of lakes, paintings equally praised royal persons and royal places. To constitute this kind of praise, painters looked at the world both empirically and platonically: they turned to both the enduring sites of architecture and the ephemeral sights of seasons, spectacles, parties, and processions. In powerfully imaginative ways and with painterly deftness, they brought together sites and histories, aesthetic ideas and epistemic genres.

Udaipur painters crafted for their courtly audience's mnemonic associations prompted by established urban vignettes—for example, the palace facade overlooking the Manek Chowk courtyard as seen in the painting of Amar Singh II watching the elephant spectacle during a monsoon downpour—that appear across various paintings. The repetition of motifs—and the resulting recognition of both commonalities among and departures from them—may have enticed the court's connoisseurs to look closely. By the 1720s, Udaipur's court painters had established as a leitmotif the image of Udaipur's rulers and citizens appreciating the beauty of their lake environs (see fig. I.4). These later painters adapted imagery from the first set of large-scale cloth paintings, such as *Maharana Amar Singh II in Udaipur during a Monsoon Downpour*, that feature the palace environs of Udaipur. By repeating the composition of the east-facing palace facade and the courtyard of the Manek Chowk, Sangram Singh II's artists established this vignette as an iconic feature of Udaipur court paintings (fig. 2.27). In the years that followed, painters cited this established palace vignette as a pictorial

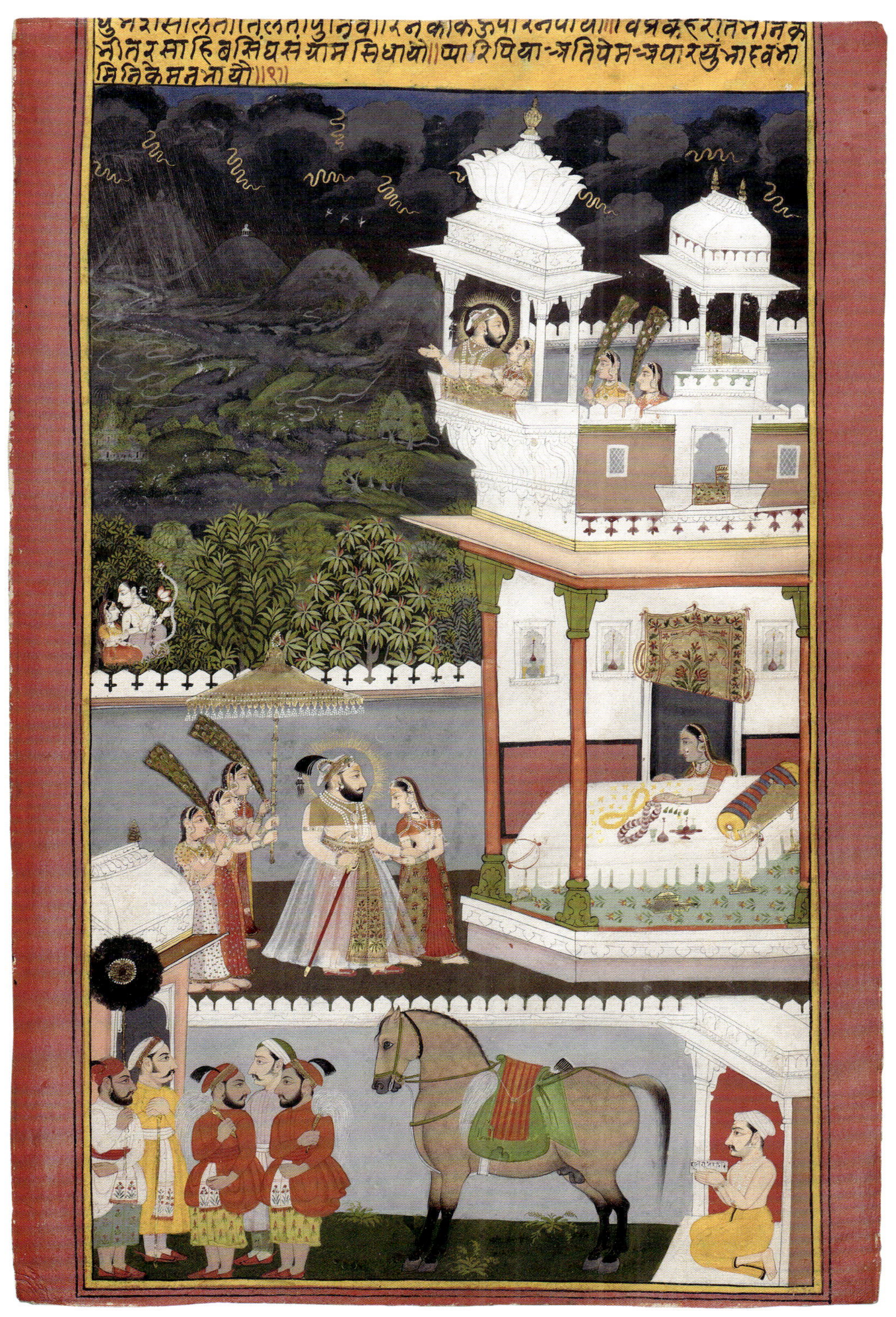

2.26. *Maharana Sangram Singh Enjoys the Monsoon*, c. 1720–25, Udaipur. Opaque watercolor on paper, 35.5 × 23.3 cm. Museum of Fine Arts, Boston; gift of John Goelet, 66.122.

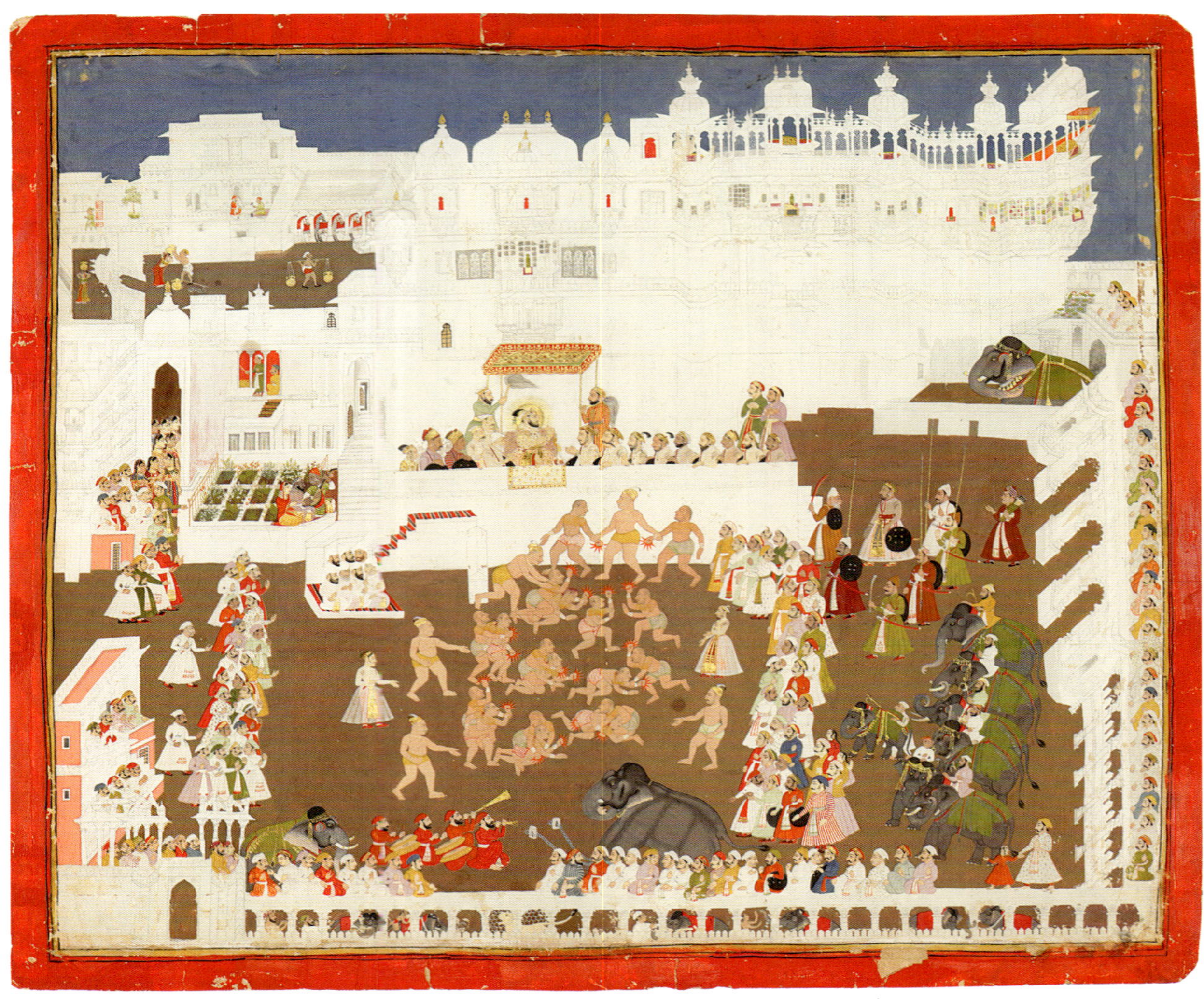

2.27. *Maharana Sangram Singh II and Durga Das Rathore of Jodhpur Watching Jethi Wrestlers at the Manek Chowk*, 1715–20, Udaipur. Opaque watercolor and gold on paper, 82 × 94 cm. The City Palace Museum, Udaipur; 2012.19.0028_R. Photography courtesy of the Freer Gallery of Art and Arthur M. Sackler Gallery, Smithsonian Institution. Photograph by Neil Greentree.

reference that attached the broader landscape, within which the ruler is shown hunting or visiting temples, to Udaipur.[54] Such paintings, made on paper, were smaller than the cloth paintings made by Amar Singh II's artists at the turn of the century. They include busier compositions, and the painters draw us to dwell on the spatial details surrounding the portraits rather than only on the portraits themselves, which the scribes nonetheless privileged in their inscriptions.

The choice to work on larger canvases, made by Udaipur patrons and painters around 1700, continues to perplex. The problem of learning and interpreting from reproductions, which inflects the field of art history, has been discussed in the literature; registering the scale of artworks presenting the city and kings of Udaipur on a large-size cloth is stymied even more by the conditions of framing, exhibition, and storage of the precious few examples that survive.[55] To develop an understanding of how historical audiences might have seen, held, and touched these paintings, I have stared at them for long periods, hoping to ascertain earlier modes of handling—which were very different from the contemporary museum context that prohibits handling. How were cloth paintings carried, folded, and unfolded? Were these paintings laid out horizontally on a floor or vertically against a wall, like a tapestry? Did court attendants hold these paintings tightly, to stretch out the canvas, or were waves on the surface of the cotton cloth present when kings saw and touched these objects? How did the experience of the paintings' size impact their interpretation compared to smaller works on paper that featured similar subjects? Surely a large painting that demands a spectator step back in order to view its entirety creates a different perception of the feel of the lake city than a small-scale painting viewed close-up. Does the intimacy of viewing water droplets and streams cheek to canvas have a stronger, if admittedly different, affective potency that needs to be accounted for?

Considering artworks of varying sizes and overlapping genres in tandem reveals how scalar specificity registers in haptic ways. In the intimately scaled painting featuring Sangram Singh on the terrace of the Manak Mahal, the king is immersed in the act of admiring the rain (fig. 2.26). Poetry on the painted page of this smaller artwork does the work of enchantment by intertwining the emotions of the king and an enthralling view of the mood of the city of lakes drenched in rain. By contrast, the audience represented in the large-scale cloth painting featuring Amar Singh II raptly admires the elephant spectacle even as the storm swoops in from the right. Such affective intermediary associations also draw attention to the expanded scale of the latter artwork. Amplification of the scale of paintings constitutes a meaningful material choice both because it made the painted subject powerful and created the radically transformed potential for the perception of—and enchantment by—the object. By enlarging the picture plane, Udaipur painters call upon the viewer to connect with the picture more on affective terms than on an isolated narrative impulse. This enhanced affect of the monumental painting would have evoked the memory of seasons past and intensified the longing for rains that were yet to arrive.

It is tempting to imagine that some connoisseurs might have ascribed efficacious power to *Maharana Amar Singh II in Udaipur during a Monsoon Downpour*, believing that it could bring their desires for a good monsoon to fruition, its affective power enhanced by its expanded scale and composition.[56] It signals the temporality of a beautiful monsoon or, in Jaichand's words, of "good times" when the earth was soaked in water. Painters entice us to imagine a courtly community savoring the *bhāva* of a cooling, water-drenched vision in the heat of the summer season—in the Manek Chowk and from its representation. If the painted monsoon downpour was commissioned for its capacity to mediate efficacious desires, then it would have equally reshaped the portrait and power of Amar Singh II. The artwork's ability to visually constitute a time that fused the present with the past or the future is contingent on criteria beyond the object's commemorative or iconographic referents. The material realization of *Maharana Amar Singh II in Udaipur during a Monsoon Downpour* itself on an impressive, monumental scale enhances the potential for attaching its image to multiple temporalities. The dialectical and flexible character of the temporality of the large-scale painted work on cloth reveals layers of potential associations.

Udaipur painters thus expanded ideas concerning acts of imagining and the relations between aesthetic emotions and empirical description on monumental material terms. If literary descriptions deploy allusions to temporal indicators, rhyme, and the sequence of words and sounds, as well as adjectives and metaphors, then painterly descriptions affix memories through palpable textures, details, and the juxtaposition of views, scales, and genres. Painters show us that they change the limits of *bhāva* as aesthetic emotion by not interpreting the passions of the monsoon solely in terms of its poetic and iconographic import. Rather, they engaged moods as a meaningful pathway through which to shape their artistic engagement with the empirical world and real emotions. Artworks depicting pleasure as aesthetic emotion, courtly ethics, and historical practice, addressed in the following chapter, reveal that Udaipur painters did not hesitate to contemplate questions of historicity and realism when foregrounding moods.

Both the patterns of pictorial choices in their affective recalling of a place and the associations established across historical and aesthetic practices are complex to trace. Nevertheless, in seeking to determine how practices of imagining were constituted in picturing the *bhāva* of a place, the tracking of parallel and intersecting artistic and intellectual enterprises can open new windows. It may not be possible to undertake such an exploration for every portrayal of the *bhāva* of a place. Each cluster of possibilities studied in the forthcoming chapters, however, begins to saliently unravel how artistic communities manipulated and realized the concept of *bhāva* in expansive terms.

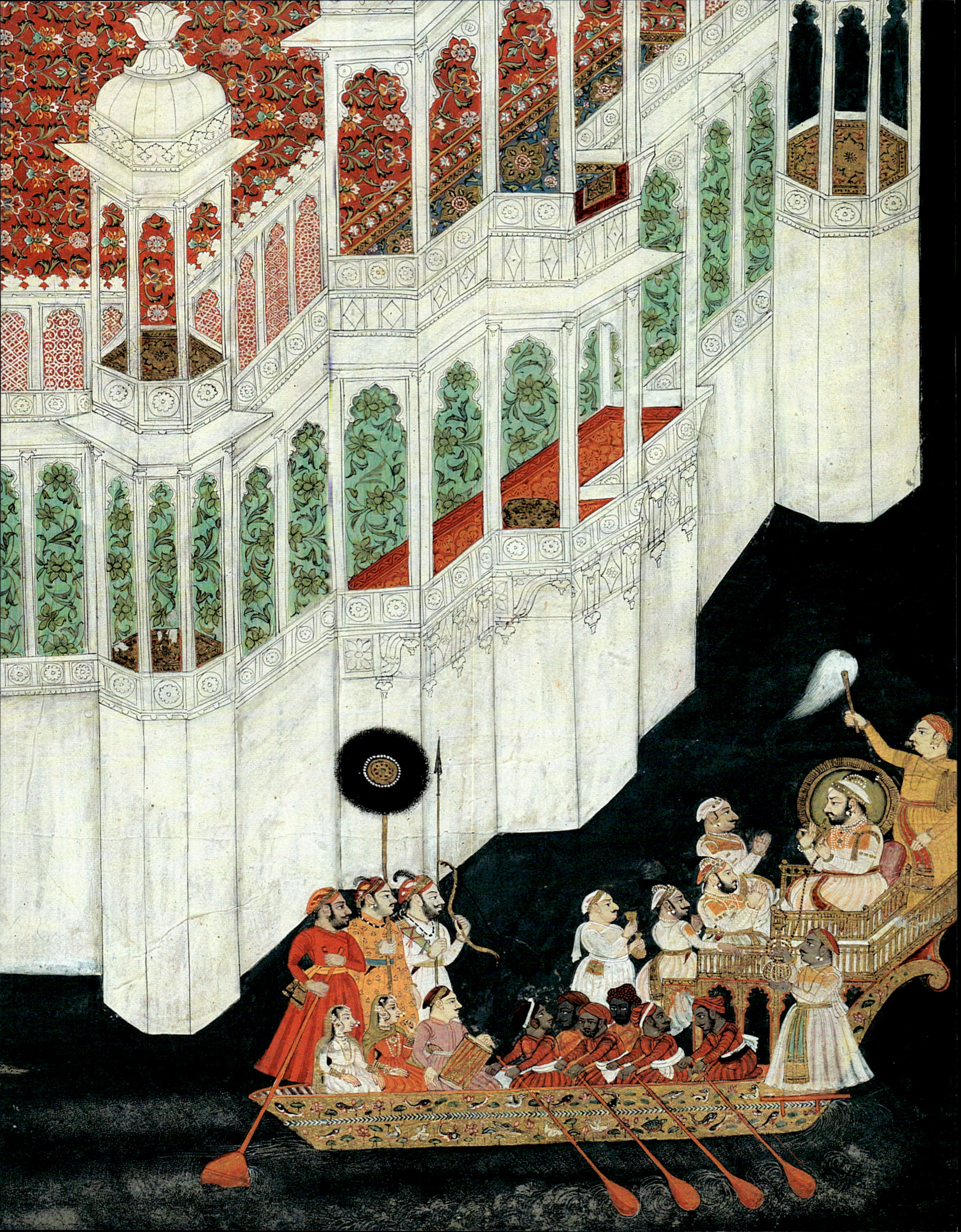

CHAPTER 3

Worlds of Pleasure and Politics of Connoisseurship

MOOD OF A PARTY

In 1751, the court painters Sukha and Syaji pictured the Jagniwas lake palace as the luxurious setting in which Maharana Jagat Singh II (r. 1734–51) partakes in the pleasures of hearing music, seeing the round dance featuring the Hindu blue god Krishna and his loving ladies, strolling the courtyards of the island palace, and shooting fish in the lake (fig. 3.1). The painters emphasized a collective aesthetic response to the depicted performance in an image of the king and the court's ladies on the terrace, raising their hands in the gesture of the dancers before them (fig. 3.2). In portraying Jagniwas as a self-contained world floating in the lake, Sukha and Syaji composed its courtyards, verandas, terraces, and pavilions from a bird's-eye view. Within every depicted space of the lake palace, the royal group is shown enjoying distinct arts and amusements. The inscription on the verso describes the artwork as a picture (*pāno*) of the likeness (*ṣūrat*) of Jagat Singh II and of the feel (or mood) of Jagniwas (*jaganivāsa ro bhāva*), associating royal portraiture and places with pleasure and allying the fine arts through collective mood.

From rain and lakes in chapter 2, we now turn our gaze toward the joyous mood of the palaces created in the middle of Lake Pichola. Just as painters and poets could dissect the aesthetic phenomenon of longing for rain, simultaneously evoking vastly different desires and affects, they also enumerated the practices of *vilāsa*, courtly pleasures. These poetic discussions of pleasure went hand in hand with deliberations on ethical kingship—and generated evocative pictures of the moods (*bhāva*) of a place. Such interrelated cultures of courtly assembly and connoisseurship played an instrumental role in shaping aesthetic practices that made pleasure central to charting histories and politics. The current chapter reorients our understanding of courtly pleasures as praise, and not simply excess, while studying places that were created to engender powerful feelings of delight. It establishes Udaipur's mid-eighteenth-century court painters as innovative interpreters of the *bhāva* of a place—especially in how they related re-presented pleasures in paintings and practiced pleasures in lake palaces.

Depictions of pleasurable parties can seem deceptively simple. Scholarship grounded in nineteenth-century historical accounts has viewed images of eighteenth-century decadence

Detail of fig. 3.14

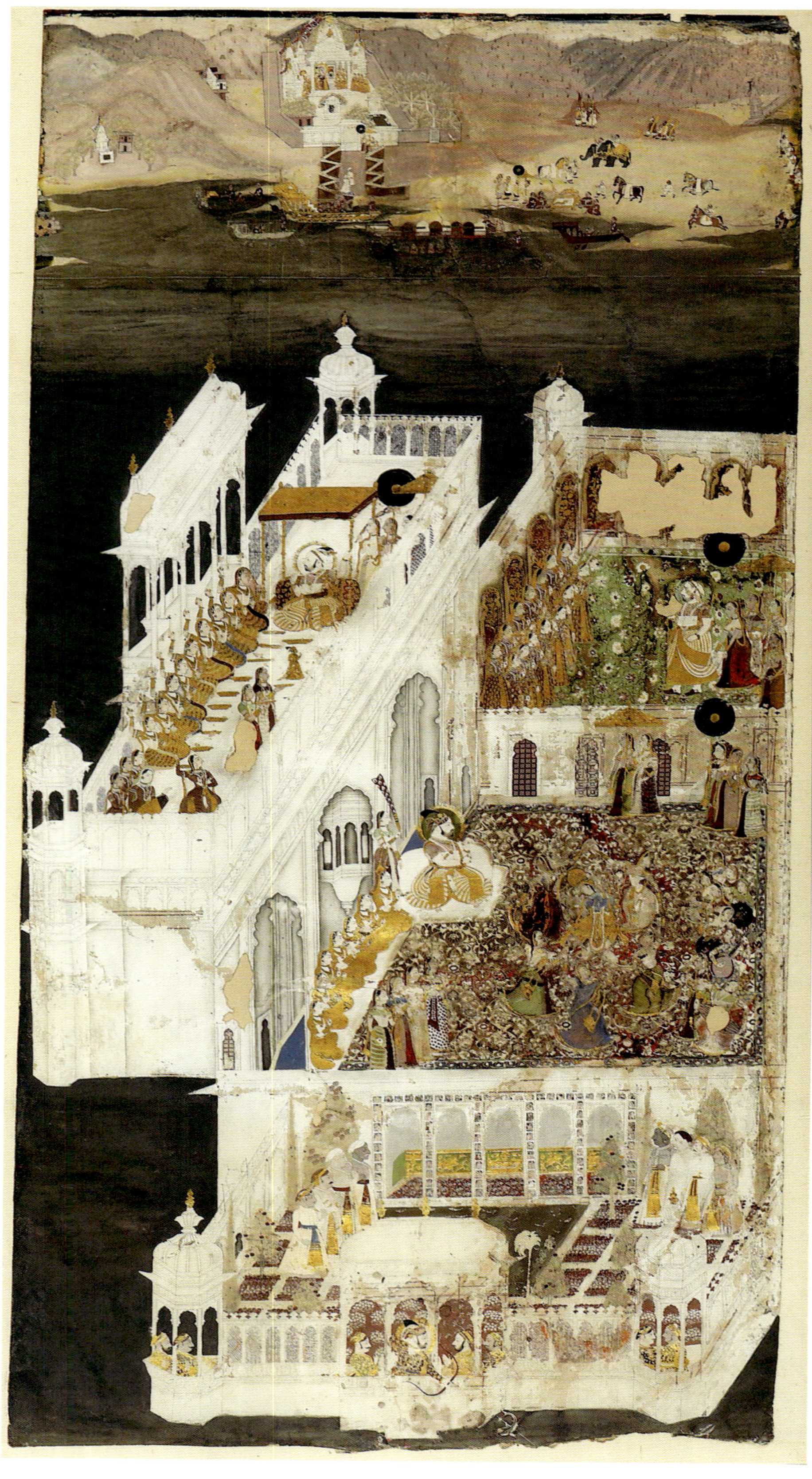

3.1. *Maharana Jagat Singh II and His Queens at Jagniwas*, Sukha and Syaji, 1751, Udaipur. Gouache with gold and silver on paper, 108 × 56.5 cm. Private collection; LI118.24.

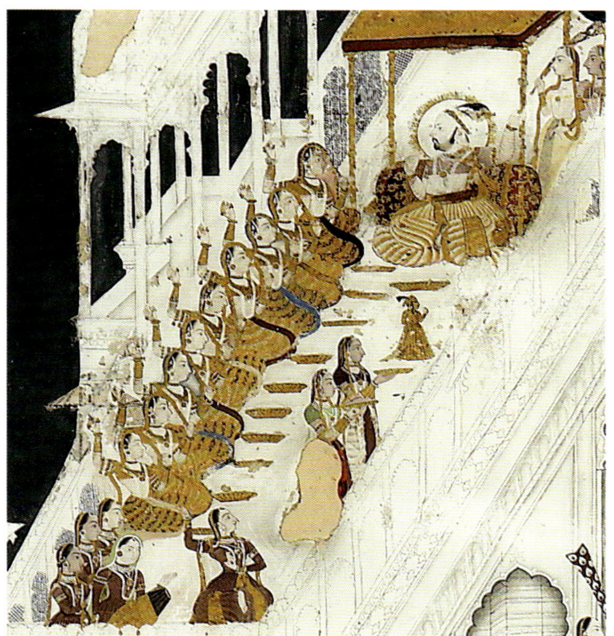

3.2. Detail of fig. 3.1. Jagat Singh II and the court's ladies raising their hands in the gesture of dancers.

3.3. View of Jagniwas Lake Palace (today the Taj Lake-Palace Hotel), inaugurated January 20, 1746, Lake Pichola, Udaipur, c. 1950–55. Gelatin silver print. The City Palace Museum, Udaipur; 2009.09.0229-00002_R.

as themselves decadent. In the *Annals and Antiquities of Rajast'han* (1829, 1832), the British colonial agent James Tod proclaimed Udaipur as a place distinct from the ruins that captivated the Romantics. Tod fixated his gaze on islands and on the palaces around the lake—where he saw Mewar's premier dynasty of Sisodia kings devolving into a line of princes immersed in "voluptuous inactivity."[1] *Vilāsa*, too, translated to indicate pleasure with overtures of excess, has largely been employed pejoratively by art historians and historians writing in both English and Hindi.[2] Characterizations of Jagat Singh II as a *vilāsī* present him as a king immersed solely in amusements related to women and wine, thereby echoing colonial tropes and narratives on decline.[3] The oversaturation of such ideas of Oriental decadence has shaped ahistorical and anachronistic understandings of the place of pleasure in early modern courts far beyond Udaipur.[4]

I elicit a different view of courtly pleasure from the eighteenth-century poem the *Jagvilās* (World of pleasure), which commemorates the commencement of the three-day inauguration ceremony of the Jagniwas lake palace on January 20, 1746 (fig. 3.3).[5] The poet Nandram presents the *bhāva* of *vilāsa*, mood of pleasure, as an idealization of real gatherings

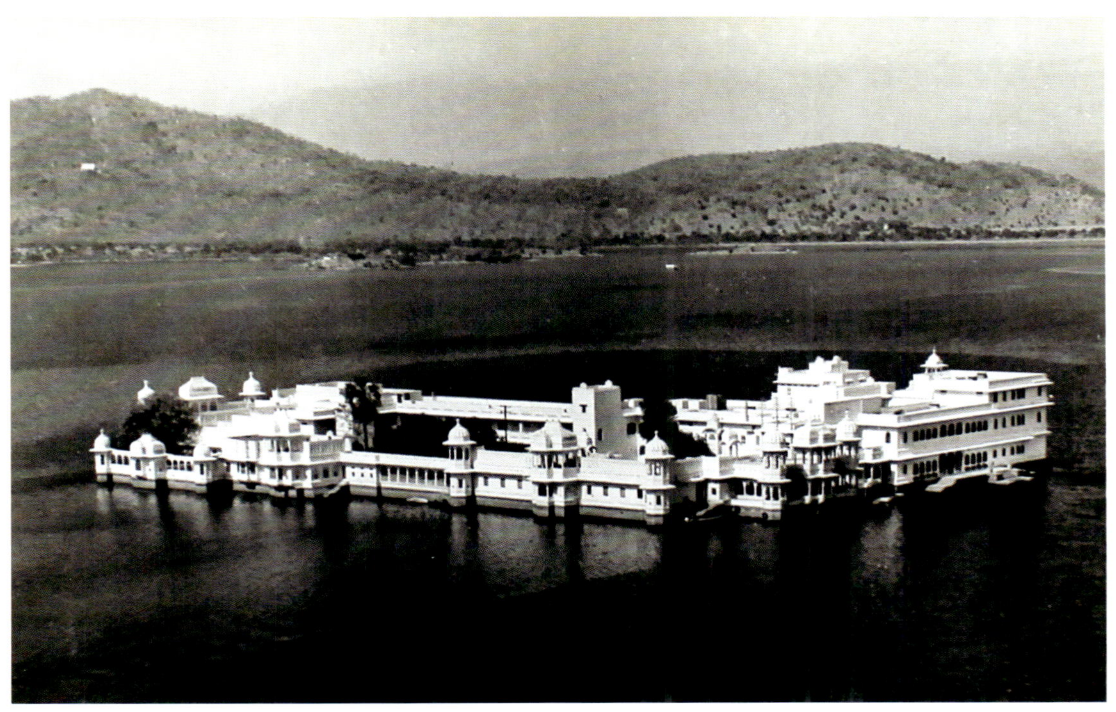

at Jagniwas, thereby inviting us to interpret the title of his praise poem not simply as "Jagat Singh's delights" but also possibly as "Pleasures offered by Jagniwas" or the "*Jaga* of *vilāsa*"—that is, "World of pleasure." Nandram's transformation of *vilāsa*, a courtly aesthetic and ethic intertwined with luxury, connoisseurship, and joyful experiences, through poetry reveals its multidimensional valence. The poetry of the *Jagvilās* emphasizes the dialectic between real and ideal as central to constructing meaning in the associated arts in early modern India and to understanding the historical appreciation of painted visions of pleasure in mid-eighteenth-century Udaipur.[6] Once divorced from the colonial topoi of pleasure and decline, the paintings of the Jagniwas lake palace become important statements in an ontology that imagined a "world of pleasure" in the mid-eighteenth century.

The preceding chapters have noted the shifting political landscape after the Mughal emperor Aurangzeb's death in 1707, which engendered a new pressure on regional courts to maintain their allies' loyalty.[7] The formation of political communities in Udaipur increasingly depended on the king's relationships with other regional kings as well as ties to the elites who populated the daily courts. The pictorial and poetic representations of Jagniwas lake palace as the "world of pleasure" enable tracking of the often-neglected perspectives of these elite men and women who surrounded Udaipur's kings and of the spatial precincts that were built in the lakeside environs of Udaipur. Thakur Sirdar Singh, Jagat Singh II's court noble and brother-in-law, was one such man, praised by the court poet Nandram for his discerning knowledge of architecture. The tenth canto of the *Jagvilās* tells us that Jagat Singh II assigned Sirdar Singh the task of hiring the best craftspeople and architects (*gajdhara*) to build Jagniwas and that the project was completed in a time span of thirty-five months.[8] The vantage point offered by Sirdar Singh, as one of the prominent court nobles who features in almost every painting depicting Jagat Singh II, allows us to imagine the mid-eighteenth-century courtly society that populated the Jagniwas palace. We register the agency of Mewar's regional thakurs, who asserted—often like more minor kings—their authority inside and outside the court and city of Udaipur. The examination of joyful moods in bonding these courtly communities opens avenues for analyzing the efficacy of re-presentations of pleasure, place, and portraiture across paintings and poetry in the social world of eighteenth-century Udaipur.

The exploration of the *bhāva* of *vilāsa* offers a deliberation on the political economy of pleasure. The attunement of communities—to bring all of the king's nobles into the mood, so to speak—required deliberate design, what Sara Ahmed calls "mood work."[9] The kind of lingering, accumulative, and settling-in qualities of getting into the right mood are especially discernable in the constitution of *vilāsa*. This important history of the emotional work of pleasure is revealed only when we shift our attention to the intersections among architecture, affect, and aesthetics—that is, the intersection between imagining the moods of a place and iterating the place of moods in courtly assemblies. The affective registers within which mimetic visions of the Jagniwas lake palace functioned reveal the enhanced agency of such imaginaries of pleasure as well as the power of ideas associated with pleasure. They offer insights into how picturing moods centrally shaped the crafting of courtly imaginaries, aesthetics, and ethics alike. When artists reiterated the pleasurable moods of architectural and urban precincts in paintings, they transformed the *bhāva* of a place. The repetition of familiar moods in multiple paintings expanded the affective work of imaginative practices infused with emotions and the material practices of pleasure. Both collective moods and consummate assemblies encountered in painted and poetic representations and created in real places expanded the potential for effective eighteenth-century political practice more than we have thus far recognized or researched.

THE AESTHETICS, ETHICS, AND SPACES OF PLEASURE

Pleasure was likely a highly subjective idea and experience for historical communities, just as it is a slippery topic for contemporary historians. As Allison Busch and Katherine Schofield both emphasize, the conversations on aesthetics and emotions within prescriptive treatises and poetry, like those surrounding paintings, raise multiple theoretical problems—including how to address the shadows of Orientalist and post-Enlightenment narratives and how to interpret and translate literary terms that relate to joy and enjoyment when expressed as an aspect of kingly ethics, within the rubric of merely pleasure.[10] The central place of Hindustani music in Mughal elite society reveals the relationship between the Mughals' pursuit of sonic pleasures and, Schofield writes, "their idea of a balanced government; government of the self, of social relations, and of the state."[11] Friends and associates performed an act of "sitting together" when they shared perfumes, foods, and scented spaces in fifteenth-century Malwa and other Deccan courts.[12] Likewise, in the *Jagvilās*, Nandram composed *vilāsa* as a historical practice and courtly ethic in eighteenth-century Udaipur. We hear about the food, poetry, and music enjoyed by the king, the visit of the royal women and princes on the day following the opening of the palace, and the king's large-scale political act of gift-giving performed at Jagniwas, including the names of nobles and poets as well as details about the horses, gems, gold, and robes they received. A verse focused on the Jagniwas lake palace's inaugural event announces that the king wished to proclaim with a "big bang" (*baḍo ganja muharata so batāo*) the invitation extended to all gentlemen (*sajjan*).[13] It expresses Jagat Singh II's capacity as king to gather Mewar's nobles at the new lake palace and his hope that it would captivate everyone's hearts. The Udaipur court poet Nandram's representations of enchanting architecture and urban environs, descriptions of the consumption of delicacies, and appreciation of dance and music as critical pleasures, as we learn through the poetry, established the bonding of this political community as a collective.

In earlier literary texts Udaipur's court poets deployed *vilāsa*—courtly pleasures—in titles of historical poems but did not engage the theme of *vilāsa* as enjoyment or delights of a specific place and time, an emphasis seen in the *Jagvilās*.[14] Nandram, like other poets of historical literary poetry, classicizes *vilāsa* by incorporating topoi of kingly praise, such as the *nakh-śikh*, head-to-toe description, and the *nagara-varṇana*, emotive descriptions of beautiful cities and plentiful settings that call upon ideal and real places alike.[15] The poet introduces the patron king, the city, and its citizens smitten by the king's beauty, as follows:

> Udaipur is like the sunrise mountain, Jagrān [Jagat Singh] is its Sun
> His body is beautiful and radiant like one thousand rays of the sun (4)
>
> The fame of Jagates is limitless; what can a poet say with his single tongue
> Sheshanaga with his one thousand tongues cannot reach the end, even if he speaks continuously (5)
>
> The poet has one mouth, the virtues and praises are numerous; [he] might describe them thus
> The ocean is perfectly full, how could it fit in a pot? (6)

Nandram's praise for Jagat Singh II echoes as a metaphor for the geographical environs of the city, evoking the expanse of Udaipur's Aravalli valley.[16] He compares the king's pace of giving gifts to the speed at which water flows into the lakes of Udaipur. Rather than opting for the detailed bourgeois verisimilitude of the novel, Nandram creates affective metaphors particular to the local topographical environs.

The building of the Jagniwas lake palace was part of a wider phenomenon in early modern architectural practice to create spaces for leisure. Historians have connected design paradigms that created settings with soothing and cooling elements in northern India's hot summers to constitute what may be called the architectures and landscapes of pleasure and leisure.[17] In Udaipur, smaller lake pavilions, like the Mohan Mandir in Lake Pichola, had been built under the patronage of Jagat Singh I (r. 1628–52). Chittorgarh, Mewar's former capital, also boasts a water palace, a building referred to as Queen Padmini's Mahal, built in the middle of what is today a small dry lake. A seventeenth-century water palace built in Bairat, northeast of Jaipur, by the Kachhwaha Raja Man Singh of Amber, was shown to have been modeled after Shah Quli Khan's late sixteenth-century water palace in Narnaul, suggesting that a deeper history of such typologies may yield other connections.[18] Water palaces became one of the preferred architectural typologies for the performing of activities of leisure, especially as planners and elites sought to exploit local environments and topographies.[19] The eighteenth century saw the building of several such structures, including the Jal Mahal (c. 1734) in Jaipur and the Sukh Mahal (1776) in Bundi.[20] The creation of monsoon-themed gardens with fountains and pavilions in Deeg and at the Saheliyon ki Bari in Udaipur in the eighteenth century sought to celebrate the joys of rain.[21] The building of the Jagniwas lake palace as a circumscribed place for Jagat Singh II's pleasures marks a momentous occasion in the development of such architecture.

Nandram's poetry within the first ten verses of the *Jagvilās* reveals Jagat Singh II's desire to build the most impressive lake palace of mid-eighteenth-century Udaipur, in order to foster affective bonds with his friends.[22] The *Jagvilās*'s introductory cantos highlight the king's enthralled reaction to the lake palace's location.

> Once upon a time, [while] enjoying a boat ride in the lake
> The whole community of courtiers [*rasikās*] enjoyed all forms of pleasures with the king
> Here is the Jalmandir [which they] admire, beautiful, delighting, and well-decorated
> There is the illuminated Jagmandir, crown upon the entire earth

The site in between is the best of the best; [let's] begin this [work] here
One that wins over, enchants everyone, Jagat, (the king and the whole world) himself, delights every heart (7)

Nandram compares the location of Jagniwas to that of the earlier Jagmandir lake palace (the Gol Mahal) on Lake Pichola, where the Mughal emperor Shah Jahan is remembered for building works that reflect sound thinking (*vivek*) and knowledge of prescribed ways (*suvidhi*) of architecture (fig. 3.4).[23] Nandram's recalling of Jagmandir's history may suggest seventeenth-century Mewar versus Mughal competition—or, more likely, refers to popular lore claiming that Jagat Singh II decided to build the Jagniwas lake palace because his father, Sangram Singh II (r. 1710–34), denied him permission to visit Jagmandir.[24] These local precedents of exceptional spaces, from water palaces to garden palaces, patronized by earlier Mewar maharanas and especially designed to delight court communities, emerge as significant nodes in Nandram's poetry. They not only locate the newly built palace but also make spaces of pleasure significant to the portrayal of Jagat Singh II's kingship. Unlike seventeenth-century court poets, Nandram created a eulogy for the king, court, and city in the mid-eighteenth century by utterly emphasizing the ethic and practice of pleasure.

The first setting of *vilāsa* in the *Jagvilās* is a garden palace in the main royal quarters on the banks of the lake.[25] The Baadi Mahal (or Shivprasana Amar Vilas Mahal), as discussed in chapter 2, includes a courtyard with soaring trees, a large raised square pool in the center, and colonnaded spaces with windowed balconies overlooking the city (fig. 3.5). The garden palace's original name, Shivprasana Amar Vilas Mahal, is allied metaphorically with the joys (*prasana*) of Lord Shiva's abode, indicating that courtly patrons and architects associated it with an ideal divine landscape.[26] Nandram equates the Shivprasana Amar Vilas Mahal with the high mountains of Mount Kailash, Shiva's dwelling place, because the garden palace was situated at the highest point in the hilly city. He imagines Jagat Singh dressing, arriving to his throne, praying to various deities, listening to devotional songs and scriptures, and giving charity on the day of the Jagniwas inauguration. The poet interweaves pleasures with kingly duties, describing the joy (*sukha*) one feels when looking at paintings and tasting food, which leads to the experience of being charmed in and by the garden palace setting itself. Nandram says:

You have made a unique gallery of paintings
In which are beautiful images that give utmost delight
Here is soul-satisfying poetry and painting
The sight of which charmed a tired mind (45)

Here assembled in the center are the Rajas and Ranas
Seems like the place of Mount Kailasha
Pure foods were called for
They were brought as per the orders (47)

All the groups of pandits and helpers
Per the rules are seated in a row
Various kinds of new foods are served
The eight flavors in constantly new combinations (48)

With the permission of his holiness [the king]
Everyone bowed his head with respect
All were absorbed sharing in the delight and entertainment
They ate with pure thoughts [virtuous mood] in their minds (49)

This set of four verses gives us a sense of how the poet interweaves joys and tastes in speaking about the king and his nobles as conjoint bodies (*rājātarāṇa*). That the verse (*chand*) on types of *vilāsa* comes after one in which the king appreciates paintings and painted rooms (*citrasālā*), and is followed by the poet's evocation of the king and his nobles sitting together enjoying a variety of delicacies, displays a compelling juxtaposition that advances our thinking about material practices and aesthetics. Concepts of taste (*rasa*) based on culinary associations inform Indian aesthetic theories in various texts. However, we have few examples that imagine the appreciation of both edible and painted delights in such located contexts.[27]

Painting seems to have inaugurated the representation of localized spaces of pleasure; the city's poets followed suit.[28] Udaipur court painters often represented Amar Singh II (r. 1698–1710) within garden spaces in which visual compositions and textual inscriptions, as seen in the painting *Maharana Amar Singh II's Holi Durbar with Sixteen Nobles in the Sarvaritu (Sarbat) Vilas Garden* (see fig. 1.35), worked together to evoke metaphorical and actual gardens. Inspired by the creation of new Islamicate gardens like that of the Shivprasana Amar Vilas Mahal, a tinted *siyah kalam* painting of the Udaipur ruler Amar Singh II depicts the king, patron of the garden palace, enjoying sex and sensorial pleasures in a Mughal-style garden with his beloved (fig. 3.6). The image evokes an idealized "*kama* world,"

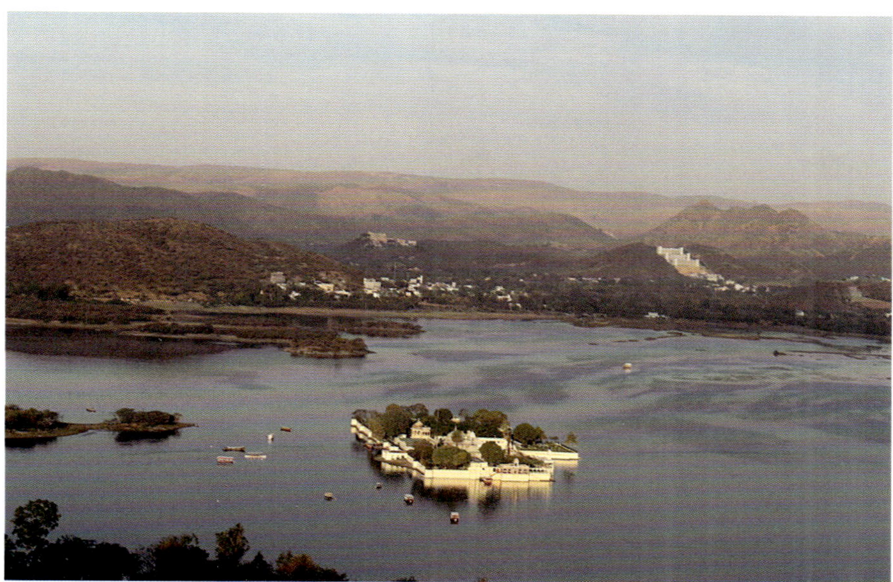

3.4. View of Jagmandir island palace, including the circular chamber Gol Mahal (c. 1620–28), Lake Pichola, Udaipur. Photograph by Emma Natalya Stein.

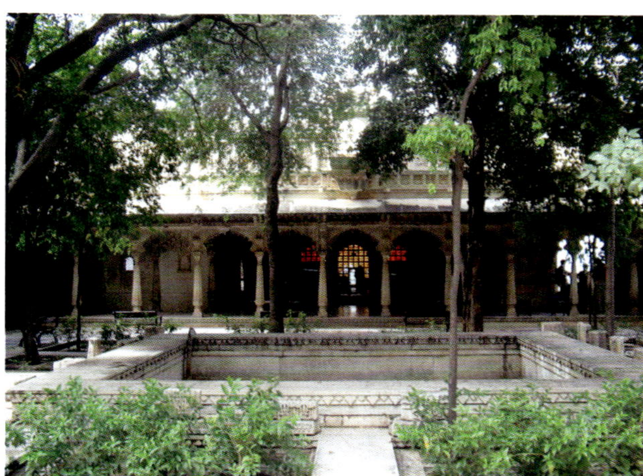

3.5. Courtyard of the Baadi Mahal (1699), the City Palace, Udaipur. Media Office, Eternal Mewar, Udaipur.

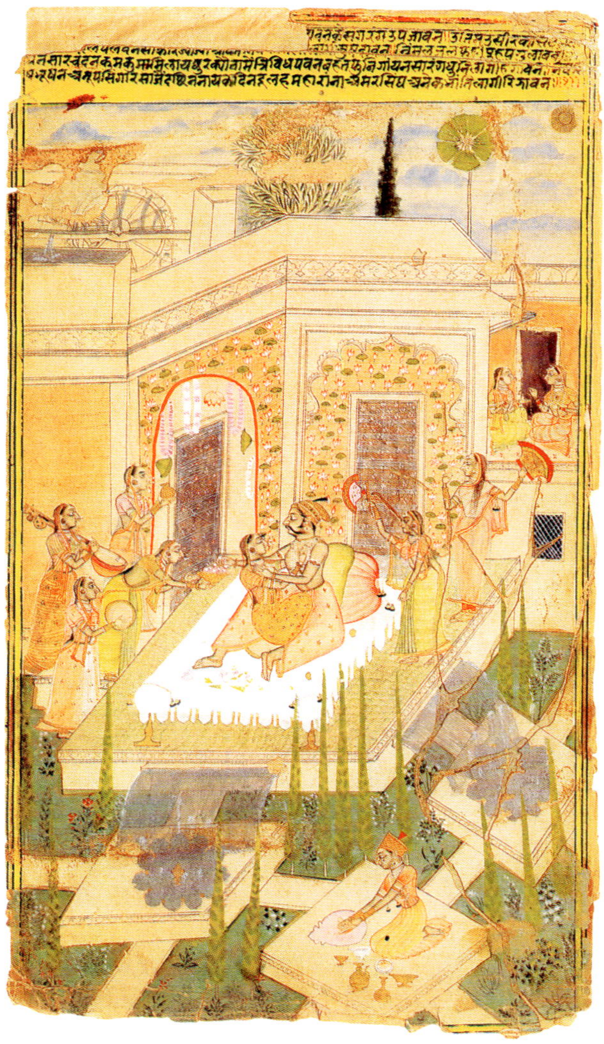

3.6. *Maharana Amar Singh II with Ladies in a Garden*, c. 1700–1705. Udaipur. Opaque watercolor on paper, 45.2 × 25.3 cm. Collection of the Trustees of the Chhatrapati Shivaji Maharaj Vastu Sangrahalaya, Mumbai; 56.32.

a place replete with delights and pleasures suited for Kamadev, the god of love and pleasure, created on earth for the king.[29] Reinforcing the painter's vision of water fountains, attendants with wine, and flowering plants, a scribe pens a verse on how material objects, wines, scents, and breeze give pleasure to the *nāyaka* (ideal man) Maharana Amar Singh.[30]

Later, Sangram Singh's painters built upon these innovations, focusing on the city's lakefront, lakeside pavilions, and lake palaces. One of the most striking uses of a palace pavilion by the lakeside appears in a portrait, thought to be by the artist Jairam, depicting the Udaipur ruler Sangram Singh II and the Jaipur ruler Sawai Jai Singh II (r. 1700–1743) in a meeting

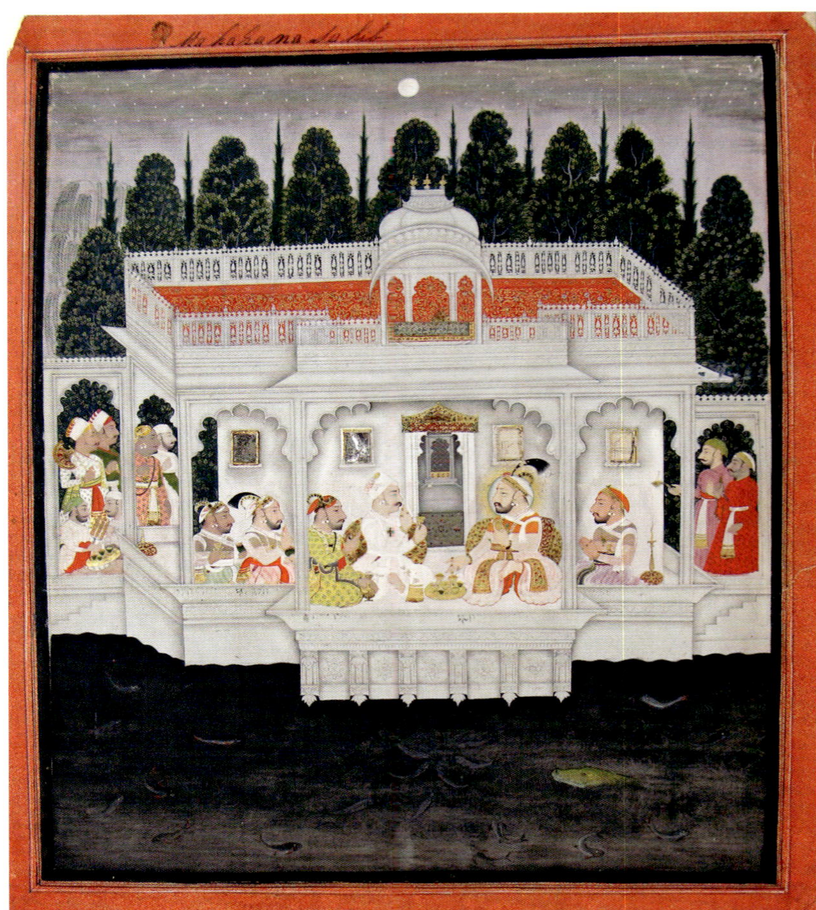

3.7. *Maharana Sangram Singh II and Sawai Jai Singh Enjoying Delicacies at Jagmandir*, attributed to Jairam, c. 1728, Udaipur. Opaque watercolor, gold, and silver on paper, 50.2 × 43.1 cm. Private collection.

held at the Jagmandir island palace that led to their shared alliance with the court of Jodhpur (fig. 3.7).[31] On the back of the painting, the scribe identifies the symmetrical setting as the windowed pavilion of Jagmandir's palace, made of twelve stones. This group portrait is quite distinct from another painting attributed to Jairam that depicts the two kings and their entourage in a camp setting, and also from a contemporaneous formal portrait of the two kings painted in the idiom of a Mughal album page at Amber (see fig. 4.25).[32] Both of these paintings commemorate the consequential meetings between the two kings that took place between 1728 and 1734, culminating in an alliance that united a combined front against the Marathas. Examined in a diplomatic context, the painter's choice to employ the spatial setting of the lake palace in the former painting (fig. 3.7) is significant. A night sky consisting of a central moon and stars painted in a uniform pattern echoes the idealized moonlit landscapes seen on the painted leaves of devotional manuscripts, which lends iconicity to this picture depicting a crucial meeting of allies. The kings and their companions partake in the collective enjoyment of food and wine in Jagmandir. Sumptuous details of the architecture, the textiles used for royal attire, and the delicacies being cooked and offered seem to prefigure the evocation of Jagniwas in *Jagvilās*, two decades later, as the lake palace where powerful men and connoisseurs gather.

This geographical shift of joyful assemblies from land to lakes and the perception of garden courtyards and lake palaces as overlapping spaces for courtly pleasure is palpable in Nandram's poetry.[33] The poet adapts classical poetic tropes to move his courtly patrons and his poetry's audience from the pleasures of the Baadi Mahal on the lake bank toward Jagniwas. Nandram shifts easily from bodily praise of the king to material praise of things that would have added grandeur to his court, including elephants and horses, drums and trumpets, and umbrellas and palanquins.[34] Rather than opting for an effect of documentary verisimilitude, Nandram describes the rousing affect of the marching horses and the shining drums. Succeeding verses in the *Jagvilās* visualize the royal procession traveling toward the city's lakefront, stopping so the king can offer homage to the Jagannath Ray deity and to the community of pandits that served as court priests. About Udaipur's citizens besotted by the king's beauty, Nandram writes,

> Here, the crowd of the men [and] women expands, as if a bed
> of flowers lay on the street
> Everyone's hearts are eager to admire, there auspicious clouds
> of joy rain down (125)

Flowers and rain acquire a local charge in the poet's imagining of Udaipur's citizens and streets as fragrant, freshened, and blessed by the sight of the king. Likewise, as discussed next, water metaphors shaped the poetic description of the pleasures inside the Jagniwas lake palace. These allusions recall trans-regional poetic tropes in early modern India describing the hearts and bodies of every man and woman captivated with the arrival of rains.[35] The poet's attention to the urban topography of Udaipur, in this water-filled panegyric poetry, equally conjures the image of a season of good rains and palaces surrounded by abundant lakes. The interweaving of metaphors and materials of joy and the attention to temporal and spatial pointers in Nandram's poetry highlight the journey from the lakeside to the middle of the lake. Each description of movement—from the garden courtyard in the palace to the streets, from the streets to the temple, from the temple back to the streets and on to the lake bank and the royal boat—provokes an imagining of the city's geography. As the party moves to ride the royal boat to Jagniwas, the poet emphasizes departure at an auspicious time. *Jagvilās* invokes a mood of anticipation of pleasure inside the lake palace.

BUILDING THE "WORLD OF PLEASURE"

In imagining Jagat Singh II at Jagniwas, poetry and painting intertwined to compose courtly communities immersed in sensorial pleasures. One strategy for rendering such immersion was interiority. Of the five paintings of Jagat Singh at Jagniwas considered here, three depict the feeling of the interiority of a lake-palace courtyard. The architectural space surrounds the king's portrait and is replete with the presence of courtly men, women, and musicians. In one example, the painters Jiva and Jugarsi show Jagat Singh walking toward a garden courtyard in the company of courtiers, who also appear seated below a canopied throne where Jagat Singh, depicted a second time, listens to female musicians (fig. 3.8). Similar framing strategies are at work in the paintings *Maharana Jagat Singh II at a Pool with Ladies at Jagniwas* (fig. 3.9) and *Maharana Jagat Singh II Bathing with His Nobles at Jagniwas* (fig. 3.10). These paintings combine planar views of a courtyard with oblique projections of arcaded spaces and elevations of walls and entranceways to depict the surrounding verandas. Nandram employed a similar emphasis on interior spaces in the *Jagvilās* to visualize Jagat Singh immersed in the lake palace's courtyards. In more than one instance, we hear that time has passed—for example, it was time for the king to be dressed and adorned for a courtly gathering, and time for him to proceed to the sitting hall (*darīkhānā*) of another courtyard in the Jagniwas. Elsewhere, we find that Nandram begins his spatial tour of the Jagniwas with the Bado Mahal's striking garden courtyard—just as the painters and viewers of the paintings, who were also the readers and listeners and the subjects of the *Jagvilās*, enjoy and admire each of the lake palace's courtyards, one at a time.[36]

> Bado Mahal, its unique building, crafted with artistry
> Beautiful garden with elegant forms, which had the name
> Dilaram ("Heart's Tranquility") (177)

> The Bado Mahal is here, lit from the east,
> Dilaram's gardens, filled with desire, beautifully made overall
> forms
> [Seated by] the unique tank in the center, the king admires
> [and] derives bliss
> [All] the paths are lined with fountains, dense rows of most-
> beautiful roses (178)

Jagat Singh II's artists had multiple models at their disposal when they created a new subgenre of topographical painting focused on the Jagniwas and the beauty of its garden courtyards. A thematic continuity can be seen between depictions of the two lake palaces; the pictorial strategies, however, are distinct. Udaipur court painters portrayed Sangram Singh II within the environs of Jagmandir in several paintings that depict this lake palace in its entirety, thereby creating a profound association between the ruler's portrait and his lake palace's image. In a painting dated to about 1720, the painter and the scribe suggest that the key concern was picturing the feeding of crocodiles at Jagmandir (fig. 3.11). The painters emphasize the garden courtyard of Jagmandir's Kunwarpada

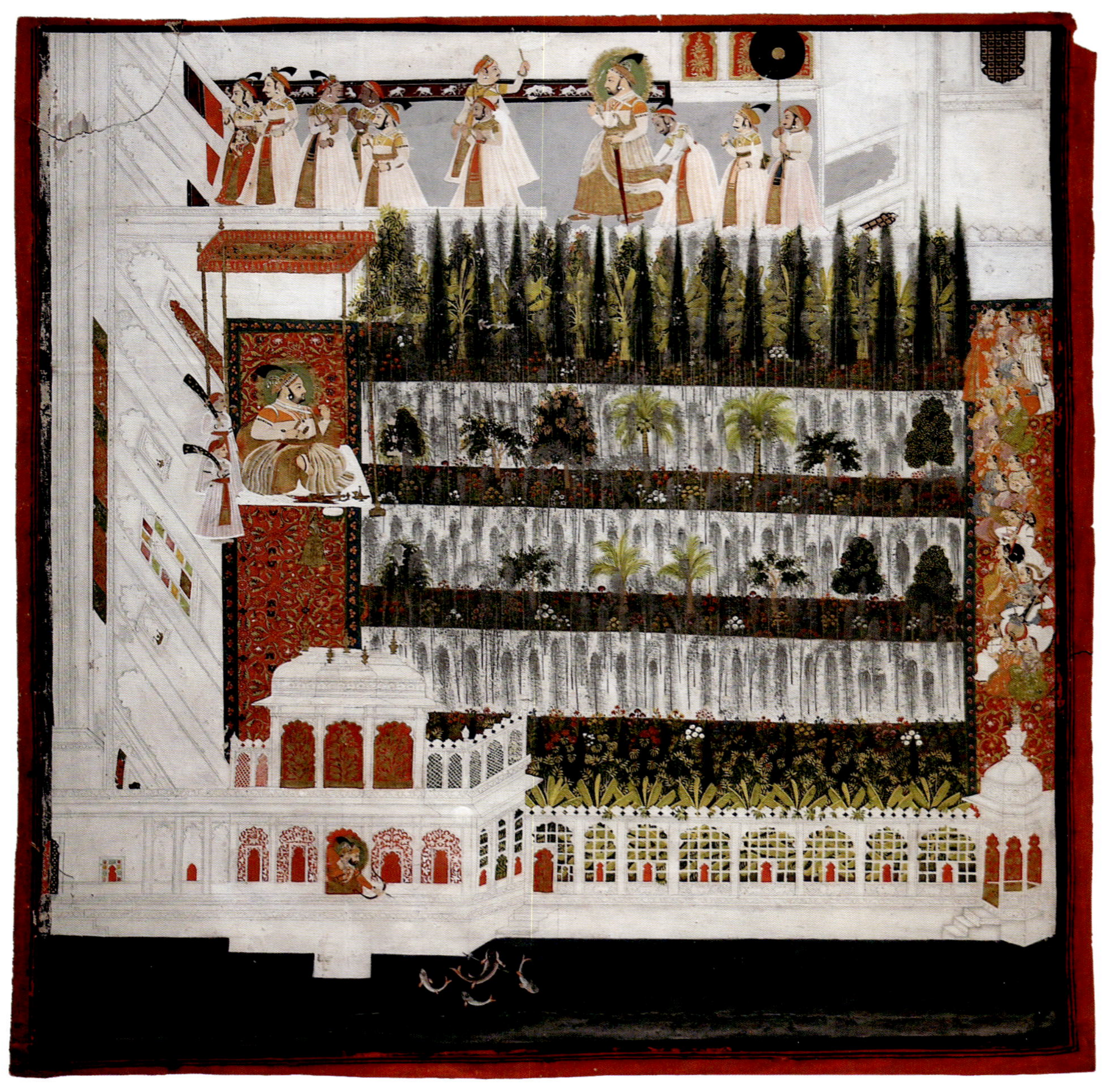

3.8. *Maharana Jagat Singh II in a Lake Palace Garden at Jagniwas*, Jiva and Jugarsi, 1751. Gouache, gold, and silver on paper, 68.6 × 68.6 cm. Private collection; LI118.20.

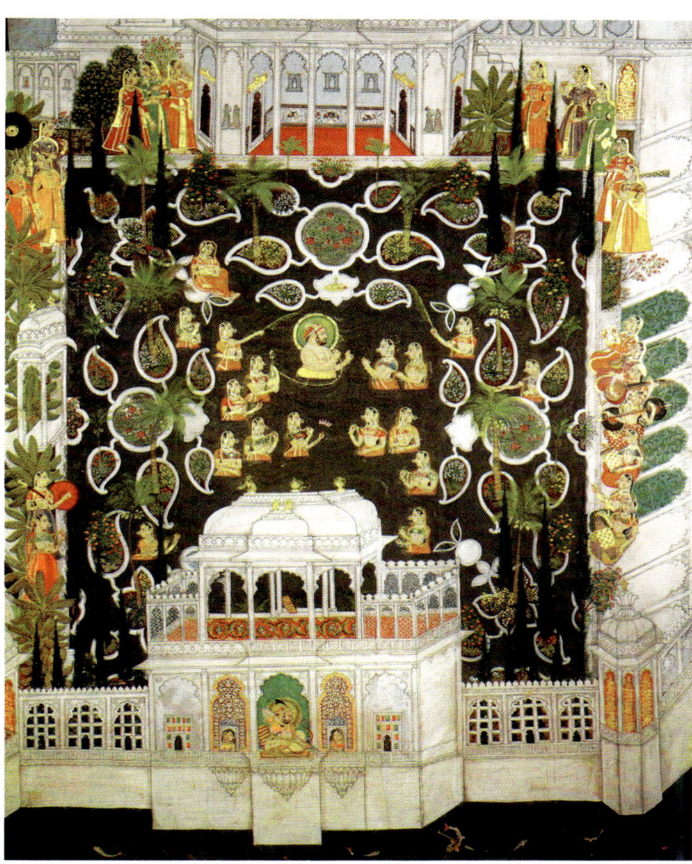

3.9. *Maharana Jagat Singh II at a Pool with Ladies at Jagniwas*. Jairam, 1751. Udaipur. Gouache, gold, and silver on paper. Location unknown.

3.10. *Maharana Jagat Singh II Bathing with His Nobles at Jagniwas*, attributed to Jairam, c. 1746–50. Udaipur. Gouache on paper, 46.9 × 81.3 cm. San Diego Museum of Art; Edwin Binney 3rd Collection; 1990:624.

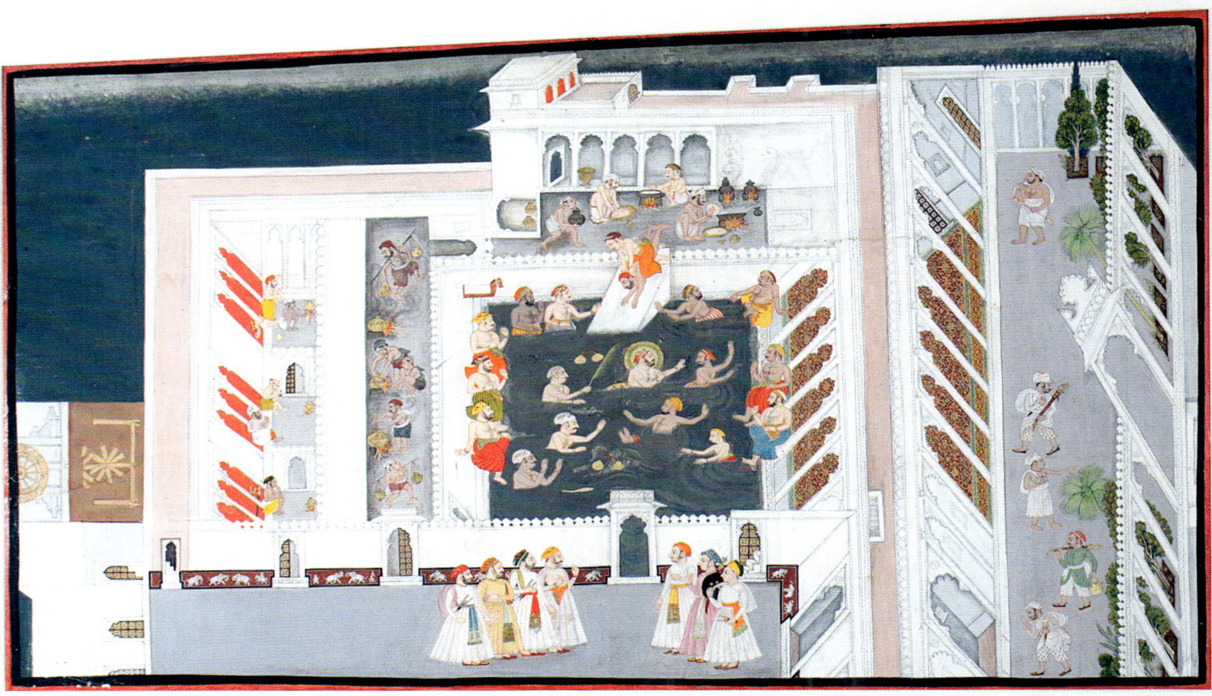

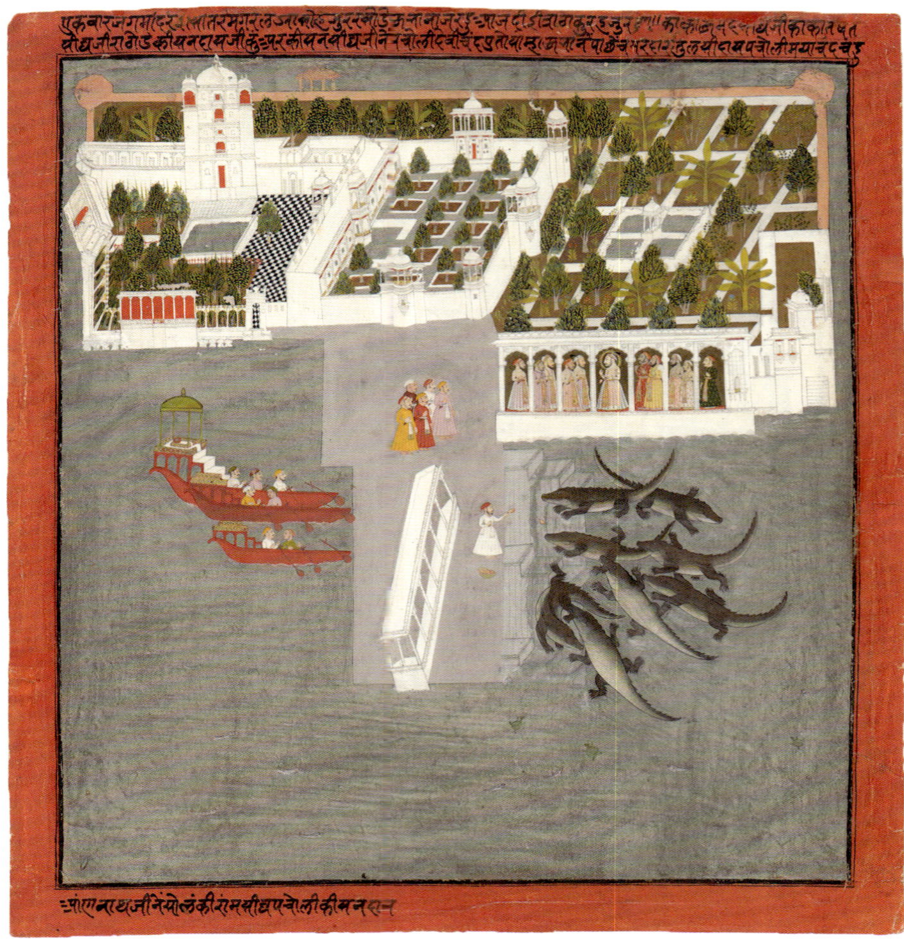

3.11. *Maharana Sangram Singh II Attending the Feeding of Crocodiles at Jagmandir*, attributed to Jairam, c. 1720. Udaipur. Opaque watercolor, gold, and silver on paper, 56.8 × 46.5 cm. National Gallery of Victoria, Melbourne; Felton Bequest, 1980, AS88- 1980.

3.12. *Maharana Jagat Singh II Amuses Himself in the Jagmandir Lake Palace*, c. 1750, Udaipur. Opaque watercolor, gold, and silver on paper, 47.5 × 60.3 cm. Philadelphia Museum of Art; Bequest of William P. Wood, 1996, 1996-120-4.

3.13. Detail of fig. 3.10. Courtly staff preparing delicacies while Jagat Singh II bathes with his nobles and Sirdar Singh leads the haloed king.

Mahal (Palace for the Princes) and the expanded gardens at the rear by making use of an oblique axis and by enlarging the size of the key pavilion in which they portrayed Sangram Singh and his courtiers. This compositional emphasis associates Sangram Singh directly with the building and gardens of the Jagmandir palace, which he expanded during his reign.[37] In front of the royal pavilion we see a group of crocodiles painted on a gigantic, highly manipulated scale. Such play with scale and the vividness of the depiction of the reptiles forge the pictorial pathways by which painters and courtly communities recalled places not simply as representations of patrons but also as the moods of memories associated with them.

By contrast, the painter Jairam's and the poet Nandram's interior visions of the architectural frame of Jagniwas's courtyards embody and embolden Jagat Singh II's portrait. A contemporaneous painting by an unknown artist of Jagat Singh II at Jagmandir is telling (fig. 3.12). The king is seen hunting water buffalo gathered by staff in proximity to the island palace and partaking in the pleasures of the pools and gardens of Jagmandir's courtyards. This painting refers to earlier portrayals of Sangram Singh at Jagmandir that privilege the depiction of the island in its entirety. It also shows that Udaipur painters' compositional move toward interiority became a preferable artistic choice for expressing the immersive experience at Jagniwas. Jairam accentuated the formal relationship between the beauty of the Bado Mahal and the beauty of the king: he surrounded the king's body on three sides with a patterned spatial vignette, thus bringing the royal portrait into central focus (figs. 3.9 and 3.10). The movement of the king configures the unfolding of the building structure. Both painted and poetic visions link the lake palace and king ontologically.

Painters equally made interiority a formal tool for expressing the *bhāva* of collective sensorial intimacy. The painting of

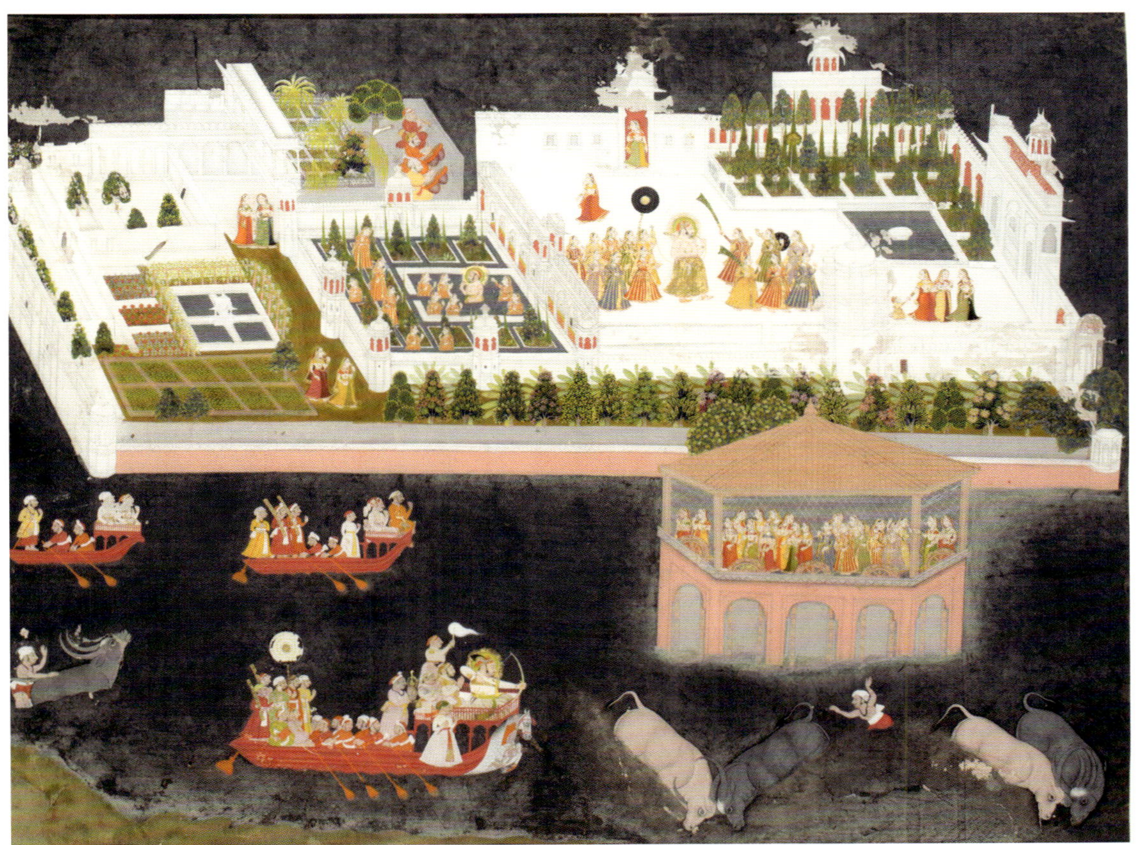

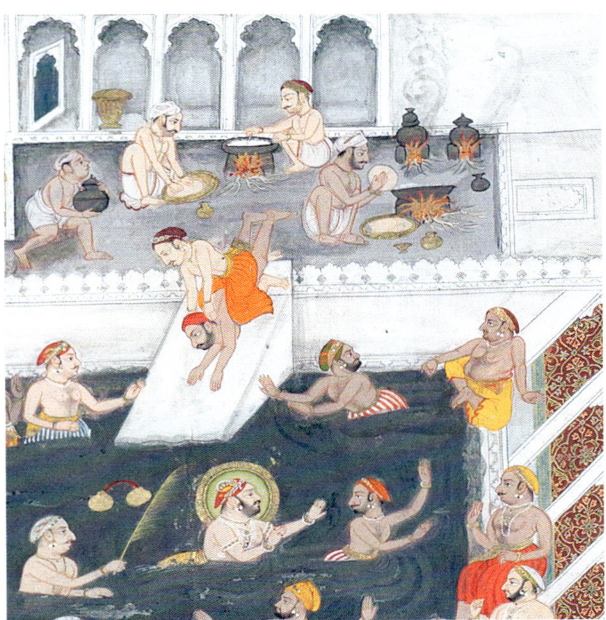

Jagat Singh bathing with his nobles (fig. 3.10) replaces the formality of the king in the earlier *Maharana Jagat Singh II at a Pool with Ladies at Jagniwas* (fig. 3.9) with bodily expressions of leisure. The men float and dip in the pool with open arms. The painter distinguishes each individual, portraying skin tones and facial hair on naked upper bodies. The figures of men relaxing poolside and swimming in the water are juxtaposed with the fully clad, standing courtly men in attendance outside the pool and the busyness of a courtly staff preparing delicacies and yet another group tending to plants and carrying goods across the complex (fig. 3.13). The smoke rising from the fires, along with an array of cooking pots, gesture to gustatory pleasures that will be ready for the swimmers. To paint in such detail images of the courtly staff engaged in cooking, cleaning, and taking care of pragmatic arrangements for their royal patrons is to use the space of the palace to make room for a vision of the work involved in creating a "world of pleasure" in Jagniwas. This composition thus stages the processes through which sensoriums were created for intimate exchanges in secluded gatherings in the middle of the lake.

Both the poetic and painted images gesture toward the evocation of feelings of intimacy that may have been possible in this world of Jagniwas in the middle of Lake Pichola—feelings of intimacy between those in attendance and the place itself that could be recalled upon seeing or hearing such evocative compositions. The *Jagvilās* similarly imagines the ambience of the inauguration party. Nandram describes the delectable tastes of fish, goat, and venison dishes prepared in a variety of ways; sweets from *laḍu* to *ghewara* and fruits such as watermelon, oranges, and lemons; sweetbreads served with milk; numerous kinds of rice and grains; and stews of lentil and rice (*khichṛi*). The verses evoke the food aromas—the smell of buttermilk mixed with crystallized sugar (*misri*) and rose (*gulāb*)—spreading to the courtyards of the Jagniwas palace. From gustatory sensory satisfactions, the poet moves to praising the mesmerizing beauty and visuality of the Jagniwas palace itself, lit by candles in the night and filled with the smells of flowers and the sounds and sights of music and dance. The lake palace thus becomes a powerfully affective frame for praising Jagat Singh's kingship as experienced through the joys of architecture, poetry, music, dance, gifts, and food.

The last of the five known paintings of Jagat Singh at Jagniwas alludes to the royal party's arrival at the lake palace (fig. 3.14). An empty throne sits in wait on a red carpet under a red canopy. The terrace balcony is composed with an angular directionality that insistently points to the throne; upon the king's arrival, the terrace of the lake palace will become the site for the re-creation of his "world of pleasure." It is difficult to ascertain whether the five paintings were made as a set.[38] The inventory numbers on the reverse sides of three of the paintings are consecutive, which may or may not imply simple contiguity in their production.[39] Such numerical evidence certainly suggests that court clerks cataloguing the paintings in the nineteenth century saw them as belonging in proximity to one another. Despite the fact that the paintings are of different sizes and were made by different painters, they evoke connections not only because they feature the same ruler but also because as a group they thematize the place and pleasures of Jagniwas. For the king and his circle of courtly audiences—the patrons of court paintings and literature—the cultivation of a shared taste for such painted visions, and of parallel poetic visions, forged affective bonds between the ruler and his city, and among courtly audiences.

As we establish a dialogue among our inquiries into painting, poetry, and architecture, the emergent intermedial imaginaries of pleasure acquire a new kind of power. Both painters and poets saw themselves as key agents in cataloguing the works of art, objects, and foods—as well as the sensorial effects of light, smells, sights, touch, taste, and sounds—that were collectively consumed and enjoyed during gatherings. Nandram directs us to his own creative talents in noting that it would take a poet with the intelligence of Pandit Vyas, the legendary author of the Vedas and Puranas, to write about the ambience and beauty of the Jagniwas inauguration. A subsection on the theme of joy in the *Jagvilās* gives us insight into the poet's conception of pleasure and its role in courtly society by layering metaphors of water and abundance. Nandram's use of the word *sukha* in each of the nearly thirty verses connects and deepens emotions of joy and contentment in describing the Jagniwas palace.[40] Let us attend to three exemplary couplets:

> Joys rain, all are delighted, singers sing songs
> Pleasure rains down like clouds; the Rana [Jagat Singh II] is absolutely charmed (194)
>
> Having seen all the spaces, now he knows them well
> After coming to the Bado Mahal, the Rana rules with joy (204)
>
> Everyone enjoys together here; they find an ocean of joy
> Laughter, joy, and pleasure continues as the clock struck four o'clock (207)

Water metaphors overflow as the poet praises the lotus-themed pool built in the courtyard of the Bado Mahal (fig. 3.15).[41] Conceptually, this segment on pleasure in the *Jagvilās* performs two key tasks. First, it provides a transition from the preceding verses on spatial description, which employ *sukha* to denote the joy derived from experiencing the material beauty of the palace, to verses that contain a thematic deliberation on pleasure connected to the king's rulership and court. Nandram suggests it would take him days to describe the Bado Mahal—and still he would be unable to do justice to the beauty of the palace.[42] The poet also uses such literary ploys to shift his gaze, and his listeners, to other spaces, in order to evoke the spatial splendor of Jagniwas's garden courtyards, the Dilkhush Mahal and the Khush Mahal—the very names of which incorporate the *khuśī* (joy) they brought to the *dil* (heart). Second, the poet develops the *bhāva*, the literary moods of pleasurable places, as discussed in chapter 2, by engaging the poetic moods of the monsoon season. Just as regional poetry describes courtly lovers and ordinary citizens

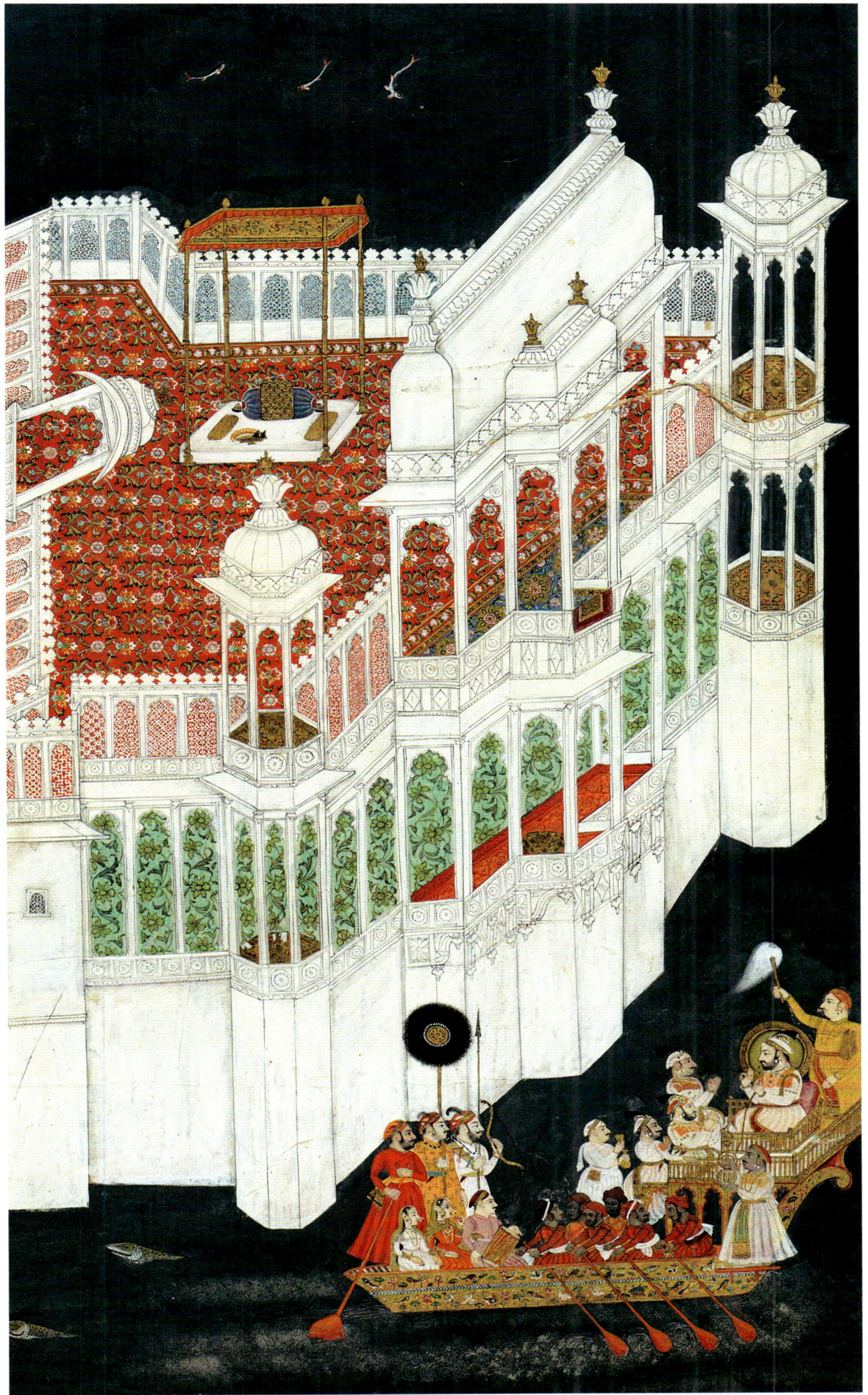

3.14. *Maharana Jagat Singh II Boating near Jagniwas*, c. 1746–50. Udaipur. Gouache on paper, 52 × 30 cm. Museum Rietberg, Zürich; gift of Balthasar and Nanni Reinhart, RVI 1832. Photograph by Rainer Wolfsberger.

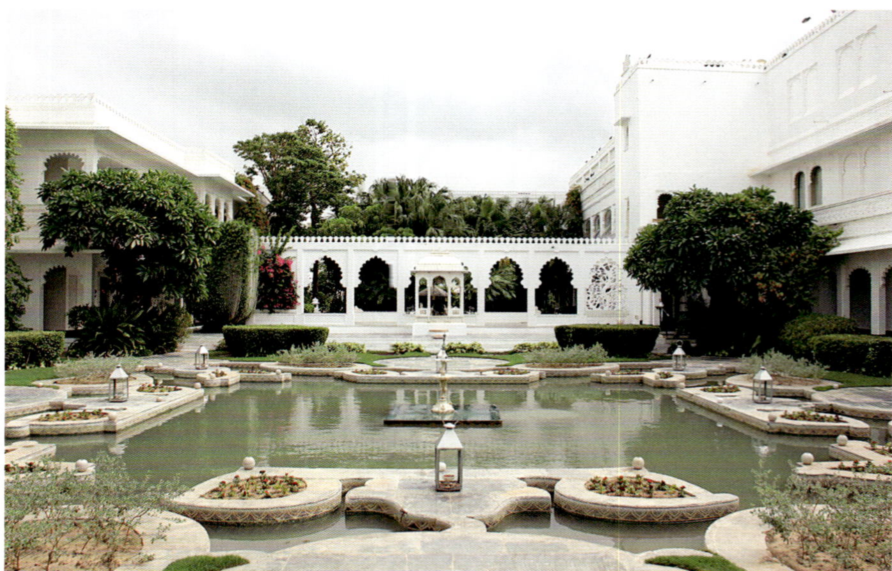

3.15. Lotus-themed pool in the courtyard of the Bado Mahal (today the lily pond of the Taj Lake-Palace Hotel), Jagniwas lake palace, Udaipur, 1746. Photograph by author.

overwhelmed by rain, the *Jagvilās* claims that the king captivated every person in the audience through the pleasures the lake palace offered. Nandram's depiction of the impact and experience of *sukha* in Jagniwas as a rain cloud (verse 194) invites us to imagine rain pouring into the city's lakes, a sight perhaps best enjoyed from the lake palaces. The pervasiveness of water in poetic imaginaries of Jagniwas denies the constant threat of drought while connecting the pleasures of the lake palace to its specifically local geography of lakes.

The bonding among nobles, possibly both allies and adversaries, in the interiors of Jagniwas must have been palpably enhanced by the corporeal experience of inhabiting the world of pleasure created within a palace bounded by water on all four sides. One's inclusion in or exclusion from a circumscribed and immersive world of sensory and material pleasure could have triggered strong emotional responses of appreciation and attachment. When Nandram says that the king "rules with joy [*sukha so rājatarāṇa*]," and that Jagniwas is where he and his companions together find an "ocean of joy [*sabahī saṁga sukha meṃ tahāṃ sukha ko sāgara pāya*]," he suggests the ways in which power was constituted through practices of pleasure—perhaps quite literally in parties. To become attuned, to be in the mood, so to speak, as Sara Ahmed points out, requires "openness" to intimacy.[43] The withdrawal of bodily expressions such as laughter or gestures can easily break the sense of intimacy. But creating the conditions for attunement inside the lake palace, the potential for such bonds was established—it did not mean that such affections were already established. This is one reason that idealizations were valued, that representing pleasurable assemblies in paintings was pertinent, that each iteration and idealization of pleasure had to perform the significant task of reinforcing the potential for affective work to take place.

One of the key histories crafted in the artworks discussed above is about the solidification of Jagat Singh II's political networks through acts of connoisseurship and the collective enjoyment and sensible appreciation of arts, architecture, delicacies, scents, and sounds in the intimate space of Jagniwas. The tastes of Udaipur's mid-eighteenth-century courtly community itself were being forged, as was the power of the king and of other members of this courtly society who partook of such pleasures not only as individuals but also as a collective.

MOBILIZING PLEASURES, IDEALIZING ABODES

Udaipur artists cast Jagniwas as the ultimate abode of pleasurable sensoriums. Their mediation of moods and pleasures in paintings suggests two critical points about imaginative practices. We learn, first, how material consumption and aesthetic ideas were mobilized to reinstate kingly authority and to renew and realize bonds among the courtly community, and second, how strategies of idealizing pleasures reshaped local places and ideal abodes alike. Both the mobilization and the idealization of pleasurable places reveal how makers and patrons viewed affect and emotion as imperative for conducting courtly politics. Paintings featuring Udaipur rulers in the mid-eighteenth century feature several other powerful nobles, some of whom can be identified both by scribes' inscriptions and by artists' careful renderings of these individuals. What happens, then, when we shift our gaze from the king's portrait toward that of one of the important political brokers and connoisseurs who participated in Jagat Singh's world of pleasure? How did painters evoke real architectural spaces of pleasure while inviting connoisseurs to imagine idealized moods of *vilāsa* and enchanted lakeside abodes beyond Udaipur? Almost two hundred verses of the *Jagvilās* are devoted to constituting the mid-century political networks of regional nobles (the thakurs of Mewar) and describing their participation in defining the courtly space of Udaipur—and thus Jagat Singh II's power. We encounter verses that describe Jagat Singh's gifting ceremony, which took place as soon as the king arrived at the new lake palace with his entourage at the planned, auspicious time. Often these thakurs followed royal ceremonials as prescribed at Udaipur, bending them per their own needs and choices, and in doing so they created new spaces for the patronage of arts and music where circulating artists could experiment more freely and thus change—from the frontiers of Mewar—the taste of connoisseurs at the center.[44]

Thakur Sirdar Singh, of the Dodia clan, was a key participant in Jagat Singh II's court and parties. Paintings of Jagniwas parties and the poetry of the *Jagvilās* both draw attention to Sirdar Singh's role in creating delightful experiences for the Udaipur king. Artists emphasized Sirdar Singh's position: he is almost always depicted immediately beside Jagat Singh II, and in some cases he is seen riding an elephant with the ruler (fig. 3.16). Sirdar Singh also accompanies Jagat Singh II in pools and gardens and on boats (fig. 3.17), and in some instances the thakur leads rather than follows the king (fig. 3.13). Painters singled out Sirdar Singh's portrait on each occasion by emphasizing his pointed chin. The tenth verse in the *Jagvilās* proclaims that Jagat Singh II assigned Sirdar Singh the task of building the Jagniwas lake palace:

> Then [he] calls Thakur Sirdar Singh near him.
> [Who is] the most intelligent and sophisticated, smiling to himself while talking to him
> All the best architects, all the well-trained workers
> [Those] with virtuosity of training and the knowledge of the architecture treatises
> Sirdar Singh took to heart all of the instructions that came [were said] to him from [Jagat Singh's] auspicious mouth,
> And on those [orders], with great acumen, has all sorts of constructions made (10)

A brief historical overview of Sirdar Singh Dodia's patronage reveals how his relationship with the Mewar court changed in the 1730s. One of Sirdar Singh's ancestors, Dodia

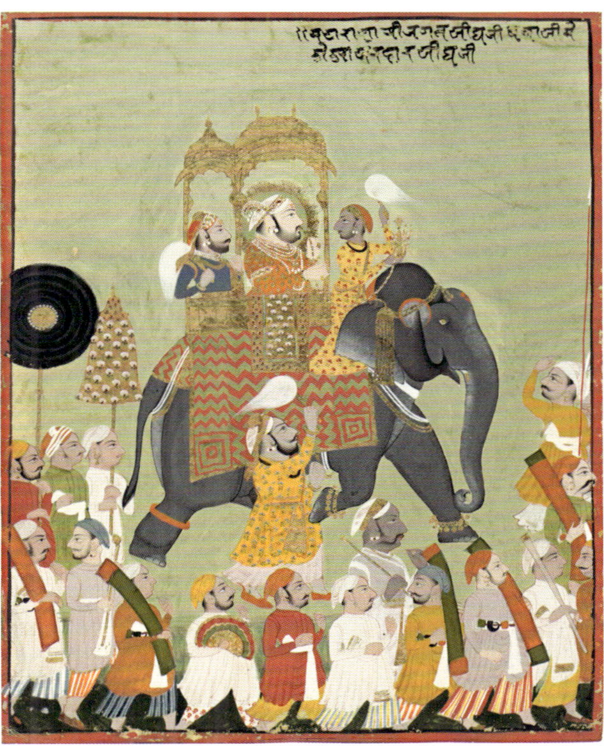

3.16. *Maharana Jagat Singh II and Thakur Sirdar Singh on an Elephant*, c. 1740–50, Udaipur. Opaque watercolor and gold on paper, 27.2 × 21.6 cm. National Gallery of Victoria, Melbourne; Felton Bequest, 1980, AS138- 1980.

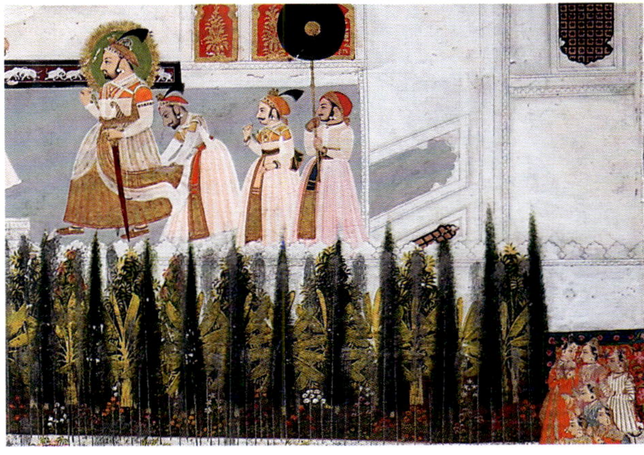

3.17. Detail of fig. 3.8. Portrait of Sirdar Singh following Jagat Singh II, holding his sash (*patkā*).

Jaskaran, came to the aid of the Mewar king Ratan Singh in 1303, which initiated the Dodia-Mewar brotherhood.[45] The Dodia clan was founded by Deipank, who came from the neighboring region of Sindh, now in Pakistan. In 1387, Dhaval Dodia was given a land grant (*jāgir*) after Rao Dodia's defense of the Udaipur ruler Lakha's mother. At this time the Dodia earned the honorable right of personally protecting the Mewar kings. Dodia lore holds that ten successive generations of clan leaders—from the fourteenth to the mid-eighteenth century—died protecting Mewar kings in various battles against the Mughals. In most cases, the succeeding Dodia clan leader was granted land in recognition of his ancestors' sacrifices. However, the literature from the late eighteenth and early nineteenth centuries does not reveal Dodia territorial establishments prior to 1738. By the 1730s, the Dodias' status in the first tier of nobles within Udaipur's hierarchy was determined not only by their sacrifices and patterns of land ownership but also by their relationship with Udaipur's royal family.

It is well known that marital alliances played a central role in defining Rajput-Mughal politics and that they were equally decisive in politics over succession within the Rajput courts.[46] Indeed, Jagat Singh II and Sirdar Singh Dodia were married to sisters, who were princesses of the court of Idar in Gujarat when Sirdar Singh began to make his presence felt at the Udaipur court, which we also infer from the above-noted courtly portraits. Clearly, Jagat Singh II sought to strengthen his brother in-law's presence at the Udaipur court when, in 1738, he awarded Sirdar Singh the estate land (*ṭhikānā*) of Lawa, fifty-eight miles north of Udaipur, just beyond Rajsamand Lake, to which he added the additional reward of prime land on the banks of Lake Pichola (in Udaipur, outside the walled city)—possibly the first such gift of its kind. In the city, Sirdar Singh constructed the Dodia *haveli*, a complex of garden courtyards and palatial rooms that sprawls over 430,000 square feet on the banks of Lake Pichola (fig. 3.18). Sirdar Singh also built an impressive rectangular fort (*gaṛh*) against the undulating hilly landscape of his estate outside the city, in Lawa; he laid its foundation in 1738 and oversaw its completion by 1743 (fig. 3.19). Jagat Singh II was invited to the opening ceremony and named the fort Sardargarh.[47] The Udaipur king must have been impressed by the fort and residential mansion, for we know that Sirdar Singh's intelligence was praised in the *Jagvilās* and that he was awarded responsibility for building the Jagniwas lake palace in 1743, the year the thakur completed both his independent building projects. As we think of the world in which the Jagniwas lake palace sought to exert its efficacy as a place that charmed associates into a "world of pleasure," Sirdar Singh's self-presentation underscores the ways in which aesthetics, patronage, and territorial expansions were intertwined.

Mobilizing spaces of pleasure to create powerful selves and powerful bonds with friends and associates in the mid-eighteenth century was not the prerogative of Udaipur's maharanas alone. Nobles such as Sirdar Singh Dodia operated "little kingdoms" on their estate lands.[48] The architecture of Sirdar Singh's fort and courtyard mansion also referenced typological spaces like the Baadi Mahal garden palace. The spatial planning of the women's quarters in the Sirdargarh fort is similar to the layout of the queens' quarters in the Udaipur palace.[49] Furthermore, the Dodia *haveli*'s prominent location on the banks of Lake Pichola, opposite the lake palace, provides a rare vantage point for the admiration of the lake and the city—and thus suggests the power and prestige of Sirdar Singh. It is quite possible that Sirdar Singh's palatial domain with garden courtyards, played a significant role in Jagat Singh II's desire for a new lake palace.[50]

A series of independent portraits of Thakur Sirdar Singh, on three vertical folios of similar size, further entice. A dispersed illustrated manuscript, titled *Sirdārvilās*, dated to about 1740, depicts the noble's world of pleasure and power (figs. 3.20–22).[51] The inscription on the frontispiece folio, entitled "Thakur Sirdar Singh Worshipping at the Krishna Temple of the Dodia *Haveli*," notes that it was commissioned by the *māhārājadhīrāja ṭhākur Sīrdar Sinġhjī* (fig. 3.20).[52] The scribe also names the poet and the painter as *citerā* Shahji, likely referring to the Udaipur artist Syaji.[53] The three folios from this manuscript, discussed below, reveal that the painter, poet, and patron all sought to display the constituents of Sirdar Singh's *vilāsa*, including the noble's portrayal as a pious person immersed in leisure and flourishing with his progeny at his lakeside residence. They present an important pictorial, architectural, and ideational precedent for the making of Jagniwas as an ideal site for the practice of courtly pleasures. This manuscript suggests the need to research further Sirdar Singh's role in innovating aesthetic ideas that established connections between poetry, painting, politics, and place while also ascertaining the agentive roles that the patron, painter, and poet played in imagining the moods of pleasure in Udaipur's lakes. The verse and image seem aligned in every folio of this manuscript to praise the piety and pleasures of Sirdar Singh. The painter Shahji's endeavor to organize his compositions around a single courtyard or temple space

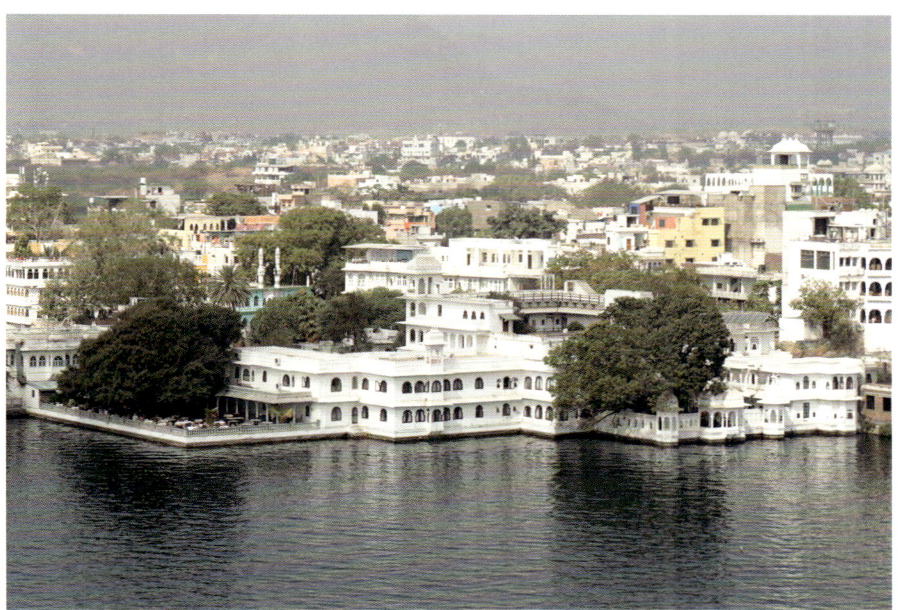

3.18. Dodia *haveli* (known today as the Hotel Amet Haveli), built by Thakur Sirdar Singh in 1743, overlooking Lake Pichola and the City Palace, Udaipur. Photograph by author.

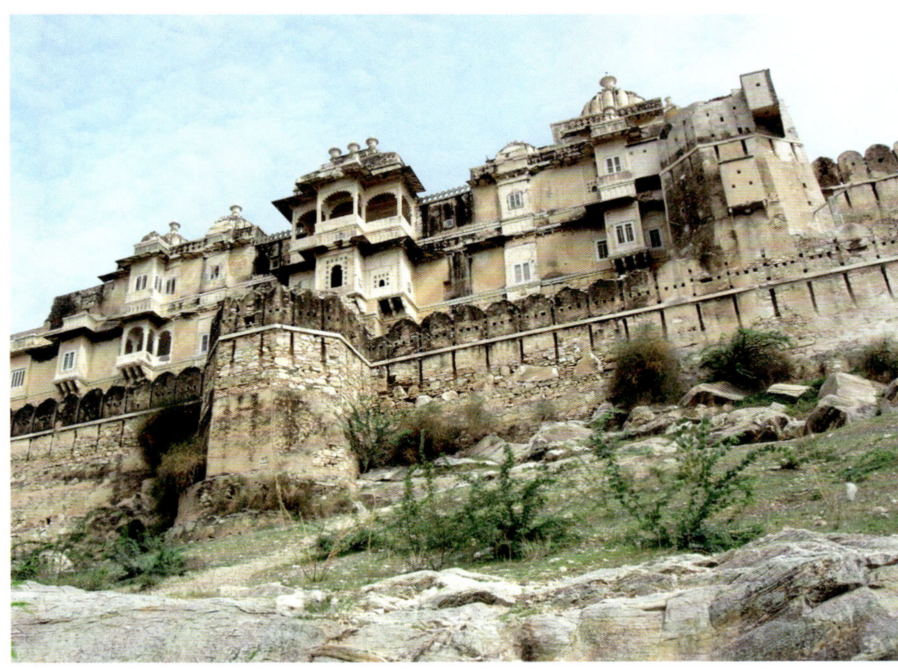

3.19. Sardargarh, fort built by Thakur Sirdar Singh in 1743, estate land of Lawa, Mewar. Photograph by author.

of the Dodia *haveli* also unites this pictorial strategy, as seen above, with the picturing of the courtyards of Jagniwas that later artists followed in the years to come. Here, I offer a pertinent glimpse into the potential of the painted *Sirdārvilās* for unraveling the phenomena of worlds of pleasure.

As with the verses of the *Jagvilās*, the painted explication of *vilāsa* in this case includes the practices of both piety and leisure. These tenets connected praise for Sirdar Singh and his portrait to other kingly panegyrics; however, the painter forcefully underscored the specificity of performing these kingly ethics in the space that iterated Sirdar Singh's territoriality on the lakefront. The frontispiece, "Thakur Sirdar Singh Worshipping at the Krishna Temple of the Dodia *Haveli*," depicts Sirdar Singh, along with his three young sons

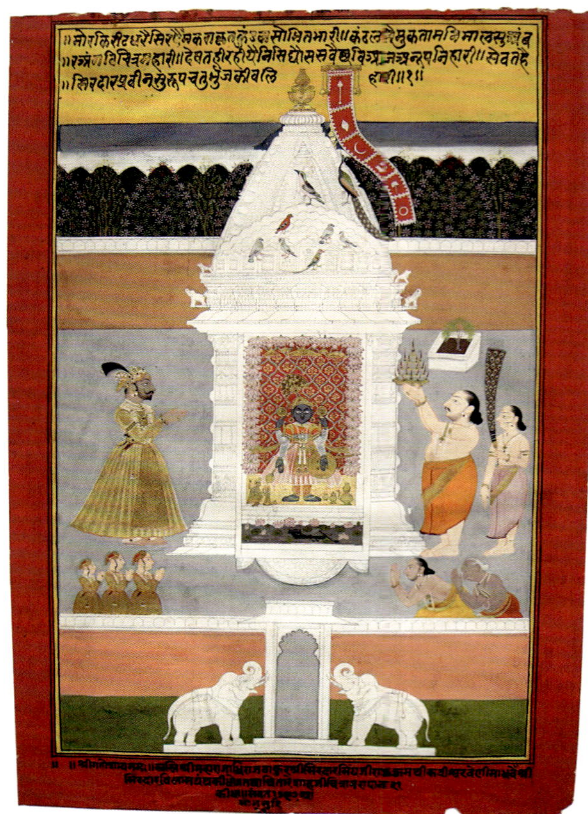

3.20. "Thakur Sirdar Singh Worshipping at the Krishna Temple of the Dodia *Haveli*," page from a dispersed illustrated manuscript of *Sirdārvilās*, Shahji, c. 1740–43. Udaipur. Opaque watercolor on paper, 36.7 × 23.5 cm. Private collection.

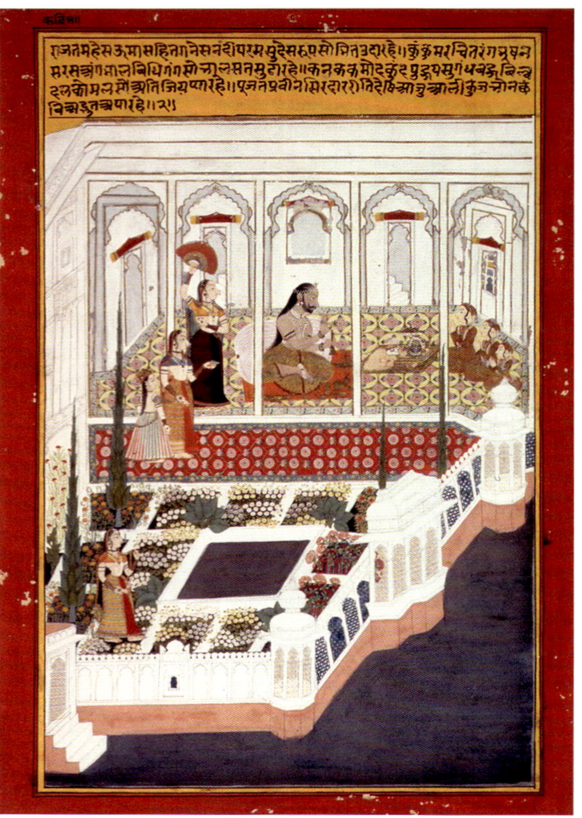

3.21. "Thakur Sirdar Singh Worshipping a Four-Faced Shiva Lingam in the Garden Courtyard of the Dodia *Haveli*," page from a dispersed illustrated manuscript of *Sirdārvilās*, attributed to Shahji, c. 1740–43, Udaipur. Opaque watercolor on paper, 36.7 × 23.5 cm. Asian Art Museum, San Francisco; gift of Mr. and Mrs. George Hopper Fitch, B84D2.

and a group of priests, offering prayers to an adorned icon of Krishna installed in a temple sanctum. The painter lavishly used gold paint to render the figure of the deity, decorated with ornaments, armor, and a peacock-feathered crown. The red and gold cloth backdrop mounted behind the deity, along with the pink fully bloomed lotuses that line the doorway of the sanctum, bring forth a painted vision that sought to praise the beauty of the blue-hued god. Shahji centralized the entrance in the frontispiece composition; this pictorial strategy creates an affinity with the way we approach the *haveli* temple, built on the axis of the entrance to the lakeside residence, as the first building in the residential complex. Because the frontispiece is the only folio of the three that does not include lake waters, likely because the lake is not directly visible from the temple, it is all the more striking to encounter a horizontal lotus-filled lake vignette with a black royal boat in the space connecting the temple to the location of Sirdar Singh's mansion. In a second folio focused on the theme of piety, "Thakur Sirdar Singh Worshipping a Four-Faced Shiva Lingam in the Garden Courtyard of the Dodia *Haveli*," the noble is shown, in the presence of his sons, offering his prayers to a *lingā* icon of Shiva, recalling the Mewar court's dynastic deity of Eklingji (fig. 3.21). It is noteworthy that Sirdar Singh is depicted independent of the Udaipur king, although he appears in an act of devotion reminiscent of those we can see in portraits of Jagat Singh II, in which the king is shown offering prayers in similar bare-chested attire (fig. 3.23). That Sirdar Singh is performing this act of devotion to the court's dynastic deity in his own lakeside residence—within a garden courtyard

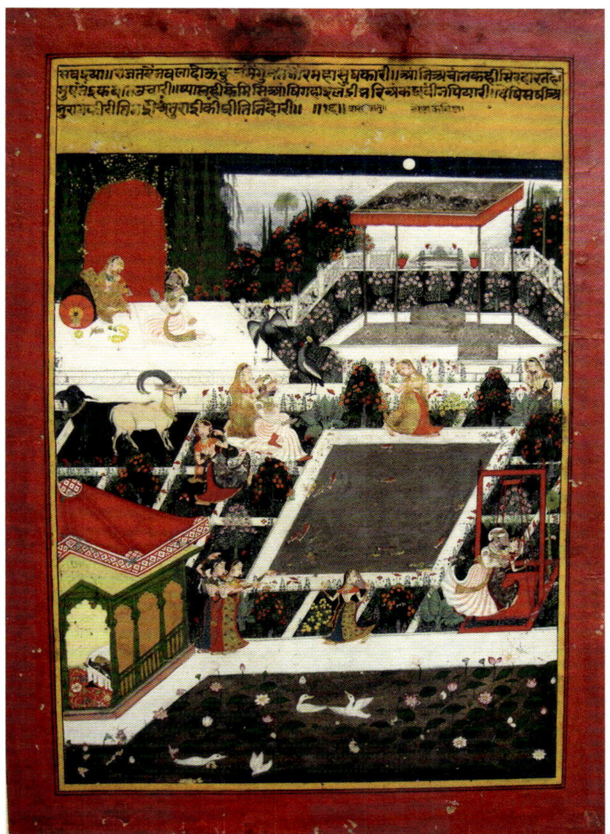

3.22. "Thakur Sirdar Singh Enjoys Pleasures with Women in the Garden Courtyard of the Dodia *Haveli*," page from a dispersed illustrated manuscript of *Sirdārvilās*, attributed to Shahji, c. 1740–43, Udaipur. Opaque watercolor on paper, 36.7 × 23.5 cm. Private collection.

overlooking lake waters—is most telling of the noble's position and power in the court and the city.

A third folio, "Thakur Sirdar Singh Enjoys Pleasures with Women in the Garden Courtyard of the Dodia *Haveli*," imagines the leisurely activities Sirdar Singh enjoyed by a beautiful lakefront under the moonlight (fig. 3.22). The painting also seems to suggest that Sirdar Singh had a menagerie, for the sounds and sights of a variety of birds and other animals are equal participants in this space of pleasure, described by the poet as a place that gives immense joy (*mahā sukhkārī*) at night. In the upper left corner of the composition, Sirdar Singh is shown seated outside a resplendent bower with a lady who offers betel leaves and flowers; in the center, the beautiful heroine (*nāyikā*) covers Sirdar Singh's eyes as if indulging in playful and loving enticement. In the lower right corner, the hero and heroine enjoy a swing by the lakeside. Both the poet and the painter included in their vignettes the figure of the intermediary female friend (*sakhī*) who admires their rituals of love and play. These images collectively evoke the devotional play (*līlā*) of the blue god Krishna and Radha accompanied by her *sakhī*s. Through the inclusion of a full moon and fully bloomed lotuses, the painter alludes to the mood of *sukha*—seduction and pleasure—created for the lovers, who are caressed by a scented and cool breeze.

While drawing a connection between changing political dynamics in the real world and practices of imagination is never simple or direct, Udaipur's unique lake-centered geography complicates the picture, for it also shaped the idealized visions of patrons, painters, and poets in powerful ways. Udaipur paintings of Shiva's abodes enable us to trace how,

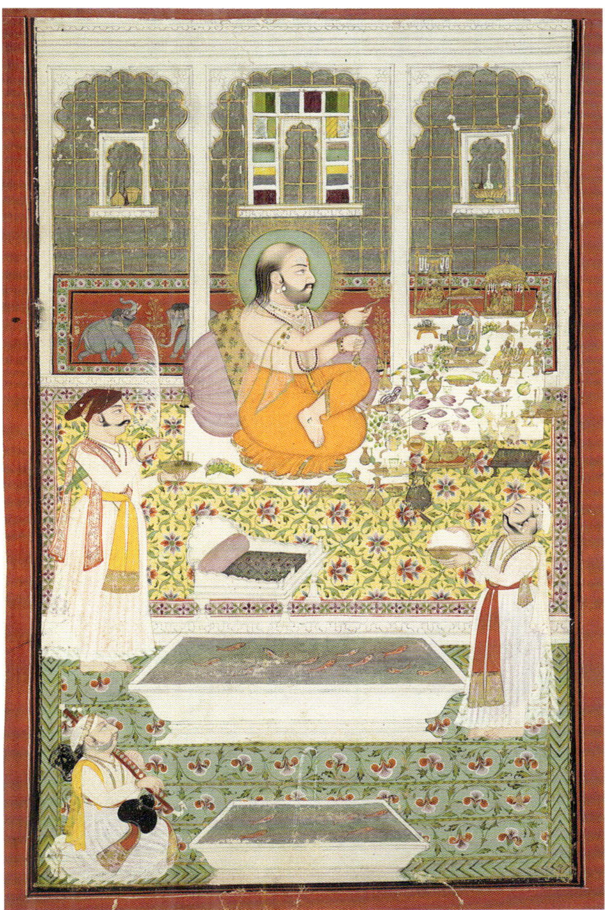

3.23. *Maharana Jagat Singh II Worshipping in the Kachari Mahal*, c. 1735–40, Udaipur. Opaque watercolor and gold on paper, 92.2 × 55.2 cm. Freer Gallery of Art, Smithsonian Institution, Washington, DC; purchase and partial gift made in 2012 from the Catherine and Ralph Benkaim Collection, Charles Lang Freer Endowment, F2012.4.6.

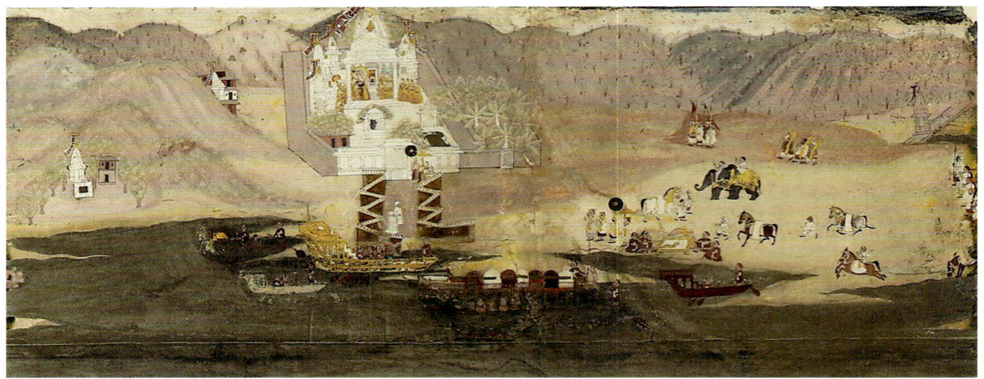

3.24. Detail of fig. 3.1. Jagat Singh II worshipping at the lakeside Vaidyanath Mahadev temple.

in poetry and in painting, the Jagniwas lake palace emerged as a heterotopia—a real space that shaped and was shaped by idealized imaginaries.[54] Another lakeside building, the Vaidyanath Mahadeva temple, built in 1716 enables us to consider why and how painters deliberately included certain specific sites in some pictures but not in others.[55] Sukha and Syaji composed the spaces of Jagniwas using a bird's-eye view (fig. 3.1), deploying a distinctive pictorial framework that depicts the *bhāva* of the lake palace's conglomeration of courtyards instead of reinforcing a singular space or mood. This team of painters also chose to expand the imaginary of the lake palace beyond its walls. They painted a smaller-scale elevation view of the hills and the Vaidyanath Mahadeva temple in the upper part of the painting (fig. 3.24), thus juxtaposing a different representational technique to highlight the temple's location, nestled between the valley and the lakeside. This vignette of the temple contrasts with another painting that depicts an Udaipur king's visit to the lakeside Vaidyanath Mahadeva temple. The latter example sets the Shiva temple among trees and mountains, by a lake filled with lotus flowers (fig. 3.25). The kingly portrait itself is unclear; we do not readily recognize the king as Jagat Singh II, despite such cues as his double-chinned face, which painters regularly highlighted. In an inscription on the front of the painting, the scribe describes the portrait as depicting Sangram Singh.[56] Perhaps this indexical gesture demonstrates that scribes saw the temple as chiefly associated with Sangram Singh, who supported its expansion from a small shrine to a temple complex, while painters gestured toward Jagat Singh II. Once the latter had built his own pleasurable abode in the lakes, meeting the challenge set by his father, painters perhaps sought to reclaim a connection with this lakeside temple in the vicinity of the Jagniwas.

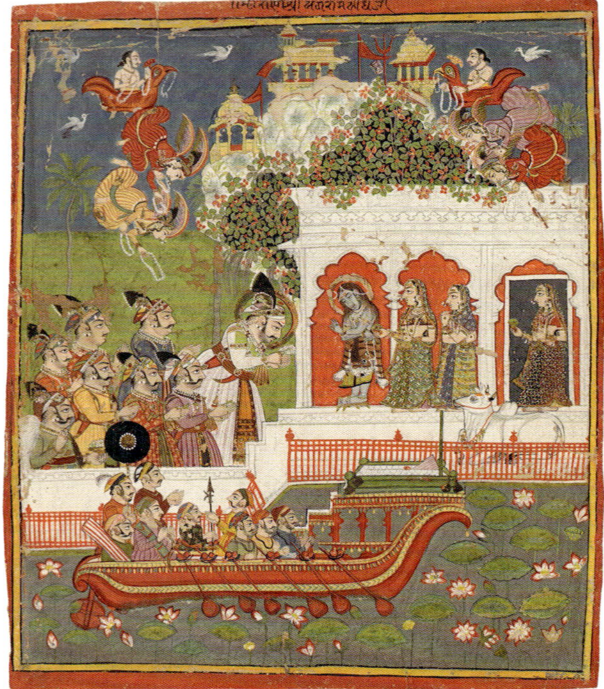

3.25. *Maharana Sangram Singh II or Jagat Singh II Worshipping Shiva*, c. 1734–40, Udaipur. Opaque watercolor and gold on paper, 35 × 29 cm. National Gallery of Victoria, Melbourne; Felton Bequest, 1980, AS103- 1980.

The earthly realm of Udaipur could be transposed to the devotional realm, and the devotional realm could be transposed to the Jagniwas lake palace. The devotional register of this painting and of the royal visit is heightened by the painter's depiction of Lord Shiva in an anthropomorphic form and by his addition of celestial beings in the sky, who bless this meeting with the king. The king's devotional encounter with the god is not imagined through ritual acts of the devotee offering his homage through material things to the sculpted aniconic Shiva lingam shrine in the temple. In his use of flatter modes and deeper colors, the painter drew on the styles of

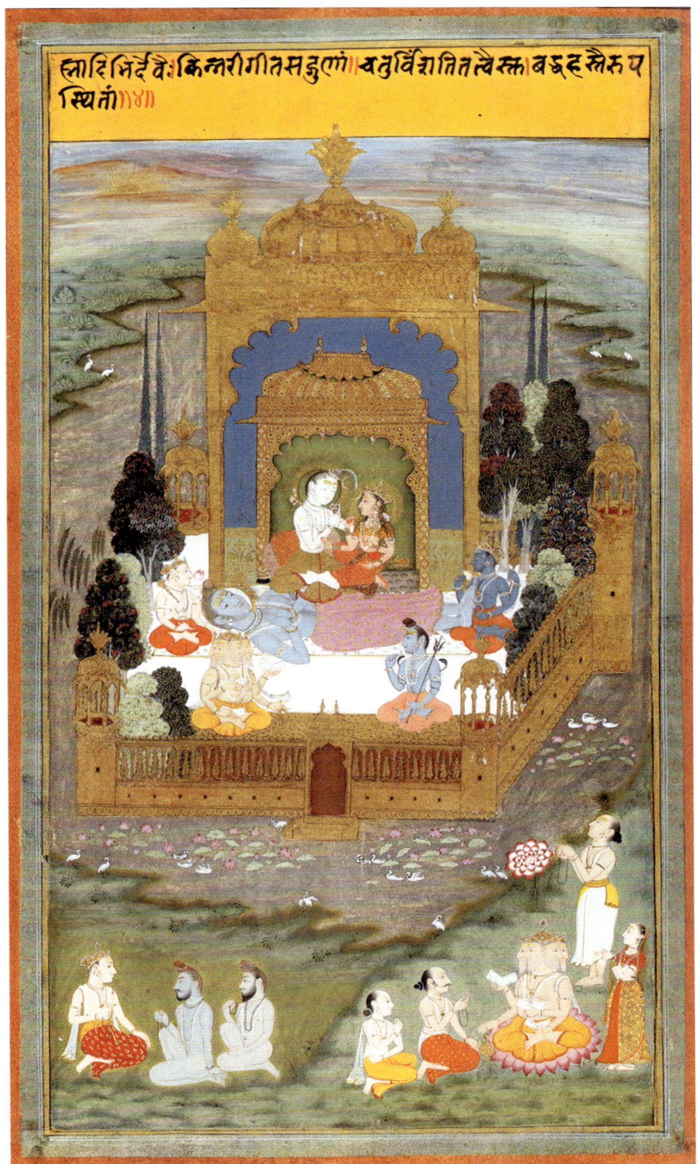

3.26. "Shiva Attended by Deities," illustration from the *Saundaryalaharī*, c. 1725–30. Udaipur. Gouache on paper, 42.2 × 22.3 cm. Museum Rietberg, Zürich; gift of Barbara and Eberhard Fischer, RVI 939. Photograph by Rainer Wolfsberger.

Mewar manuscript illustration rather than of the vignettes of Udaipur's topographical environs, thereby both emphasizing the iconic more than the mimetic and embedding a powerfully evocative image of the lakeside within the iconic genre. It is all the more striking, then, to encounter Shiva's domain in another Udaipur court painting, "Shiva Attended by Deities," as a palace pavilion in the middle of a lakelike body of water surrounded by hills and replete with lotuses (fig. 3.26). We recall that in the *Jagvilās*, the garden palace of the Shivprasana Amar Vilas Mahal was also recast as a place associated with Shiva's joys. There, the poet suggested to courtly audiences that Jagniwas, as the ultimate place for pleasure, was akin to Shiva's abode. Here, painters reverse the allusion, picturing Shiva's land and his joys in the form of Udaipur's lake pavilions.

The paintings and poetry of Jagniwas thus become less historical documents of real pleasure, as previous scholarship has understood them, than aesthetic and material means of merging the real with imagined places of pleasure. For example, while the painter Shahji, in rendering the frontispiece of the *Sirdārvilās*, drew the architectural elevation of the temple in detail, he also responded to poetic sensibilities (fig. 3.20).

By composing a gathering of a variety of birds on the temple tower, and by including a small horizontal vignette of lotus-filled lake waters with a tiny boat within the temple sanctum, the painter gestures to a wondrous and rather unreal detail. We cannot entirely decipher this miniaturized image of lake waters, except to imagine the beauty of the real lakeside environs. Another folio of the *Sirdārvilās* examined here presents Sirdar Singh immersed in a series of joyful activities (fig. 3.22). In a departure from the frontispiece, here the painter does not draw the architecture in detail. Yet, by including pictorial hints that the patron was a collector of exotic animals, the artist perhaps seeks to suggest a point about his patron's beholding of a range of awe-inspiring creatures, including the types of birds that feature in the frontispiece folio. Such inclusions and distinctions in multiple folios of a manuscript that sought to praise Sirdar Singh by describing the ethics and practices of pleasure demand further research. This exploration asserts that Udaipur's artists experimented with differing priorities in constituting *vilāsa*. Their paintings enthusiastically invited courtly connoisseurs to oscillate between empirical and expressive concerns.

Expanding beyond patronage, portraiture, and religion to explain painted subjects enables us to see the dynamic communities of men and women, allies and adversaries, that formed around the experiences of all kinds of joys—corporeal, sensorial, material, spatial, visual, and audial. By building and imagining places for the practice of pleasures, various localized artistic cultures recast familiar metaphors, moods, and memories. Paintings made at the Rajput court of Nagaur between 1729 and 1750 also engaged the theme of courtly pleasures, with patrons and painters driven to visualize plentiful, luxurious gardens and palaces to contrast their courtly world from the surrounding desert of Marwar.[57] Udaipur's artists were not alone in this approach; mid-eighteenth-century court artists in Jodhpur employed the painting palette and pleasurable themes developed earlier, at the court workshop at Nagaur, to imaginatively transform "heavenly palaces and landscapes for [depicting Krishna's] divine *līla* (play)."[58] They also take a water palace from Nagaur paintings to render Rama and Sita's idyllic realm of Ayodhya in a monumental manuscript of the epic poem *Rāmcaritmānas* (Sacred lake of the acts of Rama, c. 1775).[59] Such diverse examples and the Udaipur story invite us to further historicize the role of immersive joyful sensoriums in the making of political communities in premodern South Asia and the ways patrons and makers circulated ideas and knowledge on the aesthetic and ethic of pleasure.[60] In turn, we may learn how historical communities made meaning of allied art practices in emotionally laden ways.

ITERATING MOODS AND MEMORIES

Contemporary visitors to the Jagniwas lake palace, now the Taj Lake-Palace Hotel, arrive by motorized boat, yet the sunlight dancing over the water delights just as it would have when the palace was completed in 1746. One feels calm moving along with the cool breeze that blows from the lake bank to the lake palace. The city of Udaipur registers as an oasis within the dry desert landscape of northwestern India. Colorful squares of glass set within projecting windows punctuate the whiteness of the lake palace's walls. Once inside, unique pools and marble inlay invite us to touch and view both vertical and horizontal surfaces; fragrant air wafts from the gardens, and fountains play in the courtyards. The lake waters are visible from the windows and broad terraces. Even in the greatly adapted luxurious hotel interiors, where divisions often restrict the flow of air, light, and sound, the presence of the surrounding lake constantly inflects the moist feel and floral scent of the air inside the palace. One can also experience the erasure of such visions and sensoriums during a season of severe drought.

Sadly, in the summer of 2004, as I arrived at the temples and courtyard mansions on the opposite bank of Lake Pichola, Udaipur locals walking wearily on the dried lake bed recounted the reality of enduring the burning summer heat. They were aghast at the Taj Lake-Palace Hotel emptying water fetched in trucks and tanks into the lake pit to keep the image of the water palace afloat. Seasonal cycles and ecological crises serve as a reminder that mid-eighteenth-century paintings of the floating water palace—like the one of Udaipur as a city of lakes in a monsoon downpour (see fig. 2.1)—could also have evoked widely divergent opinions on courtly ethics, aesthetics, and associated moods and memories of elite audiences. Yet it seems rather difficult to associate Jagniwas lake palace with any mood other than pleasure and luxury—a place you admire from afar, a place that you encounter in local lore and images as a water palace, floating in a lotus-filled lake, and a place that you desire to experience from the inside.

Painted imaginings of the moods of pleasures at Jagniwas lake palace serve as palimpsests. Given the vast number of known paintings of Udaipur's lake palaces, it appears that making paintings of Udaipur kings attached to the moods and memories of pleasures at the Jagniwas and the Jagmandir retreats was absolutely pertinent to patrons and painters. The imaginings of Jagat Singh II immersed in the practice of pleasures at Jagniwas—made within a short period from 1746 to 1751—created powerful associations across paintings. Two works, both made in 1767 and featuring the Udaipur king Ari Singh (r. 1761–73) at the Jagniwas and Jagmandir, were composed as response pictures to the earlier court paintings. Painters composed the Jagmandir island yet again in its entirety (fig. 3.27) and featured only a partial view of two of the courtyards of the Jagniwas lake palace (fig. 3.28). The composition, color palette, and contiguous inventory numbers on the reverse sides of the paintings give us reasons to think that they were most likely conceived together and intended as a set. Imagining and consuming the pleasures of Jagniwas continued to delight painters and patrons. In the early years of the nineteenth century, the Udaipur painter Chokha altered the viewpoint of a painting featuring Bhim Singh in the Jagniwas lake palace.[61] He imprinted the composition with his unique stylistic preference (*chāp*) for stouter figures and included a stubbier garden courtyard. The Udaipur artist Ghasi, whose artworks are discussed in chapter 4, similarly introduced his preference for sharp and precise architectural outlines. He chose pictorial continuity in composition, as seen in his centralized portrait of the ruler Jawan Singh (r. 1828–38) painted within the environs of the lotus pool of the Jagniwas palace.[62]

While for courtly communities admiring an individual painting, textual references—such as the phrase *jaganivāsa ro bhāva* (the mood of Jagniwas), inscribed on the verso of the painting featuring Jagat Singh II's pleasures certainly played a significant descriptive and mnemonic role. The painting as an artifact demanded the act of turning it over, reading the inscription on the back, and then returning to the front to reexamine the composition and painterly effects. The mediation of moods, especially the making of collective moods through conspicuous consumption and connoisseurship, in assemblies had been central to earlier projects that included illustrated books commissioned at the pre-Mughal sultanate and Mughal courts that featured circumscribed gatherings.[63] The corporeal act of interaction with Udaipur paintings that were larger than painted books and could not be held in a single hand, however, established distinct haptic relations. The texts and seriality in books, albums, and illustrated manuscripts were more sequentially integrated, even when connoisseurs took the time to appreciate each folio independently. By contrast, the back-and-forth between the front and back of individual Udaipur paintings creates short and long synchronic periods of observation and appreciation. It may serve as a useful reminder, as discussed in chapter 1, that scribes, while usually identifying featured portraits, did not always describe depictions of the mood of a place in their inscriptions, and so a painter's iterative emphasis on the moods of historical places may have exerted a greater force than inscriptions. This possibility suggests that the affective work of recalling associated places, moods, paintings, and poetry also functioned in diachronic ways across imaginings separated by a few years or by several decades.

The multiple imaginaries of the same lake palace mediated the aesthetic delight aroused by the painted works of art and the historical memories of lake palaces built to provide the ideal experience of delight as both a courtly practice and a courtly ethic. By way of repeating similar moods, adapting older compositions, and highlighting painterly effects—such as the shimmering waters of Lake Pichola and the whiteness of Udaipur's lime-washed palaces—painters suggested that the mid-eighteenth-century lands and lakes of their city besotted them. The reinforcing of moods of pleasure enables us to track not only how paintings invited their audiences to sense *vilāsa* but also the ways in which bonding among political communities was powerfully motivated by affective experiences, and how historical memories were shaped in the sensing of moods of delight. Collectives of connoisseurs—those that artists assembled within painted representations and those that patrons assembled within real worlds of lake palaces—mutually memorialized joyful atmospheres and practices of connoisseurship. Such repetitions of aesthetic moods demand that audiences find associations among paintings, becoming alert to the intertwining of historical places, courtly assemblies, kingly ethics, and praise as motivated representational choices.

These pictorial, material, poetic, spatial, idealizing, and iterative aspects constituted the art of picturing the feelings, moods, and emotions associated with a place. Each intermedial relation enhanced the collective potential of texts, objects, and spaces infused with sentiments and desires. Each expression engendered acts of sensing moods and memories of a particular historical time in the present. Historical audiences, however, possibly recalled and connected moods and memories through a variety of paths, equally informed by idealized times and spaces that referred to other pasts and to futures.

Participation in this artistic political economy of pleasure did not require radical inventiveness, nor did the painter's

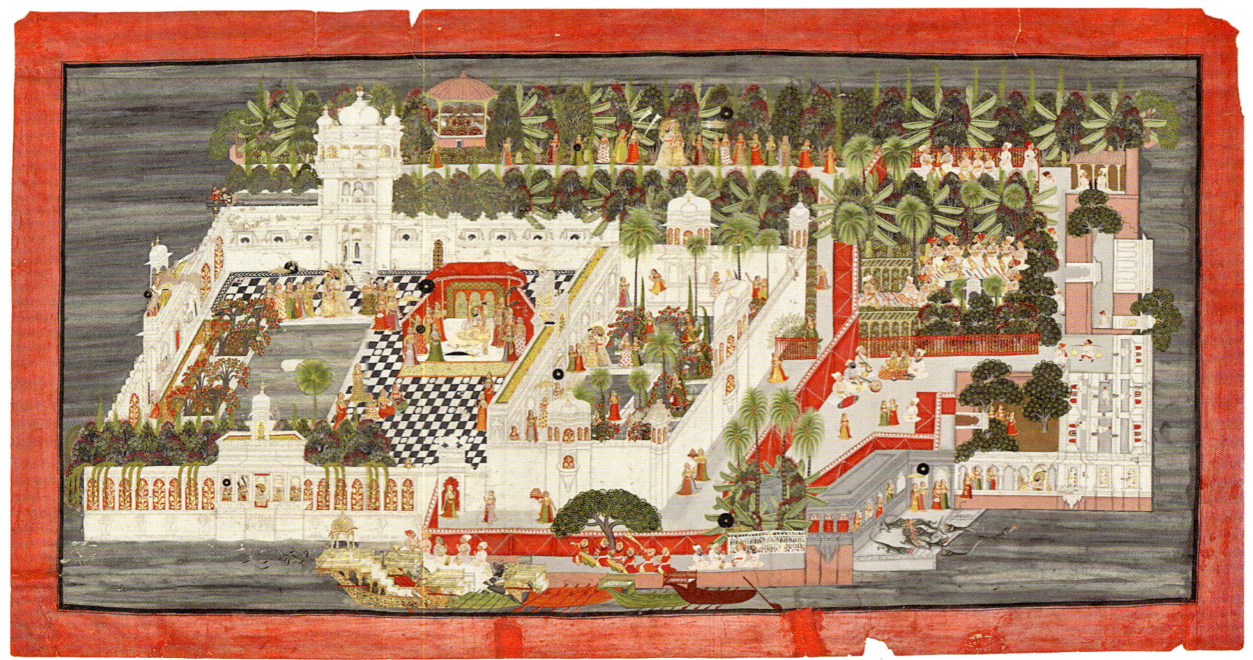

3.27. *Maharana Ari Singh II with His Ladies at Jagmandir*, attributed to Jiva and others, c. 1767, Udaipur. Gouache, gold, and silver on paper, 66.04 × 121.92 cm. The City Palace Museum, Udaipur; 2011.18.0037_R. Photography courtesy of the Freer Gallery of Art and Arthur M. Sackler Gallery, Smithsonian Institution. Photograph by Neil Greentree.

3.28. *Maharana Ari Singh II with His Courtiers Being Entertained at the Jagniwas Water Palace*, Bhima, Kesu Ram, Bhopa, and Nathu, 1767, Udaipur. Ink, opaque watercolor, and gold on paper, 67.6 × 83.5 cm. The Metropolitan Museum of Art, New York; purchase Mr. and Mrs. Herbert Irving, Mr. and Mrs. Arthur Ochs Sulzberger, and Mr. and Mrs. Henry A. Grunwald Gifts, in honor of Mr. and Mrs. Gustavo Cisneros, 1994, 1994.116.

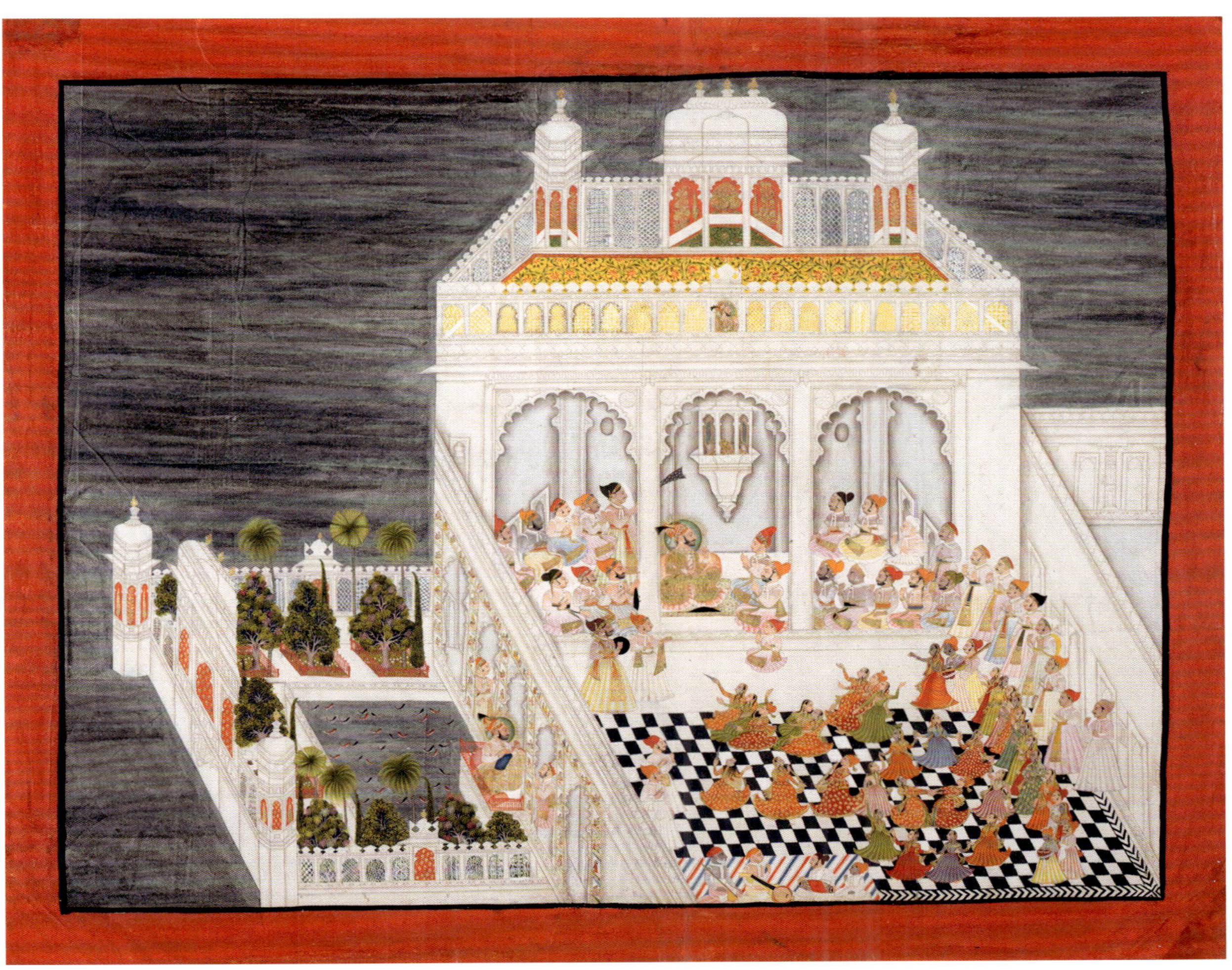

repetition of subjects display a lack of creativity. Every painting seems to endow each reconfiguration of the *bhāva* of the *vilāsa* of Jagniwas with greater power. Each recalling on behalf of the painters and patrons enforced the idealization of the lake palace as the ultimate abode of pleasure. In each of the compositions, the courtly community became a historicized gathering of sentient beings. The portrayed kings, in turn, became the ultimate conspicuous connoisseurs of the worlds of pleasure—and of pictures. Perhaps herein lies the reason that painters in the city of Udaipur to this day replicate paintings featuring the *bhāva* of the *vilāsa* of the Jagniwas lake palace. The poet Nandram perhaps best expressed the intellectual limits of imagining, iterating, and excavating the histories of pleasure:

> You have partaken in all kinds of pleasures
> I/we have tried to write about all of them in beautiful and
> varied ways
> Telling [even] just the essence of all their types
> Would take days and still not ever be compiled (46)

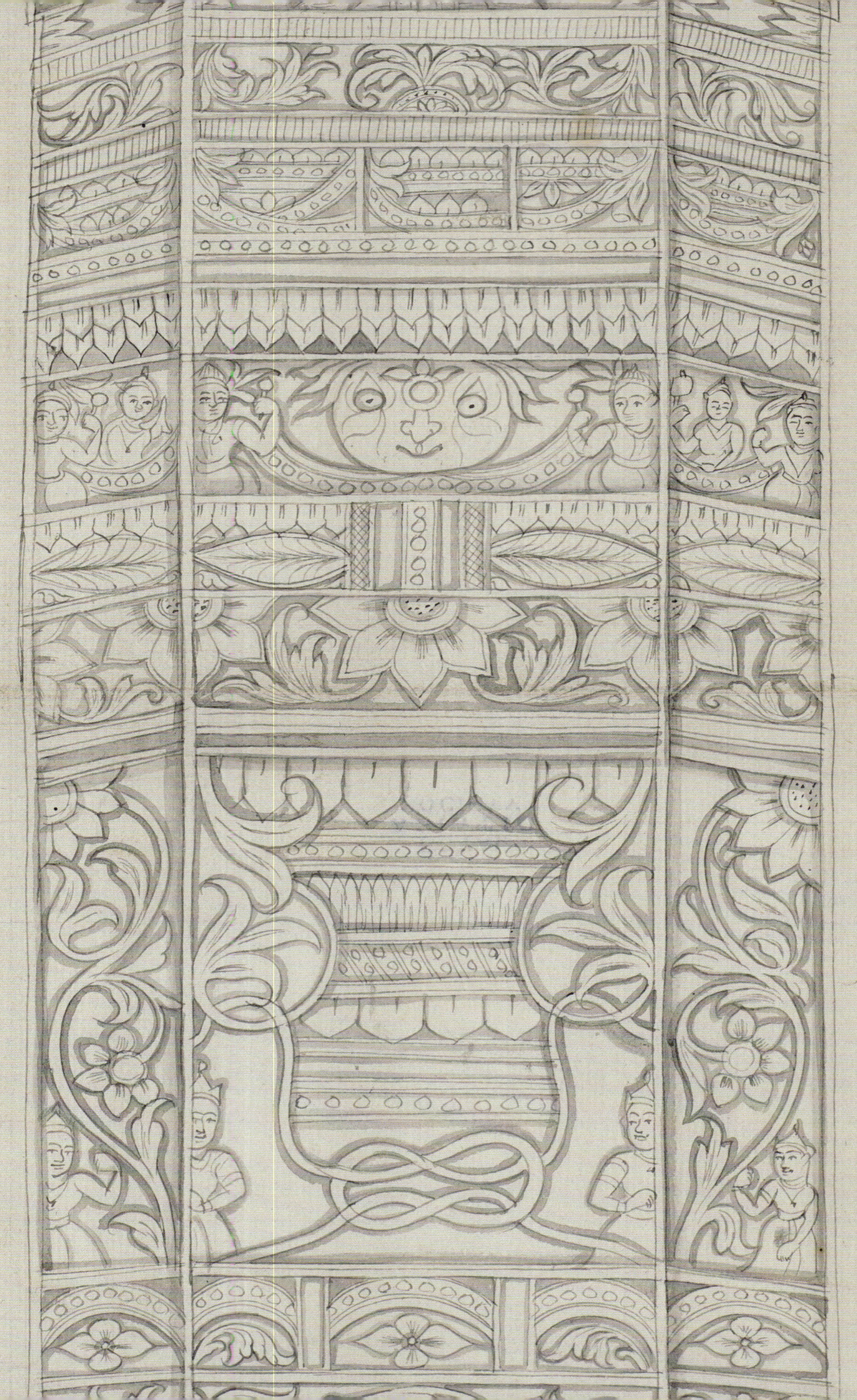

CHAPTER 4

Modes of Knowing and Skills of Drawing

COURT ARTIST/NATIVE ARTIST

Between 1820 and 1835, an artist from Udaipur named Ghasi painted under the patronage of two Indian kings and one British agent. In the early years, Ghasi created smaller portraits of the Udaipur ruler Bhim Singh (r. 1778–1828), mounted on a horse and accompanied by his entourage of men and hunting dogs, posed in a procession (*savārī*) (fig. 4.1). By around 1834–35, he had painted the Udaipur ruler Jawan Singh (r. 1828–38) in several large-scale cloth and paper paintings, picturing him within the expansive architectural environs of temples, palaces, and camps (fig. 4.2). Ghasi also made drawings, both large and small, of the elevations and architectural details of temples—rendered in fine watercolor outlines on watermarked European paper—when he traveled with Colonel James Tod, the first political agent of the British East India Company in Rajasthan (fig. 4.3). Moreover, Ghasi employed the pictorial topos of processions, found in Udaipur court paintings, to portray Tod's diplomatic encounters with Bhim Singh at the Udaipur court (fig. 4.4).

In his history of Indian princes, compiled in the two-volume *Annals and Antiquities of Rajast'han* (originally published by Smith Elder in 1829 and 1832), Tod included several engravings based on his artists' works.[1] As he traveled throughout northwestern India, Tod assigned his artists the task of documenting the architecture of the places he visited. Tod's assistant agent Patrick Waugh served as the (amateur) British artist for Tod's expeditions, and Ghasi served as the "native artist." After the departure of the British agent, Ghasi took the visual vocabulary he had used to render Rajasthan's temple architecture for a British eye and adapted it for imagining and praising the places and travels of his royal patrons in Udaipur.

Ghasi's drawings and paintings are not unknown to scholars. They exist in several collections, including those of the Royal Asiatic Society, Victoria and Albert Museum, and British Library in London; the Brooklyn Museum; and the City Palace Museum, Udaipur. Scholars have tended to explore either his work for patrons at the Udaipur court or his work for Tod, making the connection between the two spheres solely for the purpose of attribution.[2] Ghasi's works have been often interpreted as evidence of artistic decline in Udaipur court painting.[3] This prejudice comes as a corollary to Tod's construction of the eighteenth and early nineteenth centuries

Detail of fig. 4.17

in Udaipur (and northwestern India in general) as a period of political decline. Ghasi's stylistic preference for drawing precise outlines has been described as lending a kind of stiffness to his court paintings.[4] Ghasi's (and his works') transitionary status is seen as neither adequately embodying Indian tradition—specifically Udaipur court painting—nor meeting European standards of painting or architectural drawing. What has never been considered, however, is what Ghasi's translation of styles and subjects in two directions, between court and company, accomplished for his own agency as an artist.

This chapter tracks visual innovations in Ghasi's practice across genres—large-scale court paintings, portraits, and architectural drawings—and circles of making art and knowledge. The artist's travels beyond Udaipur, into northwestern India and back, and his circulation of compositional strategies and drawings of architecture, occurred during a period of critical political and artistic transition in early British India. On the one hand, this examination explores the archive of Ghasi's works and travels—across the Udaipur court and the British East India Company—to examine how the painter depicted place in relation to the demands of royal portraiture and scientific documentation. On the other hand, it presents Ghasi's intellectual engagement against the background of Tod's simultaneous representation of the geography, landscape, and architecture of northwestern India.

Tod, for his part, through the visual works of his diverse group of artist-assistants, employed rhetorical literary tropes popular in eighteenth- and nineteenth-century European travel writing as well as bardic stories and literature that circulated in the regional courts of Rajasthan to shape his deep concerns about both the historicity and the newness of mapping knowledge in northwestern India.[5] That Ghasi contributed his knowledge across image ontologies in dynamic ways, translating "both *between* and *within* cultural codes, forms, and practices," becomes apparent when we see how he chose to compose court paintings that present the mood of places associated with the Udaipur king Jawan Singh.[6] The examination of this movement between and within, as embodied in both Ghasi's and Tod's endeavors, will bring into sharp focus the choices exerted in picturing the moods of places and the relationship of visualizing moods to epistemic claims and political authority.

The multiple instances in which Ghasi's innovations shaped imperative visions for Udaipur court painting and politics in the early decades of the nineteenth century enable us to regard Ghasi not as a "figure of lack" but as one who explicitly asserted his agency.[7] Within the longer history of depicting place at the Udaipur court, Ghasi's artistic practices, especially after Tod's departure in 1822, open up a critical space for thinking about how Tod co-opted Ghasi's drawings within a narrative of ruination and, more provocatively, for reconsidering the ways in which Ghasi employed the vocabulary of drawing architecture within idioms of praise to create a picture of stability and power for Udaipur's rulers. Chapter 3 traced mid-eighteenth-century Udaipur painters' alignment of the city's urban imaginary with the mood, panegyric, and practice of pleasure. We turn now to Ghasi's large-scale paintings as highlighting the practice and panegyric of devotion for re-presenting royal authority and territory. Ghasi and his circle of artists realigned the *bhāva* of the place and royal portraiture with temple spaces and pilgrimages of the Udaipur

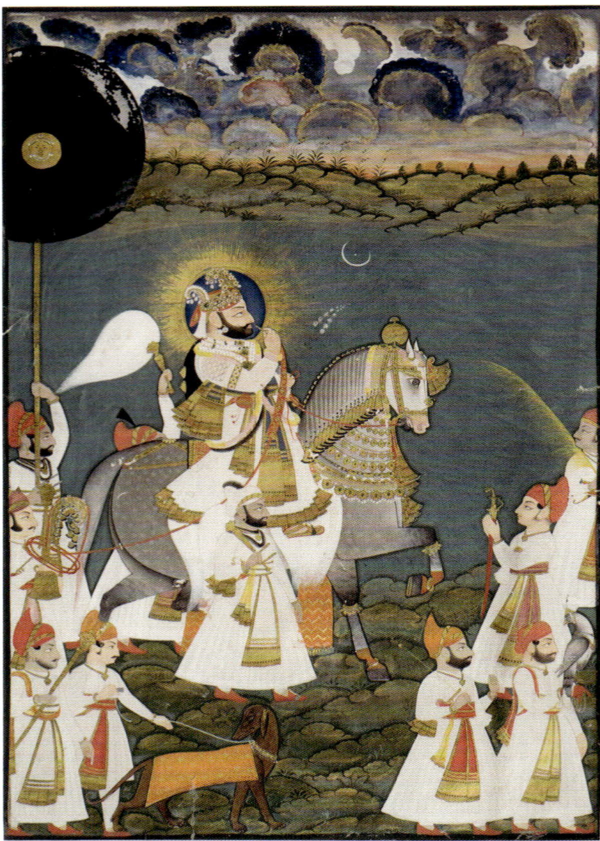

4.1. *Maharana Bhim Singh on Horseback with His Attendants*, attributed to Ghasi, c. 1820, Udaipur. Opaque watercolor and gold on paper, 34.2 × 24.8 cm. The Royal Asiatic Society, London; 63.027.

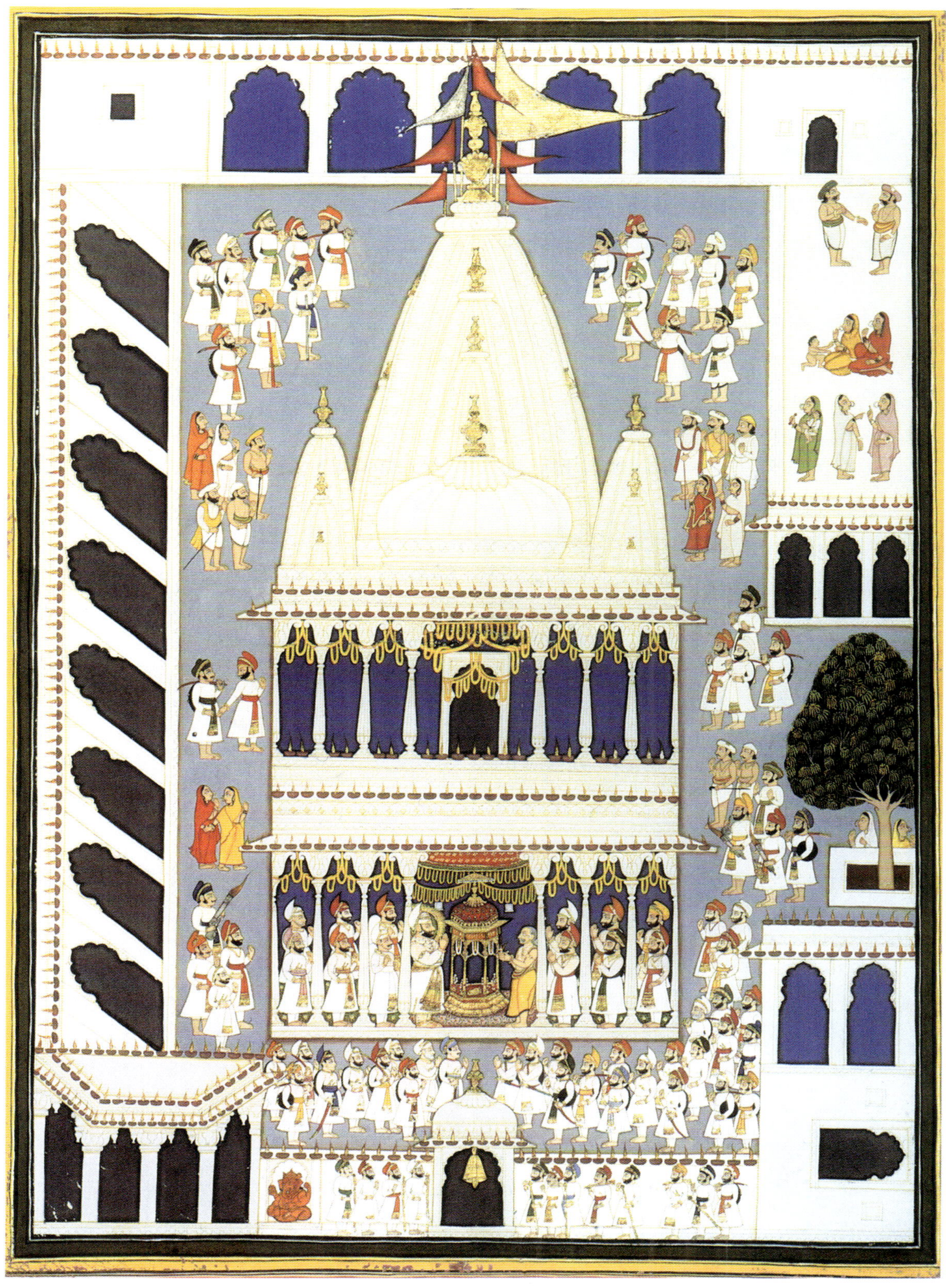

4.2. *Maharana Jawan Singh Visiting Vishnupad Temple at Gaya*, attributed to Ghasi, 1834, Udaipur. Opaque watercolor and gold on paper, 65 × 47.5 cm. Location unknown. Image from Andrew Topsfield, *Court Painting at Udaipur* (Zürich: Artibus Asiae, 2001), 246, fig. 220.

ruler Jawan Singh as a means of asserting the king's power in the wake of British colonization.[8]

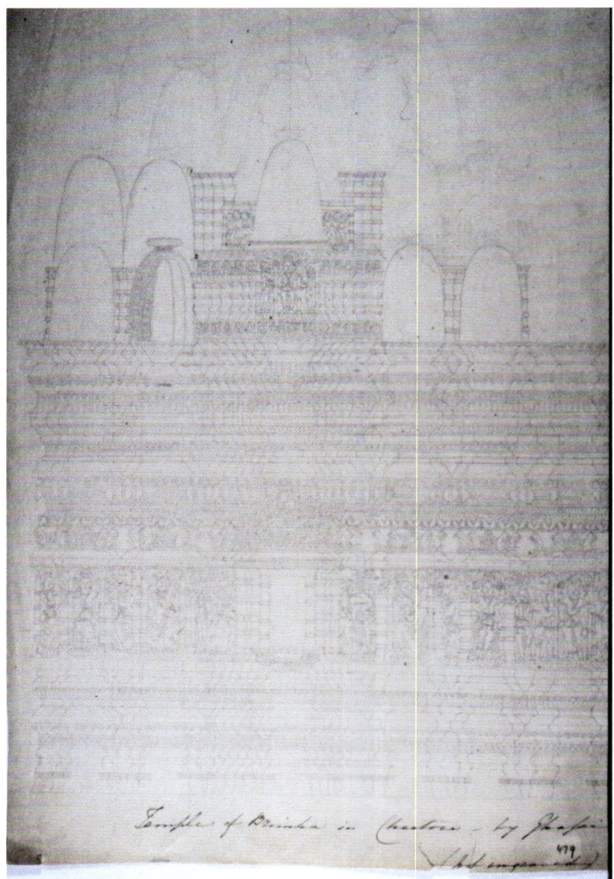

4.3. Temple at Chittor, inscribed on the front in ink by Tod "Temple of Brihma in Cheetore—by Ghassi—not engraved," Ghasi, c. 1821. Ink on paper, 43.5 × 29 cm. The Royal Asiatic Society, London; 037.161.

TOD'S *ANNALS* AND GHASI'S DRAWINGS

Tod's essay on the geography of Rajasthan in the *Annals*, along with the collections of regional manuscripts, paintings, and histories that he amassed, show that he commissioned a range of place-centric representations and deployed multiple methods of surveying to create knowledge of the topography and architecture of the region. For three key reasons, we will delve into this essay and archive.

First, the *Annals* constitute the earliest extensive English-language source in which we find assessments of early nineteenth-century visual practices that rendered northwestern India's sites and geographies onto paper—route maps used for travels, maps declaring territories, drawings of buildings that enlarged profiles of plinths and columns, architectural plans and elevations drawn on large sheets of paper, and watercolor sketches of forts, temples, towns, and cities of Rajasthan. Tod created a map of the region of northwestern India that he identified as a terra incognita; it is presented as a printed foldout in the first volume of the *Annals* and titled "Map of Rajasthan or Rajwarra, Embracing the Rajpoot Principalities of Central & Western India" (fig. 4.5). His description of the methods and persons employed in the making of maps offers insight into the nuances and politics of Tod's

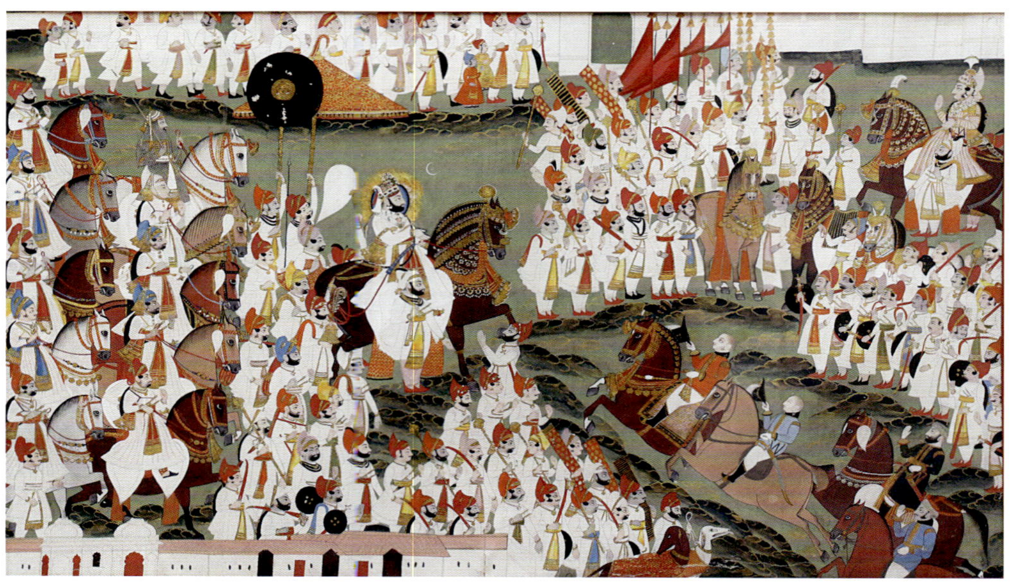

4.4. *Maharana Bhim Singh Greets Captain James Tod Outside the City*, attributed to Ghasi, c. 1820. Udaipur. Gouache and gold on paper, 66 × 100 cm. The City Palace Museum, Udaipur; 2012.19.0035_R.

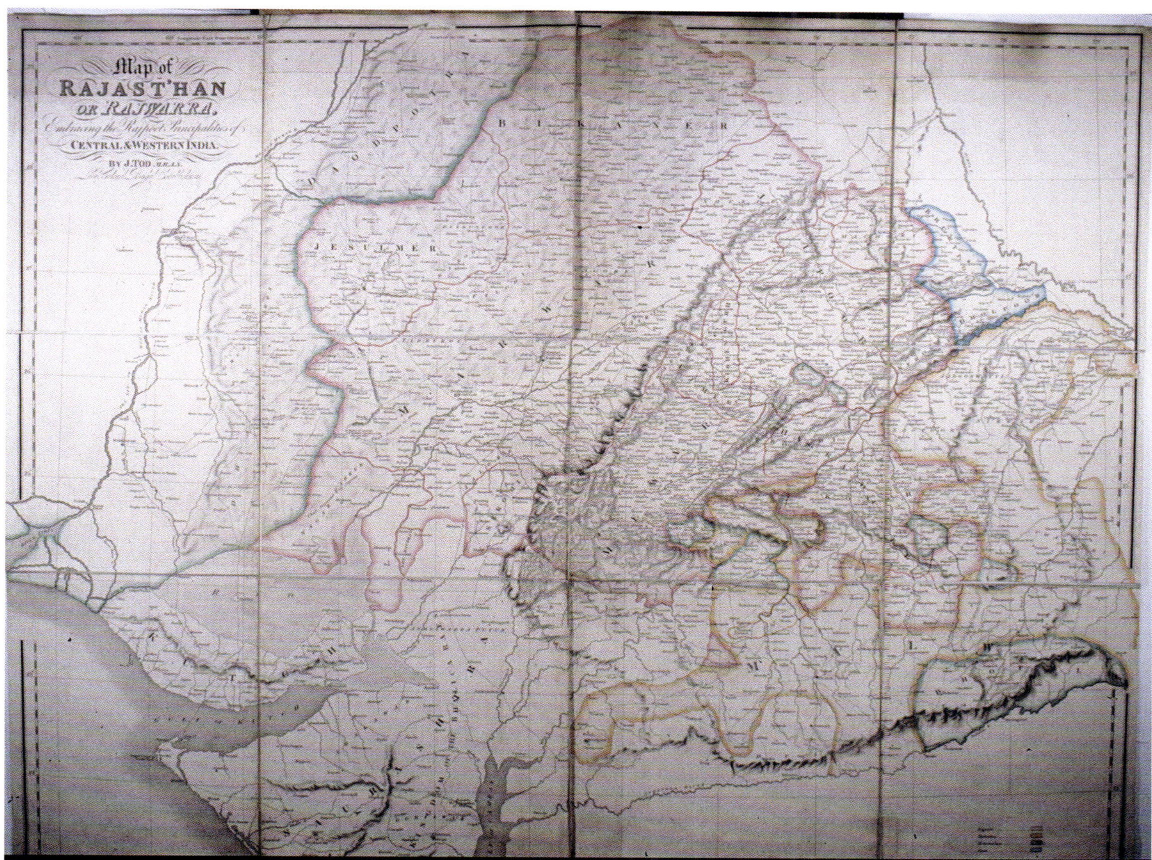

4.5. "Map of Rajasthan or Rajwarra, Embracing the Rajpoot Principalities of Central & Western India," James Tod, 1829. Engraving, 81.28 × 64.77 cm. Reproduced in James Tod, *Annals and Antiquities of Rajas'than* (London: Smith Elder, 1829), vol. 1, facing p. 1. The Royal Asiatic Society, London.

claims of accuracy—of his own endeavors and of the work of his assistants, including Ghasi.

Second, Tod's *Annals* and collections encapsulate a critical "contact zone" of knowledge making—a nineteenth-century project that compares and connects across place-centric genres.[9] Most studies have noted that Tod, a trained engineer, was the conduit through which a court painter like Ghasi would have received training in architectural drafting. This tacit assumption implies that Ghasi, as a painter, did not acquire any learning from a court workshop, whereas drawing the architecture of real places, while capturing their ambience, had in fact been central to the Udaipur court workshop since about 1700. In reconceptualizing the history of the long eighteenth century, prior to the declaration of the British Empire in the mid-nineteenth century, an aspect of scholarly work has entailed tracing the pivotal work of Indian artists and intellectuals—the "native" assistants who contributed to the making of Orientalist knowledge.[10] The enmeshed nature of the diverse intellectual histories and historical genres that proliferated before and during the colonial period, though, has received less attention.[11] Thus, examining the diverse kinds of preparatory material that contributed to the published *Annals* enables us to illuminate the very genres and expertise in drawing architecture and mapping places contributed by Indian artists and mapmakers. We find that Ghasi in particular forged critical conversations on the theme of picturing place, both within the world of the Udaipur court's visual culture of large-scale topographical paintings and between the visual and political worlds of the Udaipur court and the British company. Ghasi's paintings and drawings allow us to consider the agency of native assistants and artists from a visual perspective; that is, despite the lack of written sources acknowledging it, the visual archive of Ghasi's work enables us to think critically about his own travels rather than to focus exclusively on Tod's travels.

Third, the archive of drawings inscribed and attributed to Ghasi helps us determine the intermediary steps in visually conceiving the moods of place. How Udaipur painters carried out the practice of drawing architecture in the early decades of the nineteenth century, and how they adapted their line drawings in multiple directions for multiple communities of patrons and connoisseurs, illuminates pathways we have not been able to address previously. The preceding chapters have addressed how painters interpreted idealized aesthetic emotions that were celebrated in contemporaneous poetry—and how they evoked moods of longing and pleasure that seasons like the monsoon and spring brought and that spaces like lake palaces and lakefronts engendered in the real locales of Udaipur city. Ghasi's drawings enable us to address how Udaipur's artists created drawings of courtyards, individual palaces, street fronts, and temples to compose the moods of place in formal terms.

Recent collaborations among historians, conservation scientists, and art historians studying early modern attitudes toward "making and knowing" have pointed to the merit of reconstructing intermediate stages.[12] In the case of how-to manuals from Renaissance Europe, experiments by humanists and scientists have suggested that artisanal workshops played a key role in shaping theoretical shifts and that silences on the practical aspects of making could suggest that particular kinds of knowing were continually advanced among practitioners, even though they were not directly theorized in texts.[13] Ghasi's ways of knowing architecture and making large-scale paintings, as seen in the intermediary stages of his drawings—those prepared for the Udaipur's court workshop and for Tod's documentation projects—provide a rich and circumscribed archive to compare discursively constructed places. Tod's observations and history ultimately enable interpreting the formal innovations Ghasi brought to court paintings, especially for realigning the moods of the court and city of Udaipur in the first three decades of the ninteenth century.

MAP OF RAJASTHAN: "THE BLANK THE AUTHOR FILLED UP"

> The laborious research, in the course of which these data were accumulated, commenced in 1806, when the author was attached to the embassy sent, at the close of the Mahratta wars, to the court of Sindhia. This chieftain's army was then in Mewar, at that period almost a *terra incognita*, the position of whose two capitals, Udaipur and Chitor, in the best existing maps, was precisely reversed; that is, Chitor was inserted S.E. of Udaipur instead of E.N.E., a proof of the scanty knowledge possessed at that period.
>
> In other respects there was almost a total blank. In the maps prior to 1806 nearly all the western and central States of Rajasthan will be found wanting. It had been imagined, but a little time before, that the rivers had a southerly course into the Nerbudda; a notion corrected by the father of Indian geography, the distinguished Rennell.
>
> The blank the author filled up; and in 1815, for the first time, the geography of Rajasthan was put into combined form and presented to the Marquess of Hastings, on the eve of a general war, when the labour of ten years was amply rewarded by its becoming in part the foundation of that illustrious commander's plans of the campaign. It is a duty owing to himself to state that every map, without exception, printed since this period has its foundation, as regards Central and Western India, in the labours of the author.[14]

Tod's essay "Geography of Rajasthan or Rajputana," which opens volume one of the *Annals*, sets the spatial framework for the historical narrative that follows; it is also a compelling self-presentation of the author as an active producer of cartographic knowledge.[15] Soon after Tod's arrival in Bengal in March 1799—for his first posting in the Second European Regiment at Calcutta, where he was appointed a lieutenant in the Fourteenth Native Infantry—his skills as an engineer led to the first commission he received, to survey an "ancient canal" in Delhi in 1801. His early surveys were completed alongside British military operations against the Marathas that were focused on seizing forts and large tracts of land. Tod describes surveying as his "favorite project," for which he employed several survey teams: he notes discrepancies in previous maps; brings the reader's focus to Mewar and its capitals of Udaipur and Chittor; and connects his work to that of James Rennell, the first surveyor general of Bengal (1767–77), whose maps were celebrated among British antiquarians and East India Company officials at the time.[16] Tod divides the geographical essay into seventeen short sections, each of which includes a description of one central aspect, such as the land's mineral resources, agricultural products, or climate.[17] He lists the places, rivers, valleys, and routes that constituted his surveys, thereby amplifying the accompanying visual map. Tod also included key nuggets of information that rhetorically assert his expertise and his role in the production of new knowledge of the geography (and history) of central and western India.[18]

For Tod, claiming accuracy was imperative. The British in India promoted the ideal of systematic mapping through their great triangular survey of the subcontinent to create an imperial space that could be controlled and managed.[19] Like his British contemporaries, Tod too promoted this cartographic ideal. He gives evidence of cross-checking his own work as well as most of the work completed by his "survey parties."[20] The insistence on accuracy of the scientific methods and systematization that Tod deployed—as opposed to the methods and tools of native mapmakers—was absolutely imperative to making this new map an important geographical (and visual) artifact. His remarks on the instances of the valuable utilization of his map also read as evidence for claiming accuracy. Not only was Tod's map presented to the marquess of Hastings "on the eve of a general war," but also, according to Tod, "copies of [his] map on a reduced scale were sent to all the divisions of the armies in the field" to assist them in fighting the Marathas in 1817.[21] When copies circulated back to Europe, Tod notes, his map, which generated new cartographic information, was introduced into every recent map of India. Tod projected his discerning abilities from the very beginning of the *Annals*, which we must bear in mind as we turn to the drawings Ghasi prepared for this project.

Furthermore, Tod invokes the scientific nature of surveys as both substance and rhetoric, thereby alerting us to the role subjectivity and sentiment played in pronouncing the advanced nature of select technologies and pictorial regimes.[22] To make the terra incognita more accessible, Tod placed the reader on the peaks of the Aravalli hills and on top of Mount Abu, as well as atop several forts, including Chittorgarh and Kumbhalgarh. These bird's-eye views for imagining Rajasthan were always provided from locations within the boundaries of Mewar. To render the deserts of Rajasthan, Tod writes, "Let the reader again take post on Abu, by which he may be saved a painful journey over the Thal."[23] His projection of the journey through the desert as an uncomfortable one, which very likely corresponds to the experience of Tod and his soldiers, underwrites his "silence" and the failure to provide details on the specific resources of the desert; he characterizes this large part of northwestern India as unproductive and peripheral.[24] By contrast, Tod's prose gives the reader a visual image of moving across plateaus at Chittor and through valleys in Udaipur, making the state of Mewar central to the geography of Rajasthan and most productive. He includes a detailed account of the natural resources of minerals, stones, and metals—such as garnet, amethystine quartz, and rock crystal—thereby linking mines to the royal power of a few princely states, especially the lands of Mewar surrounding the Aravalli hills.[25] Mewar is thus proclaimed as a profitable territory with a moderate climate.[26]

In the *Annals*, history follows cartography. Tod's written account aligns with his map to create a dominance of Udaipur in multiple ways. In his "Map of Rajasthan or Rajwarra," the visuality of the shaded hills that denote the peaks of a mountainous terrain reinforces the prominence of central Rajasthan. The overabundance of the names of towns and cities connected by lines visually presents the intensity of attention that Tod's narrative bestows on the court and region of Mewar and particularly on its current capital, Udaipur. Yet Tod's map conceals as much as it reveals.

Given the embedded acknowledgments of native mapping practices within the writings of British East India Company officials like Tod and his predecessors, we can turn to Indian professionals as co-constituting and coproducing knowledge about the subcontinent in the early years of British military and mercantile expansion. In studying the emergence of modern mapping in Great Britain and early colonial India between the 1760s and 1820s, historians have located a kind of symmetry between Europe and South Asia in terms of practices and related artifacts, underscoring the link between cartographic developments and territorial expansion.[27] While describing his own investment in exhaustive and accurate survey work, Tod acknowledges "the aid of the natives," the skills of his survey parties and the knowledge of routes that letter bearers (*kāsid*) possessed. He thought that the two Indian men who led his mapping efforts, Shaikh Abu-l-Barakat and Madari Lal, were extremely proficient and understood that they could penetrate territories he personally could not.[28] Tod also invokes with admiration the recording, by "old Hindu governments," of distances between places, catalogued in bureaucratic documents. The empiricist in Tod was impressed by the use of "instruments" (tools for measuring distances), about which he learned from the *Abu Mahatamyam*, a text that praises the mountainous region of the Aravalli hills around Mount Abu, an important place for the sacred geography and pilgrimage practices of the Jain community.[29] We must therefore come to grips with both the earlier maps, such as those made in cartographic workshops of the eighteenth-century Jaipur court, as discussed in chapter 1, and the critical role played by Indian professionals—artists, mapmakers, and intellectuals—in Tod's projects.

To this end, we can look at one of the route maps found in Tod's unpublished collection, which suggests an important example of concurrent mapping practices (fig. 4.6). It likely supplied information on established routes and junctions that Tod's map of Rajasthan required in order to become a reliable cartographic artifact. This small rectangular map is composed of concentric rectangles with the names of towns and cities and the distances between them written along the vertical and horizontal axes in all four directions, as well as along the diagonal lines that indicate the directions between north, south, east, and west. Similar map diagrams, often called "charts," laid towns along the routes in each direction and in relation to a particular place in the center.[30] A mid-seventeenth-century example locates the town of Sojat—important for its religious landmarks, trading connections, and position at the center of nine forts within the boundaries of the early modern Marwar region—at its center.[31] In the example found in Tod's collection, the name of a town is missing from the central rectangle, though the maker labeled each of the directions. Because the chart's makers wrote the names of towns in a radial manner along the four directions, travelers would have continuously rotated this sheet of paper.[32] Along the northern direction, we see the names of cities and towns such as Ajmergadh, Chanderi, Payag, Kalpi, Agra, Malpur, Sirohi, and Nagor, and the list extends up to Kumaon and Kashmir within the Himalayas. When Tod describes his journey to Agra, he notes that "with a small guard I determined through untrodden fields," and the places he lists (for instance, the cities and towns of Ajmergadh, Chanderi, Payag, Kalpi, and Agra) match the sequence of towns marked in the northern direction.[33] This correspondence entices us to consider the possibility that this map was at least partially employed in Tod's own travels.[34] A second trace of this small map being used by a traveler is found in the corrections noted along the southern axis. Within the names of places listed along this axis (including Surat Ahmedavad, Vadsal, Navsari, Kankaltirth, and Porbandir), we find the evidence that new information on the names of places and corrected distances has been added in a scribal writing slightly different from that used on the rest of the map. While Tod would have us believe that he operated in a terra incognita, as in the case of historical narratives, he was not operating within a tabula rasa of either historical narratives or cartographic and architectural images.

Tod's collections reveal that the British agent's approach toward regional maps and other geographical sources departed from his approach toward regional histories. Of the several personnel who traveled with Tod, the *yati* (Jain monk) Gyanchandra, who served as Tod's tutor and intellectual informant, helped him navigate through several historical literary manuscripts, especially the *Pṛithvīrāj Rāso*, a story of the legendary king Prithviraj. The most popular recension of this story was written at the Mewar court in the early eighteenth century.[35] Tod praises Gyanchandra's intellect on several occasions in the *Annals*. Through an in-depth study of Tod's unpublished handwritten notes on the *Pṛithvīrāj Rāso*, found within a two-volume set of five large leather-bound books, Talbot has shown that Tod's translation in the published *Annals* departs only minimally from these notes.[36] This intermediary manuscript, considered alongside the dates of Gyanchandra's travels with Tod, demonstrates Tod's deep engagement with the sources he amassed, but it also leads Talbot to argue that he was likely unable to read or translate the text without the Jain intellectual's help.[37] While Tod regretted that his map of Rajasthan could not be as detailed as he had initially imagined, he desired to extend his conceptualization of geographical practices in relation to the "remains of ancient geography as can be extracted from the Puranas and other Hindu authorities."[38] Tod, therefore, must have interpreted the contemporary practices of the members of his team who surveyed the lines of route and thus enabled the production of his map of Rajasthan, either as contiguous with his own practices or as unworthy of comparing or detailing further.[39] It may be possible to consider a similar transfer of knowledge between Tod's "Map of Rajasthan or Rajwarra" and regional schematic route maps and charts that proliferated across northwestern India.

The interactions among painters working in distinct traditions and the production of multiple kinds of local knowledge gain an even stronger presence when we take into account the drawings and maps that Tod omitted from his published *Annals* and those his engravers transformed for publication. Most of the engravings published in the *Annals* were based on Waugh's watercolors of forts and palaces, represented as isolated buildings within landscapes overtaken by vegetative growth. The professional artist who prepared the drawings for the engraver Edward Finden, who is credited as the author of all the printed plates in the *Annals*, enhanced Waugh's originals; we can chart this process by examining the originals alongside the professional artist's adaptations, copies of engraving proofs, and the final published images.[40] Tod was extremely invested in decisions about how the archive of drawings he had collected would be transformed into engravings. Many annotations—"cattle to be enlarged,"[41] "ferry boats admirable,"[42] "no boats with sails," "omit the elephant,"

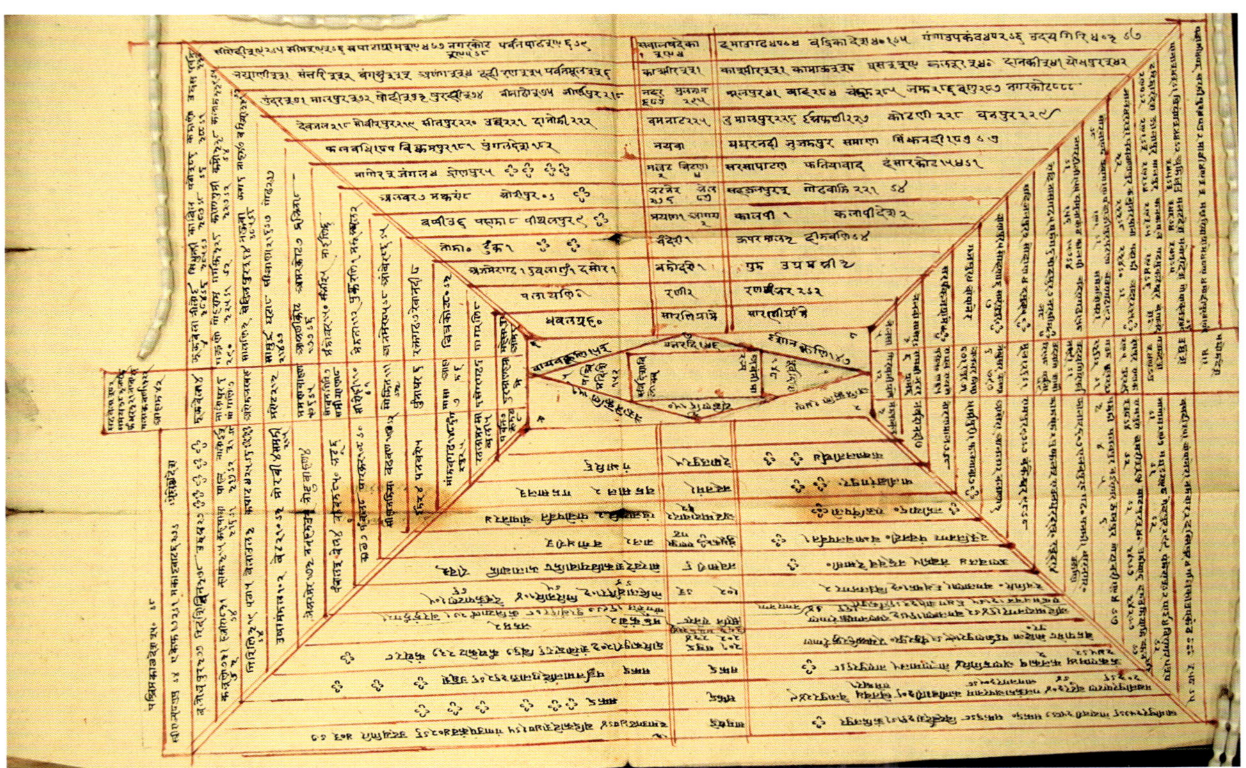

4.6. Route map/chart that includes the label "Map of Distances from Oojein as Meridian," from the collection of British agent James Tod, date unknown. Black ink on paper, 50.8 cm × 31.11 cm. The Royal Asiatic Society, London.

"the cupola to have more breadth than elevation"[43]—appear on sketches and watercolors made by Waugh. It is plausible that Tod was involved in choosing, correcting, and checking the final proofs of the visuals for his book.

The engraving "East View of the Palace of Oodipoor," which appears in the *Annals* adjacent to the opening of "Annals of Mewar," a section that recounts stories of events, conquests, and kingly achievements that Tod saw as significant in the history of the Mewar court, is instructive (fig. 4.7). It displays the choices that resulted in the engravings that ultimately appeared in the *Annals* and, in the process, the viewpoints that were eliminated. While we do not have an intermediary drawing in Tod's collections that would have served as the basis for Finden's engraving, the departures from Waugh's original seem deliberate. In his rendering, *View of the Palace of Oodipoor*, as discussed in the introduction, Waugh does not suggest the vastness of the valley and the lake or the city's reflection within waters brimming at the banks (see fig. I.5). In Finden's engraving, the reflections of Udaipur's palaces in the lake waters are highlighted, and the mountains in the backdrop are carefully recomposed to emphasize the horizon at the center of the image's horizontal axis. Also, added in the foreground are plants and trees drawn at a comparatively larger scale that heightens a sense of the lake's expanse. It is plausible that Finden, the professional artist whose image must have been the basis for this plate, or even Tod did not regard Waugh's original watercolor to be quite as picturesque as they preferred.[44] While the engraving "East View of the Palace of Oodipoor" ultimately found a formidable place in the *Annals*, Waugh's drawing is also significant in its hinting at the vantage point from which the artist made a sketch of the city's lake and palaces: Waugh included in his drawing two figures sitting on a platform on the other (near) side of the lake, but these figures are eliminated in Finden's engraving (fig. 4.8). It is tempting to imagine that the two figures depicted in the original—one in a hat holding a

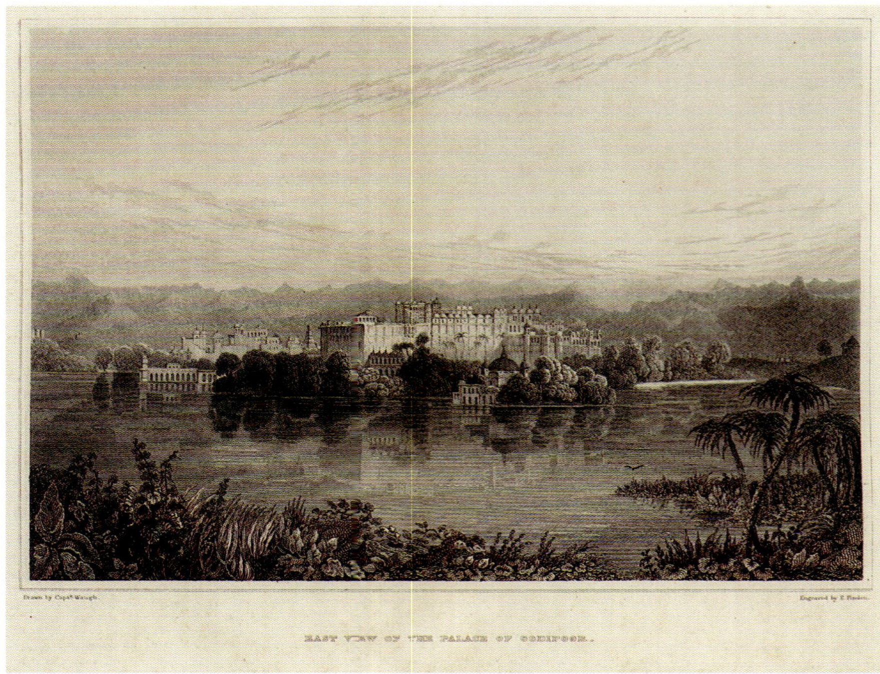

4.7. "East View of the Palace of Oodipoor," artist Patrick Waugh, engraver Edward Finden, from James Tod, *Annals and Antiquities of Rajast'han* (London: Smith Elder, 1829), vol. 1, facing p. 211. British Library Board, London; W 421/1(2).

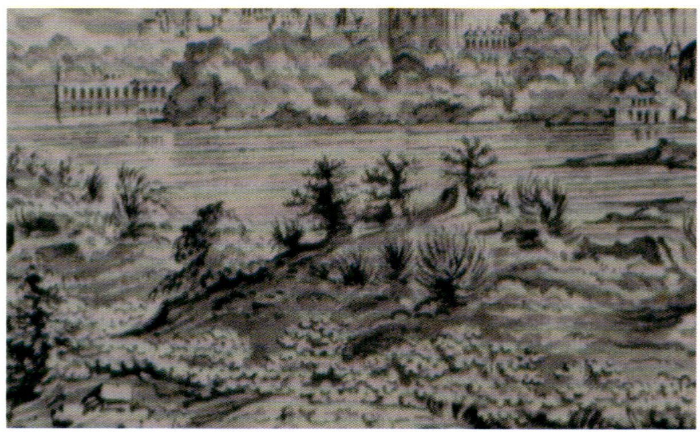

4.8. Detail of fig. I.5, *View of the Palace of Oodipoor*. Two seated figures, possibly Patrick Waugh and Ghasi sketching the view, are depicted near the painting's lower edge.

sketchpad, the other in a turban—are Waugh's portraits of himself and of Ghasi as Tod's artist-assistants.

The sketches and drawings of Tod's accompanying artists—Waugh and Ghasi—viewed alongside the published engravings tell a nuanced story of the work accomplished on the ground during their shared travels. Surveying Tod's exhaustive archive, we realize that Waugh and Ghasi are almost equally represented in his collecting enterprise, even if the presence of their works in the *Annals* remains unequal. The bulk of Ghasi's oeuvre is omitted from the *Annals*. Tod's contact with Ghasi may have alerted the British official to the value of Ghasi's drawing skills for other genres and for another kind of project he would soon undertake with Tod as his new patron; the type of skill Ghasi displayed in creating detailed drawings of architecture does not appear to have been the forte of any of Tod's team members—including Tod himself. The images—maps depicting territorial boundaries and travel routes, watercolors of forts and palaces, and line drawings constituting architectural facades and details—that appear as engravings within the *Annals* are not purely illustrative. Any interpretation of how Tod used Ghasi's and Waugh's sketches must take into account: where the visuals appear in the first edition of the printed *Annals*, the complete corpus of unpublished drawings and paintings by Waugh and Ghasi, the professional artist's watercolors that were commissioned for transforming the visuals into engravings, and the multiple proofs of the engravings themselves. Beyond their sole connection to Tod's published *Annals*, both Waugh's and Ghasi's works can be mined to consider the practices of viewing and picturing architecture that intersected in this critical contact zone.

Because we know little about Ghasi's artistic practice prior to 1820, excavating the intersecting ways in which Tod and his assistants constituted the places of Rajasthan proves fruitful on two accounts. First, we learn about the comparative role Ghasi's pictures perform inside and outside Tod's *Annals*. Second, we understand that Ghasi, like the early eighteenth-century painters and mapmakers of Jaipur's cartography workshop who painted maps and other kinds of pictorial genres, attesting to the conversations among court professionals, also encountered multiple modalities of representing places during his travels alongside Tod.[45] However, Ghasi does not seem at all invested in the pictorial possibilities presented by Waugh's landscapes. Ghasi's works display the choice to render the minutiae of the sculpted architectural forms that constituted the towers and ceilings of northwestern India's temples.

IMAGINING "THE AID OF THE NATIVES"

Nothing captures the disjunctive nature of the pictorial translations that are at play in Tod's history more fully than the impressive frontispiece, "Maharana Bheem Sing, Prince of Oodipoor," that opens volume one of the *Annals* (fig. 4.9). It is labeled as "drawn by Captain Waugh and engraved by E. Finden." Bhim Singh is portrayed riding his horse and smoking a hookah as he embarks upon a journey (*savārī*), accompanied by an entourage of courtiers, one of whom holds a fan with the striking sun emblem of the Mewar court. This depiction immediately reminds one of several portraits by Udaipur's court artists that sought to represent rulers, including Bhim Singh, within processional settings. Tod's assigning of credit for the engraving of Bhim Singh to Waugh, and not acknowledging that the image was based on the painting of a "native artist," is misleading. Indeed, Finden's engraving was based on a watercolor by a professional British artist (fig. 4.10), which in turn had used a portrait of Bhim Singh by Ghasi as its source (fig. 4.1).[46] Both of these—the original Udaipur portrait in opaque watercolor and gold on paper and the sepia copy on card—are included in Tod's collections. The delicateness with which the faces and ground are rendered in the sepia tones makes it highly unlikely that the British amateur artist Waugh, who traveled with Tod and Ghasi, made this version. Rather, this artwork appears to be the product of a professional artist, the British artist Thomas Strothard, who worked with Edward Finden and created watercolor sketches for several engravings. Finden's engraving and Stothard's rendering unmistakably adapt Ghasi's equestrian portrait that Tod had collected. Among the limited numbers of extant examples of these kinds of visual practices, the painting, drawing, and engraving that together constitute the frontispiece of Tod's *Annals* make an incisive point about the mobility of genres, artists, and authorship in early colonial India.[47]

On the level of political symbolism, the translations at play are most strongly iterated in the British artist's and the engraver's elimination of the golden halo that signals Bhim Singh's royal status within Ghasi's painting (fig. 4.11). The professional artist elongated the bodies of most of the figures and attempted to give them a three-dimensional character with the use of shading and tinting and by adapting their postures to show bodies in movement (fig. 4.12). He also transformed the landscape setting. Bhim Singh and his entourage appear against a sparse background, whereas Ghasi attempted to create the ambience of a moonlit sky with rolling, almost roaring, monsoon clouds. Ghasi's Mewar landscape of rugged earth, plants, and stones in green and gold is substituted with a tiny set of coconut trees and two human bodies or staffage in the distant background, the standard features of the picturesque landscape from this time. This particular stylization of northwestern India's landscape inserts Bhim Singh's procession in a very different time and space. The effect of the portrait's displacement from Udaipur's painted lands and emplacement into a distinct scenic landscape is further enhanced in Edward Finden's translation of the watercolor into an engraving.

Engravings of temple sites and architectural details based on Ghasi's drawings are published within Tod's "personal narrative," found at the end of volume two. This is the first instance in which we see Ghasi's works featured—and acknowledged—within the *Annals*. The engravings based on his drawings include columns, ceilings, and temple towers from buildings at the site of Chittorgarh, Mewar's former capital fort until the mid-sixteenth century, and from temples at the sites of Baroli and Chandravati, built in the seventh and tenth centuries, respectively.[48] An engraving titled "Columns of Temples at Chandravati" is embedded in Tod's writing on festivals in Rajput lands, a section that does not refer to the temple site (fig. 4.13).[49] An examination of Ghasi's drawing (as opposed to the engraving) demonstrates that his attention was focused on the details of different types of columns. He composed six types, each on individual large-scale sheets of European paper with watermarks (each sheet measuring 40.4 by 24.4 centimeters). Finden's engraving combines three column types based on Ghasi's drafts of individual columns, following Tod's instructions to "copy," written on the backs of four of the sheets of paper.[50] Ghasi's column drawings initially appear to be made in pen and ink, but a close inspection reveals that the artist deployed paint and brush in a very precise manner. He drafted extremely faint construction lines, which guided him to symmetrically draw the curves of the foliage sprouting from the pot-shaped forms represented on the upper part of each column shaft. These drawings affirm that the painter was interested in systematically drawing the architecture of

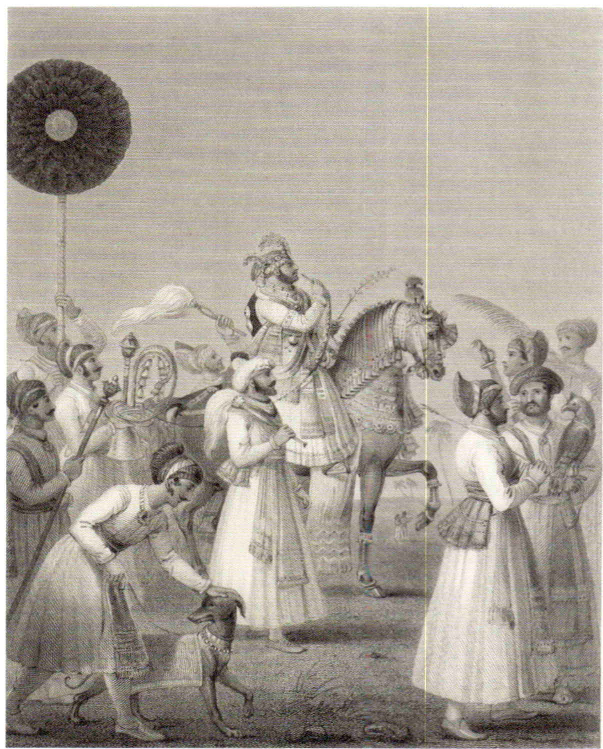

4.9. "Maharana Bheem Sing, Prince of Oodipoor," engraver Edward Finden, after Thomas Strothard's watercolor (fig. 4.10), mistakenly attributed to Patrick Waugh, from James Tod, *Annals and Antiquities of Rajast'han* (London: Smith Elder, 1829), vol. 1, frontispiece. British Library Board, London; W421/1 (frontis).

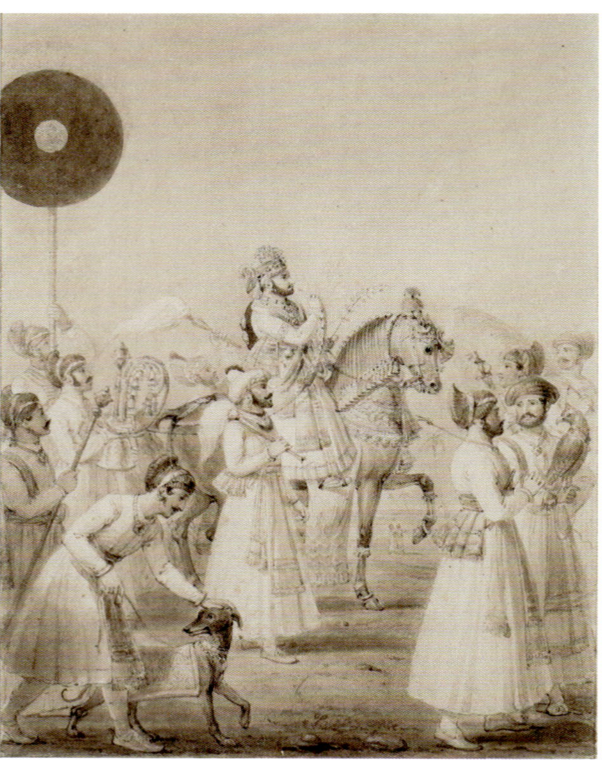

4.10. "Maharana Bheem Sing, Prince of Oodipoor," attributed to Thomas Strothard, after Ghasi's portrait (fig. 4.1), c. 1829. Sepia on card, 17.4 × 13.5 cm. The Royal Asiatic Society, London; 037.001.

the sites he visited—not from a distance but by getting up close, recording each curve, each recess, and each projection.

Together, these engravings published in the final section of the *Annals* convey architectural knowledge about the sites in a range of representational modes. To capture the architectural grandeur of Baroli, for instance, Tod includes an elevation of one of its temples. This image, titled "Outline of a Temple to Mahadeva at Barolli," depicts the sculpted figures and aedicular elements that constitute the temple tower (*śikhara*), structural elements that constitute the entrance portico of the temple, and the aniconic form of a Shiva lingam in the temple hall (fig. 4.14). The inner sanctum is drawn in a smaller size to suggest its location at the far end of the temple. Other engravings in this section based on Ghasi's originals include "Sculpted Niche on the Exterior of the Temple at Barolli," an elevation that depicts the horizontal protruding sill and the vertical columns that constitute the recesses and projections on the temple walls (fig. 4.15);[51] and "Ceiling of the Portico of Temple at Barolli," a plan depicting a section of the temple roof (as seen from inside) constituted by complex geometric patterns distributed within nesting squares (fig. 4.16).[52]

Ghasi's drawings reflect a systematic project. The artist has drawn very fine lines, as seen in the drawing of a column at Chittor, often taking the time to highlight the sculptural depth of the stone with thin parallel lines of gray wash (fig. 4.17).[53] Similarly, an elevation entitled "Entrance to the Sanctuary of a Temple at Chandravati" depicts the fine details of the animals sculpted on the lower friezes along the plinth walls and the combination of vegetal scrolling patterns and sculpted figures of deities that adorn the stone jambs of the temple entrance (fig. 4.18). Tod writes, "Ghasi is now at work upon the outline of two of the remaining shrines, and has promised to give up ten days to the details of the ceiling, the

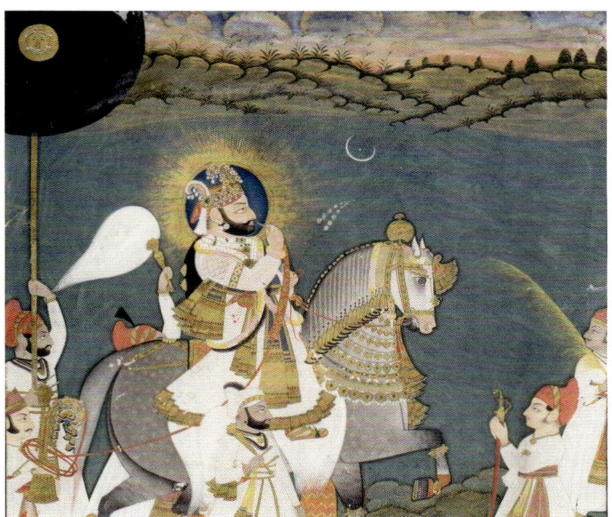

4.11. Detail of fig. 4.1. Depiction of landscape of rolling hills in opaque watercolor in tones of green and gold paint.

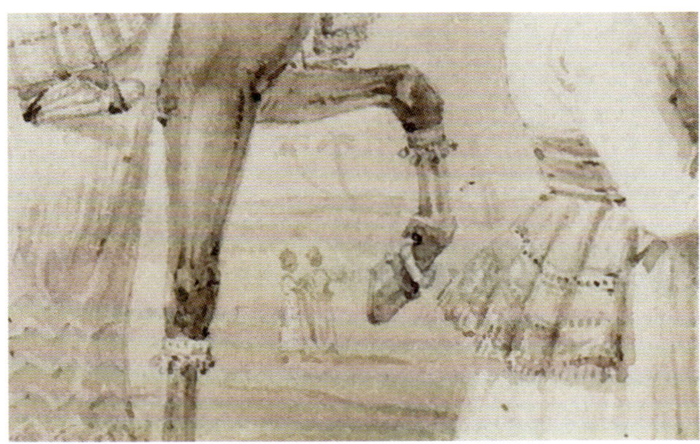

4.12. Detail of fig. 4.10. In background, depiction of landscape with palm trees and two human figures in sepia watercolor.

columns, and the rich varied ornaments, which pencil alone can represent."[54] As seen in this drawing, Ghasi's expertise in making pictures that paid careful attention to details in order to describe how sculpture was integrated with the temple walls explains why Tod's writing uncharacteristically surrendered to the efficacy of Ghasi's representations.[55] It is thus unsurprising that within Tod's vast collections we do not find a single annotation on Ghasi's drawings in Tod's handwriting that suggests corrections. Nor do we find any professional artist proofs based on Ghasi's architectural drawings. It is highly unlikely that Finden would have prepared his engravings directly from Ghasi's fine drawings, as often there is considerable difference in scale between the drawings and the engravings. Yet Finden's engravings based on Ghasi's drawings, unlike his transformations of Waugh's watercolors, as discussed above regarding the "East View of the Palace of Oodipoor," rarely depart from the Udaipur artist's renderings.

These detailed drawings of parts of temples most likely led to the production of the fine elevations Ghasi created to meet the demands of Tod's project. It is not that temple elevations are not seen in earlier Udaipur court paintings, but that Ghasi appears to have come to value finished elevation drawings in a new way as part of his understanding of which of his skills and knowledge Tod valued. To characterize the representational modes and drawings that we see at play in Ghasi's work simply as images that represent something called European "influence," operating in a single direction, completely flattens the complexity of pictorial genres and the translation and transformation of images that are embodied in Tod's collections.[56] Tod was trained as a military engineer and was engaged in drafting plans at Chittor and at the cave sites at Dhamnar in Indore;[57] however, he was most interested in applying his drafting skills to the large-scale mapping of sites as well as to the larger tracts and routes that constitute his map of Rajasthan. All the published engravings and Ghasi's drawings attest to a different skill set, best exemplified in Ghasi's depictions of the interiors and exteriors of temple architecture in various representational formats. It becomes critical to recognize that Ghasi's skills at drafting were largely based on his training as a painter in the Udaipur court painting workshop. He deployed these skills in transcultural spaces and in the process possibly realized the distinct value his drawings imparted across image ontologies and patronage circles.

Additionally, a large corpus of Ghasi's unpublished drawings exposes the artist's practices of "knowing" architectural space and mediating this knowledge by making drawings on

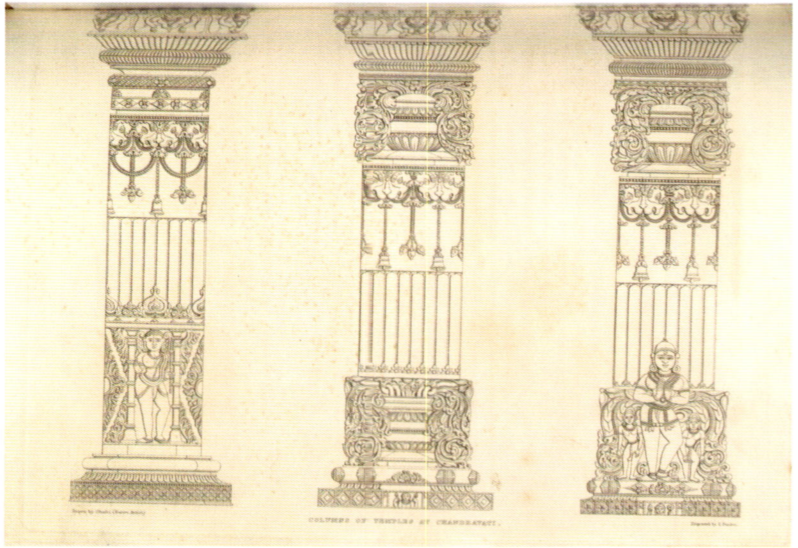

4.13. "Columns of Temples at Chandravati," artist Ghasi, engraver Edward Finden, from James Tod, *Annals and Antiquities of Rajast'han* (London: Smith Elder, 1829), vol. 1, facing p. 574. British Library Board, London; W421/1(11).

4.14. "Outline of a Temple to Mahadeva at Barolli," artist Ghasi (mistakenly attributed to Patrick Waugh), engraver Edward Finden, from Tod, *Annals and Antiquities of Rajast'han* (London: Smith Elder, 1832), vol. 2, facing p. 706. British Library Board, London; W421/2(5).

4.15. "Sculpted Niche on the Exterior of the Temple at Barolli," artist Ghasi, engraver Edward Finden, from James Tod, *Annals and Antiquities of Rajast'han* (London: Smith Elder, 1832), vol. 2, facing p. 707. British Library Board, London; W421/2 (6).

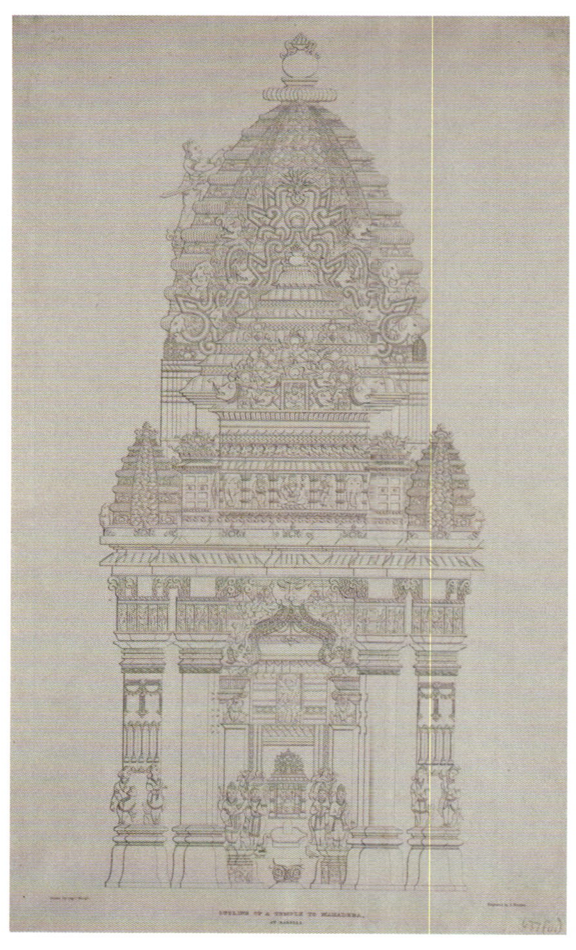

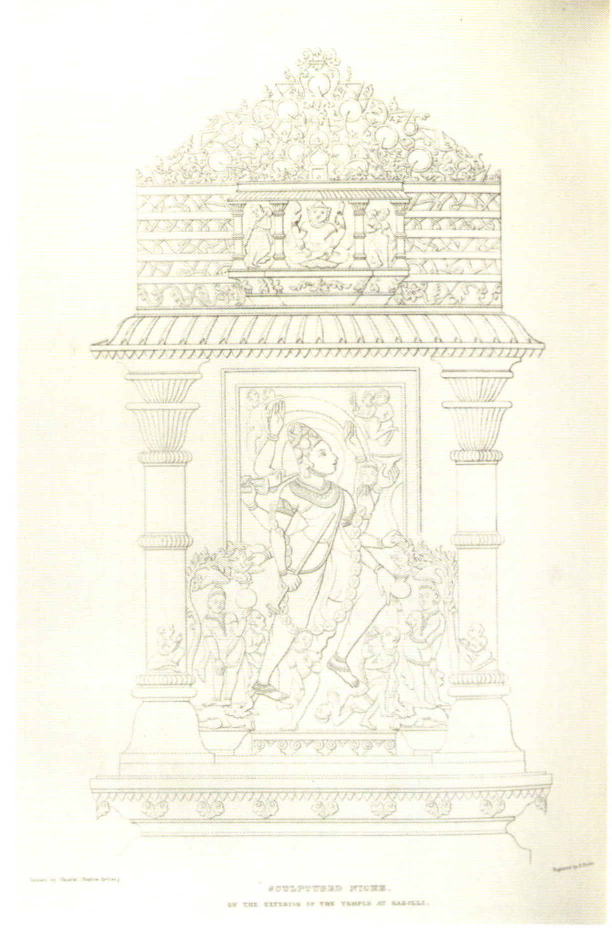

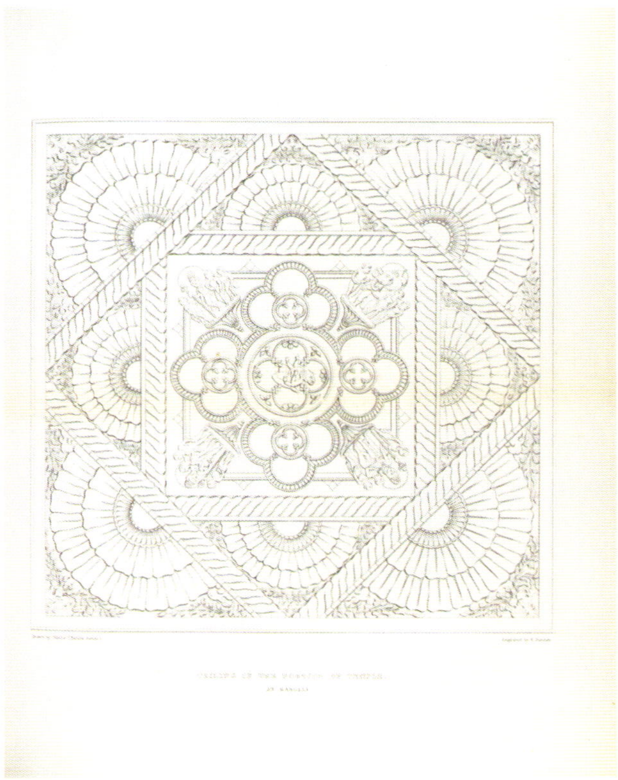

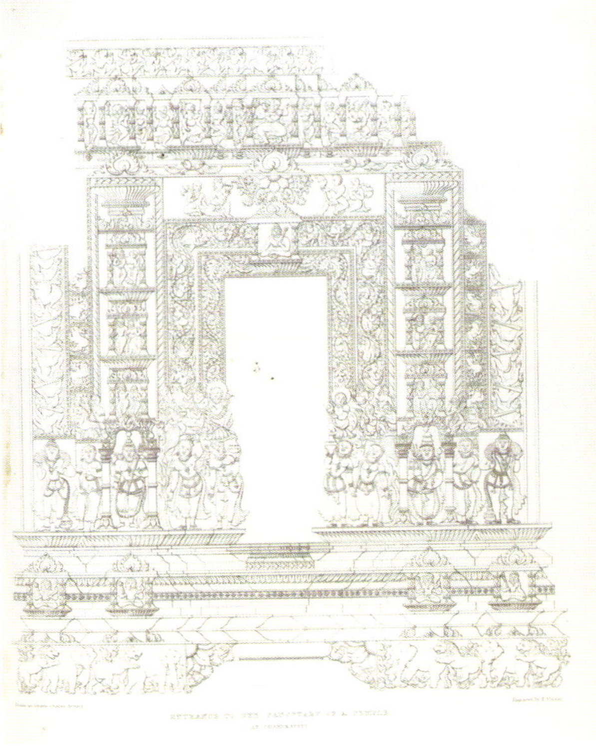

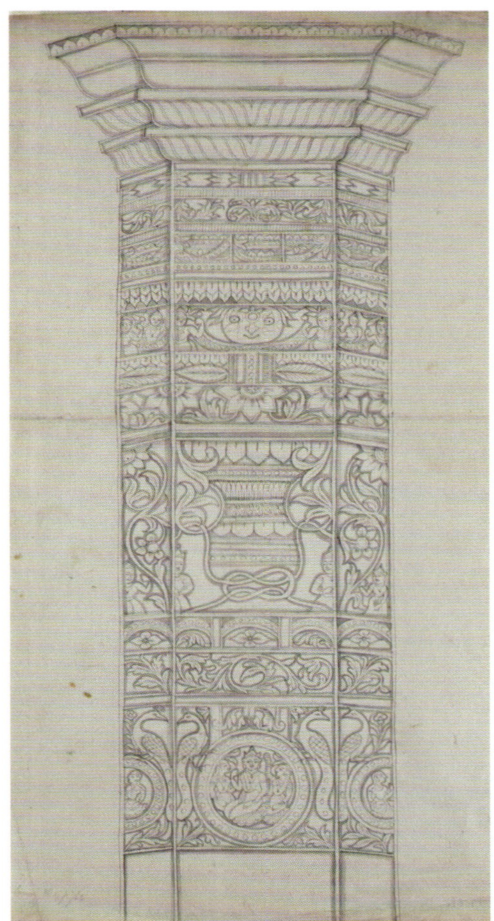

4.16. "Ceiling of the Portico of Temple at Barolli," artist Ghasi, engraver Edward Finden, from James Tod, *Annals and Antiquities of Rajast'han*, (London: Smith Elder, 1832), vol. 2, facing p. 708. British Library Board, London; W421/2(7)

4.17. Drawing of a column at Chittor, Ghasi, 1822. Pen and ink and wash, 44 × 23.2 cm. The Royal Asiatic Society, London; 037.121.

4.18. "Entrance to the Sanctuary of a Temple at Chandravati," artist Ghasi, engraver Edward Finden, from James Tod, *Annals and Antiquities of Rajast'han* (London: Smith Elder, 1832), vol. 2, facing p. 734. British Library Board, London; W421/2 (17).

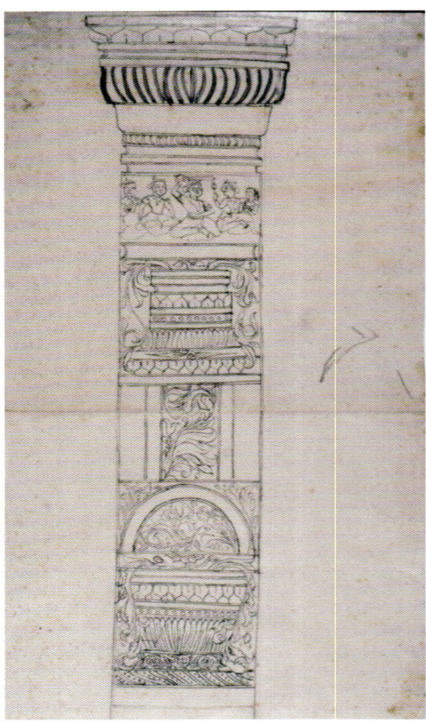

4.19. *Column in the Fortress of Cheetore*, Ghasi, c. 1820. Ink on Indian paper, 50 × 23.5 cm. The Royal Asiatic Society, London; 037.119.

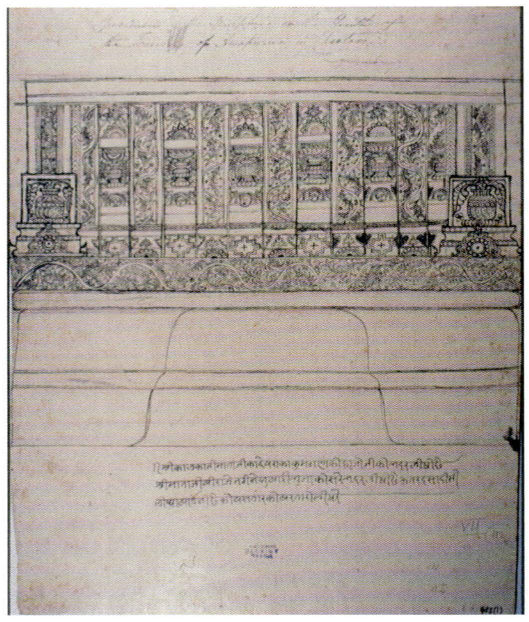

4.20. *Sculptured Frieze on a Temple at Chittor*, inscribed on the front by Tod (written upside down) "Specimen of the sculpture on the plinth of the temple of Anapurna in Cheetore . . . (fragment) . . . ," Ghasi, c. 1820. Ink on Indian paper, 24.8 × 34 cm. The Royal Asiatic Society, London; 037.171.

paper that focus on various parts of buildings as independent subjects. Most of these drawings present buildings from the site of Chittor: they include base moldings, columns, and temple towers drawn in dark, thick lines on a larger scale on sheets of thick local paper (figs. 4.19 and 4.20). In this subcorpus are also fairly finished drawings not reproduced in the *Annals*, such as an impressive elevation of Chittor's Brahma temple, done on European paper (fig. 4.3).[58] Ghasi's work betrays an interest in conveying the architectonics of the buildings in a comprehensive manner and in giving attention to the structure and proportions of the building as well as to the sculptural elements. The artist was invested in how the layers of architectural spaces—entrances that lead to main hall of the temple, for example, which further leads to the inner sanctum—could be delineated within the conventions of two-dimensional architectural drawings, particularly in the format of an elevation. These unpublished drawings on local paper in all likelihood constituted the artist's preparatory drawings of architectural elements from which he combined information to fill in details within building elevations.[59]

That Tod chose the engraving of Bhim Singh for the frontispiece of the *Annals* is metaphorical in multiple ways. Tod's use of Ghasi's composition as a frontispiece—without acknowledging him as the artist—could have been a decision that emerged from conversations with his publishers. The engraving gestures to travels and to an entourage in motion, which Tod describes in the *Annals* but in the context of his own journey through Rajasthan. Ghasi's portraits of Tod traveling with his entourage (fig. 4.4), although larger, are comparable in terms of composition to this portrait of Bhim Singh. Of course, using his own portrait as a frontispiece would have been too self-aggrandizing for Tod. The pictorial translations embodied in this engraving of Bhim Singh suggest that Ghasi's agency remains but a shadow in the printed *Annals*. Ghasi emerges in whispers in some instances and is untraceable in several others. Seen against the context of Ghasi's presence within Tod's collections—though not within the *Annals*—the anomalous figure of a man shown climbing the tower in Ghasi's sketch of the elevation of the temple at Baroli is rather intriguing (fig. 4.14). Although such a speculation cannot be substantiated, it is rather enticing to interpret this figure as a self-portrait of Ghasi climbing the temple tower to measure the curve of its lotus-shaped molding, despite the fact that the depicted person carries a sword rather than an artist's or draftsman's tools.

This chapter opened with ramifying evidence from multiple images that demonstrates how Ghasi circulated pictorial topoi and artistic skills in architectural representations across genres as he himself circulated among patronage circles and as his paintings were circulated by and among various audiences. Ultimately, Ghasi also used the ways of representing architecture that had currency within Tod's documentation project to make monumental courtly portraits, which praise the kingship, power, and devotional journeys of the Udaipur ruler Jawan Singh, successor to Bhim Singh. This wide-ranging corpus—spanning representations of architecture for projects of documentation to court paintings depicting Udaipur kings' durbars and ritual visits to temples—suggests the back-and-forth Ghasi established between idioms of praise and knowledge.

ELEVATION OF DEVOTION, C. 1830

Following Tod's departure from Rajasthan in 1822, Ghasi put the vocabulary of architectural drawing to his own distinctive uses for his next patron, Maharana Jawan Singh. Two impressive paintings depict Jawan Singh's visits to the Vishnupad temple at Gaya and to the Vishvanath temple complex at Kashi (present-day Varanasi). Both can be attributed to Ghasi, and both are commemorative in nature, related to a long pilgrimage tour of Mathura, Vrindaban, Ayodhya, Allahabad, Kashi, and Gaya that Jawan Singh undertook in 1833–34.[60] On the back of the painting *Maharana Jawan Singh Visiting Vishnupad Temple at Gaya* the scribe notes that Jawan Singh's visit to Gaya for the darshan (devotional viewing) of the temple's Vishnu icon took place on January 23, 1834 (fig. 4.2).[61] Over the course of the eighteenth century, the Marathas consolidated their power by commissioning temple repair and restoration projects as well as building temples beyond their territorial domains in the Deccan.[62] Among the Holkar Marathas based in the region of Malwa, Ahilyabai, the queen of Maheshwar, was the key patron of several temples, including both mentioned above; the Vishvanath temple in Kashi was completed in 1777, and the Vishnupad temple in Gaya was commissioned ten years later.[63] In the following section, a brief discussion of the significance of the maharana's journeys in the shifting political context of the 1830s will in turn highlight the potential modes in which Ghasi's pilgrimage paintings operated. However, a comprehensive consideration of the politics, piety, and diplomacy of Jawan Singh's pilgrimage in the early colonial period and the role temples and artworks played within these intersecting domains will be addressed in a later work. For now, I analyze Ghasi's pilgrimage paintings to a limited extent, with the aim to tease out the artist's designs of architectural compositions that evoked on paper the moods of exclusive ritual viewings of prestigious shrines and monumental temples that lay beyond the lands of Mewar.

In *Maharana Jawan Singh Visiting Vishnupad Temple at Gaya*, Ghasi evoked the feeling of a devotee inside the devotional precinct. He centralized the elevation of the temple shrine, and the picture is framed by a representation of the arched arcade that created a boundary for the temple courtyard. In the miniaturized portrait of Jawan Singh worshipping with a priest and surrounded by a group of courtiers, the king's haloed figure is only nominally larger than the depictions of the courtly nobles and laypeople—men, women, and children—who surround him and who populate the temple complex. The painter's use of oblique lines that project outward from the planimetric view of the temple courtyard, on the left side of the picture, recalls pictorial strategies adopted by Udaipur painters, as seen in chapter 3, to depict the courtyards of the Jagniwas lake palace and reinforce their interiority (see figs. 3.9 and 3.10). Here, the temple's boundary abuts the edges of the paper. Ghasi aligned the small domed entrance along the central axis of the temple's elevation and the painted composition; its threshold is emphasized by the presence of an oversize gold temple bell. Both the bodies of the represented devotees and the gaze of the painting's audience are located thus inside the bounded frame of the temple precinct.

The second, even larger painting, *Maharana Jawan Singh Visiting the Vishvanath Temple at Kashi*, demonstrates the negotiation of a similar set of pictorial choices (fig. 4.21).[64] These assert Ghasi's role in creating this monumental artwork, which is studied here on the basis of a line drawing representing the composition. The boundaries of this larger temple complex are set off by elevations of smaller shrines in the corners and by double-tier boundary walls with entrance gateways that run along the painting's bottom and top edges. The temple, with its two towers (one on either end) and open arcade hall with a domed roof (in the center), forms the focus of the composition. The horizontality of the facade of the main temple building is echoed in the painter's careful delineation of two horizontal verandas with open arcades that stack up along the length of the painting and in his placement of two smaller temple towers in the painting's lower register. The narrow strip of blue sky at the top edge of the paper, apart from such established conventions within Udaipur court painting, further urges us to connect the horizontal tiers as representing a progression of space from the main building to the arcade behind, and then on to a second layer of a boundary wall, with an entrance and another arcade behind it, most likely part of the Gyanvyapi temple located at the rear end of the Vishvanath temple. The miniature figure of Jawan Singh, depicted ten times, appears in the central hall, next to multiple shrines and icons, and in the arcade of the adjoining precinct—he is in every corner of the temple complex and the painted picture. Our eyes pursue Jawan Singh's round ceremonial umbrella held by his attendants and the group of nobles who follow him. We thus locate the king amid the architecture and the scores of people. The details of the king, garbed in deep red and gold robes, and the same noble, wearing dark blue and gold robes, accompanying him in each case, become secondary to the painted architecture.

The painter's use of monochromatic hues enhances the way in which architecture frames the royal portrait and enacts the king's devotion. In the painting *Maharana Jawan Singh Visiting Vishnupad Temple at Gaya*, gray and blue tones denote the arches of verandas and open buildings, in contrast to the white temple with its precise outlines; in the other example, burnt sienna is used to depict the temple. Most of the depicted people in this second picture, of the Vishvanath temple, apart from the king and his courtly sidekick, wear white clothing. Their groupings, in concert with their miniature scale, exaggerate the gigantic expanse of the temple precinct. Each of these pictorial strategies—form, scale, and color—embodies deliberate artistic choices. Integrated in the ways seen in both of the paintings commemorating Jawan Singh's temple visits, they create a visual effect that breaks from older depictions of royal piety. The details of architectural elements, depicted with fine brushwork in one of the final layers of paint applied to each picture, surge to the front and meet our eyes as one among the many graphic qualities the two paintings present in their depictions of devotional worlds.

Earlier generations of Udaipur artists also visualized and commemorated royal visits to temples. One of the earliest Udaipur court paintings in the topographical genre, made within the first decade of the eighteenth century, was

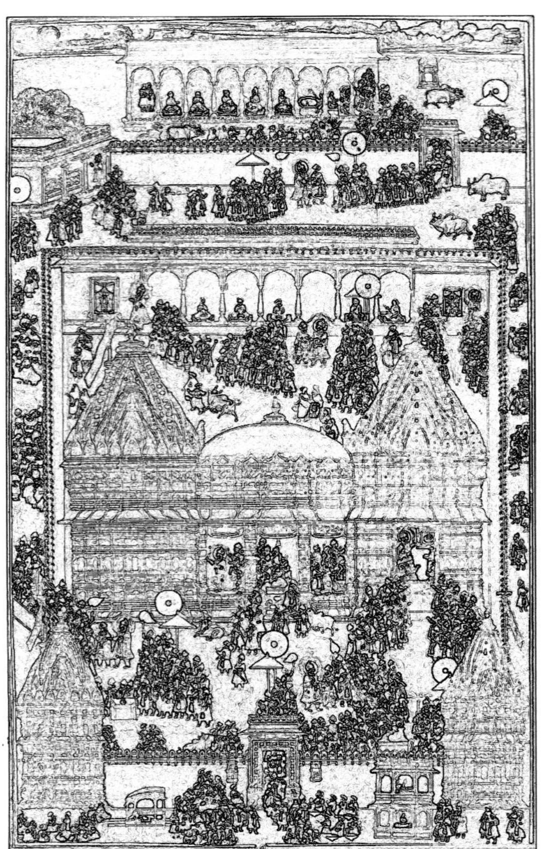

4.21. A line drawing representing the composition of a large temple with two towers and the Udaipur king's visit to the sacred precinct. Based on *Maharana Jawan Singh Visiting the Vishvanath Temple at Kashi*, attributed to Ghasi, c. 1834–35, Udaipur. Opaque watercolor, ink, and gold on paper, 134 × 95 cm. Andrew Topsfield, *Court Painting at Udaipur* (Zürich: Artibus Asiae, 2001), 248, fig. 221a.

Maharana Amar Singh II Performing Puja at Eklingji Temple, in which the painter identified as the Stipple Master rendered the elevation profile of the temple tower in his signature delicate and tinted *siyah kalam* (fig. 4.22).[65] This painting depicts Amar Singh II (r. 1698–1710) performing ritual prayers at the Eklingji temple, dedicated to the Shiva deity, who was central to the ways in which the Mewar court formulated kingship myths that linked its throne to divine authority. The drawing of the temple tower in delicate outlines highlights its elevation profile, and the use of shading and gold pigment spotlights the divine icon of the four-faced Shiva lingam. Historically, audiences would have immediately recognized

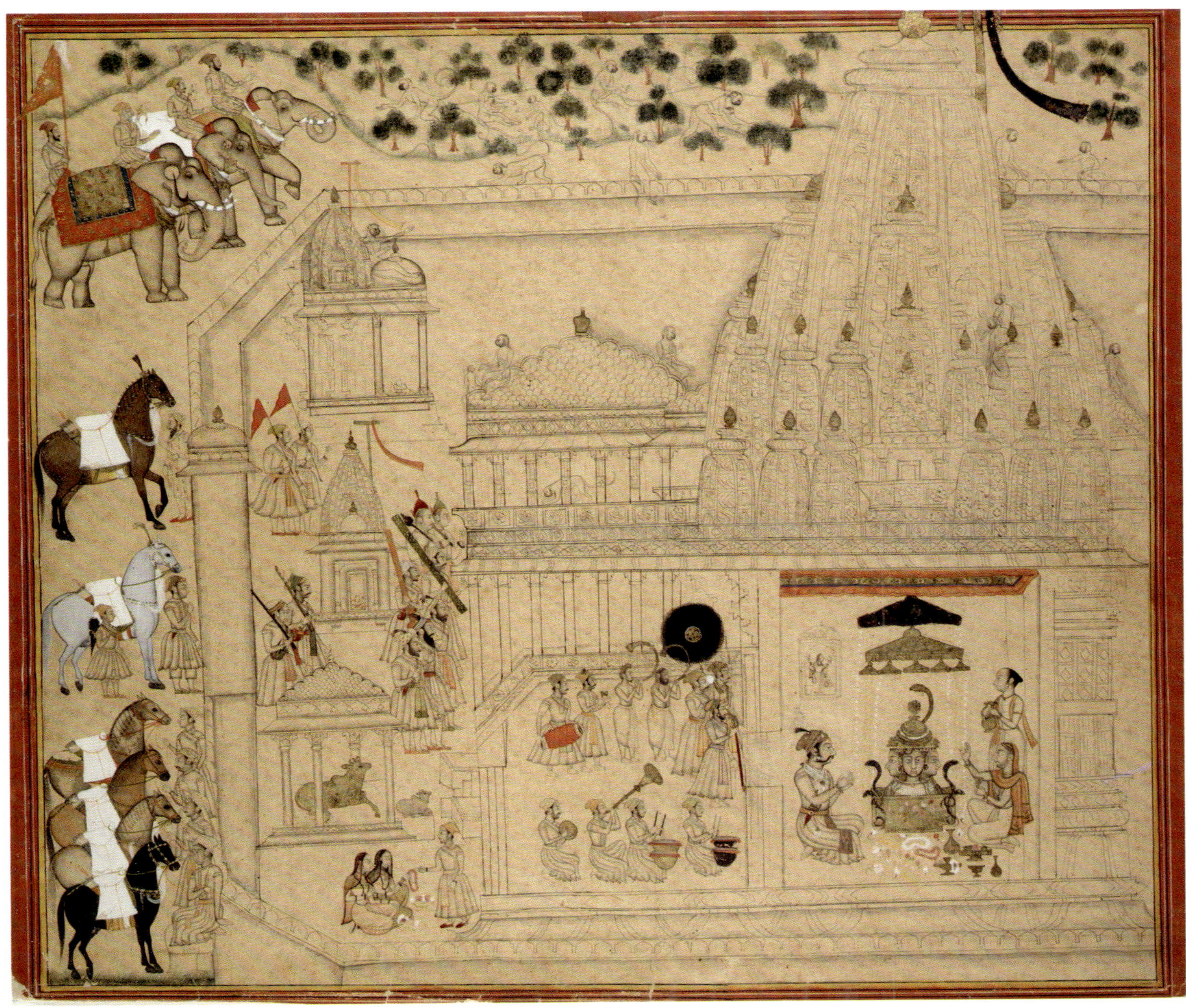

4.22. *Maharana Amar Singh II Performing Puja at Eklingji Temple*, attributed to Stipple Master, c. 1705. Gouache with gold and silver on paper, 47.5 × 54.4 cm. The Ashmolean Museum, University of Oxford; purchased with the assistance of the MLA/V&A Fund and the Friends of the Ashmolean Museum, 1989, EA1989.40.

the temple site and ritual. The towering architecture heightens the relationship between the place of worship, royal portraiture, and the power the king attains by his presence in the temple's sanctum. The composition in fine brushwork and the use of gold pigment focus the viewer's gaze on the devotional space, as if to replicate the act of devotion. The artwork invites connoisseurs to admire the temple site in its entirety. The artist's close attention to observing the details of the Eklingji temple's tower is echoed in Ghasi's focus in his pictures that engage with royal panegyrics. A precedent for the Stipple Master's mode of drawing can be found in a mid-seventeenth-century folio from Jagat Singh I's *Rāmāyaṇa* in which the Deccan Painter depicted Ravana's palatial quarters, including a temple, within the city of Lanka (see fig. 1.4). The Deccan Painter has carefully drawn a temple in white, with black outlines to emphasize the sculpted design of the tower. Its facade reads as a drafted elevation drawing, especially against the contrasting visuality of the brightly colored spatial compartments. Both precursors exemplify that more than one hundred years before Ghasi's arrival in the court workshop, Udaipur's artists had ushered in a taste for finely drafted architectural drawings. In a way, Ghasi's pictorial shifts were plausibly also engaging an archaism that became popular in the early 1700s.

The later two artists' share a sense of playfulness, seen in the Stipple Master's rendering of the endearing monkeys that populate the roof of the temple and in Ghasi's depiction of white cows in various states of slumber in *Maharana Jawan Singh Visiting the Vishvanath Temple at Kashi*. In vertically orienting the temples in his two paintings along the same axis as the doorways into the temple complex, Ghasi provided a different point of entry for the viewer, who may enter into the represented place in an imagined posture and approach that mimics the people entering and exiting at the gateways depicted on the lower and upper edges of the Vishnupad temple painting. In *Maharana Amar Singh II Performing Puja at Eklingji Temple*, the Stipple Master chose to compose a full frontal view of the deity, which can be construed as a part-sectional view of the interior of the temple, made apparent by his depiction of the wall on the right-hand side.[66] While the Stipple Master has drawn the boundaries of the devotional precinct of the Eklingji temple, he sets the inside-outside spatial relationship against the horizontal axis of the painting and not in alignment with the vertical axis of the temple's tower. Ghasi, in comparison, privileges the efficacy of the representational format of an elevation, and he aligns the boundary of the represented space with the boundary of the painting. Yet there is no mere circulation of those precise elevations of temples he drew for Tod in his court paintings. The unpublished drawing of an elevation of the Brahma temple at Chittor, discussed above (fig. 4.3), serves as evidence for thinking in this direction. It is plausible that Ghasi came to value the representational format of an elevation and renderings of architectural detail in heterogeneous ways, and thus in such a work he emulated both the court painters of the past and Tod's project in the present.

Ghasi seems to have purposefully chosen to employ drawings of temple elevations as a compositional device in the framing of the entire painting, thereby lending the temple and the ruler's portrait a quality of iconicity. Details like the systematically drawn brown earthen lamps with slender gold flames that line each wall, balcony, and the eaves, as well as the symmetrical garlands that hang from the temple, lend a uniformity to the Vishnupad image (fig. 4.2). These ornamental patterns enhance the temple's profile. The pictorial precedents found in Udaipur court painting, particularly pictures of devotional landscapes, demonstrate that when Ghasi provided Tod with elevation drawings of temples, he was adapting his artistic skills and his knowledge of a corpus of Udaipur court painting. In circulating back to the Udaipur court, in traveling with Jawan Singh, and in picturing the Udaipur king's devotional journeys, Ghasi cited both from within court painting traditions and from within the visuality of the individually framed vertical drawings of temple elevations that he prepared for Tod. His picturing of devotional temples is thus a complex translation *between* idioms, one that mediates genres, styles, conventions, and architectural knowledge across his own travels and training.

OPTICS OF THE FIRST INDO-BRITISH DURBAR, C. 1832

What work did the paintings from the 1833–34 pilgrimage accomplish for courtly audiences as they imagined a portrait of Jawan Singh attached to wider devotional and pilgrimage networks—and thus not attached only to the dynastic shrine at Eklingji or the city of Udaipur? In order to explore possible answers, we must turn to a painting that depicts the mood of the Indo-British durbar held at Ajmer in 1832 and consider how the king and his nobility would have been visually presented at this diplomatic event, a matter very likely to have been a central concern at Jawan Singh's court (fig. 4.23). This picture, *Lord William Cavendish Bentinck, Governor-General of India, Receiving Maharana Jawan Singh of Udaipur at the Ajmer Durbar, Held on February 8, 1832*, attributed to Ghasi, is a crucial case in the painter's critical application of his experiments in architectural framing. But before we explore it, we must understand the political concerns that led to the holding of British India's first imperial durbar at Ajmer, an event that led to palpable changes in territoriality and in the nature of British control in northwestern India. The durbar itself, as a highly visible form of asserting political authority, was mimetically adopted by the British from the Mughals in eighteenth-century India.[67] Rajasthan's Rajput kings were key participants in early modern Mughal durbars, where appearances, affiliations, and exchanges of gifts among elite men were the substance of political authority.[68] The exhaustive photographic record of British durbars has enabled scholars to study the British appropriation of the form of the durbar to display imperial authority, especially from the 1880s, combining features of British coronations with the bestowing of titles to Indian princes and lavish processions. The painted visualization of Indo-British durbars, specifically as they were consolidating political authority before the mid-nineteenth century, though, is barely studied.

Tod's favoritism toward Mewar and his growing sphere of influence and authority in Rajputana, especially in Mewar, was a point of contention between him and his immediate superior, Sir David Ochterlony, then resident-in-charge of

Rajputana.[69] Thus, after Tod's departure, Ochterlony applauded political agent Captain Alexander Cobbe for reducing the Mewar court's debts and getting its finances in shape.[70] In his letters to Ochterlony and others, Cobbe often expressed his differences with Tod's approach, especially in terms of the funds for personal and state expenditure that he allocated to the Udaipur rulers. After Ochterlony's tenure, the dynamics between Charles Metcalfe, the new Delhi resident-in-charge (1825–31), and Cobbe were equally tense on the question of the independent position of the Mewar maharana in his state and the extent of British interference. Both issues impacted the amount of annual tribute Mewar paid to the British government.

In tracing the changing relationship between the British East India Company and the Indian royal courts during this time period, Michael Fisher has shown that serving the "dual role" of agent and symbol of indirect British rule before 1858 was not easy for British residents.[71] He writes that while earlier residents could be seen as "[conforming] to Indian court traditions, [by] the 1820s, they sought to reshape them."[72] In fact, during his tenure, Metcalfe implemented the rule that decisions regarding the authority of each princely state in Rajputana must be made in accordance with 1818 treaties established by Tod and not on a random case-by-case basis. However, the British in Delhi continually faced challenges in asserting their authority over distant princely states and individual colonial agents. Thus, both the Udaipur and Jaipur Agencies were abolished by October 14, 1830, and merged with the Ajmer residency. The British government's inability to arbitrate between the various Rajput courts when they were in conflict—its inability to assert its "paramount" role (the key tenet in the establishment of indirect British rule in princely India at that time)—led Lord William Bentinck, governor-general at Delhi, to take a tour of Rajputana.[73] Upon Bentinck's arrival in Ajmer on January 18, 1832, he commenced a monthlong durbar and met with various Rajput princes. On February 24 of the same year, Bentinck instituted the Rajputana Agency, constituted by all the individual princely states, appointing Lieutenant Colonel A. Lockett, the superintendent and political agent at Ajmer, as its first agent to the governor-general in Rajputana.

In the minds of Rajput kings and their courtly audiences, of course, Ajmer, a key pilgrimage town since the time of the Mughal emperor Akbar (r. 1556–1605), was centrally associated with the Mughals and with the political and cultural contexts in which the Mughals and Rajputs had interacted during various Mughal durbars held there. Bentinck's declaration of the Rajputana Agency coincided with Ajmer's elevation to the status of a British territory, while the other parts of Rajputana were still governed under "indirect" British rule. Thus, by hosting the Ajmer durbar, Governor-General Bentinck put himself at the helm of the princely states—in terms of territoriality and ceremonial conduct within the space of the durbar, but also in terms of the history of the Mughals and their imperial relations with the Rajput courts. Tod's efforts at political negotiations, land surveys, and the documentation of princely genealogies, of course, had contributed not only to the eventual publication of the region's most definitive history but also to the proclamation of indirect British rule in northwestern India, in 1818, and, ultimately, to the holding of the Indo-British durbar in 1832 at Ajmer.

It appears that Ghasi traveled with Jawan Singh and his entourage from Udaipur to Ajmer. The large-scale composition of the Ajmer durbar marks the pioneering visualization of the emergent colonial state within the painted medium. This painting is one of the first visual representations we have of an Indo-British durbar held at Ajmer, far from Delhi.[74] It depicts seated officials on both sides, the Udaipur king's nobles on the left, and the governor-general's officers, along with the bounteous gifts presented to Governor-General Bentinck and his group, on the right (fig. 4.24).[75] The artist centralized the portraits of both the Udaipur ruler and the governor-general. These dignitaries are depicted as equals, yet the painter emphasizes Jawan Singh's kingly status with a green halo—an unmistakable visual code that sets his status and authority apart for regional audiences. The represented durbar embodies the hierarchical nature of the gathering, so familiar from previously established codes of Mughal and Rajput painting. Those who were the closest to the king and most powerful at court were always depicted nearest to the king's body. If we turn our attention to the painting's overall design (fig. 4.23), we find that the red tent (*qanat*) creates an architectural frame for the figures' depiction, which is so similar to temple compositions we have seen. The tent walls and their entrances are similar to the double tier of boundary walls in Ghasi's depictions of temples, and the pyramidal form of the central tent canopy, under which the king and the governor-general sit, is akin to the temple towers. The combination of planimetric and elevation views is most distinctly evoked in the horses in multiple postures at the upper edge of the painting. Toward the bottom of the painting, in a section that seeks to present the antechamber between the two entrances to the durbar, we see a planar view of horses fitted within individual cells.

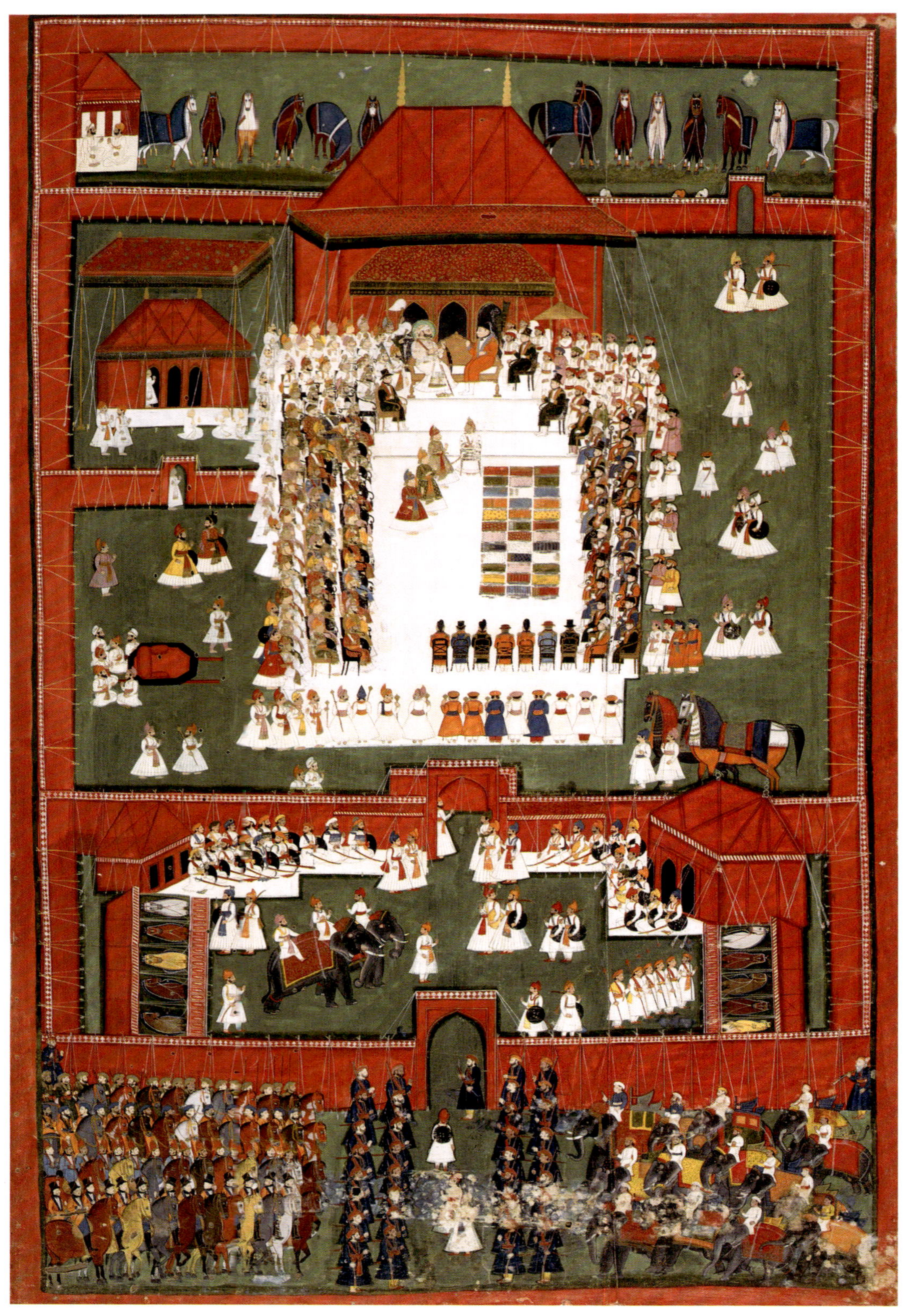

4.23. *Lord William Cavendish Bentinck, Governor-General of India, Receiving Maharana Jawan Singh of Udaipur at the Ajmer Durbar, Held on February 8, 1832*, attributed to Ghasi, c. 1832, Udaipur. Opaque watercolor, gold and silver on cloth, 189 × 128 cm. Brooklyn Museum; gift of the Alvin E. Friedman-Kien Foundation, Inc., in honor of Dr. Bertram H. Schaffner's 90th Birthday, 2002.34.

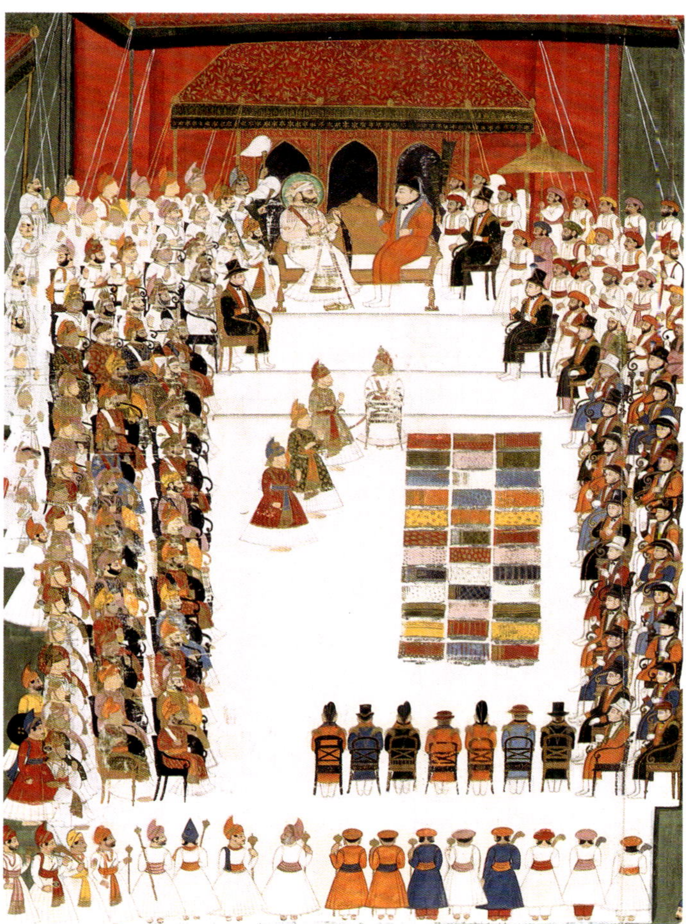

4.24. Detail of fig. 4.23. Depiction of Jawan Singh and his nobles on the left and Bentinck and his officers on the right, with the painted grid of gifts proffered by the Maharana to the governor-general's party.

The peripatetic nature of the durbars and camps held by Mughal and Rajput kings had been the subject of several earlier court paintings at Udaipur and beyond. An Udaipur court painting briefly mentioned in chapter 3 is a case in point (fig. 4.25). This work depicts the diplomatic meeting of the Udaipur ruler Sangram Singh II and the Jaipur ruler Jai Singh in a camp setting. Sangram Singh's court painter also employed red tents to depict the thresholds that lead to the inner space of the durbar inhabited by the kings.[76] He too placed the meeting at the center of the composition. The setting inside is more intimate compared to the picture presented of the 1832 Ajmer durbar. However, outside the boundaries of the tent, the painter conveys a very palpable sense of a broader landscape in pictorial elements including a slate-gray stream on the horizon and members of the entourage, who rest and converse in a manner that implies itinerancy.

Ghasi's 1832 composition lays claim to the complete pictorial plane. Gone is the essentially itinerant nature of diplomatic meetings held in durbars. A preliminary drawing for the Ajmer durbar painting, of almost the same size as the final painting, which was most likely completed on-site by Ghasi, shows that the tent was drafted as a part of the artist's original conception of this picture (fig. 4.26). The quality of line here suggests that the sketch itself was drawn quickly but also that the artist could draw the scene in several ways; this particular choice seen in the finished painting depicting the 1832 Ajmer durbar accorded value to the precisely drawn line, akin to that used in technical drawings of architectural plans and sections, for producing finished paintings at the court. In this painting, Ghasi's choices give the durbar a kind of stability.

Reams of diplomatic correspondence record the British East India Company and the Udaipur court discussing the latter's concern regarding how it would be seen in the durbar. Udaipur court records on this correspondence, written by the court official munshi Sher Singh Mehta in the regional dialect of Mewari and titled "Chronicle of the instructions on general protocols/behavior for the meeting [*bartāv sādā tarīko baiṭhak kī yād*]," note the instructions in the form of questions (*savāl*)

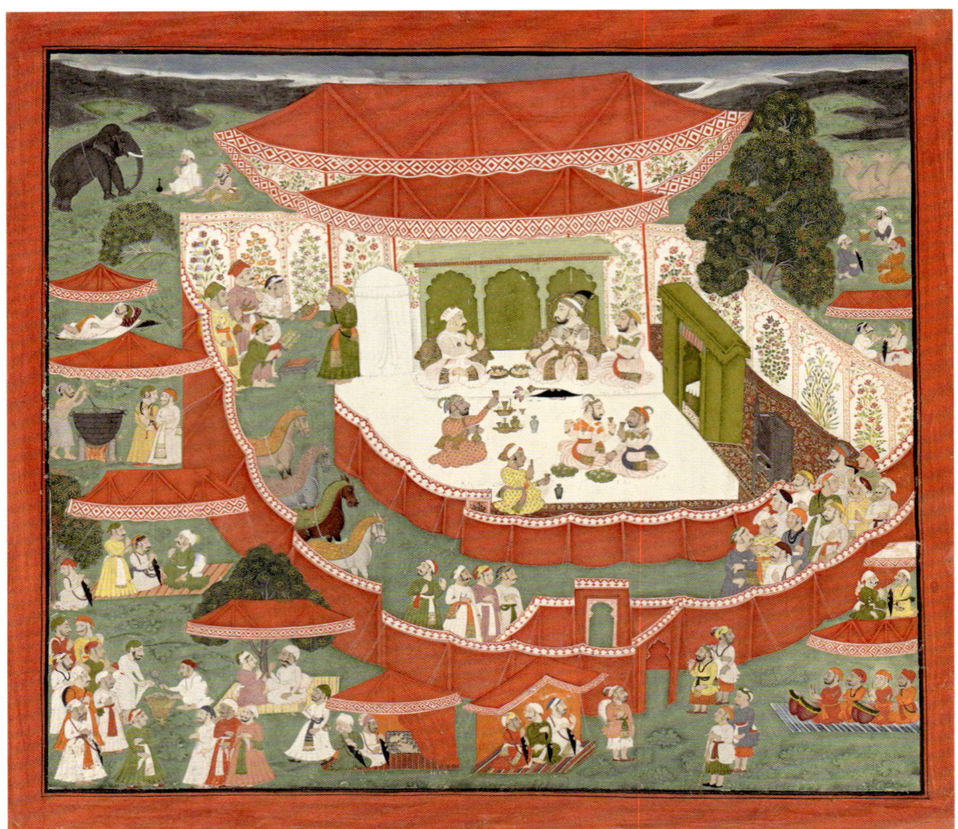

4.25. *Maharana Sangram Singh II and Maharaja Sawai Jai Singh of Jaipur in a Tent Encampment*, attributed to Jairam, c. 1732, Udaipur. Opaque watercolor and gold on paper, 45.5 × 51.4 cm. National Gallery of Victoria, Melbourne; Felton Bequest, 1980, AS100-1980.

and answers (*javāb*).[77] The first page of the document states that a copy (*nakal*) was made by munshi Chimanlalji, which most likely refers to the English version of this document authored by a person of the same name. This document, titled "Propositions submitted for the information of the Right Honorable The Governor General by Cheemanee Lal Moafmed[?] on the part of the Maha Rana's proceeding to Ajmere for the purpose of meeting the Governor General," is part of the political correspondence from 1832 in the British records.[78] Both documents focus on the layout of the durbar and the disposition of Udaipur court officers. Sher Singh Mehta, for example, insists on details of protocol concerning how Jawan Singh must be received by British officers. Most important, the question-and-answer exchange on seating instructions is pertinent to the question of what image of the Udaipur king the durbar would create. The Udaipur court, for its part, insisted that European chairs be provided for the governor-general and Jawan Singh. Sher Singh Mehta, however, stated that "the rule in the Rana's durbar is that no Sirdar is allowed to sit on equal footing. By sitting on chairs, the dignity of the Hazoor and Sirdars are rendered equal, for which reason sitting upon chairs is on no account proper."[79] In the Mewari version, the words used for the notion of "rendered equal" are *maharāṇa sāhib kī aura unkī barābarī nahī dikhegī*; that is, the equality of the Udaipur ruler and his sirdars (or thakurs/court nobles) will *not be seen* if chairs are used only for Jawan Singh and the governor-general.[80] The response from Bentinck's office to this request states,

> a separate elevated seat will be prepared for His Lordship and the Maharana. The Gentlemen of His Lordship Suite and the Sirdars, who may attend with the Maharana will sit in chairs on the right and left. By the arrangement the dignity of the Maharana will be preserved from the appear-

ance of being reduced to at par with that of his Sirdars but it is the custom of the Governor General's durbar that all who are entitled to sit shall have chairs.

The image of political power was at the heart of such contradictory concerns about custom. This anxiety about how the durbar would be visually perceived may have served as part of the impetus for Ghasi's travels with the royal party to Ajmer and thus for his detailed visualization of the durbar in the cloth painting measuring six feet by four feet.[81] His painting reveals that, ultimately, Governor-General Bentinck's custom prevailed—everyone sat on chairs. Ghasi depicts the Udaipur maharana and British governor-general sitting on a longer, throne-like seat, sharing their ceremonial space in the durbar.[82]

Aside from the concern about authority and appearance, which drives Ghasi to strategically combine realist and anti-illusionist idioms, another distinct visual focus is created by the painted grid of gifts that were proffered by the maharana to Bentinck's party.[83] Natasha Eaton has considered the valence of these kinds of material exchanges and the intercultural negotiations around gifts in the durbars of early colonial India, looking at how the British participated and transformed Mughal Hindustan's gift economy by introducing "symbolically potent portraits" in oil on canvas and, in turn, how the nawabs at the northern Indian court of Awadh used British art to display their connoisseurship and consumption in highly deliberate and self-reflexive ways.[84] While I have not been able to track the gift exchanges during the 1832 durbar

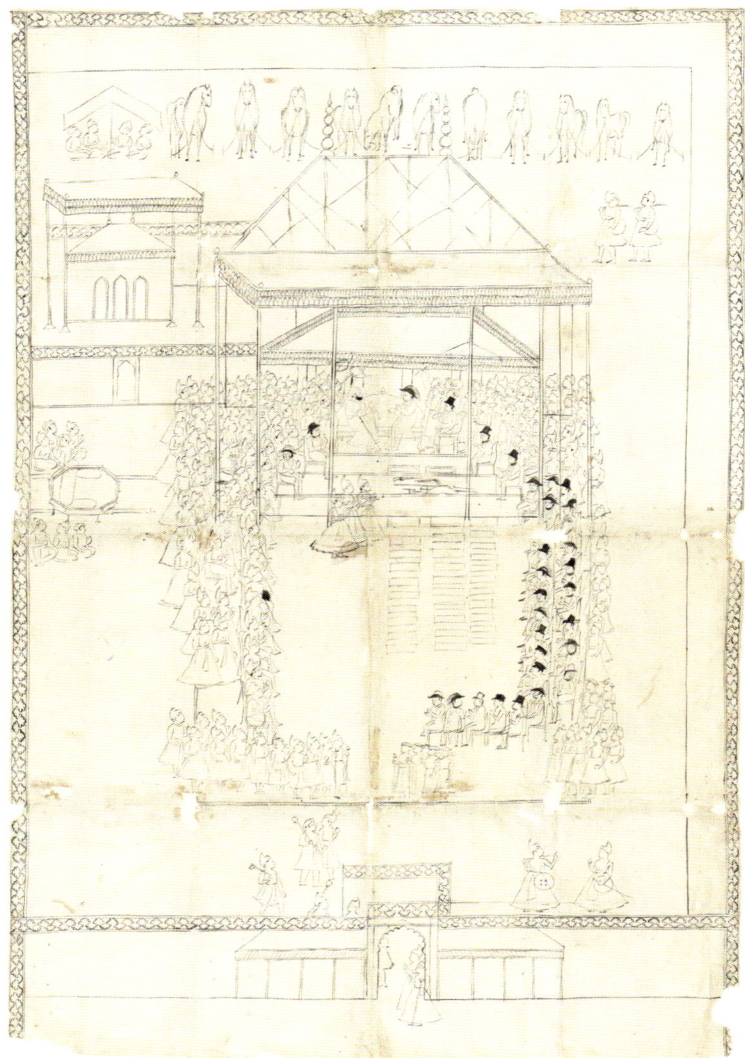

4.26. *Drawing of Lord William Cavendish Bentinck, Governor-General of India, Receiving Maharana Jawan Singh of Udaipur at the Ajmer Durbar, Held on February 8, 1832*, attributed to Ghasi, c. 1832, Udaipur. Ink on paper, 137.5 × 93 cm. The City Palace Museum, Udaipur; 2010.T.0010. Photography courtesy of the Freer Gallery of Art and Arthur M. Sackler Gallery, Smithsonian Institution. Photograph by Neil Greentree.

as yet, the represented presence introduces an ambiguity that is telling, in a way, of the uncertainty of who had greater authority in the durbar.[85] The outlines of the rectangular gifts are barely visible in Ghasi's preliminary drawing. It is in the painting, showing bright-colored cloth wraps, that their material form is fully realized. The display's geometric and abstract pattern disrupts the symmetry of the tented space, forming a block seemingly floating off the planar space. It signals the formalizing of a new political arrangement in process but remains disconnected from both parties. If Ghasi's large-scale durbar commemoration was an artwork the maharana meant to present to the governor-general, then it is worth considering that this picture of shared authority may have accorded greater power to the gift giver than the receiver. Perhaps such an intention was abandoned at a later date, which may explain why some of the portraits of nobles present in the upper left quadrant were left unfinished.

It is useful to recall Ghasi's more religiously themed paintings—made within two to three years of the 1832 durbar—in which he reinvented the use of courtly portraits within depictions of large-scale temples (figs. 4.2 and 4.21). His exploitation of this new idiom seems to assert the authority of Udaipur rulers—in a period of waning power—by drawing upon a lexicon of religious-pilgrimage networks instead of political ones. Political correspondence between the Udaipur court and British officials at Delhi and Ajmer further suggests that Jawan Singh could have commissioned these paintings as a way of asserting his power. Aligning the royal image with important temples and pilgrimage journeys beyond Udaipur could be understood as a deliberate, even calculated strategy—rather than as evidence of Jawan Singh's lack of interest in politics at the Udaipur court.[86] Jawan Singh's pilgrimage journeys were the subject of several diplomatic letters exchanged between Governor-General Bentinck and Ajmer-based agent Lieutenant Colonel A. Lockett.[87] In relation to the debt of the Udaipur court and tributes paid to the British government, discussed above, Lockett notes:

> It is the contemplation of the Rana Sahib to proceed on a pilgrimage to Giayee and Kasejee [Gaya and Kashi] the celebrated resorts of Hindoos for the purpose of offering family prayers on behalf of his deceased father Bheem Sing. In this intention, the Rana has come to a determination to set out about the time of the approaching Duseera. The affairs of the Raja are in such a low and embarrassed state that the debt due to the Sahookars alone amount to 7 or 8 Lacs of Rupess. It is therefore hoped as the liquidation of Debt is an affair of honor that through the complacency of His Lordship's arrangements the same will be discharged. It would be a bec[k]oning and praiseworthy act on the part of the Governor General and highly gratifying to the Maha Rana.[88]

When Lockett did not receive any response to the above proposition, he proposed yet again, perhaps on the urging of Jawan Singh, stating that the "Rana's pilgrimage is absolutely indispensable."[89] Governor-General Bentinck responded that, while a "qualified British Officer will be appointed to accompany him," no support of funds could be given, as that was the ruler's own responsibility.[90] Jawan Singh's father, Bhim Singh, had died in 1828. It is possible that Jawan Singh's request for funds to make a pilgrimage journey in February 1832, after the assembly at the Ajmer durbar, relates to his father's death. It is equally likely that a pilgrimage journey would offer Jawan Singh opportunities to establish alternative theo-political alliances. In chapter 5 we will see how Jawan Singh, immediately after the abolition of the independent Udaipur Agency in October 1830, attempted to establish a similar theo-political alliance with the pilgrimage networks of Jain communities. In the 1830 case, an Udaipur painter who created a vision of Udaipur as a charismatic place in order to entice powerful religious leaders to visit the city imagined that such an alliance would establish an alternative domain of authority in Udaipur, practically in the shadow of the residence of Captain Alexander Cobbe, the British colonial agent for Mewar, who was based in Udaipur. Jawan Singh finally undertook pilgrimage journeys to Mathura, Vrindaban, Ayodhya, Allahabad, Kashi, and Gaya in 1833–34, and paintings he commissioned attach his royal portrait to temples and devotional places beyond Udaipur.

MOBILITY, MOODS, MODERNITY

Ghasi appears to have become an adept traveler—crisscrossing cultural, political, and aesthetic domains as he crisscrossed northwestern India and beyond with both of his patrons. The painter belonged to groups that encountered and imagined temples in different ways, as monuments from a historical past and as devotional places that enabled pilgrimage practices. He also belonged to groups that were negotiating political power from two distinct yet closely enmeshed spaces. In critiquing a Hegelian notion of time that still dictates the questions art historians ask of images—specifically non-Euro-American works—that share *visual time*, Keith Moxey urges us to privilege contemporaneity as a temporal framework.[91] If, in Moxey's words, "synchrony, the contemporaneity of aesthetic experience, outweighs diachrony, the location of that experience in a historical continuum," then Ghasi's works suggest not artistic decline in Udaipur painting but rather artistic agency and recognition of the powerful potential of representing moods of place in the early decades of the nineteenth century.[92]

Seen against such diplomatic exchanges, and the explicit concern of the Udaipur court regarding how Jawan Singh would "look" at the 1832 Ajmer durbar, Ghasi's large-scale temple paintings must be read as generating a much-needed visual image of Jawan Singh, not simply as mere commemorations or reflections on actual events. In his temple pictures, Ghasi forcefully employs the *bhāva* of devotional places to literally and metaphorically enlarge and praise Jawan Singh's kingship and his sphere of authority. His paintings constructed effective visions of his king's power, visions that responded to the needs of the hour. In depicting Bhim Singh in the early nineteenth century, the Udaipur artist Chokha drew upon images of the blue god Krishna and Radha as idealized lovers.[93] Ghasi, for his part, turned to devotional spaces—rather than the bodies of gods—to reimagine court spaces and portraits. While he miniaturized the royal portrait and bodily presence of the king, his depiction of the architecture of temples centralized his king, imbued him with stability, and praised the ritual and political practices that constituted his rule in the 1830s.

Several small and large paintings of Jawan Singh portray him performing devotional acts. One large-scale painting, *Jawan Singh at a Vaishnava Recitation in the Baadi Mahal*, attributed to Ghasi and similar in size and composition to the artist's 1832 Ajmer durbar painting, plausibly commemorates a week-long recitation of the *Bhāgavata Purāṇa* that was held in 1835, nearly a year after Jawan Singh completed his pilgrimage journeys (fig. 4.27).[94] Almost all earlier depictions focus on the interiority of the pictured courtly space of the Shivprasana Amar Vilas Mahal (Baadi Mahal; for the architecture of the space, see figs. 1.11, 3.5); in one eighteenth-century work, depicting the Udaipur ruler Ari Singh as he offers prayers to a Shiva lingam, we see that the painter, Shambhu, was most interested in exploring one-point perspectival vision and shadows of people and trees, elements not seen in other paintings that depict the Baadi Mahal courtyard (fig. 4.28). Play with light in this fashion had not been taken up in any other Udaipur court paintings known thus far, perhaps indicating that visual interest was not what enticed Udaipur artists. Conversely, Ghasi modeled his painting of Jawan Singh enacting his devotional ethos in this courtyard upon his own earlier temple paintings. In so doing, he created a large-scale vertical painting in which the nested squares of courtly audience, the depicted courtyard, the planimetric view of the terrace, the pavilions, and the drafted nature of the drawing together reinforce the centrality of the miniaturized royal portrait. Here is the evidence of precisely how Ghasi and his circle of artists expanded the size of paintings, especially when compared to pictures that feature Bhim Singh. This expansion in size occurred first, as seen in chapter 2, within the Udaipur ruler Amar Singh II's workshop at the beginning of the eighteenth century, as artists forged the genre of large-scale topographical paintings that combined portraiture with depictions of the *bhāva* of a place, especially that of Udaipur city, its topographical environs, and its lake palaces. More than a century later, within several vertically oriented paintings approximately forty inches in width and sixty inches in height, Ghasi visualized Jawan Singh in association with the *bhāva* of visiting temples, undertaking pilgrimages and holding devotional assemblies within palatial courtyards.

Ghasi's works mediate worlds, and the painter's artistic practice refracts—rather than reflects—in layered ways his embodied experience of multiple political interests and his learning from multiple aesthetic and knowledge traditions. His pictures make statements of power for the Udaipur king Jawan Singh. Whether the Udaipur king saw pilgrimage journeys and devotional recitations as acts of idealized kingship, as an escape to another world and another place outside of Udaipur and its politics, or as a way to forge connections with broader devotional worlds and to reestablish his authority through alternative networks outside of British political circles, Ghasi and his circle of painters viewed devotional places and events as pictorial topoi within which to reimagine the intersection between visualizing places and powers at Udaipur. The drawings and paintings Ghasi imagined and drew circulated among audiences who saw them as pictures of civilizational decline and as pictures of royal praise in the early part of the nineteenth century. Ghasi's pictorial translations of architectural drawing in two genres—engravings, published in the *Annals and Antiquities of Rajast'han*, which was circulated globally as a book of authoritative history, and large-scale paintings, which were likely periodically shown to courtly audiences at Udaipur—argue for the distinct nature of the epistemic meaning his pictures make.

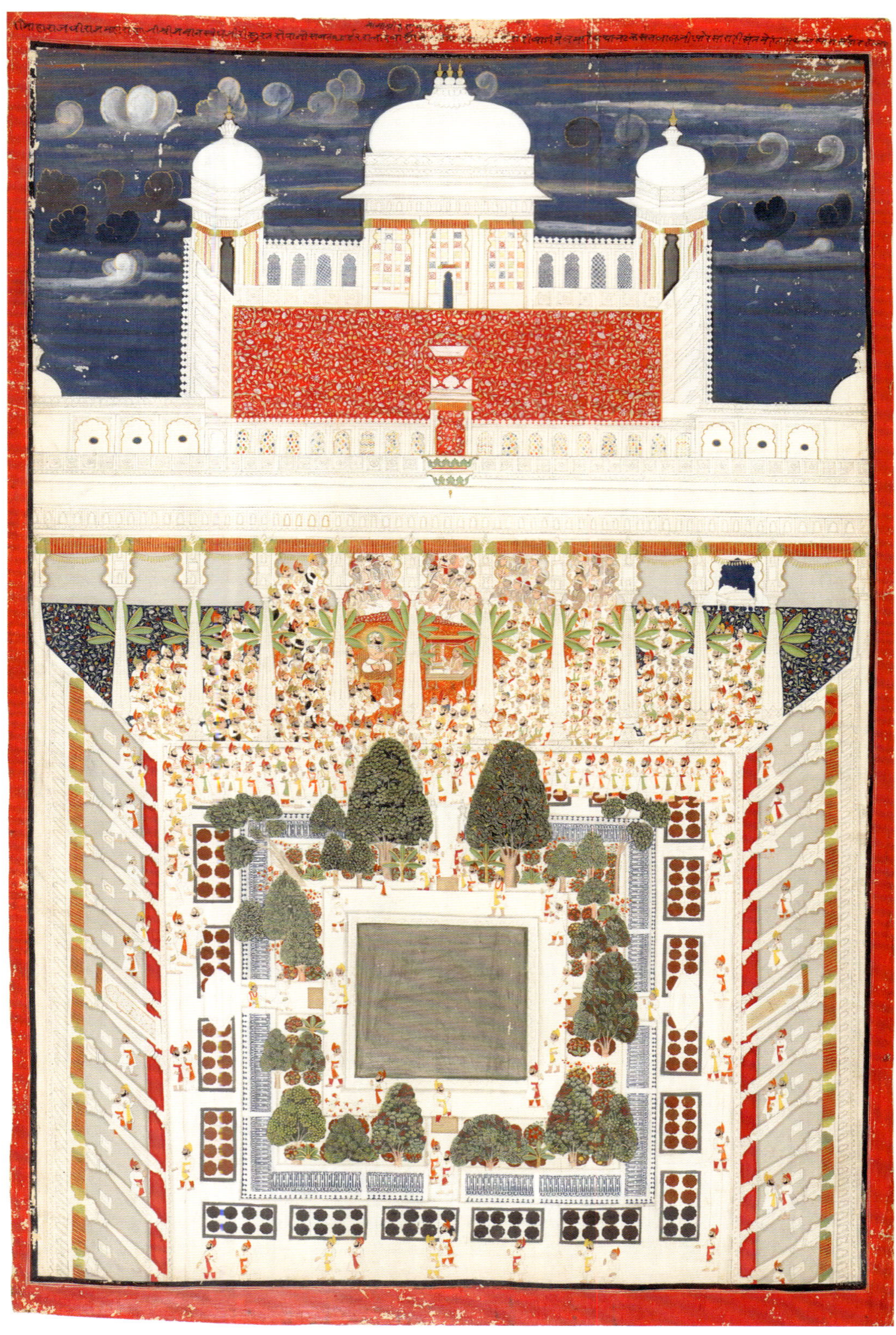

4.27. *Maharana Jawan Singh at a Vaishnava Recitation in the Baadi Mahal*, attributed to Ghasi, c. 1835, Udaipur. Gouache, gold, and silver on paper, 141 × 91.4 cm. The City Palace Museum, Udaipur; 2011.18.0033_R. Photography courtesy of the Freer Gallery of Art and Arthur M. Sackler Gallery, Smithsonian Institution. Photograph by Neil Greentree.

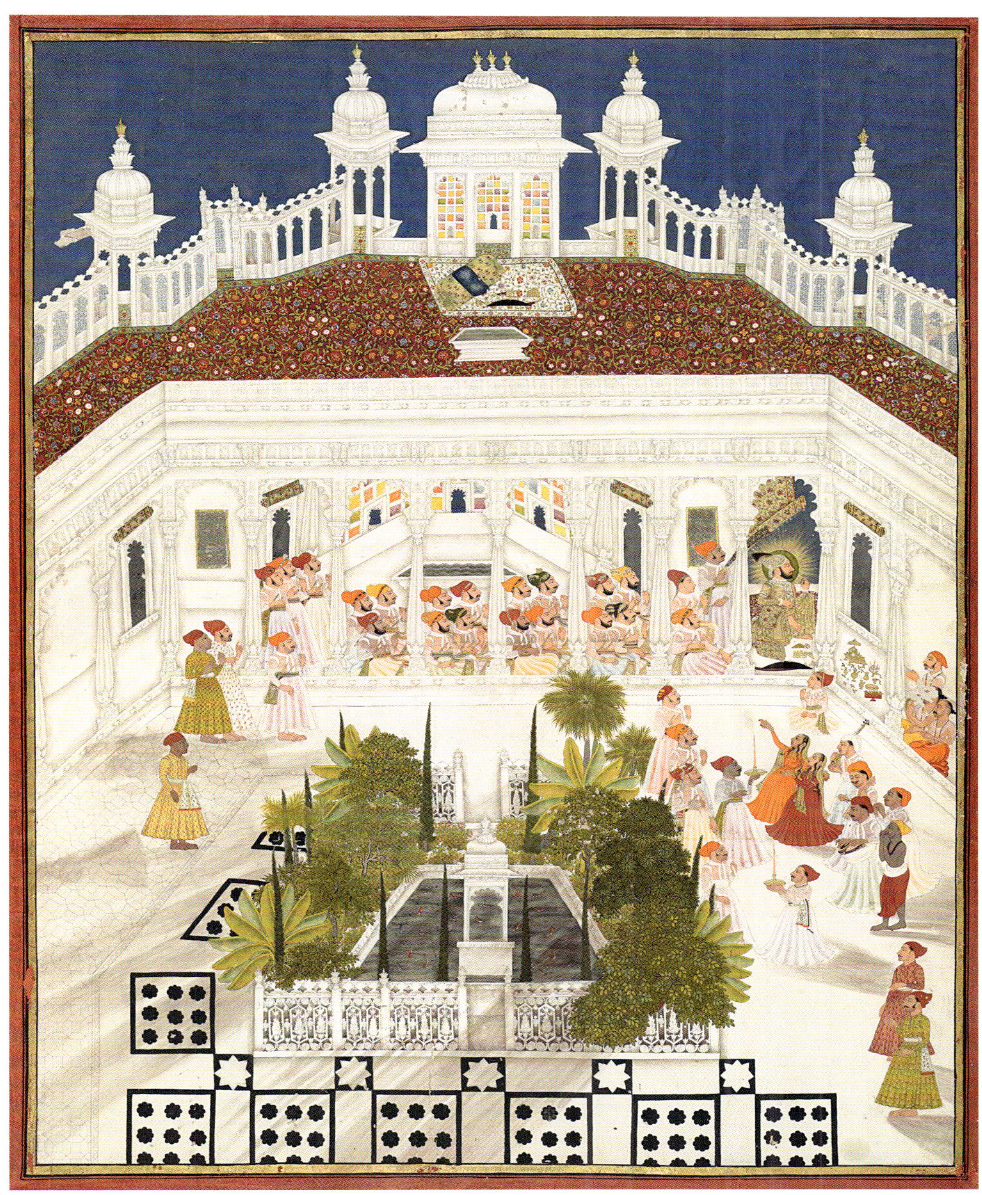

4.28. *Maharana Ari Singh Performs Puja in the Baadi Mahal*, Shambhu, 1765, Udaipur. Opaque watercolor on paper, 68 × 53 cm. Freer Gallery of Art, Smithsonian Institution, Washington, DC; purchase, Charles Lang Freer Endowment, F1986.7.

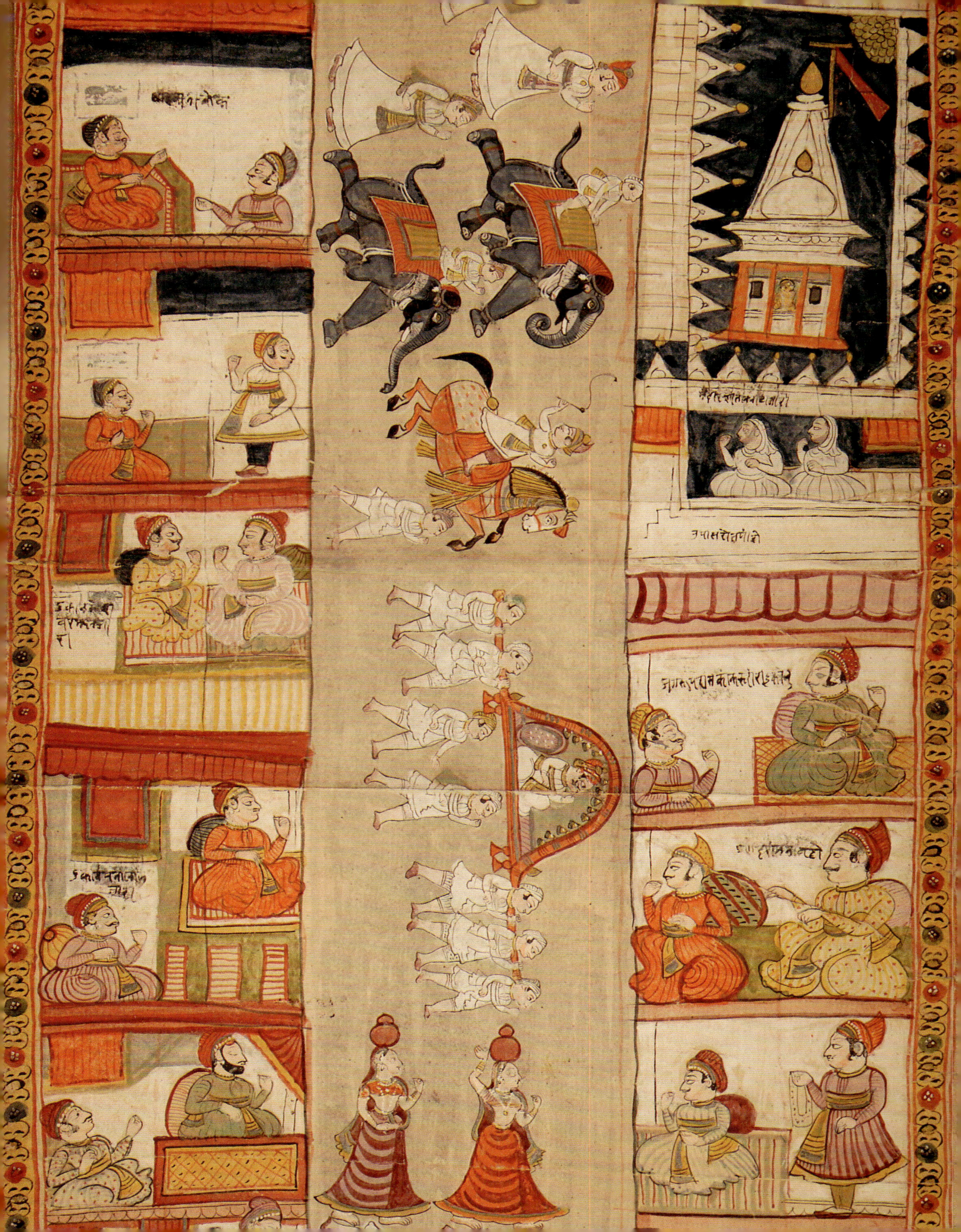

CHAPTER 5

Charismatic Places and Colonial Spaces

CIRCULATING PICTURES, LETTERS, AND PEOPLE

In 1830, the king of Mewar and a group of regional merchants jointly sent a signed painted scroll, seventy-two feet long and eleven inches wide, as an invitation letter, a *vijñaptipatra*, to the eminent monk of the Jain religious community, Shri Jinharsh Suri in Bikaner (fig. 5.1). They requested that Jinharsh Suri spend the next monsoon season in their vibrant capital city, Udaipur. Over the first sixty-five feet of this paper scroll, an unnamed artist from Udaipur creatively mapped a principal street of the city, painting its important palaces, temples, and bazaars. Although he was not a court painter, his composition shows that he was clearly knowledgeable in the pictorial style practiced by court artists. He added an elaborate procession to the center of the scroll, depicting the Udaipur ruler Jawan Singh (r. 1828–38) and the British colonial agent Alexander Cobbe, creating an unusual and innovative dual axis—a long spine that is intersected continuously by horizontal cells—along which a viewer constantly navigates in order to see and understand the work (figs. 5.2 and 5.3). In depicting the street and scenes with such realistic detail, the artist departed from earlier painted letters, which use typical metaphorical references to bazaars, temples, and regional courts in order to depict the vibrant moods of a city, such as the 1610 scroll sent by the merchants of Mughal Agra (see fig. I.1).

A *vijñaptipatra* was made in order to encourage prominent religious figures to travel to a distant city by circulating an urban imaginary of that city as a thriving place—politically, culturally, religiously, and economically. Prominent merchants of the local Jain community hoped to entice eminent Jain monks to spend the next monsoon season (*caumāsa*) in Udaipur.[1] The custom of sending *vijñaptipatra* scrolls among the Shvetambara sect of Jainism owes its origin to the traditions of asking for forgiveness for sins and vowing to perform pious deeds in the future—in this case, pilgrimages to the immobile sacred sites and the mobile holy places eminent monks created by their presence.[2] The scribes, pandits Rukhabhdas and Kushalchand, who wrote the four-foot-long invitation letter on the lower end of the scroll, reveal this desire explicitly. The last three feet of the scroll preserve the signatures of more than twenty-five prominent merchants of the city of Udaipur, each written in a distinct hand (fig. 5.4). The text of the attached letter prefacing the signatures

Detail of fig. 5.1

5.1. *Letter of Invitation (*Vijñaptipatra*) Sent to the Monk Jinharsh Suri*, 1830, Udaipur. Opaque watercolor, ink, and gold on paper, 2194.6 × 27.9 cm. Agarchand Nahata Jain Granthalaya, Bikaner. Photograph by Jonas Spinoy. To digitally scroll the Udaipur painted letter (1830) and examine its details, please see https://press.princeton.edu/books/hardcover/9780691201849/the-place-of-many-moods.

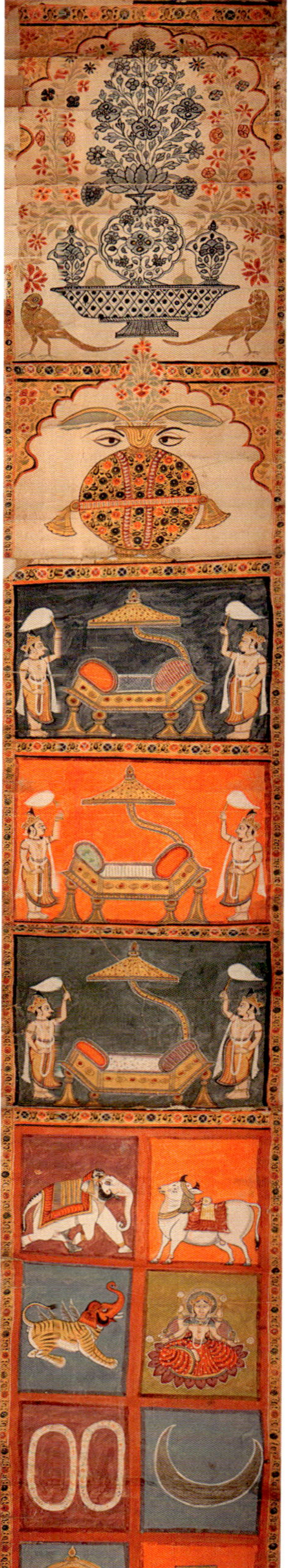

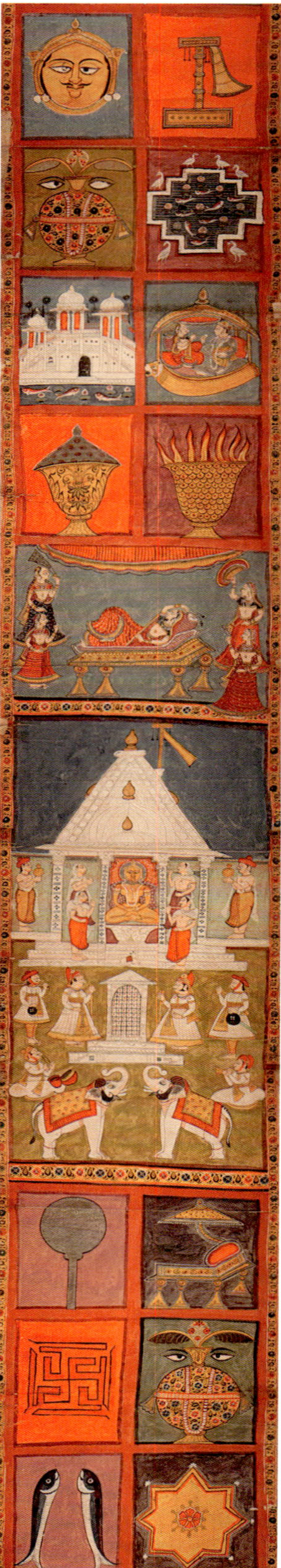

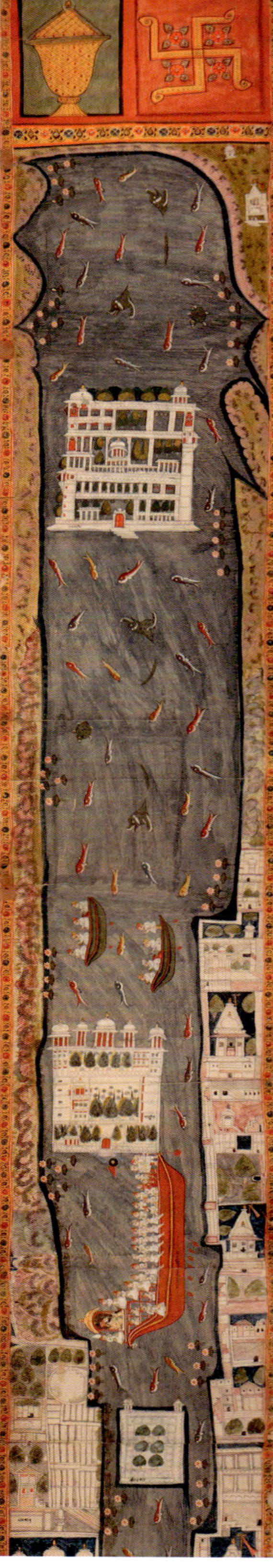

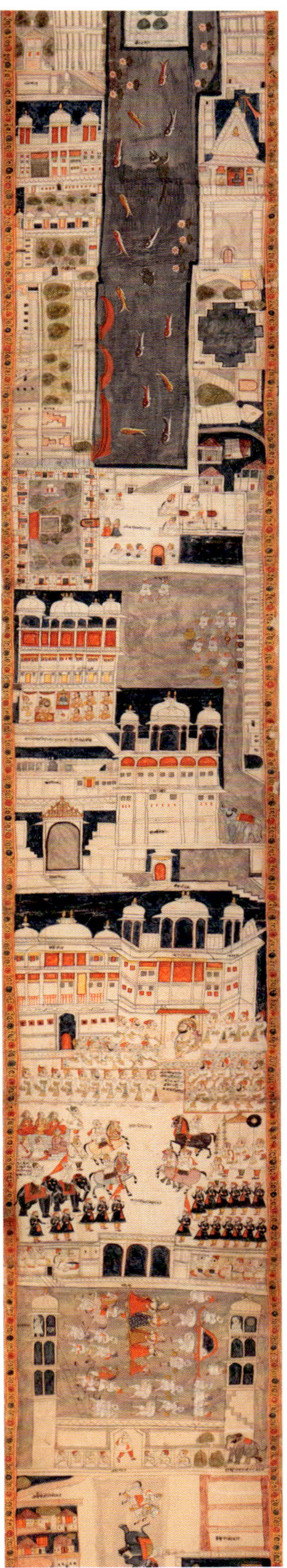
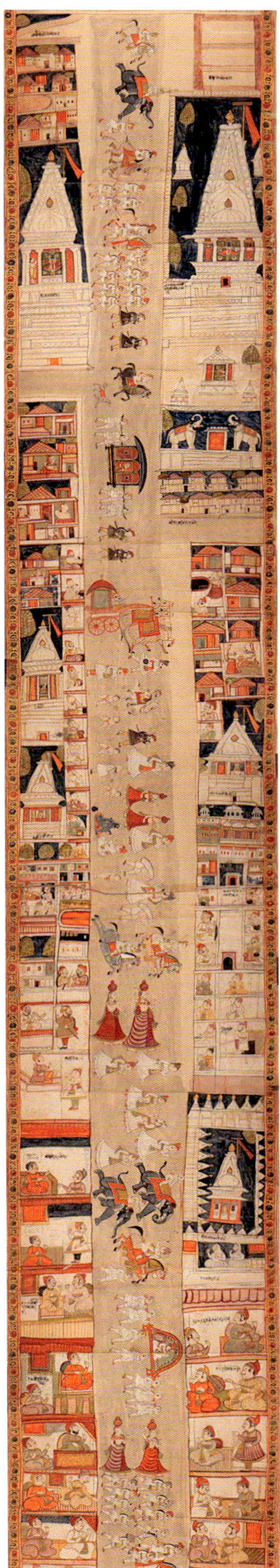
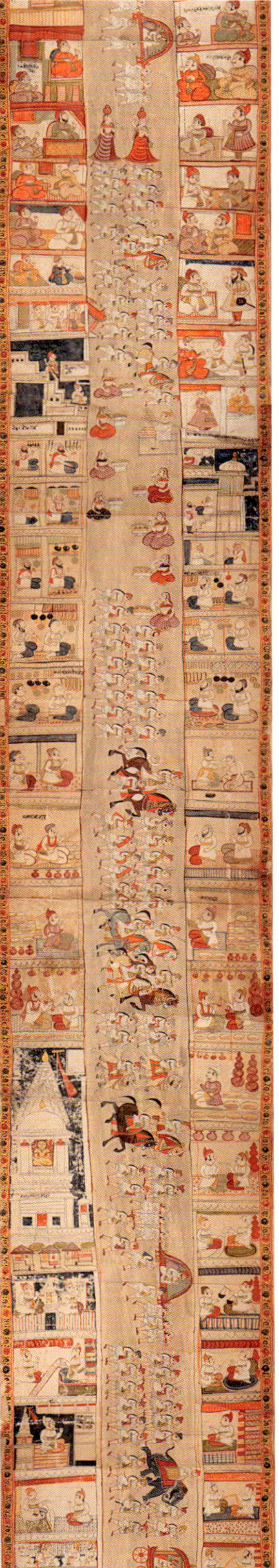

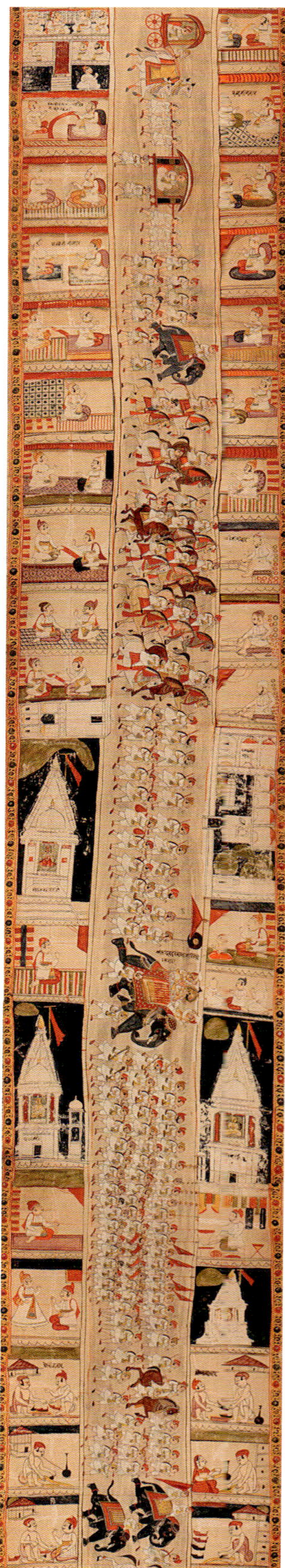
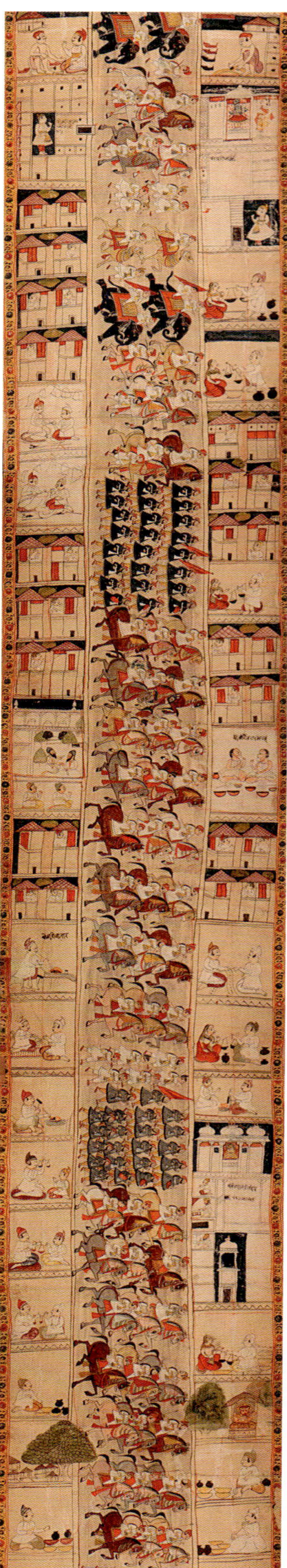
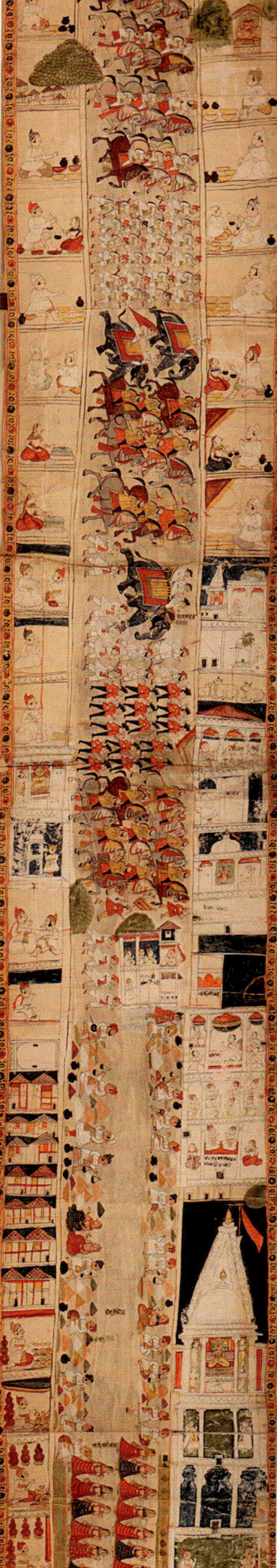

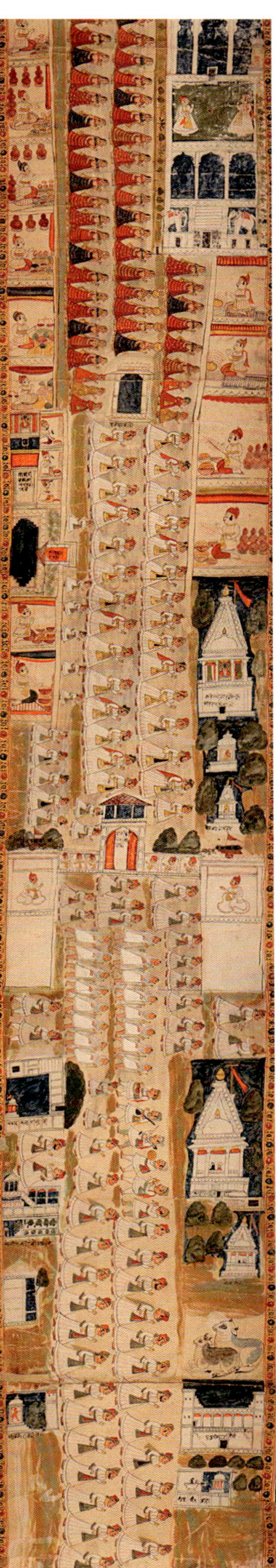

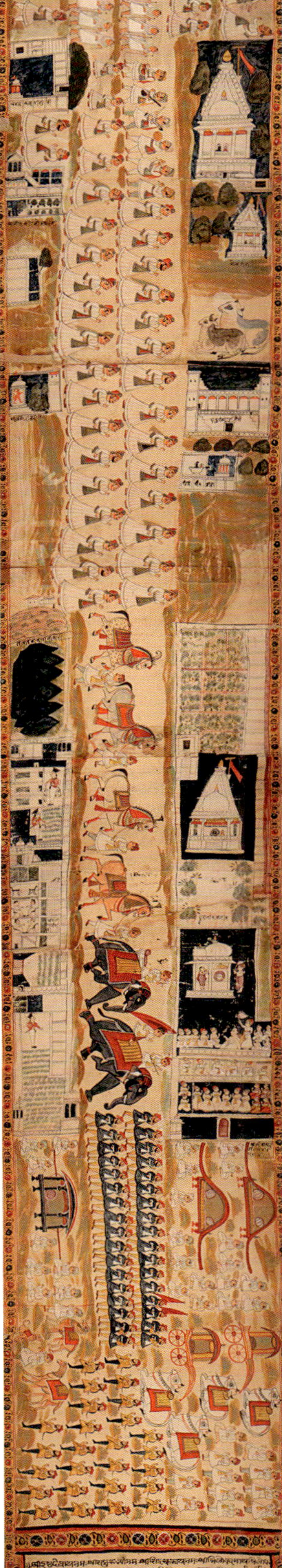

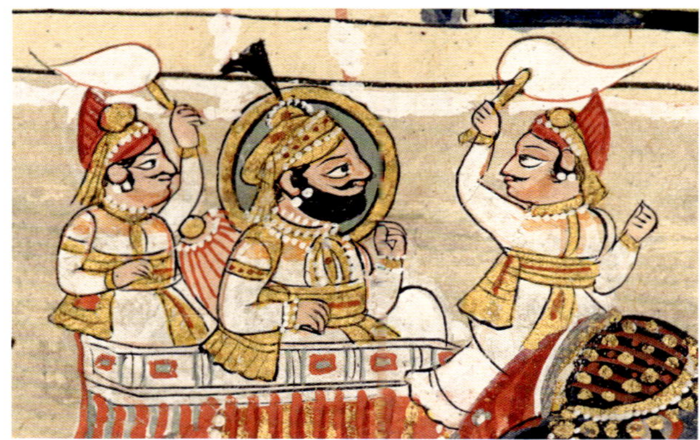

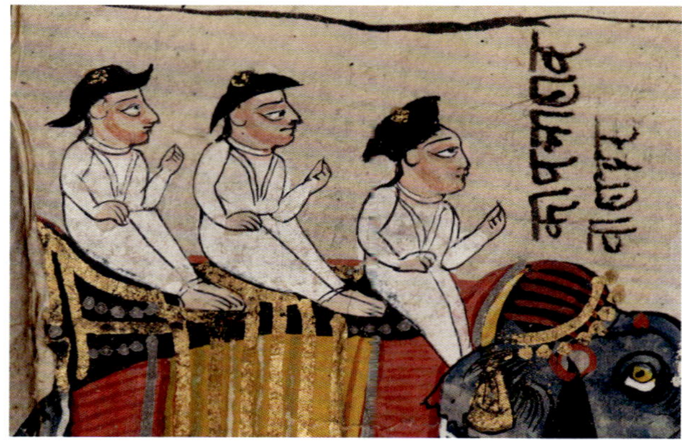

5.2. Detail of fig. 5.1. Maharana Jawan Singh in procession.

5.3. Detail of fig. 5.1. British colonial agent Captain Alexander Cobbe in procession.

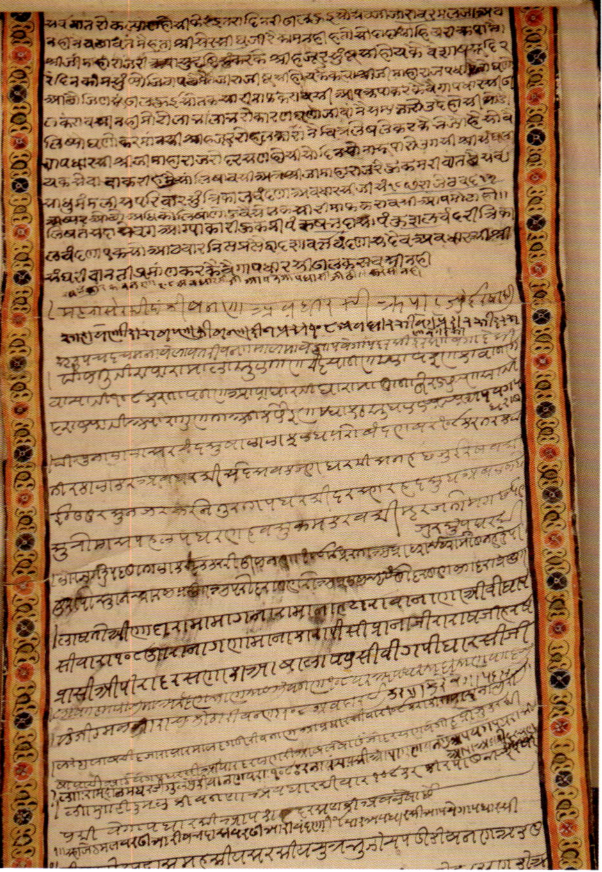

5.4. Detail of fig. 5.1. The end of the letter, written by the scroll's scribes, Pandit Rukhabhdas and Pandit Kushalchand, and individually signed by prominent Udaipur merchants.

employs poetic renditions in Sanskrit and the regional Gujarati and Rajasthani dialects to eulogize the invited monk. The letter ends by emphasizing the emotions of the devotees, the residents, and the ruler of Udaipur, all of whom were eager to welcome the eminent monk; the scribes express in writing that the "community from here remembers you day and night as a peacock awaits the arrival of the rains."[3]

The aim of the makers of the scroll was to praise Udaipur in order to present it as a charismatic and eminently attractive place, worthy of a visit. Whether Jinharsh Suri arrived during the monsoon season of 1831, bringing the change and prosperity that are projected in the pictures and the letter, is not known; however, we can establish that the neighborhood around the British residency was transformed into an important Jain neighborhood in 1832.[4] Significantly, the merchant (*seth*) Joravarmal Bapna, who played a key role in commissioning the painted invitation sent in 1830, built a temple there, and his portrait was prominently painted on the entrance wall (figs. 5.5 and 5.6).[5] This portrait was rendered in the same style as the contemporary Udaipur ruler Jawan Singh's portrait on the scroll, which suggests that the artist may have been one and the same, or at least from the same workshop or artistic milieu. What is interesting and instructive is that the artist of the scroll does not leave the question of the invitation's acceptance open-ended, as the writers of the letter did. The final pictorial vignette in the scroll imagines that this invitation would be effective—its objective realized by the pontiff's arrival (fig. 5.7). A group of elites, several palanquins, and a troop of soldiers are depicted waiting upon the monk's durbar. With this evocative image, the artist could

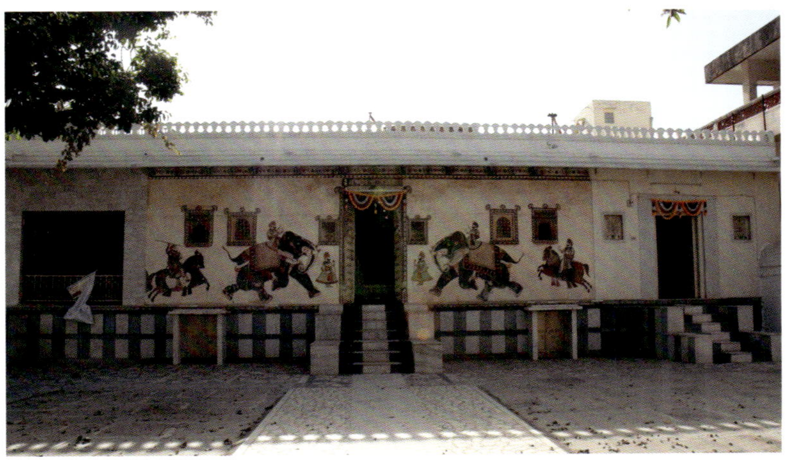

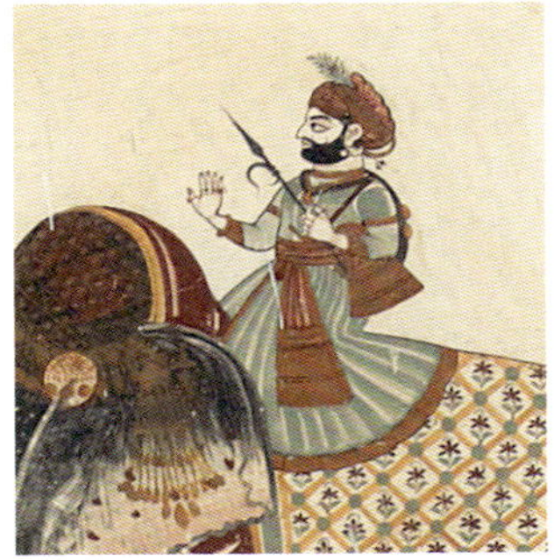

5.5. Jain temple built by the merchant Sethji Joravarmal Bapna in 1834, Udaipur. Photograph by author.

5.6. Detail of fig. 5.5. Portrait of the merchant Joravarmal Bapna, entrance wall of temple.

5.7. Detail of fig. 5.1. Imagined assembly held by the invited Jain monk Jinharsh Suri.

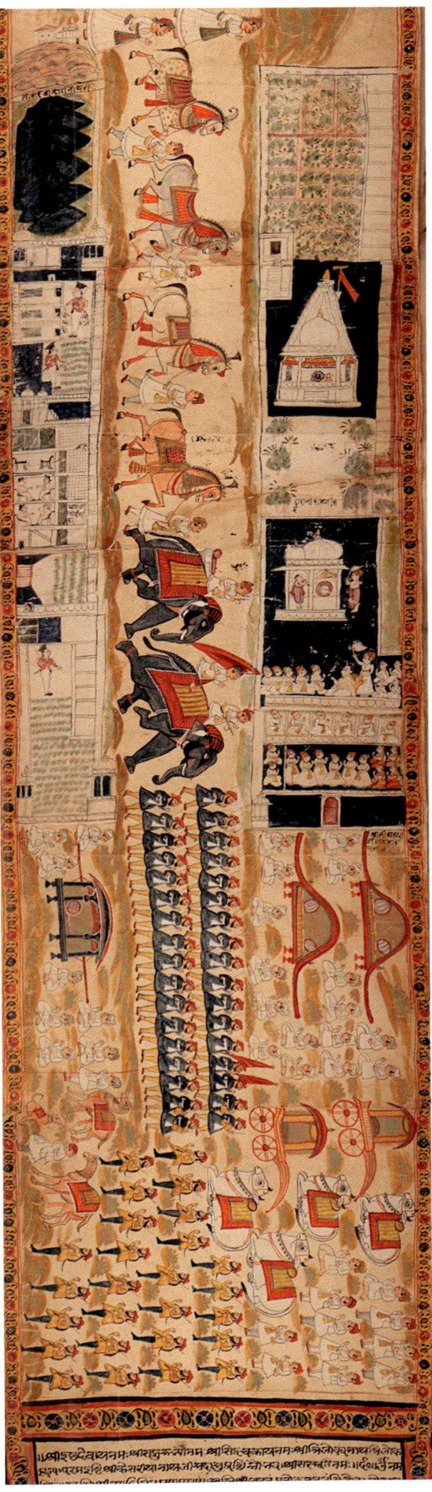

have been directing the invited Jain pontiff to imagine himself in a position of authority in Udaipur.

The 1830 scroll represents the mood of Udaipur city as a flourishing and attractive place. It invites an exploration of how artists, scribes, and poets employed urban praise to forge a mood of prosperity in present times, and how they emphasized the mood of the city in times yet to come. Previously, artifacts such as the Udaipur *vijñaptipatra* (1830) have been seen as simply another example of a Jain invitation letter and thus circumscribed to discussion within a closed religious context. Others have looked at these scrolls, such as the painted letter depicting Mughal Agra's court and city (1610) discussed in the book's introduction, as an example of Indian painting practices on the margins of court workshops, a perspective that tends to locate them in an arena of Indian art subordinate to the best-known paintings, which came from the context of royal sponsorship. Both approaches obscure the sophisticated ways in which Udaipur's patrons, painters, and scribes engaged in the artistic picturing of the moods of place and how powerful and evocative the painted letters were as enticements to travel.[6] The choices seen within this Udaipur *vijñaptipatra* underscore the dual role that such letters played. They aimed at the establishment of temporary sectarian Jain durbars in different towns and cities each year, while at the same time, in beckoning newcomers to admire a fresh place, they provided an occasion for locals to envision their own cities as ideal cityscapes of abundance in relation to realpolitik.

In citing courtly images, makers sought to create a material object that traveled from a place and embodied in various ways its connection to the represented city. At both Indo-Muslim and Hindu courts across northern and southern India, as seen in chapters 3 and 4, artists and poets visualized a king's territory as an ideal of abundance, joy, and sacredness, thus evoking a strong desire for belonging to as well as a longing for those painted lands. Chapter 2 traced how early eighteenth-century monumental paintings presented the passionate moods of monsoon season, making Udaipur the site of abundant rain gloriously coursing into its lakes. In contrast, the current chapter focuses on letter-scrolls as traveling objects that were meant to spur travel while being transported. These mobile objects enable us to examine painters and scribes operating in early modern and colonial bazaars, and to understand how they mediated praise and idealization in ontologically distinct objects—painted letters integrally connected the spaces of the bazaar, regional courts, and transregional travels. By highlighting an aspirational time when the invited monk might come, in the 1830 scroll the rainy season of the following year, they suggest possibilities for subverting established territorialities and forging alternative memories predicated on praiseworthy moods.[7]

MERCHANTS, MONKS, TRAVELERS IN THE BAZAAR

On several *vijñaptipatra* scrolls, such as a 1761 painted letter sent from Sirohi, the depiction of a merchant handing over a dated scroll to a messenger suggests an artistic consciousness of the invitation letter's connection to the bazaar (fig. 5.8). The emergence of new sovereignties and the dominance of pan-Indian mercantile networks contributed to the increased mobility of people and objects in the eighteenth and nineteenth centuries, instigating an explosion in the commissioning and circulation of even more elaborate *vijñaptipatra* scrolls. The networks and travels of pan-Indian merchants, petty traders, and itinerant religious men such as fakirs and sannyasis, as well as a range of mobile intellectuals, from artists and poets to performers and storytellers such as *bhopās* and *madārī*s, bring into question the view that "the advent of colonialism completely modified the conditions of circulation in the subcontinent."[8] In the 1610 painted letter of Agra, the artist Salivahana, made the circulation of the scroll itself a key pictorial theme (see figs. I.1–3). The makers of the 1830 Udaipur *vijñaptipatra*, in turn, allude to the audiences and objects that circulated within regional mercantile and courtly networks, drawing on charismatic and idealized landscapes and providing a visual imagining of vibrant circulatory routes. In this way, they employed art to affective and effective ends.

This integral connection of *vijñaptipatra* scrolls to the space of the bazaar, along with the mixing of pictorial practices that we will see in the Udaipur scroll, allows us to consider whether such painted invitation letters might also be seen as what Kajri Jain calls "bazaar images."[9] Late nineteenth- and twentieth-century Indian calendar *vijñaptipatra* art, featuring old devotional mythic gods and goddesses as well as new nationalistic ones, Jain argues, allude to the bazaar in colonial India as a space where domains of commerce, religiosity, and politics intersected and where inhabitants formulated their practices of devotion, exchange, and commensurability in heterogeneous ways.[10] I argue that *vijñaptipatra* scrolls are exactly these kinds of bazaar objects, which can be interpreted only at the interstices of various registers of production and consumption. They cannot be fixed to a single body of makers or patrons, nor to a single group of viewers, even if they were produced with a given recipient in mind. Because they circulated within popular domains, they offer us grounds on which to think about the reception of art and history, the power of moods and emotions for shaping memories and mobilities, and the formation of the aesthetic and historical sensibilities of a broader spectrum of people.[11]

This chapter is structured in four broad sections. The first will focus on the artist's picturing of Udaipur in this *vijñaptipatra* as well as on his citation, adaptation, and expansion of pictorial tropes from the domain of court painting and the genre of Jain painted invitation letters. The second section explores the scroll's connection to the bazaar. By interpreting scribal engagement with panegyric ideas in the writing of the invitation letter in this scroll, this section will also address how historical audiences received and perceived the places that are visualized in the scroll.

The third section proposes critical comparisons across media. We will examine contemporaneous literary practices that employed the trope of praise to construct memories of a place. Jain monks composed topographical poetry while

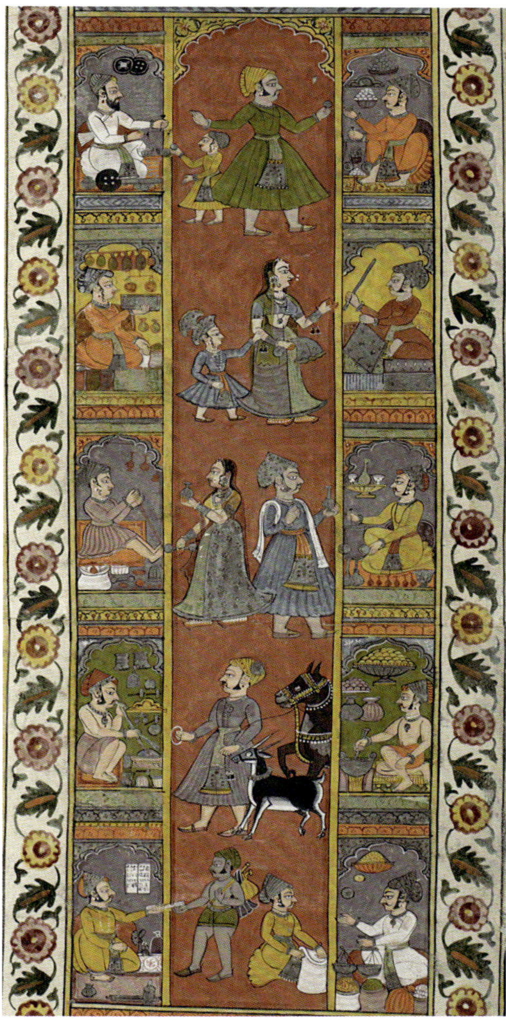

5.8. *Letter of Invitation (*Vijñaptipatra*) to a Monk*, 1761, Sirohi. Detail depicting the bazaar. Opaque watercolor and ink on paper, 246.2 × 24.6 cm. New York Public Library; Spencer Collection, Indian, MS 26.

visiting new cities with religious leaders after they had received *vijñaptipatra* scrolls as invitations to travel; both artifacts of place and praise circulated within the bazaars and religious establishments of the Jains. Both categories of artifact demonstrate that such minor and marginal traditions, thus far exclusively associated with spaces of religiosity, can be studied in order to trace how broader audiences acquired their taste for poetry and art within the overlapping social spaces of bazaars, pilgrimages, and devotional gatherings. In their mixing of aesthetic tropes and compositional strategies, both painted letter-scrolls and topographical poems are exemplary of early modern vernacular "intermediary genres" that mediate the praiseworthy moods of a city in highly motivated ways.[12] In both, artists and poets forged the moods of the city by combining a variety of circulating images with the knowledge of everyday spaces and common experiences of the city. This section raises questions about the role of tropes of praise in conjuring a world that had largely been seen as one in decline.

The final section ties together the visual and poetic imaginings of urban praise, thereby highlighting the intertwining of emotions and places within practices of imagining in colonial India. Painted letter-scrolls expand our understanding of the range of material domains within which historical viewpoints and territorial claims—maps and memories—were presented in colonial India by centralizing moods, and not merely the times and places, of events. The 1830 scroll challenges normative views on the representation of place and the production of knowledge during the long eighteenth century. It recovers the role of religious institutions, and it highlights the potential of vernacular objects, emerging from the space of local bazaars, for making interventions into the historiography of painted places and of political claims of territory. The conversations represented in such epistolary letter-scrolls, outside their defined boundary of Jain religiosity, widen our understanding of the circulatory regime of British political correspondence, which defined the nature of the emergent British territoriality in early colonial India.

PRAISING CITIES AS CHARISMATIC PLACES

The 1830 scroll is one in a line of four extravagantly long, painted *vijñaptipatra* scrolls representing Udaipur, ranging from thirty to seventy-two feet in length. As a group, these painted letters present as much of a visual and analytical quandary for the art historian today as they might have presented for the artists who visualized these long compositions and the historical audiences who viewed them. Artists joined together multiple sheets of paper of approximately two feet in length in order to create these scrolls. Considering even this simple step in the assembly of a *vijñaptipatra* scroll, one confronts multiple questions: Did a master artist draw the complete composition, to be followed by other artists from the workshop, who filled in colors in parts of the scroll? Or did the artist paint the scroll in a continuous manner, addressing a manageable length of two to three feet at a time? If artists indeed worked in this manner, how did they manage to conceive an all-encompassing cityscape as a unified picture? Was the process therefore somewhat akin to how viewers are likely to have visually explored the scroll, looking at a limited length of the city's map and streets at a time? Whether monks unrolled the complete scrolls on the floor for their primary audiences—the Jain pontiffs to whom the invitations were addressed—or the pontiffs held the scrolls themselves, it is possible to see only to two or three feet of the scroll in a focused manner at a time. Any viewing, then, is partial.

While it is nearly impossible to discuss the plethora of sites and people in this seventy-two-foot-long scroll, this section examines the idioms and styles of Udaipur court painting that were employed to praise the city pictorially to prospective visitors. These features will be considered with attention to the view from the bazaars of Udaipur and to how artists and scribes presented their subjective interpretations of urban change. It is very possible that such scrolls were created in a painting workshop in the bazaar, where the city's artists, knowledgeable of a canon of court paintings, contributed to different aspects, such as drawing the outlines, coloring the composition, and writing the labels. However, as I have been unable to attest with any degree of certainty to this kind of collaborative effort in the making of the 1830 Udaipur *vijñaptipatra*, I shall refer to the artist of this scroll as a single entity.

The artist of the 1830 Udaipur scroll adapted established conventions and maneuvered standard artistic tropes to the vertical format and genre of *vijñaptipatra* scrolls. He persuasively presented an urban landscape, intermixing universal and local images, and yet the object itself defies any notion of a complete, all-encompassing picture of a place. This challenge was not a new one in 1830. Indeed, even a cursory examination of Udaipur *vijñaptipatra* scrolls sent in 1742, 1774, and 1795 demonstrates that Udaipur artists continually adapted pictorial vignettes from horizontal court paintings to fit the vertical format of the scroll, carefully citing prevalent artistic styles and contemporary portraits of Udaipur rulers (fig. 5.9). Representation of palatial architecture was a central pictorial concern in Udaipur court painting, so it is not surprising that local artists saw a Jain *vijñaptipatra* as an apt visual space in which to experiment and to extend their interest in depicting their city. They employed various strategies to fit their compositions into these extended surfaces, in some cases using defined cells to divide the activity and in others allowing structural elements, such as architecture, to guide the eye through and around the scene—and up and down the paper scroll. The *vijñaptipatra* scroll can thus be seen as an innovative departure from the large-scale horizontal panoramas that not only had become particularly popular at the Udaipur court but also had come to globally dominate the nineteenth-century visual world.

The artist of the 1830 Udaipur *vijñaptipatra* eulogized Udaipur as an ideal place by inserting portraiture into the painting (fig. 5.10). He portrays the current ruler, Jawan Singh, engaged in a series of royal activities and cites pictorial strategies of depicting Udaipur rulers in a temporal sequence that can be found within large-scale court paintings.[13] Jawan Singh is shown, for example, enjoying a boat procession with his nobles (fig. 5.11); dining within the inner palatial domains (fig. 5.12);

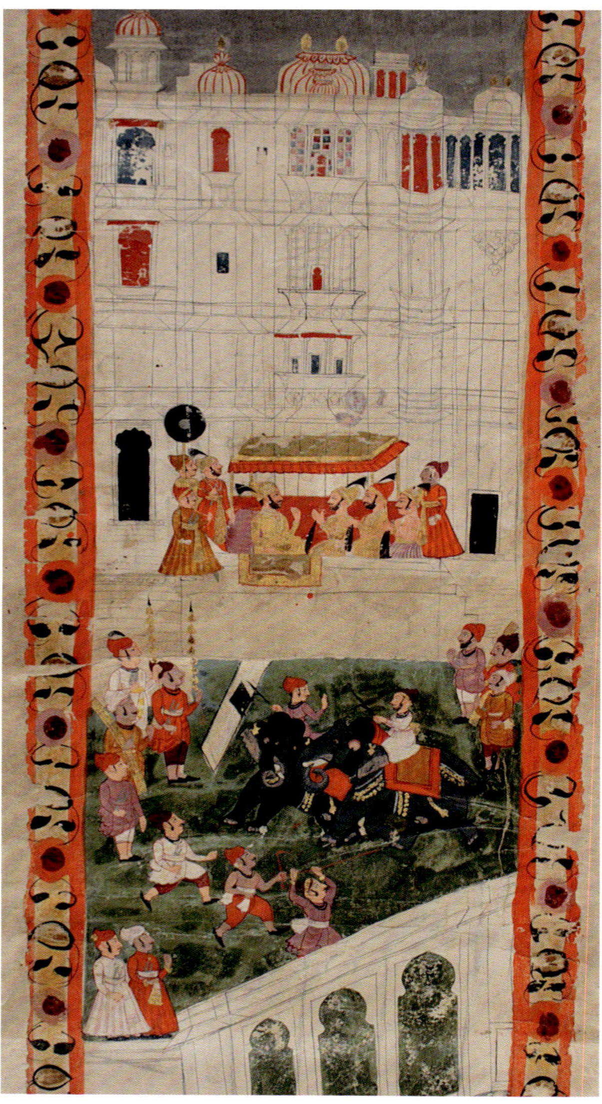

5.9. *Letter of Invitation (*Vijñaptipatra*) Sent to the Jain Monk Vijaydharma Suri*, 1774, Udaipur. Detail depicting the portrait of Maharana Ari Singh II holding a durbar, overlooking the Manek Chowk, City Palace complex, Udaipur. Opaque watercolor, gold and ink on paper, 284.7 × 32.2 cm. Lalbhai Dalpatbhai Institute of Indology, Ahmedabad; LDII.Gol.85.

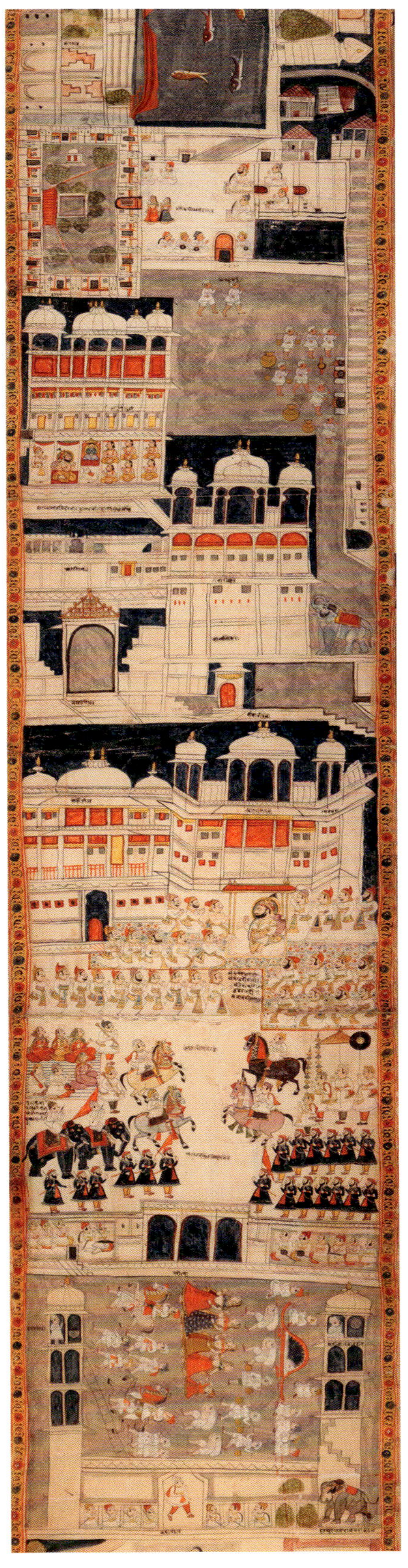

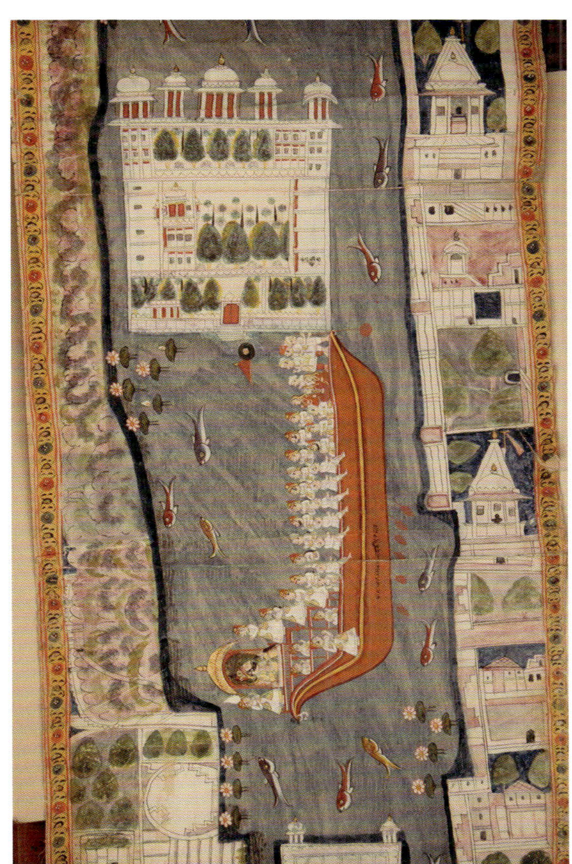

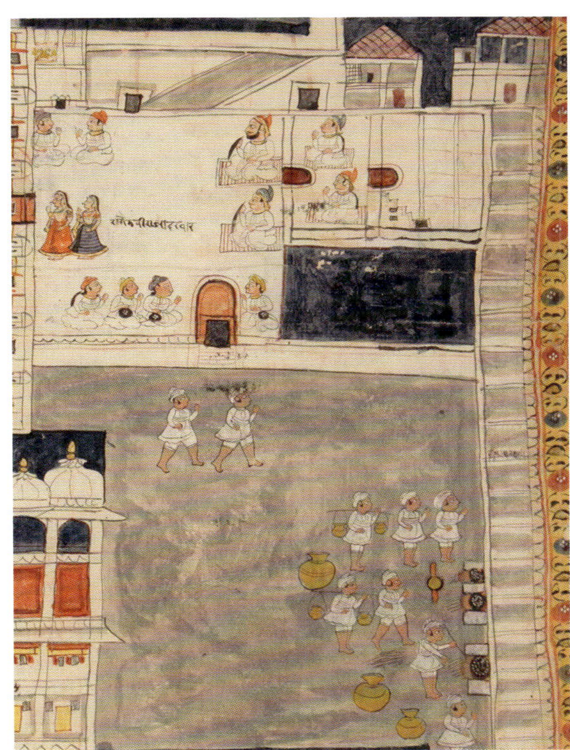

5.10. Detail of fig. 5.1. Jawan Singh performing a series of royal activities, composed within a vertical format and adapted from horizontally oriented depictions of the Udaipur palace within court paintings.

5.11. Detail of fig. 5.1. Jawan Singh enjoying a boat procession with an assembly of his nobles.

5.12. Detail of fig. 5.1. Jawan Singh dining privately in chambers adjacent to the palace kitchen.

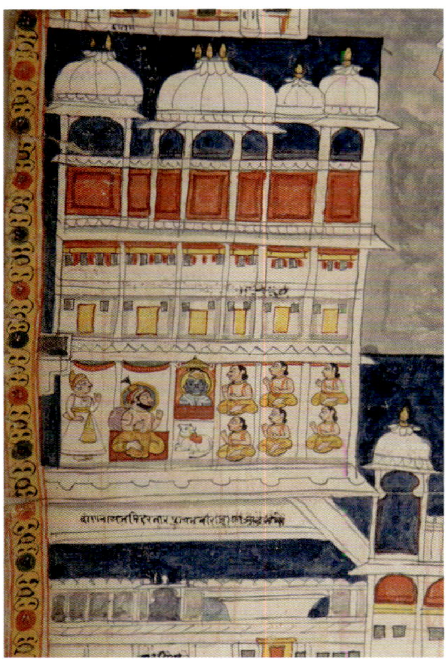

5.13. Detail of fig. 5.1. Jawan Singh performing rituals at the court temple.

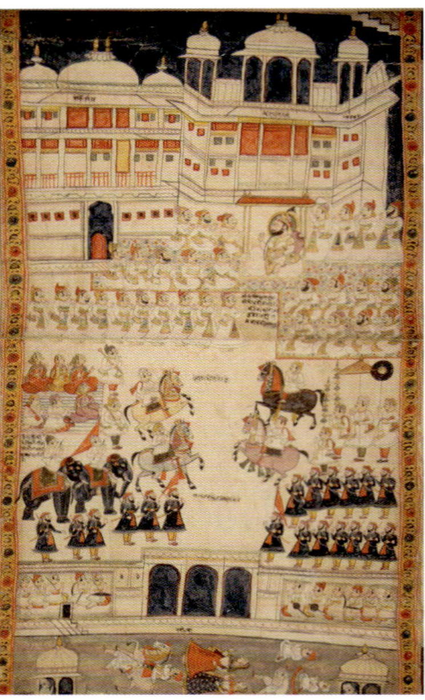

5.14. Detail of fig. 5.1. Jawan Singh with his sixteen nobles in a durbar held at the colonnaded pavilion for the Udaipur court's public assemblies.

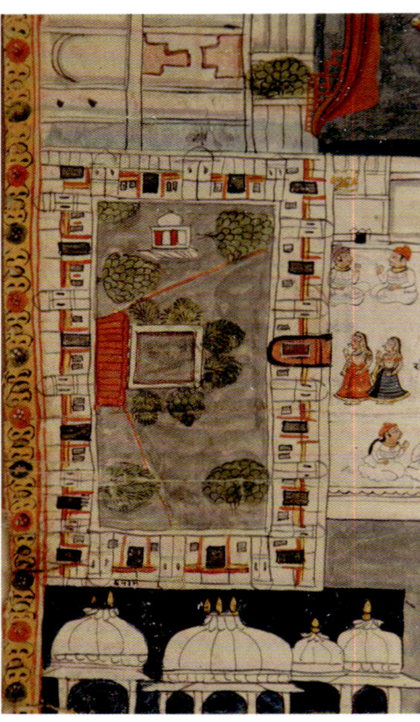

5.15. Detail of fig. 5.1. Planimetric view of the Women's Palace, Udaipur.

performing rituals, bare-chested, at the court temple (fig. 5.13); and presiding, along with his sixteen nobles, as an embodiment of the state, within the larger courtly hall of the palace (*badā darīkhānā)* (fig. 5.14). The artist's careful selection of vignettes conveys the distinctive facets of idealized kingship in action at the Udaipur court.[14] In creating these scenes, the artist eulogized Udaipur as an ideal and alluring place by specifically alluding to courtly practices that attributed to the city a royal and recognizable human element.

It is, however, in the detailed depiction of the palace environs that the scroll's artist reveals his breadth in adapting pictorial conventions of royal portraiture and praise. By depicting the iconic facade of the Udaipur palace, the artist transposed a signature architectural feature of horizontally oriented court paintings, as discussed in chapter 2, onto the narrow, vertical format of the scroll, a difficult feat of compositional reinterpretation (fig. 5.10). The local painter of an earlier Udaipur *vijñaptipatra* (1774) dealt with this challenge by painting a portrait of the contemporary ruler, Ari Singh, seated with his nobles in the Manek Chowk courtyard, against the palatial backdrop (fig. 5.9).[15] The 1774 painter carefully cites vignettes and a connection to the contemporary artistic style of Udaipur court painting; however, he does not represent the ruler's portrait multiple times in relation to the various facets of his kingship, nor does he connect the ruler to the diverse courtly spaces in his palace. By contrast, the 1830 scroll's artist reveals his facility at adapting conventions in the detailed and extensive depiction of the palace environs. The artist lent further force to his citations by painting black outlines to set off the deep blue color of the sky, which allowed him, like the court artists, to highlight the profiles, twists, and turns of domed and angular roofs. While Udaipur's court painters emphasized a visual sense of continuity in the palace facades as seen from the Manek Chowk courtyard (see fig. 2.27), the scroll's artist pictorially disaggregated this view by ingeniously dividing the horizontal palatial facade based on how the individual courtyard buildings were spatially laid out within the complex. At the same time, he established continuity within this segmented facade by employing a palette of red and yellow hues with black outlines and by writing inscriptions that identify various gateways and courtyards.

It is equally possible that the scroll artist employed this format based on circulating mapping practices, another visual source that would have been available at the time, especially for spaces that were not associated with an established iconography in court painting. For example, in representing the Women's

5.16. Detail of fig. 5.1. Sitla Mata temple.

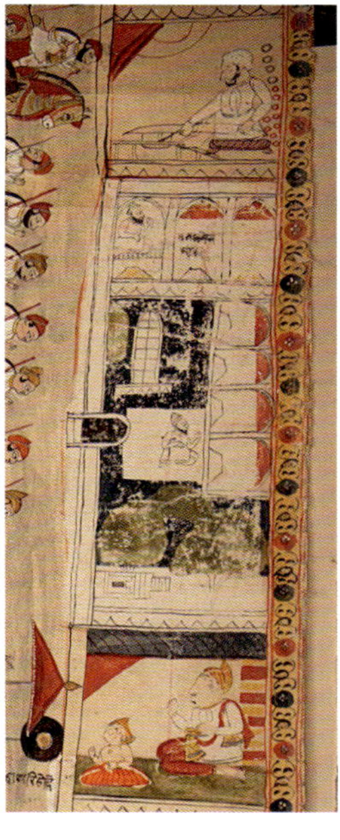

5.17. Detail of fig. 5.1. Depiction of a mosque courtyard (with a rubbed inscription).

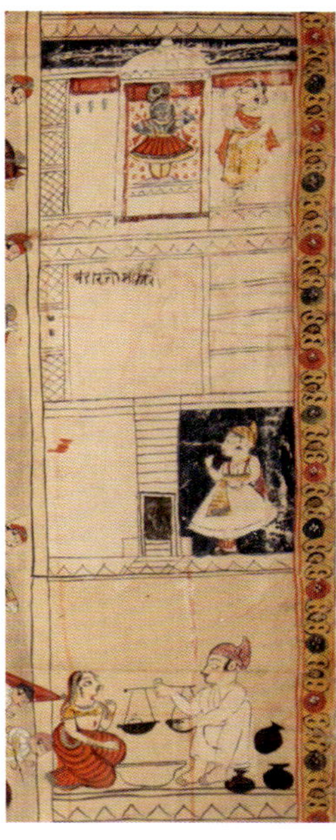

5.18. Detail of fig. 5.1. Shrinathji temple.

Palace of Udaipur, which had been pictured in a very limited number of court paintings, the artist chose to depict a plan view (fig. 5.15), which can be related to an eighteenth-century architectural drawing of the city's palace complex (see fig. 1.12).[16] Several such instances attest to the artist's interest in conveying both his knowledge and his spatial perception of the buildings he observed, in addition to displaying his aptitude for making stylistic and convention-based choices, especially in picturing temples devoted to multiple deities, mosques, and Sufi shrines along the central streets of the bazaars. The artist chose to depict some precincts by combining plan and elevation views, a convention adopted with particular enthusiasm by Udaipur's court artists. By this means, for example, in the case of the Sitla Mata temple (*sitlā mātā kā mandir*), the scroll's artist suggested the temple's greater scale and religious importance (fig. 5.16). In other cases, the artist employed this representational strategy to mark difference within his spatial typology. For example, in mapping one of the city's mosques (fig. 5.17), and while representing a temple dedicated to Shrinathji, an incarnation that celebrates the blue god Krishna as a young boy (fig. 5.18), built often as a domestic courtyard house (*haveli*), the painter highlighted the courtyard and surrounding arcades of each building. One also senses the presence of many diverse religious domains, since he also labeled the domain of the Saji saints (*sāji fakīr kā takīyā*), the Hanuman temple (*hanumān mandir*), and the premises of the Dadupanthi followers (*dādupanthi rī jāgā*). The artist's prolific labeling of precincts conspicuously reveals his proclivity for mapping Udaipur, such that the painted invitation letter must be read as an epistemic genre that contains and expresses the artist's cartographic vision.

In presenting a picture of courtly praise and cartographic knowledge as a means of constituting Udaipur as a charismatic city, the artist of the 1830 Udaipur *vijñaptipatra* also sought to expand his view of mercantile space and urban ethnography. He departed from the typical metaphorical reference to a bazaar populated with men and women, as seen in the above-discussed Sirohi scroll (fig. 5.8), by reinforcing the specificity of each trade and individual.[17] The areas occupied by dyers, barbers, arms makers, utensils sellers, cloth sellers, flower sellers, and moneylenders are all labeled, and the artist delineated each individual's turban or head scarf and facial features (figs. 5.19–22). This personalization, visible in even the smallest details of the men's beards, perhaps suggests relationships between certain trades and specific communities.

The embedding of horizontally painted processions results in the transformation of the vertical composition of the central

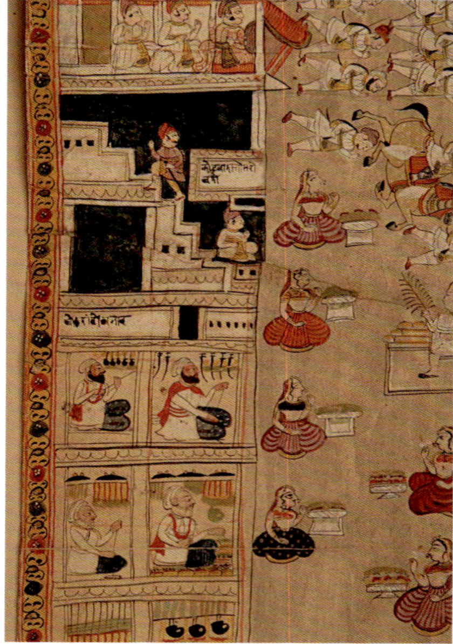

5.19. Detail of fig. 5.1. Depiction of arms shops and women selling flowers.

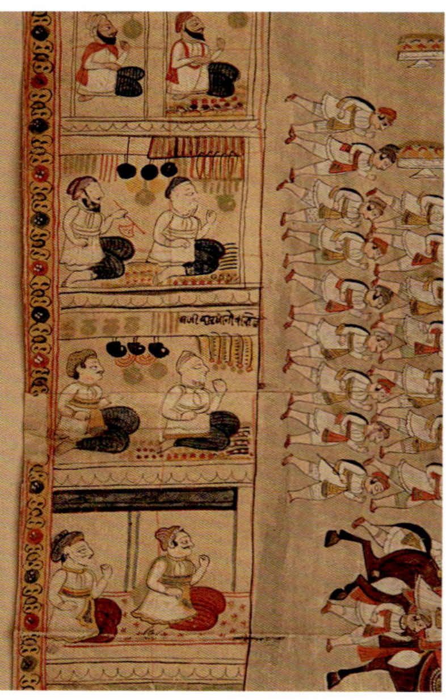

5.20. Detail of fig. 5.1. Depiction of shops of utensils sellers.

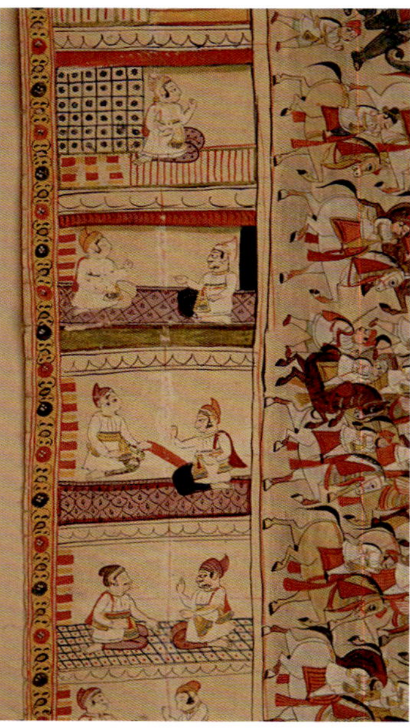

5.21. Detail of fig. 5.1. Depiction of cloth sellers.

street in the letter-scroll. It creates a perplexingly long spine for the procession, along which one could view the scroll as a horizontally oriented painting (fig. 5.1). The long retinue of footmen, horses, elephants, and troops culminates in a portrayal of the ruler Jawan Singh mounted on an elephant (fig. 5.2). Farther along the street, the artist painted another elephant, carrying three British officers. Udaipur's then-current political agent, Alexander Cobbe, is foremost, accompanied by two unnamed officers (fig. 5.3). The artist does not distinguish the political agent, unlike the Udaipur maharana, presented with a distinctive beard and halo.[18] Alongside appear sepoys and cavalry from the British Indian army. Rajasthan's colonial agent, James Tod, had recruited soldiers from Colonel James Skinner's cavalry, known as "yellow boys" due to the color of their uniforms, to his army, and Alexander Cobbe had increased their numbers in the army that the British agents maintained at Udaipur. Here the artist drew upon the aesthetic trope of processions that Udaipur court artists employed during this period to construct royal portraits and commemorate routine royal processions that took place in the city.[19] Court painters experimented with multiple scales; in some instances they miniaturized the chorography of Udaipur's environs, and in others the procession itself was miniaturized. It is important here to reiterate the singular nature of this visualization of Udaipur: processional and mercantile spaces being combined and given equal weight was unprecedented in court painting and in *vijñaptipatra* scrolls. While Udaipur's streets had been imagined as spaces for processions, we find very few examples of court artists depicting mercantile spaces and bazaars.[20] An earlier example of a manuscript leaf from the second book of Jagat Singh's *Rāmāyaṇa*, completed by the painter Sahib Din in 1650, depicts merchants decorating their shops with fine textiles and brocades and people sitting on the roofs of their houses and on the towers of temples to secure the best view of the anticipated procession for the consecration ceremony of Rama (fig. 5.23).[21] This earlier artist also situated the bazaar street amid temples—as seen in *vijñaptipatras*—specifying the presence of a Jain temple by representing an icon of a Jina. The scroll artist juxtaposed pictorial conventions, thereby extending the semantic content of the visual trope of processions.[22] His juxtaposition situates the procession within the streets of Udaipur, as if the artist sought to illuminate the mercantile space—within which the procession was performed and upon which it relied—rather than presenting a chorography of Udaipur's palaces as a panegyrical backdrop for royal or mercantile patrons.

The Udaipur scroll artist's experiments in combining pictorial idioms from courtly and sectarian contexts exemplify how established visual practices merged in painted invitation letters

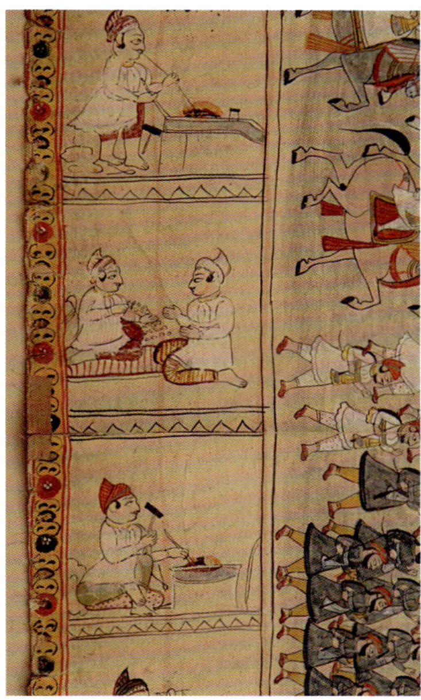

5.22. Detail of fig. 5.1. Depiction of moneylenders and blacksmiths.

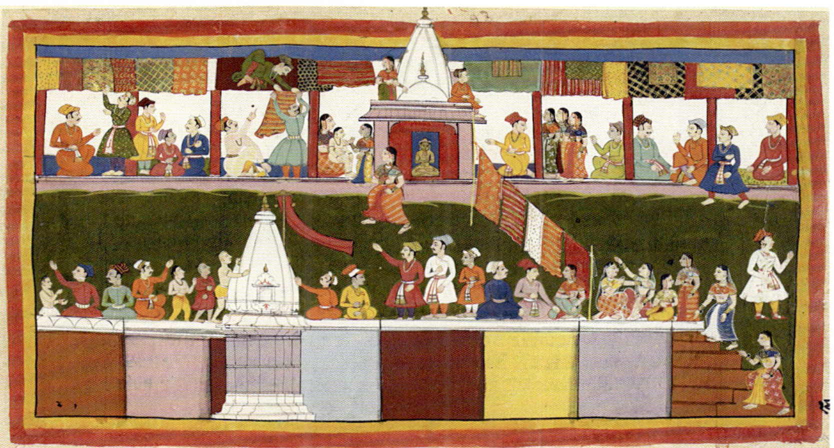

5.23. "Bazaar Street in Ayodhya," from book two of Jagat Singh's *Rāmāyaṇa*, 1649–53, Sahib Din, Udaipur. Opaque watercolor on paper, 23 × 39.9 cm. The British Library Board, London; Add. 15296(1), f.16a.

to circulate among broader audiences. These artists were the kinds of practitioners who were familiar with court styles and could link them to other visual interests and associations, such as previous scrolls and contemporary maps. This scroll recalls paintings by Jodhpur's court artists that combined conventions of devotional pictures, pilgrimage maps, and town plans in response to new theo-political alliances and new image-viewing modalities that reveal insights into what Debra Diamond characterized as the "conceptual frameworks through which historical viewers interpreted court paintings."[23] A case in point can be found in the late nineteenth-century scrolls of the Marwari desert towns of Jodhpur and Merta, where artists commenced the picturing of their towns with vignettes of lake palaces painted in white, as seen in the Udaipur *vijñaptipatra*.[24] The artists of the later scrolls may not have been citing these architectural vignettes from any of the Udaipur scrolls I have discussed thus far, but the fact that such vignettes were placed at the very beginning of the scroll, following the standardized Jain ritualistic icons, is evidence that by the end of the nineteenth century, Udaipur's lake palaces had become iconic symbols for an attractive city and could even be inserted into the pictorial presentation of a desert town as part of an idealizing vision.

The representation of Udaipur's environs outside courtly domains and the city walls is just as important as imagery of the city itself (fig. 5.7). In the case of the Udaipur *vijñaptipatra* of 1830, the artist labeled sites of the British residency, such as the "Sahab's Bungalow" and the "cantonment of the foreigner [*fīrangī*]" (fig. 5.24). Captain Alexander Cobbe had acquired a courtyard house in 1824 from one of Udaipur's prominent chieftains, and he expanded the building into his residence. The artist carefully depicted courtyards with green lawns and the home's inhabitants seated in chairs, thus marking differences between the lifestyles, furniture, and cultural protocols of the British agent and the Udaipur ruler, who was shown seated on floor cushions. Yet Udaipur's suburban frontiers are not dominated solely by the British presence. On the other side of the central street, in the most striking way, the artist pictured and labeled the assembly to be held by the invited leader, Jinharsh Suri, who is depicted as someone who was established in the city rather than as an aspirational visitor. Groups of elites, palanquins, and troops are depicted waiting upon both the monk's durbar and the British residency (fig. 5.7). While the depiction of monks holding assemblies is common in other scrolls, here, in imagining this anticipated religious assembly precisely opposite the British residency, and pictorially matching its scale, the artist presented colonial and religious powers as two equal and competing domains of authority. In the Agra *vijñaptipatra* (1610) as well, Salivahana strikingly composed the Jain monk

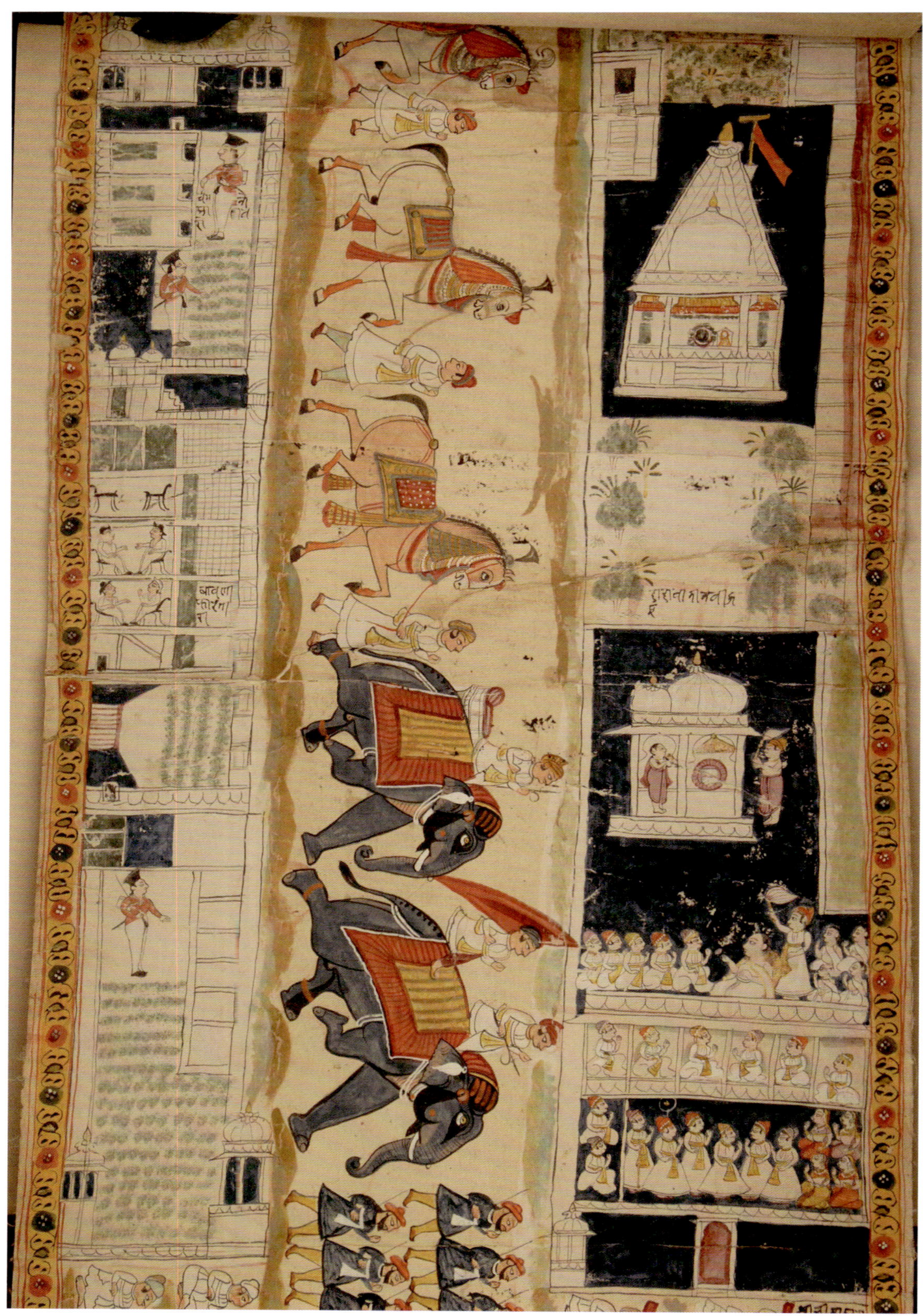

5.24. Detail of fig. 5.7. Depiction of the residency of the British colonial agent *(left)* and anticipated durbar of Jinharsh Suri *(right)*.

Vijaysena's assembly at the same scale as the assembly of the emperor Jahangir (r. 1605–1627) in his court. In both vignettes, the background is painted red; several attendees face each other and gaze upward, toward their leaders; and the leaders—political and religious—are pictured sitting under pavilions in a durbar setting (see figs. I.1–3). As I noted in the introduction to this chapter, the Udaipur artist's visualization of the invited Jain monk's assembly implies his conviction that the 1830 Udaipur *vijñaptipatra* would be effective, its objective realized by the monk's arrival. Likewise, here the depicted procession of the Udaipur ruler and the British agent can be interpreted as proceeding toward the anticipated Jain monk's assembly.

The Udaipur *vijñaptipatra* of 1830 is, therefore, simultaneously a grand representation of an ideal city, a topographical map, a picture of relational identities, and an epistle embedded in shifting territorial claims during the long eighteenth century. The artist visualizes the Jain monk's domain akin to a courtly durbar—where sophisticated men assembled for the practice of pleasure and politics. We know that a diverse and large community of monks, nuns, and laypeople traveled together on Jain pilgrimages to holy centers and during the annual establishment of itinerant religious centers in cities from which invitations were issued.[25] In almost all *vijñaptipatras*—including this Udaipur scroll—we see groups of monks, laymen, and laywomen attending assemblies held by Jain monks as well as vignettes depicting groups of drummers and trumpeters (fig. 5.25). In the Agra *vijñaptipatra* of 1610, for instance, a community of people—including merchants, laymen and laywomen, nuns, and musicians—is painted to suggest the demographic of the broader public space adjacent to the Jain monk's assembly and the key audience who witnessed the receipt of Jahangir's proclamation. In fact, the idea of publicly announcing Jahangir's *farmān* to a larger community is suggested in various ways throughout this invitation letter: for example, in the depiction of musicians beating drums and cymbals and playing the trumpet. It is quite possible that, apart from the invited monk, members of this monastic community, or its associated laypeople, were able to see and interpret this idealized pictorial image of Udaipur.[26] My understanding that *vijñaptipatra* scrolls forged an important vernacular and popular domain in the material culture of South Asia is based on the prospect of wide-ranging audiences; collective patronage; the combination and adaptation of conventions and forms that illuminated Indian painting from a defamiliarized perspective; and the annual circulation of several invitations.

The local artist of the 1830 Udaipur scroll extolled a charismatic landscape inhabited by prosperous urbanites and the powerful groups of the Udaipur court and the British East India Company, and projected a contiguous Jain landscape in relation to other religious domains throughout the length of the scroll. In recent years—by challenging the idea of the eighteenth century as a period of decline and by making a distinction between the emergence of the "early modern" and the "colonial modern" within cultural formations, especially in the early period of British rule—scholars have sought to consider the epistemic possibilities of the "vernacular" and to question how historical thinking was pursued within various early modern cultural forms, "not teleologically predetermined by the ascendancy of the colonial modern."[27] The Udaipur *vijñaptipatra* scroll forcefully demonstrates that painted letters were one such material domain wherein vernacular views, not covered within colonial and courtly sources, could be presented. It is difficult to assess whether the artist of this scroll elongated his depiction of the street to picture the procession or expanded the procession to map the street. Deploying his knowledge of the canon and style of Udaipur court painting and mapping practices in an extensive and nuanced way, he produced a scroll that exemplifies how regional imaginings of places were redefined and embedded in circulating painted invitation letters. The remarkable multiplicity of represented spaces and stakeholders provides an avenue by which we can examine the way nineteenth-century religious movements and establishments crossed the boundaries between British and princely India—a field of inquiry that requires more research.[28]

By transforming the assumed relationship through which audiences might see and perceive the scroll, the artist set interpretive processes into action. Monks probably unrolled the unwieldy seventy-two-foot-long scroll two to three feet at a time. As viewers slowly traversed the city of Udaipur, images of the densely populated procession attracted their gazes and continually disrupted their progress through the scroll. This mode of viewing would have required contemporary audiences to closely view and re-view the scroll. Its format thus literally forced audiences to see the idealized domain of the palaces after they had seen multiple interrelated domains of religiosity, commerce, and authority. The very structure of the painted invitation letter precluded engaging with the whole picture, whether as a large-scale topographical panorama, a processional painting, a bounded cartographic map, an architectural drawing, or a picturesque view. Rather,

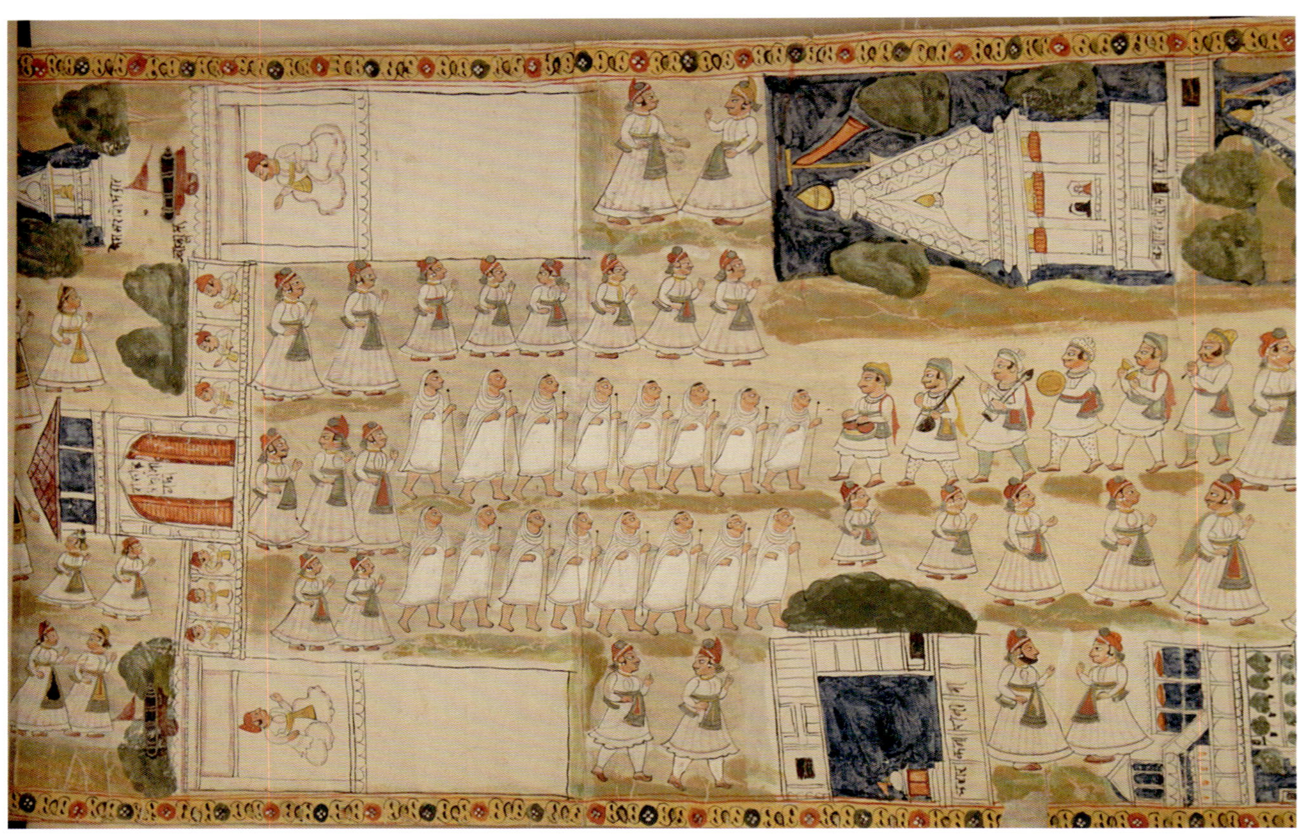

5.25. Detail of fig. 5.1. Monks, merchants, singers, and performers depicted in the procession leading to the monk Jinharsh Suri's durbar.

it constituted several pictures that stack up in the mind's eye as one unrolls it, replicating the experience of traveling or meandering through the city of Udaipur, seeing it from different angles and positions, and recalling the lingering images that evoke a sense of the place.

EPISTOLARY DESIRES

Any single example of a *vijñaptipatra* consists of two distinct yet interrelated sections, the painted images and the written letter, or *vijñapti*. Regardless of how the 1830 scroll was painted, its recipient, Jinharsh Suri, who then resided in Bikaner, must have unrolled the scroll first to read the *vijñapti* before viewing the images discussed above. On the verso of the rolled-up scroll we find evidence of a rubbed inscription that states an address in Bikaner.[29] This information provides a clue as to how the messenger carried the rolled scroll and the direction of its original spiral. It shows clearly that when the scroll was unrolled, it first presented to its audience the written letter rather than its painted counterpart. The invitation states that the Shvetambara Jain community at Kesariyaji, near Udaipur, along with Udaipur's devotees and residents as well as the city's king were eager to welcome the eminent monk. The scribes, pandits Rukhabhdas and Kushalchand, note that Jinharsh Suri's arrival would bring prosperity to the entire "Mewar country," and that the day he arrived would bring unprecedented benefaction. This panegyric note echoes the artist's careful pictorial, if aspirational, imagining of the arrived monk at a time that is yet to come. Such gestures imbue the scroll with multiple temporalities, suggesting that the charismatic landscape of Udaipur would become an ideal place only after the invited Jain monk's domain was established there. In order to fully comprehend how historical audiences might have perceived the visual and textual registers that we see within the elaborately conceived Udaipur *vijñaptipatra*, related literary and performative genres offer a critical lens. First, we turn to the textual letter.

By citing previous letters, scribes could exhibit their knowledge of other invitation letters as well as embed their own letters within an established tradition; they also referred to towns that were already located within pilgrimage networks through the circulation of letters. As a genre of letter writing, the *vijñaptipatra* was related to Sanskrit literary practices, including older Jain epistolary writing on palm-leaf manuscripts as well as the seventeenth- and eighteenth-century Sanskrit messenger poems (*dūtakāvya*) that were used to send invitations and messages to people in different locales.[30] Most scribes in the eighteenth and nineteenth centuries wrote the letters within *vijñaptipatra* scrolls partly in Sanskrit and partly in a local dialect, often combining verse and prose to compose the invitation.[31] Within the Udaipur letter (1830), pandits Rukhabhdas and Kushalchand cited several standard laudatory epithets for the invitee in Sanskrit, Prakrit, and Gujarati, and it may be possible to trace some of these to the letters within other scrolls, including parts of the text written in the 1610 Agra *vijñaptipatra*.[32] Following this pastiche of laudatory texts, the scribes of this Udaipur *vijñaptipatra* shift to writing in the local Rajasthani dialects of Mewari and Marwari in order to convey the specificities pertaining to the invitation.

The letter explicitly links the monk's arrival with prosperity (*lābha*) and good reputation (*mahīmā*). The scribes offer their sincere and humble homage to Shri Jinharsh Suri, on behalf of the entire community (*sangha*) of Udaipur, in hope that the tributes would be accepted, repeatedly emphasizing the benefits that will accrue should Jinharsh Suri visit.[33] They note that there is peace and happiness in the prominent Jain *sangha* near Udaipur that is the domain of Shri Kesariyaji Maharaja. We are told that this community prays that Jinharsh Suri (*śrijī mahārāja*) may always experience times of happiness, that his reputation may increase and expand (*āpa mōṭā ho baḍā ho*), and that he may always bless the city of Udaipur with his divine grace (*kṛipā sdṛiśtī*) and maintain a special relationship with its community (*sangha*). Having noted this collective desire, the scribes further emphasize that "rich and famous (*mōṭā mōṭā*)" merchants await his arrival in this city. The writers from the outset explicitly state that the arrival of Jinharsh Suri will be extremely beneficial to "Mewar country [*deśa*]" beyond the city of Udaipur.[34] They further elaborate that the monk's arrival will be advantageous for agricultural production, benefit the beautiful people of the place, bring fame to the administration, and ultimately propagate prosperity (*kalyāna*) in all spheres (*saṛva bāta*).[35] The eagerness of Udaipur's devout community to see Jinharsh Suri during the next monsoon (*caumāsa*) is thus expressed in intertwined emotive and economic registers. The letter invites us to imagine a community that anticipates the monk's arrival "as a peacock awaits the arrival of the rains [*jyon chātraka mōra rātra dina varśā ne rathe*]" and that is eager for growth in prosperity and piety.

Jain *vijñaptipatra* scrolls were purposefully embedded in prevailing urban politics, beyond religious concerns. In this case, while extolling the city of Udaipur and its environs, the letter also reveals certain tensions and a measure of anxiety, as reflected in its transmission details. Toward the end of the letter, before the signatures of Udaipur's merchants, the scribes recorded an apology for the delay in sending the "painted letter [*citralekh*]," as Seth Joravarmal Bapna, the city's prominent merchant, was away, and Sher Singh Mehta, his secretary (*munshi*), was on leave. They also note that the letter was being sent through the Udaipur ruler's messenger (*harkārā*), thus establishing the connection between the city's merchants and the court. In explaining this delay, the scribes note that Jinharsh Suri's arrival would help many people to "emerge [*udai hosī*]" from a plethora of problems. While such phrases could be dismissed as a common trope, scribes often used phrases such as "you may please arrive early and do not delay your trip [*āpa kṛipā karke vegā padhārsī ḍīla karāvsi nahī*]" (repeated throughout the letter and in the merchants' signatures) to indicate the sincerity of their sentiments.

It is worth considering that the scribes may be suggesting the urgency of the issues that were facing the city, as indicated by other sources, namely diplomatic letters that were circulating between the Udaipur court and British officers at this time. Already by 1818, the British colonial agent James Tod had written about the declining economic atmosphere in Udaipur, noting that he had taken it upon himself to revive the city's mercantile activity by sending his own invitation letters to merchants. The years from 1823 on were particularly stressful for the Udaipur ruler Bhim Singh, and even more so for his successor, Jawan Singh, both of whom had to negotiate their own positions and financial needs with the British East India Company and regional merchants. Yet Tod's successor, colonial agent Cobbe, depicted in the painted procession, was highly critical of his predecessor's policies. By October 14, 1830, Cobbe had ensured that the Udaipur Agency and the Jaipur Agency were abolished.[36] This abolition not only had implications for the political status of Udaipur as a princely state under indirect British rule but also suggested that Udaipur rulers would not be able to directly negotiate their rights and allowances with an exclusive British political agent residing in Udaipur. Maharana Jawan Singh immediately sent a letter to Cobbe stating that he was concerned by this treatment and the "inconvenience" the court would face due to the reduction in its revenue at a time of mounting debt.[37] This Udaipur *vijñaptipatra* appears to have been sent around the same time in 1830, and thus we can infer that it was dispatched with the diplomatic aim of propping up another sphere of authority in the city. Merchant communities that collectively commissioned such painted invitation letters not only effectively displayed their religious piety and inserted their towns into a pilgrimage economy but also reinforced their political and economic authority in the wake of British colonization. The ontology of letter-scrolls thus understood included religious, epistolary, and diplomatic functions—all deeply connected to their imagined efficacious potential.

PANEGYRIC ECHOES

Painted letters, as circulating objects that were ontologically hybrid, emerged in the space of the bazaar. They centrally mediated the present- and future-oriented moods of cities. By reading the aesthetics of praise and the tangible visuality of painted *vijñaptipatras* and poetic *gajals*—both created in the context of the traveling cultures of the Jains—we can shed light on the cross-cultural milieu within which these intervisual and intertextual artifacts were circulated and received. The panegyric modes of such painted letters and urban poetry raise questions concerning the negotiation of religious and worldly concerns within domains of sectarian travel and the expression of subjective encounters with new places. I discuss verses of the Jain monk Kavi Khetal's *Udaipur rī gajal* that evoke the city as an alluring place in order to emphasize that both the painted letter of 1830 and Khetal's sung poetry were heterogeneous cultural formations that sought to constitute a place as a charismatic landscape of urban reference. Given that a wide variety of indigenous travelers often journeyed with monks during annual monsoon pilgrimages to new temples and bazaars, both artifacts present the potential for understanding how more broad-based, popular aesthetic sensibilities, notions of territoriality, and historical memory were forged in the eighteenth and nineteenth centuries.

Poetry offered traveling monks a space to expand their gaze to subjects beyond Jain religiosity and across linguistic boundaries, toward literary genres associated with urban praise. They composed and sung *gajals*—highly repetitive poetic songs, each consisting of a series of mono-rhymed couplets—in a combination of dialects of Marwari, Brajbhasha, Persian, Awadhi, Gujarati, and Punjabi—that sought to evoke their experience of seeing new places. Persian poets composed the canonical form of the *ghazal* as a mystical poem of love and desire for a human being, divine person, or other abstract object that dominantly included a lover intoxicated with passion.[38] By the sixteenth century, poems describing public and imperial spaces, cataloguing craftsmen and professionals, and comparing subjective urban imaginaries of various cities came to be written about every major urban center in the Mughal, Iranian, Central Asian, and Ottoman regions. In the Jain monk Khetal's couplets on the city of Udaipur, discussed below, we hear the poet's evocation of the beauty of the palace and court, gardens and lakes, markets and temples, as well as the sophisticated tastes of Udaipur's diverse communities and connoisseurs. The mixing of languages puts Khetal's *gajals* in the same field as Rekhta, a Persianate term for mixed Hindi-Urdu (Khaṛi Boli).[39] Rekhta poetry exhibits strong connections with classical Brajbhasha literature and was practiced as a mixed linguistic and literary idiom across the circles of Islamicate Sufis, Krishna devotees, Mughals, Rajputs, and Sikhs. The large archive of Rekhta *gajals* on cities like Lahore, Calcutta, Bikaner, and Surat strongly suggests that Jain monks, too, participated in this multilingual literary culture that focused on crafting the regional memory of cities.[40] Jain participation in this poetic tradition thus runs counter to the vision of the Jain community as an insular world and works against scholarship that seeks to distance "Jain" *gajals* from "Muslim" *ghazals*.[41] Monks possibly saw themselves as engaging in multilingual and cosmopolitan literary dialogues with early modern Persian poets across the world—from Turkey to Iran and Central Asia to India—who composed such city poems from the beginning of the sixteenth century and well into the nineteenth century. In this regard as well, Rekhta *gajals* that were produced in the seventeenth century—including several that remained popular until the end of the nineteenth century—can be explored further to answer questions of overlapping of genres, meters, and language in northern India.

Khetal, a poet who identifies himself as a Jain monk (*yati*) belonging to the Kharatara Gaccha sect, composed the *Udaipur rī gajal* in 1718.[42] Khetal's poem had been in circulation for more than one hundred years when the 1830 Udaipur invitation was made and thus is useful for reconstructing the likely modes of urban imagining that conditioned responses to the later visual tradition. The popularity of this Udaipur *gajal* is asserted by the existence of several written copies made into the end of the nineteenth century by a variety of scribes who identify themselves as a pandit, a *yati*, or a muni and who assert their affiliations with various religious establishments across northwestern India. One of the manuscript colophons for the Udaipur *gajal* suggests that it was sung many times and written several times over. This allusion to the important sphere of orality suggests that the circulation of topographical poetry might have been facilitated not only by texts but also by recitations within urban settings and bazaars.[43] Monks, nuns, and laypeople, who traveled together during the monsoon season, were most likely the audiences who participated in this larger sphere of oral and poetic imaginings of urban towns. The differing materiality of the copies—ranging from formally copied manuscripts to small scrolls (*gutkā*) of scrap paper—also suggests the differing uses of such artifacts across monastic libraries and bazaars. The monastic collections of painted and literary manuscripts and scrolls associated with specific Jain temple establishments—and Jain monks, who were responsible for maintaining the manuscript libraries attached to Jain temples—often traveled along with monk communities during the monsoon season.[44]

It is critical to note that Jain monks perceived the Persianate genre of the *ghazal* as an apt choice, compared to models available within contemporaneous Sanskrit and vernacular literary traditions dedicated to imagining pilgrimage and sacred sites. Jain monks, such as Khetal, chose to compose Rekhta *gajals* because of the flexibility, breadth, and popularity the *shahrāshūb* topos offered across Persianate literary genres for praising and celebrating the novelty of cities in the context of travel. Poets employed *shahrāshūb* as a panegyric for urban praise in order to celebrate a place's vigor and vitality—that is, not to represent places "realistically" but rather as a topos around which they could fuse a variety of historical, ethnographic, and spatial information, including the description of a city's beautiful buildings, gardens, inhabitants, industries, and economic vitality.[45] In the Indo-Persian context, Shah Jahan's poet laureate, Abu Talib Kalim Kashani, composed a *shahrāshūb* on Akbarabad (Agra, 1640) in the literary tradition of a *masnavi*, and the poet Nurruddin Muhammad Zuhuri employed *shahrāshūb* in the *Saqīnāmah* (1616) to "produce a verbal panorama of the new city (*Nawshahr*) on the outskirts of Ahmadnagar" in the Deccan.[46] In both instances, the poet gives us a literary tour of the city and presents a striking engagement with its cosmopolitan nature, cataloguing its people engaged in various crafts and recognizing the diverse ethnicities represented in the city. For example, the Kharatara Gaccha Jain monk Jatmal Nahar—who composed the *Lahore ki gajal*, the very first known example of a Rekhta topographical poem, during the Mughal emperor Jahangir's reign—adapted his composition on Lahore from the *shahrāshūb* on Akbarabad in Kashani's Persian *ghazal*.[47] It is equally possible that Jain monks refracted the *shahrāshūb* and the topos of *nagara-varṇana*, shaped by poets of northern India in the courtly vernaculars in which Nandram's *Jagvilās* participates, for composing poetic descriptions of places.[48]

Khetal begins the Udaipur *gajal* by composing dedicatory verses to several deities that follow established formulas in Sanskrit and Braj praise poems. He fashions himself as a Kharatara Gaccha Jain *yati*, chanting the praises of and seeking protection from the Mewar court's family deity Eklingji, as well as the deity of Shrinathji and the Naths of Nathadwara, further including deities and temples in the wider region.[49] Khetal embeds the idea of seeing the city from various geographical and subjective positions—through the eyes of the ruler as well as through the eyes of both travelers to and citizens of Udaipur who may admire its beauty. He often urges his listeners and readers to turn their gaze to the area on their rear side (*pāche*) or in front of them (*āge*) or what comes first (*prathama*), elaborating on the sequence of sites. The poet shifts the visual subjects for his audience in literary and cartographic terms. Having located Udaipur within a sacred regional geography that catered to diverse beliefs, Khetal introduces Udaipur's palaces in the following manner:

> The court of *shri divan*,[50] look at the gateway and the royal doorway
> The special guards, thundering drums, hoisted flags (8)
>
> The palaces beyond rise high, new-new kinds of colored domes and pavilions
> The *jharokās* (balconied windows) offer beautiful views, the *jalis* (pierced screens) captivate hearts (9)

The above couplets describe the various architectural spaces and building features as a spectator approaching the palace from the street would see them. Simultaneously, Khetal presents the view of the city that one would be able to see from within the royal spaces of the pavilions and pierced screens. Khetal also employs the motif of the royal procession:

> The king sits in the royal boat; he watches as he tours the lake
> He proudly viewed the *chattrīs* (domed turrets), as one looks [upon] one's own sons (20)

Khetal's vision connects the city to the Udaipur ruler's body and eyes. He evokes the ruler's personal pride in and affection for Udaipur, albeit intermingled with power commanded by a king who had sons to continue his lineage. The vision imagined here is of a royal viewer seeing the city not simply as subject to his authority but as a place capable of arousing paternal pride and attachment. This vision is also one in which spectators admire royal spaces and wonder what it might mean to inhabit the vantage points from which the royal person admires the city. Khetal offers equally affective descriptions of the feel of Udaipur's urban layout in the details of architectural precincts, streets, neighborhoods, and geographical features in relation to one another, as if the poet is giving us a walking tour of the city. In another couplet, Khetal shifts from the royal gaze to the traveler's gaze, opening the way for his observations of everyday life along the lakefront, including scenes of lovers sitting by the lake—enjoying the site and taking pleasure in spending time there:

> What a rose-bodied beauty is she! One who captivates all people of the city
> A piercing presence on the *ghāt*s crowded with families, a face seen by all travelers (26)

Khetal praises the beauty of the city and the beauties seen along the lakefront, using the metaphor of the traveler, who also participates in the trope of "first vision"—love at first sight. The imaginary of the city as a beautiful woman was often seen in Persianate *shahrāshūb*. Khetal plays with the idea of the facades of Udaipur's lakefront palaces as the face of the city—and in so doing asserts his own gaze as a new and curious visitor.

Through both *gajal*s and *vijñaptipatra* scrolls, Jain identity was ultimately situated in the figure of the merchant who populated the bazaar. The evocation of the bazaar was key to Persianate *ghazal*s and Rekhta *gajal*s more than it was for descriptions of cities in Sanskrit and Brajbhasha poetry. Khetal explicitly says, "religious domains are aplenty, now please shift your gaze toward the bazaar," thus acknowledging this conceptual break in his lines.[51] He then describes bustling shops selling sweets, perfumes, and cloth, and notes the various trading communities, including the Jain Oswals and Maheshwaris among the Purohits and the Palliwals. We have seen that *vijñaptipatra*s, which facilitated the travels of Jain monk-poets, also included prominent painted vignettes of various kinds of shops and religious spaces; the 1830 example is particularly detailed in this regard. This parallel trope might have provided a key impetus for the monk-poets' adaptation of the *ghazal* form. Because their imaginings of new cities were initially formulated by the *vijñaptipatras* received as invitations to travel, these poets might have perceived evocations of bazaars and ethnographic details within Indo-Persianate *ghazals* as familiar topoi, connected to the paintings they knew well.

While Rekhta *gajals* were deeply invested in celebrating local urbanity, Jain monk-poets, like poets composing courtly works in Brajbhasha or Persianate *ghazals*, also highlighted their knowledge of broader geographies and interpretations of deeper histories. Jain merchants and monks were engaged, as discussed in the introduction, in wider cosmopolitan intellectual pursuits, thereby establishing a place for themselves and their city within a sophisticated web of cultural-religious-mercantile-political networks. Toward the end of the poem, he imagines Udaipur in relation to India's broader geography and the court's historical interests in the pride of the Hindus.[52] Khetal emphatically links Udaipur's territory and power in relation to Dillipati—the ruler of Delhi or the Mughal court—and memorializes the court's role as protector of the "boundaries of Hindustan."[53] The poet ingeniously conflates Udaipur with the whole of Hindustan and elides engagement with any specific memories of Mughal-Mewar interactions. The memory of Udaipur, and more broadly the Mewar court, as one that upheld the pride of the "Hindus" both against and in comparison with the Mughals is reinscribed here to metaphorically expand Udaipur's geographical boundaries. After all, by the time of Khetal's writing of the Udaipur *gajal*, many of the mid-seventeenth-century stories of the much-publicized Mewar submission to the Mughals were more than a half century old.[54]

The lake palaces, processions, and bazaars of the city of Udaipur, which by 1830 had been memorialized in the colonial accounts of James Tod and Alexander Cobbe as hedonistic evidence of Indian decline, were praised and celebrated as thriving in the *gajals* and *vijñaptipatra* scrolls featuring Udaipur. Khetal, like the scrolls' painters and scribes, concluded his Udaipur *gajal* with the poem's colophon as his praise (*tārif*) for the city (*sahar*), which he wished to share with the city's connoisseurs (*guṇiyana*) and worthy audiences (*lāyaka jana*). It is equally significant that authors of letters in the early nineteenth-century *vijñaptipatras* of Baroda, Sinor, and Channi in turn incorporated *gajals* within their textual letters as means of praising the beautiful city that was visualized in the painted letters, thereby recognizing and reinforcing this thematic connection.[55] Poets alluded to public proclamatory language, and several cues on singing the praises of the urbanity of Udaipur and its citizens—magnanimous Jain merchants, for example—are sprinkled throughout the poem within performative registers. Memories of hearing the Udaipur *gajal*'s couplets perhaps inflected the local artist's ways of recalling place or the viewer's perception of how to see and interpret the scroll. A *gajal*'s couplets also function independently and are often recited in a non-fixed sequence or recalled by connoisseurs in combinations triggered by affective associations and memories, thus paralleling the material nature of the scroll, which poses conditions for interrupted viewing.

The makers of the 1830 scroll layered the temporalities of the here and now and of a time one year in the future—when the monk is expected to arrive. They also relate the efficacy of the object to the expected moods and emotions of a praiseworthy place in a precise way. Such painted letter-scrolls were not only visual and religious instruments but also profoundly social, material, and political objects that moved through space, creating affection and longing for a represented place while instilling hopes for transformative urban outcomes in times of upheaval and crisis. The continuous disruptions signaled by the scroll, conditioned by its format, evoke the very challenges of imagining the city in flux that the 1830 invitation letter presents. The visual, material, and analytical quandary of deciphering the pictorial idioms and axes parallels how historical viewers and artists negotiated multiple institutions and polities. At the same time, we might read the dynamic corporeal relationship that the scroll establishes as a metaphor for the constantly shifting relationship the art historian has to the historical object.

UNSCROLLING MOODS, CONTESTING MAPS

The materiality of the 1830 Udaipur *vijñaptipatra*, with its painted images and its textual substance, reinforces a dialectic picture. The placement of the letter at the end of the scroll eliminates any possibility of reading the letter while looking at the paintings. Though both the letter and the painted vignettes, including the textual labels on the painted city precincts, praise the city of Udaipur, each cites its own set of referents and allows recipients to engage with parts of the scroll independently. Perhaps for some viewers the visual and the textual elements supplement each other. But the painted picture does not merely illustrate the text of the written letter, rather it enhances the function and charisma of the scroll object. The artist of the Udaipur *vijñaptipatra* (1830) innovates as he lays claim to and expands the genre of the invitation letter as a pictorial domain for visualizing a map and chorography of the city. This expansion suggests a desire to show the image of a city—including its key bazaars, religious sites, courtly buildings, and important personalities, as well as the procession of the regional ruler and British agent—in its entirety. Thus the artist would draw upon the affective value that a picture populated with endless details tends to evoke: a feeling of the real world. On the other hand, his radical elongation of the scroll generated an object that continuously disrupts any way of seeing a whole picture of the city. This disjunctive view of the city does not appear to be an accident of its composition but rather a structure that hinges upon a particular way of understanding urban space and, in particular, Udaipur—an emotionally and sensorially inflected mode of representing worldly places.[56]

The act of unfurling the scroll simulates the act of entering the city from its outskirts. The cultural historian Michel de Certeau critiqued the ways that artists, mapmakers, architects, and planners represent and visualize the city in tautological terms and the dominance of their viewpoints.[57] Spatial practices like walking, which are performed in a city at the ground level, he argues, illuminate perspectives that allow for formulating subjective maps of a place.[58] Walking constitutes a particular practice of everyday life that has the power to communicate plural geographies of a city, including the weaving of memories of being in the place. Such recollection of memories necessarily also includes subjective modes of forgetting. The Udaipur *vijñaptipatra* was not a route map that directed its users to turn right or left, following a particular route to reach Udaipur, nor did its artist seek to represent a measured drawing of the city's precincts, although he was clearly familiar with those types of diagrams. The scroll's artist cited tropes of Udaipur's palaces and processions from court commissions in meaningful ways while simultaneously transforming the represented street from a metaphorical pictorial position that signaled a thriving city, as seen in earlier *vijñaptipatras*, to one that marks the street with specificities. It recalls a sense of being in the place, telescoping from bird's-eye views to streetscape perspectives.

The scroll's picture of Udaipur, like Khetal's conjuring of the city in the *Udaipur rī gajal*, suggests a subjective engagement that evokes everyday practices and intimate knowledge of the place. Both artists also produced works that were intended to circulate, either physically (in the case of the letter) or orally (in the case of the *gajal*). This implicit intended mobility was embedded in both works, although it is not always visible. For that reason, it is necessary to conceive of how both were received. In the case of the scroll, the looker can gain a sense of walking into a new city and viewing its precincts and people, passing by some parts in haste and assessing others in detail. This painted invitation letter thus might have sparked the memory or imagination of its viewers in multiple subjective ways. The scroll's artist may have expected viewers of his map of the city to recall their knowledge of Udaipur, gained from fellow travelers, the city's residents, and perhaps from institutions like the guesthouses often associated with religious institutions (serais and dharmashalas) that served as resting places for pilgrims on the way to the city. An audience familiar with the city—through court paintings or other *vijñaptipatra* scrolls; from listening to or reading *gajal*s that praise the city; or through its own (vivid or fragmentary) recollections of traveling through and walking the streets of Udaipur—might have constructed the place as a palimpsest of images, maps, itineraries, and tellings of poems and stories. The scroll's innumerable images of the city aptly convey the accrued and intimate experience of knowing Udaipur through these various channels, visual, lived, heard, and remembered.

In terms of its form and content, the Udaipur *vijñaptipatra* presents an opportunity to rethink how makers and audiences in nineteenth-century India conceived of maps and mapping from vantage points not only quite different from those of British colonial agents like Tod and Cobbe but also detached from the gaze of regional rulers like Bhim Singh and Jawan Singh. The 1830 Udaipur *vijñaptipatra* scroll must be recognized as a bazaar image that formulates a vernacular mapping practice. It translates images and mixes pictorial tropes, but it also conveys a sense of the street and the everyday as well as a plethora of spatial stories that one encounters in urban places. Such cultural economies of praise for the flourishing city, and circulation of its image as charismatic, provide an alternative to the view that circumscribed popular maps in the eighteenth and nineteenth centuries, which adhered to colonial narratives of political decline and disintegration. Investigation of this *vijñaptipatra* scroll opens up an avenue for examining the bazaar and the views it offers on politics and on vernacular practices. If Khetal's Udaipur *gajal*s were repeatedly copied at the behest of several patrons as well as sung in the bazaars, they would have been capable of forging profound memories of belonging to a place. The poet's description of Udaipur not only celebrates its court, markets, temples, lakes, and people but also invokes the city's relationship to its past by mentioning the fort of Chittor and the emperor Akbar. The poem is located in the present but is open to spaces of the past.

The Udaipur city of the 1830 scroll and the *Udaipur rī gajal* is a flourishing, praiseworthy world worthy of circulation. It exists alongside and possibly contests Tod's and Cobbe's construction of Udaipur as a place that was declining economically, politically, culturally, and artistically. Udaipur's map is produced through practices of praise that are pictorially and poetically meaningful—including the citation of the local artistic style and the aesthetic trope of processions, as well as an inter-visuality and intertextuality capable of formulating and reinforcing how audiences beyond the British imagined and remembered the city and its territoriality. If Khetal's exploration of panegyric tropes enabled him to engage with cosmopolitan imaginaries of cities to adapt cross-cultural literary idioms and to formulate a gaze that privileged an urban subjectivity over a religious one, then the artist of the 1830 Udaipur scroll employed praise to subvert political and economic realities. Having pictorially praised Udaipur's thriving urbanity in the first sixty feet of the scroll, he paints into reality the fact that the city's suburban frontiers were not dominated solely by the British. On the opposite side of the street, he painted the anticipated assembly of the invited Jain leader Jinharsh Suri, on a scale that matches that of the British residency, the emblem of emergent British rule, thus imbuing the scroll with multiple temporalities and asserting that the colonial and religious powers are equal and competing domains of authority in the city.

The Udaipur Agency was abolished by the colonial agent Captain Alexander Cobbe in 1830 a few months before this invitation letter was sent. This political-economic loss drives an alternative articulation of territoriality, which imagines the counterfactual: that the charismatic landscape of Udaipur could become truly ideal after the invited Jain monk's domain was established. The complexity of networks across religious, political, and economic spheres, and the intercultural nature of artifacts point us to the irreducibility and unintelligibility of daily practices of knowledge and of the constitution of the *bhāva* of a place as a topos solely of courtly aesthetics. But such incommensurability is not a cause for denying the plurality we see in the visual engagements with the *bhāva* of a place and the potentiality painters thought pictorial moods could contain.

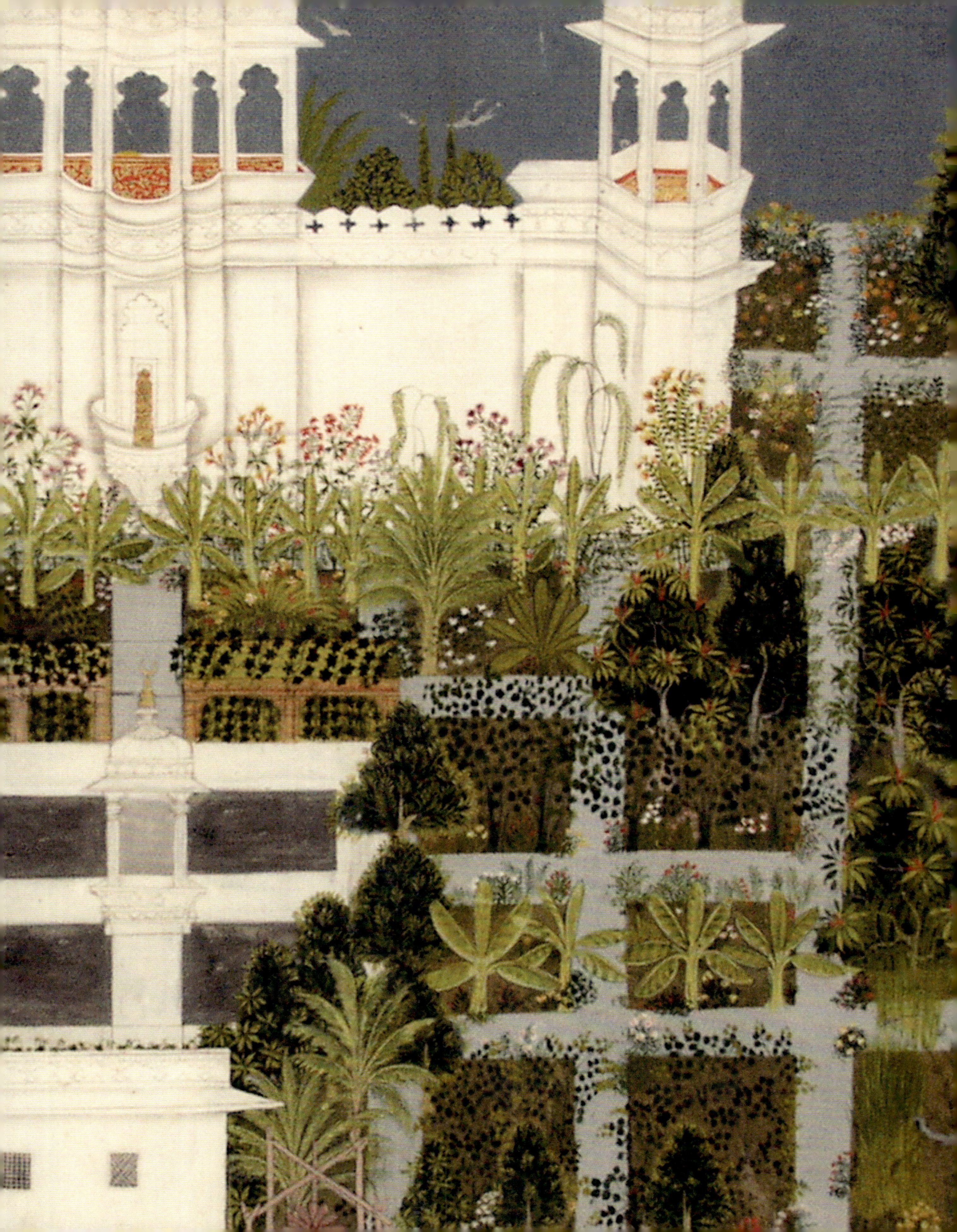

CONCLUSION

Memorializing Moods and Recovering Histories

MOODS, MATERIALITY, AND POTENTIALITY

The moods of places mattered in history. The objects that created the moods of places mattered specifically because they operated in critically supplemental ways—generating the potential for a variety of claims and conversations to occur. The moods of places emerged from painted depictions of Udaipur's lakes, palaces, streets, and lands beyond the city. The portraits of communities and connoisseurs who consumed these place-centric objects also appeared—kings, courtiers, merchants, and monks. These paintings reveal the numerous go-betweens: messengers, attendants, cooks, servants, record keepers, musicians, elephant riders, and many more, who are seen doing the work that went into creating such worlds of pleasure, spectacle, and abundance. Concomitantly, these artifacts of urban praise materially asserted the role aesthetic moods performed in the friendships forged among powerful men. The cultures of connoisseurship, immersion in beautiful places, and practice of politics are therefore bundled in one thick material bond—within objects featuring painted lands. Both the representation of moods and the presentation of such emotionally laden objects shaped affections, attachments, and imaginations in India's long eighteenth century. The localizing of moods and places was ultimately tied to pushing boundaries on real lands.

The study of the Udaipur painters' multilayered approach to picturing the moods of a place walks a tightrope between three recent approaches. At one end, art historians have emphasized the interrelations between materiality, visuality, and affect to reconceptualize the ontology of objects.[1] In the absence of textual sources elucidating the form, value, and travails of premodern artworks, these discussions extract deeply from available cues—the traces of handling and wear and tear seen on material surfaces as well as the values of affective qualities of media such as cloth, marble, bronze, and pigments. Both the agency of makers in crafting materials and ideas into objects that invited curiosity and wonderment and the agency of objects are tied to the question of efficacy. At its best, these conversations have addressed efficaciousness constituted by visual-material evidence across geographical and temporal divides but have not devolved into representing "alternate modernities," the token "global" case study, and the dehistoricized and dematerialized agency of objects.

Detail of fig. C.2

Udaipur's images of painted lands highlight the idea that *bhāva*, as an aesthetic concept with a deep intellectual history, while tied to the idealization of emotions and systematization of aesthetic experience, emerges as porous at its boundaries, open to new interpretations in the eighteenth century. Not only poets but also painters deployed an understanding of affect and aesthetics that took the concept of *bhāva* to new ends. As an affective concept that combined mental, emotional, and bodily immersion, it was shaped as much by the poetic, visual, and spatial practices as by the material presence of objects. Udaipur's artists chose material means to endow objects with affective force. Their strategy of expanding the size of paintings and iterating themes across numerous works enhances the ability of their artifacts to present the moods of places.

The second thread emerges from allied disciplines. Historians of literature, music, and art charting a new intellectual history of aesthetics have addressed beauty and panegyrics as not distinct from questions of historicity, politics, and reception in the provinces of eighteenth-century Mughal Hindustan. Thus, phenomena such as making of intellectual cultures, constitution of ethical selves, circulation across vernacular and multilingual registers, negotiation of difference, and the tracking of affective communities are seen as intimately tied in this time period. In moving away from fetishizing marginality and mobility in relation to Europe, Francesca Orsini has highlighted the importance of localizations and minor traditions in raising critical questions on itinerancy, epistemes, and disciplinary frameworks, moving beyond such generalized categories as "world literature," "world music," and "ethnomusicology."[2]

Thirdly, closely allied to these questions of aesthetics and genre, the scholarly attempts to evaluate the relation between premodern practices and colonial histories have turned to a class of native artists and scribes, men who became intermediaries/coproducers of eighteenth-century pictures, maps, and knowledge. This last historiographical strand tells stories of epistemic entanglements.

Attentive to these historiographies, I have argued for the primacy of iterating and imagining the work of moods in their own times but also considering painted moods of a place as a productive idea to think with. If the study of landscape in art history has always been tied into what Tim Barringer notes as querying the politics of its times—race, empire, ecology, identity, nationalism, global travels, and extraction of resources[3]—then, the project of figuring the *bhāva* of a place tells us that conceptualizations that may come from off-center geographies and off-center objects have much to offer.[4] The messy projects of art history do not only entail generating "knowledge" for a discipline classified into regions along a teleological model; they moreover demand the willingness to learn by not only comparing and connecting but also conceptually entering into new terminologies and archives on equal theoretical and analytical footing.

The Place of Many Moods interweaves the discussion among concepts, objects, places, and histories centered on immersive moods in India's long eighteenth century. It recovers potentiality—of efficacious desires launched onto artworks; of shifting sociability and politics in the mid-eighteenth century; and of the abilities of objects to reveal contestation of viewpoints and of painters to develop counterfactual territorial imaginaries and political communities in early colonial India. Departing from the Mewar court's rhetorical claims on a royal identity based on a divine Hindu lineage and the resistance of Muslim sultans and emperors, represented, for example, in the creation of the seventeenth-century Rajsamand Lake and the commission of Jagat Singh's *Rāmāyaṇa*, painters of the court and the city claimed pictorial genres in other kinds of aesthetic and epistemic ways as well. Udaipur painters' turn toward imagining belonging, ethics, and territorial power on distinctly local, intimate, and affective terms has barely been examined.

Medium-specific explorations of *bhāva* show that paintings make emotive demands of audiences on their own pictorial, painterly, and material terms. The painted ambience of real places and of historical times underscores the artistic adeptness in composition and brushwork, establishing associations with a wider canon. The juxtaposition of multiple conventions, such as portraits and places, planar and profile views of buildings, atmospheric naturalisms, and graphic abstractions, effectively created the palpable feel of places. The picturing of the *bhāva* of places could connect with the here and now but also with other times and other worlds. The associations across artifacts discussed in the book counter the assumption that renderings of aesthetic *rasa* and *bhāva* were largely about poetic and devotional idealizations. Instead, each chapter has revealed historically and materially contingent understandings of perception and of the role of emotions and experiences in the representations of the material world.

The painted moods of monsoons, the pleasures of lake palaces, and the prosperity of the city's bazaars all evoke *bhāva*—but in distinctive ways. The interaction between spaces and sociality in the painted depictions of the *bhāva* of Udaipur's lands and lakes denies the luxury of focusing on one medium alone. Through an exploration of urban praise and depictions of moods, this book's chapters have argued that poetic panegyrics and the visual historicity of portraits and real places seen in paintings must be studied in integrated ways, not simply as visual or textual means for relaying contexts. Scholars such as Bruno Latour have underscored finding "associations" between the material domain of things, practices, and objects to arrive at relational notions of "reality."[5] Such emphases on associations have enabled my insights into objects depicting historical moods, though they developed effectively only in the scholarly struggles of working between eighteenth-century artistic practices in the media of poetry, painting, and architecture. A focus on these intermedial practices enables the understanding of "moods of places" as a pictorial category, while also shaping insights into how the hermeneutics of affect may have worked in collective settings. The variety of genres, objects, and media that imagined the moods of real places and histories makes *bhāva* a dynamic category that shaped a new disposition to picturing lands. Udaipur's painters propelled its potential.

THE IMMERSION OF THE SPECTATOR AND THE SCHOLAR

The process of deciphering aesthetic tropes, history, and the historiography of poetic, painted, spatial, and scribal practices in distinct media insists on immersion that may develop in painstakingly slow ways, demanding time and deliberation. The scholarly self is invited to corporeally inhabit the suggested moods. Studying the associations between painted and poetic *bhāva* of places demands an attempt to historicize such sensing and the entire business of sensing moods itself. Recovering the moods invoked by dwelling in the places, and by appraising paintings and poetry, entails recalling (and mixing) memories of more than one time, medium, and sense—scents and sounds, not just sights. Thus finding intermedial associations leads to imagining and perceiving moods in more ways than one. It unravels interpretations and associations fraught with subjectivities and errors, but the process is also ripe with imagining that comes from more than one kind of source.

This heightened alertness to the relations between sociability and space reveals the role historical and scholarly collectives play(ed) in perceiving moods. For instance, the associations between the painter's and the poet's imagination of the interiority of the Jagniwas lake palace reveal the construction of moods of intimacy. The conversations among historians of poetry, painting, music, architecture, textiles, and perfumes have been foundational in making sense of such historical associations. These exchanges have underscored not simply the need for interdisciplinarity, a pursuit fraught with pitfalls, but the acknowledgment that moods always assert their presence in slightly different ways, on each occasion and in each assembly of connoisseurs and intellectuals. The increasing realization of the role scholarly sociability plays in sensing historical moods calls for not only expanding our efforts at intermedial learning but also allowing for immersion over time. Even then the *bhāva* of places may be best revealed in collectives, in lively meetings of historians of literature, painting, and music, among others.

The perception of moods likely developed over time for historical audiences as well. The iterations of familiar panegyrical tropes of pleasure, plentitude, and piousness shaped connoisseurs. It allowed them to become adept at realizing the aesthetic experience and power of moods—of pleasures created inside lake palaces, of longing for monsoons in a city of lakes, of spectacular fireworks and nighttime boat processions, of extravagant and tightly circumscribed durbars, and of kingly devotion mapped onto expansive temple complexes. Such visual and poetic iterations enable a kind of "dwelling" in the *bhāva* of places.

THE INDEPENDENCE OF ARCHITECTURE

Recuperating the "moods of places" as a pictorial category that mattered across objects, which were not necessarily described by inscribed texts in terms of moods, enables reviewing deviations and questions about the making of architectural epistemes in the long eighteenth century. The artifacts that enable us to consider the work that takes place in material, aesthetic, and epistemic borderlands have often invoked ambivalences and occupied canonical margins—as in *The Mood of Kota Palace* or Ghasi's sketches for the British agent James Tod or letter-scrolls. Each of these artifacts conveys the immediacy of itinerancy—of artworks, artists, poets, patrons, broader publics, mediums, and techniques. These objects also bear marks of experimentation of conventions and genres, and even of the urgency of drawing and finishing quickly. In a parallel manner, I will conclude with another painted set that has been relegated to the margins due to the absence of a royal portrait. This set alerts us—very much as I hope the book in its entirety does—to the role of localized practices in the creation of lingering moods and to the role of frontier objects to overturn established teleologies of artistic production.

This book has shown that paintings of temples made by artists such as Ghasi in about 1830 may have as much to do with elevations he made for Tod as they have to do with developing skills of drawing and modes of knowing from the Udaipur court workshop's entrenched practices on drawing temple towers from more than one hundred years earlier. Even so, three significant Udaipur paintings (two of which are pictured here; figs. C.1 and C.2) make the Jagmandir lake palace an independent subject of exploration in about 1740, and analysis of these works compels us to think critically about the artists' choice not to include a royal portrait in the composition. This set of paintings constitutes an important precursor to works by Ghasi that presented architectural precincts as the sole subject in response to pictorial demands expressed by the British agent James Tod in the 1820s. These mid-eighteenth-century depictions of Jagmandir complicate our understanding of early nineteenth-century conventions of architectural drawing, which has always been marked by Europe in one way or another.

These three particular paintings that feature Jagmandir—the island palace that was associated with Sangram Singh II, the father of Jagat Singh II—are so strongly parallel, we must consider the likelihood that they are specifically related works.[6] It is even possible that all three were painted in 1743, when Jagat Singh II directed his courtier Thakur Sirdar Singh to build the Jagniwas lake palace. Each of these three works depicts buildings and gardens located within a lake in a similar color palette and painting style. Their almost identical height (41, 43.8, and 44 centimeters) enables us to see that the scale at which the painters' drew the buildings is tightly aligned.[7] A dark gray band with feather-like white brushstrokes at the bottom of each painting denotes the lake and its waters, in which we see depicted fishes, crocodiles, and a red boat with boatmen. These paintings' blue skies (painted in a flat mode), tall cypresses, palms, and stubby trees (all painted in the same style and elevation view) are equally contiguous. These shared elements function as visual citations that connect the three paintings.

It is easy to draw parallels between the two paintings that feature elevation views, from two different directions, of the Gol Mahal, the circular dome-roofed building with a rectangular built form attached at one end located in the Jagmandir lake-palace complex (see fig. 3.4). The example shown here depicts the elevation of the building as seen from the eastern side (fig. C.1); the painter has strived to emphasize the building's circularity and the circular pavilions that project from the enclosed rooms on the first and second floors. He also paints details of the waterwheel, by which water was pulled up to the turrets of this building; a rectangular tank of water along the elevation perhaps denotes this action or a storage tank embedded in this wall. The corresponding painting (not shown) depicts the elevation of the facade of Gol Mahal that one encounters upon entering the largest courtyard in the island complex from the north. The linearity of the composition and extraordinary length of the painting corresponds to the Jagmandir palace complex, for the length of its east-west axis is almost twice that of its length along its north-south axis. Both of these similar paintings exhibit the use of angular lines to emphasize the three-dimensionality of some of the buildings, and the latter includes a planar view of a garden space in the foreground. Seen together, the paintings offer views of the Jagmandir palace from several different directions. Both privilege the representational format of an elevation drawing.

The third member of this set of related paintings has been described as a picture of either a different lake palace in Udaipur or the Jagniwas palace at some earlier, less-elaborated stage of the island complex, well before its completion in 1746 (fig. C.2). The building depicted here is not easily recognizable; however, the painting style, color palette, and composition, in a combination of planar and elevation views, are clearly similar. On the left-hand side of the painting, we see a depiction of the layout of smaller buildings, and in the foreground we find the layout of a larger garden space in front of an elevation of a building. An unstudied inscription on the back of this painting, most likely from the time the painting was made, labels it as a "picture of Jagmandir from the other side [*jagmaṁdar rī āthmaṇī bāju ro pāno*]." Another inscription (along the edge of the paper, in a different handwriting) notes the name of the king, Jagat Singh (*mahārāṇājī śrī jagatsīghjī*). Close and patient inspection makes it clear that the painting represents the buildings of the Jagmandir lake-palace complex as seen from the opposite end of the Kunwarpada Mahal (Palace for the Princes), a view that is not easily discernible due to the absence of the recognizable Gol Mahal. From a pictorial perspective, the maker's aim was to provide only a representation of the palace from the west, and thus to frame a unidirectional view, in spite of his combination of representational idioms of planar and elevation formats.

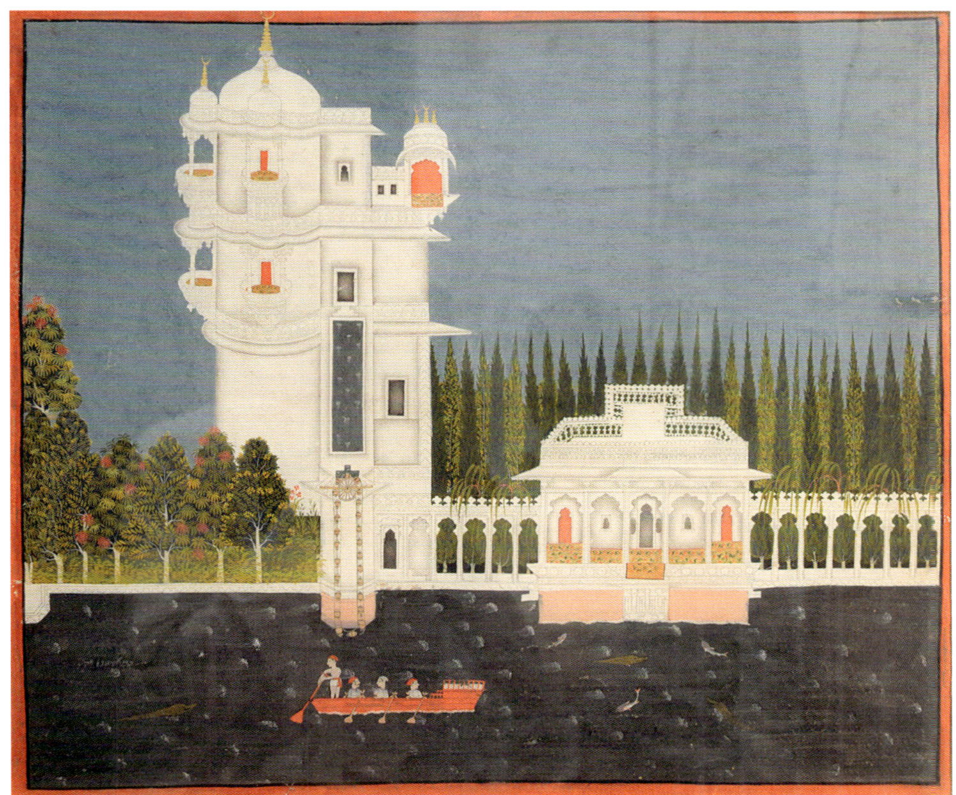

C.1. *Jagmandir Island Palace from the East Side*, c. 1740–43, Udaipur. Gouache on paper, 41 × 47 cm. National Museum, New Delhi; 57.75/52.

C.2. *Jagmandir on Lake Pichola*, c. 1740–43. The inscription notes that the picture depicts the island palace from the "other side." Opaque watercolor and gold on paper, 43.8 × 48.6 cm. Harvard Art Museums/Arthur M. Sackler Museum, Cambridge, MA; gift in gratitude to John Coolidge, gift of Leslie Cheek Jr., Anonymous Fund in memory of Henry Berg, Louise Haskell Daly, Alpheus Hyatt, Richard Norton Memorial Funds, and through the generosity of Albert H. Gordon and Emily Rauh Pulitzer; formerly in the collection of Stuart Cary Welch Jr.; 1995.79.

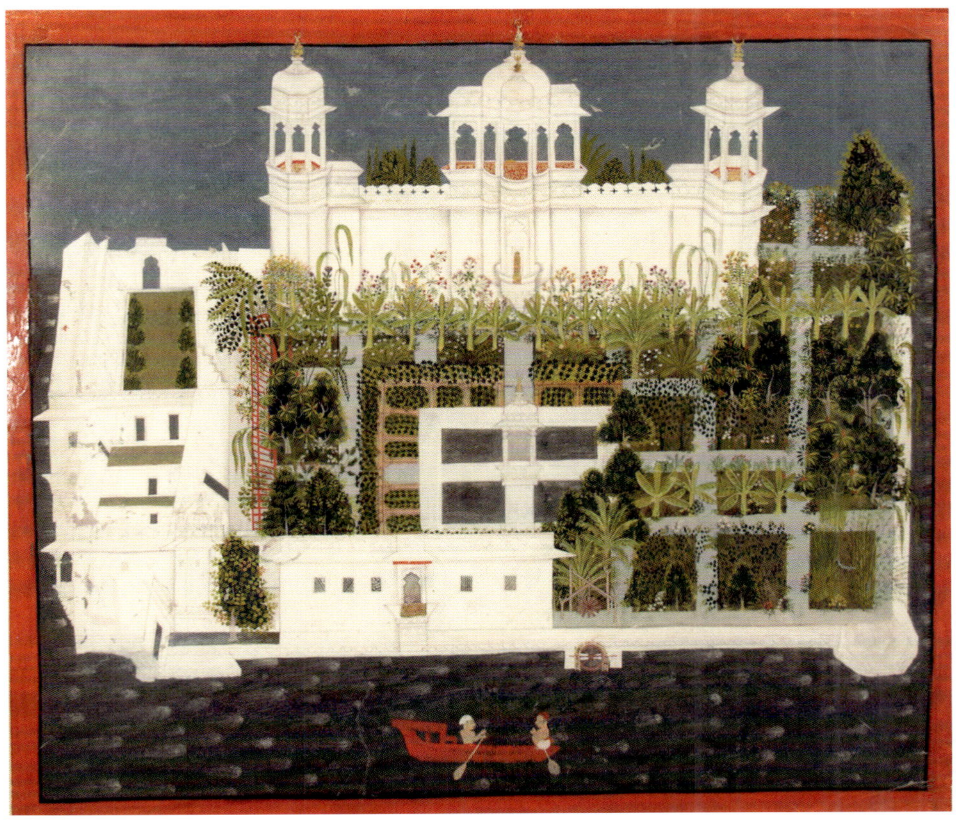

This set of paintings collectively shows us that at a certain point in mid-eighteenth-century Udaipur, painters made Jagmandir an independent subject of exploration. Each composition emphasizes details of the buildings, and the set views the complex from three directions. In the historical literary memory presented in the *Jagvilās*, we know that the beauty of the Jagmandir lake palace served as a benchmark against which Jagat Singh II imagined the Jagniwas lake palace he would see built and appreciated. Thus it is possible that this set of paintings of Jagmandir was commissioned in 1743, when it was decided that the Jagniwas lake palace would be built. Together these paintings mediate the design and details of the architecture of the place, while at the same time they constitute Jagmandir as an ideal lake palace in the context of the new lake palace of Jagniwas that was yet to be built. It is possible to conjecture that these paintings constitute a study of Jagmandir as an architectural edifice in itself—as a monument that was admired.[8]

This departure is suggestive. This set of paintings may emerge from a moment when Udaipur painters began to develop their skills in architectural drawing. Even though the combination of place and portraiture was the preferred mode—to stir emotions and mediate the moods of places—Udaipur court painters circulated their knowledge about a place in other image ontologies if and when there was a demand. The city's painters assert an insatiable appetite in knowing and re-knowing their place, in drawing and redrawing architecture. The localization and specification of knowledge here, on the one hand, operates within the traditions of court painting, where styles, repetition, and citation are valued and revalued with subtle departures and motivated interpretive eyes. On the other hand, the range of images of painted lands studied in this book, beyond court painting, shows that many of the painters at Udaipur, not just the artist Ghasi and his circle, working between about 1820 and 1835, take this penchant for localization to looking toward their city and court architecture. Differentiation and description matter in the ways they define knowing in images. These modes of knowing, however, become legible only by dwelling in the painted moods of places iterated in numerous artworks and in places over the *longue durée*. The images, places, texts, and practices infused with *bhāva* are thus continually iterated and adapted toward multiple ends, none of which sought to separate concerns of aesthetics (to praise and to idealize people and places) from epistemic aims (to depict architecture and topography and from political aims) to proclaim territoriality.

Tracing the micro-practice of artists, who circulated skills of drawing and modes of knowing among the domains of the British East India Company, Indian kings, and local bazaars in the early nineteenth century, reveals that Udaipur's painters advanced a territoriality based on the local moods of the place in India's long eighteenth century. The artistic practices that rendered these moods were far from constant, unchanging, or immobile. Itinerancy of practices—not always objects and peoples—and itinerancy of ideas (between media) point to the potentiality of aesthetic and epistemic concepts tied into structures of feeling and emotion. This quality of the practices in motion, emerging from artistic cultures invested in representing the mood of a place, enables tracking its adaptability. At the hands of new artists and in response to new demands, the moods and localizations proposed by painters in heterogeneous objects such as letter-scrolls suggest dynamic reinventions in local circles. Thus even the most spatially rooted images and moods of Udaipur's lakes and palaces were kept in motion.

Appendix

Jaichand. *Saīkī: Rājasthāna rai rajavāram ro sau sala ro itihasa*. Translated and edited by Brajmohan Jawalia. Gangashahar, Bikaner: Acharya Tulsi Rajasthani Shodh Sansthan, 2009.

The Jain monk-poet Jaichand's *Saīkī* (A history of a hundred years) offers an unusually detailed account of rainfall as it related to economics and politics during select years in the reigns of the Mughal emperor Aurangzeb and the Udaipur Maharanas Raj Singh and Amar Singh II. Almost every six-line verse in Jaichand's poem of 188 verses begins with an abbreviated reference to the years it chronicles, spanning from 1658 to 1723 (VS 1715 to 1780). There is no scholarly consensus on Jaichand's use of language. It is considered mixed, suggesting the author's plausible affiliation with the region of Mewar or Bikaner, though the relation established with the mid-seventeenth-century historical writing of Munhata Nainsi, a Jain scholar who wrote comprehensive histories of the region, suggests Jaichand's connection to the region of Marwar. Jaichand largely covers the towns and cities of Rajasthan in the northwest and he occasionally offers perspectives on places farther south in the Deccan. There is no explanation within the text as to why the chronicle stops in the year 1723. The discussion of the *Saīkī* in chapter 2, based on the select verses transliterated and translated below, notes that the history likely belongs to a wider genre of history writing by Jain monks tied to the idea of recounting one hundred years.

naiṃ panarotarai tāki mālapuro māryo phāsū
khvāje ūparāṃ khesa ajamera nai gayo uṭhā sūṃ
dhāna bāḷi pāṛyo dukāḷa prajāloka sārā pīḍāṇā
dukhī huā barasa tīna bhūkhā maratā māṇasa bīkāṇā
rāṇe rājasiṅgha patisāha sūṃ rīsa kari lokāṃ rā ghara lūṭiyā
māla na liyo patisāha ro kahī kiṇahī naiṃ kūṭiyā (8)

And by [seventeen] fifteen, the residents of Malpura were pointlessly killed
Having launched an attack on Khwaja, from there he ventured off to Ajmer
He burned the fields, a dark time struck, the common folk suffered
The next three years were distraught; all men starved and died
Rana Raj Singh, who was angry with *Padsah* Aurangzeb, looted people's homes
He did not take the wealth of the emperor, [so] tell us whom did he torture? (8)

dakṣiṇa sobe tāki auraṅgajeba avaraṅgābādai
lākha ghoḍāṃ na lei sājhī dharatī sāhijādai
murādabagasa bhaṛabhīñcha gujarāti rai giṇiyo thāṇai
sāha sūjo pūraba vāda vadī tī rāu rāṇai
dyūṃ ṭīko dārāsāha neṃ sāhijahāṁ citta vicāriyau
tīna sāhijādā mili āviyā patisāha ro māna utāriyau (9)

From Aurangabad, Aurangzeb watched provinces in the south
Bringing one *lakh* horses, established his empire on the entire earth
The brave Muradbaksh counted the posts in Gujarat
Shah Suja controlled the lands and kings in the east
I will consecrate Dara Shikoh, thus contemplated emperor Shah Jahan in his mind
The three princes joined hands, destroyed the emperor's prestige (9)

lahi avasara kari kaṭaka rākhī ṭeka rājasiṃha rāṇeṃ
mālapuro māriyo sāro sahara paṛyo bhaṅgāṇeṃ
nākhyā bāḷī nāja ṭūṅka ṭoḍā nā sagaḷā
khvājā pāḍaṇa ro mato kiyo jaisiṃha kahāyau tiṇa veḷā
patisāhī meṃ rahaṇo māharai burāī vadhai ajamera māriyāṃ
rāṇo udayapura āviyau sagaḷā kārija sāriyā (15)

He grabbed the opportunity, made his army strong; Rana Raj Singh made a pledge
He attacked Malpura, the entire city ran for refuge
He burned all the crops of Tonk and Toda
He decided to destroy the shrine of Khwajaji, at that time Jai Singh counseled
We have to live within the empire; enmity will increase with attacks on Ajmer

The Rana returned to Udaipur, [he] accomplished all his
projects (15)

panarotarai durabhikha paḍyo soḷotarai dhāna gaḷyā sagaḷā
satarotarai pāilī soḷa meha na vūṭhā pāchai pahilā
mālapurai bahu manḍi rāṇai māryā thī pahilī
lagolagi tīna barasa dhāna na rahyā duniyāṃ duhilī
jatiyāṃ rai celā juṛyā sāhū sapūta ja sāharā
jaicanda joro na kehano sukha sirajyā huvai nāha rā (16)

In [seventeen] fifteen there was famine, in sixteen all grain
decayed
In seventeen, it cost sixteen for a *pailī* weight in grain; neither
cloud nor rain from the beginning to the end
Many grain markets in Malpura were destroyed by the Rana
in those days
For three consecutive years, there were no grains and people
were pained
The sons of merchants and moneylenders became the followers of monks
Jaichand says, who can control these conditions, prosperity is
created by God (16)

aṭhārotarai meha apāra ugaṇīsai bājarī bahuḷī
bīsai na tūṭhā meha nirasī hui dharatī sagaḷī
bīsa rai tolai maṇa doḍha nāja bhāva ema jaṇāyo
aḍhī sera vali ghrita milai nahī roke rupaye mulāyo
gāi baḷada muā gayā chāchi na milī oṣadheṃ
bīkānera vaḍa desa me joti āṅkhyāṃ rī kima vadhai (17)

In [seventeen] eighteen there was abundant rain, in nineteen
there was lots of millet
In twenty the clouds did not burst, the entire earth dried up
The cost of grain for twenty *tola*s was now the same as for one
and a half *mana*
Two and a half *ser*s of ghee could not be brought even with
one rupee paid in cash
Cows and buffalos died; one does not even find buttermilk to
soothe
In the vast region of Bikaner, how do people hope for the
future? (17)

ikavīsai ghaṇa anna sarasa nīpanā sarasai
bhādrava huā doi meha tihāṁ bahuḷā varasai
sojitai na huo subhikṣa tihāṁ paṇa ghaṇā bikāṇā
dukhī huā bahu manuṣa paḍyā phiryā ghaṇū sīdāṇā
kahai jaicanda bahugyāna kari bhalā dīha vaḷiyā vaḷī
mukha sāhibī baiṭhā karo pūro nija mana nī raḷī (18)

In [seventeen] twenty-one, abundant and sweet grains flour-
ished aplenty
There were two monsoons, both poured abundant rains
Sojat did not see this abundance, there many people were sold
Many people felt pained, roamed here and there, or suffered
at home
Says Jaichand after giving deep thought, good days will come
back again
All must sit and take God's name, fulfill all your hearts' desires (18)

satāvane huo sukāḷa māruvāṛi navakoṭa majhārī
sujānasiṅgha bīkāneriyo phirai dakhiṇa meṃ asavārī
rājai rāṇo amarasiṅgha udaipura cītoṛa koṭe
jasavantasiṅgha jesalamera savāī jaisiṅgha āmbera oṭe
itarī dharatī nīpanī rāu rāṇā sagaḷā sukhī
jaicanda kahai nija bakhata sūṃ punye karī sahu meṃ sukhī (103)

[Seventeen] fifty-seven saw good times in all regions of Marwar
Sujan Singh of Bikaner embarked to the Deccan on a horse
Rana Amar Singh ruled in Udaipur and Chittor Fort
Jaswant Singh at Jaisalmer, Sawai Jai Singh controlled Amber
Crops were abundant on the earth; Raos and Ranas were happy
Says Jaichand, on their good fortune, well earned through past
deeds (103)

ikasaṭhai meha adhika jeṭha thī tūṭhau jāṇau
sarabhara huau sāvaṇeṃ bhādravai bharyā nadī nivāṇau
āsuyeṃ phaḷī adhikī āsa saraba dhānāṃ rī sarasāī
makī juāra uṛada nīpanā dhāna sagaḷāī
subhikṣa huau sāre deśa meṃ suhaṅge dhāna sukhiyā thayā
jaicanda kahai āṇanda karo cora caraṛa nāsī gayā (112)

[Seventeen] sixty-one saw extensive rains, beginning in the
months of Jyestha [May–June]
Lakes filled up in Savana [July–August], rivers and streams
were filled in Bhadon [August–September]
In the months of Asad [June–July] hopes bloomed further, all
grains were in abundance
Corn, Bajra, Udad, all the crops thrived
There was abundance in the entire country, inexpensive crops
made all people happy
Says Jaichand, do enjoy, all thieves and thugs have withdrawn!
(112)

ikasaṭhai āsū pachī māsa āṭha meha na huo dharatī māṃhem
bāsaṭhai bāhuṛyo meha eka bāra māravāṛa uchāheṃ
āsāḍha thī māsa aḍhī phiri meheṃ pācho na dīṭhau
sahu deśe paḍyo sora meha viṇa anna na lāgai mīṭhau
guḍhā huā gāma gāma rā ghara taji gāḍe ghara kiyā
ṭhākura rajapūta loka chāṇḍi ṭhika māḷave bhaṇī umāhiyā (113)

In [seventeen] sixty-one following Asad [June–July], there were no rains for eight months
In [seventeen] sixty-two rains increased, and again there was excitement in Marwar
Following Asad [June–July] after two and a half months, again rains did not arrive
The entire country was in disarray, without water food did not taste sweet
Each village shrunk into small settlements; giving up their homes, people took to the road
Even thakurs and Rajputs left their estates, desired to go toward Malwa (113)

jala rahita jīraṛo bāsaṭṭhai dīsai viruo
nadiyeṃ sūkā nīra khaṇi dharatī jotryo kuo
sīcai java lei jvāri aḍhī maṇa rupiye ekai
tola aḍhāra turatta ṭaṅka doi sera ghī ṭekai
ahamande meha huo apāra rāu ratanasiṃha rāja maiṃ
mahaṅgo dhāna mevāṛa maiṃ amarasiṃha rāṇa āvāja maiṃ (118)

Life without waters, [seventeen] sixty-two looks abandoned
Water has dried in the rivers, wells have been dug up in the earth
From that water, barley has been been irrigated, two and a half *mans* for one rupee
The cost of grain for a *tola* was eighteen [rupees?], and one *taṅka* two *sers* of ghee
In Rao Ratan Singh's Ahmadnagar there were abundant rains
In Rana Amar Singh's Mewar grains was very expensive! (118)

Nandram. *Jagvilās*. c. 1746. Rajasthan Oriental Research Institute, Udaipur. Accession no. 2216.

The eighteenth-century poetry of the *Jagvilās* (World of pleasure), commemorates the commencement of the three-day inauguration ceremony of the Jagniwas lake palace on January 20, 1746. The court poet Nandram presents the *bhāva* of *vilāsa*, mood of courtly pleasures, as an idealization of real gatherings at Jagniwas, thereby inviting us to interpret the title of his praise poem not simply as "Jagat Singh's delights" but also possibly as "Pleasures offered by Jagniwas" or the "*Jaga* of *vilāsa*"—that is, "World of pleasure." Nandram's transformation of *vilāsa*, a courtly aesthetic and ethic intertwined with luxury, connoisseurship, and joyful experiences, through poetry reveals its multidimensional valence. The select verses from the *Jagvilās*, discussed in chapter 3, are transliterated and translated here.

dohā
udayagiri sama udayapura bhāṁa manau jagarāṁna
sahasa kirana samateja tana sobhita sarasa samāna (4)

Udaipur is like the sunrise mountain, Jagrān [Jagat Singh] is its Sun
His body is beautiful and radiant like one thousand rays of the sun (4)

gāhā
jasa jagatesa anaṁto kavi ika rasnā kahaṃ lagi kahahī
sesa sahasa dive jīhā nita prati kahaṁtpāra naha pāṁī (5)

The fame of Jagates is limitless; what can a poet say with his single tongue
Sheshanaga with his one thousand tongues cannot reach the end, even if he speaks continuously (5)

dohā
kavi mukha ika gunagāna bahuta bārnauṃ yatha banāya
jalasāgara purana subhara kyauṃ gāgara su samāya (6)

The poet has one mouth, the virtues and praises are numerous; [he] might describe them thus
The ocean is perfectly full, how could it fit in a pot? (6)

chappay
ikka samaya dīvana moja dariyāva nāva madhi
rājata sakala samāja rūparati rāja su bidhi bidhi
ita jalmaṁdira nirakhi sarasa suṁdara sarsājaiṁ
uta jagamaṁdira joti dharā sārī sirtājai
duhuṁ bīca gera sarasī sarasa yātai yaha puni kijjiyeṃ
saba dikhe jīte mohai jagata āpa yekhi mana rijjīyeṃ (7)

Once upon a time, [while] enjoying a boat ride in the lake
The whole community of courtiers [*rasikās*] enjoyed all forms of pleasures with the king

Here is the Jalmandir [which they] admire, beautiful, delighting, and well-decorated
There is the illuminated Jagmandir, crown upon the entire earth
The site in between is the best of the best; [let's] begin this [work] here
One that wins over, enchants everyone, Jagat (the king and the whole world) himself, delights every heart (7)

chappay
taba ṭhākura siradāra siṁgha nija nikaṭa bulāye
sabaiṁ subidhi vyohāṁra tahāṃ kahi kahi samukāye
jite gajadhara sarasa kāmakāraka saba syaṁnae
te vidyā gunapūra silapasāstra saha jāṁnae
tin soṁ ju hukuma śri mukha tahāṃ kahata sabaiṁ vahacita dhariya
siradāra siṁgha tina ati subudhi vividhi vividhi racanā kariya (10)

Then [he] calls Thakur Sirdar Singh near him.
[Who is] the most intelligent and sophisticated, smiling to himself while talking to him
All the best architects, all the well-trained workers
[Those] with virtuosity of training and the knowledge of the architecture treatises
Sirdar Singh took to heart all of the instructions that came [were said] to him from [Jagat Singh's] auspicious mouth,
And on those [orders], with great acumen, has all sorts of constructions made (10)

chand padharī
apakariya citrasālā anūpa
ati sukhada sarasa tin mahi sarūpa
taha kavita tripada citrāṁma kīna
jihi dekhi thakita mana hota līna (45)

You have made a unique gallery of paintings
In which are beautiful images that give utmost delight
Here is soul-satisfying poetry and painting
The sight of which charmed a tired mind (45)

jei jei vilāsa apakariya tāma
tei tei sucitra lakhi gaṃma gaṃma
tinke prakāra saba kahata sāra
keteka dina na pāveṃ na pāra (46)

You have partaken in all kinds of pleasures
I/we have tried to write about all of them in beautiful and varied ways
Telling [even] just the essence of all their types
Would take days and still not ever be compiled (46)

tihi gera madhi rājatarānaṃ
jānauṃ ki īsa kailāsa ra thāṃna
parihāra saddi bhojana magāya
āgyā prmāṃna āne sutāya (47)

Here assembled in the center are the Rajas and Ranas
Seems like the place of Mount Kailasha
Pure foods were called for
They were brought as per the orders (47)

saba sūbhaṭa avara sevaka samāja
beṭhari paṁkti aga dhariya bāja
vidhi vidhi prakāra paruseṃ pravīna
ṣaṭarasa savāda nita prati navīna (48)

All the groups of pandits and helpers
Per the rules are seated in a row
Various kinds of new foods are served
The eight flavors in constantly new combinations (48)

prabhu daī sakala āgyā sutāṃma
siranāya sabahi kīnaiṃ pranāṁma
saba saṁga raṁga sukha sau sucāva
bhojana kariya mana sudha bhāva (49)

With the permission of his holiness [the king]
Everyone bowed his head with respect
All were absorbed sharing in the delight and entertainment
They ate with pure thoughts [virtuous mood] in their minds (49)

tihi tāṃ naranārina bhīra ghanī, manauṃ sāyara paiṃ phulavāri banī
sabke cita dekhana kauṃ sarasaiṃ, sukha ke subha meha tahāṁ barasaiṃ (125)

Here, the crowd of the men [and] women expands, as if a bed of flowers lay on the street
Everyone's hearts are eager to admire, there auspicious clouds of joy rain down (125)

dohā

baḍo mahala tāki suḍhiga racanā racī sukāṃma
bārī sarasa sarūpamaya dilārāma tihiṃ nāma (177)

Bado Mahal, its unique building, crafted with artistry
Beautiful garden with elegant forms, which had the name
Dilaram ("Heart's Tranquility") (177)

chand gītikā

sabataeṃ bado mahala tahā kahu puraba disa so bhanī
dilārāma bāriya kāma bhāriya rūpa besa banī dhanī
ika hoja bīca anūpa rājata dekhatae sukha pāvhī
rastāṁna meṃ nala haī ghanaīṁ gulakyāri hai susuhāvanī (178)

The Bado Mahal is here, lit from the east,
Dilaram's gardens, filled with desire, beautifully made overall forms
[Seated by] the unique tank in the center, the king admires [and] derives bliss
[All] the paths are lined with fountains, dense rows of most beautiful roses (178)

dohā

sukha barakhata harakhata hai sabai gāyana gāta gāṁa
moja barakhata megha sama saba saūṁ rījhata rāṁna (194)

Joys rain, all are delighted, singers sing songs
Pleasure rains down like clouds; the Rana [Jagat Singh II] is absolutely charmed (194)

dohā

sabahī ṭhōra dekhata tahāṃ bhaye jāṁna traya bhāna
baḍe mahala madhi āya kai sukha sau rājata rāṁna (204)

Having seen all the spaces, now he knows them well
After coming to the Bado Mahal, the Rana rules with joy (204)

dohā

sabahī saṁga sukha meṃ tahāṃ sukha ko sāgara pāya
hāsa vilāsa vinoda meṃ ghari cāra su bihāya (207)

Everyone enjoys together here; they find an ocean of joy
Laughter, joy, and pleasure continues as the clock struck four o'clock (207)

Khetal. *Udaipur rī gajal*. 1718.

I have consulted multiple manuscript copies available in the collections of the Rajasthan Oriental Research Institute, Udaipur; Rajasthan Oriental Research Institute, Jaipur; and Agarchand Nahata Jain Granthalaya, Bikaner. (See accession numbers in the bibliography.) I have also consulted the version of *Udaipur rī gajal* published within the compilation *Paramparā Rājasthānī gajala saṃgraha*, edited by Vikram Singh Rathore (Jodhpur: Chaupasani Shodh Sansthan, 1964).

Jains composed and sung *gajal*s, highly repetitive poetic songs, each consisting of a series of mono-rhymed couplets—in a combination of dialects of Marwari, Brajbhasha, Persian, Awadhi, Gujarati, and Punjabi—that sought to evoke their experience of seeing new places. Each verse is constituted of a couplet; this form defines the structure and rhythm of a *gajal*. Poetry offered traveling monks, while on their annual pilgrimage during the monsoon season (*caumāsa*), means to expand their gaze to subjects beyond Jain religiosity. They turned to associated literary genres of urban praise and across linguistic boundaries to the Persianate *ghazal*. The Jain monk-poet Kavi Khetal composed verses in the *Udaipur rī gajal* that evoke the city as an alluring place. The mixing of languages puts Khetal's *gajal*s in the same field as Rekhta, a Persianate term for mixed Hindi-Urdu (Khaṛi Boli). The select few verses transcribed and translated below have been interpreted alongside painted letter-scrolls in chapter 5.

śrī dīvāna kā durabāra, dīsai poḷa rāja dvāra
khāsā urakāra khānāka, nobata ghurata nisānāka (8)

The court of *shri divan*, look at the gateway and the royal doorway
The special guards, thundering drums, hoisted flags (8)

āgai mahila ati utaṁga, nava nava rāvaṭi navaraṁga
jhāṁkī khūba jharokāka, jālidhāra dila jokhāka (9)

The palaces beyond rise high, new-new kinds of colored domes and pavilions
The *jharokās* (balconied windows) offer beautiful views, the *jalis* (pierced screens) captivate hearts (9)

narapati baiṭhkara nāvaṁ ka, dekhata saila darīyāvāṁ ka
chaka su dekhīka chattarika, palakāṁ bīca jyu putarīka (20)

The king sits in the royal boat; he watches as he tours the lake
He proudly viewed the the *chattrīs* (domed turrets), as one looks [upon] one's own sons (20)

kyā gulabadana hai mahirīka, nija vasa karata hai saharīka
cīra rūpa ghāṭa parīvārika, surata dekha saba vaisārīka (26)

What a rose-bodied beauty is she! One who captivates all people of the city
A piercing presence on the *ghāts* crowded with families, a face seen by all travelers (26)

dillipati su yākīka, rākhata hindū kī nākīka
hindūsthāna kī sarahada, ripudala kīna chala bala rada (74)

More resolute than the ruler of Dilli, he keeps high the pride of the Hindus
[In protecting] the boundaries of Hindustan, troops of enemies have been completely slayed (74)

Notes

INTRODUCTION. MEDIUM OF MOODS AND PICTURING OF PLACE

1. These places and people are identified in the inscriptions and contemporaneous histories. See Chandra, "Ustād Sālivāhana," 25–28.
2. The letter notes that the new temple was built by the Agra merchant *sāha* Chandu, and that the inauguration will take place during the next year's holy monsoon season (*caumāsa*).
3. The scribe, who identifies himself as the "son of *sikhasā*," writes: [*jīsā*] *darīkhānā judasu tīnā samanā ye lekha māh sarab likh chhai usatā sālivāhaṇa pātisāhī chittakāra chhai teṇa tiṇa samai dekh chhai īsāhī iṇa chitta mā he bhāva rākh chhai su lekh dekh prīchhajo*. Refer to Chandra, "Ustād Sālivāhana," 28
4. Topsfield, *City Palace Museum*, 155. In the thirteen-line inscription, the scribe notes the painter's depiction of a *tamāso* (spectacle) and the Udaipur king's act of admiration of the Dhingia Gangaur festival from his boat. He also gives us the names of the other nobles, court officials, and musicians who accompany the ruler (*dhīgā gor rō tamāso dekhe nāv birājyā*).
5. Tod, *Annals* (1829), 1:433–34.
6. Ibid.
7. Ibid. Emphasis mine.
8. Tillotson, *Rajput Palaces*, 88.
9. Aquil and Chatterjee, *History in the Vernacular*, introduction, esp. 7–9.
10. Bayly, "Delhi and Other Cities," 122.
11. Markovits, *Global World*, 12.
12. Jasanoff, *Edge of Empire*, chap. 1.
13. On the nature of transitions, hybridity, and modernity of cultural practices in the eighteenth and early nineteenth centuries, see Avcıoğlu and Flood, *Globalizing Cultures*, introduction; Markovits, Pouchepadass, and Subrahmanyam, *Society and Circulation*, introduction.
14. On the significance and rise of eighteenth-century localizations, see Orsini, "Between Qasbas and Cities."
15. Rosalind O'Hanlon has suggested that, for early modern local elites, holding their communities together perhaps was even more important than holding on to land for declaring territories. See O'Hanlon, "Cultural Pluralism," 368.
16. A branch of the Guhila kings of the Mewar region possibly seized the fort in the early thirteenth century. Later, mid-fourteenth-century Sisodia kings from Rana Kumbha onward as well as Jain merchants built palaces and temples within the fort. Kapur, *State Formation in Rajasthan*, 62–63, 117–24.
17. On the role of pleasure in early medieval India, see Ali, *Courtly Culture*, chaps. 4 and 5.
18. Pernau, "Space and Emotion"; Rizvi, *Affect, Emotion, and Subjectivity*, introduction.
19. Ahmed, "Not in the Mood," 15.
20. Tuan, *Space and Place*, 149.
21. Massey, *For Space*, 130. Emphasis in original.
22. V. N. Desai, "Timeless Symbols," 321–22; Aitken, *Intelligence of Tradition*, 121.
23. Across fields scholars have reminded us of the plural nature of artifacts, and what is lost in the pursuit of a "pre-global" comparativist history of art or a "global" West-and-the-rest model that divorces concepts and thinking embedded within visual and material practices on the margins at the expense of writing art historical narratives driven by the primacy of dominant modern genres. For a recent discussion, see Purtle, "Double Take."
24. By working across genres and across visual, literary, cartographic, and spatial cultures, Pernau explores historical ways of sensing in late eighteenth-century Delhi. See Pernau, "Mapping Emotions."
25. For this methodological imperative as applied to the medieval world, see Ali, *Courtly Culture*, chap. 5.
26. Ahmed, "Affective Economies."
27. Within secondary literature on the topic, see Vila, *Cultural History of the Senses*; Stewart, "Remembering the Senses"; Jay, "In the Realm of the Senses"; Hamadeh, *City's Pleasures*; Emami, "Coffeehouses"; Babaie, *Isfahan and Its Palaces*.
28. For instance, see Elberfeld, "Sensory Dimensions."
29. Shulman, *More Than Real*, esp. chap. 1.
30. Ibid., 19.
31. Pollock, *Rasa Reader*, xv–xvi.
32. Ibid.
33. Busch, *Poetry of Kings*, chap. 2.
34. Comparing the views of contemporary poets Chintamani Tripathi and Kulapati Mishra, Busch highlights Kulapati's preface in his treatise *Rāsrahasya* (The secret of literary emotion, 1670) thus: "Poetry consists of sound and sense. It affords wondrous rapture in this world. I fashioned this definition after mastering numerous works." Ibid., 107–8.
35. The ninth *rasa*, of tranquility, was added in later centuries. See Sheldon Pollock's introduction in Bhanudatta, *Bouquet of Rasa*, xxx.
36. On emotions, Pollock further notes, "The basic ingredient is called a 'stable' or primary emotion (*sthāyibhāvas*), such as desire in the case of the erotic rasa, to which are added 'underlying factors' (*ālambana/vibhāvas*) such as the beloved, 'stimulant factors' (*uddīpana/vibhāvas*) such as a moonlit night or swinging earrings, 'transitory feelings' (*vyabhicāri/bhāvas*) such as longing or worry or shame, and 'physical reactions' (*anubhāvas*) such as perspiring or weeping. A stable emotion, when fully 'developed' or 'matured' by these factors, transforms into a rasa." Ibid.
37. For an overview, see Vatsyayana, *Kamasutra*, 3–21.
38. Ali, "Rethinking the History," 1–3.
39. O'Hanlon, "Manliness and Imperial Service," 70–83; on becoming a connoisseur, also see Brown, "If Music Be the Food of Love"; Aziz, "The British Museum Mīrzānāma."

40. Behl, *Love's Subtle Magic*, chap. 1.
41. Ibid., 31–32.
42. Bhanudatta, *Bouquet of Rasa*, introduction, xix–xlix.
43. On *nauras*, see Flatt, *Courts of the Deccan Sultanates*, 62; Hutton, *Art of the Court of Bijapur*, 110–11; Haidar and Sardar, "Kitab-i Nauras."
44. Busch, *Poetry of Kings*, chap. 4.
45. Keshavdas composed works that conversed in direct and deep ways with courtly poetry in Sanskrit and with devotional literature that located Radha and Krishna in the sacred geography of Braj. Ibid., 35–36.
46. Aitken, *Intelligence of Tradition*, 54.
47. On poetic renditions of the bower, see Snell, "Nikuñja"; and on its depiction in paintings, see Aitken, *Intelligence of Tradition*, 21.
48. See Busch, *Poetry of Kings*, 72–73.
49. I thank Dr. Prem Rajpurohit for transcribing the manuscript copy of the *Jagvilās*, Rajasthan Oriental Research Institute, Udaipur, acc. no. 2216.
50. S. Sharma, "City of Beauties"; Orsini, "How to Do Multilingual Literary History?"
51. Topsfield, "Royal Paintings Inventory," 188–99; of the three late nineteenth-century inventories, notations from two are seen behind the paintings, and the third, 1891 inventory (in the collection of the Rajasthan State Archives, Udaipur branch) follows a different classification system. Aitken, *Intelligence of Tradition*, 302n61 and n62. I am grateful to Molly Aitken for sharing her copy of the 1891 inventory, written in the format of an Udaipur court register (*bahi*), currently in the Rajasthan State Archives (Udaipur branch).
52. Busch, *Poetry of Kings*, 37–40.
53. For instance, see Pauwels, *Cultural Exchange*; Adamjee, "Artistic Agency."
54. For illustration and verse, see Topsfield, *Court Painting at Udaipur*, 147–48, 175n41 and n42.
55. On the epistemological scope of *rasa* and accounting for shifts in materiality and medium, see Pollock, "From Rasa Seen to Rasa Heard," 189–92.
56. On recognizing picturing as a visualization tool, see Kusukawa, "Drawing as an Instrument," 36.
57. Martin Jay synthesizes critiques of Cartesian Perspectivalism by several scholars, including Norman Bryson, while underscoring that this model of vision was not uniformly coercive and that several painters contested its logic. Jay, "Scopic Regimes of Modernity," 6–8; Bryson, *Vision and Painting*; also see Elkins, *Poetics of Perspective*. Michael Ann Holly argues that Jacob Burckhardt's history and map of the Renaissance world was itself depicted by the perspectival visual logic set up in the Renaissance; Holly, *Past Looking*, 56.
58. Cosgrove, "Landscape and Landschaft," 58.
59. Quilley and Bonehill, *William Hodges*; Barringer, Quilley, and Fordham, *Art and the British Empire*, introduction; on the intersection between landscape, art, and empire from a variety of local and colonial contexts, see the essays in Hallett, "Landscape Now."
60. See Vittoria Di Palma's groundbreaking genealogical account of the wasteland that leads us to eighteenth-century aesthetics and emotions of disgust and opens cross-chronological and cross-regional avenues for considering emotions and ecology; Di Palma, *Wasteland*, introduction. A recent exploration of religiosity, ecology, and art in early modern northern India can be seen in S. Ray, *Climate Change and the Art of Devotion*.
61. David Howes discusses the wide scope of Bloomsbury's four-volume *Senses and Sensation* and proposes that the concept of landscapes could be replaced by "the more neutral term 'sensescape.'" See Howes, "Expanding Field."
62. See Babur, *Bāburnāmah*.
63. Hutton and Brown, introduction, esp. 1.
64. For more on Babur's construction of gardens and their function, see Asher, "Babur and the Timurid Char Bagh."
65. On the relation between represented and real Mughal gardens, see Wescoat, "Picturing an Early Mughal Garden." It may be possible on a case-by-case basis to discern painters' ways of drawing precise terrains, such as Dust Muhammad's rendering of Humayun's assembly within a panegyric portrait. See Parodi and Wannell, "Earliest Datable Mughal Painting."
66. On the use of Michel Foucault's concept of heterotopia to describe how the gardens are operationalized in early Indian courtly society, see Ali, "Gardens in Early Indian Court Life," 225.
67. This folio is not part of a known *Bāburnāmah*. Beach, *Imperial Image*, 154.
68. For an introduction, see Titley, "Nasir Shah's Book of Delights"; and for the translated text, see Titley, *Niʿmatnāma Manuscript*.
69. For the painted scroll, see "*Vasanta Vilasa* (A Poem on Spring), (Detail)," Smithsonian, National Museum of Asian Art, https://asia.si.edu/object/F1932.24/ (accessed December 8, 2019).
70. S. Sharma, *Mughal Arcadia*.
71. For discussion of Mughal governor of Kashmir Zafar Khan's painted assemblies from the 1630s, see ibid., 36–52.
72. Hutton, "Use of Imaginary Landscapes."
73. A recent volume on the Deccan advances the conversations among sensory cultures, art history, literature, and music. See Singh, "Scent upon a Southern Breeze."
74. For a discussion on Mughal paintings as "indices of a historical encounter" rather than mimetic illustrations of historical accounts, see Rice, "Mughal Interventions."
75. Koch, "Hierarchical Principles," esp. 133, 136; Minissale, *Images of Thought*; Singh, *Real Birds in Imagined Gardens*. Also see Juneja, "Circulation and Beyond."
76. Wood, "'Curious Pictures,'" 333, 348–49.
77. Natif, *Mughal Occidentalism*, chap. 4.
78. Seventeenth-century Deccan, where discourse was ripe with conceptions of *rasa*, was also the site for innovations in *aja'ib* imagery across media. See Houghteling, "Tree of Life."
79. Padmasundar, a Jain intellectual who praised Akbar's virtues as a ruler in terms of experiencing the nine *rasas*, in a Sanskrit aesthetic treatise titled *Akbarasāhiśṛṅgāradarpaṇa* (The mirror of the erotic passion of emperor Akbar, 1569). See Truschke, *Culture of Encounters*, 31–32.
80. Busch, "Hidden in Plain View," 273–74.
81. Gadebusch, "Celestial Gardens"; Pauwels, *Mobilizing Krishna's World*, introduction.
82. Y. Sharma, "From Miniatures to Monuments."
83. See Dadlani, "'Palais Indiens' Collection," 181.
84. Diamond, "Cartography of Power."

85. R. Ray, *Under the Banyan Tree*. Diving deep into eighteenth-century formulations in England, Di Palma explores the stakes of reimagining "landscape" not as a "site, vista, picture, or garden" but rather as a "mood" for historical research and for rising to the challenge of ecological crisis. See Di Palma, "In the Mood for Landscape," 15.
86. Ibid., 24.
87. Ibid.
88. Although *Rajput* did not originally imply a singular aristocratic or military identity with the production of genealogies related to Hindu gods and their dynasties, this became the case in early modern Rajasthan and continues to the present. The term's genesis was tied to a broader category of people known for their fighting skills. See Kapur, *State Formation in Rajasthan*, 20–22.
89. On the names of all the personnel depicted in the Agra painted letter-scroll, and the use of this genre as a source for writing social histories, see Shalin Jain, *Identity, Community and State*, 34–45, 366–67.
90. Chandra, "Ustād Sālivāhana," 29–31.
91. Subrahmanyam, "Connected Histories."
92. Subrahmanyam, "Of Imarat and Tijarat."
93. Subrahmanyam, "Note on the Rise of Surat," 23–25.
94. Khera, "Arrivals at Distant Lands."
95. For instance, Cigdem Kafescioğlu has reset the question of the itinerant gaze in eastern Mediterranean and Ottoman lands by bringing cultures of cartography, poetry, and walking into conversation. See Kafescioğlu, "Viewing, Walking, Mapping Istanbul."
96. Markovits, Pouchepadass, and Subrahmanyam, *Society and Circulation*, introduction, 1–22.
97. Aitken, "Laud *Rāgamālā* Album," 34.
98. Mughal emperors Akbar, Jahangir, and Shah Jahan supported an extraordinary number of Jain intellectuals. In theological debates, Jains, more often than Hindu Brahmans, translated ideas about Islam in Sanskrit intellectual cultures. See Truschke, *Culture of Encounters*, chap. 1.
99. Banarasidas, *Ardhakathānaka*, preface, xxxi, 104–73.
100. Ibid.
101. Pollock, "Is There an Indian Intellectual History?" 536.
102. Kia, "Space, Sociality, and Sources of Pleasure," 21.
103. Asher, "Architecture of Raja Man Singh."
104. Zeigler, "Rajput Loyalties during the Mughal Period," 274–77.
105. For a discussion of the historical retelling of this defeat from both sides, see Talbot, "Justifying Defeat," 334–35.
106. Hooja, "Of Building and Books."
107. G. N. Sharma, *Mewar and the Mughal Emperors*, 120. For instance, the Mughal prince Khurram's successful campaign at Mewar is an important part of Shah Jahan's painted *Pādshāh-nāma*. See Beach, Koch, Thackston, *King of the World*, 133–34, no. 37.
108. Talbot, "Becoming Turk the Rajput Way," 215. Some court commissions in the first half of the eighteenth century continue these genealogical interests, most forcefully seen in the painted scrolls made around the 1730s–40s. Talbot, "Mewar Court's Construction of History."
109. Talbot, "Becoming Turk the Rajput Way," 218.
110. Joffee, "Art, Architecture and Politics in Mewar," chap. 4; also see Losty, *Ramayana*, 18–19.
111. Aitken identifies several pictorial instances that reflect Mewar artists' nuanced interpretations and deliberate choices, not singularly reflecting a politics of resistance or alliance. See Aitken, *Intelligence of Tradition*, chap. 2.
112. Asher and Talbot, *India before Europe*, 229–31.
113. For example, see Alam, *Crisis of Empire*; Brown, "Did Aurangzeb Ban Music?"; Pauwels and Murphy, *From Outside the Persianate Center*; Truschke, *Aurangzeb*.
114. Asher and Talbot, *India before Europe*, 231–35.
115. Hooja, *History of Rajasthan*, 660–66.
116. Taft, "Rajas and Thakurs in Rajputana," 253.
117. On the relations between Rajput kings and estate holders in eighteenth-century courts across northwestern India, see Taft, "Origins of the Shekhavat Thikanas of Jaipur"; Sahai, *Politics of Patronage and Protest*, 53–58; Saxena, *Rajput Nobility*, esp. chaps. 3 and 4. In exploring the cultural formulation of authority in precolonial India, Nicholas Dirks advanced Bernard Cohn's use of the term "little kingdom," which he deployed to describe land-based political configurations in eighteenth-century India. Both scholars sought to challenge the colonial dismissal of regional political practices. See Cohn, "Political Systems in Eighteenth Century India," 316; Dirks, *Hollow Crown*, 5–8. For a critique of Dirks' generalization of ideas related to estate holders functioning as little kings, drawing upon a range of visual and textual sources of the Kota court, see Peabody, *Hindu Kingship and Polity*, 5–8.
118. Beach, *Rajasthani Painters Bagta and Chokha*.
119. Many scholars seeking to define the centrality of the arts in producing sociability and political subjects in the early modern world have turned their attention to pleasure and friendship. For instance, see Schofield, "Learning to Taste the Emotions," 408–10; Aitken, "Laud *Rāgamālā* Album," 46–53; also see Kia, "Adab as Literary Form."
120. J. Freitag, *Serving Empire, Serving Nation*, chaps. 3 and 4.
121. Rudolph and Rudolph, "Rajputana under British Paramountcy," 138.
122. For a critical account on the misplaced emphasis on Rajputs in the understanding of the region, see Kothiyal, *Nomadic Narratives*, introduction.
123. This questioning sought to respond to the call to "provincialize Europe." See Chakrabarty, *Provincializing Europe*.
124. For example, in Topsfield, *Court Painting at Udaipur*, the chapter titled "The Great *Tamasha*" discusses the commissions of Udaipur ruler Sangram Singh II, and the chapter titled "The *Tamasha* Continues" discusses those of Jagat Singh II; see 141, 179.
125. On the inscription, see notes 3 and 4, above. In another instance, a scribal entry in the Udaipur court painting inventory from 1891 notes a painting as depicting a spectacle or entertainment of boars organized by Udaipur king Jagat Singh II (*tamāso karāyo*).
126. On the importance of tracking itinerant practices, see Rodgers, "Cultures in Motion," 3.

CHAPTER 1. ENLARGING PAINTED PLACES AND IMAGINING MOODS ANEW

1. See essays in Feld and Basso, *Senses of Place*, esp. introduction.
2. Ingold, "Temporality of the Landscape."

3. Ibid., 155.
4. Ibid.
5. Losty, *Ramayana*, 18–19.
6. Joffee, "Art, Architecture and Politics in Mewar," chap. 4.
7. Losty, *Ramayana*, 12–14.
8. Dehejia, "Treatment of Narrative."
9. Losty, "Sahib-Din's Book of Battles," 114; Aitken, *Intelligence of Tradition*, 65–67. For a discussion of translations in both directions and how the Mughal illustrated epics may have inspired Udaipur's court painters, see Adamjee and Truschke, "Reimaging the 'Idol Temple of Hindustan,'" 158–59.
10. For a comparative analysis of the three cities, particularly regarding Hanuman's arrival in Lanka as marking a geographical and emotional turning point in the poetry, see Goldman and Goldman, *Rāmāyaṇa of Vālmīki*, 5:71–74. For a discussion of Ayodhya, see Pollock, *Rāmāyaṇa of Vālmīki*, 2:10. For a comprehensive discussion on urban imaginaries in early Indian Sanskrit poetry, see Kaul, *Making of Early Kashmir*, 235–56; chap. 6 in particular discusses the cities of the *Rāmāyaṇa* and ways to interpret the sensate culture of Lanka as a space of beauty but also excess.
11. See *Ramayana*, 67–68, British Library, Online Gallery, http://www.bl.uk/onlinegallery/ttp/ramayana/accessible/pages67and68.html (accessed December 1, 2019).
12. See discussion on pleasure and gardens in introduction.
13. Losty, *Ramayana*, 18.
14. See translation especially of *sarga* (canto) 35, verses 25–34. Pollock, *Rāmāyaṇa of Vālmīki*, 2:158–59.
15. Recent digitization of the multivolume manuscript enables us to address the seriality and sequence of spatial depictions when turning from one page to the next. It can be viewed on the British Library's website: http://www.bl.uk/turning-the-pages/?id=a394c2a0-ee97-11dc-95ff-0800200c9a66 (accessed August 1, 2018).
16. For the most part, the pictorial spaces in this manuscript have been examined for the sites where the story plays out. See Dehejia, "Treatment of Narrative," 306–8.
17. Goldman and Goldman, *Rāmāyaṇa of Vālmīki*, 5:114, *sarga* 1, verse 190. For Ayodhya, see Goldman, *Rāmāyaṇa of Vālmīki*, 1:134–35, *sarga* 5, verse 1–23.
18. Ibid., 5:115–16. The translated passages, *sarga* 2, verses 9–18, are:

    The great monkey saw lovely parklands and all kinds of lakes and pleasure groves completely covered with every sort of tree that blossomed and bore fruit in all seasons. There were *saralas*, *karṇikāras*, and date palms in full blossom. There were *priyālas*, *muculindas*, *kuṭajas*, and *ketakas* as well. There were *priyaṅgus* that were filled with fragrance; there were *nīpas* and *saptacchadas* too. There were *asanas*, *kovidāras*, and flowering *karaviras*. And all these trees were thick with masses of blossoms and yet still budding. They were filled with birds, and their crowns waved gently in the breeze. And he saw ponds thronged with *haṃsas* and *kāraṇḍavas* and covered with red and blue lotuses. Approaching Laṅkā, fortunate Hanumān gazed upon that city, which was under the protection of Rāvaṇa and adorned with moats covered with red and blue lotuses. Because of the abduction of Sītā, Rāvaṇa had it especially well guarded by *rākṣasas*, who patrolled it on every side, wielding fearsome bows. It was a great and lovely fortress, surrounded by a golden rampart, bristling with hundreds of towers, and wearing a garland of banners raised on staffs. It had heavenly golden gateways decorated with vine motifs. Such was the city of Laṅkā—like the city of the gods in heaven—that Hanumān gazed upon. With its splendid white mansions, Laṅkā, set high on the mountain peak, looked to that majestic monkey like a city in the sky.

19. For another folio in which Ravana, the demon-king, is depicted to resemble the Mughal emperor Akbar and the monkey Hanuman is shown perched on a mountain surveying the bazaars of the city, see Aitken, *Intelligence of Tradition*, 67, fig. 2.5.
20. Losty notes that Jagat Singh I may have sought artists from northern Deccan when he traveled to the south during a pilgrimage in 1647. Losty, *Ramayana*, 15–16.
21. Talbot, "Mewar Court's Construction," 18–22.
22. Udaipur painters highlighted Chittor's fortified landscape in both genealogical scrolls, as did Mughal painters in the *Akbarnāmah* (Chronicle of Akbar). Ibid., 19; Stronge, *Painting for the Mughal Emperor*, 47, plate no. 73.
23. Ranawat, *Rājasthāna ke jala-saṃsādhana*, 4–6.
24. Neither of the main nearby rivers, the Berach or the Kotra, flowed for all twelve months of the year. The Debari valley was six to eight miles away from Lake Pichola. Ibid., 14–15.
25. The story is told that Lake Pichola, which today measures two and half miles from north to south and one and half miles from east to west, was created by a nomad or indigenous inhabitants of the land in the late 1380s. Ibid., 94–97.
26. Ibid., 79.
27. For an overview of historical waterworks in and around Udaipur, see Ranawat, *Rājasthāna ke jala-saṃsādhana*, chaps. 1 and 2.
28. See discussion on the history of rains and building of lakes for drought relief in chapter 2.
29. Purohit, *Mevāṛa darīkhāne*, 40–41.
30. Jain and Arora, *Living Heritage of Mewar*, 15.
31. Ibid., 48.
32. Ibid., 89.
33. For instance, in one example the setting—the elevation of the palace facade—dominates the horizontal painting, but the triple-arched gateway and the stories added above the Sabha Shiromani Darikhana, the single-level colonnaded space (*darīkhānā*), are missing (see fig. 2.20).
34. Damdama Mahal is not mentioned in any other notable text, but its location described in a seventeenth-century genealogical text is very similar to that of Jagmandir. Ranchodbhat, *Amarkāvyam*, 216.
35. The first document that organizes a class hierarchy within Mewar's *ṭhikānās* lists the seating arrangement of the thakurs in the court during the reign of Jai Singh (r. 1680–98). Amar Singh II grouped the nobles into first-class *ṭhikānās* (*solāh*), numbering sixteen nobles; second-class *ṭhikānās* (*batīs*), thirty-two nobles; and third-class *ṭhikānās* (*gol*), the remaining nobles. This seating chart is available in the private collection of the Purohit family of Udaipur, a member of which served as the principal administrator for court ceremonies. Bhati, *Rājasthāna ke ṭhikānoṃ evaṃ gharānoṃ kī purālekhīya sāmagrī*, 95–97.
36. I am unaware of genealogical poems commissioned by Sangram

Singh II; however, see earlier discussion and notes 21 and 22, above, for the two genealogical scrolls associated with his reign.

37. For an overview, see Sachdev and Tillotson, *Building Jaipur*.
38. The city's plan was at least partially inspired by the Mughal *chārbāgh*, a formal and symmetrical garden. See Johnson-Roehr, "Centering the Chārbāgh," 28–47. Sawai Jai Singh II's architects likely alluded to the Mughal imperial capital Shahjahanabad, a city with broad avenues, and to the Mughal imperial audience hall for the design of Jaipur's most important temple to house the deity Govind Deva's icon, which was relocated to the new city by 1716, even before its inauguration in 1727. See Asher, "Jaipur: City for Tolerance and Progress," esp. 416–19.
39. On the exchange of portraits as gifts, see Aitken, "Portraits, Gift Giving and the Rajput Alliance"; Aitken, *Intelligence of Tradition*, 136–41.
40. There are records of workshops devoted to arms and explosives, armor, harnesses, palanquins, printing, and painting; a variety of animal stables and associated tannery and leather stores; stores assigned for the courtly collections of gold jewelry, gems and precious stones, ivory, utensils, letters, mattresses, carpets, torches, accounting papers, costumes and clothes, eatables, perfumes, and drums; a building and construction department; and a library and dispensary. See Khan, *Art and Craft Workshops*, 7–14.
41. Mishra, "Maps and Map-Making," 147–50.
42. Ibid., 148–49.
43. To find maps across these categories, see Gole, *Indian Maps and Plans*, 14; Bahura and Singh, *Catalogue of Historical Documents*.
44. The building plans and elevations created on sheets of grid paper representing Jaipur's Jal Mahal affirm that these drawings were connected to the construction, in 1734, of the water palace within Lake Mansagar. See Mishra, "Maps and Map-Making," 142–47.
45. Bahura and Singh, *Catalogue of Historical Documents*, cat. no. 158, p. 34. I am grateful to the Maharana Mewar Charitable Foundation and to Shikha Jain for granting permission to reproduce this drawing based on an old published photograph.
46. For inscriptions, see ibid., 95–96.
47. Ibid., cat. no. 155, 34.
48. Schwartzberg, "Diwali in India," 182.
49. Bahura and Singh, *Catalogue of Historical Documents*, 2–4.
50. This map is not accessible (nor is a reproduction), but the scribal notations have been transcribed. The inscriptions convey that the Mewar king possessed lands in northern and western India beyond the capital city of Udaipur, within the towns of Ajmer, Jodhpur, Nagore, Merta, Gujarat, Jaisalmer, and Ujjain. See Bahura and Singh, *Catalogue of Historical Documents*, cat. no. 155, 15, 34, 94–95.
51. The inscriptions on this map have not been fully transcribed. I am grateful to Walter Hakala for analyzing some of the Persian inscriptions and generously sharing his insights. The correct associated record for accessing this map in the collection of the Maharaja Sawai Man Singh II Museum, City Palace, Jaipur is Potikhana (Map 119), not "(Map 110)," as listed in Bahura and Singh, *Catalogue of Historical Documents*, cat. no. 110 (old no. 55), 147; also briefly discussed in Gole, *Indian Maps and Plans*, 110–11.
52. Future in-depth study may offer insights into the mobility of trained professionals, translation practices, and the information eighteenth-century maps extracted from older ones. The scribe of the mid-seventeenth-century map of the Mewar king's territory notes that the Persian notations were translated into Hindi (*fārsī kī hindgī karī*). See Bahura and Singh, *Catalogue of Historical Documents*, 94; the later route map follows the same convention, as the scribe's writing affirms that he was more comfortable in Arabic script than Devanagari. The scribe prominently used words specific to regional terminology to label a fort, such as *gaṛh*, in Hindi, written in Devanagari script, and *kilā*, in Persian, written in Perso-Arabic script.
53. Mishra suggests that in some cases, painters such as Dwarak, apart from working across genres of portraiture and maps and media of cloth and paper, also operated as surveyors of broader regions. See Mishra, "Maps and Map-Making," 149.
54. Gole, "Size as a Measure of Importance."
55. Ibid., 102.
56. The record for the map on the website of the Metropolitan Museum of Art mentions the existence of an inscription on verso. See https://www.metmuseum.org/art/collection/search/38043 (accessed August 12, 2019).
57. There are two maps depicting the fort of Ranthambhor in the Kapad-Dwara collection. Both are no longer accessible. One of the maps entered into the palace stores record in 1753, which implies the artifact was made before the Kachhwaha kings acquired the fort in 1754 (cat. no. 320). The second, late eighteenth-century plan depicts the Ranthambhor fort's men's and women's palaces (cat no. 255). See Bahura and Singh, *Catalogue of Historical Documents*, 12, 15, 43, 49, 122.
58. The measurement of a height of ninety *gaz* noted in this inscription is not entirely clear (and deserves further research); however, we can confirm the scribal note refers to the height (*ūcao*) of the fort.
59. Koch, "Symbolic Possession," 570–75.
60. Ibid., 572–73.
61. Ibid.
62. Based on early nineteenth-century records, we know that a workshop at the Mewar court was devoted to the mantainence and procurement of new boats (*nāv rā kārkhānā*) for the king's lake excursions. See Purohit, *Mevāṛa darīkhāne*, 148–49.
63. On spatial skills acquired by walking and moving along multiple paths, see Tuan, *Space and Place*, 68–70.
64. The Kota kings were engaged in several Mughal military campaigns and peripatetic durbars, and they acquired new interests, artworks, and artists in their travels across frontiers in the Deccan and the north. Mid-seventeenth-century artists at Bundi-Kota adpated the styles and idioms of Mughal paintings to create portraits of the ruling Hada kings and their courtly spaces. Desai, "Timeless Symbols," 1:315–21.
65. On Udaipur artists' adaptations of Bundi-Kota idioms and styles seen in portraits of Amar Singh II's grandfather, Raj Singh, see Topsfield, *Court Painting at Udaipur*, 116–19.
66. One of the earliest paintings portraying Amar Singh II—as a prince (his identity documented in the inscription) hunting boars in a forest—is modeled after a Bundi example. Glynn, "'Stipple Master,'" 2:520; Topsfield, *Court Painting at Udaipur*, 121.
67. Aitken has established that *nim kalam* referred to "tinted paintings, basically siyah kalam with a hint of color, though nim kalam was often described as siyah kalam in Rajasthan's court

documents." See Aitken, *Intelligence of Tradition*, 71–72.

68. Glynn, "'Stipple Master.'"
69. Topsfield, *Court Painting at Udaipur*, 123, 128–37.
70. Bautze, "Amsterdam," 81. Based on an inscription, which has unfortunately faded away, Bautze dates at least one of the murals depicting the Chattar Mahal and the Kota court to 1700. Beach dates the mural largely to 1780, although he notes that the Chattar Mahal examples might belong to an earlier period. See Beach, *Rajput Painting at Bundi and Kota*, 42–43. This mural and the Rijksmuseum painting share the use of oblique lines for the depiction of a central courtyard, although the mural is horizontally positioned, in contrast to the Rijksmuseum painting's vertical orientation. Bautze suggests that the Rijksmuseum painting may have been made in Kota, but plausibly it is an Udaipur copy of yet another unknown painting made at the Kota workshop. However, Udaipur artists in the early eighteenth century were not painting settings in the same way as shown in the Rijksmuseum painting.
71. Chatelain, *Atlas Historique*, 114, plate no. 41.
72. Lightbown, "Oriental Art," 266–67
73. The Dutch embassy's visit was commemorated in large-scale cloth paintings. It is unknown whether these were gifted to the embassy or found their way later into collections in Amsterdam. The two paintings in the collection of the Victoria and Albert Museum in London are believed to have traveled to the United Kingdom with James Tod in 1822. The provenance and route of travel of another painting in a private collection in Amsterdam, are unknown. The embassy's arrival seems to have inspired the Udaipur court artists to make paintings depicting foreigners (*fīrangī*), and several paintings and Udaipur's palaces exhibit the use of Dutch porcelain and tiles. See Bautze, *Indian Miniature Paintings*; and Topsfield "Ketelaar's Embassy."
74. This research on Oriental art collections in Italy establishes that Picart must have made this engraving in 1715, in Amsterdam, although it was not published until 1719. See Lightbown, "Oriental Art," 266–67.
75. The speculation that the Rijksmuseum painting could have been based on Picart's engraving may be difficult to sustain. The murals in Kota depicting the same subject, and the very likely scenario that the Rijksmuseum painting arrived in the Netherlands via Udaipur, give us evidence that the engraving was made after the painting and not vice versa. Roy, *50 x India*, 102.
76. The portraits made by both the Kota and Udaipur artists also recall two smaller Udaipur portraits of the Mughal emperor Jahangir with his attendants. See Losty, *Ramayana*, 9. The artist of the current painting followed Mughal conventions, modeling the ruler as seated in the same profile pose, with one leg folded.
77. Aitken, *Intelligence of Tradition*, 103.
78. On devotional poetry praising the blue god Krishna and the depiction of the erotic mood (*śṛṅgāra*), see introduction.
79. Schwartzberg, "Diwali in India," 182.
80. Inventory numbers on the back of *The Mood of Kota Palace* are 15/125. The cost (*kīmat*) of the painting is noted as ninety rupees. The classificatory number 15 adheres to the prevalent cataloguing system of 1891 and refers to pictures of Rajput rulers "other" than those hailing from Udaipur. See Topsfield, "Royal Paintings Inventory," 192
81. I believe this confusion is a result of modern Hindi using *mehalā* as the word for palaces, whereas the regional dialect emphasizes the nasal pronunciation and eliminates the character *ha*.
82. Clifford, *Routes: Travel and Translation*, 11.
83. Sveltlana Alpers used this term to make sense of the intersections between maps and broader visual culture. See Alpers, "Mapping Impulse," 119–68.
84. Aitken, *Intelligence of Tradition*, 120–24.
85. On the 1891 painting inventory see introduction n51.
86. See introduction n4 for the inscription.
87. Koch, "Symbolic Possession," 572–74.
88. Gregg, *City Views*, 10–11.
89. Ibid.
90. See discussion on literary *bhāva* in the introduction.
91. The Gangaur festivities are featured in the record for multiple years, such as the spring of 1787; the scribe made a note of Maharana Bhim Singh's boat procession and admiration of the Gangaur spectacle (*tamāsō*).
92. Raj Singh, as prince, before he became the Udaipur king in 1652, was the patron of the gardens of Sarvaritu or Sarbat Vilas, which were built near the Rajsamand Lake outside Udaipur city and included tanks, fountains, and pavilions. In most secondary scholarship, these gardens are referred by the name "Sarvaritu Vilas" rather than "Sarbat Vilas," which is likely the reason the painting's title includes the former, even though the inscription states the latter. I have included both identifiers in the title, since the painting and place have been in circulation. However, in my discussion of the artwork, I refer to the gardens as Sarbat Vilas to adhere to the inscription. See Shyamaldas, *Vīravinoda*, 2:443.
93. Part of the inscription identifies the site and event: *śrī. bādī sarabata bilāsa re darīkhānai śrī māhārāṇā amar sīghjī phāga khele hai* (the seating pavilion in the garden of Sarbat Vilas [where] Shri Maharana Amar Singh-ji plays [the spring festival] *phag*). For the complete inscription, see Topsfield, *Paintings from Rajasthan*, 62.
94. See discussion of Amar Singh II's consolidation of thakurs in note 37, above.
95. Ten years after Amar Singh II's reign had ended, *yati* Khetal, a Jain monk who traveled to Udaipur, composed an ode to the city, *Udaipur rī gajal* (discussed at length in chapter 5). In his verse, the poet praises Amar Singh's pleasurable assemblies held in the Sarbat Vilas gardens. See Rathore, *Paramparā Rājasthānī gajala saṃgraha*, 26.

CHAPTER 2. PASSIONATE MONSOONS AND MONUMENTAL PAINTINGS

1. See the discussion of Jagat Singh I's *Rāmāyaṇa in* chapter 1.
2. On the Stipple Master, who is thought to be the artist of both small portraits of Amar Singh II, as prince and as king, seen in figs. 2.7 and 2.8, see chapter 1.
3. I draw upon the excellent essays in *Monsoon Feelings: A History of Emotions in the Rain*; the book's introduction summarizes the methodological approach to the monsoon as an emotional concept. See Rajamani, "Monsoon Feelings," esp. 25–35.
4. For a discussion on the uncertainty of rains, based on courtly records, rituals, and folk songs in seventeenth- and eighteenth-

century northern India, see Kumar, "Uncertain Monsoon," esp. 242–43, 252–57.

5. Fraser, *V. S. Naipaul Collection*, 74–75.
6. The inscription is: *sabī sāvaṇ bhādav kā do*[?] *mahīnā kī*[*che?*] (a picture of the two months of Savan and Bhadav). I have used the vernacular names for the rainy months—Savan and Bhadon in this section (sometimes spelled "Bhadav," as in the inscription)—drawing upon the Brajbhasha sources discussed here. I include diacritics for the names of the months only in the transliterations of verses or inscriptions.
7. Busch, *Poetry of Kings*, 75.
8. Keshavdas composed each verse as a six-line composite known as a *chappay*. I am grateful to Allison Busch for many discussions of Keshavdas's *bārah-māsa* poetry and painting, within workshops and beyond, and for allowing me to use her translations of the verses on Savan and Bhadon from *Kavipriyā* (1601).
9. Busch's new translation is based on the following original text, from Keshavdas, *Kavipriyā*. Busch's translation, "Selection from the Bārahmāsā or '12 month' poetry sequence in the *Kavipriyā* of Keshavas, 1601," is available on the website of the workshop "The Romance(?) of the Rainy Season," held on Saturday April 7, 2018, at Columbia University, in New York, sponsored by the South Asia Institute and the Department of Middle Eastern, South Asian, and African Studies. See http://www.columbia.edu/itc/mealac/pritchett/00urduhindilinks/workshop2018/Keshavdas_Barahmasa.pdf (accessed August 13, 2019).

   Śrāvaṇa (Sāvana)
   'Kesava' saritā sakala milita sāgara mana mohaiṃ
   Lalita latā lapaṭāta taruna tana tarabara sohaiṃ
   Ruci capalā mili megha capala camakata cahuṃorana
   Manabhāvana kahaṃ bheṃṭi bhūmi kūjata misa (nisa?) morana
   Ihi rīti ramana ramanī sakala lāge ramana ramāvana
   Priya gamana karata kī ko kahai gamana suniya nahiṃ savanna
   Bhādrapad (Bhādoṃ)
   Ghorata ghana cahuṃ ora ghoṣa nirghoṣani maṇḍahi
   Dhārādhara dhari dharani musaladhārani jala chaṇḍahi
   Jhillīgana-jhaṅkāra pavana jhuki jhuki jhakajhorata
   Bāgha siṃgha guñjarata puñja-kuñjara taru torata
   Nisidina biseṣa niraseṣa miṭi jāta su olī oṛiyai
   Nija desa piyūṣa, bidesa biṣa bhādauṃ bhāvana na choṛiyai

10. On the aspirated and alliterative sounds heard in the rainy season verses, see Orsini, "Clouds, Cuckoos and an Empty Bed," 100. On the creation of monsoon-related feelings through sung poetry, see also Williams, "Theology of Feeling."
11. Busch, "Listening for the Context," 250.
12. For a comprehensive introduction to the genre, see Dallapiccola, Glynn, and Skelton, *Ragamala: Paintings from India*.
13. For a discussion of Brajbhasha rhyme and register, see Busch, *Poetry of Kings*, 90–98.
14. Leante, "Cuckoo's Song," 262–68.
15. Lunn and Schofield, "Delight, Devotion and the Music of the Monsoon," 230.
16. Aitken, "Dark and Overwhelming, yet Joyful," esp. 159–71.
17. The partially damaged inscription on this painting deserves further examination, though I can confirm that the scribe identifies the raga. He likely pairs the word *rāginī* (the wife of the personified raga) with names of musical instruments to describe each of the depicted women shown to be playing a distinct instrument.
18. For a discussion of the dispersed manuscript and a complete translation of the inscription related to the rainy season on the back of this painting, see John Seyller's catalogue entry in Mason, *Intimate Worlds*, 68–69.
19. The short inscription in red is translated as: "While it rains, birds perch singing on the hills, and jackals appear in the fields by the banks of the River Yamuna." Mason, *Intimate Worlds*, 68–69n1.
20. Orsini, "Barahmasas in Hindi and Urdu," 143–49.
21. Orsini discusses one such case, of the early eighteenth-century Urdu poet Uzlat's imagining of a yogi's longing and the possibilities that "contamination of genres" instigated poets to bring embodied experiences into the mix. See Orsini, "Clouds, Cuckoos and an Empty Bed," 125–29.
22. All the years given in the poetry are noted per the *vikram saṃvat* (VS) calendar, so my translations of the verses include the same dates; however, in the main text I follow the Georgian/Western Christian calendar. Verses on the years after 1710 (VS 1767) are not always complete or in chronological order. All translations, unless otherwise noted, are mine. See Jaichand, *Saīkī*.
23. While the geographer Ishvar Singh Ranavat has mined this source for data on climate change and waterworks, to the best of my knowledge this genre has received limited attention from historians of literature, culture, and Jain religiosity.
24. There is no scholarly consensus on Jaichand's use of language. It is considered mixed, suggesting the author's plausible affiliation with the region of Mewar or Bikaner, though the relation established with the mid-seventeenth-century historical writing of Munhata Nainsi, a Jain scholar who wrote comprehensive histories of the region, suggests Jaichand's connection to the region of Marwar. Jaichand largely covers the towns and cities of Rajasthan in the northwest, though he occasionally also offers perspectives on places farther south in the Deccan. He describes one season of famine and drought in the Deccan as an anomaly, referring to the region as a place where there were rarely "dark times." In contrast, the yearly patterns of abundance and famines continue in his description of northern and western India. Jaichand, *Saīkī*, 148, verse 109. For an overview on the region's historical genres, including Munhata Nainsi's works, see Zeigler, "Marvari Historical Chronicles"; and Kothiyal, *Nomadic Narratives*, 52–57.
25. Jaichand, *Saīkī*, 108, verse 30.
26. For an overview of this historical source, see Jawalia, "Food Security in Rajasthan."
27. Lake Jaisamand, Raj Singh's successor Jai Singh's building project thirty-two miles southeast of Udaipur, was seven times larger than Rajsamand Lake—though its lakefront was less ambitiously inscribed and decorated. Jai Singh's aims were similar to those of his predecessor: to provide ample and reliable sources of water in case of drought. See Bhadani, *Water Harvesting*, 120–42.
28. Hooja, *History of Rajasthan*, 621–23.
29. For a summary, see Bhati, *Mevāṛa ke aitihāsika granthoṃ kā sarvekshaṇa*, 2–3.
30. The urban and historical scale of this project established a

connection for the Udaipur kings with an idealized Hindu Vedic notion of kingship, while also invoking comparison to specific waterworks projects and to the commemorative and devotional practices of Mughal kings. For an account of Raj Singh's patronage of historical manuscripts, art, and architecture, especially as they are integrated into the public site of Rajsamand Lake, see Joffee, "Art, Architecture and Politics in Mewar," chap. 4.

31. Except on one occasion, in which the poet introduces and praises King Anup Singh of Bikaner, most likely due to the context of the assembly of intellectuals the king hosted in Samovar in the years 1749 and 1750. Jaichand, *Saikī*, 130, verse 76.
32. See verse 8 in the appendix. On another occasion, in verse 92, Jaichand notes that Rajputs indulge in looting and attacks on common people. Jaichand, *Saikī*, 139 verse 92.
33. Verses 1–6 are missing from the manuscript. Verse 7, which is partially available, describes the beginning of Raj Singh's reign in Udaipur (1652). Brajmohan Jawalia, in his introduction to Jaichand's *Saikī*, suggests that verses 1–6 must have included introductory verses for the poetry as a whole and a description of the years from 1652 to 1658 (VS 1709 to 1715). The translation of verses 8 and 9 (see appendix) gives evidence on the battles for inheritance of the Mughal crown, and verse 15 shifts the focus to Raj Singh's kingship in Mewar. Jaichand, *Saikī*, introduction, 16; 96, verses 8 and 9; 101, verse 15.
34. Jaichand, *Saikī*, 101, verses 16–18.
35. Bayly, *Empire and Information*, 72–73.
36. Jaichand, *Saikī*, 101, verses 17 and 18.
37. On *rasa*, see introduction.
38. Jaichand, *Saikī*, 145, verse 103.
39. Ibid., 145, verse 101.
40. Ibid., 146–154, esp. verses 105–20.
41. Ibid., 150, verse 112.
42. Ibid., 151, verse 113; 153, verse 118. For the complete verses with translation, see appendix.
43. Topsfield, *Court Painting at Udaipur*, 111–12.
44. Ibid.
45. Ibid., 15.
46. In each of the three large cloth paintings, as well as in paintings on paper made in later years after these models, artists adopted different solutions to depict the walls of the Baadi Mahal, which overlooked the Manek Chowk courtyard. Some painters offered a view into smaller courtyard spaces that lay beyond the palace facade. Scribal notations on the fronts of the paintings often record the names of the featured elephants and bulls, as well as the cost of the works of art. Another example from this series of three is reproduced in Jain and Arora, *Living Heritage of Mewar*, 19.
47. For architectural drawings and development of the Baadi Mahal courtyard, see ibid., 80–83.
48. Water was likely drawn into the pool by a waterwheel. See Ruggles and Joffee, "Rajput Gardens and Landscape," 278–80. In chapter 3, I further discuss the courtyard's significance for the practice of courtly pleasures.
49. Jain and Arora, *Living Heritage of Mewar*, 62.
50. Di Palma, "Flow: Rivers, Roads, Routes," 37.
51. Ibid.
52. Shulman, *More Than Real*, 4–8.
53. The transliterated verse is: *mānaka bhītara sāhiba siṁgha sangrāma sidhāyo / pyāri piyā ati pema apāra su bhādava mā milike mana bhāyau.*
54. For example, see *Maharana Ari Singh Hunting Deer by a Quarry*, c. 1767, in Topsfield, *City Palace Museum*, 59, cat. no. 21.
55. See Roberts, *Scale*, esp. introduction.
56. On the efficacy of objects in relation to art history that privileges neither texts over objects nor specific temporalities or geographies, see two recent volumes, Baader and Weinryb, "Images at Work"; and Betancourt, "Introduction: The Medium before Modernism."

CHAPTER 3. WORLDS OF PLEASURE AND POLITICS OF CONNOISSEURSHIP

Parts of chapter 3 appeared in "Lakes within Lake-Palaces: A Material History of Pleasure in 18th-Century India," in *Water Histories of South Asia: The Materiality of Liquescence,* Visual and Media Histories Series, ed. Sugata Ray and Venugopal Maddipati, 60–92 (Abingdon, Oxon: Routledge, 2019); and "Jagvilasa: Picturing Worlds of Pleasure and Power in 18th-Century Udaipur Painting," in *A Magic World: New Visions of Indian Painting in Tribute to Ananda Coomaraswamy's Rajput Painting of 1916*, ed. Molly Emma Aitken, 74–87 (Mumbai: Marg Publications, 2016).

1. Tod's evocative writing on the lake palaces of Jagmandir and Jagniwas is discussed in the introduction to this volume.
2. Ojha, *Udayapura rājya kā itihāsa*, 2:609, 641.
3. For a discussion on eighteenth-century decline, see introduction.
4. The discussion of paintings made at the Rajput court of Nagaur presents an exception. See Glynn, "Rathore and Mughal Interactions."
5. For *Jagvilās* manuscript repository, see introduction n49.
6. Khera, "Jagvilasa: Picturing Worlds," 83–86.
7. On this point, see introduction.
8. See a further discussion on *Jagvilās* verse 10 later in this chapter. The foundation of Jagniwas was laid on April 22, 1743. See Shyamaldas, *Vīravinoda*, 2:443.
9. Ahmed, "Not in the Mood." On attunement, see introduction.
10. Schofield, "Sense and Sensibility," 1–5. On postcolonial discomfort with court cultures, see Busch, *Poetry of Kings*, 11–17.
11. Schofield, "Sense and Sensibility," 7.
12. Flatt, "Social Stimulants"; Flatt, "Sitting Together."
13. Nandram, *Jagvilās*, verse 17.
14. Earlier works of Sanskrit and Brajbhasha (classical Hindi) poetry commissioned at the Udaipur court, such as *Jaisiṅghvilāsa* (n.d.) and *Rājvilāsa* (1689), explore themes of royal praise and portraiture by privileging genealogy. See Joffee, "Art, Architecture and Politics," 104–8. For a summary of *Rājvilāsa*, see Bhati, *Mevāṛa ke aitihāsika granthoṃ kā sarvekshaṇa*, 2–3.
15. For seventeenth-century examples of *nagara-varṇana* from Bundi, Orchha, and Shahjahanabad, where poets have paid attention to "local inflections" but not necessarily composed poetry focused on one space, see Busch, *Poetry of Kings*, 148–51, 181, 191–92.
16. On the city's lakes and locale, see chapter 1.
17. Michell, *Royal Palaces of India*, 52–60; Asher, *Architecture of Mughal India*, 123–27; Brookshaw, "Palaces, Pavilions and Pleasure-Gardens," 199–223. For an overview of pools related to

courtly spaces and pleasure, see Hegewald, *Water Architecture in South Asia*, chap. 7.

18. Asher, *Architecture of Mughal India*, 84.
19. However, lakes, water tanks, and water palaces that made up eighteenth-century Jaipur highlight both secular and devotional concerns. See Horstmann, "Jaipur's Waterscape," 96–107.
20. Sachdev and Tillotson, *Building Jaipur*, 70. Future research may yield connections with Udaipur's lake palaces since we have contemporaneous depictions of Sawai Jai Singh II participating in assemblies held at the Jagniwas.
21. On Deeg's gardens, see Asher, "'It Is a Day for Enjoyment and Revelry,'" 203–9.
22. Likewise, Chandar Bhan Brahman, the state secretary and poet in the Mughal emperor Shah Jahan's court, revealed that "political business and literary pleasure" were inextricably linked during parties. See Kinra, *Writing Self, Writing Empire*, esp. chap. 1, 43–44.
23. Modern histories often recount that Prince Khurram, before becoming emperor Shah Jahan, built and lived in the Gol Mahal (circular chamber), the most iconic building on the Jagmandir island. My research suggests that *Jagvilās* is the first historical literary source that associates Shah Jahan with Jagmandir. On the chronology in which the various palaces in the Jagmandir lake-palace complex were built, see Khera and Mansukhani, *The City within a City*.
24. Shyamaldas, *Vīravinoda*, 3:1233. For Mewar's seventeenth-century history, see my introduction.
25. For courtly pleasures of and in gardens, see this volume's introduction.
26. Shyamaldas, *Vīravinoda*, 2:790.
27. See discussion on *rasa* in the introduction.
28. However, we may be missing key texts by Udaipur poets that make architecture an object of affection.
29. For discussion of "*kama* world," see introduction.
30. Topsfield, *Court Painting at Udaipur*, 130.
31. See ibid., 160–61. The 1891 Mewar royal collection inventory also describes a painting related to the 1708 political and marital alliance among the courts of Udaipur, Jaipur, and Jodhpur (discussed in the introduction) as "the three rulers meeting by the lake." See Aitken, "Portraits, Gift Giving and the Rajput Alliance," 359.
32. For a discussion of diplomacy and depiction of bonding, as seen in Jairam's camp painting, see Khera, "Joys of Bonding," 112–14; for the Mughal album page, see Los Angeles County Museum of Art, accession no. M.2001.24, https://collections.lacma.org/node/203164 (accessed September 1, 2019).
33. For a longer discussion on this shift, see Khera, "Lakes within Lake-Palaces."
34. Nandram, *Jagvilās*, verses 55–109.
35. On this point, refer to chapter 2.
36. In one instance (verse 204), Nandram refers to the Bado Mahal as the "Bade Mahal." Nandram used *bado* and *bade*, both meaning "big/large," to describe the Bado Mahal as "large palace." Given the closeness in the sounds of the words *bado*, *bade*, and *bādi* (garden), and the garden courtyard around which the palatial space was built, the name Bado Mahal also evokes the image of a large garden palace.
37. Similarly, two other paintings depict Sangram Singh in the environs of the Jagmandir lake-palace complex. One of them, last seen in the collection of the Kunwar Sangram Singh Museum, is related to the previously discussed painting in terms of the composition of the architecture. The other painting is unusual because the lake palace is oriented vertically, a composition that is not seen in any other known painting depicting either of Udaipur's lake palaces. See Topsfield, "Jagmandir and the Other Royal Palaces," 108.
38. Topsfield ascertained that the paintings depicting the *rāslīlā* (dance and drama enacting Krishna's divine play with Radha and her friends) were made in the 1740s by artists working in Jagat Singh II's court workshop. They share a theme and feature similar compositions; additionally, the inventory numbers on the versos of this set of *rāslīlā* paintings are consecutive. Topsfield, "Udaipur Paintings of the Raslila," 59n2.
39. The inventory numbers on the reverse sides of two of the Jagniwas paintings are J 1/257 (fig. 3.9) and J 1/258 (fig. 3.14). The 1891 Udaipur painting inventory states that a painting titled *Jagnivās ro bhāva*, numbered 259, was priced at 150 rupees; this entry could refer to the painting that opened this chapter (fig. 3.1). Additionally, these three paintings with consecutive inventory numbers share the date of November 1751 (*kārtik badi 7, vikram saṃvat* 1808), which indicates a posthumous date, as Jagat Singh II died in June 1751. This sequence, however, is complicated by the fact that the painting *Maharana Jagat Singh II Hawking and Boar Hunting*, in the Edwin Binney 3rd Collection of the San Diego Museum of Art, depicting the lake environs (not the lake palaces), was assigned the same inventory number (J 1/259) as *Maharana Jagat Singh II and His Queens at Jagniwas* (fig. 3.1); see http://collection.sdmart.org/Obj5719 (accessed December 8, 2019). See Topsfield, *Court Painting at Udaipur*, 192, 209–210n21, n23–n26, n58.
40. Nandram, *Jagvilās*, verses 176–204.
41. On the relationship between water metaphors and the lotus motif deployed to design the pool, see Khera, "Lakes within Lake-Palaces," 77–81.
42. Nandram, *Jagvilās*, verse 181 concludes the description of the Bado Mahal.
43. Ahmed, "Not in the Mood," 17.
44. For example, the Udaipur court painter Bakhta and his son Chokha changed the workshop's direction in the last quarter of the eighteenth century by adapting painting styles and genres developed in working for the Mewar thakurs in another regional *ṭhikānā*, of Devgarh. See Beach, *Rajasthani Painters Bagta and Chokha*, chap. 5.
45. The history of the Dodia clan was written in verse form between 1855 and 1876 in the *Dīpaṅgakulaprakāśa*, which commemorated the clan's founder. In 1855, after Sirdar Singh's grandson succeeded in regaining control of the Sardargarh fort, the Mewar king Swaroop Singh (r. 1842–61) proclaimed Sardargarh as a second-class estate of Mewar. Following Sardargarh's reincorporation within Mewar's *ṭhikānās* in 1855, Maharana Shambhu Singh (r. 1861–74), during his visit to the fort, commissioned Kayamdan Dadhivariya, father of Kaviraj Shyamaldas, the author of *Vīravinoda* (1886), the first narrative history of the court, to write the history of the Dodias in recognition of their services to the Mewar court. Based on court records detailing Kaviraj Shyamaldas's years of service at the Mewar court, Braj-

mohan Jawalia suggests in his foreword to *Dīpaṅgakulaprakāśa* that Shyamaldas completed most parts of this composition after his father's death in 1870. I use this primary source and history of the Dodias recounted in Shyamaldas's *Vīravinoda* to present the Dodia clan's history in brief. Future research on this source is planned. Dadhivariya, *Dīpaṅgakulaprakāśa*, foreword (*prastāvanā*), 5–17; historical summary (*aitihāsik sār*), 18–46.

46. Taft, "Honor and Alliance."
47. Shyamaldas, *Vīravinoda*, 3:1929.
48. For discussion on eighteenth-century "little kingdoms," see introduction n117.
49. Man Singh Dodia, the late patriarch of the Dodia clan, who died in 2012, claimed during a personal conversation in July 2003 that the same architects and craftsmen who were responsible for the design and building of Sirdargarh and the Dodia *haveli* designed the Jagniwas lake palace as well. This topic will be addressed in the future. For a discussion of the development of the courtyard mansion as a dwelling type in Rajasthan, see Shikha Jain, *Havelis*, 13–36.
50. A currently inaccessible topographical painting from c. 1762–65 depicting an elaborate procession of the Udaipur king Ari Singh also shows the city of Udaipur beyond the palace complex. Based on what I can discern from the image of the painting generously shared by Andrew Topsfield, it offers extraordinary details of the lake's waterfront architecture from which to explore how the Dodia *haveli* provides a rare vantage point for the admiration of Lake Pichola and Udaipur's palaces. Apart from the elevation of the eastern facade of the main palace, the painters selectively highlighted specific buildings (presumably those that were deemed most important by courtly audiences). By combining a bird's-eye view with planimetric and elevation views, the painters provided the complete layouts of Jagniwas and Jagmandir as well as the complete complex of the courtyard mansion of Sirdar Singh Dodia.
51. The *Sirdārvilās* folios, including the relation between verse and image in each instance, will be treated at length elsewhere; in this book I simply gesture toward the manuscript's significance, since it was created before the inception of the Jagniwas lake palace and allied paintings and poetry.
52. The scribe of the illustrated manuscript spells the noble's name as "Sirdar" Singh, not "Sardar" Singh, as he is known today. In the terms of the fort built by the noble, I have adhered to Sardargarh, rather than Sirdargarh. Given the paucity of scholarship on this key figure and place, I want to ensure that contemporary visitors and historians can find the place and its discussion in recent scholarship.
53. From the three folios discussed here, we know that there may have been thirty-one paintings in the illustrated *Sirdārvilās*. Two more folios, one, numbered 16 (in a yet unknown repository), and, second, numbered 28 (in the Pierpont Morgan Library, Gift; Paul F. Walter; 1985. MS M.1075.6), show that the aesthetics of seasons were also part of the manuscript's vision of *vilāsa*. These aspects, including tracking the painters who participated in this project, will be researched in the future. Shahji (or Sahaji) and Syaji were likely the same artist. I have used both spellings in this book, based on each painting's inscriptional evidence; thus I credit "Shahji" as the painter of the *Sirdārvilās* folios (figs. 3.20–22) and "Syaji" as the painter of the artwork discussed earlier (fig. 3.1). For discussion on the artist, see Topsfield, *Court Painting at Udaipur*, 208n13.
54. See the discussion on spaces of pleasure functioning as heterotopias in the introduction.
55. Sangram Singh II generously supported the building of the temple, though his mother led the inauguration. Her family, of the Mewar thakurs of Dungarpur, was also involved in this project. Ojha, *Udayapura rājya kā itihāsa*, 2:620–21.
56. Though the scribe identifies the portrait of the king as Sangram Singh, the painter allies it with portraits of Jagat Singh II. Topsfield, *Paintings from Rajasthan*, 83.
57. Glynn, "Rathore and Mughal Interactions," 11, 16–19. Also see Diamond et al., *Garden and Cosmos*, 72–73, plate 10; 91–97, plates 18–20.
58. Mid-eighteenth-century Jodhpur court painters also employed the Nagaur palette to meld royal imaginaries and Krishna's heavenly landscapes. See Diamond, "Maharaja Vijai Singh," 21.
59. Diamond et al., *Garden and Cosmos*, 134–35, plate 29.
60. Other regional artworks—like the intriguing example of Jaipur's Sawai Madho Singh I (r. 1750–68) in a boat procession, in the collection of the City Palace Museum, Jaipur, which stands apart in its somewhat singular status—merit further research. I thank Shailka Mishra for bringing this example to my attention. Additional regional artworks by a painter from Kutch, on the coast of Gujarat, feature depictions of festive boat processions and lakes based on those in Udaipur paintings. See Goswamy and Dallapiccola, *A Place Apart*, 32, 77, plate XI.
61. The painting, *Maharana Bhim Singh Frolics with Noblemen in the Palace Pool*, can be viewed on the website of the San Diego Museum of Art; http://collection.sdmart.org/Obj5066 (accessed December 8, 2019).
62. The painting, *Maharana Jawan Singh Bathing with His Sardars*, can be viewed on the website of the National Gallery of Victoria, Melbourne; https://www.ngv.vic.gov.au/explore/collection/work/53640/ (accessed December 8, 2019).
63. See introduction for the discussion on gardens and assemblies, especially within the painted *Bāburnāmah* and *Niʿmatnāmah-i Nāṣirshāhī*.

CHAPTER 4. MODES OF KNOWING AND SKILLS OF DRAWING

1. Hereafter, I will refer to the publication *Annals and Antiquities of Rajast'han* as *Annals*. I have consulted the first edition of the *Annals*, published in 1829 (volume 1) and 1832 (volume 2), to discuss the engravings and their placing in relation to Tod's narrative. For the text, I have referred the later edition published in 1920.
2. Topsfield brings attention to two inscribed works on paper by Ghasi. One painting, dated to 1825, depicts Bhim Singh at a hunting picnic; its inscription notes that Ghasi was given an award of a gold bracelet for his work. Another painting (undated but also from around 1825), which also notes Ghasi's name, depicts Jawan Singh as a prince, seated on a swing bed in a courtly setting. Topsfield, *Court Painting at Udaipur*, 234–38.
3. For Tod's description of Ghasi as "a native artist (who labours at Udaipur for the same daily pay as a tailor, carpenter, or any other artisan)" and his dismissive opinion of Ghasi's under-

standing of linear perspective as indicative of an Udaipur court artist's skill, see Tod, *Annals* (1920), 3:1297. This view is iterated in Topsfield, *Court Painting at Udaipur*, 235.

4. The Udaipur court artists Bakhta and his son Chokha, who was Ghasi's contemporary at Udaipur for a few years, have been applauded for bringing an innovative freshness to compositions of portraits and royal hunts. In traveling between, and painting in, the court workshops at Udaipur and Devgarh, one of Mewar's estate lands (a *ṭhikānā*, like Sardargarh, discussed in chapter 3), Bakhta and Chokha experimented with and combined pictorial models and artistic styles developed at other Rajasthan courts. By contrast, Ghasi's skill in making "detailed delineations" of architecture for Tod and for the Udaipur court are certainly recognized but not necessarily interpreted as innovative. See Topsfield, *Court Painting at Udaipur*, chap. 8; Beach, *Rajasthani Painters Bagta and Chokha*; and Aitken, *Intelligence of Tradition*, chap. 5.
5. On the connection to European narratives, see D'Souza, "Tod as an Observer of Landscape in Rajasthan"; and on the relation to bardic stories, see Talbot, "Recovering the Heroic History of Rajasthan."
6. Flood, *Objects of Translation*, 9 (emphasis in original).
7. On the formulation of distinct figures of "lack" and "inadequacy" within colonial histories, see Chakrabarty, *Provincializing Europe: Postcolonial Thought*, 35–40.
8. Here I use "circle of artists" to alert us to the problem of authorship and attribution, especially as it pertains to discussions of artistic agency in court workshops. See Aitken, *Intelligence of Tradition*, 272–73.
9. Based on Mary Louise Pratt's usage of the term "contact zone" in Pratt, *Imperial Eyes: Travel Writing and Transculturation*, Kapil Raj deployed the term to examine the "intercultural 'contact zone'" where South Asians and Europeans interacted and worked together, to reexamine "the nature of scientific knowledge making in the globalized space of early modernity in the context of European expansion." See Raj, *Relocating Modern Science*, 10–11.
10. By tracing the role and work of Indian intellectuals, including "native" assistants and artists who feature within the accounts and collections of British political agents and antiquarians (for instance, Tod's contemporary Colin Mackenzie, based in Madras), scholars such as Cynthia Talbot and Thomas Trautmann have sought to shift the account of the production of knowledge and history to include not only British agents but also Indian assistants. See Talbot, *Last Hindu Emperor*, esp. chap. 6; also see essays in Trautmann, *Madras School of Orientalism*.
11. Henry Noltie has highlighted the work of the Indian artists Rungiah and Govindoo and how they shaped the corpus of botanical drawings produced by the British East India Company surgeon-botanist Robert Wight between 1826 and 1853. See Noltie, *Robert Wight*. Holly Shaffer has highlighted the artist Gangram Tambat's critical role in the making of British watercolors and the drawings of architectural sites represented in collections of Sir Charles Warre Malet, British East India Company resident in Poona between 1785 and 1798. See Shaffer, *Adapting the Eye*. Also, Chanchal Dadlani's and Yuthika Sharma's tracking of late Mughal artists for multiple patrons and the creation of hybrid genres is noted in the introduction.
12. Smith, "In the Workshop of History," esp. 7.
13. Bilak et al., "The Making and Knowing Project," 37, 42.
14. Tod, *Annals* (1920), 1:3.
15. The *Annals* were originally published in two volumes, each composed of eleven books. For details on the relationship between the structure of the books and the construction of history in the volumes, see J. Freitag, *Serving Empire, Serving Nation*, chap. 5.
16. On Rennell, see Edney, *Mapping an Empire*, chap. 1.
17. The sections are as follows: Boundaries of Rajasthan; The States of Rājputāna; History of Geographical Surveys; The Author's Surveys; Survey Parties; The Author's Map—1814; Physiography of Rājputāna; The Aravalli Range; Views from the Aravalli Hills; Geology of the Aravallis; The Patār Plateau; The Mountain System of Central India; The Chambal River; The Western Desert; The Luni River; The Mirage; The Desert.
18. Tod, *Annals* (1920), 1:4–9.
19. On the relation between mapping as a process, rhetoric of accuracy, and conception of empire, see Edney, "The Patronage of Science," 64.
20. Tod notes that "after having laid down these varied lines in the outline described," he was "determined to check and confirm its accuracy by recommencing the survey on a new plan, viz. trigonometrically." See Tod, *Annals* (1920), 1:7.
21. Tod, *Annals* (1920), 1:3n2.
22. J. Freitag, *Serving Empire, Serving Nation*, 34–36.
23. Tod identifies "the Thal" as "the general term for the sand ridges of the desert." Tod, *Annals* (1920), 1:19, 19n5.
24. Tod, *Annals* (1920), 1:19–22. On maps as artifacts that point to the importance of not only making meanings of the visible in maps but also carefully evaluating the "silences," see Harley, "Deconstructing the Map," 4; Harley, "Maps, Knowledge and Power," 289–92.
25. Tod, *Annals* (1920), 1:14.
26. Although his work is indebted to Harley's and Edney's frameworks, Ian Barrow argues that in the project of colonial mapping, the construction of territory is related to ideas of possession and profitability. Barrow, *Making History, Drawing Territory*, 9–14.
27. Raj, *Relocating Modern Science*, 7–11.
28. Tod, *Annals* (1920), 1:6–7.
29. Ibid., 1:6.
30. Gole, *Indian Maps and Plans*, 49–53.
31. This small chart (19 × 16.5 cm), part of the collection of the Rajasthani Shodh Sansthan, Jodhpur, was included in the history of the region (*Mārwāra rā pargānana rī vigata*) written in 1646 by Sundarsi, brother of Marwar's foremost court historian, Munhata Nainsi. The making of such charts continued to the mid-twentieth century, as Gole notes a later chart, made in 1941 (current location unknown), that locates Jaipur at its center. Ibid., 24, 52, cat. no. 231.
32. North is at the bottom of the image in the orientation of the map reproduced here.
33. Tod, *Annals* (1920), 1:15–16.
34. In the future, I hope to trace Tod's travel routes (as documented in the personal narrative at the end of the *Annals*) using geographic information system to juxtapose them with Tod's map of Rajasthan.

35. Babb, "Tod and Traders," 110–21.
36. Talbot, "Recovering the Heroic History," 104.
37. Talbot asserts that Tod's "greatest legacy is not his collection . . . rather [it is] the research into Rajasthan's history that he carried out using the various texts and artifacts he had amassed." Ibid., 99.
38. Tod, *Annals* (1920), 1:2. Tod's conceptions were most likely based on the essays on historical geography written by Sir William Jones, published during this time period in the volumes of *Asiatic Researches*. Tod mentions this source on multiple occasions in his essay "History of Rajpoot Tribes." Tod, *Annals* (1920), 1:23–38.
39. Tod, *Annals* (1920), 1:7.
40. Tod's comments on Waugh's original sketches and my research into the various versions of Finden's engravings suggest that inquiry into the role of professional artists and engravers in translating and transforming watercolors into published images remains a largely under-researched topic in evaluating the circulation of landscape and architectural imagery of eighteenth- and nineteenth-century South Asia.
41. Head and Royal Asiatic Society, *Catalogue*, 115 (accession no. 037.077).
42. Royal Asiatic Society accession no. 037.007A. The remarks on the sails and ferry boats are noted on the reverse of a depiction of the same view by a professional British artist. This detail is not noted in the current catalogue. Head and Royal Asiatic Society, *Catalogue*, 110.
43. Head and Royal Asiatic Society, *Catalogue*, 112 (accession no. 037.022).
44. On the assumptions of a singular "picturesque," see R. Ray, *Under the Banyan Tree*.
45. On Jaipur's cartography workshop, see chapter 1.
46. Topsfield, "Tod's Collection of Rajasthani Paintings," 23.
47. In another instance, in a book published in 1800 on the siege of Srirangapatnam in southern India, the frontispiece is an engraving of "Tippoo Sultaun" made by S. W. Reynolds. While the native artist's name is not mentioned, the caption explicitly states that the original drawing was in the possession of the marquis Wellesley. We see Tipu Sultan, the ruler of the princely state of Mysore, depicted in a profile view, gazing at a horizon filled with hints of smoke and dust that suggest the context of the siege of Srirangapatnam. It appears that the original artist may have drawn in detail his costume, jewelry, and accessories, as the engraver attempted to evoke a palpable sense of the profuse nature and variety of textiles and ornamentation. See Beatson, *View of the Origin and Conduct of the War*, frontispiece.
48. Ghasi traveled to these sites with Tod in November 1821, December 1822, and February 1822, toward the end of Tod's stay in the region. For an introduction to Tod's travels and their intersection with the visual works in his collection and those published in the *Annals*, see Topsfield, "Tod's Collection of Rajasthani Paintings"; Tillotson, "Illustrating the Annals."
49. Tod, *Annals* (1829), 1:facing p. 574. Also reproduced in the section on Chandravati temples in vol. 2, facing p. 732.
50. Royal Asiatic Society accession nos. 037.011, .012, .013, and .014 carry these instructions. Head and Royal Asiatic Society, *Catalogue*, 111.
51. Ghasi's drawing that forms the basis for the engraving is in the collection of the Royal Asiatic Society, London, accession no. 037.087. See Head and Royal Asiatic Society, *Catalogue*, 111.
52. Ghasi's drawing that forms the basis for the engraving is accession no. 037.090, Royal Asiatic Society, London. Ibid.
53. See drawings by Ghasi in the Royal Asiatic Society: *Two Niches at Barolli* (accession no. 037.154) and *Column in the Fortress of Chitor* (037.121). Head and Royal Asiatic Society, *Catalogue*, 116, 120.
54. Tod, *Annals* (1920), 3:1786.
55. Tod, *Annals* (1832), 2:734.
56. Topsfield, *Court Painting at Udaipur*, 238.
57. Tod, *Annals* (1920), 3:1815. Plans of temples from this site are available in the British Library and are attributed to Tod (accession no. WD1480–6). Head and Royal Asiatic Society, *Catalogue*, 116.
58. Head and Royal Asiatic Society, *Catalogue*, 161 (accession number 037.161).
59. We find versions made in fine lines with watercolor and brush based on the rougher drawings. For instance, the drawing of the base structure with molding discussed above (fig. 4.20) was copied by Ghasi in finer lines (037.172). See Head and Royal Asiatic Society, *Catalogue*, 121. Some of the drawings also include inscriptions, very likely recorded by the painter or by accompanying scribes and assistants.
60. Topsfield, *Court Painting at Udaipur*, 246–49. The travel route Jawan Singh followed for this pilgrimage is well documented. There is limited information on the maharana's Kashi journey, but Purohit's summary confirms that the Vishvanath temple was the primary precinct he visited. For details on the rituals, donations, and meetings Jawan Singh completed in each city during the pilgrimage, based on court archives, see Purohit, *Mevāṛa darīkhāne*, 168–71.
61. Cimino, *Vita di corte*, 111, 30 (v).
62. There is extensive scholarship on the emergence of Varanasi (referred to as Kashi in the Udaipur archive and as Banaras in scholarship on the city's importance in the time period under discussion) as a Hindu pilgrimage city and political center in the eighteenth and nineteenth centuries. For example, on Maratha pandits and their forging of knowledge networks in Banaras, which assisted the Marathas to consolidate political power, see O'Hanlon, "Letters Home"; for discussions that account for urban and architectural change, see S. Freitag, "Power and Patronage," M. Desai, *Banaras Reconstructed*, and Michell, *Late Temple Architecture*.
63. Michell, *Late Temple Architecture*, 31–33.
64. Neither the painting depicting the Vishvanath temple nor the inscription are accessible. However, a study of the painting based on Andrew Topsfield's book and photograph and the above line drawing is insightful. The temple's design, of "clustered shikhara towers," confirms that the depiction is indeed the Vishvanath temple. I thank Joshua Kwassman and Nita Roberts for creating line drawings of this painting, and Catherine Asher and Heeryoon Shin for help with identifying the temple. On the temples depicted in both paintings (figs. 4.2 and 4.21), see Michell, *Late Temple Architecture*, 155, 163.
65. On Stipple Master, see chapter 1.
66. Note that we may also construe this vignette as a part-sectional view combined with a planimetric view of the inner sanctum,

given that the steps leading to this space are depicted in plan format on the left-hand side of Amar Singh II's portrait.

67. See the essays in Codell, *Power and Resistance*, esp. introduction, 8–9.
68. See discussion on Mughal durbars in the introduction.
69. Freitag, *Serving Empire, Serving Nation*, 38.
70. See British Library, Political Correspondence and Private Papers of James Tod, 1927, Mss Eur F144/73; Tod departed for Europe in June 1822 and handed over his responsibilities to assistant agent Patrick Waugh, who was political agent for about one year after Tod departed. On April 15, 1823, Cobbe took charge from Patrick Waugh. For a brief period in 1826, Captain J. Sutherland was the officiating agent. Vashishtha, *Rajputana Agency*, 15–40. I borrow heavily from Vashishtha's work on the constitution of the Rajputana Agency in this paragraph.
71. Fisher, "The Resident in Court Ritual," 419–58.
72. Ibid., 452.
73. The British ruled the princely states through a special form of indirect rule, paramountcy. The imprecise limits on the exercise of power within paramountcy worked to the British advantage. See Rudolph and Rudolph, "Rajputana under British Paramountcy," 139.
74. That the first British durbar of political importance was held in Ajmer and not in Delhi is of great significance, considering the cachet and symbolic capital of this Mughal town in the early nineteenth century for the British. A future project in this direction will comprehensively examine the diplomatic correspondence concerning the event (a source that I briefly explore later in this chapter), paintings made by other court artists (apart from Ghasi) who traveled to Ajmer, and the work of French traveler Victor Jacquemont, who wrote an eyewitness account. We know that painters traveled to this durbar with Maharao Ram Singh of Kota and that they made large paintings depicting the meeting of the Kota king with Bentinck. See Bautze, "Ajmer Darbar," 71–73.
75. Paintings attributed to Ghasi and dated to about 1826 depict Jawan Singh's father, Bhim Singh, in a durbar setting with the British official Charles Metcalfe and his entourage within interior spaces of Udaipur palaces. These works also set a precedent for Ghasi's Ajmer durbar painting. Topsfield, *Court Painting at Udaipur*, 237.
76. Khera, "Joys of Bonding," 112–14.
77. Mehta, *Bartāv sādā tarīko baiṭhak kī yād*, Maharana Mewar Charitable Foundation, Udaipur, MS 2692. I am grateful to the archivist Sarita Srimal, who corrected my transcriptions and helped me read this document.
78. National Archives of India, New Delhi, Political Correspondence, April 2, 1832, no. 29.
79. Ibid.
80. Mehta, *Bartāv sādā tarīko baiṭhak kī yād*, Maharana Mewar Charitable Foundation, Udaipur, MS 2692.
81. In writing about Jacquemont's impression of the meeting between Jawan Singh and Governor-General Bentinck, Bautze also makes note of the French traveler's sense that the Udaipur ruler was unhappy with his meeting at the durbar because protocol had been violated. Bautze, *Interaction of Cultures*, 160–61.
82. Another painting depicting a meeting of the Udaipur ruler Jawan Singh and the Jaipur ruler Jai Singh in their own tent precincts at Ajmer during Bentinck's monthlong durbar, made by a Jaipur artist, displays adherence to the custom of seating nobles on the floor and seating their rulers against cushions on the carpet. It is striking that the artist (who does not appear to be Ghasi, as the portrait of Jawan Singh is rendered in a very different style than in the Ghasi paintings seen thus far) in this case also aligns the boundaries of the tent with the boundaries of the painting. The depicted chintz tent connects the painting to Jaipur. The painting's current location is unknown, but scholars think that at least two copies exist. Bautze, "Ajmer Darbar," 71.
83. I thank Kajri Jain for the suggestion to pay attention to the painted gifts.
84. Eaton, "Between Mimesis and Alterity," 818–19, 833.
85. The gifts exchanged between Governor-General Bentinck and the Rajput king of Kota after the conclusion of the 1832 Ajmer durbar, however, are now known. See Ramaswamy, *Terrestrial Lessons*, 56–57.
86. Topsfield, *Court Painting at Udaipur*, 247.
87. National Archives of India, New Delhi, Political Correspondence, "24 December 32," no. 11–13.
88. Ibid.
89. Ibid.
90. Ibid.
91. Moxey, *Visual Time*, 18. He writes, "Unlike modernity, contemporaneity is both multiple and not multiple at the same time. Dominant cultures export and disseminate such temporal structures . . . [the] time that matters, that on which the artistic canon depends, has always favored the cultures of the powerful."
92. Ibid., 28.
93. Aitken, *Intelligence of Tradition*, chap. 5.
94. Topsfield, *City Palace Museum*, 81n2.

CHAPTER 5. CHARISMATIC PLACES AND COLONIAL SPACES

Parts of chapter 5 appeared in "Marginal, Mobile, Multilayered: Painted Invitation Letters as Bazaar Objects in Early Modern India," *Journal18*, no. 1 (Spring 2016), http://www.journal18.org/527.

1. The Udaipur scroll (1830) belongs to the Agarchand Nahata Jain Granthalaya, a private library and archive set up by the Nahata family, which was one of the most important mercantile families in Bikaner in the eighteenth and nineteenth centuries. It is unclear whether Agarchand Nahata acquired this scroll at a later date or if it had been part of the family collection since the 1830s. The latter prospect raises the possibility that the Nahata family hosted the monk Jinharsh Suri.
2. Shvetambara monks as mendicants on a lifelong pilgrimage were expected to be mobile for eight months of the year. See Cort, "Twelve Chapters from the Guidebook to Various Pilgrimage Places" 288–89. *Vijñaptipatra* scrolls were largely sent by Shvetambara Jains, who owe religious alliances to "white-clad" ascetics, unlike the other Jain sect, Digambara, whose members follow "sky-clad," or naked, ascetics. On epistolary aspects of letters, see H. Shastri, *Ancient Vijñaptipatras*. For an overview of the genre, see Shalin Jain "Inviting the Lords."
3. The transliterated excerpt of the letter is:

śri jī mahārāja rā sadā sukha ānanda rī ghaḍi sadā sarvadā cāhije jī āpa mōṭā ho baḍā ho udayapura na śri sangha sāthe sadā kṛipā sdṛiśtī rākhavo jīṇsū viśeśa rakhāvsi jī atra no śri sangha rātrā din smaraṇa karrayo[?] che jyon chātraka mōra rātra dina varśā ne rathe jyon śri sangha smae[?] rat[?]raiya[?] che so śri sangha māthe kṛipā karke abke caumāsa udayapura no karāvsi āpre to vaḍā vaḍā śrāvaka vāta dēkha raiyā che śri sangha māthe pūrṇa kṛipā huve.

4. Neither the English documents of Cobbe's agency nor the daily diaries of the court's activities during Jawan Singh's reign reveal information on the monk's arrival.
5. Jain merchants and monks occupied the neighborhood (*sethjī rī bāṛī*) near the British residency in Udaipur in the nineteenth century. It appears that the expansion of Udaipur city in the outskirts was spurred by Joravarmal Bapna's building of the temple near the residency. The temple has been expanded and renovated in recent years; however, the original entrance to the main shrine is largely unaltered.
6. On marginalized objects and cultures of mobility, see the introductory section in Khera, "Marginal, Mobile, Multilayered."
7. In recent years, scholars have turned to regional-language sources from the sixteenth through nineteenth centuries to explore how historical memory was embedded in literary genres. For example, see Busch "Hidden in Plain View"; Chatterjee, "Communities, Kings and Chronicles"; Sreenivasan, *Many Lives*; Deshpande, *Creative Pasts*; Rao, Shulman, and Subrahmanyam, *Textures of Time*. On situating geographical perspectives from the margins, see Ramaswamy, *Lost Land of Lemuria*.
8. Markovits, Pouchepadass, and Subrahmanyam, *Society and Circulation*, introduction, 8.
9. K. Jain, *Gods in the Bazaar*, 13–16.
10. Calendars, as objects, did not simply represent the new technology of chromolithographs but also complicated the categories of "fine art" and "history." Their makers combined images from across visual domains, which were embraced by a very broad spectrum of people in India. See ibid.
11. However, I maintain that the domain of the "popular" that *vijñaptipatra* scrolls forge is still quite distinct—in terms of materiality, visual technologies, numbers, and the thematic conceptualization of public space—from the later "popular" art of chromolithographed bazaar images.
12. On the value of intermediary genres in early modern India for studying history, before colonial notions of literature and history became dominant, see Orsini, *Before the Divide*, introduction, 11–13.
13. For instance, see the discussion in chapter 2 on the repetition of the elephant to denote its swift movements and chapter 3 for the repetition of Jagat Singh II's portrait in the spaces of the Jagniwas lake palace.
14. See fig. 3.23 for a court painting depicting a portrait of a bare-chested Maharana Jagat Singh II worshipping in his palatial quarters, c. 1735–40.
15. For the 1774 scroll painter's depiction of the Baadi Mahal elevation, see Andhare and Bhojak, *Jain Vastrapatas*, 146–49.
16. See chapter 1 for my discussion on Jaipur's cartographic workshops and Udaipur's mid-seventeenth-century maps.
17. All known Sirohi *vijñaptipatra* scrolls depict a central street with a single example of a cloth or utensil seller to denote each type of trade.
18. Vashishtha, *Rajputana Agency*, 20–22.
19. The court poet Nandram describes the king's procession from the palace to the lakefront on the inauguration day of the Jagniwas lake palace. See chapter 3.
20. For example, in Mewar's genealogical scroll dated to around 1730–40 (Victoria and Albert Museum, accession no. 07964/1 [IS]), we see vignettes that hint at the visualization of a marketplace; however, how this subsection of the scroll narrates Mewar's history is unclear.
21. Losty, *Ramayana*, 11.
22. Another vertical pictorial vignette representing a bazaar scene in the double page from Nusrati's *Gulshan-i-'ishq*, attributed to a Deccan court artist in Hyderabad, generates a dramatic juxtaposition of courtly space and city space (1710). See Leach, *Paintings from India*, 244–47.
23. Diamond, "The Cartography of Power," 279.
24. *Vijñaptipatra* depicting Jodhpur, late nineteenth century, 844 × 31 cm, Rajasthan Oriental Research Institute, Jodhpur branch (accession no. 20114); *vijñaptipatra* depicting Merta, 1861, dimensions unknown, Rajasthan Oriental Research Institute, Jodhpur branch (accession no. 8470), currently exhibited at the Sardar Government Museum, Jodhpur.
25. Granoff, "Jain Pilgrimage in Memory," 67–68.
26. It is difficult to ascertain whether this practice of performers showing the scroll was followed in the case of Jain painted invitation letters. For examples of contemporaneous painted scrolls, wherein the "art" object functioned as a "cultural" prop, see essays in J. Jain, *Picture Showmen*; and Ghosh, "Story of a Storyteller's Scroll," 175–77.
27. Aquil and Chatterjee, *History in the Vernacular*, esp. 9–10.
28. For example, see Bangha, "Courtly and Religious Communities"; Urban, "Marketplace and the Temple"; Ramusack, "Punjab States"; and Saha, "Movement of Bhakti."
29. The location of the delivery address on this scroll, and the damage to the paper edge in many other scrolls on the part where the letter concludes, indicate this part was subject to wear and tear due to the direction in which *vijñaptipatras* were rolled.
30. My larger, ongoing project on letter-scrolls builds upon Hiranand Shastri's multiple insights on the literary aspects of *vijñaptipatra* scrolls. These include the importance of messenger poems (*dūtakāvya*), largely modeled on the ancient Sanskrit classic by Kalidasa, *Meghadūta* (The cloud messenger), for exploring the poetic imagining of geography, topography, and route maps; and the poetry of the *Indudūta* (and its eighteenth-century manuscript copies), in which the moon (*indu*) serves as the messenger. H. Shastri, *Ancient Vijñaptipatras*, 5–8; see also Satyavrat Shastri, "Critical Survey of Dutakavyas."
31. While we have Sanskrit treatises outlining the rules and tropes for writing and decorating letters as literary compositions, no prescriptive text for writing letters within a *vijñaptipatra* has been found. The pastiche of laudatory texts in several scrolls indicates that a letter-writing guide or handbook must have existed. Several examples suggest that conventions for composing such letters were somewhat standardized by the eighteenth century—similar to the standardization, noted earlier in this chapter, of the visual icons referring to symbols of faith and

prosperity in the Jain religious canon that open painted scrolls. H. Shastri, *Ancient Vijñaptipatras*, 9–18.

32. I am grateful to Phyllis Granoff for advising me on the introductory laudatory passages, in which the scribes seem to cite parts of the introductory text in the Agra *vijñaptipatra* (1610). Personal communication with Phyllis Granoff, e-mail, August 24, 2010.
33. The scribes address Jinharsh Suri as *śri śri jī mahārāja* in most parts of the letter, repeating honorifics such as *śri* to emphasize the monk's exalted stature. They also formulate various forms of collective and individual respectful homage (*vaṇdanā, trikāl vaṇdanā, vaṇdanā ek sau āth vāra*), adhering to standardized tenets of letter writing within *vijñaptipatra*. In contrast to the address in other letter-scrolls, the writers do not employ several different epithets to describe the monk.
34. Although by the first quarter of the eighteenth century several Mewar court nobles ruled fairly independently, contemporaneous writers employ the term *Mewar* to refer to a historical imaginary and territoriality of Udaipur's kings that extends beyond the capital city.
35. For example, see the following passage:

    āchau punyā huve jinī thikāne śrijī mahārāja ro paḍārno huve phēra mewāḍa deśa mein makī jawāro bant[?] *hai*[?] *jiṇi sāmo dekhāvsī nahī dina sankaḍi*[?] *āya hai ghanā bhāvya jīva*[?] *ne samyā*[?] *ro lābha hosī jina śāsana*[?] *rī ghaṇī mahīmā hosī śri ganaghar*[?] *mahārāja padhārsī jaṭhe*[?] *saṛva bāta ro kalyāna hosī.*

    Good deeds happen in the places where Shriji Maharaja proceeds. Now the production of grains has ended[?] in the Mewar country, and changing times are not in sight. Days of problems are here thus . . . [?] many beautiful lives would be benefited by the [this] timely opportunity, the rule[r] of this place would be famous, where . . . Maharaja would proceed. All spheres would benefit.

36. National Archives, New Delhi, Political Correspondence, 14 October 1830, no. 1–2. See also, British Library, Political Correspondence, March–August 1831, IOR/F/4/1384/55168, and February–December 1831, IOR/F/4/1402/55504, which describes the termination of the letter-writing offices at Udaipur and Jaipur and the revision of tributes under Cobbe. On the transferring of the Udaipur Agency and the neighboring Jaipur Agency to the Ajmer Agency, see Vashishtha, *Rajputana Agency*, 15–40.
37. National Archives of India, New Delhi, Political Correspondence, March 11, 1831, no. 44.
38. Each two-line verse of a *ghazal*, based on Urdu examples, affirms that its "verses share meter, rhyme, and usually end-refrain as well, [and that] it has a powerful symmetry and cohesion"; however, each line can be an independent, freestanding poem. See Pritchett and Faruqi, "Lyric Poetry in Urdu," 9.
39. Bangha, "Rekhta: Poetry in Mixed Language," 21–83. For the relationship of Rekhta to Urdu poetry in eighteenth-century Delhi, see Faruqi, "Conventions of Love," 3–32.
40. On the use of *gajals* praising the region of Marwar as an archive of crafts, craftsmen, and non-courtly sociocultural perspectives in the early modern city, see Sahai, *Politics of Patronage and Protest*, 28–29, 178–80.
41. For example, in the first published compilation (1964), these Rekhta *gajals* are described as Jain examples associated with Hindu Sanskrit classical poetry describing cities (*nagara-varṇana*); Rathore, *Paramparā Rājasthānī gajala saṃgraha*, vii. For an overview of Rekhta-language poetry's problematic reception and classification, see Bangha, "Rekhta: Poetry in Mixed Language," 62.
42. Khetal, *Udaipur rī gajal*, 1718, Agarchand Nahata Jain Granthalaya, MS 7677. Khetal also composed *gajals* on Mewar's former capital Chittor Fort (1691) and the city of Ajmer (1730).
43. Orsini and Schofield, *Tellings and Texts*, introduction, 12–16.
44. Cort, "Jain Knowledge Warehouses," 80–84. I have not come across other literary works that were authored by the monk-poets who composed topographical *gajals*.
45. Poets employed the term *shahrāshūb* originally as an "appellation for a beautiful beloved in a lyric poem" and also as "a short bawdy lyric addressed to a young boy who is engaged in a trade or craft and coquettishly offers his wares to the love-struck poet." See S. Sharma, "City of Beauties," 73–74.
46. Ibid., 75.
47. In the *Lahore ki gajal*, the poet Jatmal Nahar praises the physical traits of this city and situates it within a broader geography. Along with describing its palaces, gardens, and bazaars; craftsmen and tradesmen; and intellectuals ranging from mullahs to pandits, he recounts the beautiful women of the city in multiple couplets. While the poet enumerates the temples, mosques, and shrines in the city, he does not give any specific importance to Jain temples. He idealizes the emperor Akbar's reign by comparing it to the idea of a *rāmrājya*, the god-king Rama's ethical and just rule, and concludes by describing the imagery of an idealized place, the beautiful gardens and their flora and fauna, on the outskirts of the city. While it is difficult to suggest that Jatmal Nahar translated and adapted any specific Persianate *gajal* on Lahore into this Rekhta example, the poet does not see this literary approach as being antithetical to the description of travels related to Jain pilgrimage. My interpretations are based on the manuscript copy in the Agarchand Nahata Jain Granthalaya (MS 7674).
48. On Nandram's *Jagvilās*, see introduction and chapter 3.
49. It is rather surprising that Khetal incorporates neither Mount Abu nor Kesariyaji (an important Shvetambara Jain community near Udaipur, which is specifically mentioned in the textual letter of the 1830 Udaipur *vijñaptipatra*).
50. The Udaipur rajas presented themselves as the *dīvān*, the administrative representatives, of the family deity Eklingji.
51. Khetal devotes only three verses to some of the city's temples before moving his gaze to the bazaars in verse 32. He does not seek to describe any of the Jain temples in particular.
52. I am grateful to Allison Busch for alerting me to the use of this trope from Rajput court poetry, which suggests the need for further research on Khetal's combining of literary models. The entire couplet (74) appears in the appendix.
53 See Appendix, Khetal, *Udaipur rī gajal*, couplet 74.
54. On Mewar's history of resisting the Mughals, see introduction.
55. For other examples of letter writers' use of literary tropes of urban praise and the *gajal*'s couplets within painted scrolls, see H. Shastri, *Ancient Vijñaptipatras*, 55–61.
56. The relations between the unrolling of early modern Japanese scrolls and the exploration of collective versus individual

viewing of these artworks may provide valuable comparative insights for examining the interpretations that the material form of a scroll engenders. See McKelway, *Capitalscapes*; and McCormick, *Tosa Mitsunobu and the Small Scroll*.

57. Certeau, *Practice of Everyday Life*, 91–110.
58. Ibid., 93.

CONCLUSION. MEMORIALIZING MOODS AND RECOVERING HISTORIES

1. Baader and Weinryb, "Images at Work."
2. Orsini, "Between Qasbas and Cities."
3. Barringer, "Landscape Then and Now," n.p.
4. Dave-Mukherji, "Whither Art History."
5. Latour, *Reassembling the Social*, 3–5.
6. See chapter 3 for the shift from Jagmandir to Jagniwas lake palace as the idealized place for courtly pleasures. For an image of the third painting depicting Jagmandir, in the Birla collection, see Khandalavala, *Collector's Dream*, 132.
7. Fig. C.1 measures 41 × 47 cm; fig. C.2, 43.8 × 48.6 cm. The third painting, depicting the island palace from the north (not reproduced in this volume; see note 6, above), is *Jagmandir*, c. 1740–43, artist unknown, 44 × 99 cm.
8. The use of fine gray lines to denote the depth of building surfaces and the gold and red for windows reminds us of the mastery of architectural rendering seen in the Udaipur painter Jairam's works, including other works related to Jagniwas and Jagmandir discussed above (see figs 3.7, 3.9, 3.10, 3.11, 4.25). Works ascribed and/or currently attributed to Jairam evince his keen interest in the picturing of places in Udaipur court painting. He could have taken his knowledge of depicting architecture in multiple directions.

APPENDIX

All translations of the poetry are mine. I am very grateful to Allison Busch, Prem Rajpurohit, and Dalpat Rajpurohit for comments on my initial transliterations and translations of *Jagvilās* and *Udaipur rī gajal*, and to Tyler Williams for offering critical thoughts and corrections on key verses. I thank Justin Ben-Hain for feedback on transliterations and translations of Jaichand's *Saīkī*. Any remaining errors are mine. All the years in the poetry are noted per the Indian calendar, so the translation includes the dates per the *vikram saṃvat* (VS); however, in the main text I have followed the Georgian/Western Christian calendar for the convenience of the reader.

Bibliography

MANUSCRIPT SOURCES

British Library. Political Correspondence, February–December 1831. "The Maharana of Oodeypoor pays tribute to the conduct of Major Thomas Alexander Cobbe when Political Agent at Udaipur." Asia, Pacific and Africa Collections (formerly Oriental and India Office Collections). India Office Records. IOR/F/4/1402/55504.

British Library. Political Correspondence, March–August 1831. "Following the abolition of the Oodeypoor and Jeypoor Political Agencies, establishments of News writers and Harkaras are to bet set up in both places." Asia, Pacific and Africa Collections (formerly Oriental and India Office Collections). India Office Records. IOR/F/4/1384/55168.

British Library. Political Correspondence and Private Papers of James Tod, 1927. "The Residency, Udaipur—an account of the buildings and surroundings of the Residency at Udaipur; with additions made to the list of Residents up to 1943." Asia, Pacific and Africa Collections (formerly Oriental and India Office Collections). India Office Records. MSS Eur F144/73.

Haqīqat Bahīdā of Maharana Bhim Singh. Part 1 (1778–93). Maharana Mewar Research Institute, Udaipur. BH 664.

Haqīqat Bahīdā of Maharana Bhim Singh. Part 2 (1794–1807). Maharana Mewar Research Institute, Udaipur. BH 672.

Haqīqat Bahīdā of Maharana Bhim Singh. Part 3 (1808–19). Maharana Mewar Research Institute, Udaipur. BH 679.

Haqīqat Bahīdā of Maharana Bhim Singh. Part 4 (1820–24). Maharana Mewar Research Institute, Udaipur. BH 686.

Haqīqat Bahīdā of Maharana Bhim Singh. Part 5 (1824–27). Maharana Mewar Research Institute. BH 688.

Jatmal Nahar. *Lahore kī gajal*. 1605–1718. Agarchand Nahata Jain Granthalaya, Bikaner. MS 7674.

Khetal. *Chittor rī gajal*. 1718. Rajasthan Oriental Research Institute, Udaipur. 2611.

Khetal. *Udaipur rī gajal*. 1718. Agarchand Nahata Jain Granthalaya, Bikaner. MS 7677, MS 7671.

Khetal. *Udaipur rī gajal*. 1718. Rajasthan Oriental Research Institute, Jaipur. 1883 (22, 23).

Khetal. *Udaipur rī gajal*. 1718. Rajasthan Oriental Research Institute, Udaipur. 4361.

Mehta, Sher Singh. *Bartāv sādā tarīko baiṭhak kī yād* (Chronicle of the instructions on general protocols for the assembly). 1832. Maharana Mewar Research Institute, Udaipur. MS 2692.

Nandram. *Jagvilās*. c. 1746. Rajasthan Oriental Research Institute, Udaipur. 2216.

National Archives of India, New Delhi. Political Correspondence. "Maharana's desire to make a pilgrimage to Giayee, 24 December 32." Foreign and Political Department, no. 11–13.

National Archives of India, New Delhi. Political Correspondence. "Oodeypoor and Jeypoor Agencies placed under Agent at Ajmer, 14 October 1830." Foreign and Political Department, no. 1–2.

National Archives of India, New Delhi. Political Correspondence. "Oodeypoor Maharana's programme of reception at the Durbar at Ajmer, 2 April 1832." Foreign and Political Department, no. 29.

National Archives of India, New Delhi. Political Correspondence. "Oodeypore Rana's khureetas for the retention of Alexander Cobbe at his capital, 11 March 1831." Foreign and Political Department, no. 44.

Udaipur Painting Inventory, 1891, Rajasthan State Archives, Udaipur.

PRINTED PRIMARY SOURCES

Babur. *The Bāburnāmah: Memoirs of Babur, Prince and Emperor*. Translated and edited by W. M. Thackston. New York: Modern Library, 2002.

Banarasidas. *Ardhakathānaka: A Half Story*. Translated and introduction by Rohini Chowdhury. Preface by Rupert Snell. New Delhi: Penguin Books, 2009.

Beatson, Alexander. *A View of the Origin and Conduct of the War with Tippoo Sultaun: Comprising a Narrative of the Operations of the Army under the Command of Lieutenant-General George Harris, and of the Siege of Seringapatam*. London: G. and W. Nicol, 1800.

Bhanudatta. *Bouquet of Rasa and River of Rasa*. Translated and introduction by Sheldon Pollock. The Clay Sanskrit Library 41. New York: New York University Press and JJC Foundation, 2009.

Bhati, Hukum Singh, ed. *Mevāṛa ke aitihāsika granthoṃ kā sarvekshaṇa*. Jodhpur: Rajasthani Granthaghar, 1996.

———. *Mevāṛa ṭhikānoṃ ke abhilekha: Ṭhikānā Baneṛā, Bhiṇḍara, Saradāragaṛha, Gogundā, Kānoṛa*. Udaipur: Pratap Shodh Pratishthan, 1994.

———. *Rājasthāna ke ṭhikānoṃ evaṃ gharānoṃ kī purālekhīya sāmagrī*. Udaipur: Pratap Shodh Pratishthan, 1996.

Chatelain, Henri Abraham. *Atlas historique; ou, Nouvelle introduction à l'histoire, à la chronologie & à la geographie ancienne & moderne. . . .* Vol. 5. Amsterdam: L'Honore & Chatelain, 1719.

Dadhivariya, Kayamdan, and Kaviraj Shyamaldas. *Dīpaṅgakulaprakāśa: Saradāragaṛha ke Ḍoḍiyoṃ kā itihāsa*. Translated and edited by Brajmohan Jawalia. Udaipur: Pratap Shodh Pratishthan, 1995.

Goldman, Robert P., ed. and trans. *The Rāmāyaṇa of Vālmīki: An Epic of Ancient India*. Vol. 1: *Balakāṇḍa*. Introduction by Robert P. Goldman. Annotation by Robert P. Goldman and Sally J. Sutherland. Princeton, NJ: Princeton University Press, 1984.

Goldman, Robert P., and Sally J. Sutherland Goldman, eds. and trans. *The Rāmāyaṇa of Vālmīki: An Epic of Ancient India*. Vol. 5: *Sundarakāṇḍa*. Princeton, NJ: Princeton University Press, 1996.

Hodges, William. *Travels in India, during the Years 1780, 1781, 1782, and 1783*. London: printed for the author, and sold by J. Edwards, 1793.

Jahangir. *The Jahāngīrnāmah: Memoirs of Emperor Jahangir*. Translated and edited by W. M. Thackston. Washington DC: Freer Gallery of Art, Arthur M. Sackler Gallery / New York: Oxford University Press, 1999.

Jaichand. *Saikī: Rājasthāna rai rajavāram ro sau sala ro itihasa*. Translated and edited by Brajmohan Jawalia. Gangashahar, Bikaner: Acharya Tulsi Rajasthani Shodh Sansthan, 2009.

Keshavdas. *Kavipriyā*. In *Keśavgranthāvalī*, vol. 1. Edited by Vishvanathprasad Mishra. Allahabad: Hindustani Academy, 1954.

Munhata Nainsi. *Muṃhatā Naiṇasīrī Khyāta*. Edited by Badariprasad Sakariya. 4 vols. Jodhpur: Rajasthan Oriental Research Institute, 1960.

Nahata, Agarchand, ed. *Aitihasik Jain Kavya Samgraha*. Calcutta: Shankardan Shubhairaj Nahata, 1937.

Pollock, Sheldon I., trans. *The Rāmāyaṇa of Vālmīki: An Epic of Ancient India*. Vol. 2: *Ayodhyakāṇḍa*. Introduction by Sheldon I. Pollock. Edited by Robert P. Goldman. Princeton, NJ: Princeton University Press, 1986.

Ranchodbhat. *Amarkāvyam*. Edited by Dev Kothari, Shaktikumar Sharma, and Rajendraprakash Bhatnagar. Udaipur: Rajasthan Vidyapeth Sahitya Santhan.

Rathore, Vikram Singh, ed. *Paramparā Rājasthānī gajala saṃgraha*. Jodhpur: Chaupasani Shodh Sansthan, 1964

Tod, James. *Annals and Antiquities of Rajast'han, or the Central and Western Rajpoot States of India*. Vol. 1. London: Smith Elder, 1829.

———. *Annals and Antiquities of Rajast'han, or the Central and Western Rajpoot States of India*. Vol. 2. London: Smith Elder, 1832.

———. *Annals and Antiquities of Rajasthan, or The Central and Western Rajput States of India*. Edited by William Crooke. Vol. 1. London and New York: Humphrey Milford, Oxford University Press, 1920.

———. *Annals and Antiquities of Rajasthan, or The Central and Western Rajput States of India*. Edited by William Crooke. Vol. 3. London and New York: Humphrey Milford, Oxford University Press, 1920.

———. *Travels in Western India, Embracing a Visit to the Sacred Mounts of the Jains and the Most Celebrated Shrines of Hindu Faith Between Rajputana and the Indus: With an Account of the Ancient City of Nehrwalla*. London: William H. Allen and Co., 1839.

Vatsyayana. *The Kamasutra*. Translated and introduction by Wendy Doniger and Sudhir Kakar. Oxford University Press: New York, 2002.

SECONDARY SOURCES

Adamjee, Qamar. “Artistic Agency in Painted Narratives: The Case of Chandayan Manuscripts.” In *A Magic World: New Visions of Indian Painting*, edited by Molly Emma Aitken, 116–29. Mumbai: Marg Publications, 2017.

Adamjee, Qamar, and Audrey Truschke. “Reimagining the ‘Idol Temple of Hindustan’: Textual and Visual Translation of Sanskrit Texts in Mughal India.” In *Pearls on a String: Artists, Patrons, and Poets at the Great Islamic Courts*, edited by Amy Landau, 141–65. Baltimore: Walters Art Museum / Seattle: University of Washington Press, 2015.

Ahmad, Aziz. “The British Museum Mīrzānāma and the Seventeenth Century Mīrzā in India.” *Iran* 13 (1975): 99–110.

Ahmed, Sara. “Affective Economies.” *Social Text* 22, no. 2 (2004): 117–39.

———. “Not in the Mood.” *New Formations: A Journal of Culture/Theory/Politics* 82 (2014): 13–28.

Aitken, Molly Emma. “Dark and Overwhelming, yet Joyful: The Monsoon in Rajput Painting.” In *Monsoon Feelings: A History of Emotions in the Rain*, edited by Imke Rajamani, Margrit Pernau, and Katherine Butler Schofield, 137–84. New Delhi: Niyogi Books, 2018.

———. *The Intelligence of Tradition in Rajput Court Painting*. New Haven, CT: Yale University Press, 2010.

———. “The Laud *Rāgamālā* Album, Bikaner, and the Sociability of Subimperial Painting.” *Archives of Asian Art* 63, no. 1 (2013): 27–58.

———. “Parataxis and the Practice of Reuse, from Mughal Margins to Mīr Kalān Khān.” *Archives of Asian Art* 59 (2009): 81–103.

———. “Portraits, Gift Giving and the Rajput Alliance of 1708.” In *The Ananda-Vana of Indian Art: Dr. Anand Krishna Felicitation Volume*, edited by Naval Krishna and Manu Krishna, 355–66. Varanasi: Indica Books; Abhidha Prakashan, 2004.

Alam, Muzaffar. *The Crisis of Empire in Mughal North India: Awadh and the Punjab, 1707–48*. Delhi and New York: Oxford University Press, 1986.

Ali, Daud. *Courtly Culture and Political Life in Early Medieval India*. Cambridge Studies in Indian History and Society. New York: Cambridge University Press, 2004.

———. “Gardens in Early Indian Court Life.” *Studies in History* 19, no. 2 (August 1, 2003): 221–52.

———. “Rethinking the History of the Kama World in Early India.” *Journal of Indian Philosophy* 39, no. 1 (February 1, 2011): 1–13.

Alpers, Svetlana. “The Mapping Impulse in Dutch Art.” In *The Art of Describing: Dutch Art in the Seventeenth Century*, 119–68. Chicago: University of Chicago Press, 1983.

Andhare, Shridhar, and Late Pandit Lakshmanbhai Bhojak. *Jain Vastrapatas: Jain Paintings on Cloth and Paper*. Ahmedabad, India: Lalbhai Dalpatbhai Institute of Indology, Bhulabhai and Dhirajlal Desai Memorial Trust, and Sheth Dalpatbhai Maganbhai (Hutheesing) Shardabhuvan Jain Pathshala Trust, 2015.

Aquil, Raziuddin, and Partha Chatterjee, eds. *History in the Vernacular*. Ranikhet and Bangalore: Permanent Black, 2008.

Asher, Catherine B. *Architecture of Mughal India*. New Cambridge History of India, 1:4. Cambridge and New York: Cambridge University Press, 1992.

———. “The Architecture of Raja Man Singh: A Study of Sub-Imperial Patronage.” In *The Powers of Art: Patronage in Indian Culture*, edited by Barbara Stoler Miller, 183–201. Delhi: Oxford University Press, 1992.

———. “Babur and the Timurid Char Bagh: Use and Meaning.” In *Environmental Design: Journal of the Islamic Environmental Design Research Centre*, edited by Attilo Petruccioli, 1–2:46–55. Rome: Dell'oca Editore, 1991.

———. “‘It Is a Day for Enjoyment and Revelry’: The Monsoon Garden.” In *Monsoon Feelings: A History of Emotions in the Rain*, edited by Imke Rajamani, Margrit Pernau, and Katherine Butler Schofield, 185–218. New Delhi: Niyogi Books, 2018.

———. “Jaipur: City of Tolerance and Progress.” *South Asia: Journal of South Asian Studies* 37, no. 3 (September 2014): 410–30.

Asher, Catherine B., and Cynthia Talbot. *India before Europe*. Cambridge and New York: Cambridge University Press, 2006.

Avcıoğlu, Nebahat, and Finbarr Barry Flood. Introduction. In *Globalizing Cultures: Art and Mobility in the Eighteenth Century*, edited by Finbarr Barry Flood and Nebahat Avcıoğlu, 7–38. Ann Arbor: Dept. of the History of Art, University of Michigan / Washington, DC: Freer Gallery of Art, 2010.

Baader, Hannah, and Ittai Weinryb. "Images at Work." *Representations* 133, no. 1 (February 1, 2016): 1–19.
Babaie. *Isfahan and Its Palaces: Statecraft, Shi'ism and the Architecture of Conviviality in Early Modern Iran*. Edinburgh: Edinburgh University Press, 2008.
Babb, Lawrence A. "Tod and Traders." In *James Tod's Rajasthan: The Historian and His Collection*, edited by Giles Tillotson, 110–21. Mumbai: Marg Publications, 2007.
Bahura, Gopal Narayan, and Chandramani Singh. *Catalogue of Historical Documents in Kapad-Dwara Jaipur, Maps and Plans*. Jaipur: Jaipur Printers, 1990.
Bangha, Imre. "Courtly and Religious Communities as Centres of Literary Activity in Eighteenth-Century India: Anandghan's Contacts with the Princely Court of Kishengarh-Rupnagar and with the Math of the Nimbarkar Smapraday in Salemabad." In *Indian Languages and Texts Through the Ages: Essays of Hungarian Indologists in Honour of Prof. Csaba Töttössy*, edited by Csaba Dezsö, 307–54. New Delhi: Manohar, 2007.
———. "Rekhta: Poetry in Mixed Language: The Emergence of Khari Boli Literature in North India." In *Before the Divide: Hindi and Urdu Literary Culture*, edited by Francesca Orsini, 21–83. New Delhi: Orient BlackSwan, 2010.
Barringer, Tim. "Landscape Then and Now." *British Art Studies*, iss. 10 (November 2018), n.p. https://doi.org/10.17658/issn.2058-5462/issue-10/tbarringer/p1.
Barringer, T. J., Geoff Quilley, and Douglas Fordham. *Art and the British Empire*. Manchester: Manchester University Press, 2007.
Barrow, Ian J. *Making History, Drawing Territory: British Mapping in India, c. 1756–1905*. New Delhi and Oxford: Oxford University Press, 2003.
Bautze, J. "The Ajmer Darbar of 1832 and Kota Painting." *South Asian Studies* 6, no. 1 (1990): 71–91.
———. "Amsterdam and the Earliest Published Kota Painting." In *Panels of the VIIth World Sanskrit Conference*, edited by Ellen M. Raven, K. R. van Kooij, and Johannes Bronkhorst, 78–93. Kern Institute, Leiden, August 23–29, 1987. Leiden, Netherlands: Brill, 1992.
———. *Indian Miniature Paintings, c. 1590–c. 1850*. Amsterdam: Galerie Saundarya Lahari, 1987.
———. *Interaction of Cultures: Indian and Western Painting, 1780–1910; The Ehrenfeld Collection*. Alexandria, VA: Art Services International, 1998.
Bayly, C. A. "Delhi and Other Cities of North India during the 'Twilight.'" In *Delhi through the Ages: Essays in Urban History, Culture, and Society*, edited by Robert E. Frykenberg, 121–36. New Delhi: Oxford University Press, 1986.
———. *Empire and Information: Intelligence Gathering and Social Communication in India, 1780–1870*. Cambridge: Cambridge University Press, 1996.
———. *Origins of Nationality in South Asia: Patriotism and Ethical Government in the Making of Modern India*. Delhi: Oxford University Press, 1998.
———. *Rulers, Townsmen, and Bazaars : North Indian Society in the Age of British Expansion, 1770–1870*. Vol. 1. Cambridge South Asian Studies. Cambridge and New York: Cambridge University Press, 1983.
Beach, Milo Cleveland. *The Imperial Image: Paintings for the Mughal Court*. Rev. and expanded ed. Washington, DC: Freer Gallery of Art, Arthur M. Sackler Gallery, Smithsonian Institution, 2012.
———. "The Masters of the Chunar Ragamala and the Hada Master." In *Masters of Indian Painting*, edited by B. N. Goswamy, Milo Cleveland Beach, and Eberhard Fischer, 1:291–304. [Zürich]: Artibus Asiae, 2011.
———. *Mughal and Rajput Painting*. The New Cambridge History of India, 1:3. Cambridge: Cambridge University Press, 1992.
———. *Rajasthani Painters Bagta and Chokha: Master Artists at Devgarh*. Artibus Asiae, supplementum 46. Zürich: Artibus Asiae, 2005.
———. *Rajput Painting at Bundi and Kota*. Artibus Asiae, supplementum. Ascona, Switzerland: Artibus Asiae, 1974.
Beach, Milo Cleveland, Ebba Koch, and W. M. Thackston, eds. *King of the World: The Padshahnama: An Imperial Mughal Manuscript from the Royal Library, Windsor Castle*. London: Azimuth Editions, 1997.
Behl, Aditya. *Love's Subtle Magic: An Indian Islamic Literary Tradition, 1379–1545*. New York: Oxford University Press, 2012.
Betancourt, Roland. "Introduction: The Medium before Modernism." *West 86th: A Journal of Decorative Arts, Design History, and Material Culture* 23, no. 2 (September 1, 2016): 163–67.
Bhadani, Bhanwar L. *Water Harvesting, Conservation, and Irrigation in Mewar (800–1700)*. New Delhi: Manohar, 2012.
Bilak, Donna, Jenny Boulboullé, Joel Klein, and Pamela H. Smith. "The Making and Knowing Project: Reflections, Methods, and New Directions." *West 86th: A Journal of Decorative Arts, Design History, and Material Culture* 23, no. 1 (March 1, 2016): 35–55.
Brookshaw, Dominic P. "Palaces, Pavilions and Pleasure-Gardens: The Context and Setting of the Medieval Majlis." *Middle Eastern Literatures* 6, no. 2 (2003): 199–223.
Brown, Katherine Butler [Schofield]. "Did Aurangzeb Ban Music? Questions for the Historiography of His Reign." *Modern Asian Studies* 41, no. 1 (2007): 77–120.
———. "If Music Be the Food of Love: Masculinity and Eroticism in the Mughal 'Mehfil.'" In *Love in South Asia: A Cultural History*, edited by Francesca Orsini, 61–86. Cambridge and New York: Cambridge University Press, 2006.
Bryson, Norman. *Vision and Painting: The Logic of the Gaze*. New Haven, CT: Yale University Press, 1983.
Busch, Allison. "The Classical Past in the Mughal Present." In *Innovations and Turning Points: Toward a History of Kāvya Literature*, edited by Yigal Bronner, David Shulman, and Gary A Tubb, 648–90. Oxford: Oxford University Press, 2014.
———. "Hidden in Plain View: Brajbhasha Poets at the Mughal Court." *Modern Asian Studies* 44, no. 2 (2010): 267–309.
———. "Listening for the Context: Tuning into the Reception of Rīti Poetry." In *Tellings and Texts*, edited by Francesca Orsini and Katherine Schofield, 249–82. Cambridge, UK: Open Book Publishers, 2015.
———. *Poetry of Kings: The Classical Hindi Literature of Mughal India*. South Asia Research. New York: Oxford University Press, 2011.
Certeau, Michel de. *The Practice of Everyday Life*. Berkeley: University of California Press, 1984.
Chakrabarty, Dipesh. *Provincializing Europe: Postcolonial Thought and Historical Difference*. Princeton Studies in Culture/Power/History. Princeton, NJ: Princeton University Press, 2000.
Chandra, Pramod. "Ustād Sālivāhana and the Development of Popular Mughal Style." *Lalitkalā* 8 (1960): 27–46.

Chatterjee, Kumkum. "Communities, Kings and Chronicles: The Kulagranthas of Bengal." *Studies in History* 21, no. 2 (September 1, 2005): 173–213.

Chaudhuri, K. N. "Surat Revisited: A Tribute to Ashin Das Gupta." *Journal of the Economic and Social History of the Orient* 43, no. 1 (2000): 18–22.

Cimino, Rosa Maria. *Vita di corte nel Rajasthan: Miniature indiane dal XVII al XIX secolo.* Exhibition catalogue. Palazzo Reale, Turin, March 22–May 22, 1985. Florence: M. L. Giusti, 1985.

Clifford, James. *Routes: Travel and Translation in the Late Twentieth Century.* Cambridge, MA: Harvard University Press, 1997.

Codell, Julie F., ed. *Power and Resistance: The Delhi Coronation Durbars, 1877, 1903, 1911.* Ahmedabad, India: Mapin, 2012.

Cohn, Bernard S. "Political Systems in Eighteenth Century India: The Banaras Region." *Journal of the American Oriental Society* 82, no. 3 (1962): 312–20.

Cooper, Frederick. "What Is the Concept of Globalization Good For? An African Historian's Perspective." *African Affairs* 100, no. 399 (2001): 189–213.

Copland, Ian. *The British Raj and the Indian Princes: Paramountcy in Western India, 1857–1930.* London: Sangam Books, 1982.

———. *The Princes of India in the Endgame of Empire, 1917–1947.* Cambridge Studies in Indian History and Society. Cambridge and New York: Cambridge University Press, 1997.

Cort, John E. "The Jain Knowledge Warehouses: Traditional Libraries in India." *Journal of the American Oriental Society* 115, no. 1 (January 1, 1995): 77–87.

———. "Twelve Chapters from the Guidebook to Various Pilgrimage Places, the Vividhatīrthakalpa of Jinaprabhāsūri." In *The Clever Adultress and the Hungry Monk*, edited by Phyllis Granoff, 245–90. New York: Mosaic Press, 1990.

Cosgrove, Denis E. "Landscape and Landschaft." *German Historical Institute Bulletin* 35 (Fall 2004): 57–71.

Dadlani, Chanchal. "The 'Palais Indiens' Collection of 1774: Representing Mughal Architecture in Late Eighteenth-Century India." In *Globalizing Cultures: Art and Mobility in the Eighteenth Century*, edited by Nebahat Avcıoğlu and Finbarr Barry Flood, 175–97. Ann Arbor: Dept. of the History of Art, University of Michigan / Washington, DC: Freer Gallery of Art, 2010.

Dallapiccola, Anna L., Catherine Glynn, and Robert Skelton, eds. *Ragamala: Paintings from India.* London and New York: Philip Wilson Publishers, 2011.

Dalrymple, William, and Yuthika Sharma, eds. *Princes and Painters in Mughal Delhi, 1707–1857.* New York: Asia Society Museum / New Haven, CT: Yale University Press, 2012.

Dave-Mukherji, Parul. "Whither Art History in a Globalizing World." *Art Bulletin* 96, no. 2 (2014), 151–55.

———. "Who Is Afraid of Mimesis? Contesting the Common Sense of Indian Aesthetics through the Theory of 'Mimesis' or Anukaraṇa Vâda." In *The Bloomsbury Research Handbook of Indian Aesthetics and the Philosophy of Art*, 1st ed., edited by Arindam Chakrabarti, 71–91. Bloomsbury Research Handbooks in Asian Philosophy. London: Bloomsbury Academic, 2016.

Dehejia, Vidya. "The Treatment of Narrative in Jagat Singh's 'Rāmāyaṇa': A Preliminary Study." *Artibus Asiae* 56, no. 3/4 (1996): 303–24.

Desai, Madhuri. *Banaras Reconstructed: Architecture and Sacred Space in a Hindu Holy City.* Seattle: University of Washington Press, 2017.

Desai, Vishakha N. "Timeless Symbols: Royal Portraits from Rajasthan, 17th–19th Centuries." In *The Idea of Rajasthan: Explorations in Regional Identity*, edited by Karine Schomer, Joan L. Erdman, Lodrick O. Deryck, and Lloyd I. Rudolph, 1:313–42. New Delhi: Manohar and American Institute of Indian Studies, 1994.

Deshpande, Prachi. *Creative Pasts: Historical Memory and Identity in Western India, 1700–1960.* Cultures of History. New York: Columbia University Press, 2007.

Diamond, Debra. "The Cartography of Power: Mapping Genres in Jodhpur Painting." In *Arts of Mughal India: Studies in Honour of Robert Skelton*, edited by Rosemary Crill, Andrew Topsfield, and Susan Stronge, 278–85. London: Victoria and Albert Museum / Ahmedabad, India: Mapin Publications, 2004.

———. "Holi in the Zenana: Genre, Style and Sociability." In *A Magic World: New Visions of Indian Painting*, edited by Molly Emma Aitken, 100–115. Mumbai: Marg Publications, 2017.

———. "Maharaja Vijai Singh and the Epic Landscape, 1752–93." In *Garden and Cosmos: The Royal Paintings of Jodhpur*, edited by Debra Diamond, Catherine Glynn, and Karni Singh Jasol, 21–30. Washington, DC: Arthur M. Sackler Gallery, Smithsonian Institution, 2008.

———. "Sarayu Palace from the *Ramcharitmanas* of Tulsidas." In *Garden and Cosmos: The Royal Paintings of Jodhpur*, edited by Debra Diamond, Catherine Glynn, and Karni Singh Jasol, 134. Washington, DC: Arthur M. Sackler Gallery, Smithsonian Institution, 2008.

Diamond, Debra, Catherine Ann Glynn, and Karni Singh Jasol, eds. *Garden and Cosmos: The Royal Paintings of Jodhpur.* Washington, DC: Arthur M. Sackler Gallery, Smithsonian Institution, 2008.

Di Palma, Vittoria. "Flow: Rivers, Roads, Routes, and Cartographies of Leisure." In *Routes, Roads and Landscapes*, edited by Mari Hvattum, Brita Brenna, Beate Elvebakk, and Janike Kampevold Larsen, 27–43. Farnham, Surrey: Ashgate, 2011.

———. "In the Mood for Landscape." In *Thinking the Contemporary Landscape*, edited by Christophe Girot and Dora Imhof, 15–29. New York: Princeton Architectural Press, 2017.

———. *Wasteland: A History.* New Haven, CT, and London: Yale University Press, 2014.

Dirks, Nicholas B. *The Hollow Crown: Ethnohistory of an Indian Kingdom.* Cambridge and New York: Cambridge University Press, 1988.

D'Souza, Florence. "Tod as an Observer of Landscape in Rajasthan." In *James Tod's Rajasthan: The Historian and His Collection*, edited by Giles Tillotson, 48–57. Mumbai: Marg Publications, 2007.

Eaton, Natasha. "Between Mimesis and Alterity: Art, Gift, and Diplomacy in Colonial India, 1770–1800." *Comparative Studies in Society and History* 46, no. 4 (2004): 816–44.

Edney, Matthew H. *Mapping an Empire: The Geographical Construction of India, 1765–1843.* Chicago : University of Chicago Press, 1997.

———. "The Patronage of Science and the Creation of Imperial Space: The British Mapping of India, 1799–1843." *Cartographica: The International Journal for Geographic Information and Geovisualization* 30, no. 1 (October 1, 1993): 61–67.

Ehnbohm, Daniel. "Masters of the Dispersed Bhagavata Purana." In *Masters of Indian Painting*, edited by B. N. Goswamy, Milo Cleveland Beach, and Eberhard Fischer, 1:77–88. [Zürich]: Artibus Asiae, 2011.

Elberfeld, R. "Sensory Dimensions in Intercultural Perspective and the Problem of Modern Media and Technology." In *Technology and Cultural Values*, edited by P. Hershock, M. Stepaniants, and R. Ames. Honolulu: University of Hawaii Press, 478–90.

Elkins, James. *The Poetics of Perspective*. Ithaca, NY: Cornell University Press, 1994.

Emami, Farshid. "Coffeehouses, Urban Spaces, and the Formation of a Public Sphere in Safavid Isfahan." *Muqarnas Online* 33, no. 1 (November 14, 2016): 177–220.

Faruqi, Shamsur Rehman. "Conventions of Love, Love of Conventions: Urdu Love Poetry in the Eighteenth Century." *Annual of Urdu Studies* 14 (1999): 3–32.

Feld, Steven, and Keith H. Basso, eds. *Senses of Place.* Santa Fe, NM: School of American Research Press, 1996.

Fisher, Michael H. "The Resident in Court Ritual, 1764–1858." *Modern Asian Studies* 24, no. 3 (July 1, 1990): 419–58.

Flatt, Emma J. *The Courts of the Deccan Sultanates: Living Well in the Persian Cosmopolis*. Cambridge and New York: Cambridge University Press, 2019.

———. "Sitting Together: A Practice of Friendship in Indo-Persian Courtly Societies." Unpublished paper.

———. "Social Stimulants: Perfuming Practices in Sultanate India." In *The Arts of the Deccan*, edited by Kavita Singh. Mumbai: Marg Publications, forthcoming.

Flood, Finbarr Barry. *Objects of Translation: Material Culture and Medieval Hindu-Muslim Encounter*. Princeton, NJ: Princeton University Press, 2009.

Fraser, Marcus. *The V. S Naipaul Collection of Indian Paintings, Drawings and Watercolours*. [London]: Andrew Clayton-Payne, 2014.

Freitag, Jason. *Serving Empire, Serving Nation: James Tod and the Rajputs of Rajasthan*. European Expansion and Indigenous Response. Leiden, Netherlands, and Boston: Brill, 2009.

Freitag, Sandria. "Power and Patronage: Banaras in the 18th and 19th Century." In *Banaras: The City Revealed*, edited by George Michell and Rana Singh, 30–41. Mumbai: Marg Publications, 2005.

Gadebusch, Raffael Dedo. "Celestial Gardens: Mughal Miniatures from an Eighteenth Century Album." *Orientations* 31, no. 9 (2000): 69–74.

Geertz, Clifford. "Thick Description: Towards an Interpretive Theory of Culture." In *The Interpretation of Cultures: Selected Essays*, 3–30. New York: Basic Books, 1973.

Ghosh, Pika. "The Story of a Storyteller's Scroll." *RES: Anthropology and Aesthetics*, no. 37 (2000): 166–85.

Glynn, Catherine. "Rathore and Mughal Interactions: Artistic Development at the Nagaur Court, 1600–1751." In *Garden and Cosmos: The Royal Paintings of Jodhpur*, edited by Debra Diamond, Catherine Glynn, and Karni Singh Jasol, 11–19. Washington, DC: Arthur M. Sackler Gallery, Smithsonian Institution, 2008.

———. "The 'Stipple Master.'" In *Masters of Indian Painting*, edited by B. N. Goswamy, Milo Cleveland Beach, and Eberhard Fischer, 2:515–30. [Zürich]: Artibus Asiae, 2011.

Gole, Susan. *Indian Maps and Plans: From Earliest Times to the Advent of European Surveys*. New Delhi, India: Manohar, 1989.

———. "Size as a Measure of Importance in Indian Cartography." *Imago Mundi* 42 (1990): 99–105.

Goswamy, B. N., and Anna L. Dallapiccola. *A Place Apart: Painting in Kutch, 1720–1820*. Bombay and New York: Oxford University Press, 1983.

Granoff, Phyllis E. "Jain Pilgrimage in Memory and Celebration of the Jinas." In *The Peaceful Liberators: Jain Art from India*, edited by Pratapaditya Pal, 63–77. Los Angeles: Los Angeles County Museum of Art / New York: Thames and Hudson, 1994.

Gregg, Ryan E. *City Views in the Habsburg and Medici Courts: Depictions of Rhetoric and Rule in the Sixteenth Century*. Leiden, Netherlands: Brill, 2019.

Guha-Thakurta, Tapati. *Monuments, Objects, Histories: Institutions of Art in Colonial and Postcolonial India*. Cultures of History. New York: Columbia University Press, 2004.

Haidar, Navina Najat, and Marika Sardar, eds. "'The Kitab-i Nauras, Key to Bijapur's Golden Age.'" In *Sultans of the South: Arts of India's Deccan Courts, 1323–1687*, 26–43. New York: Metropolitan Museum of Art, 2011.

Hallett, Mark, ed. "Landscape Now." *British Art Studies* 10 (November 29, 2018). https://www.britishartstudies.ac.uk/issues/issue-index/issue-10/landscape-now.

Hamadeh, Shirine. *The City's Pleasures: Istanbul in the Eighteenth Century*. Seattle: University of Washington Press, 2008.

Harley, J. B. "Deconstructing the Map." *Cartographica: The International Journal for Geographic Information and Geovisualization* 26, no. 2 (October 1, 1989): 1–20.

———. "Maps, Knowledge and Power." In *The Iconography of Landscape: Essays on the Symbolic Representation, Design, and Use of Past Environments*, edited by Dennis Cosgrove and Stephen Daniels, 277–312. Cambridge and New York: University of Cambridge Press, 1988.

Head, Raymond, and Royal Asiatic Society. *Catalogue of Paintings, Drawings, Engravings and Busts in the Collection of the Royal Asiatic Society*. London: Royal Asiatic Society, 1991.

Hegewald, Julia A. B. *Water Architecture in South Asia: A Study of Types, Developments and Meanings.* Leiden, Netherlands: Brill, 2002.

Holly, Michael Ann. *Past Looking: Historical Imagination and the Rhetoric of the Image*. Ithaca, NY: Cornell University Press, 1996.

Hooja, Rima. *A History of Rajasthan*. New Delhi: Rupa & Co., 2006.

———. "Of Building and Books: The Theory and Practice of the Architect Mandan." *Marg* 52, no. 4 (June, 2001): 12–27.

Horstmann, Monika. "Jaipur's Waterscape: A Cultural Perspective." In *Water Design: Environment and Histories*, edited by Jutta Jain-Neubauer, 96–107. Mumbai: Marg Publications, 2016.

Houghteling, Sylvia. "The Tree of Life and the World of Wonder: Aja'ib Imagery on 17th-Century Kalamkaris." In *The Arts of the Deccan*, edited by Kavita Singh, 88–107. Mumbai: Marg Publications, 2018.

Howes, David. "The Expanding Field of Sensory Studies." *Sensory Studies*, August 2013 (vers. 1.0). https://www.sensorystudies.org/sensorial-investigations/the-expanding-field-of-sensory-studies/.

Hutton, Deborah S. *Art of the Court of Bijapur*. Contemporary Indian Studies. Bloomington: Indiana University Press, 2006.

———. "The Use of Imaginary Landscapes in Paintings from Bijapur." In *Garden and Landscape Practices in Precolonial India: Histories from the Deccan*, edited by Daud Ali and Emma J. Flatt, 127–47. New Delhi: Routledge, 2012.

Hutton, Deborah S., and Rebecca M. Brown. "Introduction: In and Out of Place: Engagements in South Asian and Islamic Art History." In *Rethinking Place in South Asian and Islamic Art,*

1500–Present, edited by Deborah S. Hutton and Rebecca M. Brown, 1–13. Abingdon, UK: Routledge / New York: Taylor & Francis, 2017.

Ingold, Tim. "The Temporality of the Landscape." *World Archaeology* 25, no. 2 (1993): 152–74.

Jain, Jyotindra. *Picture Showmen: Insights into the Narrative Tradition in Indian Art*. Mumbai: Marg Publications, on behalf of National Centre for the Performing Arts, 1998.

Jain, Kajri. *Gods in the Bazaar: The Economies of Indian Calendar Art*. Objects/Histories. Durham, NC: Duke University Press, 2007.

Jain, Shalin. *Identity, Community and State: The Jains under the Mughals.* Delhi: Primus Books, 2017.

———. "Inviting the Lords: *Vigyaptipatras* as a Source of Medieval Indian History." In *Proceedings of the Indian History Congress*, 264–75. Delhi: 2012.

Jain, Shikha. *Havelis: A Living Tradition of Rajasthan*. Gurgaon: Shubhi Publications, 2004.

Jain, Shikha, and Vanicka Arora. *Living Heritage of Mewar: Architecture of the City Palace, Udaipur*. Ahmedabad, India: Mapin Publishing in association with Maharana Mewar Historical Publications Trust, 2017.

Jasanoff, Maya. *Edge of Empire: Lives, Culture, and Conquest in the East, 1750–1850*. New York: Vintage Books, 2005.

Jawalia, B[rajmohan]. M. "Food Security in Rajasthan with Specific Reference to the Marwar Region during the 17th and 18th Centuries." *Asian Agri-History* 5, no. 4 (December 2001): 265–82.

Jay, Martin. "In the Realm of the Senses: An Introduction." *American Historical Review* 116, no. 2 (April 1, 2011): 307–15.

———. "Scopic Regimes of Modernity." In *Vision and Visuality*, edited by Hal Foster, 3–28. Discussions in Contemporary Culture, no. 2. Seattle: Bay Press, 1988.

Joffee, Jennifer Beth. "Art, Architecture and Politics in Mewar, 1628–1710." PhD diss., University of Minnesota, 2005.

Johnson-Roehr, Susan N. "Centering the Chārbāgh: The Mughal Garden as Design Module for the Jaipur City Plan." *Journal of the Society of Architectural Historians* 72, no. 1 (March 2013): 28–47.

Juneja, Monica. "Circulation and Beyond: The Trajectories of Vision in Early Modern Eurasia." In *Circulations in the Global History of Art*, edited by Thomas DaCosta Kaufmann, 69–78. London: Ashgate, 2015.

Kafescioğlu, Cigdem. "Viewing, Walking, Mapping Istanbul, ca. 1580." *Mitteilungen des Kunsthistorischen Institutes in Florenz* 56, no. 1 (2014): 16–35.

Kapur, Nandini Sinha. *State Formation in Rajasthan: Mewar during the Seventh–Fifteenth Centuries*. New Delhi: Manohar, 2002.

Kaul, Shonaleeka. *The Making of Early Kashmir: Landscape and Identity in the Rajatarangini*. New Delhi: Oxford University Press, 2018.

Khan, Sumbul Halim. *Art and Craft Workshops under the Mughals: A Study of Jaipur Karkhanas*. New Delhi: Primus Books, 2015.

Khandalavala, Karl J. *A Collector's Dream: Indian Art in the Collections of Basant Kumar and Saraladevi Birla and the Birla Academy of Art and Culture*. Bombay: Marg Publications, 1987.

Khera, Dipti. "Arrivals at Distant Lands: Artful Letters and Entangled Mobilities in the Indian Ocean Littoral." In *The Nomadic Object*, edited by Christine Göttler and Mia Mochizuki, 571–605. Leiden, Netherlands: Brill, 2018.

———. "Fortified Memories: Picturing Chitor in Eighteenth Century Poems and Paintings." Paper presented at College Art Association Annual Conference, New York, February 13, 2013.

———. "Jagvilasa: Picturing Worlds of Pleasure and Power in 18th-Century Udaipur Painting." In *A Magic World: New Visions of Indian Painting in Tribute to Ananda Coomaraswamy's Rajput Painting of 1916*, edited by Molly Emma Aitken, 74–87. Mumbai: Marg Publications, 2017.

———. "The Joys of Bonding." In *Visions of Paradise: Indian Paintings in the National Gallery*, edited by Wayne Crothers, 108–17. Melbourne: National Gallery of Victoria, 2018.

———. "Lakes within Lake-Palaces: A Material History of Pleasure in 18th-Century India." In *Water Histories of South Asia: The Materiality of Liquescence,* Visual and Media Histories Series, edited by Sugata Ray and Venugopal Maddipati, 60–92. Abingdon, Oxon: Routledge, 2019.

———. "Marginal, Mobile, Multilayered: Painted Invitation Letters as Bazaar Objects in Early Modern India." *Journal18*, no. 1 (Spring 2016). http://www.journal18.org/527.

Khera, Dipti, and Raju Mansukhani. *The City within a City*. Vol. 1: *Jagmandir on Lake Pichola*. New Delhi: Penguin Enterprise, 2002.

Kia, Mana. "Adab as Literary Form and Social Conduct: Reading the Gulistan in Late Mughal India." In *"No Tapping around Philology": A Festschrift in Celebration and Honor of Wheeler McIntosh Thackston Jr.'s 70th Birthday*, edited by Alireza Korangy and Daniel J. Sheffield, 281–308. Wiesbaden, Germany: Harrassowitz, 2014.

———. "Space, Sociality, and Sources of Pleasure: A Response to Sanjay Subrahmanyam," *Journal of the Economic and Social History of the Orient* 61, no. 1–2 (2018): 257–60.

Kinra, Rajeev. *Writing Self, Writing Empire: Chandar Bhan Brahman and the Cultural World of the Indo-Persian State Secretary*. South Asia across the Disciplines. Oakland: University of California Press, 2015.

Koch, Ebba. "The Hierarchical Principles of Shah-Jahani Painting." In *King of the World: The Padshahnama: An Imperial Mughal Manuscript from the Royal Library, Windsor Castle*, edited by Milo Cleveland Beach and Ebba Koch, 130–43. London: Azimuth Editions, 1997.

———. *Mughal Architecture: An Outline of Its History and Development, 1526–1858*. Munich and New York: Prestel, 1991.

———. "The Symbolic Possession of the World: European Cartography in Mughal Allegory and History Painting." *Journal of the Economic and Social History of the Orient* 55, no. 2–3 (January 1, 2012): 547–80.

Kothiyal, Tanuja. *Nomadic Narratives: A History of Mobility and Identity in the Great Indian Desert*. Cambridge: Cambridge University Press, 2016.

Kumar, Mayank. "The Uncertain Monsoon: Perceptions and Experiences in North-West India in Seventeenth and Eighteenth Centuries." In *Revisiting the History of Rajasthan: Essays for Professor Dilbagh Singh*, edited by Mayank Kumar, Rameshwar Prasad Bahuguna, and Surajbhan Bharadwaj, 240–63. New Delhi: Primus Books, 2017.

Kusukawa, Sachiko. "Drawing as an Instrument of Knowledge: The Case of Conrad Gessner." In *Vision and Its Instruments: Art, Science, and Technology in Early Modern Europe*, edited by Alina Payne, 36–48. University Park: Pennsylvania State University Press, 2015.

Latour, Bruno. *Reassembling the Social: An Introduction to Actor-Network-Theory*. Clarendon Lectures in Management Studies. Oxford and New York: Oxford University Press, 2007.

Leach, Linda York. *Paintings from India*. Nasser D. Khalili Collection of Islamic Art, vol. 8. London and New York: Nour Foundation in association with Azimuth Editions and Oxford University Press, 1998.

Leante, Laura. "The Cuckoo's Song: Imagery and Movement in Monsoon *Ragas*." In *Monsoon Feelings: A History of Emotions in the Rain*, edited by Imke Rajamani, Margrit Pernau, and Katherine Butler Schofield, 255–90. New Delhi: Niyogi Books, 2018.

Lightbown, R. W. "Oriental Art and the Orient in Late Renaissance and Baroque Italy." *Journal of the Warburg and Courtauld Institutes* 32 (1969): 228–79.

Losty, Jeremiah P. *The Ramayana: Love and Valour in India's Great Epic: The Mewar Ramayana Manuscripts*. London: British Library, 2008.

———. "Sahib-Din's Book of Battles: Rana Jagat Singh's Yuddhakanda." In *The Legend of Rama: Artistic Visions*, edited by Vidya Dehejia, 101–16. Bombay: Marg Publications, 1994.

Lunn, David, and Katherine Butler Schofield. "Delight, Devotion and the Music of the Monsoon at the Court of Emperor Shah'Alam II." In *Monsoon Feelings: A History of Emotions in the Rain*, edited by Imke Rajamani, Margrit Pernau, and Katherine Butler Schofield, 219–54. New Delhi: Niyogi Books, 2018.

Markel, Stephen, and Tushara Bindu Gude. *India's Fabled City: The Art of Courtly Lucknow*. Los Angeles: Los Angeles County Museum of Art, 2010.

Markovits, Claude. *The Global World of Indian Merchants, 1750–1947: Traders of Sind from Bukhara to Panama*. Cambridge: Cambridge University Press, 2000.

Markovits, Claude, Jacques Pouchepadass, and Sanjay Subrahmanyam, eds. *Society and Circulation: Mobile People and Itinerant Cultures in South Asia, 1750–1950*. Delhi and Bangalore: Permanent Black, 2003.

Mason, Darielle, ed. *Intimate Worlds: Indian Paintings from the Alvin O. Bellak Collection*. Philadelphia, PA: Philadelphia Museum of Art, 2001.

Massey, Doreen. *For Space*. London: Sage Publications, 2005.

Maurya, Anubhuti. "Of Tulips and Daffodils: Kashmir Jannat Nazir as a Political Landscape in the Mughal Empire." *Economic and Political Weekly* 52, no. 15 (April 15, 2017): 37–44.

McCormick, Melissa. *Tosa Mitsunobu and the Small Scroll in Medieval Japan*. Seattle: University of Washington Press, 2009.

McKelway, Matthew P. *Capitalscapes: Folding Screens and Political Imagination in Late Medieval Kyoto*. Honolulu: University of Hawaii Press, 2006.

Michell, George. *Late Temple Architecture of India 15th to 19th Centuries: Continuities, Revivals, Appropriations, and Innovations.* New Delhi: Oxford University Press, 2015.

———. *The Royal Palaces of India*. London: Thames & Hudson, 1994.

Minissale, Gregory. *Images of Thought: Visuality in Islamic India, 1550–1750*. Newcastle-upon-Tyne, UK: Cambridge Scholars, 2006.

Mishra, Shailka. "Maps and Map-Making at the Amber-Jaipur Suratkhana in the 18th Century." *Jnana-Pravaha Research Journal* 18 (2015).

Moxey, Keith. *Visual Time: The Image in History*. Durham, NC: Duke University Press, 2013.

Nair, Janaki. *Mysore Modern: Rethinking the Region under Princely Rule*. Minneapolis: University of Minnesota Press, 2011.

Natif, Mika. *Mughal Occidentalism: Artistic Encounters between Europe and Asia at the Courts of India, 1580–1630*. Leiden, Netherlands: Brill, 2018.

Noltie, Henry J. *Robert Wight and the Botanical Drawings of Rungiah and Govindoo*. Edinburgh: Royal Botanic Garden, 2007.

O'Hanlon, Rosalind. "Cultural Pluralism, Empire and the State in Early Modern South Asia." *Indian Economic Social History Review* 44, no. 3 (2007): 363–81.

———. "Letters Home: Banaras Pandits and the Maratha Regions in Early Modern India." *Modern Asian Studies* 44, no. 2 (2010): 201–40.

———. "Manliness and Imperial Service in Mughal North India." *Journal of the Economic and Social History of the Orient* 42, no. 1 (1999): 47–93.

Ojha, Gaurishankar Hirachand. *Udayapura rājya kā itihāsa*. Vols. 1 and 2. Jodhpur: Rajasthani Granthaghar, 1999.

Orsini, Francesca. "Barahmasas in Hindi and Urdu." In *Before the Divide: Hindi and Urdu Literary Culture*, edited by Francesca Orsini, 142–77. New Delhi: Orient BlackSwan, 2010.

———. *Before the Divide: Hindi and Urdu Literary Culture*. New Delhi: Orient BlackSwan, 2010.

———. "Between Qasbas and Cities: Language Shifts and Literary Continuities in North India in the Long Eighteenth Century." *Comparative Studies of South Asia, Africa and the Middle East* 39, no. 1 (2019): 68–81.

———. "Clouds, Cuckoos and an Empty Bed: Emotions in Hindi-Urdu *Barahmasas*." In *Monsoon Feelings: A History of Emotions in the Rain*, edited by Imke Rajamani, Margrit Pernau, and Katherine Butler Schofield, 97–136. New Delhi: Niyogi Books, 2018.

———. "How to Do Multilingual Literary History? Lessons from Fifteenth- and Sixteenth-Century North India." *Indian Economic and Social History Review* 49 (2012): 225–46.

Orsini, Francesca, and Katherine Butler Schofield, eds. *Tellings and Texts: Music, Literature and Performance in North India*. n.p.: OpenBook Publishers, 2015. http://crossasia-repository.ub.uni-heidelberg.de/3820/1/Tellings-and-Texts.pdf.

Parodi, Laura, and Bruce Wannell. "The Earliest Datable Mughal Painting: An Allegory of the Celebrations for Akbar's Circumcision at the Sacred Spring of Khwaja Seh Yaran near Kabul (1546 AD)." AsianArt.com, November 18, 2011. https://www.asianart.com/articles/parodi/index.html#10.

Patel, Alka, and Karen Isaksen Leonard, eds. *Indo-Muslim Cultures in Transition*. Brill's Indological Library, vol. 38. Leiden, Netherlands, and Boston: Brill, 2012.

Pauwels, Heidi Rika Maria. *Cultural Exchange in Eighteenth-Century India: Poetry and Paintings from Kishangarh*. Berlin: EB-Verlag, 2015.

———. *Mobilizing Krishna's World: The Writings of Prince Savant Singh of Kishangarh*. Seattle: University of Washington Press, 2017.

Pauwels, Heidi, and Anne Murphy, eds. *From Outside the Persianate Center: Vernacular Views of Aurangzeb/"Alamgir."* Special issue of *Journal of the Royal Asiatic Society* 28, no. 3 (2018).

Peabody, Norbert. *Hindu Kingship and Polity in Precolonial India*. Cambridge Studies in Indian History and Society, 9. Cambridge and New York: Cambridge University Press, 2003.

Peck, Amelia, ed. *Interwoven Globe: The Worldwide Textile Trade, 1500–1800*. New York: Metropolitan Museum of Art, 2013.

Pernau, Margrit. "Mapping Emotions, Constructing Feelings." *Journal of the Economic and Social History of the Orient* 58, no. 5 (November 23, 2015): 634–67.

———. "Space and Emotion: Building to Feel." *History Compass* 12 (July 28, 2014): 541–49.

Philon, Helen. "Deccani Gardens and Architectural Landscapes in the Fourteenth and Fifteenth Centuries." *South Asian Studies* 27, no. 2 (September 1, 2011): 157–84.

Pollock, Sheldon. "From Rasa Seen to Rasa Heard." In *Aux Bords de La Clairière*, edited by Caterina Guenzi and Sylvia d'Intino, 189–207. Collections Érudites de l'École Pratique des Hautes Études. Paris: Brepols, 2012.

———. "Is There an Indian Intellectual History? Introduction to 'Theory and Method in Indian Intellectual History.'" *Journal of Indian Philosophy* 36, no. 5–6 (October 1, 2008): 533–42.

———. "Pretextures of Time." *History and Theory* 46, no. 3 (October 1, 2007): 366–83.

———. *A Rasa Reader: Classical Indian Aesthetics.* Historical Sourcebooks in Classical Indian Thought. New York: Columbia University Press, 2016.

Pratt, Mary Louise. *Imperial Eyes: Travel Writing and Transculturation.* London and New York: Routledge, 1992.

Pritchett, Frances W., and Shamsur Rehman Faruqi. "Lyric Poetry in Urdu: The Ghazal." *Delos* 3, no. 3–4 (Winter 1991): 7–12.

Purohit, Rajendra Nath. *Mevāṛa darīkhāne ke rīti-rivāja evaṃ saṃskāra*. Jodhpur, Rajasthan Granthaghar, 2005.

Purtle, Jennifer. "Double Take: Chinese Optics and Their Media in Postglobal Perspective." *Ars Orientalis* 48 (2018): 71–117.

Quilley, Geoff, and John Bonehill. *William Hodges, 1744–1797: The Art of Exploration*. Exhibition catalogue. National Maritime Museum, Greenwich, UK, July–November 2004; Yale Center for British Art, January–April 2005. New Haven, CT, and London: Yale University Press, 2004.

Raj, Kapil. *Relocating Modern Science: Circulation and the Construction of Knowledge in South Asia and Europe, 1650–1900*. Basingstoke, UK, and New York: Palgrave Macmillan, 2007.

Rajamani, Imke. "Monsoon Feelings: Introduction." In *Monsoon Feelings: A History of Emotions in the Rain*, edited by Imke Rajamani, Margrit Pernau, and Katherine Butler Schofield. New Delhi: Niyogi Books, 2018.

Raman, Bhavani. *Document Raj: Writing and Scribes in Early Colonial South India*. Chicago and London: University of Chicago Press, 2012.

———. "Itinerancy and Power." In *Cultures in Motion*, edited by Daniel T. Rodgers, Bhavani Raman, and Helmut Reimitz, 267–69. Princeton, NJ, and Oxford: Princeton University Press, 2017.

Ramaswamy, Sumathi. *The Lost Land of Lemuria: Fabulous Geographies, Catastrophic Histories*. Berkeley: University of California Press, 2004.

———. *Terrestrial Lessons: Conquest of the World as a Globe*. Chicago: University of Chicago Press, 2017.

Ramusack, Barbara N. *The Indian Princes and Their States*. The New Cambridge History of India, 3:6. Cambridge and New York: Cambridge University Press, 2004.

———. *The Princes of India in the Twilight of Empire: Dissolution of a Patron-Client System, 1914–1939*. Columbus: Published for the University of Cincinnati by the Ohio State University Press, 1978.

———. "Punjab States: Maharajas and Gurudwaras: Patiala and the Sikh Community." In *People, Princes, and Paramount Power: Society and Politics in the Indian Princely States*, edited by Robin Jeffrey, 170–204. Delhi: Oxford University Press, 1978.

Ranawat, Ishwar Singh. *Rājasthāna ke jala-saṃsādhana: Mevāṛa ke sandarbha meṃ; 16 vīṃ evaṃ 17 vīṃ śatābdī*. Udaipur: Chirag Prakashan, 2004.

Rao, Velcheru Narayan, David Dean Shulman, and Sanjay Subrahmanyam. *Textures of Time : Writing History in South India, 1600–1800*. Delhi and Bangalore: Permanent Black, 2001.

Ray, Romita. *Under the Banyan Tree: Relocating the Picturesque in British India.* New Haven, CT: Yale University Press, 2013.

Ray, Sugata. *Climate Change and the Art of Devotion: Geoaesthetics in the Land of Krishna, 1550–1850*. Seattle: University of Washington Press, 2019.

Rice, Yael. "The Brush and the Burin: Mogul Encounters with European Engravings." In *Crossing Cultures: Conflict, Migration and Convergence*, edited by Jaynie Anderson, 305–10. Proceedings of the 32nd International Congress of the History of Art. Carlton, Victoria: Miegunyah Press, Melbourne University Publishing, 2009.

———. "Mughal Interventions in the Rampur Jami' Al-Tavarikh." *Ars Orientalis* 42 (2012): 150–64.

Rizvi, Kishwar, ed. *Affect, Emotion, and Subjectivity in Early Modern Muslim Empires: New Studies in Ottoman, Safavid, and Mughal Art and Culture*. Leiden, Netherlands, and Boston: Brill, 2018.

Roberts, Jennifer L. *Scale*. Chicago: Terra Foundation for American Art, 2016.

Rodgers, Daniel T. "Cultures in Motion: An Introduction." In *Cultures in Motion*, edited by Daniel T. Rodgers, Bhavani Raman, and Helmut Reimitz, 1–20. Princeton, NJ; Oxford: Princeton University Press, 2017.

Roy, Malini. *50 x India: De 50 mooiste Miniaturen van het Rijksmuseum / The 50 Most Beautiful Miniatures from the Rijksmuseum*. Amsterdam: Nieuw Amsterdam, 2008.

Rudolph, Lloyd I., and Susanne Hoeber Rudolph. "Rajputana under British Paramountcy: The Failure of Indirect Rule." *Journal of Modern History* 38, no. 2 (June 1, 1966): 138–60.

Ruggles, D. Fairchild, and Jennifer Beth Joffee. "Rajput Gardens and Landscape." In *Middle East Garden Traditions: Unity and Diversity; Questions, Methods and Resources in a Multicultural Perspective*, edited by Michel Conan. Washington, DC: Dumbarton Oaks Research Library and Collection, 2007.

Sachdev, Vibhuti, and Giles Henry Rupert Tillotson. *Building Jaipur: The Making of an Indian City*. London: Reaktion Books, 2002.

Saha, Shandip. "The Movement of Bhakti along a North-West Axis: Tracing the History of the Puṣṭimārg between the Sixteenth and Nineteenth Centuries." *International Journal of Hindu Studies* 11, no. 3 (2007): 299–318.

Sahai, Nandita Prasad. *Politics of Patronage and Protest: The State, Society, and Artisans in Early Modern Rajasthan*. New Delhi: Oxford University Press, 2006.

Saxena, R. K. *Rajput Nobility: A Study of 18th Century Rajputana*. Jaipur: Publication Scheme, 1996.

Schofield, Katherine Butler. "Learning to Taste the Emotions: The Mughal Rasika." In *Tellings and Texts: Music, Literature and Performance in North India*, edited by Francesca Orsini and Katherine Butler Schofield, 407–22. n.p.: OpenBook Publishers, 2015.

———. "Sense and Sensibility: The Domain of Pleasure and the Place of Music in Mughal Society," 1–31. Talk presented at School of Oriental and African Studies, London, March 6, 2009.

Schwartzberg, Joseph E. "Diwali in India." In *The Map Book*, edited by Peter Barber, 182. New York: Levenger Press, 2005.

Shaffer, Holly. *Adapting the Eye: An Archive of the British in India, 1770–1830*. Exhibition catalogue. Yale Center for British Art, October 11–December 31, 2011. New Haven, CT: Yale Center for British Art, 2011.

Sharma, G. N. *Mewar and the Mughal Emperors (1526–1707 A.D.)*. 1st ed. Agra, India: S. L. Agarwala, 1954.

Sharma, Sunil. "The City of Beauties in Indo-Persian Poetic Landscape." *Comparative Studies of South Asia, Africa and the Middle East* 24, no. 2 (2004): 73–81.

———. *Mughal Arcadia: Persian Poetry at an Indian Court*. Cambridge, MA: Harvard University Press, 2017.

Sharma, Yuthika. "From Miniatures to Monuments: Picturing Shah Alam's Delhi (1771–1806)." In *Indo-Muslim Cultures in Transition*, edited by Alka Patel and Karen Leonard, 111–38. Brill's Indological Library, vol. 38. Leiden, Netherlands, and Boston: Brill, 2012.

Shastri, Hiranand. *Ancient Vijñaptipatras*. Baroda, India: Baroda State Press, 1942.

Shastri, Satyavrat. "Critical Survey of Dutakavyas." In *Essays on Indology*, 1st. ed., 82–138. Delhi: Meharchand Lachhmandass, 1963.

Shulman, David Dean. *More Than Real: A History of the Imagination in South India*. Cambridge, MA: Harvard University Press, 2012.

Shyamaldas, Kaviraj. *Vīravinoda: Mevāṛa kā itihāsa; Mahārāṇāoṃ kā ādi se lekara san 1884 takak kā vistr̥ta vr̥ttānta ānushaṅgika sāmagrī sahita*. 4 vols. Delhi: Motilal Banarsidass, 1986. Originally published 1886.

Singh, Kavita. "Congress of Kings: Notes on a Painting of Mohammad Shah Rangeela Having Sex." In *A Magic World: New Visions of Indian Painting*, edited by Molly Emma Aitken, 38–49. Mumbai: Marg Publications, 2017.

———. *Real Birds in Imagined Gardens: Mughal Painting Between Persia and Europe*. Los Angeles: Getty Research Institute, Getty Publications, 2017.

———. "Scent upon a Southern Breeze: The Synaesthetic Arts of the Deccan." In *The Arts of the Deccan*, edited by Kavita Singh, 8–23. Mumbai: Marg Publications, 2018.

Skelton, Robert. "Farrokh Beg." *Ars Orientalis* 2 (1957): 393–411.

———. "Farrukh Beg in the Deccan: An Update." In *Sultans of the South: Arts of India's Deccan Courts, 1323–1687*, edited by Navina Najat Haidar and Marika Sardar, 12–25. New York: Metropolitan Museum of Art, 2011.

Smith, Pamela. "In the Workshop of History: Making, Writing, and Meaning." *West 86th: A Journal of Decorative Arts, Design History, and Material Culture* 19, no. 1 (Spring–Summer 2012): 4–31.

Snell, Rupert. "The Nikuñja as Sacred Space in Poetry of the Rādhāvallabhī Tradition." *Journal of Vaiṣṇava Studies* 7, no. 1 (Fall 1998): 63–84.

Sreenivasan, Ramya. *The Many Lives of a Rajput Queen: Heroic Pasts in India, c. 1500–1900*. Seattle: University of Washington Press, 2007.

Stewart, Susan. "Remembering the Senses." In *Empire of the Senses: The Sensual Culture Reader*, edited by David Howes, 59–69. Sensory Formations Series. Oxford and New York: Berg, 2005.

Stronge, Susan. *Painting for the Mughal Emperor: The Art of the Book, 1560–1660*. London: Victoria and Albert Museum / New York: Harry N. Abrams, 2002.

Subrahmanyam, Sanjay. "Connected Histories: Notes Towards a Reconfiguration of Early Modern Eurasia." *Modern Asian Studies* 31, no. 3 (July 1, 1997): 735–62.

———. "A Note on the Rise of Surat in the Sixteenth Century." *Journal of the Economic and Social History of the Orient* 43, no. 1 (January 1, 2000): 23–33.

———. "Of Imarat and Tijarat: Asian Merchants and State Power in the Western Indian Ocean, 1400 to 1750." *Comparative Studies in Society and History* 37, no. 4 (1995): 750–80.

Taft, Frances. "Honor and Alliance: Reconsidering Mughal-Rajput Marriages." In *The Idea of Rajasthan: Explorations in Regional Identity*, edited by Karine Schomer, Joan L. Erdman, Lodrick O. Deryck, and Lloyd I. Rudolph, 2:217–41. New Delhi: Manohar / American Institute of Indian Studies, 1994.

———. "The Origins of the Shekhavat Thikanas of Jaipur." In *Religion, Ritual, and Royalty*, edited by Narendra Kumar Singhi and Rajendra Joshi, 284–303. Jaipur: Rawat Publications, 1999.

———. "Rajas and Thakurs in Rajputana: The Case of Bikaner." In *Folk, Faith and Feudalism: Rajasthan Studies*, edited by Narendra Kumar Singhi and Rajendra Joshi, 241–56. Jaipur: Rawat Publications, 1995.

Talbot, Cynthia. "Becoming Turk the Rajput Way: Conversion and Identity in an Indian Warrior Narrative." *Modern Asian Studies* 43, no. 1 (2009): 211–43.

———. "Justifying Defeat: A Rajput Perspective on the Age of Akbar." *Journal of the Economic and Social History of the Orient* 55, no. 2–3 (2012): 329–68.

———. *The Last Hindu Emperor: Prithviraj Chauhan and the Indian Past, 1200–2000*. Cambridge: Cambridge University Press, 2016.

———. "The Mewar Court's Construction of History." In *Kingdom of the Sun: Indian Court and Village Art from the Princely State of Mewar*, 12–33. San Francisco, CA: Asian Art Museum / Chong-Moon Lee Center for Asian Art and Culture, 2007.

———. "Recovering the Heroic History of Rajasthan: Tod and the Prithviraj Raso." In *James Tod's Rajasthan: The Historian and His Collection*, edited by Giles Tillotson, 98–109. Mumbai: Marg Publications, 2007.

Tillotson, Giles H. R. "Illustrating the Annals: The Architectural Views of Waugh and Ghasi." In *James Tod's Rajasthan: The Historian and His Collection*, edited by Giles Tillotson, 58–69. Mumbai: Marg Publications, 2007.

———. *The Rajput Palaces: The Development of an Architectural Style, 1450–1750*. New Haven, CT: Yale University Press, 1987.

Titley, Norah. "Nasir Shah's Book of Delights." Asian and African Studies blog, British Library, November 21, 2016. https://blogs.bl.uk/asian-and-african/2016/11/nasir-shahs-book-of-delights.html (accessed December 6, 2019).

———. *The Niʿmatnāma Manuscript of the Sultans of Mandu: The Sultan's Book of Delights*. Routledge Curzon Studies in South Asia. London and New York: RoutledgeCurzon, 2005.

Topsfield, Andrew. "City Palace and Lake Palaces: Architecture and Court Life in Udaipur Painting." In *Stones in the Sand: The Architecture of Rajasthan*, edited by G. H. R. Tillotson, 54–67. Mumbai: Marg Publications, 2001.

———. *The City Palace Museum, Udaipur: Paintings of Mewar Court Life*. Museums of India. Ahmedabad, India: Mapin / Middletown, NJ: Grantha, 1990.

———. *Court Painting at Udaipur: Art under the Patronage of the Maharanas of Mewar*. Artibus Asiae, supplementum. Zürich: Artibus Asiae, 2001.

———. "Jagmandir and the Other Royal Palaces in Udaipur Painting." In *The City within a City*, vol. 1, *Jagmandir on Lake Pichola*,

edited by Dipti Khera and Raju Mansukhani, 117–41. New Delhi: Penguin Enterprise, 2002.
———. "Ketelaar's Embassy and the Farangi Theme in the Art of Udaipur." *Oriental Art* 30, no. 4 (Winter 1984): 350–67.
———. *Paintings from Rajasthan in the National Gallery of Victoria: A Collection Acquired Through the Felton Bequests' Committee*. Melbourne: National Gallery of Victoria, 1980.
———. "The Royal Paintings Inventory at Udaipur." In *Indian Art and Connoisseurship: Essays in Honour of Douglas Barrett*, edited by Douglas E. Barrett and John Guy, 188–99. Chidambaram Ahmedabad, India: Indira Gandhi National Centre for the Arts, in association with Mapin / Middletown, NJ: Grantha, 1995
———. "Tod's Collection of Rajasthani Paintings." In *James Tod's Rajasthan: The Historian and His Collection*, edited by Giles Tillotson, 18–35. Mumbai: Marg Publications, 2007.
———. "Udaipur Paintings of the Raslila." *Art Bulletin of Victoria* 28 (1987): 55–70.
Trautmann, Thomas R., ed. *The Madras School of Orientalism: Producing Knowledge in Colonial South India*. New Delhi: Oxford University Press, 2009.
Truschke, Audrey. *Aurangzeb: Life and Legacy of India's Most Controversial King.* Stanford, CA: Stanford University Press, 2017.
———. *Culture of Encounters: Sanskrit at the Mughal Court*. New York: Columbia University Press, 2016.
Tuan, Yi-Fu. *Space and Place: The Perspective of Experience.* Minneapolis: University of Minnesota Press, 1977.
Urban, Hugh B. "The Marketplace and the Temple: Economic Metaphors and Religious Meanings in the Folk Songs of Colonial Bengal." *Journal of Asian Studies* 60, no. 4 (2001): 1085–1114.
Vashishtha, Vijay Kumar. *Rajputana Agency, 1832–1858: A Study of British Relations with the States of Rajputana during the Period with Special Emphasis on the Role of Rajputana Agency*. Jaipur, India: Aalekh, 1978.
Vaudeville, Charlotte. *Barahmasa in Indian Literatures: Songs of the Twelve Months in Indo-Aryan Literatures*. Delhi: Motilal Banarsidass, 1986.
Vila, Anne C. *A Cultural History of the Senses in the Age of Enlightenment*. Cultural History of the Senses, vol. 4. London and New York: Bloomsbury Academic, 2014.
Welch, Stuart Cary. "Kotah's Lively Patrons and Artists." In *Gods, Kings, and Tigers: The Art of Kotah*, 15–38. Munich and New York: Prestel, 1997.
Wescoat, James. "Picturing an Early Mughal Garden." *Asian Art* 4, no. 2 (Fall 1989): 59–79.
Williams, Richard. "A Theology of Feeling: The Radhavallabhi Monsoon in the Eighteenth Century." In *Monsoon Feelings: A History of Emotions in the Rain*, edited by Imke Rajamani, Margrit Pernau, and Katherine Butler Schofield, 71–96. New Delhi: Niyogi Books, 2018.
Wood, Christopher S. "'Curious Pictures' and the Art of Description." *Word and Image* 11, no. 4 (1995): 332–52.
Zeigler, Norman P. "Marvari Historical Chronicles: Sources for the Social and Cultural History of Rajasthan." *Indian Economic and Social History Review* 13. no. 2 (1976): 219–50.
———. "Rajput Loyalties during the Mughal Period." In *Kingship and Authority in South Asia*, edited by John F. Richards, 274–77. Delhi and New York: Oxford University Press, 1998.

Index

Image Credits

© Art Gallery of New South Wales, Sydney (fig. 2.12)
© Ashmolean Museum, University of Oxford, Oxford (fig. 3.1, fig. 3.8, fig. 4.22)
© Asian Art Museum, San Francisco (fig. 3.21)
© The British Library Board, London (fig. 1.1, fig. 1.2, fig. 1.3, fig. 1.4, fig. 4.7, fig. 4.9, fig. 4.13, fig. 4.14, fig. 4.15, fig. 4.16, 4.18, fig. 5.23)
© British Museum, London (fig. 2.10, fig. 2.11)
© Brooklyn Museum, Brooklyn (fig. 4.23)
© Collection of the Trustees of the Chhatrapati Shivaji Maharaj Vastu Sangrahalaya, Mumbai (fig. 3.6)
© Fondation Custodia, Collection Frits Lugt, Paris (fig. 2.8)
© Freer Gallery of Art, Washington, DC (fig. I.8, I.11, fig. 2.1, fig. 2.7, fig. 3.23, fig. 4.28)
© Freer Gallery of Art and Arthur M. Sackler Gallery Archives, Washington, DC (fig. 1.24)
© President and Fellows of Harvard College, Cambridge (fig. C.2)
© Lalbhai Dalpatbhai Institute of Indology, Ahmedabad (fig. I.1, fig. 5.9)
© Los Angeles County Museum of Art, Los Angeles (fig. 2.13, fig. 2.14)
© Maharaja Sawai Man Singh II Museum, City Palace Museum, Jaipur (fig. 1.13)
© Maharana of Mewar Charitable Foundation, The City Palace Museum, Udaipur. Photography courtesy of the Freer Gallery of Art and Arthur M. Sackler Gallery, Smithsonian Institution. Photographer: Neil Greentree (fig. I.4, fig. 2.27, fig. 3.27, fig. 4.26, fig. 4.27)
© Maharana of Mewar Charitable Foundation, The City Palace Museum, Udaipur (fig. 1.7, fig. 1.9, fig. 1.10, fig. 1.11, fig. 2.20, fig. 3.3, fig. 4.4)
© Maharana of Mewar Charitable Foundation, Media Office, Eternal Mewar, The City Palace, Udaipur (fig. I.7, fig. 1.8, fig. 2.21, fig. 2.22, fig. 2.23, fig. 2.24, fig. 2.25, fig. 3.5)
© The Metropolitan Museum of Art, New York (fig. I.9, fig. 1.16, fig. 3.28)
© Museum of Fine Arts, Boston (fig. 2.16, fig. 2.26)
© Museum Rietberg, Zürich (fig. 3.14, fig. 3.26)
© National Gallery Victoria, Melbourne (fig. 1.19, fig. 1.35, fig. 3.11, fig. 3.16, fig. 3.25, fig. 4.25)
© National Museum, New Delhi (fig. C.1)
© New York Public Library, New York (fig. 5.8)
© Philadelphia Museum of Art, Philadelphia (fig. 2.17, fig. 2.18, fig. 3.12)
© The Rjiksmuseum, Amsterdam (fig. 1.20)
© The Royal Asiatic Society, London (fig. I.5, fig. 4.1, fig. 4.3, fig. 4.5, fig. 4.6, fig. 4.10, fig. 4.17, fig. 4.19, fig. 4.20)
© San Diego Museum of Art, San Diego (fig. 2.15, fig. 3.10)
© Victoria and Albert Museum, London (fig. I.10, fig. 1.6)
© Virginia Museum of Fine Arts, Richmond (fig. 2.9)
Image courtesy of Shikha Jain and Vanicka Arora, *Living Heritage of Mewar: Architecture of the City Palace, Udaipur* (Ahmedabad, India: Mapin Publishing in association with Maharana Mewar Historical Publications Trust, 2017) (fig. 1.12)
Image courtesy of Private Collection (fig. 2.19, fig. 3.7, fig. 3.20, fig. 3.22)
Image courtesy of Emma Natalya Stein (fig. I.6, fig. 3.4)
Image courtesy of Andrew Topsfield (fig. 3.9)
Image courtesy of Andrew Topsfield, *Court Painting of Udaipur* (Zürich: Artibus Asiae, 2001) (fig. 4.2)